Dimensions of the Writing Process

CHOOSING
Purpose and

COLL

Observing

Sensory details
Comparisons and images
Changes
What is not there

Remembering

Specific scenes
Changes and conflict
Connections between past and present

Reading

Active reading
Annotating
Summarizing
Responding

Investigating

Asking questions
Interviews
Questionnaires
Library research

SHAPING

Chronological order
Spatial order
Comparison/contrast
Definition
Example

Focusing and narrowing subject
Introductions
Body paragraphs
Conclusions

Causal analysis
Process analysis
Dialogue
Image
Voice and persona

DRAFTING

Planning
Re-reading
Talking

Reconsidering purpose and audience
Starting at the beginning
Starting at the middle

Writing nonstop
Stopping when you know what comes next

REVISING AND EDITING

Major Changes

Changing purpose or audience
Collecting new information, ideas, evidence, examples
Reshaping paragraphs or reorganizing an essay
Choosing a new point of view

Minor Changes

Revising sentences, transitions, word choice
Editing for grammar, punctuation, usage
Proofreading for spelling and mechanics

THE PRENTICE HALL GUIDE FOR COLLEGE WRITERS

ANNOTATED INSTRUCTOR'S EDITION

THE PRENTICE HALL GUIDE FOR COLLEGE WRITERS

THIRD EDITION

STEPHEN REID

COLORADO STATE UNIVERSITY

PRENTICE HALL, ENGLEWOOD CLIFFS, NJ 07632

Library of Congress Cataloging-in-Publication Data
Reid, Stephen,
The Prentice Hall guide for college writers/Stephen Reid. —3rd ed.
p. cm.
Includes index.
ISBN 0-13-073677-5 (Brief Edition)—ISBN 0-13-073669-4 (Full Edition)
1. English language—Rhetoric. I. Title. II. Title: Guide for college writers
PE1408.R424 1994b 94-23222 (Full Edition)
808'.042—dc20 94-32196 (Brief Edition)
CIP

Acquisitions Editor: *Alison Reeves*
Development Editor: *Ronald Librach*
Editorial/Production Supervision: *Tony VenGraitis*
Design Director: *Paula Martin*
Interior and Cover Design: *Louise Fili*
Electronic Formatting: *Yvette Raven*
Manufacturing Buyer: *Mary Ann Gloriande*
Photo Editor: *Lorinda Morris-Nantz*
Photo Researcher: *Kathy Ringrose*

Cover Art & Back Cover (Detail): Thomas McKnight, "Wall Street Office, Manhattan Suite" serigraph 14" x 16" © Thomas McKnight 1994 courtesy of Chalk & Vermilion Fine Arts.

A Simon & Schuster Company
Englewood Cliffs, New Jersey 07632

Printed in the United States of America

10 9 8 7 6 5 4 3 2 1

ISBN 0-13-073669-4
0-13-073677-5 (Brief Edition)
0-13-122557-X (Annotated Instructor's Edition)

Prentice-Hall International (UK) Limited, *London*
Prentice-Hall of Australia Pty. Limited, *Sydney*
Prentice-Hall Canada Inc., *Toronto*
Prentice-Hall Hispanoamericana, S.A., *Mexico*
Prentice-Hall of India Private Limited, *New Delhi*
Prentice-Hall of Japan, Inc., *Tokyo*
Simon & Schuster Asia Pte. Ltd., *Singapore*
Editora Prentice-Hall do Brasil, Ltda., *Rio de Janeiro*

Brief Contents

ONE
Writing Myths and Rituals
2

TWO
Purposes and Processes for Writing
18

THREE
Observing
50

FOUR
Remembering
100

FIVE
Reading
142

SIX
Investigating
200

SEVEN
Explaining
252

EIGHT
Evaluating
306

NINE
Problem Solving
358

TEN
Arguing
416

ELEVEN
Responding to Literature
474

TWELVE
Writing a Research Paper
520

Appendix: Writing under Pressure
575

Handbook
587

Contents

PREFACE
XIX

ONE

Writing Myths and Rituals

2

Writing Fitness: Rituals and Practice 6

Place, Time, and Tools 7 Energy and Attitude 9

Keeping a Journal 10

Warming Up: Journal Exercises 14

"On Keeping a Journal" by Roy Hoffman 14

TWO

Purposes and Processes for Writing

18

"Writing for Myself" by Russell Baker 22

Purposes for Writing 23

Writer-Based Purposes 24 Subject- and Audience-Based Purposes 24

Combination of Purposes 25 Subject, Purpose, and Thesis 25

Purpose and Audience 26

Audience Analysis 27 The Writing Situation 28

Purpose and Audience in Two Essays 29

"The Struggle to Be an All-American Girl" by Elizabeth Wong 29

"I'm OK, but You're Not" by Robert Zoellner 31

Dimensions of the Processes 33

Collecting 33 Shaping 34

Drafting 34 Revising 34 The Whole Process 35

Writing with a Computer 36

Warming Up: Journal Exercises 38

A WRITING PROCESS AT WORK: COLLECTING AND SHAPING 40

"Athletes and Education" by Neil H. Petrie 40

"On Writing 'Athletes and Education'" by Neil H. Petrie 43

A WRITING PROCESS AT WORK: DRAFTING AND REVISING 46

From "The Declaration of Independence" 47

THREE

OBSERVING

50

TECHNIQUES FOR WRITING ABOUT OBSERVATIONS 54

Observing People 56 Observing Places 56

Observing Objects 58 Observing Events 59

Warming Up: Journal Exercises 60

OBSERVING: PROFESSIONAL WRITING 62

"Take This Fish and Look at It" by Samuel H. Scudder 62

"The Snake" by Annie Dillard 66

"Observing Wolves" by Farley Mowat 70

OBSERVING: THE WRITING PROCESS 78

Choosing a Subject 78 Collecting 80

Shaping 82 Drafting 89 Revising 90

OBSERVING: STUDENT WRITING 93

"A New Leaf" by Mark Skelton 93 "Empty Windows" by Stephen White 96

FOUR

REMEMBERING

100

TECHNIQUES FOR WRITING ABOUT MEMORIES 104

Remembering People 106 Remembering Places 106

Remembering Events 107

Warming Up: Journal Exercises 108

REMEMBERING: PROFESSIONAL WRITING 110

"The Day Language Came into My Life" by Helen Keller 110

"Under the Influence" by Scott Russell Sanders 113

"Beauty: When the Other Dancer Is the Self" by Alice Walker 116

REMEMBERING: THE WRITING PROCESS 124

Choosing a Subject 124 Collecting 125

Shaping 126 Drafting 132 Revising 132

REMEMBERING: STUDENT WRITING 134

"The Wind Catcher" by Todd Petry 134

"Kit Carson" by Brooke Selby 137

FIVE

READING

142

TECHNIQUES FOR WRITING ABOUT READING 146

How Readers Read 147

SUMMARIZING AND RESPONDING TO AN ESSAY 148

"Teach Diversity—with a Smile" by Barbara Ehrenreich 149

Summarizing 151 Responding 153

Summarizing and Responding to an Advertisement 156

"Some Don't Like Their Blues at All" by Karyn Lewis 156

Warming Up: Journal Exercises 158

READING: PROFESSIONAL WRITING 162

"Animal Rights and Beyond" by David Quammen 162

"Masters of Desire: The Culture of American Advertising" by Jack Solomon 168

READING AND WRITING PROCESSES 172

Choosing a Subject 173

"Children and Violence in America" by Dudley Erskine Devlin 173

Collecting 175 Shaping 180

Drafting 186 Revising 187

READING: STUDENT WRITING 188

"Drawing the Line" by Paula Fisher 188

"Two Responses to Deborah Tannen" by Jennifer Koester and Sonja H. Browe 192

SIX

INVESTIGATING

200

TECHNIQUES FOR INVESTIGATIVE WRITING 203

Summary of a Book or Article 204 Investigation Using Multiple Sources 206 Profile of a Person 209

Warming Up: Journal Exercises 210

INVESTIGATING: PROFESSIONAL WRITING 211

"Triumph of the Wheel" by Lewis Grossberger 211

"The Homeless and Their Children" by Jonathan Kozol 219

INVESTIGATING: THE WRITING PROCESS 242

Choosing a Subject 227 Collecting 228

Shaping 236 Drafting 240 Revising 241

INVESTIGATING: STUDENT WRITING 226

"See Dick Run, Run Dick Run, Why, Why, Why?" by Jan Peterson 242

"My Friend, Michelle: An Alcoholic" by Bridgid Stone 248

SEVEN

EXPLAINING

252

TECHNIQUES FOR EXPLAINING 256

Explaining *What* 257 Explaining *How* 259 Explaining *Why* 261

Warming Up: Journal Exercises 263

EXPLAINING: PROFESSIONAL WRITING 264

"Is Sex Necessary? Virgin Birth and Opportunism in the Garden" by David Quammen 264

"To Dispel Fears of Live Burial" by Jessica Mitford 270

"How Male and Female Students Use Language Differently" by Deborah Tannen 276

EXPLAINING: THE WRITING PROCESS 282

Choosing a Subject 282 Collecting 283

Shaping 286 Drafting 292 Revising 293

EXPLAINING: STUDENT WRITING 296

"The Police Were Calling Me Names": An Explanation of Hard-Core Punk Rock" by Dennis Alexander 296

"Anorexia Nervosa" by Nancie Brosseau 302

EIGHT

EVALUATING

306

TECHNIQUES FOR WRITING EVALUATIONS 310

Evaluating Commercial Products or Services 312 Evaluating Works of Art 314

Evaluating Performances 316

Warming Up: Journal Exercises 318

EVALUATING: PROFESSIONAL WRITING 322

"The Gettysburg Address" by Gilbert Highet 323

"Armageddon, Complete and Uncut" by Robert Kiely 329

EVALUATING: THE WRITING PROCESS 334

Choosing a Subject 334 Collecting 334

Shaping 337 Drafting 341 Revising 342

EVALUATING: STUDENT WRITING 344

"Borrowers Can Be Choosy" by Linda Meininger 344

"The Big Chill" by Kent Y'Blood 354

NINE

PROBLEM SOLVING

358

TECHNIQUES FOR PROBLEM SOLVING 362

Demonstrating that a Problem Exists 362 Proposing a Solution and Convincing Your Readers 364

Warming Up: Journal Exercises 366

PROBLEM SOLVING: PROFESSIONAL WRITING 367

"Solving for Pattern" by Wendell Berry 367

"Sex, Lies, and Advertising" by Gloria Steinem 371

"The Agony Must End" by Paul Zimmerman 383

PROBLEM SOLVING: THE WRITING PROCESS 388

Choosing a Subject 388 Collecting 390

Shaping 394 Drafting 399 Revising 399

PROBLEM SOLVING: STUDENT WRITING 401

"No Parking" by Kristy Busch, Steve Krause, and Keith Wright 401

"Who Should Take Charge?" by Eui Young Hwang 408

TEN

ARGUING

416

TECHNIQUES FOR WRITING ARGUMENT 420

Claims for Written Argument 421 Appeals for Written Argument 425 Rogerian Argument 430

Warming Up: Journal Exercises 432

ARGUING: PROFESSIONAL WRITING 434

"Darwin's Middle Road" by Stephen Jay Gould 434

"The Damnation of a Canyon" by Edward Abbey 443

ARGUING: THE WRITING PROCESS 448

Choosing a Subject 450 Collecting 450

Shaping 452 Drafting 457 Revising 458

ARGUING: STUDENT WRITING 463

"Protect Yourself—Buckle Up!" by Jim Haas 463

"Games the Military Plays" by David Thomas 468

ELEVEN

Responding to Literature

474

"The Story of an Hour" by Kate Chopin 479

Techniques for Responding to Literature 481

Warming Up: Journal Exercises 482

Purposes for Responding to Literature 483

Responding to Short Fiction 485

Responding as a Reader 485 Reading with a Writer's Eye 486

Short Fiction: Professional Writing 488

"A Worn Path" by Eudora Welty 488

"The Lesson" by Toni Cade Bambara 496

Responding to Literature: The Writing Process 504

Collecting 505 Shaping 507 Drafting 510 Revising 510

Responding to Literature: Student Writing 512

"A Worn Path" by Julia MacMillan and Brett MacFadden 512

"Death: The Final Freedom" by Pat Russell 518

TWELVE

Writing a Research Paper

520

Techniques for Writing a Research Paper 524

Using Purpose, Audience, and Form as Guides 525 Finding the Best Sources 526

Using Sources to Make Your Point 527 Documenting Your Sources 527

Preparing Yourself for the Research Process 527

Warming Up: Journal Exercises 528

Research Notebook 529 Research Timetable 533

Documentation Format: MLA and APA Styles 534

RESEARCH PAPER: THE WRITING PROCESS 534

Choosing a Subject 535 Collecting 538

Shaping 547 Drafting 551

Revising 556

RESEARCH PAPER: STUDENT WRITING 568

"Foreign Language Study: An American Necessity" by Kate McNerny 568

APPENDIX

WRITING UNDER PRESSURE

575

KNOW YOUR AUDIENCE 577

ANALYZE KEY TERMS 577

MAKE A SKETCH OUTLINE 578

KNOW THE MATERIAL 581

PRACTICE WRITING 581

PROOFREAD AND EDIT 582

SAMPLE ESSAY QUESTIONS AND RESPONSES 582

HANDBOOK

587

SECTION 1–REVIEW OF BASIC SENTENCE ELEMENTS 594

SECTION 2–SENTENCE STRUCTURE AND GRAMMAR 604

SECTION 3–DICTION AND STYLE 622

SECTION 4–PUNCTUATION AND MECHANICS 636

INDEX

653

Thematic Contents

The Prentice Hall Guide for College Writers, third edition, contains excerpts and selections from over 50 writers. Thematic clusters are indicated below.

Race and Cultural Diversity

Barbara Ehrenreich, "Teach Diversity—with a Smile" 149

Jeanne Wakatsuke Houston, "Farewell to Mansanar" 106

Eui Young Hwang, "Who Should Take Charge?" 408

Martin Luther King, Jr., from "Letter from Birmingham Jail" 436

N. Scott Momaday, from *The Way to Rainy Mountain* 106

Patricia Raybon, from "A Case of Severe Bias" 422

Peter Travers, "The Year of Malcolm X" 317

Alice Walker, "Beauty: When the Other Dancer Is the Self" 116

Stephen White, "Empty Windows" 96

Elizabeth Wong, "The Struggle to Be an All-American Girl" 29

Robert Zoellner, "I'm OK, but You're Not" 31

Gender Roles

Sonja H. Browe and Jennifer Koester, "Two Responses to Deborah Tannen" 192

Kate Chopin, "The Story of an Hour" 479

Charlene Muehlenhard and Melaney Linton, "Date Rape: Familiar Strangers" 205

Richard Rodriguez, "The Boy's Desire" 107

Gloria Steinem, "Sex, Lies, and Advertising 371

Deborah Tannen, "How Male and Female Students Use Language Differently" 276

Elizabeth Wong, "The Struggle to Be an All-American Girl" 29

Families

Jonathan Kozol, "The Homeless and Their Children" 219

Richard Rodriguez, "The Boy's Desire" 107

Scott Russell Sanders, "Under the Influence" 113

Brooke Selby, "Kit Carson" 137

Alice Walker, "Beauty: When the Other Dancer is the Self" 116

Eudora Welty, "A Worn Path" 488

Animal Rights

Paula Fisher, "Drawing the Line" 188

David Quammen, "Animal Rights and Beyond" 162

Albert Rosenfeld, from "Animal Rights versus Human Health" 431

Environmental Issues

Edward Abbey, "The Damnation of a Canyon" 443

Wendell Berry, "Solving for Pattern" 367

Annie Dillard, "The Snake" 66

Isak Dinesen, "The Iguana" 55

Farley Mowat, "Observing Wolves" 70

Education

Toni Cade Bambara, "The Lesson" 496

Caroline Bird, from, "College Is a Waste of Time and Money" 424

Kate McNerny, "Foreign Language Study: An American Necessity" 568

Neil H. Petrie, "Athletes and Education" 40

Samuel H. Scudder, "Take This Fish and Look at It" 62

James Thurber, :"University Days" 129

Literacy and Language

Russell Baker, "Writing for Myself" 22

Gilbert Highet, "The Gettysburg Address" 323

Roy Hoffmann, "On Keeping a Journal" 10

Helen Keller, "The Day Language Came into My Life" 110

Jonathan Kozol, from *Illiterate America* 262

Jonathan Kozol, "The Homeless and Their Children" 219

Neil H. Petrie, "On Writing 'Athletes and Education'" 43

Advertising and the Media

Dudley Erskine Devlin, "Children and Violence in America" 173

Lewis Grossberger, "The Triumph of the Wheel" 211

Andrea Lee, "Mayakovsky Square" 105

Karyn Lewis, "Some Don't Like Their Blues at All" 156

Patricia Raybon, from "A Case of Severe Bias" 422

Jack Solomon, "Masters of Desire: The Culture of American Advertising" 168

Gloria Steinem, "Sex, Lies, and Advertising" 371

David Thomas, "Games the Military Plays" 468

Marie Winn, from *The Plug-In Drug* 423

Dependency and Dysfunction

Nancie Brosseau, "Anorexia Nervosa" 302

Sukie Colgrave, "Projection" 257

Jan Peterson, "See Dick Run, Run Dick Run, Why, Why, Why?" 242

Patricia Raybon, from "A Case of Severe Bias" 422

Scott Russell Sanders, "Under the Influence" 113

Anne Wilson Schaef, from *When Society Becomes an Addict* 425

Bridgid Stone, "My Friend, Michelle: An Alcoholic" 248

Anastasia Toufexis, "The Personality Pill" 206

Violence and Society

Dudley Erskine Devlin, "Children and Violence in America" 173

Robert Kiely, "Armageddon, Complete and Uncut" 329

Mark Stevens, "The Third of May, 1808" 314

Frank Trippett, "A Red Light for Scofflaws" 363

Paul Zimmerman, "The Agony Must End" 383

Preface

We aim to make better writers, not
necessarily—or immediately—better texts.
Stephen North

The writer may write to inform, to explain, to entertain,
to persuade, but whatever the purpose there should be,
first of all, the satisfaction of the writer's own learning.
Donald Murray

Few things give teachers—and textbook writers—more satisfaction than helping students learn to become better writers. Strategies, classroom activities, professional and student essays—all are merely means to achieve those moments of excitement and learning that propel writers to transform themselves through reading and writing. I hope that this textbook continues to offer students and their teachers contexts for those transformations.

In its third edition, *The Prentice Hall Guide for College Writers* retains an emphasis on aims and purposes for writing, on a clear sequence of chapters that move from expressive to argumentative writing, and on extensive, integrated writing-process advice that helps students learn. Providing ongoing support for both students and teachers during the invention, composing, and revising processes remains the overriding goal of this text.

New to the third edition is an increased emphasis on reading and responding to texts. Chapter Five, "Reading," uses the summary/response essay as a means to teach active and critical reading, accurate summarizing, and focused responding to texts. Drawing on reader-response theories and psycho-linguistic research, Chapter Five demonstrates how discussion activities promote active reading and response. The new chapter prepares students to use their reading as an invention strategy to complement the other major sources of invention—observing, remembering, and investigating.

In addition to the new chapter on reading, the third edition has eight new selections by professional writers such as Farley Mowat, Scott Russell Sanders, Barbara Ehrenreich, Jack Solomon, Deborah Tannen, Wendell Berry, and Toni Cade Bambara. The additional essays in each chapter create thematic clusters of topics that reappear throughout the text: cultural diversity, gender roles, the environment, literacy, advertising and the media, and animal rights. See the Thematic Contents (following the table of contents) for a complete listing.

Eight new essays by student writers—on topics such as gender-based learning, advertising tactics, the media and the military, alcoholism, and interracial conflicts—provide students with realistic models for their own essays. *The Prentice Hall Guide for College Writers* continues to showcase student writing, featuring the work of over 40 student writers from several colleges and universities. The third edition contains 23 full-length student essays and 10 essays with sample prewriting materials and drafts.

KEY FEATURES

Continuing in the third edition of *The Prentice Hall Guide for College Writers* is a wide range of noteworthy features:

LOGICAL SEQUENCE OF PURPOSE-BASED CHAPTERS Aims and purposes, not rhetorical strategies, guide each writing assignment. Early chapters focus on invention strategies (observing, remembering, reading, and investigation), while later chapters emphasize exposition and argumentation (explaining, evaluating, problem solving, and arguing).

FOCUS ON WRITING PROCESSES Every major chapter contains techniques, professional and student samples, journal exercises, reading and writing activities, collaborative activities, peer-response guidelines, and revision suggestions designed to assist students with their work-in-progress.

JOURNAL WRITING Throughout the text, write-to-learn activities help writers improve their critical reading skills, "warm up" for each assignment, and practice a variety of invention and shaping strategies.

MARGINAL QUOTATIONS Nearly a hundred short quotations by composition teachers, researchers, essayists, novelists, and poets personalize for the inexperienced writer a larger community of writers still struggling with the same problems that each student faces.

ANNOTATED INSTRUCTOR'S EDITION (AIE) In the margins of the teacher's annotated edition are hundreds of teaching tips, reference citations, and suggestions for assignments and group activities.

Designed to accompany the Annotated Instructor's Edition is a teacher's manual containing sections on composition theory, policy statements, lesson plans, collaborative writing, group learning, write-to-learn exercises, reading/writing exercises, assignments, student conferences, responding to and evaluating writing, and an annotated bibliography of articles about teaching writing. Also included are chapter commentaries and answers to discussion questions.

An Introduction to Myths and Rituals for Writing. Chapter One, "Writing Myths and Rituals," discounts some common myths about college writing courses, introduces the notion of writing rituals, and outlines the variety of journal writing used throughout the text. Rituals are crucial for all writers but especially so for novice writers. Effective rituals are simply those behavioral strategies that complement the cognitive and social strategies of the writing process. Illustrating a variety of possible writing rituals are quotations from a dozen professional writers on the nature of writing. These short quotations continue throughout the book, reminding students that writing is not some magical process, but rather a madness that has a method to it, a love that is built from labor, and a learning that is born of reading, thinking, observing, remembering, discussing, and writing.

An Orientation to Rhetorical Situation and to Writing Processes. Chapter Two, "Purposes and Processes for Writing," bases the writing process in the rhetorical situation (writer, subject, purpose, text, and audience). It restores the writer's intent or purpose (rather than a thesis sentence or a rhetorical strategy) as the driving force during the writing process. It demonstrates how meaning evolves from a variety of recursive, multidimensional, and hierarchical activities that we call the writing process. Finally, it reassures students that, because individual writing and learning styles differ, they will be encouraged to discover and articulate their own processes from a range of appropriate possibilities.

Aims and Purposes for Writing. The text then turns to specific purposes and assignments for writing. Chapters Three through Six ("Observing," "Remembering," "Reading," and "Investigating") focus on invention strategies. These Chapters illustrate how writing to learn is a natural part of learning to write. To promote reading, writing, discussing, revising, and learning, these chapters introduce four sources of invention—observing people, places, events, and objects; remembering people, places, and events; reading and responding to texts; and investigating information through interviews, surveys, and written sources. Although students write essays intended for a variety of audiences in each of these chapters, the emphasis is on invention strategies and on writer-based purposes for writing. Although this text includes expressive and transactional elements in every assignment, the direction of the overall sequence of assignments is from the more personal forms of discourse to the more public forms.

Chapters Seven through Ten ("Explaining," "Evaluating," "Problem Solving," and "Arguing") emphasize subject- and audience-based purposes. The sequence in these chapters moves the student smoothly from exposition to argumentation (acknowledging the obvious overlapping), building on the skills and cognitive strategies of the previous chapters. The teacher may, in fact, use Chapters Seven through Ten as a minicourse in argument, teaching students how to develop and argue claims of fact, claims of cause and effect, claims about values, and claims about solutions or policies.

Responding to Literature. Chapter Eleven guides students through the process of writing interpretive essays about short fiction, using many of the critical reading strategies, invention techniques, and shaping strategies practiced in the earlier chapters. This chapter contains three short fiction works and two student essays.

Research Paper. Chapter Twelve ("Writing a Research Paper") draws on all the cognitive and social strategies presented in the first eleven chapters. Research papers are written for a purpose and audience too, but the invention, composing, and revising processes are more extended. This chapter helps students select and plan their projects, use the library, evaluate and document sources, record their progress, and test ideas in research logs—learning all the while to integrate the information they gather with their own experiences and ideas.

ACKNOWLEDGMENTS

This textbook builds on the work of hundreds of teachers and researchers. Its most obvious and immediate debts are to James Kinneavy, Frank D'Angelo, Donald Murray, Rise Axelrod and Charles Cooper, Jeanne Fahnestock and Marie Secor, Linda Flower and John Hayes, Patricia Bizzell, Maxine Hairston, Frank Smith, Louise Rosenblatt, and Lynn Troyka. Beyond those are many other writers whose theories and practices contribute to this textbook: David Barholomae, Ann Berthoff, James Britton, Kenneth Bruffee, Richard Coe, Robert Connors, Edward Corbett,

Peter Elbow, Caroline Eckhardt and David Stewart, Janet Emig, Richard Fulkerson, Toby Fulwiler, George Hillocks, Richard Larson, Erika Lindemann, Stephen North, Mina Shaughnessy, and Stephen Toulmin.

In addition, the following teachers offered excellent advice about changes and additions for the third addition; Sue V. Lape–Columbus State Community College; Jim Moody–South Suburban College; Clayton G. Holloway–Hampton University; Winifred Morgan– Edgewood College; Michael Hogan–A.E. Missouri State University; James C. McDonald–University of S. Louisiana; Sarah Liggett–Louisiana State University; Paula Gillespie–Marquette University.

For the expert crew at Prentice Hall, I am especially grateful. Phil Miller, a fine editor and friend, has enthusiastically supported this text from the first edition. Alison Reeves provided ongoing editorial and organizational assistance while Ron Librach clarified the manuscript at every turn. To Gina Sluss and Tracy Augustine, I can only say thanks for being such professionals—and for being such good friends.

Finally, I wish to thank my family—Joy, Shelley, Michael, Gus and Loren—for their continued patience and active support.

THE NEW YORK TIMES and PRENTICE HALL are sponsoring THEMES OF THE TIMES: a program designed to enhance student access to current information of relevance in the classroom.

Through this program, the core subject matter provided in the text is supplemented by a collection of time-sensative articles from one of the world's most distinguished newspapers, THE NEW YORK TIMES. These articles demonstrate the vital, ongoing connection between what is learned in the classroom and what is happening in the world around us.

To enjoy the wealth of information of THE NEW YORK TIMES daily, a reduced subscription rate is available in deliverable areas. For information, call toll-free: 1-800-631-1222.

PRENTICE HALL and THE NEW YORK TIMES are proud to co-sponsor THEMES OF THE TIMES. We hope it will make the reading of both textbooks and newspapers a more dynamic, involving process.

ABC News/Prentice Hall Video Library for Composition, Volume II (013-149030-3)

This text is accompanied by a videocassette from ABC NEWS and PRENTICE HALL which contains nine video segments, one for each of the nine chapters on purposes for writing. These videos were selected from such award-winning news programs as *20/20, World News Tonight/American Agenda, Nightline* and *Primetime Live*.

ABC NEWS annotations in the Annotated Instructor's Edition indicate ite-ins between the video library and the text and show professors how to use the videos as springboards for writing and/or as "texts" for analyzing rhetorical strategies.

A video guide, the *ABC News/Prentice Hall Video Guide for Composition* (0-13-122649-5) by William Costanzo of Westchester Community College, provides a synopsis for and transcripts of each video; an overview of how to use the video library in class and teaching notes organized three ways: by textbook chapter, by video selection, and by rhetorical strategies.

Acknowledgments

Edward Abbey, excerpt from "The Damnation of a Canyon," from *Beyond the Wall* by Edward Abbey. Copyright © 1984 by Edward Abbey. Reprinted by permission of Henry Holt and Company, Inc. **Vicki Alexander and Grace Lyu-Volckhausen,** excerpt from "Black–Asian Conflict: Where Do We Begin?" Originally appeared in *Ms. Magazine*, November/December 1991 issue. Reprinted by permission of Ms. Magazine. © 1991. **Russell Baker,** "Writing for Myself" (editor's title), excerpt from *Growing Up*, © 1982 by Russell Baker. Reprinted by permission of Congdon & Weed, Inc. **Toni Cade Bambara,** "The Lesson," from *Gorilla, My Love* by Toni Cade Bambara. Copyright © 1972 by Toni Cade Bambara. Reprinted by permission of Random House, Inc. **Wendell Berry,** excerpt from "Solving for Pattern," from *The Gift of Good Land* by Wendell Berry. Copyright © 1981 by Wendell Berry. Reprinted by permission of North Point Press, a division of Farrar, Straus & Giroux, Inc. **Consumers Reports** excerpt from "How Much Car for $3990?" Copyright 1986 by Consumers Union of United States, Inc., Mount Vernon, NY 10553. Excerpt by permission of *Consumers Reports*, February 1986. **Annie Dillard,** "The Snake," selected excerpt from *Pilgrim at Tinker Creek*. Copyright © 1974 by Annie Dillard. Reprinted by permission of HarperCollins Publishers, Inc. **Barbara Ehrenreich,** "Teach Diversity—with a Smile," from *Time* magazine, April 08, 1991. Copyright 1991 Time Inc. Reprinted by permission. **James Gorman,** "Man, Bytes, Dog." Reprinted by permission; © 1984 James Gorman. Originally in *The New Yorker*. **Stephen Jay Gould,** "Darwin's Middle Road." Reprinted from *The Panda's Thumb: More Reflections in Natural History* by Stephen Jay Gould, with the permission of W. W. Norton & Company, Inc. Copyright © 1980 by Stephen Jay Gould. **Lewis Grossberger,** "The Triumph of the Wheel," from *Rolling Stone*, December 04, 1986 by Straight Arrow Publishers Company, L.P. 1986. All rights reserved. Reprinted by permission. **Gilbert Highet,** "The Gettysburg Address." excerpt from *A Clerk of Oxenford*. Reprinted by permission of Curtis Brown, Ltd. Copyright © 1954 by Gilbert Highet. **Roy Hoffman,** "On Keeping a Journal," *Newsweek On Campus*, October 1983, Newsweek, Inc. All rights reserved. **Marjorie Hope and James Young,** excerpt from "Making the Case for Full Employment," *The Christian Century*, August 26, 1987. Reprinted by permission of *The Christian Century* magazine. **Gary Larson,** "The Far Side" cartoon is reprinted by permission of Chronicle Features, San Francisco. **Robert Kiely,** "Armageddon, Complete and Uncut," from *The New York Times*, June 05, 1990. Copyright © 1990 by The New York Times Company. Reprinted by permission. **Martin Luther King, Jr.,** excerpt from "Letter from Birmingham Jail–April 16, 1963," from *Why We Can't Wait*. Reprinted by arrangement with the heirs to the estate of Martin Luther King, Jr., c/o Joan Daves Agency as agent for the proprietor. Copyright 1963 by Martin Luther King, Jr., copyright renewed 1991 by Coretta Scott King. **Jonathan Kozol,** excerpt from *Illiterate America*. Reprinted by permission of Anchor Press, a division of Bantam, Doubleday, Dell Publishing Group, Inc. **Jeff Meer,** "Date Rape: Familiar Strangers." Reprinted with permission from *Psychology Today Magazine*, Copyright © 1987 (Sussex Publishers, Inc.). **Jessica Mitford,** "To Dispel Fears of Live Burial" (editor's title) from *The American Way of Death*. Reprinted by permission of Jessica Mitford. All rights reserved. Copyright © 1963, 1978 by Jessica Mitford. **Lance Morrow,** excerpt from "The Start of a Plague Mentality," from *Time* magazine, September 23, 1985. Copyright 1985 Time Inc. Reprinted by permission. **Farley Mowat,** "Observing Wolves," from *Never Cry Wolf*. Copyright © 1963 by Farley Mowat Limited. By permission of Little, Brown and Company. **Neil H. Petrie,** "Athletes and Education." Originally appeared as "Colleges Give Their Student Athletes an Especially Reprehensible Form of Hypocrisy," in *The Chronicle of Higher Education*, February 24, 1988. Copyright 1988, Chronicle of Higher Education. Reprinted with permission. **George Orwell,** excerpt from "Shooting an Elephant" in *Shooting an Elephant and Other Essays* by George Orwell, copyright 1950 by Sonia Brownell Orwell; renewed 1978 by Sonia Pitt-Rivers. Reprinted by permission of Harcourt Brace Jovanovich, Inc. and the estate of the late Sonia Brownell Orwell and Secker & Warburg Ltd. **David Quammen,** "Animal Rights and Beyond" from *Natural Acts.* Reprinted by permission of David Quammen. All rights reserved. Copyright © 1982 by David Quammen. "Is Sex Necessary: Virgin Birth and Opportunism in the Garden," from *Natural Acts.* Reprinted by permission of David Quammen. All rights reserved. Copyright © 1982 by David Quammen. **James Rachels,** excerpt from "Active and Passive Euthanasia," *The New England Journal of Medicine*, vol. 292, pp. 78–80, 1975. Copyright 1975 Massachusetts Medical Society. Reprinted by permission. **Patricia Raybon,** excerpt from "*My Turn*—A Case of Severe Bias" in *Newsweek*, October 1989. © 1989 by Patricia Raybon. Reprinted by permission of the author. **Phyllis Richman,** excerpt from "Hunan Dynasty." Reprinted by permission of *The Washington Post.* **Richard Rodriguez,** excerpt from "The Boy's Desire," copyright © 1983 by Richard Rodriguez. Reprinted by permission of Georges Borchardt, Inc. for the author. First published in *California Magazine.* **Albert Rosenfeld,** excerpt from "Animal Rights vs. Human Health" *Science81*, June 1981. Reprinted by permission of American Association for the Advancement of Science, and the author. **Scott Russell Sanders,** "Under the Influence," copyright © 1989 by *Harper's Magazine.* All rights reserved. Reprinted from the November issue by special permission. **Jack Solomon,** "Masters of Desire: The Culture of American Advertising." Reprinted by permission of The Putnam Publishing Group/Jeremy P. Tarcher, Inc. from *The Signs of Our Times* by Jack Solomon, Ph.D. Copyright © 1988 by Jack Fisher Solomon, Ph.D. **Gloria Steinem,** excerpt from "Sex, Lies and Advertising," in *Ms. Magazine*, July/August 1990. Reprinted by permission of Gloria Steinem. **Mark Stevens,** excerpt from "Goya's Third of May, 1808." Reprinted by permission of the author. **Deborah Tannen,** "How Male and Female Students Use Language Differently" from *The Chronicle of Higher Education*, June 19, 1991. Reprinted by permission of International Creative Management, Inc. Copyright 1991 by Deborah Tannen. **Lewis Thomas,** excerpt from *Lives of a Cell.* Copyright © 1974 by Lewis Thomas. All rights reserved. Reprinted by permission of Viking Penguin Inc. **James Thurber,** excerpt from "University Days." Copyright © 1933, 1961 by James Thurber. From *My Life and Hard Times*, published by Harper & Row and Hamish Hamilton Ltd. **Anastasia Toufexis,** "The Personality Pill" from *Time* magazine, October 11, 1993. Copyright 1993 Time Inc. Reprinted by permission. **Peter Travers,** "The Year of Malcolm X" from *Rolling Stone*, December 10, 1992 by Straight Arrow Publishers Company, L.P. 1992. All rights reserved. Reprinted by permission. **Frank Trippet,** excerpt from "A Red Light for Scofflaws," from *Time* magazine, January 24, 1983. Copyright 1983 Time Inc. Reprinted by permission. **Alice Walker,** "Beauty: When the Other Dancer Is the Self." Copyright © 1983 by Alice Walker, reprinted from her volume *In Search of Our Mothers' Gardens* by permission of Harcourt Brace Jovanovich, Inc. **Eudora Welty,** "A Worn Path" from *A Curtain of Green, and Other Stories*, copyright 1941 and renewed 1969 by Eudora Welty, reprinted by permission of Harcourt Brace Jovanovich, Inc. **Elizabeth Wong,** "The Struggle to Be an All-American Girl." Originally appeared in the *Los Angeles Times.* Reprinted by permission of the author. **Paul Zimmerman,** excerpt from "The Agony Must End." The article is reprinted courtesy of *Sports Illustrated* from the November 10, 1986 issue. Copyright © 1986, Time Inc. All rights reserved. **Robert Zoellner,** "I'm OK, but You're Not," from *The Coloradoan.* Reprinted by permission.

THE PRENTICE HALL GUIDE FOR COLLEGE WRITERS

ONE / WRITING MYTHS AND RITUALS

A writer is someone who writes, that's all.

GORE VIDAL,

NOVELIST AND SOCIAL COMMENTATOR

❧

I've always disliked words like inspiration. Writing is probably like a scientist thinking about some scientific problem or an engineer about an engineering problem.

DORIS LESSING,

AUTHOR OF ESSAYS AND FICTION, INCLUDING THE GOLDEN NOTEBOOK

❧

I always worked until I had something done and I always stopped when I knew what was going to happen next. That way I could be sure of going on the next day.

—ERNEST HEMINGWAY,

JOURNALIST AND NOVELIST, AUTHOR OF THE OLD MAN AND THE SEA

ONE MYTH ABOUT WRITING I HAVE BELIEVED MY WHOLE LIFE IS THAT "GOOD WRITERS ARE BORN, NOT MADE." My attitude when beginning this writing course was one of apprehension and dread. I wondered if I *could* improve my writing, or if I was destined to receive B's and C's on every essay for the rest of my life. This writing class has given me concrete examples and suggestions for improvement—not just grammar or essay maps. The freewriting is such a great help that whenever I'm stuck I immediately turn to my ten-minute freewriting to open up blocked passages. Once I get past my writer's block, I see that I can be a good writer.

❧

FOR ME, THE MOST EFFECTIVE WRITING RITUAL IS TO GATHER UP ALL OF MY STUFF—LEGAL PAD AND PENCIL, NOTES, DICTIONARY, AND THESAURUS—AND GET ON MY BIKE, RIDE TO CAMPUS, AND SET MYSELF UP IN THE ART LOUNGE IN THE STUDENT CENTER. During the week, I'll do this in the evening after dinner. On a weekend, I go any time from 10 A.M. to midnight. I don't write effectively at home because there are always distractions. Some people will be moving around and I'll go see who they are and what they're doing, or I'll go get a cup of coffee or a piece of toast, or I'll snap on the TV, ignoring that tiny voice inside saying, "Get busy—you have to get this done!" So what makes the art lounge better? Simple—no distractions. I can lay out all of my stuff, get a cup of coffee, and go to work. All around me people are doing the same thing, and somehow all of those hard-working people are an encouragement. The art lounge is always quiet, too—quieter than the library—and it doesn't smell like the library.

Grandma Moses, *Catching the Thanksgiving Turkey*. Courtesy of Grandma Moses Properties Co.

AS YOU BEGIN A COLLEGE WRITING COURSE, YOU NEED TO GET RID OF SOME MYTHS ABOUT WRITING THAT YOU MAY HAVE BEEN PACKING AROUND FOR SOME TIME. Don't allow misconceptions to ruin a good experience. Here are a few common myths about writing, followed by some facts compiled from the experiences of working writers.

MYTH "Good writers are born, not made. A writing course really won't help my writing."
FACT: *Writers acquire their skills the same way athletes do—through practice and hard work.* There are very few "born" writers. Most writers—even professional writers and journalists—are not continually inspired to write. In fact, they often experience "writer's block"—the stressful experience of staring helplessly at a piece of paper, unable to think or to put words down on paper. A writing course will teach you how to cope with your procrastination, anxiety, lack of "inspiration," and false starts by focusing directly on solving the problems that occur during the writing process.
MYTH: "Writing courses are just a review of boring grammar and punctuation. When teachers read your writing, the only thing they mark is that stuff, anyway."
FACT: *Learning and communicating—not grammar and punctuation—come first in college writing courses.* Knowledge of grammar, spelling, punctuation, and usage is essential to editing, but it is secondary to discovering ideas, thinking, learning, and communicating. In a writing course, students learn to revise and improve the content and organization of each other's writing. *Then* they help each other edit for grammar, punctuation, or spelling errors.
MYTH: "College writing courses are really 'creative writing,' which is not what my major requires. If I wanted to be another Shakespeare and write poetry, I'd change my major."
FACT: *Writing courses emphasize rhetoric, not poetry.* Rhetoric involves practicing the most effective means or strategies for informing or persuading an audience. All writing—even technical or business writing—is "creative." Deciding what to write, how to write it, how best to get your reader's attention, and how to inform or persuade your reader requires creativity and imagination. Every major requires the skills that writing courses teach: exploring new ideas, learning concepts and processes, communicating with others, and finding fresh or creative solutions to problems.
MYTH "Writing courses are not important in college or the real world. I'll never have to write, anyway."
FACT *Writing courses do have a significant effect on your success in college,*

I work at my writing as an athlete does at... training, taking it very seriously. What is important is the truth in it and the way that truth is expressed.
—EDNA O'BRIEN, NOVELIST AND PLAYWRIGHT

BACKGROUND ON MYTHS

Discussing myths about writing is the first step in probing how your students translate plans into writing. The whole point of teaching "writing process" is to shift from responding only to written products to responding to how writers' plans and intentions translate into written documents. Discussing writing myths at the beginning of the course, discussing writing plans during a workshop, and reviewing writing in postscripts are all strategies to help students translate plans into written discourse.

TEACHING TIP

Students often don't believe that writing skills are necessary in their majors. Two activities may change that attitude. First, discuss typical essay questions from other classes (see the Appendix on "Writing Under Pressure"). Second, invite an instructor in history, business, animal science, or engineering to speak to your class for ten minutes about the importance of writing in his or her discipline. Ask this instructor to bring some examples of good and poor writing to illustrate the importance of effective writing.

on the job, and in life. Even if you don't have frequent, formal writing assignments in other courses, writing improves your note taking, reading comprehension, and thinking skills. When you do have other written tasks or assignments, a writing course teaches you to *adapt* your writing to a variety of different purposes and audiences—whether you are writing a lab report in biology, a letter to an editor, a complaint to the Better Business Bureau, or a memorandum to your boss. Taking a writing course helps you express yourself more clearly, confidently, and persuasively—a skill that comes in handy whether you're writing a philosophy essay, a job application, or a love letter.

The most important fact about writing is that *you are already a writer.* You have been writing for years. A writer is someone who writes, not someone who writes a nationally syndicated newspaper column, publishes a bestseller, or wins a Pulitzer Prize. To be an effective writer, you don't have to earn a million dollars; you just have to practice writing often enough to get acquainted with its personal benefits for you and its value for others.

■ **WARM-UP EXERCISE: FREEWRITING** Put this book aside—right now—and take out pencil or pen and a piece of paper. Use this free exercise (private, unjudged, ungraded) to remind yourself that you are already a writer. Time yourself for five minutes. Write on the first thing that comes to mind—*anything whatsoever.* Write *nonstop.* Keep writing even if you have to write, "I can't think of anything to say. This feels stupid!" When you get an idea, pursue it.

When five minutes are up, stop writing and reread what you have written. Whether you write about a genuinely interesting topic or about the weather, freewriting is an excellent way to warm up, to get into the habit of writing, and to establish a writing ritual.

Remind students that they are also readers—of print and visual media. The *ABC News/Prentice Hall Video Guide* will help to link your students' television literacy to their goals as writers. The focus is on common principles of good communication.

WRITING FITNESS: RITUALS AND PRACTICE

Writing is no more magic or inspiration than any other human activity that you admire: figure skating at the Olympics, rebuilding a car engine, cooking a gourmet meal, or acting in a play. Behind every human achievement are many unglamorous hours of practice—working and sweating, falling flat on your face, and picking yourself up again. You can't learn to write just by reading some chapters in a textbook or by memorizing other people's advice. You need help and advice, but you also need practice. Consider the following parable about a Chinese painter:

> A rich patron once gave money to the painter Chu Ta, asking him to paint a picture of a fish. Three years later, when he still had not received the painting, the patron went to Chu Ta's house to ask why the picture was not done. Chu Ta did not answer but dipped a brush in ink and with a few strokes drew a splendid fish. "If it is so easy," asked the patron, "why didn't you give me the picture three years ago?" Again, Chu Ta did not answer. Instead, he opened the door of a large cabinet. Thousands of pictures of fish tumbled out.

Most writers develop little rituals that help them practice their writing. A ritual is a *repeated pattern of behavior* that provides structure, security, and a sense of progress to the one who practices it. Creating your own writing rituals and making them part of your regular routine will help reduce that dreaded initial panic and enable you to call upon your writing process with confidence when you need it.

Place, Time, and Tools

Some writers work best in pen and ink, sprawled on their beds in the afternoon while pets snooze on nearby blankets. Others start at 8 A.M. and rely on hard chairs, clean tables, and a handful of Number 2 pencils sharpened to needle points. Still others are most comfortable with the blinking amber or green lights of word processors at midnight. Legal-sized pads help some writers produce, while others feel motivated by spiral notebooks with pictures of mountain streams on the covers. Only you can determine which place, time, and tools give you the best support as a writer.

The place where you write is also extremely important. If you are writing in a computer lab, you have to adapt to that place, but if you write a draft in longhand, on a typewriter, or on your own word processor, you can choose the place yourself. In selecting a place, keep the following tips in mind:

- *Keep distractions minimal.* Some people simply can't write in the kitchen, where the refrigerator is distractingly close, or in a room that has a TV in it. On the other hand, a public place—a library, an empty classroom, a cafeteria—can be fine as long as the surrounding activity does not disturb you.
- *Control interruptions.* If you can close the door to your room and work without interruptions, fine. But even then, other people often assume that you want to take a break when *they* do. Choose a place where *you* can decide when it's time to take a break.
- *Have access to notes, journal, textbooks, sources, and other materials.* If the place is totally quiet but you don't have room to work or

Writing is [like] making a table. With both you are working with reality, a material just as hard as wood. Both are full of tricks and techniques. Basically very little magic and a lot of hard work are involved.... What is a privilege, however, is to do a job to your own satisfaction.
—GABRIEL GARCÍA MARQUEZ, NOBEL PRIZE-WINNING AUTHOR OF <u>ONE HUNDRED YEARS OF SOLITUDE</u>

TEACHING TIP

A ritual is a ceremonial behavior performed not for its own sake but for some other goal. Fastening a car seat belt is a habit, but it becomes a ritual if we regularly use that act to remind us to drive defensively. In writing, even avoidance rituals—sharpening pencils, fixing coffee, cleaning your desk—can lead to successful writing.

Writers are notorious for using any reason to keep from working: overresearching, retyping, going to meetings, waxing the floors—anything.
—GLORIA STEINEM, FORMER EDITOR OF MS. MAGAZINE

access to important notes or sources, you still may not make much progress. Whatever you need—a desk to spread your work out on, access to notes and sources, a pencil sharpener—make sure your place has it.

The time of day you write and the tools you write with can also affect your attitude and efficiency. Some people like to write early in the morning, before their busy days start; others like to write in the evening, after classes or work. Whatever time you choose, try to write *regularly*—at least three days a week—at about the same time. If you're trying to get in shape by jogging, swimming, or doing aerobics, you wouldn't exercise for five straight hours on Monday and then take four days off. Like exercise, writing requires regular practice and conditioning.

Your writing tools—pen, pencil, paper, legal pads, four-by six-inch notecards, notebooks, computer—should also be comfortable for you. Some writers like to make notes with pencil and paper and write drafts on computers, some like to do all composing on computers. As you try different combinations of tools, be aware of how you feel and whether your tools make you more effective. If you feel comfortable, it will be easier to establish rituals that lead to regular practice.

Rituals are important because they help you with the most difficult part of writing—getting started. So use your familiar place, time, and tools to trick yourself into getting some words down on paper. Your mind will devise clever schemes to avoid writing those first ten words—watching TV, balancing your checkbook, drinking some more coffee, or calling a friend and whining together about all the writing you have to do. But if your body has been through the ritual before, it will walk calmly to your favorite place, where all your tools are ready (perhaps bringing the mind kicking and screaming all the way). Then, after you get the first ten words down, the mind will say, "Hey, this isn't so bad—I've got something to say about that!" And off you'll go.

Each time you perform your writing ritual, the *next* time you write will be that much easier. Soon, your ritual will let you know: "*This is where you write. This is when you write. This is what you write with.*" No fooling around. Just writing.

Energy and Attitude

Once you've tricked yourself into the first ten words, you need to keep your attitude positive and your energy high. When you see an intimidating wall starting to form in front of you, don't ram your head into it; figure out a way to sneak around it. Try these few tricks and techniques:

- *Start anywhere, quickly*. No law says that when you sit down to write a draft, you have to "begin at the beginning." If the first sentence is hard to write, begin with the first thoughts that come to mind. Or begin with a good example from your experience. Use that to get you going; then come back and rewrite your beginning after you've figured out what you want to say.
- *Write the easiest parts first*. Forcing yourself to start a piece of writing by working on the hardest part first is a sure way to make yourself hate writing. Take the path of least resistance. If you can't get your thesis to come out right, jot down more examples. If you can't think of examples, go back to brainstorming.
- *Keep moving*. Once you've plunged in, write as fast as you can—whether you are scribbling ideas out with a pencil or hitting the keys of a typewriter or a computer. Maintain your momentum. Reread if you need to, but then plunge ahead.
- *Quit when you know what comes next*. When you do have to quit for the day, stop at a place where you know what comes next. Don't drain the well dry; stop in the middle of something you know how to finish. Make a few notes about what you need to do next and circle them. Leave yourself an easy place to get started next time.

One of the most important strategies for every writer is to *give yourself a break from the past and begin with a fresh image*. In many fields—mathematics, athletics, art, engineering—some people are late bloomers. Don't let that C or D you got in English back in the tenth grade hold you back now like a ball and chain. Imagine yourself cutting the chain and watching the ball roll away for good. Now you are free to start fresh with a clean slate. Your writing rituals should include only positive images about the writer you are right now and realistic expectations about what you can accomplish.

I am by nature lazy, sluggish and of low energy. It constantly amazes me that I do anything at all.
—MARGARET ATWOOD,
WHO HAS MANAGED TO PRODUCE NUMEROUS BOOKS OF FICTION AND POETRY

Since I began writing I have always played games. . . . I have a playful nature; I have never been able to do things because it is my duty to do them. If I can find a way to do my duty by playing a game, then I can manage.
—MARIA IRENE FORNES,
OBIE AWARD-WINNING PLAYWRIGHT

Film and television offer strong visual models for the activities of composing. *The Video Guide* shows how to relate familiar roles like "news anchor", "talk show host", and "investigative reporter" to student-writing tasks.

- *Visualize yourself writing.* Successful athletes know how to visualize a successful tennis swing, a basketball free throw, or a baseball swing. When you are planning your activities for the day, visualize yourself writing at your favorite place. Seeing yourself doing your writing will enable you to start writing more quickly and maintain a positive attitude.
- *Discover and emphasize the aspects of writing that are fun for you.* Emphasize whatever is enjoyable for you—discovering an idea, getting the organization of a paragraph to come out right, clearing the unnecessary words and junk out of your writing. Concentrating on the parts you enjoy will help you make it through the tougher parts.
- *Set modest goals for yourself.* Don't aim for the stars; just work on a sentence. Don't measure yourself against some great writer; be your own yardstick. Compare what you write to what *you* have written before.
- *Congratulate yourself for the writing you do.* Writing is hard work; you're using words to create ideas and meanings literally out of nothing. So pat yourself on the back occasionally. Keep in mind the immortal words of comedian and playwright Steve Martin: "I think I did pretty well, considering I started out with nothing but a bunch of blank paper."

Keeping a Journal

"I carry a journal with me almost all the time . . ."
—NTOZAKE SHANGE, AUTHOR OF THE PLAY FOR COLORED GIRLS WHO HAVE CONSIDERED SUICIDE WHEN THE RAINBOW IS ENUF

Many writers keep some kind of notebook in which they write down their thoughts for later use. Some writers call it a "journal," a place for their day-to-day thoughts. Other writers call it a "daybook," a place to record ideas, collected information, possible outlines, titles, questions—anything related to the process of writing, thinking, and learning. Scientists and social scientists keep daily logs in which they record data or describe behavior. The word "journal" is the general term referring to "a place for daily writing." Whatever you call it, it should become part of your writing ritual. In it should go all kinds of writing. Bits and pieces of experience or memory that might come in handy later. Summary/responses of essays you read. In-class write-to-learn entries. Plans for writing your essays. A log of your writing plans and the writing problems you face. Postscripts on your writing process. Your journal is a place to practice, a closet where all your "fish paintings" go.

As the following list indicates, there are many kinds of journal entries, but they fall into three categories: *Reading Entries*, *Write-to-Learn Entries*, and *Writing Entries*. Reading entries help you understand

and actively respond to student or professional writing. Write-to-learn entries help you summarize, react to, or question ideas or essays discussed in class. Writing entries help you warm up, test ideas, make writing plans, practice rhetorical strategies, or solve specific writing problems. All three kinds of journal writing, however, take advantage of the unique relationship between thinking, writing, and learning. Simply put, writing helps you learn what you know (and don't know) by shaping your thoughts into language.

"The most valuable writing tool I have is my daybook. . . . I write in my lap, in the living room or on the porch, in the car or an airplane, in meetings at the university, in bed, or sitting down on a rock wall during a walk. . . . It is always a form of talking to myself, a way of thinking on paper.

—DONALD MURRAY, JOURNALIST, AUTHOR OF BOOKS AND ESSAYS ABOUT WRITING

Reading Entries

- *Prereading journal entries.* Before you read an essay, read the headnote and write for five minutes on the topic of the essay—what you know about the subject, what related experiences you have had, and what opinions you hold. After you write your entry, the class can discuss the topic before you read the essay. The result? Your reading will be more active, engaged, and responsive.
- *Double-entry logs.* Draw a line vertically down a sheet of paper. On the left-hand side, summarize key ideas as you reread an essay. On the right-hand side, write down your reactions, responses, and questions. Writing while you read helps you understand and respond more thoroughly.
- *Essay annotations.* Writing your comments in the margin as you read is sometimes more efficient than writing separate journal entries. Also, in a small group in class, you can share your annotations and collaboratively annotate a copy of the essay.
- *Vocabulary entries.* Looking up unfamiliar words in a dictionary and writing out definitions in your journal will make you a much more accurate reader. Often an essay's thesis, meaning, or tone will hinge on the meanings of a few key words.
- *Summary/response entries.* Double-entry logs help you understand while you reread, but a short one-paragraph summary and one-paragraph response after you finish your rereading helps you focus on both the main ideas of a passage and your own key responses.

Students can also use double-entry Viewing Logs to become more active, critical "readers" of television. See Chapter 1 of the *Video Guide*.

Write-to-Learn Entries

- *Lecture/discussion entries.* At key points in a class lecture or discussion, your teacher may ask you to write for five minutes by responding to a few questions: What is the main idea of the discussion? What one question would you like to ask? How does the topic of discussion relate to the essay that you are currently writing?

RESOURCE NOTE

This list represents only the tip of the iceberg of possibilities for journal entries. Three good sources for other journal ideas are Peter Elbow, *Writing Without Teachers;* Donald Murray, *Write to Learn*; and Toby Fulwiler, *The Journal Book.* (See *Teacher's Guide* for complete citations.)

- *Responses to essays.* Before discussing an essay, write for a few minutes to respond to the following questions: What is the main idea of this essay? What do you like best about the essay? What is confusing, misleading, or wrong in this essay? What strategies illustrated in this essay will help you with your own writing?
- *Time-out responses.* During a controversial discussion or argument about an essay, your teacher may stop the class, take time-out, and ask you to write for five minutes to respond to several questions: What key issue is the class debating? What are the main points of disagreement? What is your opinion? What evidence, either in the essay or in your experience, supports your opinion?

Writing Entries

- *Warming up.* Writing, like any other kind of activity, improves when you loosen up, stretch, get the kinks out, practice a few lines. Any daybook or journal entry gives you a chance to warm up.
- *Collecting and shaping exercises.* Some journal entries will help you collect information by observing, remembering, or investigating people, places, events, or objects. You can also record quotations or startling statistics for future writing topics. Other journal entries suggested in each chapter of this book will help you practice organizing your information. Strategies of development, such as comparison/contrast, definition, classification, or process analysis will help you discover and shape ideas.
- *Writing for a specific audience.* In some journal entries, you need to play a role. Imagine that you are in a specific situation, writing for a defined audience. For example, you might write a letter of application for a job or letter to a friend explaining why you've chosen a certain major.
- *Identifying and solving writing problems.* Your journal is also the place to keep a log—a running account of your writing plans, problems, and solutions. Include your research notes and postscripts on your writing process in this log.
- *Imitating styles of writers.* Use your journal to copy passages from writers you like. Practice imitating their styles on different topics. Also, try simply transcribing a few paragraphs. Even copying effective writers' words will reveal some of their secrets for successful writing.
- *Making free journal entries.* Use your journal to record ideas, reactions to people on campus, events in the news, reactions to controversial articles in the campus newspaper, conversations after class or work, or just your private thoughts.

For each of these writing entries, let your ideas flow easily. Don't stop to fix spelling or punctuation. Focus on key images from your train of thought.

Below is a sample of a freewriting entry. The author, Terri Ciccarello, had originally decided to write about a bumper sticker that she had seen, but the more she wrote, the more it suggested related ideas to her. Although she never wrote an essay about that bumper sticker, the theme of being an individual and wanting to make the world a better place was an undercurrent in several of her essays. Articulating these questions helped her discover what she wanted to write about.

I just bought a bumper sticker, white writing on black that reads, "Are we having fun yet?" It struck me as funny. The purpose of that bumper sticker for those who display it is to make a statement about a way of life. Are we having fun yet? It conveys a sense of dissatisfaction at the way life is supposed to be. It's an attitude. Why does it have to be structured the way it is? Does everyone have to fit in? Is this it? Is this all? Are we having fun yet? Are we supposed to be? When do I get to do what I want to do? Why don't things go my way? Can't I play by my own rules?

That seems like a lot of "message" in one little saying, but when I read it for the first time, that's what it brought to my mind. So, I was part of the audience. I think a lot of people, especially young people are the intended audience for this sticker. Young people who are still idealistic; who think that maybe there is still time to change the world. Young people who are brought into a society they didn't organize and if they had, it would have been done differently. Young people who want to be individuals when they "grow up", not just another nameless faceless joe blow on the street. Are we having fun yet? When is it our turn to run the show?

— Terri Ciccarello

TEACHING TIP

Teachers may prefer to assign one or two journal suggestions that relate to an upcoming class discussion. The students' response to suggestion 2 is a good lead-in to a discussion of writing processes; suggestion 3 may point to problems that students have—or *think* they have. Suggestion 4 is vital: Do they think all essays have five paragraphs? Should they use big words, write in complicated sentences, and avoid using "I"? Ask each student to bring in one piece of "good" writing so that the class has specific examples of various styles, purposes, and genres of writing to illustrate their preconceptions or preferences.

■ **WARMING UP: JOURNAL EXERCISES** Choose three of the exercises below and write for ten minutes on each. Date and number each entry.

1. Make an "authority" list of activities, subjects, ideas, places, people, or events that you already know something about. List as many topics as you can. If your reaction is, "I'm not really an *authority* on anything," then imagine you've met someone from another school, state, country, or historical period. Regarding that person as your audience, what are you an "authority" on?

2. Choose one activity, sport, or hobby that you do well and that others might admire you for. In the form of a letter to a friend, describe the steps or stages of the process through which you acquired that skill or ability.

3. In two or three sentences, complete the following thought: "I have trouble writing because . . ."

4. In a few sentences, complete the following thought: "In my previous classes and from my own writing experience, I've learned that the three most important rules about writing are . . ."

5. Describe your own writing rituals. *When*, *where*, and *how* do you write best?

6. Write an open journal entry. Describe events from your day, images, impressions, bits of conversation—anything that catches your interest. For possible ideas for open journal entries, read the following essay by Roy Hoffman.

ON KEEPING A JOURNAL

ROY HOFFMAN

In a Newsweek On Campus *essay, Roy Hoffman describes his own experience, recording events and trying out ideas just as an artist doodles on a sketch pad. Your own journal entries about events, images, descriptions of people, and bits of conversation will not only improve your writing but will also become your own personal time capsule, to dig up and reread in the year 2020.*

Wherever I go I carry a small notebook in my coat or back pocket for thoughts, observations and impressions. As a writer I use this notebook as an artist would a sketch pad, for stories and essays, and as a sporadic journal of my comings and goings. When I first started keeping notebooks, though, I was not yet a professional writer. I was still in college.

I made my first notebook entries in the summer of 1972, just after my freshman year, in what was actually a travel log. A buddy and I were setting out to trek from our Alabama hometown to the distant tundra of Alaska. With unbounded enthusiasm I began: "Wild, crazy ecstasy wants to wrench my head from my body". The log, written in a university composition book, goes on to chronicle our adventures in the land where the sun never sets, the bars never close and the prepipeline employment prospects were so bleak we ended up taking jobs as night janitors.

When I returned to college that fall I had a small revelation: the world around me of libraries, quadrangles, Frisbees and professors was as rich with material for my journals and notebooks as galumphing moose and garrulous fishermen.

These college notebooks, which built to a pitch my senior year, are gold mines to me now. Classrooms, girlfriends, cups of coffee and lines of poetry—from mine to John Keats's—float by like clouds. As I lie beneath these clouds again, they take on familiar and distinctive shapes.

Though I can remember the campus's main quadrangle, I see it more vividly when I read my description of school on a visit during summer break: "the muggy, lassitudinal air . . . the bird noises that can not be pointed to, the summer emptiness that grows emptier with a few students squeaking by the library on poorly oiled bicycles." An economics professor I fondly remember returns with less fondness in my notebooks, "staring down at the class with his equine face." And a girl I had a crush on senior year, whom I now recall mistily, reappears with far more vitality as "the ample, slightly-gawky, whole-wheat, fractured object of my want gangling down the hall in spring heat today."

When, in reading over my notebooks, I am not peering out at quadrangles, midterm exams, professors or girlfriends, I see a portrait of my parents and hometown during holidays and occasional weekend breaks. Like a wheel, home revolves, each turn regarded differently depending on the novel or political essay I'd been most influenced by the previous semester.

Mostly, though, in wandering back through my notebooks, I meet someone who could be my younger brother: the younger version of myself. The younger me seems moodier, more inquisitive, more fun-loving and surprisingly eager to stay up all night partying or figuring out electron orbitals for a 9 a.m. exam. The younger me wanders through a hall of mirrors of the self, writes of "seeing two or three of myself on every corner," and pens long meditations on God and society before scribbling in the margin, "what a child I am." The younger me also finds

Encourage students to think of a notebook as a camera as well as a sketch pad, an instrument for recording the moving sights and sounds around them.

humor in trying to keep track of this hall of mirrors, commenting in ragged verse.

I hope that one day
Some grandson or cousin
Will read these books,
And know that I was
Once a youth
Sitting in drugstores with
Anguished looks.
And poring over coffee,
And should have poured
The coffee
Over these lines.

I believe that every college student should attempt to keep some form of notebook, journal or diary. A notebook is a secret garden in which to dance, sing, muse, wander, perform handstands, even cry. In the privacy of this little book, you can make faces, curse, turn somersaults and ask yourself if you're *really* in love. A notebook or journal is one of the few places you can call just your own.

. . . Journal writing suffers when you let someone, in your mind, look over your shoulder. Honesty wilts when a parent, teacher or friend looms up in your imagination to discourage you from putting your *true* thoughts on the page. Journal writing also runs a related hazard: the dizzying suspicion that one day your private thoughts, like those of Samuel Pepys or Virginia Woolf, will be published in several volumes and land up required reading for English 401. How can you write comfortably when the eyes of all future readers are upon you? Keep your notebooks with the abandon of one who knows his words will go up in smoke. Then you might really strike fire a hundred years or so from now if anyone cares to pry.

By keeping notebooks, you improve your writing ability, increasing your capacity to communicate both with yourself and others. By keeping notebooks, you discover patterns in yourself, whether lazy ones that need to be broken or healthy ones that can use some nurturing. By keeping notebooks, you heighten some moments and give substance to others: even a journey to the washateria offers potential for some offbeat journal observations. And by keeping notebooks while still in college, you chart a terrain that, for many, is more dynamically charged with ideas and discussions than the practical, workaday world just beyond. Notebooks, I believe, not only help us remember this dynamic charge, but also help us sustain it.

Not long ago, while traveling with a friend in Yorktown, Va., I passed by a time capsule buried in the ground in 1976, intended to be dug up in

2076. Keeping notebooks and journals is rather like burying time capsules into one's own life. There's no telling what old rock song, love note, philosophical complaint or rosy Saturday morning you'll unearth when you dig up these personal time capsules. You'll be able to piece together a remarkable picture of where you've come from, and may well get some important glimmers about where you're going.

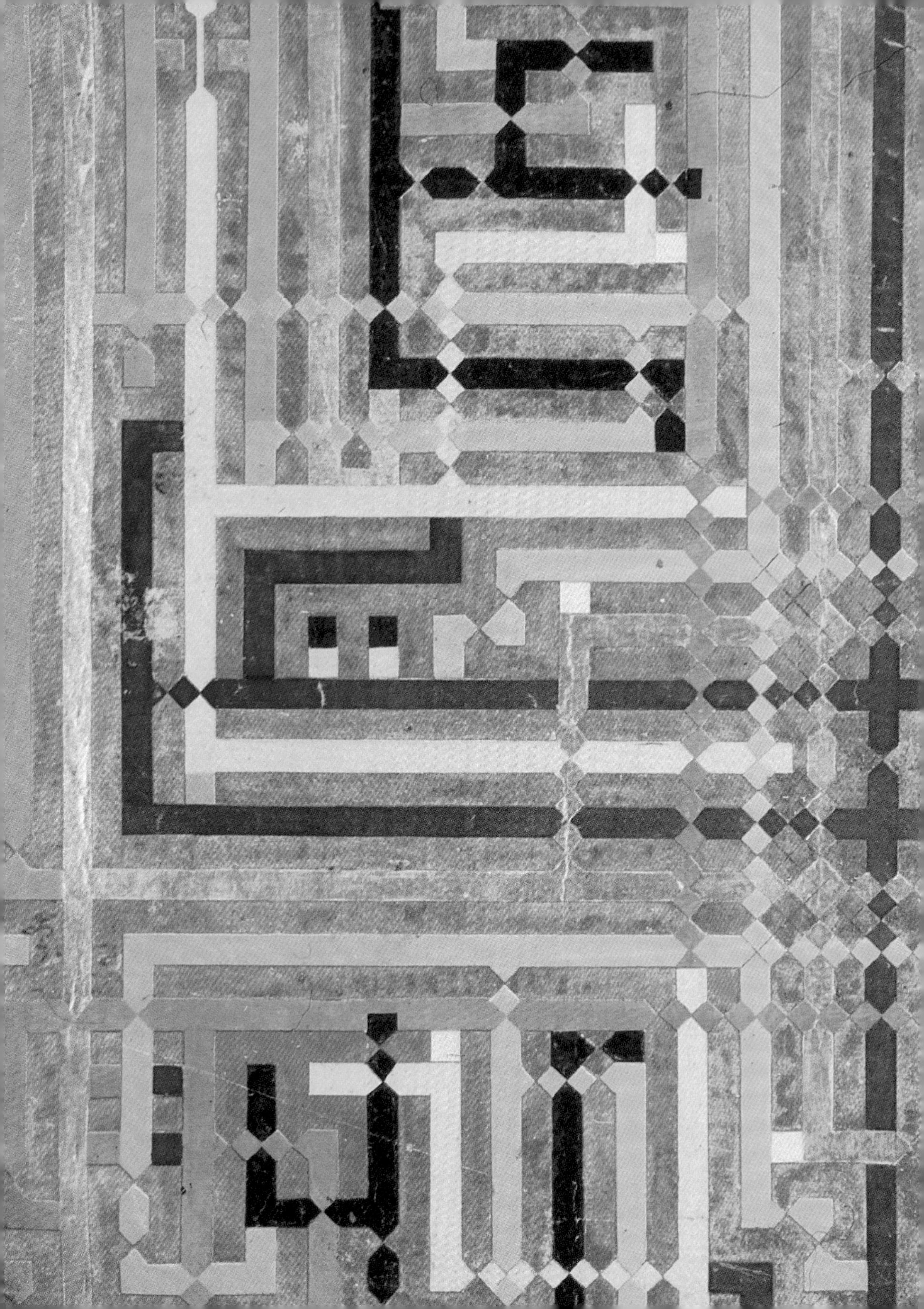

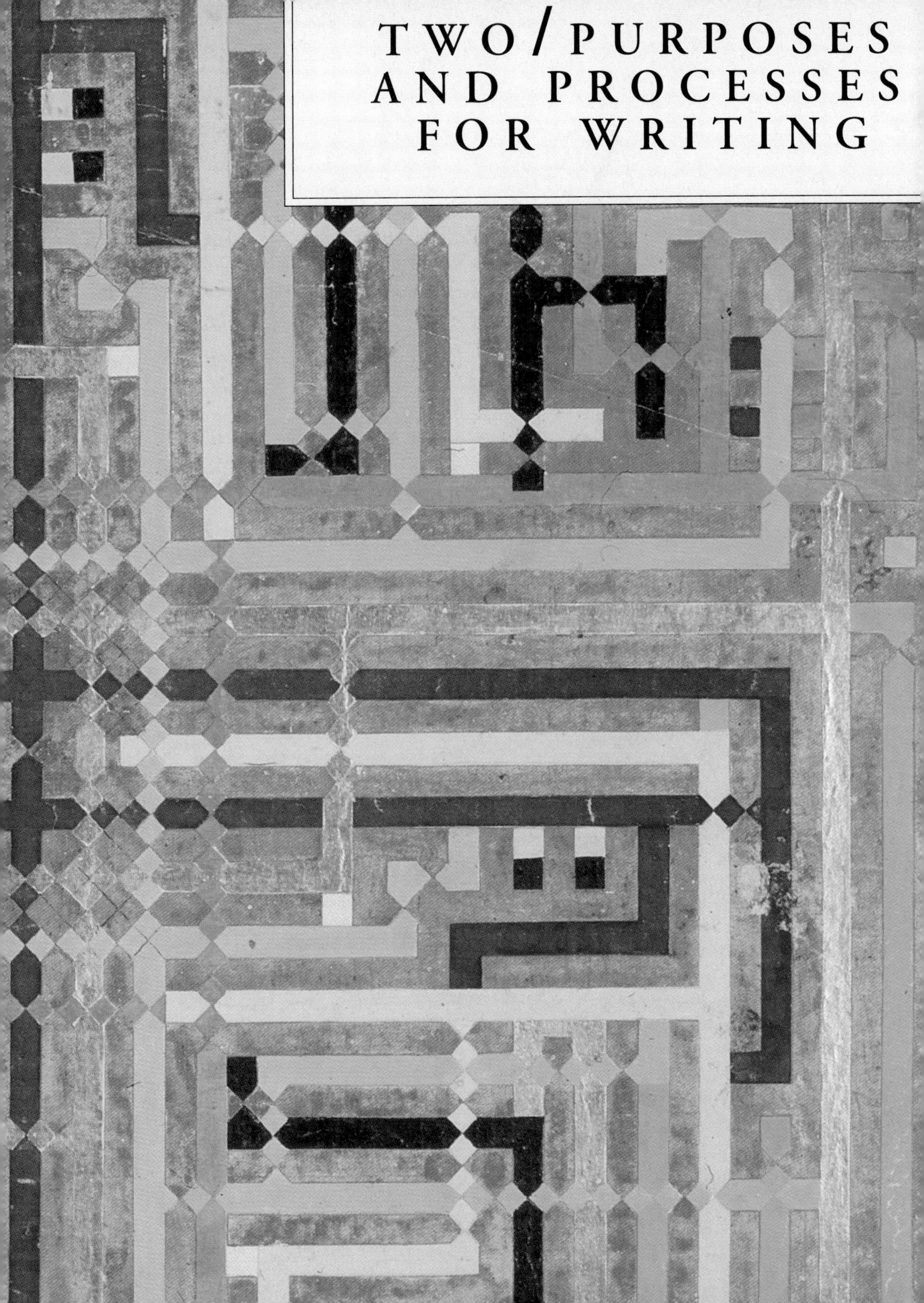

TWO / PURPOSES AND PROCESSES FOR WRITING

First and foremost I write for myself. Writing has been for a long time my major tool for self-instruction and self-development.

—TONI CADE BAMBARA, AUTHOR OF THE SALT EATERS

How do I know what I think until I see what I say?

—E.M. FORSTER, AUTHOR OF A PASSAGE TO INDIA

AS A CHINESE AMERICAN WOMAN GROWING UP IN AMERICA, YOU DECIDE TO WRITE ABOUT THE DIFFICULTY OF LIVING IN TWO CULTURES. You recall how, during your childhood, you rebelled against your mother when she insisted that you learn about your Chinese heritage. You remember how much you hated your Chinese school and how embarrassed you were that your mother could not speak English properly. As you grew older, however, you realized the price you paid for your assimilation into American culture. After discussing this conflict with your friends, you decide to describe your experiences to others who share them or who may want to know what you learned. At that point, you write an autobiographical account of your experiences and send it to a metropolitan newspaper.

A VETERAN SMOKER, YOU HAVE BECOME INCREASINGLY IRRITATED AT THE NONSMOKING REGULATIONS THAT HAVE APPEARED IN RESTAURANTS, BUSINESSES, AND OTHER PUBLIC PLACES. And it's not just the laws that are irritating, but the holier-than-thou attitude of people who presume that what's good for them should be good for you. Nonsmoking laws seem to give people license to censure your behavior while totally ignoring their own offensive behavior: polluting the atmosphere with hydrocarbons, fouling the aquifers with fertilizers, and generally corrupting the social air with odors of false superiority. So after one particularly memorable experience, you write a letter to the editor of the local paper, intending not only to express your own frustration but also to satirize all those smug do-gooders.

Page from the Album of the Conqueror (Topkapu Palace Museum, Istanbul)

THE WRITING FOR THIS COURSE (AND THE STRUCTURE OF THIS TEXTBOOK) STARTS WITH THE PREMISE THAT EFFECTIVE COMMUNICATION BEGINS WITH LEARNING. It also assumes that learning results—at least in part—from your written efforts to make connections and see relationships between your own observations and experience and the written or collected knowledge of others. There are four important sources for learning, writing, and communication:

- observing and describing the world around you
- remembering and drawing on your experiences
- reading and responding to textual material
- investigating knowledge through interviews, surveys, and library sources.

Writing, as a means of learning and communicating, begins with what you see and have experienced. It then makes use of what you're reading in texts, hearing in lectures, finding out at work, or learning from friends and family.

■ **Freewriting: Inventory of Your Writing** Before you read further in this chapter, take out a pen or pencil and a piece of paper and inventory what you have written in the last year or two. Brainstorm a list of everything you can think of: grocery lists, letters, wedding invitations, reports, school essays, notes to friends, applications for jobs, memos to your boss. Then for *one* of your longer writing projects, jot down several sentences describing the situation that called for that piece of writing—*when* you did it, *whom* you wrote it for, *what* its purpose was, *where* you wrote it, and *how* you went about writing it.

Most good writing has a personal dimension. It may be about the writer personally or it may address a subject or an idea the writer cares about. It begins with honesty, curiosity, inquiry, and even vulnerability. Good writers assert themselves, knowing that they are vulnerable to other people's criticism. They take risks—sometimes writing on subjects they don't completely understand—knowing that taking their thoughts to a public forum is one way to actively engage the information that threatens to overwhelm them. By continually probing and learning, being honest with themselves, and accepting risks, writers can use their writing to teach themselves as well as their readers.

Write to Learn

A write-to-learn activity occurs when writers write for themselves—to record what they think, feel, see, remember, and read. The audience for such activities is the individual writer. The purpose is to help the writer learn, think, discover, and remember. In the classroom, one advantage of a write-to-learn activity is that writing, unlike lecture or discussion, requires *active engagement of a topic by every student.* Write-to-learn activities include freewriting, clustering, taking double-entry notes, writing two-minute summaries of class discussion, writing questions during class, describing people and behavior, recalling past events, annotating written texts, recording consensus ideas from small groups, and writing plans for essays. This textbook assumes that observing, remembering, and investigating are also write-to-learn strategies, not just rhetorical forms (description, narration, investigation).

WRITING FOR MYSELF

RUSSELL BAKER

For many years, Russell Baker wrote humorous essays for The New York Times. *Before that, however, he was just a writer—someone who wrote about his experiences, what he was learning or was curious about, or what he found amusing or absurd. In this selection from his autobiography,* Growing Up, *Baker describes how bored he was as a student required to write "compositions," until he found a topic that had a personal dimension for him. The essay he wrote for his composition class, on the art of eating spaghetti, taught Baker an important truth: Writers should write honestly about topics that are important—even fun—for them.*

The notion of becoming a writer had flickered off and on in my head since the Belleville days, but it wasn't until my third year in high school that the possibility took hold. Until then I'd been bored by everything associated with English courses. I found English grammar dull and baffling. I hated the assignments to turn out leaden, lackluster paragraphs that were agonies for teachers to read and for me to write. The classics thrust on me to read seemed as deadening as chloroform.

When our class was assigned to Mr. Fleagle for third-year English I anticipated another grim year in that dreariest of subjects. Mr. Fleagle was notorious among City students for dullness and inability to inspire. He was said to be stuffy, dull, and hopelessly out of date. To me he looked to be sixty or seventy and prim to a fault. He wore primly severe eyeglasses, his wavy hair was primly cut and primly combed. He wore prim vested suits with neckties blocked primly against the collar buttons of his primly starched white shirts. He had a primly pointed jaw, a primly straight nose, and a prim manner of speaking that was so correct, so gentlemanly, that he seemed a comic antique.

I anticipated a listless, unfruitful year with Mr. Fleagle and for a long time was not disappointed. Late in the year we tackled the informal essay. Mr. Fleagle distributed a homework sheet offering us a choice of topics. None was quite so simpleminded as "What I Did on My Summer Vacation," but most seemed to be almost as dull. I took the list home and dawdled until the night before the essay was due. Sprawled on the sofa, I finally faced up to the grim task, took the list out of my notebook, and scanned it. The topic on which my eye stopped was "The Art of Eating Spaghetti."

This title produced an extraordinary sequence of mental images. Surging up out of the depths of memory came a vivid recollection of a night in Belleville when all of us were seated around the supper table—

Uncle Allen, my mother, Uncle Charlie, Doris, Uncle Hal—and Aunt Pat served spaghetti for supper. Spaghetti was an exotic treat in those days. Neither Doris nor I had ever eaten spaghetti, and none of the adults had enough experience to be good at it. All the good humor of Uncle Allen's house reawoke in my mind as I recalled the laughing arguments we had that night about the socially respectable method for moving spaghetti from plate to mouth.

Suddenly I wanted to write about that, about the warmth and good feeling of it, but I wanted to put it down simply for my own joy, not for Mr. Fleagle. It was a moment I wanted to recapture and hold for myself. I wanted to relive the pleasure of an evening at New Street. To write it as I wanted, however, would violate all the rules of formal composition I'd learned in school, and Mr. Fleagle would surely give it a failing grade. Never mind. I would write something else for Mr. Fleagle after I had written this thing for myself.

When I finished it the night was half gone and there was no time left to compose a proper, respectable essay for Mr. Fleagle. There was no choice next morning but to turn in my private reminiscence of Belleville. Two days passed before Mr. Fleagle returned the graded papers, and he returned everyone's but mine. I was bracing myself for a command to report to Mr. Fleagle immediately after school for discipline when I saw him lift my paper from his desk and rap for the class's attention.

"Now, boys," he said. "I want to read you an essay. This is titled, 'The Art of Eating Spaghetti.'"

And he started to read. My words! He was reading my words out loud to the entire class. What's more, the entire class was listening. Listening attentively. Then somebody laughed, then the entire class was laughing, and not in contempt and ridicule, but with openhearted enjoyment. Even Mr. Fleagle stopped two or three times to repress a small prim smile.

I did my best to avoid showing pleasure, but what I was feeling was pure ecstasy at this startling demonstration that my words had the power to make people laugh. In the eleventh grade, at the eleventh hour as it were, I had discovered a calling. It was the happiest moment of my entire school career. When Mr. Fleagle finished he put the final seal on my happiness by saying, "Now that, boys, is an essay, don't you see. It's—don't you see—it's of the very essence of the essay, don't you see. Congratulations, Mr. Baker."

The writer may write to inform, to explain, to entertain, to persuade, but whatever the purpose there should be first of all, the satisfaction of the writer's own learning. . . .

—DONALD MURRAY, TEACHER AND PULITZER PRIZE-WINNING JOURNALIST

PURPOSES FOR WRITING

Getting a good grade, making a million dollars, or contributing to society may be among your motives for writing. However, as a writer, you also have more specific purposes for writing. These purposes help you make key decisions about content, structure, and style. When your main purpose is to express your feelings, you may write a private entry in your journal. When your main purpose is to explain how your sales promotion increased the number of your company's customers, you may write a factual report to your boss. When your main purpose is to persuade others to see a movie that you like, you may write a review for the local newspaper. In each case, the intended use or impact of what you write helps determine what you write and how you write it.

TEACHING TIP

Class discussions are more effective if students initially write about the subject. Draw on the "Freewriting" exercise in this chapter: Ask eight or ten students to select one piece of writing inventory and, at the board, briefly describe the subject, the situation, and the main purpose of that particular piece of writing. Their examples will illustrate a variety of purposes for writing.

WRITER-BASED PURPOSES

Because writing is, or should be, for yourself first of all, everything you write involves at least some purpose that benefits you. Of course, expressing yourself is a fundamental purpose of all writing. Without the satisfaction of expressing your thoughts, feelings, reactions, knowledge, or questions, you might not make the effort to write in the first place.

A closely related purpose is learning: Writing helps you discover what you think or feel, simply by using language to identify and compose your thoughts. Writing not only helps you form ideas, but actually promotes observing and remembering. If you write down what you observe about people, places, or things, you can actually "see" them more clearly. Similarly, if you write down facts, ideas, experiences, or reactions to your readings, you will remember them longer. Writing and rewriting facts, dates, definitions, impressions, or personal experiences will improve your powers of recall on such important occasions as examinations and job interviews.

I think writing is really a process of communication. . . . It's the sense of being in contact with people who are part of a particular audience that really makes a difference to me in writing.

—SHERLEY ANN WILLIAMS,
POET, CRITIC, AND NOVELIST

SUBJECT- AND AUDIENCE-BASED PURPOSES

Although some writing is intended only for yourself—such as entries in a diary, lists, class notes, reminders—much of your writing will be read by others, by those readers who constitute your "audience."

- You may write to inform others about a particular subject—to tell them about the key facts, data, feelings, people, places, or events.
- You may write to explain to your readers what something means, how it works, or why it happens.
- You may write to persuade others to believe or do something—to convince others to agree with your judgment about a book, record, or restaurant, or to persuade them to take a certain class, vote for a certain candidate, or buy some product you are advertising.
- You may write to explore ideas and "truths," to examine how your

ideas have changed, to ask questions that have no easy answers, and then to share your thoughts and reflections with others.

- You may write to entertain—as a primary purpose in itself or as a purpose combined with informing, explaining, persuading, or exploring. Whatever your purposes may be, good writing both teaches and pleases. Remember, too, that your readers will learn more, remember more, or be more convinced when your writing contains humor, wit, or imaginative language.

Combinations of Purposes

In many cases, you write with more than one purpose in mind. Purposes may appear in combinations, connected in a sequence, or actually overlapping. Initially, you may take notes about a subject to learn and remember, but later you may want to inform others about what you have discovered. Similarly, you may begin by writing to express your feelings about a movie that you loved or that upset you; later, you may wish to persuade others to see it—or not to see it.

Purposes can also contain each other, like Chinese boxes, or overlap, blurring the distinctions. An explanation of how an automobile works will contain information about that vehicle. An attempt to persuade someone to buy an automobile may contain an explanation of how it handles and information about its body style or engine. Usually, writing to persuade others will contain explanations and basic information, but the reverse is not necessarily true; you can write simply to give information, without trying to persuade anyone to do anything.

Subject, Purpose, and Thesis

The *thesis, claim,* or *main idea* in a piece of writing is related to your purpose. As a writer, you usually have a purpose in mind that serves as a guide while you gather information about your subject and think about your audience. However, as you collect and record information, impressions, and ideas you gradually narrow your subject to a specific topic and thus clarify your purpose. You bring your purpose into sharper and sharper focus—as if progressing on a target from the outer circles to the bull's-eye—until you have narrowed your purpose down to a central thesis. The thesis is the dominant idea, explanation, evaluation, or recommendation that you want to impress upon your readers.

The following examples illustrate how a writer moves from a general subject, guided by purpose, to a specific thesis or claim.

Invite students to see how the purposes for writing are also purposes for other forms of communication, like television. The Video Guide demonstrates how television news seeks to inform, persuade, and entertain specific audiences.

Writing, as a rhetorical act, is carried out within a web of purpose.
—LINDA FLOWER, TEACHER AND RESEARCHER IN COMPOSITION

Teaching Tip

This textbook uses several terms to describe the main idea of an essay: dominant idea is the key term for observing and remembering essays; thesis is used for explaining essays; and claim is used most frequently for evaluating, problem-solving, and arguing essays. Whatever term the writer or teacher uses, however, the main idea helps both writer and

TEACHING TIP (CON'T)

reader: The writer selects or rejects material based on the main idea (or the writer discovers the main idea while selecting material); the reader uses the stated main idea (or guesses about the implied main idea) in constructing meaning.

SUBJECT	PURPOSE	THESIS, CLAIM, OR MAIN IDEA
childhood experiences	To *express* your feelings and explain how one childhood experience was important.	The relentless competition between me and my sisters distorted my easygoing personality
heart disease	To *inform* readers about relationships between Type A personalities and heart attacks.	Type A personalities do not necessarily have an abnormally high risk of suffering heart attacks.
AIDS	To *persuade* readers not to quarantine AIDS victims.	Children afflicted with AIDS should not be prevented from attending school.

PURPOSE AND AUDIENCE

Writing for yourself is relatively easy; after all, you already know your audience and can make spontaneous judgments about what is essential and what is not. However, when your purpose is to communicate to other readers you need to analyze your audience. Your writing will be more effective if you can anticipate what your readers know and need to know, what they are interested in, and what their beliefs or attitudes are. As you write for different readers, you will select different kinds of information, organize it in different ways, or write in a more formal or less formal style.

■ FREEWRITING: WRITING FOR DIFFERENT AUDIENCES

Before you read further, get a pen or pencil and several sheets of paper and do the following exercise:

1. For your eyes only, write about what you did at a recent party. Write for four minutes.

2. On a second sheet of paper, describe for the members of your writing class what you did at this party; you will read it aloud to the class. Stop after four minutes.

3. On a third sheet of paper, write a letter to one of your parents describing what you did at the party. Stop after four minutes.

Students often can identify the intended audiences for specific television commercials and news programs, a good introduction to the value of audience analysis. See Chapter 2 of the *Video Guide*.

AUDIENCE ANALYSIS

If you are writing to communicate to other readers, analyzing your probable audience will help you answer some basic questions:

- How much information or evidence is enough? What should I assume my audience already knows? What should I not tell them? What do they believe? Will they readily agree with me or will they be antagonistic?
- How should I organize my writing? How can I get my readers' attention? Can I just describe my subject and tell a story or should I analyze everything in a logical order? Should I put my best examples or arguments first or last?
- Should I write informally, with simple sentences and easy vocabulary, or should I write in a more elaborate or specialized style, with technical vocabulary?

Analyze your audience by considering the following questions. As you learn more about your audience, the possibilities for your own role as a writer will become clearer.

1. **Audience profile.** How narrow or broad is your audience? Is it a narrow and defined audience—a single person, such as your Aunt Mary, or a group with clear common interests, such as the zoning board in your city or the readers of Organic Gardening? Is it a broad and diverse audience: educated readers who wish to be informed on current events, American voters as a whole, or residents of your state? Do your readers have identifiable roles? Can you determine their age, sex, economic status, ethnic background, or occupational category?

2. **Audience-subject relationship.** Consider what your readers know about your subject. If they know very little about it, you'll need to explain the basics; if they already know quite a bit, you can go straight to more difficult or complex issues. Also estimate their probable attitude toward this subject. Are they likely to be sympathetic or hostile?

3. **Audience-writer relationship.** What is your relationship with your readers? Do you know each other personally? Do you have anything in common? Will your audience be likely to trust what you say or will they be skeptical about your judgments? Are

TEACHING TIP

You may wish to collect—or better yet, have your students collect—samples of writing that illustrate a *variety* of audiences. Magazines and journals are an excellent source of writings aimed at particular audiences. List the titles of fifteen magazines available in the library or at local stores. (See *Writer's Digest* for a brief description of each magazine's audience.) Require each student to bring to class a photocopy of one piece of magazine writing. In small groups, students can then practice analyzing the audiences for articles in magazines ranging from, say, *Prevention to The New England Journal of Medicine*.

you the expert on this particular subject and the readers the novices? Or are you the novice and your readers the experts?

4. **Writer's role.** To communicate effectively with your audience, you should also consider your own role or perspective. Of the many roles that you could play (friend, big sister or brother, student of psychology, music fan, employee of a fast-food restaurant, and so on), choose one that will be effective for your purpose and audience. If, for example, you are writing to sixth-graders about nutrition, you could choose the perspective of a concerned older brother or sister. Your writing might be more effective, however, if you assume the role of a person who has worked in fast-food restaurants for three years and knows what goes into hamburgers, french fries, and milkshakes.

Writers may write to real audiences, or they may create audiences. Sometimes the relationship between writer and reader is real (sister writing to brother); so then the writer starts with a known audience and writes accordingly. Sometimes, however, writers begin and gradually discover or create an audience in the process of writing. Knowing the audience guides the writing, but the writing may create an audience as well.

RESOURCE NOTES

Writers don't always address particular audiences; sometimes they construct, create or invoke audiences. Articles by Wayne C. Booth, Douglas B. Park, and Lisa Ede and Andrea Lunsford in *Tate and Corbett, The Writing Teacher's Sourcebook*, discuss the important concept of audience and its role in the writing process.

Compare the writer's role to familiar television personalities such as Barbara Walters, Ted Koppel, Oprah Winfrey, or John Quiñones.

THE WRITING SITUATION

Taken together, the writer's purpose or aim, the subject, and the probable audience (whether yourself or others) define the writing situation. Sometimes an instructor or employer assigns you a specific writing situation. At other times, you yourself construct a situation from scratch.

The components of the writing situation—subject, purpose, thesis, and audience—are so interrelated that a change in one may affect the other three. As you write, therefore, you do not always follow a step-by-step order. You may begin, for example, with a specific audience on which you wish to make an impression; as you analyze the audience, you decide what subject and purpose would be most appropriate. Conversely, you may start with an interesting subject but no clear sense of purpose or audience. Or you may be asked to write for a certain audience and discover that its needs and expectations have led you to discover or modify your purpose or subject. In short, subject, purpose, thesis, and audience are all modified, reconsidered, and revised as you write.

The following examples illustrate how subject, purpose, and audience combine to define a writing situation.

In response to a request by an editor of a college recruiting pamphlet, a student decides to write an essay explaining the advantages of the social and academic life at his university. According to the editor, the account needs to be realistic but should also promote the university. It shouldn't be too academic and stuffy—the college catalogue itself contains all the basic information—but it should give high school seniors a flavor of college life. The student decides to write a narrative account of his most interesting experiences during his first week at college.

A student majoring in journalism reads about correspondents' accounts of restrictions during the Persian Gulf conflict. The military limited reporters to carefully controlled "pools," and during the ground offensive, television journalists' tapes were mysteriously delayed or lost until after the ground war was over. Following a class debate on the public's right to know versus the military's need to maintain secrecy in times of war, the student investigates specific incidents to see if the military exercised unnecessary or excessive censorship. The student researches these incidents and reports her findings in a letter to her congressional representative, asking for a further investigation of certain cases of alleged censorship.

Purpose and Audience in Two Essays

The two short essays that follow appeared as columns in newspapers. Both relate the writers' own experiences. They are similar in form but have different purposes and appeal to different kinds of readers. As you read each essay, decide which one you find more interesting—and why.

The Struggle to Be an All-American Girl

Elizabeth Wong

It's still there, the Chinese school on Yale Street where my brother and I used to go. Despite the new coat of paint and the high wire fence, the school I knew 10 years ago remains remarkably, stoically the same.

Every day at 5 p.m., instead of playing with our fourth- and fifth-grade friends or sneaking out to the empty lot to hunt ghosts and animal bones, my brother and I had to go to Chinese school. No amount of kicking, screaming, or pleading could dissuade my mother, who was solidly determined to have us learn the language of our heritage.

Forcibly, she walked us the seven long, hilly blocks from our home to school, depositing our defiant tearful faces before the stern principal. My only memory of him is that he swayed on his heels like a palm tree, and

CRITICAL READING

Use the essays by Wong and Zoellner to teach critical reading through annotation of texts. Ask students to choose one of these essays and annotate for three features: (1) sentences that illustrate either effective or ineffective writing, (2) sentences that suggest the purpose of the essay, and (3) sentences that suggest the author's intended audience. Students can then meet in groups of three or four and collate their annotations before discussing these essays with the whole class. A group recorder or spokesperson should be prepared to defend and explain each group's choices.

Compare Elizabeth Wong's struggle in Chinatown to Maya Angelou's experience in the segregated South, described in "Maya Angelou, Inaugural Poetess" in the *Video Library*.

he always clasped his impatient twitching hands behind his back. I recognized him as a repressed maniacal child killer, and knew that if we ever saw his hands we'd be in big trouble.

We all sat in little chairs in an empty auditorium. The room smelled like Chinese medicine, and imported faraway mustiness. Like ancient mothballs or dirty closets. I hated that smell. I favored crisp new scents. Like the soft French perfume that my American teacher wore in public school.

Although the emphasis at the school was mainly language—speaking, reading, writing—the lessons always began with an exercise in politeness. With the entrance of the teacher, the best student would tap a bell and everyone would get up, kowtow, and chant, "sing san ho," the phonetic for "How are you, teacher?"

Being ten years old, I had better things to learn than ideographs copied painstakingly in lines that ran right to left from the tip of a *moc but*, a real ink pen that had to be held in an awkward way if blotches were to be avoided. After all, I could do the multiplication tables, name the satellites of Mars, and write reports on "Little Women" and "Black Beauty." Nancy Drew, my favorite book heroine, never spoke Chinese.

The language was a source of embarrassment. More times than not, I had tried to disassociate myself from the nagging loud voice that followed me wherever I wandered in the nearby American supermarket outside Chinatown. The voice belonged to my grandmother, a fragile woman in her seventies who could outshout the best of the street vendors. Her humor was raunchy, her Chinese rhythmless, patternless. It was quick, it was loud, it was unbeautiful. It was not like the quiet, lilting romance of French or the gentle refinement of the American South. Chinese sounded pedestrian. Public.

In Chinatown, the comings and goings of hundreds of Chinese on their daily tasks sounded chaotic and frenzied. I did not want to be thought of as mad, as talking gibberish. When I spoke English, people nodded at me, smiled sweetly, said encouraging words. Even the people in my culture would cluck and say that I'd do well in life. "My, doesn't she move her lips fast," they would say, meaning that I'd be able to keep up with the world outside Chinatown.

My brother was even more fanatical than I about speaking English. He was especially hard on my mother, criticizing her, often cruelly, for her pidgin speech—smatterings of Chinese scattered like chop suey in her conversation. "It's not 'What it is,' Mom," he'd say in exasperation. "It's 'What is it, what is it, what is it!" Sometimes Mom might leave out an occasional "the" or "a," or perhaps a verb of being. He would stop her in mid-sentence: "Say it again, Mom. Say it right." When he tripped over his own tongue, he'd blame it on her: "See, Mom, it's all your fault. You set a bad example."

After two years of writing with a *moc but* and reciting words with multiples of meanings, I finally was granted a cultural divorce. I was permitted to stop Chinese school.

I thought of myself as multicultural. I preferred tacos to egg rolls; I enjoyed Cinco de Mayo more than Chinese New Year.

At last, I was one of you; I wasn't one of them.

Sadly, I still am.

I'M O.K., BUT YOU'RE NOT

ROBERT ZOELLNER

The American novelist John Barth, in his early novel, *The Floating Opera,* remarks that ordinary, day-to-day life often presents us with embarrassingly obvious, totally unsubtle patterns of symbolism and meaning—life in the midst of death, innocence vindicated, youth versus age, etc.

The truth of Barth's insight was brought home to me recently while having breakfast in a lawn-bordered restaurant on College Avenue near the Colorado State University campus. I had asked to be seated in the smoking section of the restaurant—I have happily gone through three or four packs a day for the past 40 years.

As it happened, the hostess seated me—I was by myself—at a little two-person table on the dividing line between the smoking and non-smoking sections. Presently, a well-dressed couple of advanced years, his hair a magisterial white and hers an electric blue, were seated in the non-smoking section five feet away from me.

It was apparent within a minute that my cigarette smoke was bugging them badly, and soon the husband leaned over and asked me if I would please stop smoking. As a chronic smokestack, I normally comply, out of simple courtesy, with such requests. Even an addict such as myself can quit for as long as 20 minutes.

But his manner was so self-righteous and peremptory—he reminded me of Lee Iacocca boasting about Chrysler—that the promptings of original sin, always a problem with me, took over. I quietly pointed out that I was in the smoking section—if only by five feet—and that that fact meant that I had met my social obligation to non-smokers. Besides, the idea of morning coffee without a cigarette was simply inconceivable to me—might as well ask me to vote Republican.

The two of them ate their eggs-over-easy in hurried and sullen silence, while I chain-smoked over my coffee. As well as be hung for a sheep as a lamb, I reasoned. Presently they got up, paid their bill, and stalked out in an ambiance of affronted righteousness and affluent propriety.

And this is where John Barth comes in. They had parked their car—a diesel Mercedes—where it could be seen from my table. And in the car, waiting impatiently, was a splendidly matched pair of pedigreed poodles, male and female.

Both dogs were clearly in extremis, and when the back door of the car was opened, they made for the restaurant lawn in considerable haste. Without ado (no pun intended), the male did a doo-doo that would have done credit to an animal twice his size, and finished off with a leisurely, ruminative wee-wee. The bitch of the pair, as might be expected of any well-brought-up female of Republican proclivities, confined herself to a modest wee-wee, fastidious, diffident, and quickly executed.

Chapter 2 of the *Video Guide* describes how these four stages—collecting, shaping, drafting, and revising—also characterize the processes for producing television shows.

Having thus polluted the restaurant lawn, the four of them marshalled their collective dignity and drove off in a dense cloud of blue smoke—that lovely white Mercedes was urgently in need of a valve-and-ring job, its emission sticker an obvious exercise in creative writing.

As I regretfully watched them go—after all, the four of them had made my day—it seemed to me that they were in something of a hurry, and I uncharitably wondered if the husband was not anxious to get home in order to light the first Fall fire in his moss-rock fireplace, or apply the Fall ration of chemical fertilizer to his doubtlessly impeccable lawn, thus adding another half-pound of particulates to the local atmosphere and another 10 pounds of nitrates and other poisons to the regional aquifers. But that, of course, is pure and unkindly speculation.

In any case, the point of this real-life vignette, as John Barth would insist, is obvious. The current controversy over public smoking in Fort Collins is a clear instance of selective virtue at work, coming under the rubric of, what I do is perfectly OK, but what you do is perfectly awful.

TEACHING TIP

One successful discussion strategy for these questions is to divide the class into five small groups and assign each group one question. Ask each group to select a recorder to write down key ideas or examples. After a short group session, ask each recorder (or group) to report to the class.

QUESTIONS FOR WRITING AND DISCUSSION

1. Choosing only one adjective to describe your main reaction to each essay, answer the following question: "When I finished the ___________ [Wong, Zoellner] essay, I was ___________ [intrigued, bored, amused, irritated, curious, confused, or ___________] because ___________. Explain your choice of adjectives in one or two sentences.

2. Referring to specific passages, explain the purpose and state the thesis or main point of each essay.

3. What personality or role does each writer project? Drawing from evidence in the essay, describe what you think both writers would be like if you met them.

4. Both of these essays appeared in newspapers. What kind of reader would find each essay interesting? What kind of reader would not enjoy each essay? For each essay, find examples of specific sentences, word choices, vocabulary, experiences, or references to culture or politics that would appeal to one reader but perhaps irritate another.

5. These two essays are similar in form—(they are both informal essays narrating personal experiences and explaining what each writer discovered or learned). There are differences, however, in structure and style. What differences do you notice in the way each essay begins and concludes, in the order of the paragraphs, and in vocabulary or style of the sentences?

I don't see writing as communication of something already discovered, as "truths" already known. Rather, I see writing as a job of experiment. It's like any discovery job; you don't know what's going to happen until you try it.
—WILLIAM STAFFORD,
TEACHER, POET, AND ESSAYIST

Dimensions of the Process

Processes for writing vary from one writer to the next and from one writing situation to the next. Most writers, however, can identify four basic stages, or dimensions, of their writing process: collecting, shaping, drafting, and revising. The writing situation may precede these stages—particularly if you are assigned a subject, purpose, audience, and form. Usually, however, you continue to narrow your subject, clarify your purpose, meet the needs of your audience, and modify your form as you work through the dimensions of your writing process.

Collecting

Mark Twain, author of *Huckleberry Finn,* once observed that if you attempt to carry a cat around the block by its tail, you'll gain a whole lot of information about cats that you'll never forget. You may collect such firsthand information, or you may rely on the data, experience, or expertise of others. In any case, writers constantly collect facts, impressions, opinions, and ideas that are relevant to their subjects, purposes, and audiences. Collecting involves observing, remembering, imagining, thinking, reading, listening, writing, investigating, talking, taking notes, and experimenting. Collecting also involves thinking about the relationships among the bits of information that you have collected.

Teaching Tip

Two other frequently used schemes for the writing process are prewriting/writing/rewriting and inventing/planning/drafting/revising. This text uses Donald Murray's term "collecting" and the common term "shaping" rather than "prewriting" (misnamed because writing does occur during invention) or "planning" (not particularly useful because the term is so broad). Remind students that collecting and shaping are not distinct linear operations: Collecting (invention) leads to possible shapes, but shaping (arrangement) also assists with collecting. The two operations are often inseparable.

Teaching Tip

A note of caution: Teaching the "writing process" is not the goal of a writing class. Writing processes are flexible means to achieve a goal: a piece of writing that meets its purpose for a specific audience or situation. As teachers, we are not "teaching writing process." Instead, we use writing process to teach. Our modeling and response during the writing process should teach writers how to recognize and solve the problems they face during the composing process.

Shaping

Writers focus and organize the facts, examples, and ideas that they have collected into the recorded, linear form that is written language. When a hurricane hits the Gulf Coast, for example, residents of Texas, Louisiana, Mississippi, Alabama, and Florida are likely to collect an enormous amount of data in just a few hours. Rain, floods, tree limbs snapping in the wind, unboarded windows shattering, sirens blaring—all of these events occur nearly simultaneously. If you try to write about such devastation, you need to narrow your focus (you can't describe everything that happened) and organize your information (you can't describe all of your experiences at the same time).

A chronological order is just one of the shapes that a writer may choose to develop and organize experience. Such shaping strategies also help writers collect additional information and ideas. Reconstructing a chronological order, for example, may suggest some additional details—perhaps a wet, miserable-looking dog running through the heavy downpour—that you might not otherwise have remembered.

Drafting

At some point, writers actually write down a rough version of what will evolve into the finished piece of writing. Drafting processes vary widely from one writer to the next. Some writers prefer to reread their collecting and shaping notes, find a starting point, and launch themselves—figuring out what they want to say as they write it. Other writers start with a plan—a mental strategy, a short list, or an outline—of how they wish to proceed. Whatever approach you use in your draft, write down as much as possible: You want to see whether the information is clear, whether your overall shape expresses and clarifies your purpose, and whether your content and organization meet the needs and expectations of your audience.

In film and television work, revising is literally a matter of "reseeing" a visual text, often with a preview audience to give objective feedback.

Revising

When writers revise rough drafts, they literally "resee" their subjects—and then modify drafts to fit new visions. Revision is more than just tinkering with a word here and there; revision leads to larger changes—new examples or details, a different organization, or a new perspective. You accomplish these changes by adding, deleting, substituting, or reordering words, sentences, and paragraphs. Although revision begins the moment you get your first idea, most revisions are based on the reactions—or anticipated reactions—of the audience to your draft. You often play the role of audience yourself by putting the draft aside and rereading it later when you have some distance from your writing. Wherever you feel readers might not get your point, you revise to make it clearer. You may also get feedback from readers in a class workshop, suggesting that you collect more or different information, alter the shape of your draft to improve the flow of ideas, or clarify your terminology. As a result of your rereading and your readers' suggestions, you may change your thesis or write for an entirely different audience.

Editing—in contrast to revising—focuses on the minor changes that you make to improve the accuracy and readability of your language. You usually edit your essay to improve word choice, grammar, usage, or punctuation. You also use a computer spell check program and proofread to catch typos and other surface errors.

The writing process is not linear, moving smoothly in one direction from start to finish. It is messy, recursive, convoluted, and uneven. Writers write, plan, revise, anticipate, and review throughout the writing process. . . .
—MAXINE HAIRSTON, TEACHER AND AUTHOR OF ARTICLES AND TEXTBOOKS ON WRITING

THE WHOLE PROCESS

In practice, a writer's process rarely follows the simple, consecutive order that these four stages or dimensions suggest. The writing process is actually recursive: It begins at one point, goes on to another, comes back to the first, jumps to the third, and so forth. A stage may last hours or only a second or two. While writing a letter to a friend, you may collect, shape, revise, and edit in one quick draft; a research paper may require repeated shaping over a two-week period. As writers draft, they may correct a few mistakes or typos, but they may not proofread until many days later. In the middle of reorganizing an essay, writers often reread drafts, go back and ask more questions, and collect more data. Even while editing, writers may throw out several paragraphs, collect some additional information, and draft new sections.

We must and do write each our own way.
—EUDORA WELTY, NOVELIST AND ESSAYIST

In addition to the recursive nature of the writing process, keep in mind that writing often occurs during every stage, not just during drafting and revising. During collecting, you will be recording information and jotting down ideas. During shaping, you will be writing out trial versions that you may use later when you draft or revise. Throughout the writing process, you use your writing to modify your subject, purpose, audience, and form.

The most important point to keep in mind is that the writing process is unique to each writer and to each writing situation. What works for one writer may be absolutely wrong for you. Some writers compose nearly everything in their heads. Others write only after discussing the subject with friends or drawing diagrams and pictures.

During the writing process, you need to experiment with several collecting, shaping, and drafting strategies to see what works best for you and for a particular piece of writing. As long as your process works, however, it's legitimate—no matter how many times you backtrack and repeat stages. When you are struggling with a piece of writing, remember that numerous revisions are a normal part of the writing process—even for most professionals.

Circling back over what you have already written—to sharpen your thesis, improve the organization, tighten up a paragraph, or add specific details to your examples—is likely to be the most time-consuming, yet worthwhile, part of your writing process. Most professional writers testify to the necessity and value of writing numerous drafts. When you are reworking a piece of writing, scrawling revisions over what you had hoped would be your finished product, remember what Nobel laureate Isaac Bashevis Singer once pointed out: "The wastepaper basket is the writer's best friend."

RESOURCE NOTES

Eudora Welty's point that we "write each our own way"is not just a statement that writers compose idiosyncratically. Composing processes often relate to a writer's basic learning style: visual, auditory, kinesthetic, tactile, or some combination. Dunn's "Learning Style: State of the Scene" in *Theory into Practice* is a good introduction to the subject. A learning-styles inventory may help your students assess their learning and composing preferences.

WRITING WITH A COMPUTER

Many students who are taking college writing courses have never used computers for writing essays or papers. If you are one of those students, don't panic. Most schools have computer laboratories with well-trained, knowledgeable staff who will help you learn how to write with a computer. Over the period of the semester, you'll become more comfortable at a keyboard and less worried when you press the wrong key or accidentally delete a sentence or paragraph. Gradually, you'll learn when you still want to use a pencil and paper and when you want to compose and revise on the computer. In the long run, the computer's revision capabilities and high-quality printing will make your writing faster, easier, and more professional-looking.

Some students, however, already have experience with computers. They have written papers on personal computers with one of the popular word processing programs, such as Microsoft Word or WordPerfect. They have struggled through the frustration of learning to type, learning a word-processing program, and revising on a computer screen because they know the potential benefits are great. Now, they can create files for each of their courses or papers, and they know how to find information, draft, reorganize, revise, and edit their essays. If you are one of those students, you may learn how to make your writing even more efficient and productive by using your computer lab's updated equipment.

Usually, college computer writing laboratories or classrooms provide additional software programs to assist with the writing and revising processes. First, the lab computers may have some composing software—such as Blue Pencil, Writer's Helper, or Daedelus—that prompts writers to freewrite, brainstorm, dialogue, question, outline, organize, and revise.

RESOURCE NOTES

Five introductory sources for ideas about using computers in composition are Wresch, *The Computer in Composition Instruction;* Halpern and Liggett, *Computers & Composing;* Rodrigues and Rodrigues, *Teaching Writing with a Word Processor;* Hawisher and Selfe, *Evolving Perspectives on Computers & Composition Studies;* and Meyers, *Approaches to Computer Writing Classrooms.*

In addition the lab computers have spelling checkers, thesauruses, and even style checkers to help with editing. The most technologically advanced college computer labs or classrooms, however, have added two new capabilities that transform the computer from a writing tool into a high-tech communicating and information gathering tool. These two technologies are *networks* and *hypertext.*

Writing with Computers

The computer can assist you both as a writing tool and as a networking tool. Listed in the left-hand column are writing activities that a stand-alone computer provides. Listed in the right-hand column are the additional capabilities of computers tied into a network.

The Computer as a Writing Tool	**The Computer as a Networking Tool**
Freewriting	Access to bulletin boards
Brainstorming	E-mail messages
Double-entry reading log	E-mail essays or files
Answers to "Wh" questions	"Chat" dialogues
Insert/delete sentences	Access to on-line library catalogs
Move paragraphs	Access to the information superhighway through programs such as Gopher and World Wide Web hypertext
Style/usage checkers	
Thesaurus	
Spelling checker	
Print preview	

For better or worse, less of me will remain unsaid because of the speed and ease and even intimacy of computer-assisted writing.
—PETER R. STILLMAN, TEACHER AND ESSAYIST

Networks are created when several computers are linked so that they can communicate with each other. Compared to a stand-alone computer, networked computers offer special advantages both within the writing classroom and outside of the classroom. In the writing classroom or laboratory, writers can communicate with each other and with their teachers in a variety of ways. First, they can use electronic mail (e-mail) to send messages or even entire files to their peers or to teachers. Teachers and students can read drafts and offer suggestions while a student is revising. In addition, some networked classrooms allow writers to send typewritten messages or "chat" with each other on their computers, just as they might sit and talk across a table. Finally, some classrooms or labs have electronic bulletin boards available for public comment and reaction. A writer can electronically send his or her essay draft to a bulletin board and have students in the class comment on his or her work-in-progress. If the class agrees, a writer's essay or his or her bulletin board comments can be anonymous or identified by a fictional name.

In addition to facilitating communication within a classroom, networked computers provide access to an incredible array of information sources across the campus and around the world. With immediate access to library on-line catalogs, writers don't have to make repeated trips across campus to the library to find information for their essays. In a few minutes, they can check the holdings of their library and—if they wish—the holdings of dozens of other libraries. In some cases, they can print out bibliographic information, abstracts of articles, or even entire articles without leaving their computer. Networked computers also help writers reach beyond the campus. Networked computers offer access to the so-called information superhighway through programs such as Gopher or World Wide Web hypertext. Overall, networked computers offer several key advantages for writers: They save time, paper, and printing costs; they give writers quick access to information; and they electronically reinforce the idea that a writing class is a supportive, interactive learning community.

While networks already exist in most colleges and universities, hypertext environments are still in a developing phase. A hypertext is simply a computer-based system that allows readers and writers to take multiple paths through a network of available passages or texts. For example, if you were learning about computer technology in a hypertext format, you might be able to select the word "hypertext" from a menu on your screen and get any of the following: A short history of hypertexts; a comment on the difference between hypertext and hypermedia (hypermedia usually adds graphics, sound, and/or animation); a definition of "virtual reality"; or a bibliography of articles about the uses of hypertext in computer classrooms. Instead of having to read through a whole chapter in conventional print format, hypertexts allow you to select what you want to learn next. As the separate technologies of television, compact disks (CDs), networks, and computers merge, hypertexts will change how we access information, how we learn, and even how we communicate with other people. Thanks to the creative potential of networks and hypertexts, your computer writing lab or classroom may soon operate like something out of a *Star Trek* episode.

■ **Warming Up: Journal Exercises** The following exercises will help you review and practice the topics the lab covered in this chapter. In addition, you may discover a subject for your own writing. Choose three of the following entries, and write for ten minutes on each.

1. Reread your "authority" list from Chapter 1. Choose one of those subjects and then explain your purpose and a possible audience for that subject.

2. Find a sample of writing from a magazine or newspaper article, an advertisement, a letter, or even from graffiti on walls. What is the purpose of that writing? Who is the intended audience? Why is the writing effective or ineffective?

3. Read Neil Petrie's essay and postscript at the end of this chapter. Then find the best paper you've written during the past year or two and write a "postscript" for it. Describe (a) the writing situation, (b) your purpose, and (c) the process you used to write it.

4. If you have already been given a writing assignment in another course, explain the purpose and the intended audience for that assignment. What might be your process for writing that essay?

5. During the first week of the term, one of your friends, Mark Lindstrom, is in an accident and is hospitalized. While still under the effects of anesthesia, he scribbles the following note for you to mail to his parents.

Dear Mom and Dad,

I arrived here last week. The trip was terrible. Dr. Stevens says that my leg will be better soon. My roommate is very strange. The police say my money is gone forever.

Please send $1,500 to my new address right away.

Thanks!

Your loving son
Mark

Because you were at the accident and can fill in the details, Mark asks you to explain everything to his parents. Write a short letter to them. Next, write a paragraph to your best friend that describes what happened to Mark.

6. Write an open-journal entry. Writing for yourself, describe one event from your week that upset or angered you. What did you learn from this event?

7. Explore the availability of computers on your campus. Where is the English Department computer lab? What services does it offer? What other computer facilities are available?

A Writing Process at Work: Collecting and Shaping

ATHLETES AND EDUCATION

NEIL H. PETRIE

In the following essay that appeared in The Chronicle of Higher Education, *Neil H. Petrie argues that colleges have a hypocritical attitude toward student-athletes. Although most universities claim that their athletes—both male and female—are in college to get a good education, in reality, the pressures on athletes compromise their academic careers. The problem, Petrie argues, is not the old cliché that jocks are dumb, but that the endless hours devoted to practice or spent on road trips drain even the good student-athlete's physical and mental energies. Colleges point with pride to a tiny number of athletes who become professionals, but much more frequently the collegiate system encourages athletes to settle for lower grades and incomplete programs. In far too many cases, athletes never graduate. These are the students that, as Petrie says, "the system uses and then discards after the final buzzer."*

I have spent all my adult life in academe, first as a student and then as a professor. During that time I have seen many variations in the role of intercollegiate athletics in the university, and I've developed sharply split opinions on the subject. On one hand, I despise the system, clinging as it does to the academic body like a parasite. On the other hand, I feel sympathy and admiration for most of the young athletes struggling to balance the task of getting an education with the need to devote most of their energies to the excessive demands of the gym and the field. **(1)**

My earliest experiences with the intrusion of athletics into the classroom came while I was still a freshman at the University of Colorado. While I was in my English professor's office one day, a colleague of hers came by for a chat. Their talk turned to the football coach's efforts to court the favor of the teachers responsible for his gladiators by treating them to dinner and a solicitous discussion of the academic progress of the players. I vividly recall my professor saying, "He can take me out to dinner if he wants, but if he thinks I'll pass his knuckleheads just because of that, he'd better think again." **(2)**

Later, as a graduate teaching fellow, a lecturer, and then an assistant professor of English, I had ample opportunity to observe a Division I university's athletics program. I soon discovered that the prevailing stereotypes did not always apply. Athletes turned out to be as diverse as any other group of students in their habits, tastes, and abilities, and they showed a wide range of strategies for coping with the stress of their dual roles. **(3)**

Some of them were poor students. An extreme example was the All-American football player (later a successful pro) who saw college only as a step to a six-figure contract and openly showed his disdain for the educational process. Others did such marginal work in my courses that I got the feeling they were daring me to give them D's or F's. One woman cross-country star, who almost never attended my composition class, used to push nearly illiterate essays under my office door at odd hours. **(4)**

Yet many athletes were among the brightest students I had. Not so surprising, when you consider that, in addition to physical prowess, success in athletics requires intelligence, competitive drive, and dedication—all qualities that can translate into success in the classroom as well as on the field. The trouble is that the grinding hours of practice and road trips rob student athletes of precious study time and deplete their reserves of mental and physical energy. A few top athletes have earned A's; most are content to settle for B's or C's, even if they are capable of better. **(5)**

The athletes' educational experience can't help being marred by their numerous absences and divided loyalties. In this respect, they are little different from the students who attempt to go to college while caring for a family or working long hours at an outside job. The athletes, however, get extra help in juggling their responsibilities. Although I have never been bribed or threatened and have never received a dinner invitation from a coach, I am expected to provide extra time and consideration for athletes, far beyond what I give other students. **(6)**

Take the midterm grade reports, for example. At my university, the athletic department's academic counselor sends progress questionnaires to every teacher of varsity athletes. While the procedure shows admirable concern for the academic performance of athletes, it also amounts to preferential treatment. It requires teachers to take time from other teaching duties to fill out and return the forms for the athletes. (No other students get such progress reports.) If I were a cynic it would occur to me that the athletic department might actually be more concerned with athletes' eligibility than with their academic work. **(7)**

Special attendance policies for athletes are another example of preferential treatment. Athletes miss a lot of classes. In fact, I think the road trip is one of the main reasons that athletes receive a deficient education. You simply can't learn as much away from the classroom and the library as on the campus. Nevertheless, professors continue to provide make-up tests, alternative assignments, and special tutoring sessions to accommodate athletes. Any other student would have to have been very sick or the victim of a serious accident to get such dispensations. **(8)**

It is sad to see bright young athletes knowingly compromise their potential and settle for much less education than they deserve. It is infuriating, though, to see the ones less gifted academically exploited by a system that they do not comprehend and robbed of any possible chance to grow intellectually and to explore other opportunities. **(9)**

One specific incident illustrates for me the worst aspects of college athletics. It wasn't unusual or extraordinary—just the all-too-ordinary case of an athlete not quite good enough to make a living from athletics and blind to the opportunity afforded by the classroom. **(10)**

I was sitting in my office near the beginning of a term, talking to a parade of new advisees. I glanced up to see my entire doorway filled with the bulk of a large young man, whom I recognized as one of our basketball stars from several seasons ago who had left for the pros and now apparently come back. **(11)**

Over the next hour I got an intensive course on what it's like to be a college athlete. In high school, John had never been interested in much outside of basketball, and, like many other indifferent students, he went on to junior college on an athletic scholarship. After graduating, he came to the university, where he played for two more years, finishing out his eligibility. He was picked in a late round of the N.B.A. draft and left college, but in the end he turned out to be a step too slow for the pros. By that time he had a family to support, and when he realized he could never make a career of basketball, he decided to return to college. **(12)**

We both knew that his previous academic career hadn't been particularly focused, and that because of transferring and taking minimum course loads during the basketball season, he wouldn't be close to a degree. But I don't think either one of us was prepared for what actually emerged from our examination of his transcripts. It was almost as if he had never gone beyond high school. His junior-college transcript was filled with remedial and non-academic courses. **(13)**

Credit for those had not transferred to the university. Over the next two years he had taken a hodgepodge of courses, mostly in physical education. He had never received any advice about putting together a coherent program leading to a degree. In short, the academic side of his college experience had been completely neglected by coaches, advisers, and, of course, John himself. **(14)**

By the time we had evaluated his transcripts and worked out a tentative course of study, John was in shock and I was angry. It was going to take him at least three years of full-time study to complete a degree. He thanked me politely for my time, picked up the planning sheets, and left. I was ashamed to be a part of the university that day. Why hadn't anyone in the athletic department ever told him what it would take to earn a degree? Or at least been honest enough to say, "Listen, we can keep you eligible and give you a chance to play ball, but don't kid yourself into thinking you'll be getting an education, too." **(15)**

I saw John several more times during the year. He tried for a while. He took classes, worked, supported his family, and then he left again. I lost track of him after that. I can only hope that he found a satisfying job or completed his education at some other institution. I know people say the situation has improved in the last few years, but when I read about the shockingly low percentages of athletes who graduate, I think of John. **(16)**

Colleges give student athletes preferential treatment. We let them cut classes. We let them slide through. We protect them from harsh realities. We applaud them for entertaining us and wink when they compromise themselves intellectually. We give them special dorms, special meals, special tutors, and a specially reprehensible form of hypocrisy. **(17)**

I can live with the thought of the athletes who knowingly use the college-athletics system to get their pro contracts or their devalued degrees. But I have trouble living with the thought of the ones whom the system uses and then discards after the final buzzer. **(18)**

ON WRITING "ATHLETES AND EDUCATION"

In the following postscript on his writing process, Neil Petrie describes why he wanted to write the paper, how he collected material to support his argument, and how he shaped and focused his ideas as he wrote. His comments illustrate how his purpose—to expose the hypocrisies of collegiate athletics—guided his writing of the essay. In addition, Petrie explains that other key questions affected the shape of his essay: how he should begin, where he should use his best example, and what words he should choose.

This essay has its origin, as all persuasive writing should, in a strongly held opinion. I'm always more comfortable if I care deeply about my subject matter. As a teacher, I hold some powerful convictions about the uneasy marriage of big-time athletics and higher education, and so I wanted to write an essay that would expose what I think are the dangers and hypocrisies of that system.

At the beginning of my essay, I wanted to establish some authority to lend credibility to my argument. Rather than gather statistics on drop-out rates of student athletes or collect the opinions of experts, I planned to rely on my own experiences as both a student and teacher. I hoped to convince my readers that my opinions were based on the authority of firsthand knowledge. In this introduction I was also aware of the need to avoid turning off readers who might dismiss me as a "jock hater." I had to project my negative feelings about the athletic system while maintaining my sympathy with the individual student athletes involved in that system. The thesis, then, would emerge gradually as I accumulated the evidence; it would be more implied than explicitly stated.

Gathering the material was easy. I selected a series of examples from my personal experiences as a college student and instructor, as well as anecdotes I'd heard from other instructors. Most of these stories were ones that I had shared before, either in private discussions with friends or in classrooms with students.

Shaping the material was a little tougher. As I began thinking about my examples and how to order them, I saw that I really wanted to make two main points. The first was that most colleges give preferential treatment to athletes. The second point was that, despite the extra attention, the success of the athlete's academic career is often ignored by all parties involved. Many of my examples, I realized, illustrated the varieties of pressures put upon both athletes and instructors to make sure that the students at least get by in class and remain eligible. These examples seemed to cluster together because they showed the frustrations of teachers and the reactions of athletes trying to juggle sports and academics. This group would make a good introduction to my general exposé of the system. But I had one more example I wanted to use that seemed to go beyond the cynicism of some athletes or the hypocrisy of the educators. This was the case of John, an athlete who illustrated what I thought were the most exploitative aspects of varsity athletics. I originally planned on devoting the bulk of my essay to this story and decided to place it near the end where it would make my second point with maximum emotional effect.

A two-part structure for the essay now emerged. In the first segment following my introductory paragraph, I gave a series of shorter examples, choosing to order them in roughly chronological order (paragraphs 2–4). I then moved from these specific details to a more general discussion of the demands placed upon both students and teachers, such as lengthy practice time, grade reports, road trips and special attendance policies. This concluded my description of the way the system operates (paragraphs 5–8).

Then it was time to shift gears, to provide a transition to the next part of my essay, to what I thought was my strongest example. I wanted the story of John to show how the system destroyed human potential. To do this, I needed to increase the seriousness of the tone in order to persuade the reader that I was dealing in more than a little bureaucratic boondoggling. I tried to set the tone by my word choice: I moved from words such as "sad," "compromise," and "settle" to words with much stronger emotional connotations such as "infuriating," "exploited," and "robbed," all in a single short transitional paragraph (paragraph 9).

I then introduced my final extended example in equally strong language, identifying it as a worst-case illustration (paragraph 10). I elaborated on John's story, letting the details and my reactions to his situation carry the more intense outrage that I was trying to convey in this second part of the essay (paragraphs 10–16). The first version that I tried was a rambling narrative that had an overly long recounting of John's high school and college careers. So I tightened this section by eliminating such items as his progress through the ranks of professional basketball and his dreams of million-dollar contracts. I also cut down on a discussion of the various courses of study he was considering as options. The result was a sharper focus on the central issue of John's dilemma: the lack of adequate degree counseling for athletes.

After my extended example, all that was left was the conclusion. As I wrote, I was very conscious of using certain devices, such as the repetition of key words and sentence patterns in paragraph seventeen ("We let them . . . We let them . . . We protect them . . . We applaud them . . . We give them . . .") to maintain the heightened emotional tone. I was also conscious of repeating the two-part structure of the essay in the last two paragraphs. I moved from general preferential treatment (paragraph 17) to the concluding and more disturbing idea of devastating exploitation (paragraph 18).

On the whole, I believe that this essay effectively conveys its point through the force of accumulated detail. My personal experience was the primary source of evidence, and that experience led naturally to the order of the paragraphs and to the argument I wished to make: that while some athletes knowingly use the system, others are used and exploited by it.

QUESTIONS FOR WRITING AND DISCUSSION

1. In your journal, describe how your extracurricular activities (athletics, jobs, clubs, or family obligations) have or have not interfered with your education. Recall one specific incident that illustrates how these activities affected your classwork—either positively or negatively.

2. Describe Petrie's audience and purpose for this essay. What sentences reveal his intended audience? What sentences reveal his purpose? What sentences contain his thesis, claim, or main idea? Do you agree with that thesis? Why or why not?

3. Reread Petrie's postscript. Based on his comments and on your reading of the essay, how does Petrie describe or label each of the following sections of his essay:

paragraphs 1–4
paragraphs 5–8
paragraphs 9
paragraphs 10–16
paragraphs 17–18.

4. Who do you think is most to blame for the situation that Petrie describes: The athletes themselves? The colleges for paying their scholarships and then ignoring them when they drop out? The students and alumni who pay to see their teams win?

5. Petrie does not explicitly suggest a solution to the problem that he describes. Assume, however, that he has been asked by the president of his university to propose a solution. Write the letter that you think Petrie would send to the president.

TEACHING TIP

Although students may be intrigued by drafts of historical documents, they also need to see the *reasons* for the writer's revisions. Writing teachers should create real contexts for revision by modeling their own revision processes with the class. Illustrate the revision process by bringing a draft of something you are writing. Put your double-spaced draft of a paragraph or two on an overhead (or at the chalkboard or on a projected computer screen) and ask students to suggest revisions, based on your intended purpose, audience, and writing situation. Create alternative phrases and sentences. Ask students to explain which version is most effective and why.

A Writing Process at Work: Drafting and Revising

While drafting and revising, writers frequently make crucial changes in their ideas and language. The first scribbled sentences, written primarily for ourselves, are often totally different from what we later present to other people in final, polished versions. Take, for example, the final version of Abraham Lincoln's Gettysburg Address. It begins with the famous lines "Four score and seven years ago our fathers brought forth on this continent a new nation. . . ." But his first draft might well have begun, "Eighty-seven years ago, several politicians and other powerful men in the American Colonies got together and decided to start a new country . . . ." It is difficult to imagine that language ingrained in our consciousness was once drafted, revised, drafted again, and edited, as the author or authors added, deleted, reordered, and otherwise altered words, sentences, and ideas. In fact, it usually was.

Carl Becker's study of the American Declaration of Independence assembles the early drafts of that famous document and compares them with the final version. Shown below is Thomas Jefferson's first draft, with revisions made by Benjamin Franklin, John Adams, and other members of the Committee of Five that was charged with developing the new document.

Thomas Jefferson's Rough Draft of the Opening Sentences of the Declaration of Independence

one
When in the course of human events it becomes necessary for ~~a~~ ^
dissolve the political bonds which have
people to ^ ~~advance from that subordination in which they have hitherto~~
connected them with another, and to
~~remained, & t~~o assume among the powers of the earth the ~~equal & inde-~~
separate and equal
~~pendent~~ ^station to which the laws of nature & of nature's god entitle
them, a decent respect to the opinions of mankind requires that they
the separation.
should declare the causes which impel them to ~~the change.~~ ^

self-evident
We hold these truths to be ^ ~~sacred & undeniab~~le; that all men are
they are endowed by their creator
created equal ~~& independent;~~ that ^ ~~from that equal creation they derive~~
with rights; that these
~~in right~~s inherent & inalienable ^among ~~which~~ ^are ~~the preservation of~~
life, ~~&~~ liberty, & the pursuit of happiness. . . .

The Final Draft of the Opening Sentences of the Declaration of Independence, as Approved on July 4, 1776.

When in the Course of human events, it becomes necessary for one people to dissolve the political bands, which have connected them with another, and to assume among the powers of the earth, the separate and equal station to which the Laws of Nature and of Nature's God entitle them, a decent respect to the opinions of mankind requires that they should declare the causes which impel them to the separation.

We hold these truths to be self-evident, that all men are created equal, that they are endowed by their Creator with certain unalienable Rights, that among these are Life, Liberty and the pursuit of Happiness.

Questions for Writing and Discussion

1. Describe your reaction to the "rough draft" of the Declaration of Independence. Where did it seem strange or make you feel uncomfortable?

2. Select one change in a sentence that most improved the final version. Explain how the revised wording is more effective.

3. Find one change in a word or phrase that constitutes an alteration in meaning rather than just a choice of "smoother" or more appropriate language. How does this change affect the meaning?

4. Upon rereading this passage from the Declaration of Independence, one reader wrote, "I was really irritated by that 'all men are created equal' remark. The writers were white, free, well-to-do, Anglo-Saxon, mostly Protestant males discussing their own 'unalienable rights.' They sure weren't discussing the 'unalienable rights' of female Americans or of a million slaves or of nonwhite free Americans!" Revise the passage from the Declaration of Independence using this person as your audience.

THREE/OBSERVING

My task . . . is, by the power of the written word, to make you hear, to make you feel—it is, before all, to make you see.

—JOSEPH CONRAD, AUTHOR OF HEART OF DARKNESS AND OTHER NOVELS

Seeing is of course very much a matter of verbalization. Unless I call my attention to what passes before my eyes, I simply won't see it.

—ANNIE DILLARD, NATURALIST AND AUTHOR OF PILGRIM AT TINKER CREEK

IN THE FAR CORNER OF A FRIEND'S LIVING ROOM IS A LIGHTED AQUARIUM. Instead of water, the aquarium has a few inches of white sand, a dish of water, and a small piece of pottery. When you ask about the aquarium, your friend excitedly says, "You mean you haven't met Nino?" In a matter of seconds, you have a small, tannish-brown snake practically in your lap, and your friend is saying, "This is Nino. She—or he—is an African sand boa." You imagined that all boa constrictors were those huge snakes that suffocated and then swallowed babies. "Actually, "replies your friend," Nino is very shy. She prefers to burrow in the sand." The snake is fascinating. It is only fifteen inches long, with a strong, compact body and a stub tail. Before it burrows into your coat pocket, you observe it closely so you can describe it to your younger brother, who loves all kinds of snakes.

IN THE PHYSICS LABORATORY, YOU'RE DOING AN EXPERIMENT ON LIGHT REFRACTION. You need to observe how light rays bend as they go through water, so you take notes describing the procedure and the results. During each phase of the experiment, you observe and record the angles of refraction. The data and your notes will help you write up the lab report that is due next Monday.

Leonardo da Vinci, Mona Lisa (detail), Louvre, Paris, France

OBSERVING IS ESSENTIAL TO GOOD WRITING. Whether you are writing in a journal, doing a laboratory report for a science class, dashing off a memo at work, or writing a letter to the editor of a newspaper, keen observation is essential. Writing or verbalizing what you see helps you discover and learn more about your environment. Sometimes your purpose is limited to yourself: You observe and record to help you understand your world or yourself better. At other times, your purpose extends to a wider audience: You want to share what you have learned with others to help them learn as well. No matter who your audience is or what your subject may be, however, your task is to *see* and to help your readers *see*.

Of course, observing involves more than just "seeing." Good writers draw on all their senses: sight, smell, touch, taste, hearing. In addition, however, experienced writers also notice what is *not* there. The smell of food that should be coming from the kitchen but isn't. A friend who usually is present but now is absent. The absolute quiet in the air that precedes an impending storm. Writers should also look for *changes* in their subjects—from light to dark, from rough to smooth, from bitter to sweet, from noise to sudden silence. Good writers learn to use their previous *experiences* and their *imaginations* to draw comparisons and create *images*. Does a sea urchin look and feel like a pincushion with the pins stuck in the wrong way? Does the room feel as cramped and airless as the inside of a microwave oven? Finally, good writers write from a specific *point of view* or role: a student describing basic laws of physics or an experienced worker in a mental health clinic describing the clientele.

Depending on your purpose and audience, writing from observation can be relatively *objective*, as when you record what is actually, demonstrably there; or it can be more *subjective*, as when you suggest how you feel, think, or react to a subject. For example, you might describe a bicycle objectively as a "secondhand 1992 blue Bridgestone MB-3 mountain bike with a 25-inch Ritchey Logic frame, Shimano Deore DX derailleurs, a Shimano crank, Dia Compe brakes, and an Avocet saddle." You might need to communicate that kind of objective information to a prospective buyer or to an employee in a cycle repair shop. On the other hand, you may wish to communicate the bicycle's subjective feel—how easily it pedals, how it cranks up steep, rocky trails, or how solid it feels on rough terrain. In most situations, however, good writers describe their subjects both objectively and subjectively. They use some objectivity for accuracy and specific detail and some subjectivity to suggest the value or relevance of subjects in a human environment.

BACKGROUND ON OBSERVING

The observing chapter serves three important functions at the beginning of a writing course. It encourages writers to discover and learn by drawing on their senses. It provides early practice in selecting and focusing information so that all observed details relate to or help create some *dominant idea*. Finally, it provides practice in observing as an *invention* technique that will be used in the following chapters of this text.

Use the camera-pen analogy to focus your students' attention on significant visual detail. Observe how good film and television accomplish the writer's task "to make you see." The program on "Lyme Disease" in the *Video Guide*, for example, helps its audience to visualize the cause and symptoms of the disease.

The key to effective observing is to *show* your reader the person, place, event, or object through *specific detail.* Good description allows the reader to draw general conclusions based on specific detail. Rather than just telling a reader, "This bicycle has good technical components," the writer should *show* or describe how it feels as she rides it. If your reader is going to learn from your observations, you need to give the *exact details that you learned from*, not just your conclusions or generalizations. Even in writing, experience is the best teacher, so use specific details to communicate the feel, the data, the sights and sounds and smells. Whether you are a tourist describing the cliff dwellings at Mesa Verde, a salesperson analyzing consumer preferences for your boss, a physicist presenting data on a new superconducting material to other physicists, or a social worker putting together the details of a child-abuse case, your first task is to describe your subject—to show your readers, to make them *see.*

■ **FREEWRITING: OBSERVING** Before reading further in this chapter, do this exercise. Close your eyes and relax. Then turn your head slightly up, down, or to the right or left. Open your eyes and focus on the first thing you see. Writing nonstop for five minutes, describe this thing in as much sensory detail as possible. After five minutes, stop writing. Now move closer. If possible, pick the thing up, turn it over, touch it, shake it, smell it, and reexamine it. Then write for five more minutes, nonstop, describing everything else you noticed.

TECHNIQUES FOR WRITING ABOUT OBSERVATIONS

... Not that it's raining, but the feel of being rained upon.

—E. L. DOCTOROW, AUTHOR OF RAGTIME AND OTHER NOVELS

The short passages that follow all use specific techniques for observing people, places, objects, or events. Some emphasize objective detail; some re-create subjective reactions or feelings. In all the passages, however, the writer *narrows* or *limits* the scope of the observation and selects specific details. The result is some *dominant idea.* The dominant idea reflects the writer's purpose for that particular audience. As you read these excerpts, notice how the authors use the following six techniques for recording vivid observations:

- **Giving sensory details (sight, sound, smell, touch, taste).** Also include *actual dialogue* and *names of things* where appropriate. Good writers often "zoom in" on crucial details.
- **Using comparisons and images.** To help readers visualize the unfamiliar (or see the commonplace in a new light), writers often draw comparisons and use evocative images.

- **Describing what is not there.** Sometimes keen observation requires stepping back and noticing what is absent, what is not happening, or who is not present.
- **Noting changes in the subject's form or condition.** Even when the subject appears static—a landscape, a flower, a building—good writers look for evidence of changes, past or future: a tree being enveloped by tent worms, a six-inch purple-and-white iris that eight hours earlier was just a green bud, a sandstone exterior of a church being eroded by acid rain.
- **Writing from a distinct point of view.** Good writers assume distinct roles; in turn, perspective helps clarify what they observe. A lover and a botanist, for example, see entirely different things in the same red rose. *What* is seen depends on *who* is doing the seeing.
- **Focusing on a dominant idea.** Good writers focus on those details and images that clarify the main ideas or discoveries. Discovery often depends on the *contrast* between the reality and the writer's expectations.

Note how many writing terms are borrowed from the filmmaker's lexicon: focus, close up, zoom, angle, point of view. Note also how filmmakers reinforce rhetorical strategies with visual techniques: framing to narrow attention, split screens to compare, time-lapse photography to record change, off-screen sound to suggest what is not there.

These six techniques are illustrated in the following two paragraphs by Karen Blixen, who wrote *Out of Africa* under the pen name Isak Dinesen. A Danish woman who moved to Kenya to start a coffee plantation, Blixen knew little about the animals in Kenya Reserve. In this excerpt from her journals, she describes a startling change that occurred when she shot a large iguana. **The annotations in the margin identify all six observing techniques.**

> In the Reserve I have sometimes come upon the Iguana, the big lizards, as they were sunning themselves upon a flat stone in a riverbed. They are not pretty in shape, but nothing can be imagined more beautiful than their coloring. They shine like a heap of precious stones or like a pane cut out of an old church window. When, as you approach, they swish away, there is a flash of azure, green and purple over the stones, the color seems to be standing behind them in the air, like a comet's luminous tail.

Role: A newcomer to the Reserve

Comparisons and images
Sensory details
Comparisons and images

> Once I shot an Iguana. I thought that I should be able to make some pretty things from his skin. A strange thing happened then, that I have never afterwards forgotten. As I went up to him, where he was lying dead upon his stone, and actually while I was walking the few steps, he faded and grew pale, all color died out of him as in one long sigh, and by the time that I touched him he was grey and dull like a lump of concrete. It was the live impetuous blood pulsating within the animal, which had radiated out all that glow and splendor. Now that the flame was put out, and the soul had flown, the Iguana was as dead as a sandbag.

Changes in condition

Sensory detail

What is not there
Dominant idea: now colorless and dead

For a small-group activity or class discussion, ask students to annotate marginally—in their journals—each of the following illustrations (observing people, places, objects, and events). Using the Karen Blixen passage as a model, marginal annotations for this passage might be as follows:

Role: writer is an outsider looks objectively at jobs, is probably older

Dominant idea: youth

Sensory detail: visual description

Comparison and image

What is not there: facial hair

What is not there: tact

Comparison

Observing People

Observing people—their dress, facial features, body language, attitudes, behavior, skills, quirks, habits and conversation—is a pastime that we all share. When writers describe people, however, they zero in on specific details that fit overall patterns or impressions. In an *Esquire* magazine article, for example, Joseph Nocera profiles Steven Jobs, the co-creator of the Apple and Macintosh computers, ex-chairman of the board of Apple Computer, and now head of Next, Inc., another Silicon Valley firm. All of Nocera's details reinforce his dominant idea that Steven Jobs is a temperamental boy genius.

> With personal computers so ubiquitous today, you tend to forget that the industry is still barely ten years old; the Apple II, the machine that began it all, was unleashed upon an unsuspecting world in 1977. You forget, that is, until you sit in a room full of people who have built them and realize how young they are. Jobs himself is only thirty-one. If anything, he looks younger. He is lithe and wiry. He is wearing faded jeans (no belt), a white cotton shirt (perfectly pressed), and a pair of brown suede wing-tipped shoes. There is a bounce to his step that betrays a certain youthful cockiness; the quarterback of your high school football team used to walk that way. His thin, handsome face does not even appear to need a daily shave. And that impression of eternal youth is reinforced by some guileless, almost childlike traits: by the way, for instance, he can't resist showing off his brutal, withering intelligence whenever he's around someone he doesn't think measures up. Or by his almost willful lack of tact. Or by his inability to hide his boredom when he is forced to endure something that doesn't interest him, like a sixth grader who can't wait for class to end.

Observing Places

In the following excerpt from *Brown Girl, Brownstones*, Paule Marshall creates a catalog of the sights, sounds, and smells of a Brooklyn street during the Great Depression of the 1930s. In this paragraph, she records a typical Saturday night on Fulton Street: the bright lights, the clamorous street activity, the mixed odors of foods, and the faces of the street people. The specific details contribute to the overall idea of vibrant, chaotic energy.

> Unlike Chauncey Street, Fulton Street this summer Saturday night was a whirling spectrum of neon signs, movie marquees, bright-lit

store windows and sweeping yellow streamers of light from the cars. It was canorous voices, hooted laughter and curses ripping the night's warm cloak; a welter of dark faces and gold-etched teeth; children crying high among the fire escapes of the tenements; the subway rumbling below; the unrelenting wail of a blues spilling from a bar; greasy counters and fish sandwiches and barbecue and hot sauce; trays of chitterlings and hog maws and fat back in the meat stores; the trolley's insistent clangor; a man and woman in a hallway bedroom, sleeping like children now that the wildness had passed; a drunken woman pitching along the street; the sustained shriek of a police car and its red light stabbing nervously at faces and windows. Fulton Street on Saturday night was all beauty and desperation and sadness.

Compare Marshall's portrait of the clamorous activity on Fulton Street with Wendell Berry's tranquil description of a barn on a family farm. Berry, author of *The Unsettling of America* and other books on America's agricultural crisis, gives us a simple but effective portrait of Elmer Lapp's Place. Because one of Berry's purposes is to argue that the family farm is worth saving, the details that he selects create a positive dominant idea about farm life.

The thirty cows come up from the pasture and go one by one into the barn. Most of them are Guernseys, but there are also a few red Holsteins and a couple of Jerseys. They go to their places and wait while their neck chains are fastened. And then Elmer Lapp, his oldest son, and his youngest daughter go about the work of feeding, washing, and milking.

In the low, square room lighted by a row of big windows, a radio is quietly playing music. Several white cats sit around waiting for milk to be poured out for them from the test cup. Two collie dogs rest by the wall, out of the way. Several buff Cochin bantams are busily foraging for whatever waste grain can be found in the bedding and in the gutters. Overhead, fastened to the ceiling joists, are many barn swallow nests, their mud cups empty now at the end of October. Two rusty-barrelled .22 rifles are propped in window frames, kept handy to shoot English sparrows, and there are no sparrows to be seen. Outside the door a bred heifer and a rather timeworn pet jenny are eating their suppers out of feed boxes. Beyond, on the stream that runs through the pasture, wild ducks are swimming. The shadows have grown long under the low-slanting amber light.

These writing exercises on observing have familiar counterparts in television programming: profiles that focus on individuals, travelogues on places, commercials on objects, documentaries on events (See "Maya Angelou," "Lyme Disease," and "Jack Smith's Vietnam Diary" in the *Video Library*).

COLLABORATIVE ACTIVITY

Bring a group of unfamiliar objects (abstract paintings or sculpture, scientific utensils, sports equipment) to class for observation. Ask students to work in groups of three or four, brain storming sensory details (or taking double-entry notes) and collaboratively writing a paragraph of description. Based on their writing, what guesses can they make about the purpose, function, and context for their object? (Students who immediately identify the object should switch to another group.) The purpose of the activity is to practice using sensory detail to discover a dominant idea or the identity of their object.

OBSERVING OBJECTS

In observing an inanimate object such as a cookie, Paul Goldberger brings his special point of view—architecture critic for *The New York Times*—to his description. He totally ignores the cookie's taste, ingredients, and calories, focusing instead on the architectural relationships of function and form. Goldberger's architectural perspective helps focus his observations, creating a dominant idea for each passage.

Sugar Wafer (Nabisco) There is no attempt to imitate the ancient forms of traditional, individually baked cookies here—this is a modern cookie through and through. Its simple rectangular form, clean and pure, just reeks of mass production and modern technological methods. The two wafers, held together by the sugar-cream filling, appear to float, and the Nabisco trademark, stamped repeatedly across the top, confirms that this is a machine-age object.

Fig Newton (Nabisco) This, too, is a sandwich but different in every way from the Sugar Wafer. Here the imagery is more traditional, more sensual even; a rounded form of cookie dough arcs over the fig concoction inside, and the whole is soft and pliable. Like all good pieces of design, it has an appropriate form for its use, since the insides of Fig Newtons can ooze and would not be held in place by a more rigid form. The thing could have had a somewhat different shape, but the rounded tip is a comfortable, familiar image, and it's easy to hold. Not a revolutionary object but an intelligent one.

Observing Events

Observing events requires weaving specific details about people, places, and objects into some chronological order, as in the following account of a rhythm-and-blues performance by Bobby "Blue" Bland. The paragraph, taken from Peter Guralnick's *Lost Highway: Journeys and Arrivals of American Musicians*, demonstrates how vivid, specific details (names of singers, a description of barefoot dancing, titles of songs, the recording of actual dialogue and lyrics) create a dominant idea: a single night's performance blurs into an endless series of one-night stands.

> Every night it is exactly the same. The band, a brass-heavy ten pieces with dilapidated reading stands that say "Mel Jackson/MFs Bobby Bland's Revue," does a desultory thirty-minute set. Then Burnett Williams, singer, valet, bus driver, and all-around good fellow, swings affably into a succession of Al Green numbers and current soul hits. The band plays dispiritedly behind him; even the bandleader, Mel Jackson, has disappeared from the stand; but Burnett always works up a sweat, finishing out his segment with shoes kicked off, doing the barefoot to the strains of "Love and Happiness." This invariably cracks up Mel Jackson, who reappears precisely at this point, dapper, diminutive, very much in charge. His eyes gleam and dart skittishly about the room as he laughs out loud, proclaims, "That boy doing some barefooting!" and gives Burnett a soul slap and quick little hug as the warm-up singer departs from the stage, his shoes held delicately aloft. Then it's Show Time, Ladies and Gentlemen, a Young Man Who Needs No Introduction, he'll Take Care of You, Further on Up the Road, won't let you Cry No More, cause when you Cry Cry Cry he just wants to Turn On Your Lovelights, well he's a Good-Time Charlie, and You're the One (That He Adores), but now The Feeling is Gone and he's Two steps From the Blues. The string of hits becomes a litany, a numbing incantation. Audience talk becomes louder and more distracted, and then Bobby "Blue" Bland appears, big, shambling, sleepy-eyed, a cigarette between his fingers, tongue licking at the edge of his lips. He plays aimlessly for a moment with the microphone, his eyes cast upwards as if for inspiration, the band kicks off, and that smooth, mellow, almost hornlike voice slides in among the three trumpets, trombone, and saxophone (guitar, bass, two drummers, and occasionally a piano round out the band). "I pity the fool/I pity the fool that falls in love with you. . . ." It is ten-thirty, and Bobby "Blue" Bland is just going to work.

For Godsake, keep your eyes open. Notice what's going on around you.
—WILLIAM BURROUGHS, NOVELIST

■ **Warming Up: Journal Exercises** The following topics will help you practice close, detailed observation and may possibly suggest a subject for your assignment on observing. Read the following exercises and then write on the two or three that interest you the most.

1. Go to a public place (library, bar, restaurant, hospital emergency room, gas station, laundromat, park, shopping mall, hotel lobby, police station, beach, skating rink, beauty salon, city dump, tennis court, church, etc.). Sit and observe everything around you. Use your pencil to help you see, both by drawing sketches and by recording sensory details in words. What do you see that you haven't noticed before? Then *narrow* your attention to a single person, *focus* on a restricted place, or *zoom in* on a single object. What do you see that you haven't noticed before?

2. Buy a piece of fruit or a vegetable. An apple, orange, pear, carrot, or onion will do, but if possible find a persimmon, pawpaw, mango, pineapple, guava, pomegranate, coconut, passion fruit, artichoke, cauliflower, broccoli, jicama, bok choy, or rutabaga. Sit down somewhere and look at it. Record your impressions. Hold it close to your ear and shake it. Record your impressions. Scrape your fingernail over the surface. Rub it against your cheek. Record your impressions. Close your eyes and sample it with your tongue. Record your impressions. Scratch the surface with a utensil. Now close your eyes and smell it. Record your impressions. Peel it or take it apart. Describe what it looks like now. Take a bite out of it. Record your impressions.

3. Find a place where people (either friends or strangers) are talking (over lunch, at a bar, at a party). For ten or fifteen minutes, record the conversation word for word. To keep friends from being self-conscious, tell them that you're doing homework. If you're eavesdropping on strangers, be as inconspicuous as possible. Your purpose is to record as much of the dialogue as possible, with the pauses, interruptions, *uh*'s and *er*'s, unfinished sentences, slang—everything *exactly* as you hear it.

4. Go to a private place that is away from the rush of everyday life (a field, a lake, a grove of trees, a hill, a desert, a seashore, or even an oasis in the city that is quiet and peaceful). Sit for a few minutes until you are accustomed to the quiet and the silence. Then observe the place around you and describe what's happening. You'll have to be attentive, noticing the little things, minor events, or subtle changes. Record your observations.

5. In one of your classes, use your repeated observations of the total learning environment (the room, the seating arrangements, the blackboards, the audio-visual or computer equipment, the teacher, the daily teaching or learning rituals, and the students) to speculate on who has authority, how knowledge is created or communicated, and what the learning goals are for this course.

6. "Obnoxious," the dictionary says, means "highly disagreeable, offensive, irritating, odious." Describe the most obnoxious person you know by giving at least two detailed examples of his or her behavior. Or do just the reverse: Tell how the most obnoxious person you know would describe you.

7. Go to a gallery, studio, or museum where you can observe sculpture, paintings, or other works of art. Choose one work of art and draw it. Then describe it as fully as possible. Return to the gallery the next day, reread your first description, observe the work again, and add details that you didn't notice the first time.

8. As you sit in a lecture class, restaurant, student lounge, library, department store, airport, or bar, describe the three or four most common *types* of people you observe there. In a class, for example, you might describe the Fanatic Scribbler, the Whisperer, and the Sleeper. In a department store, you might describe *types* of shoppers: the Look-but-Never-Buy Customer, the Complainer/Whiner, the Price-Haggler, and the Bet-You-Can't-Fit-Me Customer. Describe their behavior using specific detail.

9. Visit a local park. Pretend that you are a landscape architect, a photographer, a bird-watcher, an entomologist, an engineer building a road, a jogger, or a mother with two small children. Describe what you see. Now choose another role—you're a social worker, a woman alone in a park at night, a person without a home, a Secret Service agent assigned to protect the President of the United States, a Saint Bernard, or a sixth-grader just out of school for the day. Describe what you see. Then reread both descriptions. Compare them. Briefly, explain how and why they are similar or dissimilar.

WRITE TO LEARN

Observing journal entries are one of the most important write-to-learn strategies. To reinforce the sense that journals are not busywork but are critical to the observing and learning process, discuss their purpose when you make an assignment. When students complete an activity, have a few volunteers read their entries aloud. Ask the writer to explain what he or she learned by writing that entry. Ask other class members what they learned as they listened.

Observing: Professional Writing

Take This Fish and Look at It

Samuel H. Scudder

In this essay, Samuel H. Scudder (1837–1911), an American entomologist, narrates his early attempts at scientific observation. Scudder recalls how a famous Swiss naturalist, Louis Agassiz, taught him to learn by observing closely, carefully, and repeatedly. Agassiz, a professor of natural history at Harvard, taught his students that both factual details and general laws are important. "Facts are stupid things," he said, "until brought into connection with some general law." Scudder, writing about his studies under Agassiz, suggests that repeated observation can help us connect facts or specific details with general laws. This essay shows us what Scudder learned: To help us see, describe, and connect, "a pencil is one of the best of eyes."

Teaching Tip

Early in your discussion of this essay, make sure your students realize that while Scudder's essay does contain observation of the fish (see paragraphs 7–12), the framework for the essay is largely narrative. In contrast, the following essay by Annie Dillard is almost entirely descriptive. Although students need to hear Scudder's advice about repeated observation, their own essays for this chapter should emphasize extended observation, not extended narration.

It was more than fifteen years ago that I entered the laboratory of Professor Agassiz, and told him I had enrolled my name in the Scientific School as a student of natural history. He asked me a few questions about my object in coming, my antecedents generally, the mode in which I afterwards proposed to use the knowledge I might acquire, and, finally, whether I wished to study any special branch. To the latter I replied that, while I wished to be well grounded in all departments of zoology, I purposed to devote myself specially to insects. **(1)**

"When do you wish to begin?" he asked. **(2)**

"Now," I replied. **(3)**

This seemed to please him, and with an energetic "Very well!" he reached from a shelf a huge jar of specimens in yellow alcohol. "Take this fish," he said, "and look at it; we call it a haemulon; by and by I will ask what you have seen." **(4)**

With that he left me, but in a moment returned with explicit instructions as to the care of the object entrusted to me. **(5)**

"No man is fit to be a naturalist," said he, "who does not know how to take care of specimens." **(6)**

I was to keep the fish before me in a tin tray, and occasionally moisten the surface with alcohol from the jar, always taking care to replace the stopper tightly. Those were not the days of ground-glass stoppers and elegantly shaped exhibition jars; all the old students will recall the huge neckless glass bottles with their leaky, wax-besmeared corks, half eaten by insects, and begrimed with cellar dust. Entomology was a cleaner science than ichthyology, but the example of the Professor, who had unhesitatingly plunged to the bottom of the jar to produce the fish, was infectious; and though this alcohol had a "very ancient and fishlike smell," I really dared not show any aversion within these sacred precincts, and treated the alcohol as though it were pure water. Still I was conscious of a passing feeling of disappointment, for gazing at a fish did not commend itself to an ardent entomologist. My friends at home, too, were annoyed when they discovered that no amount of eau-de-Cologne would drown the perfume which haunted me like a shadow. **(7)**

In ten minutes I had seen all that could be seen in that fish, and started in search of the Professor—who had, however, left the Museum; and when I returned, after lingering over some of the odd animals stored in the upper apartment, my specimen was dry all over. I dashed the fluid over the fish as if to resuscitate the beast from a fainting fit, and looked with anxiety for a return of the normal sloppy appearance. This little excitement over, nothing was to be done but to return to a steadfast gaze at my mute companion. Half an hour passed—an hour—another hour; the fish began to look loathsome. I turned it over and around; looked it in the face—ghastly; from behind, beneath, above, sideways, at three-quarters' view—just as ghastly. I was in despair; at an early hour I concluded that lunch was necessary; so, with infinite relief, the fish was carefully replaced in the jar, and for an hour I was free. **(8)**

On my return, I learned that Professor Agassiz had been at the Museum, but had gone, and would not return for several hours. My fellow-students were too busy to be disturbed by continued conversation. Slowly I drew forth that hideous fish, and with a feeling of desperation again looked at it. I might not use a magnifying-glass; instruments of all kinds were interdicted. My two hands, my two eyes, and the fish: it seemed a most limited field. I pushed my finger down its throat to feel how sharp the teeth were. I began to count the scales in the different rows, until I was convinced that was nonsense. At last a happy thought struck me—I would draw the fish; and now with surprise I began to discover new features in the creature. Just then the Professor returned. **(9)**

"That is right," said he; "a pencil is one of the best of eyes. I am glad to notice, too, that you keep your specimen wet, and your bottle corked." **(10)**

With these encouraging words, he added: "Well, what is it like?" **(11)**

He listened attentively to my brief rehearsal of the structure of parts whose names were still unknown to me: the fringed gill-arches and movable operculum; the pores of the head, fleshy lips and lidless eyes; the lateral line, the spinous fins and forked tail; the compressed and

CRITICAL READING

Use Question 2 under "Questions for Writing and Discussion" to teach basic critical-reading strategies. Give students time in class to annotate Scudder's observing techniques by *actually marking in their texts*. If time permits, have students in groups of three or four collate their annotations. What students discover about the essay during their rereading should, if possible, generate the focus for class discussion.

arched body. When I finished, he waited as if expecting more, and then, with an air of disappointment: "You have not looked very carefully; why," he continued more earnestly, "you haven't even seen one of the most conspicuous features of the animal, which is plainly before your eyes as the fish itself; look again, look again!" and he left me to my misery. **(12)**

I was piqued; I was mortified. Still more of that wretched fish! But now I set myself to my task with a will, and discovered one new thing after another, until I saw how just the Professor's criticism had been. The afternoon passed quickly; and when, towards its close, the Professor inquired: "Do you see it yet?"**(13)**

"No," I replied, "I am certain I do not, but I see how little I saw before." **(14)**

"That is next best," said he, earnestly, "but I won't hear you now; put away your fish and go home; perhaps you will be ready with a better answer in the morning. I will examine you before you look at the fish." **(15)**

This was disconcerting. Not only must I think of my fish all night, studying, without the object before me, what this unknown but most visible feature might be; but also, without reviewing my discoveries, I must give an exact account of them the next day. I had a bad memory; so I walked home by Charles River in a distracted state, with my two perplexities. **(16)**

The cordial greeting from the Professor the next morning was reassuring; here was a man who seemed to be quite as anxious as I that I should see for myself what he saw. **(17)**

"Do you perhaps mean," I asked, "that the fish has symmetrical sides with paired organs?" **(18)**

His thoroughly pleased "Of course! of course!" repaid the wakeful hours of the previous night. After he had discoursed most happily and enthusiastically—as he always did—upon the importance of this point, I ventured to ask what I should do next. **(19)**

"Oh, look at your fish!" he said, and left me again to my own devices. In a little more than an hour he returned, and heard my new catalogue. **(20)**

"That is good, that is good!" he repeated; "but that is not all; go on"; and so for three long days he placed that fish before my eyes, forbidding me to look at anything else, or to use any artificial aid. "Look, look, look," was his repeated injunction. **(21)**

This was the best entomological lesson I ever had—a lesson whose influence has extended to the details of every subsequent study; a legacy the Professor had left to me, as he has left it to so many others, of inestimable value, which we could not buy, with which we cannot part. **(22)**

A year afterward, some of us were amusing ourselves with chalking outlandish beasts on the Museum blackboard. We drew prancing starfishes; frogs in mortal combat; hydra-headed worms; stately craw-fishes, standing on their tails, bearing aloft umbrellas; and grotesque fishes with gaping mouths and staring eyes. The Professor came in shortly after, and was as amused as any at our experiments. He looked at the fishes. **(23)**

"Haemulons, every one of them," he said; Mr.—drew them." **(24)**

True; and to this day, if I attempt a fish, I can draw nothing but haemulons. **(25)**

The fourth day, a second fish of the same group was placed beside the first, and I was bidden to point out the resemblances and differences between the two; another and another followed, until the entire family lay before me, and a whole legion of jars covered the table and surrounding shelves; the odor had become a pleasant perfume; and even now, the sight of an old, six-inch worm-eaten cork brings fragrant memories. **(26)**

The whole group of haemulons was thus brought in review; and, whether engaged upon the dissection of the internal organs, the preparation and examination of the bony framework, or the description of the various parts, Agassiz's training in the method of observing facts and their orderly arrangement was ever accompanied by the urgent exhortation not to be content with them. **(27)**

"Facts are stupid things," he would say, "until brought into connection with some general law." **(28)**

At the end of eight months, it was almost with reluctance that I left these friends and turned to insects; but what I had gained by this outside experience has been of greater value than years of later investigation in my favorite groups. **(29)**

Vocabulary

In your journal, write down the meanings of the following words:

- my *antecedents* generally (1)
- *entomology* was a cleaner science than *ichthyology* (7)
- dared not show any *aversion* (7)
- to *resuscitate* the beast (8)
- instruments of all kinds were *interdicted* (9)
- movable *operculum* (12)
- I was *piqued* (13)
- with my two *perplexities* (16)

- his repeated *injunction* (21)
- *hydra-headed* worms (23)
- the urgent *exhortation* (27)

Questions for Writing and Discussion

1. Without looking again at the essay, record in writing what you found to be the most memorable parts of the essay. What parts seemed most vivid? Explain.

2. Apply Scudder's technique of *repeated observation* to his own essay. Read the essay a second time, carefully, looking for techniques for recording observations. Use a pencil to help you read, by underlining or making brief notes. What do you notice on the *second* reading that you did not see on the first?

3. What is the purpose of this essay? To *inform* us about fish? To *explain* how to learn about fish? To *persuade* us to follow Professor Agassiz's method? To *entertain* us with his college stories? In your estimation what is the primary purpose?

4. Describe the intended audience for this essay. Which *sentences* most clearly address the intended audience?

5. "Facts are stupid things," Agassiz says, "until brought into connection with some general law." Reread paragraph 8. What is the "general law"—or, in this case, the *dominant idea*—created by the specific details describing Scudder's first session with his fish? Are his descriptive details objective, subjective, or a combination of both? Explain.

THE SNAKE

ANNIE DILLARD

Annie Dillard was born in Pittsburgh in 1945 and received her B.A. and M.A. degrees from Hollins College. She has published a book of poetry, Tickets for a Prayer Wheel *(1974), columns and essays for* Living Wilderness, Harpers, *and the* Atlantic, *and several books, including (1984),* An American Childhood *(1987), and* A Writing Life *(1989). In the following selection from* Pilgrim at Tinker Creek, *Dillard carefully observes a snake, a poisonous copperhead, as it lies on a sandstone quarry ledge at twilight. To her surprise, a mosquito alights on the snake and goes about its business of drilling through the scaly skin and sucking the snake's blood. Observing this bizarre episode, Dillard wonders about the laws of biological survival: "A little blood here, a chomp there, and still we live, trampling the grass? Must everything whole be nibbled?"*

There was a snake at the quarry with me tonight. It lay shaded by cliffs on a flat sandstone ledge above the quarry's dark waters. I was thirty feet away, sitting on the forest path overlook, when my eye caught the dark scrawl on the rocks, the lazy sinuosity that can only mean snake. I approached for a better look, edging my way down the steep rock cutting, and saw that the snake was only twelve or thirteen inches long. Its body was thick for its length. I came closer still, and saw the unmistakable undulating bands of brown, the hourglasses: copperhead. **(1)**

I never step a foot out of the house, even in winter, without a snakebite kit in my pocket. Mine is a small kit in rubber casing about the size of a shotgun shell; I slapped my pants instinctively to fix in my mind its location. Then I stomped hard on the ground a few times and sat down beside the snake. **(2)**

The young copperhead was motionless on its rock. Although it lay in a loose sprawl, all I saw at first was a camouflage pattern of particolored splotches confused by the rushing speckles of light in the weeds between us, and by the deep twilight dark of the quarry pond beyond the rock. Then suddenly the form of its head emerged from the confusion: burnished brown, triangular, blunt as a stone ax. Its head and the first four inches of its body rested on airy nothing an inch above the rock. I admired the snake. Its scales shone with newness, bright and buffed. Its body was perfect, whole and unblemished. I found it hard to believe it had not just been created on the spot, or hatched fresh from its mother, so unscathed and clean was its body, so unmarked by any passage. **(3)**

Did it see me? I was only four feet away, seated on the weedy cliff behind the sandstone ledge; the snake was between me and the quarry pond. I waved an arm in its direction: nothing moved. Its low-forehead glare and lipless reptile smirk revealed nothing. How could I tell where it was looking, what it was seeing? I squinted at its head, staring at those eyes like the glass eyes of a stuffed warbler, at those scales like shields canted and lapped just so, to frame an improbable, unfathomable face. **(4)**

Yes, it knew I was there. There was something about its eyes, some alien alertness . . . what on earth must it be like to have scales on your face? All right then, copperhead. I know you're here, you know I'm here. This is a big night. I dug my elbows into rough rock and dry soil and set-

CRITICAL READING

In a writing class, the lessons and discoveries made through critical reading should be *transferred* to the student's own writing. For example, after students annotate Dillard's essay for the six observing techniques, ask them to annotate occurrences of these techniques in each other's drafts. If one or more techniques is absent, the writer and peer editor should decide whether more sensory detail, dialogue, or images would be effective.

Teaching Tip

Immediately following this selection, Dillard writes, "When I reached home, I turned first to the bookshelf, to see if I could possibly have seen what I thought I had. All I could find was this sentence in Will Barker's book *Familiar Insects of North America*: 'The bite of the female [Mosquito, *Culex pipiens*] is effected with a little drill that can puncture many types of body covering—even the leathery skin of a frog or the overlapping scales on a snake.' All right then; maybe I had seen it. Anything can happen in any direction; the world is more chomped on than I'd dreamed." Read this passage to your students and then ask them what they might read about *their* subjects to help them revise their own drafts. As in Dillard's case, what they read may help clarify their discovery or their dominant idea.

tled back on the hillside to begin the long business of waiting out a snake. **(5)**

The only other poisonous snake around here is the timber rattler, *Crotalus horridus horridus*. These grow up to six feet long in the mountains, and as big as your thigh. I've never seen one in the wild; I don't know how many have seen me. I see copperheads, though, sunning in the dust, disappearing into rock cliff chinks, crossing dirt roads at twilight. Copperheads have no rattle, of course, and, at least in my experience, they do not give way. You walk around a copperhead—if you see it. Copperheads are not big enough or venomous enough to kill adult humans readily, but they do account for far and away the greatest number of poisonous snakebites in North America: there are so many of them, and people, in the Eastern woodlands. It always interests me when I read about new studies being done on pit vipers; the team of herpetologists always seems to pick my neck of the woods for its fieldwork. I infer that we have got poisonous snakes as East Africa has zebras or the tropics have orchids—they are our specialty, our stock-in-trade. So I try to keep my eyes open. But I don't worry: you have to live pretty far out to be more than a day from a hospital. And worrying about getting it in the face from a timber rattler is like worrying about being struck by a meteorite: life's too short. Anyway, perhaps the actual bite is painless. . . . **(6)**

The copperhead in front of me was motionless; its head still hung in the air above the sandstone rock. I thought of poking at it with a weed, but rejected the notion. Still, I wished it would do something. Marston Bates tells about an English ecologist, Charles Elton, who said, with his Britishness fully unfurled, "All cold-blooded animals . . . spend an unexpectedly large proportion of their time doing nothing at all, or at any rate nothing in particular." That is precisely what this one was doing. **(7)**

I noticed its tail. It tapered to nothingness. I started back at the head and slid my eye down its body slowly: taper, taper, taper, scales, tiny scales, air. Suddenly the copperhead's tail seemed to be the most remarkable thing I had ever seen. I wished I tapered like that somewhere. What if I were a shaped balloon blown up through the tip of a finger? **(8)**

Here was this blood-filled, alert creature, this nerved rope of matter, really here instead of not here, splayed soft and solid on a rock by the slimmest of chances. It was a thickening of the air spread from a tip, a rush into being, eyeball and blood, through a pin-hole rent. Every other time I had ever seen this rock it had been a flat sandstone rock over the quarry pond; now it hosted and bore this chunk of fullness that parted the air around it like a driven wedge. I looked at it from the other direction. From tail to head it spread like the lines of a crescendo, widening from stillness to a turgid blast; then at the bulging jaws it began contracting again, diminuendo, till at the tip of its snout the lines met back at the infinite point that corners every angle, and that space once more ceased being a snake. **(9)**

While this wonder engaged me, something happened that was so unusual and unexpected that I can scarcely believe I saw it. It was ridiculous. **(10)**

Night had been rising like a ground vapor from the blackened quarry pool. I heard a mosquito sing in my ear; I waved it away. I was looking at the copperhead. The mosquito landed on my ankle; again, I idly brushed it off. To my utter disbelief, it lighted on the copperhead. It squatted on the copperhead's back near its "neck," and bent its head to its task. I was riveted. I couldn't see the mosquito in great detail, but I could make out its lowered head that seemed to bore like a well drill through surface rock to fluid. Quickly I looked around to see if I could find anyone—any hunter going to practice shooting beer cans, any boy on a motorbike—to whom I could show this remarkable sight while it lasted. **(11)**

To the best of my knowledge, it lasted two or three full minutes; it seemed like an hour. I could imagine the snake, like the frog sucked dry by the giant water bug, collapsing to an empty bag of skin. But the snake never moved, never indicated any awareness. At last the mosquito straightened itself, fumbled with its forelegs about its head like a fly, and sluggishly took to the air, where I lost it at once. I looked at the snake; I looked beyond the snake to the ragged chomp in the hillside where years before men had quarried stone; I rose, brushed myself off, and walked home. **(12)**

Is this what it's like, I thought then, and think now: a little blood here, a chomp there, and still we live, trampling the grass? Must everything whole be nibbled? Here was a new light on the intricate texture of things in the world, the actual plot of the present moment in time after the fall: the way we the living are nibbled and nibbling—not held aloft on a cloud in the air but bumbling pitted and scarred and broken through a frayed and beautiful land. **(13)**

Vocabulary

In your journal, write down the meanings of the following words:

- the lazy *sinuosity* (1)
- *undulating* bands (1)
- team of *herpetologists* (6)
- *splayed* soft and solid (9)
- lines of a *crescendo* (9)
- *diminuendo* (9)
- in time after the *fall* (13)

Questions for Writing and Discussion

1. If you have ever seen a snake or reptile up close, describe the snake (and the experience) in a paragraph.

2. Using only the details and description provided by Dillard, write a paragraph describing and characterizing the copperhead. Now, compare the paragraph you wrote in question 1 (above) with the details that Dillard gives. What does she describe that you did not? What did you notice that she doesn't?

3. Reread Dillard's essay, annotating for sensory details, images, descriptions of what is not there, and changes in her subject. Cite two specific examples (phrases or sentences) for each of these four observing techniques. Which of these techniques does she use most frequently? Which does she use most effectively?

4. In addition to observing her subject, Dillard describes herself and her relationship to the snake. Find three specific instances of this strategy. If she omitted these descriptions of herself, would her essay be more effective? Explain.

5. Observing essays focus on a discovery, a dominant idea, or a perceived general law. In Scudder's essay, Professor Agassiz says, "Facts are stupid things until brought into connection with some general law." What "facts" does Dillard observe? What general law does she perceive? In which sentences does Dillard *connect* observed facts with her general law or dominant idea?

OBSERVING WOLVES

FARLEY MOWAT

Farley Mowat was born in Ontario in 1921 and received a B. A. from the University of Toronto. He has published over fifty books of fiction and nonfiction, including People of the Deer *(1952),* Never Cry Wolf *(1963), and* Woman in the Mists: The Story of Dian Fossey and the Mountain Gorillas of Africa *(1987).* Never Cry Wolf, *from which "Observing Wolves" was taken, describes how the Canadian Government sent Mowat to the Keewatin Barren Lands in the Northwest Territories to prove that the wolves were decimating the caribou herds—and thus should be exterminated. After observing wolves for a few short days, however, Mowat realized that "the centuries-old and universally accepted human concept of wolf character was a palpable lie. . . . I made my decision that, from this hour onward, I would go open-minded into the lupine world and learn to see and know the wolves, not for what they were supposed to be, but for what they actually were." In the first scene, Mowat learns how wolves establish territories; in the second, he discovers something about their diet. Mowat also gives names to each wolf that he observes: Angeline is a female wolf, George is her mate, and Uncle Albert is a male attached to the group.*

I

During the next several weeks I put my decision into effect with the thoroughness for which I have always been noted. I went completely to the wolves. To begin with I set up a den of my own as near to the wolves as I could conveniently get without disturbing the even tenor of their lives too much. After all, I *was* a stranger, and an unwolflike one, so I did not feel I should go too far too fast. **(1)**

Abandoning Mike's cabin (with considerable relief, since as the days warmed up so did the smell) I took a tiny tent and set it up on the shore of the bay immediately opposite to the den esker. I kept my camping gear to the barest minimum—a small primus stove, a stew pot, a teakettle, and a sleeping bag were the essentials. I took no weapons of any kind, although there were times when I regretted this omission, even if only fleetingly. The big telescope was set up in the mouth of the tent in such a way that I could observe the den by day or night without even getting out of my sleeping bag. **(2)**

During the first few days of my sojourn with the wolves I stayed inside the tent except for brief and necessary visits to the out-of-doors which I always undertook when the wolves were not in sight. The point of this personal concealment was to allow the animals to get used to the tent and to accept it as only another bump on a very bumpy piece of terrain. Later, when the mosquito population reached full flowering, I stayed in the tent practically all of the time unless there was a strong wind blowing, for the most bloodthirsty beasts in the Arctic are not wolves, but the insatiable mosquitoes. **(3)**

My precautions against disturbing the wolves were superfluous. It had required a week for me to get their measure, but they must have taken mine at our first meeting; and, while there was nothing overtly disdainful in their evident assessment of me, they managed to ignore my presence, and indeed my very existence, with a thoroughness which was somehow disconcerting. **(4)**

Quite by accident I had pitched my tent within ten yards of one of the major paths used by the wolves when they were going to, or coming from, their hunting grounds to the westward; and only a few hours after I had

Reading against the Text

Farley Mowat is a partisan observer and apologist for all of nature's species, including wolves. Ask students to find passages in this text where Mowat's bias is apparent. Do his sympathies for the wolf affect his observations or conclusions? Is he ignoring scientific information that might present the wolf in a less favorable light?

taken up residence one of the wolves came back from a trip and discovered me and my tent. He was at the end of a hard night's work and was clearly tired and anxious to go home to bed. He came over a small rise fifty yards from me with his head down, his eyes half-closed, and a preoccupied air about him. Far from being the preternaturally alert and suspicious beast of fiction, this wolf was so self-engrossed that he came straight on to within fifteen yards of me, and might have gone right past the tent without seeing it at all, had I not banged my elbow against the teakettle, making a resounding clank. The wolf's head came up and his eyes opened wide, but he did not stop or falter in his pace. One brief, sidelong glance was all he vouchsafed to me as he continued on his way. **(5)**

It was true that I wanted to be inconspicuous, but I felt uncomfortable at being so totally ignored. Nevertheless, during the two weeks which followed, one or more wolves used the track past my tent almost every night—and never, except on one memorable occasion, did they evince the slightest interest in me. **(6)**

By the time this happened I had learned a good deal about my wolfish neighbors, and one of the facts which had emerged was that they were not nomadic roamers, as is almost universally believed, but were settled beasts and the possessors of a large permanent estate with very definite boundaries. **(7)**

The territory owned by my wolf family comprised more than a hundred square miles, bounded on one side by a river but otherwise not delimited by geographical features. Nevertheless there *were* boundaries, clearly indicated in wolfish fashion. **(8)**

Anyone who has observed a dog doing his neighborhood rounds and leaving his personal mark on each convenient post will have already guessed how the wolves marked out *their* property. Once a week, more or less, the clan made the rounds of the family lands and freshened up the boundary markers—a sort of lupine beating of the bounds. This careful attention to property rights was perhaps made necessary by the presence of two other wolf families whose lands abutted on ours, although I never discovered any evidence of bickering or disagreements between the owners of the various adjoining estates. I suspect, therefore, that it was more of a ritual activity. **(9)**

In any event, once I had become aware of the strong feeling of property rights which existed amongst the wolves, I decided to use this knowledge to make them at least recognize my existence. One evening, after they had gone off for their regular nightly hunt, I staked out a property claim of my own, embracing perhaps three acres, with the tent at the middle, and *including a hundred-yard long section of the wolves' path.* **(10)**

Staking the land turned out to be rather more difficult than I had anticipated. In order to ensure that my claim would not be overlooked, I felt obliged to make a property mark on stones, clumps of moss, and patches of vegetation at intervals of not more than fifteen feet around the circumference of my claim. This took most of the night and required frequent returns to the tent to consume copious quantities of tea; but before dawn brought the hunters home the task was done, and I retired, somewhat exhausted, to observe results. **(11)**

I had not long to wait. At 0814 hours, according to my wolf log, the leading male of the clan appeared over the ridge behind me, padding homeward with his usual air of preoccupation. As usual he did not deign to glance at the tent; but when he reached the point where my property line intersected the trail, he stopped as abruptly as if he had run into an invisible wall. He was only fifty yards from me and with my binoculars I could see his expression very clearly. **(12)**

His attitude of fatigue vanished and was replaced by a look of bewilderment. Cautiously he extended his nose and sniffed at one of my marked bushes. He did not seem to know what to make of it or what to do about it. After a minute of complete indecision he backed away a few yards and sat down. And then, finally, he looked directly at the tent and at me. It was a long, thoughtful, considering sort of look. **(13)**

Having achieved my object—that of forcing at least one of the wolves to take cognizance of my existence—I now began to wonder if, in my ignorance, I had transgressed some unknown wolf law of major importance and would have to pay for my temerity. I found myself regretting the absence of a weapon as the look I was getting became longer, yet more thoughtful, and still more intent. **(14)**

I began to grow decidedly fidgety, for I dislike staring matches, and in this particular case I was up against a master, whose yellow glare seemed to become more baleful as I attempted to stare him down. **(15)**

The situation was becoming intolerable. In an effort to break the impasse I loudly cleared my throat and turned my back on the wolf (for a tenth of a second) to indicate as clearly as possible that I found his continued scrutiny impolite, if not actually offensive. **(16)**

He appeared to take the hint. Getting to his feet he had another sniff at my marker, and then he seemed to make up his mind. Briskly, and with an air of decision, he turned his attention away from me and began a systematic tour of the area I had staked out as my own. As he came to each boundary marker he sniffed it once or twice, then carefully placed *his* mark on the outside of each clump of grass or stone. As I watched I saw where I, in my ignorance, had erred. He made his mark with such economy that he was able to complete the entire circuit without having to reload once, or, to change the simile slightly, he did it all on one tank of fuel. **(17)**

The task completed—and it had taken him no longer than fifteen minutes—he rejoined the path at the point where it left my property and

Teaching Tip

"Facts are stupid things," Scudder says, "until brought into connection with some general law." Ask students to locate specific passages in part II of Mowat's essay in which he connects observed "facts" with some general law. In Mowat's case, how do the facts subvert the conventional wisdom or law about wolves? If students have drafts of their own essays, have them check each other's essays to make sure they have passages that connect their observations either with some general law or with their discovered knowledge.

trotted off towards his home—leaving me with a good deal to occupy my thoughts. **(18)**

II

After some weeks of study I still seemed to be as far as ever from solving the salient problem of how the wolves made a living. This was a vital problem, since solving it in a way satisfactory to my employers was the reason for my expedition. **(19)**

Caribou are the only large herbivores to be found in any numbers in the arctic Barren Lands. Although once as numerous as the plains buffalo, they had shown a catastrophic decrease during the three or four decades preceding my trip to the Barrens. Evidence obtained by various Government agencies from hunters, trappers and traders seemed to prove that the plunge of the caribou toward extinction was primarily due to the depredations of the wolf. It therefore must have seemed a safe bet, to the politicians-cum-scientists who had employed me, that a research study of wolf-caribou relationships in the Barrens would uncover incontrovertible proof with which to damn the wolf wherever he might be found, and provide a more than sufficient excuse for the adoption of a general campaign for his extirpation. **(20)**

I did my duty, but although I had searched diligently for evidence which would please my superiors, I had so far found none. Nor did it appear I was likely to. **(21)**

Toward the end of June, the last of the migrating caribou herds had passed Wolf House Bay heading for the high Barrens some two or three hundred miles to the north, where they would spend the summer.

Whatever my wolves were going to eat during those long months, and whatever they were going to feed their hungry pups, it would not be caribou, for the caribou were gone. But if not caribou, what *was* it to be? **(22)**

I canvassed all the other possibilities I could think of, but there seemed to be no source of food available which would be adequate to satisfy the appetites of three adult and four young wolves. Apart from myself (and the thought recurred several times) there was hardly an animal left in the country which could be considered suitable prey for a wolf. Arctic hares were present; but they were very scarce and so fleet of foot that a wolf could not hope to catch one unless he was extremely lucky. Ptarmigan and other birds were numerous; but they could fly, and the wolves could not. Lake trout, arctic grayling and whitefish filled the lakes and rivers; but wolves are not otters. **(23)**

About this time I began having trouble with mice. The vast expanses of spongy sphagnum bog provided an ideal milieu for several species of small rodents who could burrow and nest-build to their hearts' content in the ready-made mattress of moss. **(24)**

They did other things too, and they must have done them with great frequency, for as June waned into July the country seemed to become alive with little rodents. The most numerous species were the lemmings, which are famed in literature for their reputedly suicidal instincts, but which, instead, *ought* to be hymned for their unbelievable reproductive capabilities. Red-backed mice and meadow mice began invading Mike's cabin in such numbers that it looked as if *I* would soon be starving unless I could thwart their appetites for my supplies. *They* did not scorn my bread. They did not scorn my bed, either; and when I awoke one morning to find that a meadow mouse had given birth to eleven naked offspring inside the pillow of my sleeping bag, I began to know how Pharaoh must have felt when he antagonized the God of the Israelites. **(25)**

I suppose it was only because my own wolf indoctrination had been so complete, and of such a staggeringly inaccurate nature, that it took me so long to account for the healthy state of the wolves in the apparent absence of any game worthy of their reputation and physical abilities. The idea of wolves not only eating, but actually thriving and raising their families on a diet of mice was so at odds with the character of the mythical wolf that it was really too ludicrous to consider. And yet, it was the answer to the problem of how my wolves were keeping the larder full. **(26)**

Angeline tipped me off. **(27)**

Late one afternoon, while the male wolves were still resting in preparation for the night's labors, she emerged from the den and nuzzled Uncle Albert until he yawned, stretched and got laboriously to his feet. Then she left the den site at a trot, heading directly for me across a broad expanse of grassy muskeg, and leaving Albert to entertain the pups as best he could. **(28)**

There was nothing particularly new in this. I had several times seen her conscript Albert (and on rare occasions even George) to do duty as a babysitter while she went down to the bay for a drink or, as I mistakenly thought, simply went for a walk to stretch her legs. Usually her peregrinations took her to the point of the bay farthest from my tent where she was hidden from sight by a low gravel ridge; but this time she came my way in full view and so I swung my telescope to keep an eye on her. **(29)**

She went directly to the rocky foreshore, waded out until the icy water was up to her shoulders, and had a long drink. As she was doing so, a small flock of Old Squaw ducks flew around the point of the Bay and pitched only a hundred yards or so away from her. She raised her head and eyed them speculatively for a moment, then waded back to shore, where she proceeded to act as if she had suddenly become demented. **(30)**

Yipping like a puppy, she began to chase her tail; to roll over and over among the rocks; to lie on her back; to wave all four feet furiously in the air; and in general to behave as if she were clean out of her mind. **(31)**

I swung the glasses back to where Albert was sitting amidst a gaggle of pups to see if he, too, had observed this mad display, and, if so, what his reaction to it was. He had seen it all right, in fact he was watching Angeline with keen interest but without the slightest indication of alarm. **(32)**

By this time Angeline appeared to be in the throes of a manic paroxysm, leaping wildly into the air and snapping at nothing, the while uttering shrill squeals. It was an awe-inspiring sight, and I realized that Albert and I were not the only ones who were watching it with fascination. The ducks seemed hypnotized by curiosity. So interested were they that they swam in for a closer view of this apparition on the shore. Closer and closer they came, necks outstretched, and gabbling incredulously among themselves. And the closer they came, the crazier grew Angeline's behavior. **(33)**

When the leading duck was not more than fifteen feet from shore, Angeline gave one gigantic leap towards it. There was a vast splash, a panic-stricken whacking of wings, and then all the ducks were up and away. Angeline had missed a dinner by no more than inches. **(34)**

This incident was an eye-opener since it suggested a versatility at food-getting which I would hardly have credited to a human being, let alone to a mere wolf. However, Angeline soon demonstrated that the charming of ducks was a mere side line. **(35)**

Having dried herself with a series of energetic shakes which momentarily hid her in a blue mist of water droplets, she padded back across the grassy swale. But now her movements were quite different from what they had been when she passed through the swale on the way to the bay. **(36)**

Angeline was of a rangy build, anyway, but by stretching herself so that she literally seemed to be walking on tiptoe, and by elevating her neck like a camel, she seemed to gain several inches in height. She began to move infinitely slowly upwind across the swale, and I had the impression that both ears were cocked for the faintest sound, while I could see her nose wrinkling as she sifted the breeze for the most ephemeral scents. **(37)**

Suddenly she pounced. Flinging herself up on her hind legs like a horse trying to throw its rider, she came down again with driving force, both forelegs held stiffly out in front of her. Instantly her head dropped; she snapped once, swallowed, and returned to her peculiar mincing ballet across the swale. Six times in ten minutes she repeated the straight-armed pounce, and six times she swallowed—without my having caught a glimpse of what it was that she had eaten. The seventh time she missed her aim, spun around, and began snapping frenziedly in a tangle of cotton grasses. This time when she raised her head I saw, quite unmistakably, the tail and hind quarters of a mouse quivering in her jaws. One gulp, and it too was gone. **(38)**

Although I was much entertained by the spectacle of one of this continent's most powerful carnivores hunting mice, I did not really take it seriously. I thought Angeline was only having fun; snacking, as it were. But when she had eaten some twenty-three mice I began to wonder. Mice are small, but twenty-three of them adds up to a fair-sized meal, even for a wolf. **(39)**

It was only later, by putting two and two together, that I was able to bring myself to an acceptance of the obvious. The wolves of Wolf House Bay, and, by inference at least, all the Barren Land wolves who were raising families outside the summer caribou range, were living largely, if not almost entirely, on mice. **(40)**

Vocabulary

In your journal, write down the meanings of the following words:

the den *esker* (2)
superfluous (4)
somehow *disconcerting* (4)
preternaturally (5)
evince the slightest interest (6)
lupine (9)
extirpation (20)
her *peregrinations* (29)

Questions for Writing and Discussion

1. Describe what you knew about wolves before you read Mowat's description. Which parts of Mowat's description agree with your preconceptions? Which parts give you new information or a different opinion?

2. What equipment and habits of observation does the narrator employ in his study of wolves?

3. *What* is observed depends on *who* is doing the observing. Describe the narrator's behavior and personality. How do his preconceptions affect what he observes? Should a scientific observer interfere with the lives of the wolves, as the narrator does? What does the narrator learn?

4. Four keys to effective description are repeated observation, attention to sensory details, noticing changes in the subject or the subject's behavior, and noticing what is not present. Find examples of each of these four strategies in this essay.

5. Reread Dillard's "The Snake." What are the similarities and differences between Mowat's and Dillard's methods of observation, their voices as observers, and their discoveries?

6. Some naturalists are currently advocating the reintroduction of wolves in Yellowstone National Park. Nearby ranchers, however, are fearful that the wolves will leave the park and kill livestock. How would Mowatt respond to this debate? Write a letter that Mowat might send to a rancher whose lands adjoin the park and who is worried about losing livestock to marauding wolves. You may wish to read additional chapters from *Never Cry Wolf.*

OBSERVING: THE WRITING PROCESS

TEACHING TIP

Some teachers prefer a more restricted assignment that is both easier to manage during workshops and easier to evaluate. The scenarios at the beginning of the chapter, the journal suggestions, and the ideas under "Choosing a Subject" offer possible topics. Another alternative is to coordinate this assignment with a later chapter. For example, students could use extended observation to begin evaluating a class, restaurant, place of work, social service, or person. The purpose of this piece of writing would be only to *inform* readers about the place, activity, thing, or person. Later, in Chapter 8, the student would complete the evaluation.

■ ASSIGNMENT FOR OBSERVING Do a piece of writing in which you observe a specific person, place, object, or event. Your goal is to show how specific, observed details create dominant ideas about the person, place, object, or event. Your initial purpose is to use your writing to help you observe, discover, and learn about your subject; your final purpose will be to show your reader what you have seen and learned.

Important: Repeated observation is essential. Choose some *limited* subject—a person or small group of people, a specific place, a single object or animal, or a recurring event—that *you can reobserve over a period of several days during the writing process.*

CHOOSING A SUBJECT

If one of your journal entries suggested an interesting subject, try the collecting and shaping strategies. If none of those exercises caught your interest, consider the following ideas:

- Think about your current classes. Do you have a class with a laboratory—chemistry, physics, biology, engineering, animal science, horticulture, industrial sciences, physical education, social work, drawing, pottery—in which you have to make detailed observations? Use this assignment to help you in one of those classes: Write about what you observe and learn during one of your lab sessions.
- Seek out a new place on campus that is off your usual track. Check the college catalog for ideas about places you haven't yet seen: a

"Write about dogs!"

theater where actors are rehearsing, a greenhouse, a physical education class in the martial arts, a studio where artists are working, a computer laboratory, or an animal research center. Or visit a class you wouldn't take for credit. Observe, write, and learn about what's there and what's happening.

- Get a copy of the Yellow Pages for your town or city. Open to a page at random and place your finger on the page. If it lands on an advertisement for a nearby store, take your notebook there for a visit. Describe the chocolate mousse at a restaurant, an expensive wine at a liquor store, a new car at a dealership, a headstone at a burial-monument company, a twelve-string guitar at a music shop—whatever you would like to learn about through careful observation.

We don't take in the world like a camera or a set of recording devices. The mind is an agent, not a passive receiver. . . . The active mind is a composer and everything we respond to, we compose.
—ANN BERTHOFF, AUTHOR AND TEACHER

As you write on your subject, consider a tentative audience and purpose. Who might want to know what you learn from your observations? What do you need to explain? What will readers already know? Jot down tentative ideas about your subject, audience, and purpose. Remember, however, that these are not cast in concrete: You may discover some new idea, focus, or angle as you write.

COLLECTING

Once you have chosen a subject from your journal or elsewhere, begin collecting information. Depending on your purpose, your topic, or even your personal learning preferences, some activities will work better than others. However, you should *practice* all of these activities to determine which is most successful for you and most appropriate to your topic. During these collecting activities, go back and *reobserve your subject.* The second or third time you go back, you may see additional details or more actively understand what you're seeing.

Sketching Begin by *drawing* what you see. A pen or pencil can be "the best of eyes," as Scudder's essay demonstrates. Your drawing doesn't have to be great art to suggest other details, questions, or relationships that may be important. Instead of trying to cover a wide range of objects, try to narrow and focus on one limited subject and draw it in detail.

Here's an example. Writing student Brad Parks decided to visit an Eskimo art display at a local gallery. As part of his observing notes, he drew the following sketches of Eskimo paintings. As he drew, he made notes in the margins of his sketches and zoomed in for more detail on one pair of walruses.

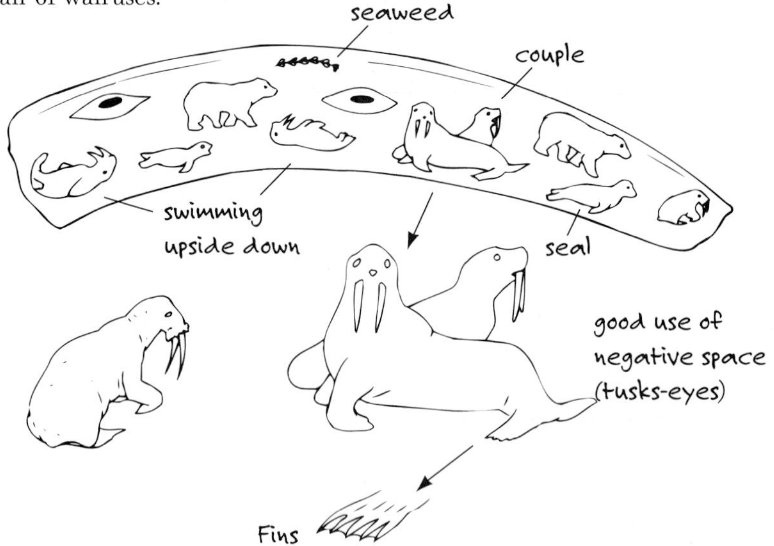

Computer Tips: Collecting

1. Computers are perfectly tailored to freewriting. As you type, for example, you don't have to hit a "Return" key because the text file keeps expanding as long as your ideas are flowing. You never have a dull pencil or run out of paper.

2. If your computer has split-screen capability, keep your double-entry log on the computer. On a computer, you can expand any one point as much as you like, without having to write in the margins or on the back of a page.

3. Try *invisible writing*. If you are freewriting and you find that you keep stopping to fix spelling or sentence errors as you write, turn down the contrast on the screen and then type as you normally would. At first, writing with a blank screen will seem a bit strange. As you practice, however, you will become more comfortable. Invisible writing imitates the spontaneous process of thinking to yourself, without the distraction of typos or misspelled words. After you are finished writing, turn up the contrast and read what you have written.

In cinematic terms, the double-entry log can be compared to the two-tiered format of documentary film: what you perceive (visuals, sound effects) depicted on the left and what it means (commentary) explained on the right.

Taking Double-Entry Notes Taking notes in a double-entry format is a simple but effective system for recording observed details. Draw a vertical line down the middle of a page in your journal. On the left-hand side, record bits of description and sensory details. On the right-hand side, jot down your reactions, thoughts, or ideas. On the left-hand side, make your observed details as objective as possible. Comments on the right-hand side will be more *subjective,* noting your impressions, reactions, comparisons, and images, as well as additional questions and ideas.

Sensory details, facts, data	Impressions, reactions, ideas, questions
size, color, shape, sounds, smell, touch, taste, actions, behavior	impressions, associations, feelings, reactions, ideas, images, comparisons, related thoughts, questions

Teaching Tip

Answering questions will not work as an invention strategy unless students *actually write out their responses* in their journals. Give your students a few minutes in class to apply these questions to their individual topics. Ask a few students to report on which strategies might help shape their essays.

Answering Questions To help you describe the person, place, object, or event, write a short response in your journal to each of the following questions:

- What exactly is it? Can you *define* this person, place, object, or event? If it's an object, are its parts related? Who needs it, uses it, or produces it?
- How much could it change and still be recognizable?
- Compare and contrast it. How is it similar to or different from other comparable people, places, things, or events?
- From what points of view is it usually seen? From what point of view is it rarely seen?

RESOURCE NOTE

For a full discussion of freewriting techniques, see Elbow, *Writing Without Teachers*, or Lindemann, *A Rhetoric for Writing Teachers*.

Freewriting Freewriting means exactly what it says. Write about your subject, nonstop, for five to ten minutes. Sometimes you may have to write, "I can't think of anything" or "This is really stupid," but keep on writing. Let your words and ideas suggest other thoughts and ideas. For observing, the purpose of freewriting is to let your *imagination* work on the subject, usually *after* you have observed and recorded specific details. Freewriting on your subject will also develop more *associations* or *comparisons* for the right-hand side of your double-entry log. It should also help you to identify a dominant idea for your details.

SHAPING

To focus once again on the shaping process, consider your subject, purpose, and audience. Has your purpose changed? Can you narrow your subject to a specific topic? You may know the answers to some questions immediately; others you may not know until after you complete your first draft. Jot down your current responses to the following questions:

- *Subject*: What is your general subject?
- *Specific topic*: What aspect of your subject are you interested in? Try to *narrow* your field or *limit* your focus.
- *Purpose*: Why is this topic interesting or important to you or to others? From what point of view will you be writing? What is the dominant idea you are trying to convey?
- *Audience*: Who are your readers? What are these readers like and why might they be interested in this topic? How can you direct your description of your subject to your particular audience?

Your audience is one single reader. I have found that sometimes it helps to pick out one person—a real person you know, or an imagined person and write to that one.
—JOHN STEINBECK, NOVELIST

With answers to these questions in mind, you should experiment with several of the following shaping strategies. These strategies will not only organize your specific examples but may also suggest related ideas to improve your description.

As you practice these strategies, try to *focus* on your subject. In a profile of a person, for example, focus on key facial features or revealing habits or mannerisms. If you're writing about a place or an event, narrow the subject. Describe, for instance, the street at night, a spider spinning a web in a windowsill, a man in a laundromat banging on a change machine, a bird hovering in midair, a photograph, a fish. Write in depth and detail about a *limited* subject.

With a limited subject, a shaping strategy such as spatial order, classification, or comparison/contrast will organize all the specific details for your audience. Shaping strategies give you ways of seeing relationships among the many bits of your description and of presenting them in an organized manner for your reader. Seeing these relationships will also help you discover and communicate the *dominant idea* to your reader.

Spatial Order Spatial order is a simple way to organize your descriptive details. Choose some sequence—left to right, right to left, bottom to top—and describe your observed details in that sequence. In the following description of his "trashed" dorm room, Dale Furnish, a student who was the victim of a prank, uses spatial order. The italicized words illustrate the spatial order.

> As I walked in the door, I could hardly believe that this scene of destruction used to be my room. *Along the left hand wall*, nearly hiding my desk and mirror, was a pile of beer cans and bottles, paper cups and old crumpled newspapers. The small window *on the far wall* was now covered with the mattress of the bed, and the frame of the bunk bed stood on end. The clothes closet, *to the right of the window*, looked as though it were a giant washing machine which had just gone through spin cycle—clothes were plastered all over, and only four hangers remained, dangling uselessly on the pole. *On the right wall*, where the bed had been, was the real surprise. Tied to the heating pipe was a mangy looking sheep. I swear. It was a real sheep. As I looked at it, it turned to face me and loudly and plaintively said, "Baaaa." *Behind me*, in the hall, everyone began laughing. I didn't know whether to laugh or cry.

Chronological Order Chronological order is simply the time sequence of your observation. In the following passage, Gregory Allen, writing from his point of view as a five-foot-six-inch guard on a basketball team, describes sights, sounds, and his feelings during a pickup game. The italicized words emphasize the chronological order.

> The game *begins*. The guy checking me is about 6′1″, red hair, freckles, and has no business on the court. He looks slow, *so* I decide to run him to tire him. I dribble twice, pump fake, and the guy goes

WRITE TO LEARN

To make full use of shaping strategies, students must *practice* applying them to their own topics. First, students should explain, in their journals or on their drafts, which three shaping strategies they might use to develop their topics. Then, imitating each of these three strategies, they should write on their own topics. To help students practice these strategies, *model* this exercise with your own observing topic or notes.

Since films, like essays, are sequential texts, they often use visual conventions to signal shifts from one segment to another. To clarify spatial relationships, the camera may pan horizontally, tilt vertically, or track through space. To contrast objects or events, the screen may be split into two. Ask your students to compare these visual strategies to the conventions available to writers.

for it, thinking that he's going to block this much smaller guy's shot. *Then* I leap, flick my wrist, and the ball glides through the air and flows through the net with a swish as the net turns upside down. I come down and realize that I have been scratched. *Suddenly*, I feel a sharp pain as sweat runs into the small red cut. I wipe the blood on my shorts and *continue playing* the game. *After* that first play, I begin to hear the common song of the game. There's the squeak of the high-top Nike sneakers, the bouncing ball, the shuffle of feet. *Occasionally*, I hear "I'm open!" "Pass the ball!" "Augghh!" And *then*, "Nice play, man!"

Comparison/Contrast If what you've observed and written about your subject so far involves seeing similarities or differences, you may be able to use comparison/contrast as a shaping strategy—either for a single paragraph or for a series of paragraphs. The following two paragraphs, for example, are taken from Albert Goldman's biography of Elvis Presley, entitled *Elvis*. In these paragraphs, Goldman's dominant idea depends on the striking contrast between what he finds on the front lawn of Graceland, the rock star's mansion in Memphis, and what he notices when he steps through the front door.

> Prominently displayed on the front lawn is an elaborate créche. The stable is a full-scale adobe house strewn with straw. Life-sized are the figures of Joseph and Mary, the kneeling shepherds and Magi, the lambs and ewes, as well as the winged annunciatory angel hovering over the roof beam. Real, too, is the cradle in which the infant Jesus sleeps.
>
> When you step through the ten-foot oak door and enter the house, you stop and stare in amazement. Having just come from the contemplation of the tenderest scene in the Holy Bible, imagine the shock of finding yourself in a *whorehouse*! Yet there is no other way to describe the drawing room of Graceland except to say that it appears to have been lifted from some turn-of-the-century bordello down in the French Quarter of New Orleans. . . . The room is a gaudy melange of red velour and gilded tassels, Louis XV furniture and porcelain bric-a-brac, all informed by the kind of taste that delights in a ceramic temple d'amour housing a miniature Venus de Milo with an electrically simulated waterfall cascading over her naked shoulders.

Examine once again your collecting notes about your subject. If there are striking similarities or differences between the two parts or between various aspects of your subject, perhaps a comparison or contrast structure will organize your details.

PEER RESPONSE

Peer response should not be limited to reading completed drafts of essays. Have students bring their observing notes to class. In small groups of two or three, students should trade their notes and identify one or two shaping strategies that might help them organize and develop their descriptions. Following this activity, give students three minutes to write on the ideas suggested by their peers' response. **Note:** Before you divide into groups, *model* this peer response activity by using a handout or overhead of your own observing notes and drafts. Describe what you were observing. Explain what your discovery or dominant idea is. Have class members identify the strategies that you are already using and suggest one or two strategies that you might use as you develop your notes.

Classification Classifying people, events, or things by ***types*** may provide a shape that you can use for either a paragraph or a whole essay. In the following paragraph from "Speedway," an essay on racing at the Indianapolis 500, cultural critic Paul Fussell categorizes spectators into three social classes: the middle classes, or "middles"; the high proletarians, or "high proles"; and the "uglies."

> I'd say the people can be divided into three social classes: the middles, who on race day tend, in homage to the checkered flag, to dress all in black and white and who sit in reserved seats; the high proles, who watch standing or lolling in the infield, especially at the turns, "where the action is"; and the uglies, the overadvertised, black-leathered, beer-sodden, pot-headed occupiers of that muddy stretch of ground in the infield at the first turn, known as the Snake Pit. These are the ones who, when girls pass, spiritlessly hold up signs reading "Show Us Your T—s." The uglies are sometimes taken to be the essence of Indy, and they are the people who, I think Frank Deford has in mind when he speaks of "barbarians." But they are not the significant Indy audience. The middle class is all those people arriving at the Speedway in cars bearing Purdue and Indiana State stickers.

Classification is often a useful method of shaping description. To see if it is appropriate for your subject, ask "What types do you observe?" The answer may lead to categories or types that you had failed to observe, and the categories may provide a shape you can adopt.

Definition Definition is the essence of observation. Defining a person, place, or object requires stating its exact meaning and describing its basic qualities. Literally, a definition sets the boundaries, indicating, for example, how an apple is distinct from an orange or how a canary is different from a sparrow. Definition, however, is a catchall term for a variety of strategies. It uses classification and comparison as well as description. It often describes a thing by negation—by saying what it is not. For example, Sidney Harris, a columnist for many years for the *Chicago Daily News,* once defined a "jerk" by referring to several types of people ("boob," "fool," "dope," "bore," "egotist" "nice person," "clever person") and then compared or contrasted these terms to show where "jerk" leaves off and "egotist" begins. In the following excerpt, Harris also defines by negation, saying that a jerk has no grace and is tactless. The result, when combined with a description of qualities he has observed in jerks, is definition.

> Thinking it over, I decided that a jerk is basically a person without insight. He is not necessarily a fool or a dope, because some extremely

> clever persons can be jerks. In fact, it has little to do with intelligence as we commonly think of it; it is, rather, a kind of subtle but persuasive aroma emanating from the inner part of the personality.
>
> I know a college president who can be described only as a jerk. He is not an unintelligent man, or unlearned, nor even unschooled in the social amenities. Yet he is a jerk *cum laude*, because of a fatal flaw in his nature—he is totally incapable of looking into the mirror of his soul and shuddering at what he sees there.
>
> A jerk, then, is a man (or woman) who is utterly unable to see himself as he appears to others. He has no grace, he is tactless without meaning to be, he is a bore even to his best friends, he is an egotist without charm. All of us are egotists to some extent, but most of us—unlike the jerk—are perfectly and horribly aware of it when we make asses of ourselves. The jerk never knows.

At this stage in the writing process, you have already been defining your subject simply by describing it. But you may want to use a deliberately structured definition, as Harris does, to shape your observations.

Simile, Metaphor, and Analogy Simile, metaphor, and analogy create vivid word pictures or *images* by making *comparisons*. These images may take up only a sentence or two, or they may shape several paragraphs.

- A *simile* is a comparison using "like" or "as": A is like B. "George eats his food like a vacuum cleaner."
- A *metaphor* is a direct or implied comparison suggesting that A *is* B: "At the dinner table, George is a vacuum cleaner."
- An *analogy* is an extended simile or metaphor that builds a point-by-point comparison into several sentences, a whole paragraph, or even a series of paragraphs. Writers use analogy to explain a difficult concept, idea, or process by comparing it with something more familiar or easier to understand.

If the audience, for example, knows about engines but has never seen a human heart, a writer might use an analogy to explain that a heart is like a simple engine, complete with chambers or cylinders, intake and exhaust valves, and hoses to carry fuel and exhaust.

As an illustration of simile and metaphor, notice how Joseph Conrad, in the following brief passage from *Heart of Darkness*, begins with a simile and then continues to build on his images throughout the paragraph. Rather than creating a rigid structural shape for his details (as classification or comparison/contrast would do), the images combine and flow like the river he is describing.

> Going up that river was like travelling back to the earliest beginnings of the world, when vegetation rioted on the earth and the big trees were kings. An empty stream, a great silence, an impenetrable forest. The air was warm, thick, heavy, sluggish. There was no joy in the brilliance of sunshine. The long stretches of the waterway ran on, deserted, into the gloom of overshadowed distances. On silvery sandbanks hippos and alligators sunned themselves side by side. The broadening waters flowed through a mob of wooded islands; you lost your way on that river as you would in a desert, and butted all day long against shoals, trying to find the channel, till you thought yourself bewitched and cut off for ever from everything you had known once—somewhere—far away—in another existence perhaps.

An analogy helps shape the following paragraph by Carl Sagan, author of *The Dragons of Eden* and *Cosmos.* To help us understand a difficult concept, the immense age of the Earth—(and, by comparison, the relatively tiny span of human history)—Sagan compares the lifetime of the universe to something simple and familiar: the calendar of a single year.

> The most instructive way I know to express this cosmic chronology is to imagine the fifteen-billion year lifetime of the universe . . . compressed into the span of a single year. . . . It is disconcerting to find that in such a cosmic year the Earth does not condense out of interstellar matter until early September; dinosaurs emerge on Christmas Eve; flowers arise on December 28th; and men and women originate at 10:30 P.M. on New Year's Eve. All of recorded history occupies the last ten seconds of December 31; and the time from the waning of the Middle Ages to the present occupies little more than one second.

Consider whether a good analogy would help you shape one or more paragraphs in your essay. Ask yourself: "What is the most difficult concept or idea I'm trying to describe?" Is there an extended point-by-point comparison—an analogy—that would clarify it?

Title, Introduction, and Conclusion Depending on your purpose and audience, you may want a *title* for what you're writing. At the minimum, titles—like labels—should accurately indicate the contents in the package. In addition, however, good titles capture the reader's interest with some catchy phrasing or imaginative language—something to make the reader want to "buy" the package. Writing primarily for himself, Mark Skelton uses a simple label, "A New Leaf," for his description, something which appears at the end of this chapter. Samuel H. Scudder's title, however, is both a good label (the essay is about looking at fish) and features catchy phrasing: "Take This Fish and Look at It." If a title is appropriate for your observation, write out several possibilities in your journal.

The introduction should set up the context for the reader—*who, what, when, where,* and *why*—so that readers can orient themselves. Depending on your audience and purpose, introductions can be very

Computer Tips: Collecting and Shaping

Transfer the following shaping strategies directly to your computer file. After you have done that, reread your journal or collecting notes, adding your details in the blank parts. If the shaping strategy is appropriate for your subject and purpose, you may generate more details and, at the same time, organize your ideas. On the computer, play with the possibilities for each shaping strategy.

1. Spatial Order. Enter a series of transition words in your file and then complete the sentences, noting what you saw. For example, for a line-of-sight description, enter:

From where I was sitting, at first I saw . . .
As I raised my eyes just slightly . . .
Only a few feet ahead was . . .
Beyond that, I noticed . . .
Finally, I saw . . .

2. Chronological Order. Enter a series of transition words, filling in the necessary details after each prompt: First . . . Next . . . After that . . . Then . . . Shortly thereafter . . . Soon . . . At last . . .

As you add details, you are actually shaping a trial version.

3. Comparison/Contrast. Enter the subjects (A and B) and then enter your observations. As you write, you will be experimenting with a possible structure for your observations.

Subject A___________
Observations about point one . . .
point two . . .
point three . . .
Subject B___________
Observations about B and similarities/differences between A and B on point one . . .
point two . . .
point three . . .

4. Classification. List the types within a single group that you observe, and then add your observed details about each.

First type:__________. Observing details:__________.
Second type __________. Observing details:__________.
Third type:__________. Observing details:__________.

As you add details, you will be testing your subject to see if classification is appropriate.

brief, pushing the reader quickly into the scene, or they can take more time, easing readers into the setting: "It was more than fifteen years ago that I entered the laboratory of Professor Agassiz," Scudder begins, giving us both background information and context. Stephen White, in his essay about Mesa Verde at the end of this chapter, begins more mysteriously: "It is difficult for me to say exactly what it was that drew me to this solitary place. . . ." White doesn't tell his reader that he's talking about Mesa Verde until the second paragraph. Writing primarily for himself, however, Mark Skelton is content with an abrupt beginning: "My potted plant sits on my desk at home."

Conclusions should bring the observation to a close, giving a sense of completeness. Conclusions depend upon a writer's purpose and audience, but they tend to be of two types or have two components: a *summary* and a *reference* to the introduction. Scudder both summarizes his dominant idea that his experiences were of great value and refers back to his introduction: "At the end of eight months, it was almost with reluctance that I left these friends and turned to insects." Skelton concludes by reemphasizing the dominant idea of his description: The plant is really a *family* of leaves.

As you work on shaping strategies and drafting, make notes about possible titles, appropriate introductions, or effective conclusions for your written observations.

Drafting

Reread Journal Entries and Notes from Collecting and Shaping
Before you start drafting, review your material so you aren't writing cold. Stop and reread everything you've written on your subject. You're not trying to memorize particular sentences or phrases; you're just getting it

all fresh in your mind, seeing what you still like and discarding details that are no longer relevant.

Reobserve Your Subject If necessary, go back and observe your subject again. One more session may suggest an important detail or idea that will help you get started writing.

Re-examine Purpose, Audience, Dominant Idea, and Shape After all your writing and rereading, you may have some new ideas about your purpose, audience, or dominant idea. Take a minute to jot these down in your journal. Remember that your specific details should *show* the main point or dominant idea, whether you state it explicitly or not.

Next, if the shaping strategies suggested an order for your essay, use it to guide your draft. You may, however, have only your specific details or a general notion of the dominant idea you're trying to communicate to your reader. In that case, you may want to being writing and work out a shape or outline as you write.

The idea is to get the pencil moving quickly.
—BERNARD MALAMUD, NOVELIST

Create a Draft With the above notes as a guide, you are ready to start drafting. Work on establishing your ritual: Choose a comfortable, familiar place with the writing tools you like . Make sure you'll have no interruptions. Try to write nonstop. If you can't think of a word, substitute a dash. If you can't remember how to spell a word, don't stop to look it up now—keep writing. Write until you reach what feels like the end. If you do get stuck, *reread* your last few lines or some of your writing process materials. Then go back and pick up the thread. Don't stop to count words or pages. You should shoot for more material than you need because it's usually easier to cut material later, when you're revising, than to add more if you're short.

REVISING

All the stuff you see back there on the floor is writing I did last week that I have to rewrite this week.
—ERNEST J. GAINES, AUTHOR OF THE AUTOBIOGRAPHY OF MISS JANE PITTMAN

Gaining Distance and Objectivity Revising, of course, has been going on since you put your first sentence down on paper. You've changed ideas, thought through your subject again, and observed your person, place, object, or event. After your rough draft is finished, your next step is to revise again to *resee* the whole thing. But before you do, you need to let it sit at least twenty-four hours, to get away from it for a while, to gain some distance and perspective. Relax. Congratulate yourself.

About the time you try to relax, however, you may get a sudden temptation—even an overwhelming urge—to have someone else read it—immediately! Usually, it's better to resist that urge. Chances are, you will want to have someone else read it either because you're bubbling with enthusiasm and you want to share it or because you're certain that it's all garbage and you want to hear the bad news right away. Most readers will not find it either as great as you hope *or* as awful as you fear. As a result, their offhand remarks may seem terribly insensitive or condescending. In a day or so, however, you'll be able to see your writing more objectively: Perhaps it's not great yet, but it's not hopeless, either. At that point, you're ready to get some feedback and start your revisions.

Rereading and Responding to Your Readers When you've been away from the draft for a while, you are better able to see the whole piece of writing. Start by rereading your own draft and making marginal notes. Don't be distracted by spelling errors or typos; concentrate on the quality of the details and the flow of the sentences. Focus on the overall effect you're creating, see if your organization still makes sense, and check to make sure that all the details support the dominant idea. If you have feedback from a workshop session, think about the comments and suggestions you've received. Depending on the reactions of your readers, you may need to change the point of view, add a few specific examples or some comparisons or images, fix the organization of a paragraph, reorder some details, delete some sentences, or do several of the above. Be prepared, however, to rewrite several paragraphs to help your readers really ***see*** what you are describing.

TEACHING TIP

For a revision workshop in class, choose the three or four items most relevant to the problems your students have with their drafts. In addition, these guidelines can be the basis for an evaluation sheet indicating how you will grade this essay. Students should have the evaluation sheet as they revise.

Guidelines for Revision As you revise your essay, keep the following tips and checklist questions in mind:

- **Re-examine your purpose and audience.** Are you doing what you intended? If your purpose or audience has changed, what other changes do you need to make as you revise?
- **Pay attention to the advice your readers give you, but don't necessarily make all the changes they suggest.** Ask them *why* something should be changed. Ask them specifically *where* something should be changed.
- **Consider your point of view.** Would changing to another point of view clarify what you are describing?
- **Consider your vantage point.** Do you have a bird's-eye view, or are you observing from a low angle? Do you zoom in for a close-up of a person or object? Would a different vantage point fit your purpose and audience?

- **Make sure you are using sensory details where appropriate.** Remember, you must *show* your reader the details you observe. If necessary, *reobserve* your subject.
- **Do all your details and examples support your *dominant idea?*** Reread your draft and omit any irrelevant details.
- **What is *not*** present in your subject that might be important to mention?
- **What *changes*** occur in the form or function of your subject? Where can you describe those changes more vividly?
- **Make comparisons if they will help you or your reader understand your subject better.** Similes, metaphors, or analogies may describe your subject more vividly.
- **Does what you are observing belong to a class of similar objects?** Would classification organize your writing?
- **Be sure to cue or signal, your reader with appropriate transition words.** Transitions will improve the coherence or flow of your writing.

  - *Spatial Order:* on the left, on the right, next, above, below, higher, lower, farther, next, beyond
  - *Chronological Order:* before, earlier, after, afterward, thereafter, then, from then on, the next day, shortly, by that time, immediately, slowly, while, meanwhile, until, now, soon, within an hour, first, later, finally, at last
  - *Comparison/Contrast:* on one hand, on the other hand, also, similarly, in addition, likewise, however, but, yet, still, although, even so, nonetheless, in contrast.

- **Revise sentences for clarity, conciseness, emphasis, and variety.**
- **When you have revised your essay, edit your writing for correct spelling and appropriate word choice, punctuation, usage, and grammar.**

I went for years not finishing anything. Because, of course, when you finish something you can be judged....
—ERICA JONG, AUTHOR OF FEAR OF FLYING

TEACHING TIP

In this journal entry, students review their writing processes to see how they write and how they can make the process more efficient. In addition, teachers often relate their evaluative comments on an essay *to the student's writing process.* If the writing is still too vague and general, for example, the entry may show that the student needs more time for collecting activities.

■ **POSTSCRIPT ON THE WRITING PROCESS** When you've finished writing this assignment, do one final journal entry. Briefly, answer the following three questions:

1. What was the hardest part of this writing assignment for you?
2. What exercise, practice, strategy, or workshop was the "break-

through" for you? What led you to your discovery or dominant idea?

3. State in one sentence your discovery or the dominant idea of your essay.

4. What did you learn about your writing ritual and process? What did you learn about observing?

Observing: Student Writing

A New Leaf

MARK SKELTON

Mark Skelton decided to write a description of his potted plant, an impatiens, *which he kept in his room. His initial purpose was to learn, through careful scrutiny, exactly how the plant looked. Following Agassiz's advice, Skelton observed his plant on three different occasions, each time taking notes, drawing pictures, and then writing a draft. What follows are his notes for the first two observing sessions, his first draft, and then a revised version. As you read his drafts, notice how his focus changes as he zooms in closer for more detail. Look also for an interesting discovery that he makes about his plant.*

Observing Notes

Observation 1

9:40 pm

2-4-95

*combination of light green and dark green

*shaped like a dog's head with ears sticking up

*about an inch and a half long

Observation 2

3:00 pm

2-5-95

*small dust particles dull some of the shine

*hidden beneath the large leaves like a shy child behind his mother's leg

*tilted more toward the

Observing Notes (continued)

*crinkled appearance like someone wadded it up and then straightened it out
*can tell it's younger by the shiny appearance (shinier than the older leaves)
*deeper in color than the older leaves
*no brown tips or yellow spots like the old leaves that need to be cut off
*no smell
*top is smooth
*underneath is rough because of the little veins
*Characteristics of each half are different (like fingerprints)
*shape is symmetrical

left side
more light green color
less dark green

right side
more dark green color
less light green

sun nourishing its ~~gro~~ growth
*supported by a long stem which looks too shiny to hold it up
*veins which are not visible on the top side can be seen running like a spider web on the underneath side
*If held in your fingertips and wedged gently a small popping sound is made from the small ~~bald~~ bulges in the surface as they pop in and out
*Light green color running through the middle looks like the shape of a ~~[illegible] with it stead and then a pointed tips)~~ maple leaf
~~*~~The light green runs along the main veins which are larger.

Peer Response

Students' drafts typically have sensory details and description but frequently leave the reader asking, "What's the point? So what?" As Scudder suggests, without some general law or dominant idea, "facts are stupid things." Use Skelton's first draft to illustrate what you mean by a "So what?" description. After discussing how Skelton incorporates a dominant idea (based on his parent-child imagery) in his revised draft, have students work in groups of two or three, reading each other's drafts and suggesting ways to clarify the writer's discovery or dominant idea.

First Draft

My Potted Plant

My potted plant is not a particularly spectacular specimen but it at least brightens up my otherwise surgically practical room. The plant is about eighteen inches high and is planted in a two-gallon pot made of wooden slats held together with a pair of brass rings. The plant is a light green, similar to the green of a Cox's apple. It has one solitary pink flower perched delicately on the end of one limb. The flower is only about half an inch in diameter and has six petals centered around a white middle. The plant is densely leafed with various sizes of oval shaped leaves. It has no hard, woody, sections of stem but rather a soft, watery stem. When it needs water, it droops like a marathon runner overcome with exhaustion, gasping for breath. During the summer, the plant springs to life, and several tiny, bright flowers appear, randomly decorating its foliage like distant stars in the night sky. Occasionally it sheds its leaves and is left barren for a number of days until it returns to its normal perkiness.

Revised Version

A New Leaf

A potted plant sits on my desk at home. It is not a particularly spectacular specimen, but it adds a human touch to my otherwise surgically sterile room. The plant, called an *impatiens* or a Busy Lizzie, is about eighteen inches high and sits in a two-gallon pot made from several slats of wood held together with a pair of brass rings. The plant is light green, similar to the green of a Cox's apple. Nestled among all of the larger, more mature leaves of the plant is a sign of new growth: a young leaf. Like a small, shy child peering from behind his mother's leg, this inch-and-a-half baby leaf is just barely visible. At first appearance the shape of this combined greenish-yellow and deep green leaf looks like a dog's head, with its ears sticking straight up. Up the center of the leaf runs a larger vein the width of a straight pin, separating the leaf into two symmetrically-shaped sides, each looking like a wafer-thin orange slice. Because of its youth, the new leaf has not fully straightened out, and it looks like a piece of wadded up paper that has been flattened out. Shinier and a deeper green than the older leaves, this young leaf has no brittle brown tips and is dulled by only a few minute dust particles. A smooth top, like that of a vinyl seat cover, hides the rougher texture found underneath, and the waxy surface repels water just like a slicker on a rainy day. Supporting this dogeared leaf is a very slender, deep green stem that looks as if it has to struggle to support the leaf. Due to phototropism, the fragile-looking stem leans towards the beam of morning sunlight like wheat bending in a breeze. The leaf gives off no apparent smell, but because of its youthful appearance, a feeling of springtime fills the air in my room. Hidden there among the duller, more mature leaves of the plant, the new leaf looks remarkably like a young child in a family. In fact, the rest of the *impatiens'* leaves do support this young leaf, giving their energy to the new growth. This family of leaves, a plant, goes quietly about its business of generating new life, brightening my room. All I have to do is notice.

Questions for Writing and Discussion

1. *Without looking again at either draft*, describe what you remember about Skelton's plant. List all the details you can remember. Reread your list of details and then look again at the drafts: From which version did you remember the details?

2. Of the six strategies for observing discussed at the beginning of this chapter, which does Skelton use? Which are most effective? Which are least effective?

3. What does Skelton learn or discover while observing his plant? Where in the revised draft does he reveal his discovery? Do his images lead naturally to this discovery? What details or images would you suggest *adding* or *deleting* in order to sharpen the focus or dominant idea of the paragraph?

EMPTY WINDOWS

STEPHEN WHITE

In this essay, Stephen White describes both what his senses tell him and what he can only imagine about the Anasazi, the ancient Native Americans who more than a thousand years ago built the cliff dwellings at Mesa Verde in southwestern Colorado. Writing about those empty dwellings with their darkened windows, White says, "Perhaps there lurks, behind every blackened window, a certain unexplainable something we can never understand."

It is difficult for me to say exactly what it was that drew me to this solitary place and held me here, virtually entranced, the entire day. It's the silence, maybe, or the empty houses perched precariously on the canyon wall below me. Or, could it be the knowledge that something seemingly nonexistent does indeed exist? **(1)**

I awoke this morning with a sense of unexplainable anticipation gnawing away at the back of my mind, that this chilly, leaden day at the Mesa Verde would bring something new and totally foreign to any of my past experiences. It was a sensation that began to permeate my entire being as I sat crouched before my inadequate campfire, chills running up my spine. Chills which, I am certain, were due not entirely to the dreary gray of a winter "sunrise." **(2)**

It had been my plan to travel the so-called Ruins Road early today, and then complete my visit here, but as I stopped along the road and stood scanning the opposite wall of the canyon for ruins, I felt as if some force had seized control of my will. I was compelled to make my way along the rim. **(3)**

Starting out upon the rock, I weaved in and out repeatedly as the gaping emptiness of the canyon and the weathered standstone of the rim battled one another for territory. At last arriving here, where a narrow peninsula of canyon juts far into the stone, I was able to peer back into the darkness of a cave carved midway in the vertical wall opposite, within whose smoke blackened walls huddle, nearly unnoticeable, the rooms of a small crumbled ruin. **(4)**

They are a haunting sight, these broken houses, clustered together down in the gloom of the canyon. It presents a complete contrast to the tidy, excavated ruins I explored yesterday, lost within a cluster of tourists and guided by a park ranger who expounded constantly upon his wealth of knowledge of excavation techniques and archaeological dating methods. The excavated ruins seemed, in comparison, a noisy, almost modern city, punctuated with the clicking of camera shutters and the bickering of children. Here it is quiet. The silence is broken only by the rush of the wind in the trees and the trickling of a tiny stream of melting snow springing from ledge to ledge as it makes its way down over the rock to the bottom of the canyon. And this small, abandoned village of tiny houses seems almost as the Indians left it, reduced by the passage of nearly a thousand years to piles of rubble through which protrude broken red adobe walls surrounding ghostly jet black openings, undisturbed by modern man. **(5)**

Those windows seem to stare back at me as my eyes are drawn to them. They're so horribly empty, yet my gaze is fixed, searching for some sign of the vitality they must surely have known. I yearn for sounds amidst the silence, for images of life as it once was in the bustling and prosperous community of cliff dwellers who lived here so long ago. It must have been a sunny home when the peaceful, agrarian Anasazi, or ancient ones, as the Navajo call them, lived and dreamed their lives here, wanting little more than to continue in their ways and be left alone, only to be driven away in the end by warring people with whom they could not contend. **(6)**

I long to hear, to see, and to understand, and though I strain all my senses to their limits, my wishes are in vain. I remain alone, confronted only by the void below and the cold stare of those utterly desolate windows. I know only an uneasy sensation that I am not entirely alone, and a quick, chill gust gives birth once again to that restless shiver tracing its path along the length of my spine. **(7)**

As a gray afternoon fades into a gray evening, I can find neither a true feeling of fear nor one of the quiet serenity one would expect to experience here. It is comforting for me to believe that it was the explorer in me which brought me here, to feel that I was lured to stand above this lonely house by that same drive to find and explore the unknown which motivated the countless others who have come here since seeking knowledge and understanding of the ancient people of the "Green Table." Yet as I begin the journey back to my car and the security of an evening fire, I remain uncomfortably unconvinced. **(8)**

Perhaps the dreariness of a cloudy day united with my solitude to pave a mental pathway for illusion and mystery. Or perhaps all homes are never truly empty, having known the multitude of experience which is human life. Perhaps there lurks, behind every blackened window, a certain unexplainable something we can never understand. I know only that the Indian has long respected these places and given them wide berth, leaving their sanctity inviolate. **(9)**

Questions for Writing and Discussion

1. Describe a similar experience you have had with an empty room or vacant house. White says that "perhaps all homes are never truly empty, having known the multitude of experience which is human life." Based on your experience, do you agree with him?

2. Through his description, what did White help you "see" about the Anasazi and their cliff dwellings? What did you learn?

3. Consider once again the basic techniques for observing—using sensory detail, comparisons, and images; describing what is not there; noting changes; and writing from a clear point of view. Which ones does White use most effectively? Cite an example of each technique from his essay.

4. In which paragraphs does White use each of the following shaping strategies: spatial order, chronological order, comparisons or contrasts, and simile, metaphor, or analogy? Which strategies did you find most effective in organizing the experience for you as a reader?

FOUR / REMEMBERING

For me the initial delight is in the surprise of remembering something I didn't know I knew.

—ROBERT FROST, POET

The fact is that there's no understanding the future without the present, and no understanding where we are now without a glance, at least, to where we have been.

—JOYCE MAYNARD, COLUMNIST AND AUTHOR OF <u>LOOKING BACKWARD: A CHRONICLE OF GROWING UP OLD IN THE SIXTIES</u>

THIS MORNING YOU ACCIDENTALLY RAN INTO A CERTAIN PERSON WHOM YOU KNEW SEVERAL YEARS AGO, AND FOR SEVERAL HOURS YOU'VE BEEN IN A BAD MOOD. You called your best friend, but no one answered the phone. You went to class and then for your usual jog, but you pooped out after only half a mile. You even watched a game show on television in the middle of the afternoon and ate half a bag of potato chips, but you still felt lousy. You yell at the television: "Why do I always react this way when I see that person?" But the television has no reply. So you grab some paper and begin scrawling out every memory you have of your experiences with the person you ran into this morning, hoping to understand your feelings.

YOU AND SEVERAL CO-WORKERS HAVE FORMED A COMMITTEE TO DRAFT A REPORT FOR YOUR COMPANY'S VICE-PRESIDENT IN CHARGE OF PERSONNEL. You have grievances about workload, pay scale, daily procedures, and the attitudes of supervisors. Your report needs to recommend changes in current policies. The committee decides that each person will contribute part of the report by describing actual incidents that have had negative effects on efficiency and human relations. You decide to describe a day last June when your immediate supervisor expected you to learn a new word-processing system and at the same time meet a 3:00 P.M. deadline for a thirty-seven-page budget analysis.

Georges Seurat, France, 1859–1891, A Sunday on La Grande Jatte—1884, oil on canvas, 1884–86, 207.6 x 308 cm, Helen Birch Bartlett Memorial Collection, 1926.224.

THE HUMAN BRAIN IS A PACK RAT: NOTHING IS TOO SMALL, OBSCURE, OR MUNDANE FOR THE BRAIN'S COLLECTION. Bits and pieces in the collection may seem useless, but they may be important. Often the brain collects and discards information without regard to our wishes. Out of the collection may arise, with no warning, the image of windblown whitecaps on a lake you visited more than five years ago, the recipe for Uncle Joe's incomparable chili, or even the right answer to an exam question that you've been starting at for the past fifteen minutes.

Remembering is sometimes easy, sometimes difficult. Often careful concentration yields nothing, while the most trivial occurrence—an old song on a car radio, the acrid smell of diesel exhaust, the face of a stranger—will trigger a flood of recollections. Someone tells a story and you immediately recall incidents, funny or traumatic, from your own life. Some memories, however, are nagging and troublesome, keeping you awake at night, daring you to deal with them. You pick at these memories. Why are they so important? You write about them, usually to probe that mystery of yesterday and today. Sights, sounds, or feelings from the present may draw you to the past, but the past leads, just as surely, back to the present.

Direct observations are important to learning and writing, but so are your memories, experiences, and stories. You may write an autobiographical account of part of your life, or you may recall a brief event, a person, or a place just as an example to illustrate a point. Whatever form your writing from memory takes, however, your initial purpose is to remember experiences so that you can understand yourself and your world. The point is not to write fiction, but to practice drawing on your memories and to write vividly enough about them so that you and others can discover and learn.

The value of remembering lies exactly here: Written memories have the power to teach you and, through *empathy* with your readers, to inform or convince them as well. At first, you may be self-conscious about sharing your personal memories. But as you reveal these experiences, you realize that your story is worth telling—not because you're such an egotist, but because sharing experiences helps everyone learn.

■ **FREEWRITING: FIRST MEMORIES** Turn to a blank page in your journal or open a computer file. What are your earliest memories? Choose one particular event. How old were you? What was the place? Who were the people around you? What happened? Write nonstop for ten minutes.

BACKGROUND ON REMEMBERING

In this chapter, autobiographical writing is an end in itself, but in later chapters, "remembering" becomes an invention strategy for expository and argumentative writing. This chapter builds on the observing skills from Chapter 3 and shows how writers can use specific examples from their own experiences in a variety of writing situations.

Time passes and the past becomes the present. . . . These presences of the past are there in the center of your life today. You thought . . . they had died, but they have just been waiting their chance.

—CARLOS FUENTES, ESSAYIST, DRAMATIST, AND DIPLOMAT

Techniques for Writing About Memories

Many of these techniques for writing about memories are illustrated in the *ABC News/Prentice Hall Video Library* for Composition. "Jack Smith's Vietnam Diary" is an excellent example.

Teaching Tip

Although all five of these strategies are important, two are critical for writing remembering essays. In their own essays, encourage students to focus on *specific scenes* that occurred at a defined time and place. Narrating a past event in the present tense, as Alice Walker does, may help students focus and develop their scenes. Second, be sure to stress the importance of *focusing* on some main idea, point, or discovery. A remembering essay should clearly answer the question, "So what?" or "What's the point?"

Writing vividly about memories includes all the skills of careful observing, but it adds additional techniques that are described below. Not all writing about memories uses all five techniques, but one or two of them will often transform a lifeless or boring account into an effective narrative.

- **Using *detailed observation* of people, places, and events.** Writing vividly about memories requires many of the skills of careful observation. Give *actual dialogue* where appropriate.
- **Creating specific scenes set in time and space.** *Show* your reader the actual events; don't just *tell* about events. Narrate specific incidents as they actually happened. Avoid monotonously summarizing events or presenting just the conclusions (for instance, "those experiences really changed my life").
- **Noting *changes, contrasts*, or *conflicts*.** Changes in people or places, contrasts between two different memories or between memories of expectations and realities or conflicts between people or ideas—any of these may lead to the meaning or importance of a remembered person, place, or event.
- **Making *connections* between past events, people, or places and the present.** The main idea of a narrative often grows out of changes and conflicts or arises from the *connections* you make between past and present.
- **Discovering and focusing on a main idea.** A remembering essay is not a random narrative of the writer's favorite memories. A narrative should have a clear main point, focus on a main idea, or make a discovery. The essay should clearly show *why* the memories are important.

All of these techniques are important, but you should also keep several other points in mind. Normally, you should write in the *first person*, using "I" or "we" throughout the narrative. Although you will usually write in *past tense*, sometimes you may wish to lend immediacy to the events by retelling them in the *present tense*, as if they are happening now. Finally, you may choose straightforward *chronological order*, or you may begin near the end and use a *flashback* to tell the beginning of the story.

The key to effective remembering, however, is to get beyond *generalities and conclusions* about your experiences ("I had a lot of fun—those days really changed my life"). Your goal is to recall *specific incidents set in time and place* that *show* how and why those days changed your life. The specific incidents should show your *main point* or *dominant idea.*

The following passage by Andrea Lee began as a journal entry during a year she spent in Moscow and Leningrad following her graduation from college. She then combined these firsthand observations with her memories and published them in a collection called *Russian Journal.* She uses first person and, frequently, present tense as she describes her reactions to the sights of Moscow. In these paragraphs, she weaves observations and memories together to show her main idea: The contrast between American and Russian advertising helped her understand both the virtues and the faults of American commercialism.

Remembering is usually handled differently than direct observation by the visual media. Consider how file footage, flashbacks, and voice-over narration are used to recall and reflect on the past, often with a steady focus on specific incidents.

> In Mayakovsky Square, not far from the Tchaikovsky Concert Hall, a big computerized electric sign sends various messages flashing out into the night. An outline of a taxi in green dots is accompanied by the words: "Take Taxis—All Streets are Near." This is replaced by multicolored human figures and a sentence urging Soviet citizens to save in State banks. The bright patterns and messages come and go, making this one of the most sophisticated examples of advertising in Moscow. Even on chilly nights when I pass through the square, there is often a little group of Russians standing in front of the sign, watching in fascination for five and ten minutes as the colored dots go through their magical changes. The first few times I saw this, I chuckled and recalled an old joke about an American town so boring that people went out on weekends to watch the Esso sign.
>
> Advertising, of course, is the glamorous offspring of capitalism and art: why advertise in a country where there is only one brand, the State brand, of anything, and often not enough even of that? There is nothing here comparable to the glittering overlay of commercialism that Americans, at least, take for granted as part of our cities; nothing like the myriad small seductions of the marketplace, which have led us to expect to be enticed. The Soviet political propaganda posters that fill up a small part of the Moscow landscape with their uniformly cold red color schemes and monumental robot-faced figures are so unappealing that they are dismissable.
>
> I realize now, looking back, that for at least my first month in Moscow, I was filled with an unconscious and devastating disappointment. Hardly realizing it, as I walked around the city, I was looking for the constant sensory distractions I was accustomed to in America. Like many others my age, I grew up reading billboards and singing advertising jingles; my idea of beauty was shaped—perniciously, I think—by the models with the painted eyes and pounds of shining hair whose beauty was accessible on every television set and street corner.

Specific scene

Detailed observation

Connections past and present

Contrast

Main idea

Detailed observation

Connections past and present

Contrast and change

Main idea

Remembering People

A writer is a reader moved to emulation.
—SAUL BELLOW, AUTHOR OF HENDERSON THE RAIN KING

In the following passage from the introduction to *The Way to Rainy Mountain*, N. Scott Momaday remembers his grandmother. While details of place and event are also re-created, the primary focus is on the character of his grandmother as revealed in several *specific*, recurring actions. Momaday does not give us generalities about his feelings (for instance, "I miss my grandmother a lot, especially now that she's gone"); instead, he begins with specific memories of scenes that *show* how he felt.

> Now that I can have her only in memory, I see my grandmother in the several postures that were peculiar to her: standing at the wood stove on a winter morning and turning meat in a great iron skillet; sitting at the south window, bent above her beadwork, and afterwards, when her vision failed, looking down for a long time into the fold of her hands; going out upon a cane, very slowly as she did when the weight of age came upon her; praying. I remember her most often at prayer. She made long, rambling prayers out of suffering and hope, having seen many things. I was never sure that I had the right to hear, so exclusive were they of all mere custom and company. The last time I saw her she prayed standing by the side of her bed at night, naked to the waist, the light of a kerosene lamp moving upon her dark skin. Her long, black hair, always drawn and braided in the day, lay upon her shoulders and against her breasts like a shawl. I do not speak Kiowa, and I never understood her prayers, but there was something inherently sad in the sound, some merest hesitation upon the syllables of sorrow. She began in a high and descending pitch, exhausting her breath to silence; then again and again—and always the same intensity of effort, of something that is, and is not, like urgency in the human voice. Transported so in the dancing light among the shadows of her room, she seemed beyond the reach of time. But that was illusion; I think I knew then that I should not see her again.

Remembering Places

In the following passage from *Farewell to Manzanar*, Jeanne Wakatsuke Houston remembers the place in California where, as Japanese Americans, her family was imprisoned during World War II. As you read, look for specific details and bits of description that convey her main idea.

> In Spanish, Manzanar means "apple orchard." Great stretches of Owens Valley were once green with orchards and alfalfa fields. It has been a desert ever since its water started flowing south into Los Angeles, sometime during the twenties. But a few rows of untended

pear and apple trees were still growing there when the camp opened, where a shallow water table had kept them alive. In the spring of 1943 we moved to block 28, right up next to one of the old pear orchards. That's where we stayed until the end of the war, and those trees stand in my memory for the turning of our life in camp, from the outrageous to the tolerable.

Papa pruned and cared for the nearest trees. Late that summer we picked the fruit green and stored it in a root cellar he had dug under our new barracks. At night the wind through the leaves would sound like the surf had sounded in Ocean Park, and while drifting off to sleep, I could almost imagine we were still living by the beach.

Remembering Events

In the following essay, called "The Boy's Desire," Richard Rodriguez recalls a particular event from his childhood that comes to mind when he remembers Christmas. In his memory, he sorts through the rooms in his house on 39th street in Sacramento, recalling old toys: a secondhand bike, games with dice and spinning dials, a jigsaw puzzle, and a bride doll. In this passage, Rodriguez describes both the effort to remember and the memory itself—the one memory that still "holds color and size and shape." Was it all right, he wonders, that a boy should have wanted a doll for Christmas?

> The fog comes to mind. It never rained on Christmas. It was never sharp blue and windy. When I remember Christmas in Sacramento, it is in gray: The valley fog would lift by late morning, the sun boiled haze for a few hours, then the tule fog would rise again when it was time to go into the house.
>
> The haze through which memory must wander is thickened by that fog. The rooms of the house on 39th Street are still and dark in late afternoon, and I open the closet to search for old toys. One year there was a secondhand bike. I do not remember a color. Perhaps it had no color even then. Another year there were boxes of games that rattled their parts—dice and pegs and spinning dials. Or perhaps the rattle is of a jigsaw puzzle that compressed into an image . . . of what? of Paris? a litter of kittens? I cannot remember. Only one memory holds color and size and shape: brown hair, blue eyes, the sweet smell of styrene.
>
> That Christmas I announced I wanted a bride doll. I must have been seven or eight—wise enough to know not to tell anyone at school, but young enough to whine out my petition from early November.

Collaborative Activity

The selection by Rodriguez offers an excellent opportunity to show how observing and remembering strategies work together. Have students from one half of the class divide into groups of three or four and annotate this passage for observing techniques while groups from the other half of the class annotate for remembering techniques. Each group should write its collaborative annotations on a transparency made from a photocopy of this passage. Allow ten minutes for group annotations. Then one member from each group should place his or her group's transparency on an overhead projector and explain the group's annotations to the rest of the class. (Note: Provide each group's recorder with a special marking pen for the transparencies.)

My father's reaction was unhampered by psychology. A shrug—"*Una muñeca*?"—a doll, why not? Because I knew it was my mother who would choose all the presents, it was she I badgered. I wanted a bride doll! "Is there something else you want?" she wondered. No! I'd make clear with my voice that nothing else would appease me, "We'll see," she'd say, and she never wrote it down on her list.

By early December, wrapped boxes started piling up in my parents' bedroom closet, above my father's important papers and the family album. When no one else was home, I'd drag a chair over and climb up to see . . . Looking for the *one*. About a week before Christmas, it was there. I was so certain it was mine that I punched my thumb through the wrapping paper and the cellophane window on the box and felt inside—lace, two tiny, thin legs.

I got other presents that year, but it was the doll I kept by me. I remember my mother saying I'd have "to share her" with my younger sister—but Helen was four years old, oblivious. The doll was mine. My arms would hold her. She would sleep on my pillow.

And the sky did not fall. The order of the universe did not tremble. In fact, it was right for a change. My family accommodated itself to my request. My brother and sisters played round me with their own toys. I paraded my doll by the hands across the floor.

The other day, when I asked my brother and sisters about the doll, no one remembered. My mother remembers. "Yes," she smiled. "One year there was a doll."

The closet door closes. (The house on 39th Street has been razed for a hospital parking lot.) The fog rises. Distance tempts me to mock the boy and his desire. The fact remains: One Christmas in Sacramento I wanted a bride doll, and I got one.

Some very small incident that takes place today may be the most important event that happens to you this year, but you don't know that when it happens. You don't know it until much later.
—TONI MORRISON, NOBEL PRIZE–WINNING AUTHOR OF BELOVED AND SONG OF SOLOMON

■ **WARMING UP: JOURNAL EXERCISES** The following topics will help you practice writing about your memories. Read all of the following exercises, and then write on three that interest you the most. If another idea occurs to you, write a free entry about it.

1. Select one moment in your past that either changed your life or showed you how your life had already changed. What was the event? What were you like before and afterward?

2. Go through old family photographs and find one of yourself, taken at least five years ago. Describe the person in the photograph—what he or she did, thought, said, or hoped. How is that person like or unlike the person you are now?

3. Remember a place, a sanctuary, where you used to go to be alone. What was it like? When did you go there? Have you been back there recently? If so, how had it (or you) changed?

4. Remember the first job you had. How did you get it, and what did you do? What mistakes did you make? What did you learn? Were there any humorous or serious misunderstandings between you and others?

5. You and a friend are trading stories about sensitive times in your lives. You want to tell a story about a particularly embarrassing or sensitive moment, but you don't want your friend's sympathy. So you decide to tell the story through some imaginary person. You change a few details about the story so your friend won't recognize you, but the basic story is still yours. Using the third person, write the story you'd tell your friend.

6. Pick a favorite record from your collection—one that you've owned for a few years—and play one track. As you listen, write down the associations or memories that come to mind. What were you doing when you first heard the song? What other people, places, or events does it remind you of?

7. Reread your freewriting exercise from the beginning of this chapter. Then call members of your family and interview them for their memories of this incident. How does what you actually remember differ from what your family tells you? Revise your first memory to incorporate additional details provided by your family.

8. At some point in the past, you may have faced a conflict between what was expected of you—by parents, friends, family, coach, or employer—and your own personality or abilities. Describe one occasion when these expectations seemed unrealistic or unfair. Was the experience entirely negative or was it, in the long run, positive?

9. At at least one point in our lives, we have felt like an outsider. In a selection earlier in this chapter, for instance, both Richard Rodriguez recalls feelings of being different, rejected, or outcast. Write about an incident when you felt alienated from your family, peers, or social group. Focus on a key scene or scenes that show what happened, why it was important, and how it affects you now.

10. Read Helen Keller's essay in this chapter and write your own literacy narrative. What are your early memories about learning to read and write? At what points did you struggle or fail? When did you most enjoy reading or writing?

TEACHING TIP

Journal entries can often serve as a prereading activity. Students' answers to Questions 1 to 3 and a discussion or small-group activity using their entries will prepare students for an active reading of Helen Keller's or Alice Walker's essay.

LITERACY NARRATIVES

Helen Keller's essay provides an excellent model for a literacy narrative assignment. Ask students to write about one or two key events in their lives that focused on language—writing, reading, and/or learning. Other model essays for literacy narratives are Roy Hoffman's "On Keeping a Journal" (Chapter 1) and Russell Baker's "Writing for Myself" (Chapter 2). Discussion Question #1 following this essay asks students to recall an early reading/writing incident that might also become the subject for a literacy narrative.

REMEMBERING: PROFESSIONAL WRITING

THE DAY LANGUAGE CAME INTO MY LIFE

HELEN KELLER

At the age of eighteen months, Helen Keller (1880–1968) lost her sight and hearing as a result of illness. During the next five years of her childhood, Keller became increasingly wild and unruly as she struggled against her dark and silent world. In "The Day Language Came into My Life," Keller remembers how, at age seven, her teacher Anne Sullivan arrived and taught her the miracle of language. After learning sign language and Braille, Keller began her formal schooling and—with continued help from Sullivan—eventually graduated with honors from Radcliffe College. In her adult years, Keller became America's best-loved ambassador for the blind and disabled. She met nearly every American president, traveled to dozens of countries to speak on behalf of blind and deaf people, and wrote several books, including The Story of My Life *(1903),* The World I Live In *(1908), and* Midstream: My Later Life *(1930). The story of Anne Sullivan's teaching is told in William Gibson's Pulitzer Prize-winning play,* The Miracle Worker.

The most important day I remember in all my life is the one on which my teacher, Anne Mansfield Sullivan, came to me. I am filled with wonder when I consider the immeasurable contrast between the two lives which it connects. It was the third of March 1887, three months before I was seven years old. **(1)**

On the afternoon of that eventful day, I stood on the porch, dumb, expectant. I guessed vaguely from my mother's signs and from the hurrying to and fro in the house that something unusual was about to happen, so I went to the door and waited on the steps. The afternoon sun penetrated the mass of honeysuckle that covered the porch and fell on my upturned face. My fingers lingered almost unconsciously on the familiar leaves and blossoms which had just come forth to greet the sweet southern spring. I did not know what the future held of marvel or surprise for me. Anger and bitterness had preyed upon me continually for weeks and a deep languor had succeeded this passionate struggle. **(2)**

Have you ever been at sea in a dense fog, when it seemed as if a tangible white darkness shut you in, and the great ship, tense and anxious, groped her way toward the shore with plummet and sounding-line, and you waited with beating heart for something to happen? I was like that ship before my education began, only I was without compass or sounding-line and had no way of knowing how near the harbor was. "Light! give me light!" was the wordless cry of my soul, and the light of love shone on me in that very hour. **(3)**

I felt approaching footsteps. I stretched out my hand as I supposed to my mother. Someone took it, and I was caught up and held close in the arms of her who had come to reveal all things to me, and, more than all things else, to love me. **(4)**

The morning after my teacher came she led me into her room and gave me a doll. The little blind children at the Perkins Institution had sent it and Laura Bridgman had dressed it; but I did not know this until afterward. When I had played with it a little while, Miss Sullivan slowly spelled into my hand the word "d-o-l-l." I was at once interested in this finger play and tried to imitate it. When I finally succeeded in making the letters correctly I was flushed with childish pleasure and pride. Running downstairs to my mother I held up my hand and made the letters for doll. I did not know that I was spelling a word or even that words existed; I was simply making my fingers go in monkeylike imitation. In the days that followed I learned to spell in this uncomprehending way a great many words, among them *pin*, *hat*, *cup* and a few verbs like *sit*, *stand* and *walk*. But my teacher had been with me several weeks before I understood that everything has a name. **(5)**

One day, while I was playing with my new doll, Miss Sullivan put my big rag doll into my lap also, spelled "d-o-l-l" and tried to make me understand that "d-o-l-l" applied to both. Earlier in the day we had had a tussle over the words "m-u-g" and "w-a-t-e-r." Miss Sullivan had tried to impress it upon me that "m-u-g" is *mug* and that "w-a-t-e-r" is *water*, but I persisted in confounding the two. In despair she had dropped the subject for the time, only to renew it at the first opportunity. I became impatient at her repeated attempts and, seizing the new doll, I dashed it upon the floor. I was keenly delighted when I felt the fragments of the broken doll at my feet. Neither sorrow nor regret followed my passionate outburst. I had not loved the doll. In the still, dark world in which I lived there was no strong sentiment or tenderness. I felt my teacher sweep the fragments to one side of the hearth, and I had a sense of satisfaction that the cause of my discomfort was removed. She brought me my hat, and I knew I was going out into the warm sunshine. This thought, if a wordless sensation may be called a thought, made me hop and skip with pleasure. **(6)**

We walked down the path to the well-house, attracted by the fragrance of the honeysuckle with which it was covered. Someone was drawing water and my teacher placed my hand under the spout. As the cool stream gushed over one hand she spelled into the other the word

CRITICAL READING

Essays by Helen Keller and Alice Walker work nicely as a pair to teach critical reading skills. With the Helen Keller essay, model for students how to do reader response annotations. At the chalkboard or on an overhead, show your paragraph-by-paragraph responses: the parts you liked best or least, the questions you wrote, your own experiences that Keller's essay triggered, the other essays or fiction that you recalled, and so forth. Ask each class member to practice writing his or her own reader response annotations. Then shift to reading with a writer's eye by annotating Keller's essay for a few remembering techniques and shaping strategies. Modeling the critical reading process with the Helen Keller essay will prepare students to annotate Alice Walker's more complex essay.

water, first slowly, then rapidly. I stood still, my whole attention fixed upon the motions of her fingers. Suddenly I felt a misty consciousness as of something forgotten—a thrill of returning thought; and somehow the mystery of language was revealed to me. I knew then that "w-a-t-e-r" meant the wonderful cool something that was flowing over my hand. The living word awakened my soul, gave it light, hope, joy, set it free! There were barriers still, it is true, but barriers that could in time be swept away. **(7)**

I left the well-house eager to learn. Everything had a name, and each name gave birth to a new thought. As we returned to the house every object which I touched seemed to quiver with life. That was because I saw everything with the strange, new sight that had come to me. On entering the door I remembered the doll I had broken. I felt my way to the hearth and picked up the pieces. I tried vainly to put them together. Then my eyes filled with tears; for I realized what I had done, and for the first time I felt repentance and sorrow. **(8)**

I learned a great many new words that day. I do not remember what they all were; but I do know that *mother, father, sister, teacher* were among them—words that were to make the world blossom for me, "like Aaron's rod, with flowers." It would have been difficult to find a happier child than I was as I lay in my crib at the close of that eventful day and lived over the joys it had brought me, and for the first time longed for a new day to come. **(9)**

Vocabulary

In your journal, write the meaning of the following words:

- I stood on the porch, *dumb* **(2)**
- a deep *languor* **(2)**
- with *plummet* and *sounding-line* **(3)**
- no strong *sentiment* **(6)**
- like *Aaron's rod* **(9)**

Questions for Writing and Discussion

1. Write for five minutes, recalling your earliest memories with reading, speaking, or writing. Focus on *one specific incident.* How old were you? Where were you? What were you reading or writing?

2. Helen Keller's books have been translated into more than fifty languages. Explain why you believe her story, as illustrated in this essay, has such universal appeal.

3. In paragraph 3, Keller uses an analogy to explain her feelings and her state of mind before language opened her life. Identify the extended comparison. What "difficult concept" does Keller explain through her analogy?

4. In paragraph 8, Keller says, "Everything had a name, and each name gave birth to a new thought." Explain what Keller means by using examples of the *names* of things from your own life.

5. Contrast Keller's actions and feelings before she discovers language to her actions and feeling afterward. In addition to learning words, how do her feelings and personality change?

6. A century ago, when Helen Keller was learning to read and speak, people who were blind and deaf were classified by the law as "idiots." Describe one experience you have had with a disabled person. Based on that experience, explain how Americans' attitudes toward people with some disability have (or have not) improved.

UNDER THE INFLUENCE

SCOTT RUSSELL SANDERS

Scott Russell Sanders was born in Memphis in 1945, attended Brown University, and received a Ph.D. from Cambridge University in 1971. He has published dozens of essays and works of fiction and nonfiction, including Hear the Wind Blow: American Folksongs Retold *(1985),* Stone Country *(1985),* Audubon Reader: The Best Writings of John James Audubon *(1986), and* The Invisible Company *(1989). In "Under the Influence," taken from a longer essay published in Harper's Magazine in 1989, Sanders remembers the shame, anger, and guilt he felt about his father's lifelong—and losing—battle with alcoholism. "Every day without the furtive glint of bottles," Sanders recalls, "every meal without a fight, every bedtime without sobs encouraged us to believe that such bliss might go on forever."*

My father drank. He drank as a gut-punched boxer gasps for breath, as a starving dog gobbles food—compulsively, secretly, in pain and trembling. I use the past tense not because he ever quit drinking but because he quit living. That is how the story ends for my father, age sixty-four,

CLASS ACTIVITY

As students draft their remembering essays, conduct a dialogue-writing workshop. Have students practice writing dialogue for at least one scene in their remembering essays. (They don't necessarily have to use this scene in their final version.) Since many students wonder how to punctuate dialogue, use the dialogue in Sanders's essay as a model.

heart bursting, body cooling, slumped and forsaken on the linoleum of my brother's trailer. The story continues for my brother, my sister, my mother, and me, and will continue as long as memory holds. **(1)**

In the perennial present of memory, I slip into the garage or barn to see my father tipping back the flat green bottles of wine, the brown cylinders of whiskey, the cans of beer disguised in paper bags. His Adam's apple bobs, the liquid gurgles, he wipes the sandy-haired back of a hand over his lips, and then, his bloodshot gaze bumping into me, he stashes the bottle or can inside his jacket, under the workbench, between two bales of hay, and we both pretend the moment has not occurred. **(2)**

"What's up, buddy?" he says, thick-tongued and edgy. **(3)**

"Sky's up," I answer, playing along. **(4)**

"And don't forget prices," he grumbles. "Prices are always up. And taxes." **(5)**

In memory, his white 1951 Pontiac with the stripes down the hood and the Indian head on the snout lurches to a stop in the driveway; or it is the 1956 Ford station wagon, or the 1963 Rambler shaped like a toad, or the sleek 1969 Bonneville that will do 120 miles per hour on straight-aways; or it is the robin's-egg-blue pickup, new in 1980, battered in 1981; the year of his death. He climbs out, grinning dangerously, unsteady on his legs, and we children interrupt our game of catch, our building of snow forts, our picking of plums, to watch in silence as he weaves past us into the house, where he drops into his overstuffed chair and falls asleep. Shaking her head, our mother stubs out a cigarette he has left smoldering in the ashtray. All evening, until our bedtimes, we tiptoe past him, as past a snoring dragon. Then we curl fearfully in our sheets, listening. Eventually he wakes with a grunt, Mother slings accusations at him, he snarls back, she yells, he growls, their voices clashing. Before long, she retreats to their bedroom, sobbing—not from the blows of fists, for he never strikes her, but from the force of his words. **(6)**

Left alone, our father prowls the house, thumping into furniture, rummaging in the kitchen, slamming doors, turning the pages of the newspaper with a savage crackle, muttering back at the late-night drivel from television. The roof might fly off, the walls might buckle from the pressure of his rage. Whatever my brother and sister and mother may be thinking on their own rumpled pillows, I lie there hating him, loving him, fearing him, knowing I have failed him. I tell myself he drinks to ease the ache that gnaws at his belly, an ache I must have caused by disappointing him somehow, a murderous ache I should be able to relieve by doing all my chores, earning A's in school, winning baseball games, fixing the broken washer and the burst pipes, bringing in the money to fill his empty wallet. He would not hide the green bottles in his toolbox, would not sneak off to the barn with a lump under his coat, would not fall

CRITICAL READING

The section on "Techniques for Writing about Memories" encourages students to "set scenes in time and space" and "narrate the actual events." Have students reread the last sentence in paragraph 2 and then discuss how Sanders creates one scene out of multiple memories ("inside his jacket, under the workbench, between two bales of hay"). Then have students analyze—individually or in groups—how and where Sanders uses the same strategy in paragraphs 6 and 7. If time permits, encourage students to reread their own drafts to see if Sanders' strategy would work for them.

asleep in the daylight, would not roar and fume, would not drink himself to death, if only I were perfect. **(7)**

I am forty-four, and I know full well now that my father was an alcoholic, a man consumed by disease rather than by disappointment. What had seemed to me a private grief is in fact, of course, a public scourge. In the United States alone, some ten or fifteen million people share his ailment, and behind the doors they slam in fury or disgrace, countless other children tremble. I comfort myself with such knowledge, holding it against the throb of memory like an ice pack against a bruise. Other people have keener sources of grief: poverty, racism, rape, war. I do not wish to compete to determine who has suffered most. I am only trying to understand the corrosive mixture of helplessness, responsibility, and shame that I learned to feel as the son of an alcoholic. I realize now that I did not cause my father's illness, nor could I have cured it. Yet for all this grown-up knowledge, I am still ten years old, my own son's age, and as that boy I struggle in guilt and confusion to save my father from pain. **(8)**

Vocabulary

In your journal, write the meanings of the following words:

- *compuslively* **(1)**
- the *perennial* present **(2)**
- late-night *drivel* **(7)**
- *corrosive* mixture **(8)**

Questions for Writing and Discussion

1. Everyone knows the two faces of alcohol—the happy, feeling-no-pain clown entertaining the party and the angry, out-of-control drunk on the edge of violence. Describe an experience with one or both of these faces. Explain how these memories help you understand Sanders' experiences.

2. Effective remembering essays build on detailed descriptions. Review the observing techniques from Chapter 3. Of the techniques discussed there (using sensory details and images, describing what is not present, noting changes, writing from a point of view, and focusing on a dominant idea), which does Sanders use most effectively? To support your choice, find examples for each of these techniques in Sanders' essay.

3. Where in his essay does Sanders use each of the following remembering techniques: using details and dialogue, creating specific scenes, noting changes and conflicts, and making connections between the past and the present? Which of these techniques were most effective? Why?

4. Reread Helen Keller's essay. Both Keller and Sanders re-create key scenes, but they do so differently. Analyze each essay for verb tense, scenes set in time and place, dialogue, and tone. Which style would work best for the essay you are writing?

5. Choose one of the scenes that Sanders describes and rewrite it from the point of view of another family member—the father, mother, brother, or sister. Use detailed description, dialogue, and contrasts between past and present to re-create the scene.

BEAUTY: WHEN THE OTHER DANCER IS THE SELF

ALICE WALKER

Diversity Issues

The essays by Keller and Walker provide an excellent opportunity to discuss how social attitudes about gender, race, and culture limit and stereotype people. After students discuss how key characters and events in these two essays affect the narrators' lives, have them reread the drafts of their own remembering essays. Which characters and scenes from their essays illustrate the negative power of gender, race, or cultural stereotyping and limiting? How did that power affect them, as the narrator? (How did their attitudes affect others?)

The author of the Pulitzer Prize-winning novel The Color Purple *(1983), Alice Walker has written works of fiction and poetry, including* Love and Trouble: Stories of Black Women *(1973),* Meridian *(1976), and* Revolutionary Petunias and Other Poems *(1973). "Beauty: When the Other Dancer Is the Self" originally appeared in* Ms. *magazine and was revised and published in her collection of essays* In Search of Our Mother's Gardens *(1983). Walker, a former editor of Ms., refers in this essay to Gloria Steinem and an interview published in* Ms. *entitled, "Do You Know This Woman? She Knows You—A Profile of Alice Walker." As you read the essay reprinted below, consider Walker's purpose: Why is she telling us—total strangers—about a highly personal and traumatic event that shaped her life?*

It is a bright summer day in 1947. My father, a fat, funny man with beautiful eyes and a subversive wit, is trying to decide which of his eight children he will take with him to the county fair. My mother, of course, will not go. She is knocked out from getting us ready: I hold my neck stiff against the pressure of her knuckles as she hastily completes the braiding and then beribboning of my hair. **(1)**

My father is the driver for the rich old white lady up the road. Her name is Miss Mey. She owns all the land for miles around, as well as the house in which we live. All I remember about her is that she once offered to pay my mother thirty-five cents for cleaning her house, raking up piles of her magnolia leaves, and washing her family's clothes, and that my mother—she of no money, eight children, and a chronic earache—refused it. But I do not think of this in 1947. I am two-and-a-half years old. I want to go everywhere my daddy goes. I am excited at the prospect of riding in a car. Someone has told me fairs are fun. That there is room in the car for only three of us doesn't faze me at all. Whirling happily in my starchy frock, showing off my biscuit polished patent leather shoes and lavender socks, tossing my head in a way that makes my ribbons bounce, I stand, hands on hips, before my father. "Take me, Daddy," I say with assurance, "I'm the prettiest!" **(2)**

Later, it does not surprise me to find myself in Miss Mey's shiny black car, sharing the backseat with the other lucky ones. Does not surprise me that I thoroughly enjoy the fair. At home that night I tell all the unlucky ones about the merry-go-round, the man who eats live chickens, and the abundance of Teddy bears, until they say: that's enough, baby Alice. Shut up now, and go to sleep. **(3)**

It is Easter Sunday, 1950. I am dressed in a green, flocked scalloped-hem dress (handmade by my adoring sister Ruth) that has its own smooth satin petticoat and tiny hot-pink roses tucked into each scallop. My shoes, new T-strap patent leather, again highly biscuit polished. I am six years old and have learned one of the longest Easter speeches to be heard in church that day, totally unlike the speech I said when I was two: "Easter lilies / pure and white / blossom in / the morning light." When I rise to give my speech I do so on a great wave of love and pride and expectation. People in the church stop rustling their new crinolines. They seem to hold their breath. I can tell they admire my dress, but it is my spirit, bordering on sassiness (womanishness), they secretly applaud. **(4)**

"That girl's a little *mess*," they whisper to each other, pleased. **(5)**

Naturally I say my speech without stammer or pause, unlike those who stutter, stammer, or, worst of all, forget. This is before the word "beautiful" exists in people's vocabulary, but "Oh, isn't she the *cutest* thing!" frequently floats my way. "And got so much sense!" they gratefully add . . . for which thoughtful addition I thank them to this day. **(6)**

It was great fun being cute. But then, one day, it ended. **(7)**

I am eight years old and a tomboy. I have a cowboy hat, cowboy boots, checkered shirt and pants, all red. My playmates are my brothers, two and four years older than I. Their colors are black and green, the only difference in the way we are dressed. On Saturday nights we all go to the picture show, even my mother; Westerns are her favorite kind of movie. Back home, "on the ranch," we pretend we are Tom Mix, Hopalong Cassidy, Lash LaRue (we've even named one of our dogs Lash LaRue); we chase each other for hours rustling cattle, being outlaws, delivering damsels from distress. Then my parents decide to buy my

DIVERSITY ISSUES (CONT'D)

Does the central conflict or discovery of their narrative hinge on these conflicts of social attitude and power? After rereading each other's drafts for diversity issues, have students revise their essays. A possible focus or main idea for their essays may become clearer.

See the *Video Library* for other instances of traumatic memories. Maya Angelou stopped speaking for five and a half years after she was raped at the age of seven. Jack Smith and his battle comrades suffered deep mental scars in Vietnam.

CRITICAL READING

If you have used the Helen Keller essay (or some other essay) to model critical reading, have the class practice (as a whole or in small groups) both reader response annotations and reading with a writer's eye. (Class discussions are more effective if you begin with the students' *own* annotations and questions rather than with set study questions.) If students already have tentative topics or drafts of their own essays, follow the essay discussion with a workshop session on their own essays. Encourage students to apply what they learn from reading to their own writing: Which of Alice Walker's strategies could they use in their own essays?

brothers guns. These are not "real" guns. They shoot "BBs," copper pellets my brothers say will kill birds. Because I am a girl, I do not get a gun. Instantly I am relegated to the position of Indian. Now there appears a great distance between us. They shoot and shoot at everything with their new guns. I try to keep up with my bow and arrows. **(8)**

One day while I am standing on top of our makeshift "garage"—pieces of tin nailed across some poles—holding my bow and arrow and looking out toward the fields, I feel an incredible blow in my right eye. I look down just in time to see my brother lower his gun. **(9)**

Both brothers rush to my side. My eye stings, and I cover it with my hand. "If you tell," they say, "we will get a whipping. You don't want that to happen, do you?" I do not. "Here is a piece of wire," says the older brother, picking it up from the roof; "say you stepped on one end of it and the other flew up and hit you." The pain is beginning to start. "Yes," I say. "Yes, I will say that is what happened." If I do not say this is what happened, I know my brothers will find ways to make me wish I had. But now I will say anything that gets me to my mother. **(10)**

Confronted by our parents we stick to the lie agreed upon. They place me on a bench on the porch and I close my left eye while they examine the right. There is a tree growing from underneath the porch, that climbs past the railing to the roof. It is the last thing my right eye sees. I watch as its trunk, its branches, and then its leaves are blotted out by the rising blood. **(11)**

I am in shock. First there is intense fever, which my father tries to break using lily leaves bound around my head. Then there are chills: my mother tries to get me to eat soup. Eventually, I do not know how, my parents learn what has happened. A week after the "accident" they take me to see a doctor. "Why did you wait so long to come?" he asks, looking into my eye and shaking his head. "Eyes are sympathetic," he says. "If one is blind, the other will likely become blind too." **(12)**

This comment of the doctor's terrifies me. But it is really how I look that bothers me most. Where the BB pellet struck there is a glob of whitish scar tissue, a hideous cataract, on my eye. Now when I stare at people—a favorite pastime, up to now—they will stare back. Not at the "cute" little girl, but at her scar. For six years I do not stare at anyone because I do not raise my head. **(13)**

Years later, in the throes of a mid-life crisis, I ask my mother and sister whether I changed after the "accident." "No," they say, puzzled. "What do you mean?" **(14)**

What do I mean? **(15)**

I am eight, and for the first time, doing poorly in school, where I have been something of a whiz since I was four. We have just moved to the place where the "accident" occurred. We do not know any of the people around us because this is a different county. The only time I see the friends I knew is when we go back to our old church. The new school is the former state penitentiary. It is a large stone building, cold and drafty, crammed to overflowing with boisterous, ill-disciplined children. On the third floor there is a huge circular imprint of some partition that has been torn out. **(16)**

"What used to be here?" I ask a sullen girl next to me on our way past it to lunch. **(17)**

"The electric chair," says she. **(18)**

At night I have nightmares about the electric chair, and about all the people reputedly "fried" in it. I am afraid of the school, where all the students seem to be budding criminals. **(19)**

"What's the matter with your eye?" they ask, critically. **(20)**

When I don't answer (I cannot decide whether it was an "accident" or not), they shove me, insist on a fight. **(21)**

My brother, the one who created the story about the wire, comes to my rescue. But then brags so much about "protecting" me, I become sick. **(22)**

After months of torture at the school, my parents decide to send me back to our old community to my old school. I live with my grandparents and the teacher they board. But there is no room for Phoebe, my cat. By the time my grandparents decide there *is* room, and I ask for my cat, she cannot be found. Miss Yarborough, the boarding teacher, takes me under her wing, and begins to teach me to play the piano. But soon she marries an African—a "prince," she says—and is whisked away to his continent. **(23)**

At my old school there is at least one teacher who loves me. She is the teacher who "knew me before I was born" and bought my first baby clothes. It is she who makes my life bearable. It is her presence that finally helps me turn on the one child at the school who continually calls me "one-eyed bitch." One day I simply grab him by his coat and beat him until I am satisfied. It is my teacher who tells me my mother is ill. **(24)**

My mother is lying in bed in the middle of the day, something I have never seen. She is in too much pain to speak. She has an abscess in her ear. I stand looking down on her, knowing that if she dies, I cannot live. She is being treated with warm oils and hot bricks held against her cheek. Finally a doctor comes. But I must go back to my grandparents' house. The weeks pass, but I am hardly aware of it. All I know is that my mother might die, my father is not so jolly, my brothers still have their guns, and I am the one sent away from home. **(25)**

"You did not change," they say. **(26)**

Did I imagine the anguish of never looking up? **(27)**

I am twelve. When relatives come to visit I hide in my room. My

COLLABORATIVE ACTIVITY

For a focused and efficient discussion of Alice Walker's essay, divide the class into groups of three to five and assign each group one of the "Questions for Writing and Discussion" that follow this essay. Each group should then report its findings to the class as a whole. Again, if students have a tentative idea or draft of their own essay, connect their reading with their writing by giving them ten minutes to read their own rough drafts and find one place where they can use one of Alice Walker's remembering techniques or shaping strategies. Following this activity, ask students to report to the class on which strategies were most applicable to their own essays.

cousin Brenda, just my age, whose father works in the post office and whose mother is a nurse, comes to find me. "Hello," she says. And then she asks, looking at my recent school picture which I did not want taken, and on which the "glob" as I think of it is clearly visible, "You still can't see out of that eye?" **(28)**

"No," I say, and flop back on the bed over my book. **(29)**

That night, as I do almost every night, I abuse my eye. I rant and rave at it, in front of the mirror. I plead with it to clear up before morning. I tell it I hate and despise it. I do not pray for sight. I pray for beauty. **(30)**

"You did not change," they say. **(31)**

I am fourteen and baby-sitting for my brother Bill who lives in Boston. He is my favorite brother and there is a strong bond between us. Understanding my feelings of shame and ugliness, he and his wife take me to a local hospital where the "glob" is removed by a doctor named O. Henry. There is still a small bluish crater where the scar tissue was, but the ugly white stuff is gone. Almost immediately I become a different person from the girl who does not raise her head. Or so I think. Now that I've raised my head, I win the boyfriend of my dreams. Now that I've raised my head, I have plenty of friends. Now that I've raised my head, classwork comes from my lips as faultlessly as Easter speeches did, and I leave high school as valedictorian, most popular student and *queen*, hardly believing my luck. Ironically, the girl who was voted most beautiful in our class (and was) was later shot twice through the chest by a male companion, using a "real" gun, while she was pregnant. But that's another story in itself. Or, is it? **(32)**

"You did not change," they say. **(33)**

It is now thirty years since the "accident." A beautiful journalist comes to visit and to interview me. She is going to write a cover story for her magazine that focuses on my last book. "Decide how you want to look on the cover," she says. "Glamorous, or whatever." **(34)**

Never mind "glamorous," it is the "whatever" that I hear. Suddenly all I can think of is whether I will get enough sleep the night before the photography session: if I don't, my eye will be tired and wander, as blind eyes will. **(35)**

At night in bed with my lover I think up reasons why I should not appear on the cover of a magazine. "My meanest critics will say I've sold out," I say. "My family will now realize I write scandalous books." **(36)**

But what's the real reason you don't want to do this?" he asks. **(37)**

"Because in all probability," I say in a rush, "my eye won't be straight." (38)

"It will be straight enough," he says. Then, "Besides, I thought you'd made your peace with that." **(39)**

And I suddenly remember that I have. **(40)**

I remember:

I am talking to my brother Jimmy, asking if he remembers anything unusual about the day I was shot. He does not know I consider that day the last time my father, with his sweet home remedy of cool lily leaves, "chose" me, and that I suffered and raged inside because of this. "Well," he says, "all I remember is standing by the side of the highway with Daddy, trying to flag down a car. A white man stopped, but when Daddy said he needed somebody to take his little girl to the doctor, he drove off." **(41)**

I remember:

I am in the desert for the first time. I fall totally in love with it. I am so overwhelmed by its beauty, I confront for the first time, consciously, the meaning of the doctor's words years ago: "Eyes are sympathetic. If one is blind, the other will likely become blind too." I realize I have dashed about the world madly, looking at this, looking at that, storing up images against the fading of the light. *But I might have missed seeing the desert*! The shock of that possibility—and gratitude for over twenty-five years of sight—sends me literally to my knees. Poem after poem comes—which is perhaps how poets pray.

On Sight

I am so thankful I have seen
The Desert
And the creatures in the desert
And the desert Itself.
The desert has its own moon
Which I have seen
With my own eye
There is no flag on it.
Trees of the desert have arms
All of which are always up
That is because the moon is up
The sun is up
Also the sky
The stars
Clouds
None with flags.
If there were flags, I doubt
the trees would point.
Would you? ***(42)***

But mostly, I remember this:

I am twenty-seven, and my baby daughter is almost three. Since her birth I have worried over her discovery that her mother's eyes are different from other people's. Will she be embarrassed? I wonder. What will she say? Every day she watches a television program called "Big Blue Marble." It begins with a picture of the earth as it appears from the moon. It is bluish, a little battered-looking, but full of light, with whitish clouds swirling around it. Every time I see it I weep with love, as if it is a picture of Grandma's house. One day when I am putting Rebecca down for her nap, she suddenly focuses on my eye. Something inside me cringes, gets ready to try to protect myself. All children are cruel about physical differences, I know from experience, and that they don't always mean to be is another matter. I assume Rebecca will be the same. **(43)**

But no-o-o-o. She studies my face intently as we stand, her inside and me outside her crib. She even holds my face maternally between her dimpled little hands. Then, looking every bit as serious and lawyerlike as her father, she says, as if it may just possibly have slipped my attention: "Mommy, there's a *world* in your eye." (As in, "Don't be alarmed, or do anything crazy.") And then, gently, but with great interest: "Mommy, where did you *get* that world in your eye?" **(44)**

For the most part, the pain left then. (So what if my brothers grew up to buy even more powerful pellet guns for their sons and to carry real guns themselves. So what if a young "Morehouse man" once nearly fell off the steps of Trevor Arnett Library because he thought my eyes were blue.) Crying and laughing I ran to the bathroom, while Rebecca mumbled and sang herself off to sleep. Yes indeed, I realized, looking into the mirror. There *was* a world in my eye. And I saw that it was possible to love it; that in fact, for all it had taught me, of shame and anger and inner vision, I *did* love it. Even to see it drifting out of orbit in boredom, or rolling up out of fatigue, not to mention floating back at attention in excitement (bearing witness, a friend has called it), deeply suitable to my personality, and even characteristic of me. **(45)**

That night I dream I am dancing to Stevie Wonder's song "Always" (the name of the song is really "As," but I hear it as "Always"). As I dance, whirling and joyous, happier than I've ever been in my life, another bright-faced dancer joins me. We dance and kiss each other and hold each other through the night. The other dancer has obviously come through all right, as I have done. She is beautiful, whole and free. And she is also me. **(46)**

TEACHING TIP

Don't ignore the value of vocabulary in teaching students to read critically. In addition to clarifying a sentence, studying vocabulary words can help readers actively construct meaning. In context, probing the meanings of *sympathetic*, *cataract*, and even *witness* leads naturally to a discussion of the central image of blindness (see Question 6).

VOCABULARY

In your journal, write the meaning of the following words:

- a *subversive* wit **(1)**

- rustling their new *crinolines* (4)
- Eyes are *sympathetic* (12)
- a hideous *cataract* (13)
- *boisterous*, ill-disciplined children (16)
- bearing *witness* (45)

Questions for Writing and Discussion

1. Why does Alice Walker share this story with us? What memories from your own life did her story trigger? Write them down.

2. What does Walker discover or learn about herself? As a reader, what did you learn about your own experiences by reading this essay?

3. Reread the essay, looking for examples of the following techniques for writing about memories: (1) using detailed observations; (2) creating specific scenes; (3) noting changes, contrasts, or conflicts; and (4) seeing relationships between past and present. In your opinion, which of these techniques does she use most effectively?

4. What is Walker's main idea in this autobiographical account? State it in your own words. Where in the essay does she state it most explicitly?

5. How many scenes or episodes does Walker recount? List them according to her age at the time. Explain how each episode relates to her main idea.

6. Walker also uses images of sight and blindness to organize her essay. The story begins with a description of a father who has "beautiful eyes" and ends with her dancing in her dream to a song by Stevie Wonder. Catalogue the images of sight and blindness from each scene or episode. Explain how, taken together, these images reinforce Walker's main idea.

7. Walker writes her essay in the present tense, and she uses italics not only to emphasize ideas but to indicate the difference between past thoughts and events and the present. List the places where she uses italics. Explain how the italicized passages reinforce her main point.

TEACHING TIP

Writers often have problems with the subjects and the focus for remembering essays. Although Keller, Sanders, and Walker write about highly dramatic moments in their lives, often the *seemingly ordinary* events make good topics as well. (See Todd Petry's essay about his cowboy hat.) To help students limit and focus their topics, ask them to narrate only *one or two key scenes* rather than describe a long series of events. Remind students that their audience will not want to read a series of unconnected personal anecdotes.

TEACHING TIP

To screen those topics that may be overly emotional or excessively personal, have students write their tentative topics at the board. For any topics that seem highly personal, traumatic, or sexually explicit, have your class discuss the key issues of *approriateness* and the *other students' rights to privacy*. Although remembering essays are personal and expressive, they must still consider the rights and sensibilities of readers

Memory is more indelible than ink.
—ANITA LOOS, AUTHOR OF KISS HOLLYWOOD GOODBYE

TEACHING TIP

Try small-group brainstorming for memories. Groups can focus on families, trips, school memories, or personal discoveries. Ask students to brainstorm individually in their journals for five minutes, share their memories in the group for eight to ten minutes, and then record ideas for five more minutes in their journals.

REMEMBERING: THE WRITING PROCESS

■ **ASSIGNMENT FOR REMEMBERING** Write an essay about an important person, place, and/or event in your life. Your purpose is to recall and then use specific examples that *re-create* this memory and *show why* it is so important to you.

As you begin writing, assume that you are writing for yourself or for a small audience of good friends who are interested in your life. Let your writing re-create the experience vividly enough so that your readers can see the main idea that you wish to convey.

CHOOSING A SUBJECT

If one of the journal-entry exercises suggested a possible subject, try the collecting and shaping strategies below. If none of those exercises led to an interesting subject, consider the following ideas:

- Interview (in person or over the phone) your parents, a brother or sister, or a close friend. What events or experiences do they remember that were important to you?
- Get out a map of your town, city, state, or country and spend a few minutes doing an inventory of places you have been. Make a list of trips you have taken, with dates and years. Which of those places is the most memorable for you?
- Dig out a school yearbook and look through the pictures and the inscriptions that your classmates wrote. Whom do you remember most clearly? What events do you recall most vividly?
- Go to the library and look through news magazines or newspapers from five to ten years ago. What were the most important events of those years? What do you remember about them? Where were you and what were you doing when these events occurred? Which events had the largest impact on your life?
- Choose an important moment in your life, but write from the *point of view* of another person—a friend, family member, or stranger who was present. Let this person narrate the events that happened to you.

Note: Avoid choosing overly emotional topics such as the recent death of a close friend or family member. If you are too close to your subject, responding to your reader's revision suggestions may be difficult. Ask yourself if you can emotionally distance yourself from that subject. If you received a *C* for that essay, would you feel devastated?

COLLECTING

Once you have chosen a subject for your essay, try the following collecting strategies:

Brainstorming Brainstorming is merely jotting down anything and everything that comes to mind which is remotely connected to your subject: words, phrases, images, or complete thoughts. You can brainstorm by yourself or in groups, with everyone contributing ideas and one person recording them.

Looping Looping is a method of controlled freewriting that generates ideas and provides focus and direction. Begin by freewriting about your subject for eight to ten minutes. Then pause, reread what you have written, and *underline* the most interesting or important idea in what you've written so far. Then, using that sentence or idea as your starting point, write for eight to ten minutes more. Repeat this cycle, or "loop," one more time. Each loop should add ideas and details from some new angle or viewpoint, but overall you will be focusing on the most important ideas that you discover.

Clustering Clustering is merely a visual scheme for brainstorming and free-associating about your topic. It can be especially effective for remembering because it helps you sketch relationships among your topics and subtopics. As you can see from the sample sketch below, the sketch that you make of your ideas should help you see relationships between ideas or get a rough idea about an order or shape you may wish to use.

RESOURCE NOTE

For additional information about looping and cubing, see Cowan Neeld, *Writing*. For more on clustering, see Rico, *Writing the Natural Way*. Lindemann, *A Rhetoric for Writing Teachers* explains other invention strategies, such as the classical *topoi*, Burke's pentad, and tagmemics from Young, Becker, and Pike

TEACHING TIP

Some writers may prefer to read this section, devise plans using several of these strategies, and then draft their essays. Others may want to read this section for ideas, start drafting, and after finishing the drafts, reread this section to see which of these strategies they intuitively chose. Then they can amplify those shaping strategies already suggested by their drafts. Short workshop sessions asking students to *identify* the shaping strategies they find in each other's drafts may help both kinds of writers revise their essays.

SHAPING

First, reconsider your purpose; perhaps it has become clearer or more definite since you recorded it in your journal entry. In your journal, jot down tentative answers for the following questions. If you don't have an answer, go on to the next question.

- *Subject:* What is your general subject?
- *Specific Topic:* What aspect of your subject are you interested in?
- *Purpose:* Why is this topic interesting or important to you or your readers?
- *Main idea:* What might your main idea be?
- *Audience:* For whom are you writing this? What is your reader like, and why might he or she be interested in this topic?

WRITE TO LEARN

Encourage your students to write a "discovery draft" or "zero draft" to get their ideas on paper. Collecting and shaping strategies can be effective invention strategies, but actual drafts may help—if students know that the purpose is to let their writing lead them to *discover the focus for their memories*. Some teachers have students trade "zero drafts" with peers, discuss what the writer discovered and learned, have each writer make written plans based on the draft and the discussion, and then hand in the drafts. Teachers may read the drafts and return them later, in time for a revision activity *after* students have written a complete draft.

Narrow and focus your subject. If you're going to write a three-page essay, don't try to cover everything in your life. Focus on one person, one episode, one turning point, one day, even one *part* of one day, and do that in depth and detail.

As you start your shaping activities, use the observing strategies discussed in Chapter 3. *Spatial order* may help you shape your description of a place you are remembering; *classification* or *definition* can shape your memories of people, places, or events. *Similes, metaphors*, and *analogies* will make your writing more vivid and may also suggest a shape or help you develop your subject.

In addition, use the following strategies for shaping written memories. Try each strategy to see if it works for your subject. Although some strategies may not be appropriate, others will work naturally, suggesting ways to shape and develop your writing.

Chronological Order If you are writing about remembered events, you will probably use some form of chronological order. Try making a *chronological list of the major scenes or events*. Then go through the list, deciding what you will emphasize by telling about each item in detail and what you will pass over quickly. Normally, you will be using a straightforward chronological order, but you may wish to use a flashback, starting in the middle or near the end and then returning to tell the beginning. In his paragraph about a personal relationship, for example, student writer Gregory Hoffman begins the story at the most dramatic point, returns to tell how the relationship began, and then concludes the story.

> Her words hung in the air like iron ghosts. "I'm pregnant," she said as they walked through the park, the snow crackling beneath their feet. Carol was looking down at the ground when she told him, somewhat ashamed, embarrassed and defiant all at once. Their rela-

tionship had only started in September, but both had felt the uneasiness surrounding them for the past months. She could remember the beginning so well and in such favor, now that the future seemed so uncertain. The all-night conversations by the bay window, the rehearsals at the university theatre—where he would make her laugh during her only soliloquy, and most of all the Christmas they had spent together in Vermont. No one else had existed for her during those months. Yet now, she felt duped by her affections—as if she had become an absurd representation of a tragic television character. As they approached the lake he put his arm around her, "Just do what you think is best, babe. I mean, I think you know how I feel." At that moment, she knew it was over. It was no longer "their" decision. His hand touched her cheek in a benedictorial fashion. The rest would only be form now. Exchanging records and clothes with an aside of brief conversation. She would see him again, in the market or at a movie, and they would remember. But like his affection in September, her memory of him would fade until he was too distant to see.

Computer Tips: Shaping

If you are remembering an event, test your essay to see if a *flashback* might work. Open a file and brainstorm a list of specific incidents within the event that you want to write about. Arrange this list in chronological order. Now, use your MOVE feature to reorder the events in the list to create a flashback effect. Choose one crucial incident *near* the end and move it to the top of the list. See if you could begin your story at this point and then flash back to tell earlier incidents. You can then conclude your story with the incidents at the end of the list.

Comparison/Contrast Although you may be comparing or contrasting people, places, or events from the past, you will probably also be comparing or contrasting the past to the present. You may do that at the beginning, noting how something in the present reminds you of a past person, place, or event. You may do it at the end, as Andrea Lee does in *Russian Journal.* You may do it both at the beginning and at the end, as Richard Rodriguez does in "The Boy's Desire." You may even contrast past and present throughout, as Alice Walker does in "Beauty: When the Other Dancer Is the Self." Comparing or contrasting the past with the present will often clarify your dominant idea.

Your students can learn about rhetorical economy and force by studying how news programs represent complex concepts in a single image. See the *Video Guide* for examples.

Image Sometimes a single mental picture or recurring image will shape a paragraph or two in an essay. Consider how novelist George Orwell, in his essay "Shooting an Elephant," uses the image of a puppet or dummy to describe his feeling at a moment when he realized that, against his better judgment, he was going to have to shoot a marauding elephant in order to satisfy a crowd of two thousand Burmese who had gathered to watch him. The italicized words emphasize the recurring image.

> Suddenly I realized that I should have to shoot the elephant after all. The people expected it of me and I had got to do it; I could feel their *two thousand wills pressing me forward*, irresistibly. And it was at this moment, as I stood there with the rifle in my hands, that I first grasped the hollowness, the futility of the white man's dominion in the East. Here was I, the white man with his gun, standing in front of the unarmed native crowd—*seemingly the leading actor* of the piece; but in reality I was only an absurd *puppet pushed to and fro* by the will of those yellow faces behind. I perceived in this moment that when the white man turns tyrant it is his own freedom that he destroys. He becomes a sort of *hollow, posing dummy*, the *conventionalized figure* of a sahib. For it is the condition of his rule that he shall spend his life in trying to impress the "natives" and so in every crisis he has got to do what the "natives" expect of him. He *wears a mask*, and his face grows to fit it. I had got to shoot the elephant. I had committed myself to doing it when I sent for the rifle. *A sahib has got to act like a sahib*; he has got to appear resolute, to know his own mind and do definite things.

Voice and Tone When you have a personal conversation with someone, the way you look and sound—your body type, your voice, your facial expressions and gestures—communicates a sense of personality and attitude, which in turn affects how the other person reacts to what you say. In written language, although you don't have those gestures, expressions, or the actual sound of your voice, you can still create the sense that you are talking directly to your listener.

The term *voice* refers to a writer's personality as revealed through language. Writers may use emotional, colloquial, or conversational language to communicate a sense of personality. Or they may use abstract, impersonal language either to conceal their personalities or to create an air of scientific objectivity.

Tone is a writer's attitude toward the subject. The attitude may be positive or negative. It may be serious, humorous, honest, or ironic; it may be skeptical or accepting; it may be happy, frustrated, or angry. Often voice and tone overlap, and together they help us hear a writer talking to us. In the following passage, we hear student writer Kurt Weekly talking to us directly; we hear a clear, honest voice telling the story. His tone is not defensive or guilty: He openly admits he has a "problem."

> Oh no, not another trash day. Every time I see all those trash containers, plastic garbage bags and junk lined up on the sidewalks, it drives me crazy. It all started when I was sixteen. I had just received my driver's license and the most beautiful Ford pickup. It was Wednesday as I remember and trash day. I don't know what happened. All of a sudden I was racing down the street swerving to the right, smashing into a large green Hefty trash bag filled with grass clippings. The bag exploded, and grass clippings and trash flew everywhere. It was beautiful and I was hooked. There was no stopping me.
>
> At first I would smash one or two cans on the way to school. Then I just couldn't get enough. I would start going out the night before trash day. I would go down the full length of the street and wipe out every garbage container in sight. I was the terror of the neighborhood. This was not a bad habit to be taken lightly. It was an obsession. I was in trouble. There was no way I could kick this on my own. I needed help.
>
> I received that help. One night after an evening of nonstop can smashing, the Arapahoe County Sheriff Department caught up with me. Not just one or a few but the whole department. They were willing to set me on the right path, and if that didn't work, they were going to send me to jail. It was a long, tough road to rehabilitation, but I did it. Not alone. I had the support of my family and the community.

Persona Related to voice and tone is the *persona*—the "mask" that a writer can put on. Sometimes in telling a story about yourself, you may want to speak in your own "natural" voice. At other times, however, you may change or exaggerate certain characteristics in order to project a character different from your "real" self. Writers, for example, may project themselves as braver and more intelligent than they really are. Or to create a humorous effect, they may create personas who are more foolish or clumsy than they really are. This persona can shape a whole passage. In the following excerpt, James Thurber, a master of autobiographical humor, uses a persona—along with chronological narrative—to shape his account of a frustrating botany class.

> I passed all the other courses that I took at my university, but I could never pass botany. This was because all botany students had to spend several hours a week in a laboratory looking through a microscope at plant cells, and I could never see through a microscope. I never once saw a cell through a microscope. This used to enrage my instructor. He would wander around the laboratory pleased with the

Ask your students to describe the screen personae of well-known film and television personalities. How do these public masks differ from real people behind them? What purposes do they serve?

TEACHING TIP

Many beginning writers have trouble revising because they believe that the words of their remembering essay are exactly equivalent to their experiences. Changing a draft thus means altering or even falsifying their experiences. Asking students to adopt a persona, or mask, to tell their story not only gives them a new perspective, but it may enable them to take revision suggestions more objectively.

PEER RESPONSE

Revision requires at least three steps. Writers must first become aware that a bit of text is deficient or could be *improved*. Then they need to create *alternative* versions of that portion of the text. Finally, they must *choose* among those alternative versions, based on the purpose, audience, and context. Too often, teachers focus revision workshops primarily on step one, without giving students sufficient time to create alternative language or without showing students how to choose one version based on purpose, audience, or context. Using your own draft of a remembering essay on an overhead transparency or projected computer screen, model all three steps for your students before you assign revision workshops.

progress all the students were making in drawing the involved and, so I am told, interesting structure of flower cells, until he came to me. I would just be standing there. "I can't see anything," I would say. He would begin patiently enough, explaining how anybody can see through a microscope, but he would always end up in a fury claiming that I could too see through a microscope but just pretended that I couldn't. "It takes away from the beauty of flowers anyway," I used to tell him. "We are not concerned with beauty in this course," he would say. "We are concerned solely with the mechanics of flowers." "Well," I'd say, "I can't see anything." "Try it just once again," he'd say, and I would put my eye to the microscope and see nothing at all, except now and again a nebulous milky substance—a phenomenon of maladjustment. You were supposed to see a vivid, restless clockwork of sharply defined plant cells. "I see what looks like a lot of milk," I would tell him. This, he claimed, was the result of my not having adjusted the microscope properly, so he would readjust it for me, or rather, for himself. And I would look again and see milk.

I finally took a deferred pass, as they called it, and waited a year and tried again. (You had to pass one of the biological sciences or you couldn't graduate.) The professor had come back from vacation brown as a berry, bright-eyed, and eager to explain cell-structure again to his classes. "Well," he said to me, cheerily, when we met in the first laboratory hour of the semester, "we're going to see cells this time, aren't we?" "Yes, sir," I said. Students to the right of me and to the left of me and in front of me were seeing cells; what's more, they were quietly drawing pictures of them in their notebooks. Of course, I didn't see anything.

"We'll try it," the professor said to me, grimly, "with every adjustment of the microscope known to man. As God is my witness, I'll arrange this glass so that you see cells through it or I'll give up teaching. In twenty-two years of botany, I—" He cut off abruptly for he was beginning to quiver all over, like Lionel Barrymore, and he genuinely wished to hold onto his temper; his scenes with me had taken a great deal out of him.

So we tried it with every adjustment of the microscope known to man. With only one of them did I see anything but blackness or the familiar lacteal opacity, and that time I saw, to my pleasure and amazement, a variegated constellation of flecks, specks, and dots. These I hastily drew. The instructor, noting my activity, came back from an adjoining desk, a smile on his lips and his eyebrows high in hope. He looked at my cell drawing. "What's that?" he demanded, with a hint of a squeal in his voice. "That's what I saw," I said. "You didn't, you didn't, you didn't!" he screamed, losing control of his

> temper instantly, and he bent over and squinted into the microscope. His head snapped up. "That's your eye!" he shouted. "You've fixed the lens so that it reflects! You've drawn your eye!"

Dialogue Dialogue, which helps to *re-create* people and events rather than just tell about them, can become a dominant form and thereby shape your writing. Re-creating an actual conversation, you could possibly write a whole scene using nothing but dialogue. More often, however, writers use dialogue occasionally for dramatic effect. In the account of his battle with the microscope, for instance, Thurber uses dialogue in the last two paragraphs to dramatize his conclusion:

> "We'll try it," the professor said to me, grimly, "with every adjustment known to man. As God is my witness, I'll arrange this glass so that you see cells through it or I'll give up teaching. In twenty-two years of teaching botany, I—" . . . "What's that?" he demanded. . . . "That's what I saw," I said. "You didn't, you didn't, you didn't!" he screamed. . . . "You've fixed the lens so that it reflects! You've drawn your eye!"

Title, Introduction, and Conclusion In your journal, sketch out several possible *titles* you might use. You may want a title that is merely an accurate label, such as *Russian Journal* or "The Boy's Desire," but you may prefer something less direct that gets your reader's attention. For example, for his essay about his hat that appears at the end of this chapter, student writer Todd Petry uses the title "The Wind Catcher." As a reader, what do you think about Alice Walker's title, "Beauty: When the Other Dancer Is the Self?"

Introductions or beginning paragraphs take several shapes. Some plunge the reader immediately into the action—as Gregory Hoffman does—and then later fill in the scene and context. Others are more like Kurt Weekly's, announcing the subject—trash cans—and then taking the reader from the present to the past and the beginning of the story: "It all started when I was sixteen. . . . " At some point, however, readers do need to know the context—the *who, what, when*, and *where* of your account.

Conclusions are also of several types. In some, writers will return to the present and discuss what they have learned, as Andrea Lee does in *Russian Journal*. Some, like Alice Walker, end with an image or even a dream. Some writers conclude with dramatic moments, as James Thurber does, or with an emotional scene, as student writer Brooke Selby does in the essay on Kit Carson that appears at the end of this chapter. But many writers will try to tie the conclusion back to the beginning, as Richard Rodriguez does at the end of "The Boy's Desire": "The closet door closes . . . the fog rises." In your journal, experiment with several possibilities until you find one that works for your subject.

I start at the beginning, go on to the end, then stop.
—GABRIEL GARCÍA MARQUEZ

I always know the ending; that's where I start.
—TONI MORRISON, NOBEL PRIZE-WINNING NOVELIST

Drafting

When you have experimented with the above shaping strategies, reconsider your purpose, audience, and main idea. Have they changed? In your journal, re-examine the notes you made before trying the shaping activities. If necessary, revise your statements about purpose, audience, or main idea based on what you have actually written.

Working from your journal material and from your collecting and shaping activities, draft your essay. It is important *not* to splice different parts together or just recopy and connect segments, for they may not fit or flow together. Instead, reread what you have written, and then start with a clean sheet of paper. If you're working on a computer file, you can start with your list of events or one of your best shaping strategies and expand that file as you draft. Concentrate on what you want to say and write as quickly as possible.

To avoid interruptions, choose a quiet place to work. Follow your own writing rituals. Try to write nonstop. If you cannot think of the right word, put a line or a dash, but keep on writing. When necessary, go back and reread what you have previously written.

PEER RESPONSE

If you plan to have a peer-response workshops on your students' remembering essay drafts, see the instructor's manual for a sample guide. Also, you may wish to adapt the sample peer-response sheets included in Chapters 7–10. Or use several of the questions from the Revising Guidelines. To encourage your students to respond actively, have them review and revise your workshop sheet the day *before* the workshop. Especially for the first peer-response workshop, be sure to *model* the use of those guidelines with a sample student essay.

Revising

Revising begins, of course, when you get your first idea and start collecting and shaping. After you have a draft and some feedback from other readers, however, you need to distance yourself and objectively reread what you have written. Especially for this remembering essay, make sure your memories are *re-created* on paper. Don't be satisfied with suggesting incidents that merely trigger your own memories: You must *show* people and events vividly for your reader.

The difference between the right word and the nearly right word is the same as that between lightning and the lightning bug.
—MARK TWAIN, AUTHOR OF THE ADVENTURES OF HUCKLEBERRY FINN

Guidelines for Revision

- **Re-examine your purpose and audience.** Are you doing what you intended?
- **Revise to make the main idea of your account clearer.** You don't need a "moral" to the story or a bald statement saying "This is why this person was important." Your reader, however, should know clearly why you wanted to write about the memory that you chose.
- **Revise to clarify the important *relationships* in your story.** Consider relationships between past and present, between you and the people in your story, between one place and another place, between one event and another event.

- **Close and detailed observation is crucial.** *Show*, don't just tell. Can you use any of the collecting and shaping strategies for observing discussed in Chapter 3?
- **Revise to show crucial changes, contrasts, or conflicts more clearly.** Keller's and Walker's essays, for instance, illustrate how *conflict* and *change* are central to an effective remembering essay. See if their strategies will work in your essay.
- **Have you used a straight chronological order?** If it works, keep it. If not, would another order be better? Should you begin in the middle and do a flashback? Do you want to move back and forth from present to past or stay in the past until the end?
- **If you are using a chronological order,** cue your reader by occasionally using transitional words to signal changes:

  then, when, first, next, last, before, after, while, as, sooner, later, initially, finally, yesterday, today
- **Be clear about point of view.** Are you looking back on the past from a viewpoint in the present? Are you using the point of view of yourself as a child or at some earlier point in your life? Are you using the point of view of another person or object in your story?
- **What are the key images in your account?** Should you add or delete an image to show the experience more vividly?
- **What voice are you using?** Does it support your purpose? If you are using a persona, is it appropriate for your audience and purpose?
- **Revise sentences to improve clarity, conciseness, emphasis, and variety.**
- **Check your dialogue for proper punctuation and indentation.** See the essay by Scott Russell Sanders in this chapter for a model.
- **When you are relatively satisfied with your draft, edit for correct spelling, appropriate word choice, punctuation, and grammar.**

Postscript on the Writing Process

After you finish writing, revising, and editing your essay, you will want to breathe a sigh of relief and turn it in. But before you do, think about the problems that you solved as you wrote this essay. *Remember*: One of your goals in this course is to discover your style of writing or composing. What approaches work best for you? And, just as important, **what doesn't work**? Take a few minutes to answer the following questions:

TEACHING TIP

Question 4 asks students to evaluate, in general terms, the final versions of their essays. If teachers intend to help students learn how to revise, *the student's perception of strengths and weaknesses should be the focus of a teacher's written or oral response.* If the student correctly says, for example, that the first scene needs more detail but the final scene is effective, then the teacher can verify the student's judgment. If the student mistakenly thinks that a key scene is effective when it is narrated too hurriedly, then the teacher can explain what the problem is and suggest how to fix it.

1. Review your writing process. Which collecting, shaping, and revising strategies helped you remember and describe incidents most quickly and clearly? What problems were you unable to solve?

2. Reread your essay. With a small asterisk [*], identify in the margin of your essay sentences where you used sensory details, dialogue, or images to show or re-create the experience for your reader.

3. If you received feedback from your peers, identify one piece of advice that you followed and one bit of advice that you ignored. Explain your decisions.

4. Rereading your essay, what do you like best about it? What parts of your essay need work? What would you change if you had another day to work on this assignment?

REMEMBERING: STUDENT WRITING

THE WIND CATCHER

TODD PETRY

Todd Petry decided to write about his cowboy hat, observing it in the present and thinking about some of the memories that it brought back. His notes, his first short draft paragraphs, and his revised version demonstrate how observing and remembering work together naturally: The details stimulate memories, and memories lead to more specific details.

NOTES AND DETAILS

DETAILS	MORE SPECIFIC DETAILS
Gray	Dirty, dust coated, rain stained cowdung color
Resistol	The name is stained and blurred
Size 7 3/8	
Diamond shape	Used to be diamond shape, now battered, looks abandoned

4" brim	Front tipped down, curled up in back
1" sweat band	blackish
5 yrs. old	still remember the day I bought it
4x beaver	
What it is not:	it is unlike a hat fresh out of the box
What it compares to:	point of crown like the north star like a pancake with wilted edges battered like General Custer's hat
What I remember:	the day I bought the hat a day at Pray Mesa

First Draft

THE WIND CATCHER

The other day while I was relaxing in my favorite chair and listening to Ian Tyson, I happened to notice my work cowboy hat hanging on the wall. Now I look at that old hat no less than a dozen times a day without too much thought, but on that particular day, my eyes remained fixed on it and my mind went to remembering.

I still remember I had $100 cash in my pocket the day I went hat shopping. The local tack, feed, and western wear CO-OP was my first and only stop. Finding a hat to meet my general specifications was no big deal. I wanted a gray Resistol, size 7 3/8, with a 4-inch brim and diamond shaped crown. From there on, though, my wants became very particular. I took 30 minutes to find the one that had the right fit, and five times that long to come to terms with the hat shaper. Boy, but I was one proud young fellow the next day when I went to school sporting my new piece of head gear. I've had that wind catcher five years through rough times, but in a way, it really looks better now, without any shape, dirty, and covered with dust and cowdung.

Revised Version

THE WIND CATCHER

The other day while I was relaxing in my favorite chair and listening to Ian Tyson, I happened to notice my work cowboy hat hanging on the wall. Now I look at that old hat no less than a dozen times a day without too much thought, but on that particular day, my eyes remained fixed on it and my mind went to remembering. **(1)**

I was 15 years old and had $100 cash in my pocket the day I went hat shopping 5 years ago. The local tack, feed, and western wear CO-OP was my first and only stop. Finding a hat to meet my general specifications was no big deal. I wanted a gray 4X Resistol, size 7 3/8, with a 4-inch brim and diamond shaped crown. I wanted no flashy feathers or gaudy hatbands, which in my mind were only for pilgrims. From there on, though, my wants became very particular. I took 30 minutes to find the one that had the right fit, and five times that long to come to terms with the hat shaper. Boy, but I was one proud young fellow the next day when I went to school sporting my new piece of head gear. **(2)**

About that time, Ian Tyson startled me out of my state of reminiscence by singing "Rose in the Rockies," with that voice of his sounding like ten cow elk cooing to their young in the springtime. As I sat there listening to the music and looking at that old hat, I had to chuckle to myself because that wind catcher had sure seen better days. I mean it looked rode hard and put up wet. The gray, which was once as sharp and crisp as a mountain lake, was now faded and dull where the sun had beat down. Where the crown and brim met, the paleness was suddenly transformed into a gritty black which ran the entire circumference of the hat. This black was unlike any paint or color commercially available, being made up of head sweat, dirt, alfalfa dust, and powdered cow manure. Water blemishes from too much rain and snow mottled the brim, adding to the colors' turbidity. Inside the crown and wherever the slope was less than ninety degrees, dust had collected to hide the natural color even more. **(3)**

After awhile, my attention lost interest in the various colors and began to work its way over the hat's shape, which I was once so critical of. General Custer's hat itself could not have looked worse. All signs of uniformity and definite shape had disappeared. The diamond shaped crown, which was once round and smooth, now bowed out on the sides and had edges as blunt as an orange crate. The point, which once looked like the North Star indicating the direction, now was twisted off balance from excessive right hand use. Remembering last spring, how I threw that hat in the face of an irate mother cow during calving, I had to chuckle again.

Throwing that hat kept my horse and me out of trouble but made the "off balance look" rather permanent. As I looked at the brim, I was reminded of a three-day-old pancake with all its edges wilted. The back of that brim curled upward like a snake ready to strike, and the front had become so narrow and dipped, it looked like something a dentist would use on your teeth. **(4)**

For probably half an hour I sat looking at the wear and tear on that ancient hat. Awhile back, I remember, I decided to try to make my old hat socially presentable by having it cleaned and blocked, removing those curls and dips and other signs of use. However, when a hat shop refused to even attempt the task, I figured I'd just leave well enough alone. As I scanned my eyes over the hat, I noticed several other alterations from its original form, such as the absent hat band which was born off in the brush on Pray Mesa and the black thread that drew together the edges of a hole in the crown. However, try as I might, I could not for the life of me see where any character had been lost in the brush, or any flair had been covered with cowdung. **(5)**

QUESTIONS FOR WRITING AND DISCUSSION

1. Close observation often leads to specific memories. In the opening paragraph of his revised version, Todd Petry says that "on that particular day, my eyes remained fixed on it and my mind went to remembering." He then recalls the time when he was fifteen years old and bought his hat. Identify two other places where observation leads Petry to remember specific scenes from the past.

2. Petry chose "The Wind Catcher" as the title for his essay. Reread the essay and then brainstorm a list of five other titles that might be appropriate for this short essay. Which title do you like best?

3. Where does Petry most clearly express the main idea of his essay? Write out the main idea in your own words.

KIT CARSON

BROOKE SELBY

In the following essay, Brooke Selby remembers an Easter reunion that turned out to be a celebration of life in a small western town. As she wrote, Selby says, she tried to "paint a prose portrait of a place which

COLLABORATIVE ACTIVITY

Two proven strategies for writing introductions to remembering essays are to throw the reader immediately into a scene, as Alice Walker does, or to begin at a distance and gradually zoom in on a specific scene and time, as Selby does. Have pairs of students trade drafts of their essays, read each other's introductions, and together, write alternate introductions to both of their essays. Writers should then decide which introduction (their original or their alternate version) works best.

always held an almost spiritual 'specialness' for my family. I closed my eyes and tried to recall actual snapshots from the day; I used those mental images as I searched for the words to describe it."

The town of Kit Carson is often omitted from Colorado maps. One sees just a glimpse from the highway, a square cluster of peeling white frame houses and dingy brown buildings, long bathed in the eastern Colorado dust. To the two hundred and eighty persons who call Kit Carson their home, it is the very center of existence, but to outsiders it is a curious, tattered remnant from farming days: a slow-moving, wind-blown apparition from the past. **(1)**

The highway bisects Kit Carson, seeming almost an incongruity amidst the time-worn face of the town. The only motel lies on the northernmost edge, gaudy and commercial amidst the waving plains grasses. From the road one catches a glimpse of a one room museum, an old red brick drug store, some tired stone churches, rusted screen doors which lead into the musty quiet of the few surviving shops, some deserted buildings with splintered boards nailed across the windows . . . all this in a rapid blur like an old newsreel, flashed by too quickly to grasp any more than a vague impression of deteriorating quiet. Yet from the road, one sees also black windmills, the sentinels of surrounding farms, and huge fields, opulent with crops, so that one knows that there are those who still prosper in this town. **(2)**

My mother was fifteen years old when she left Kit Carson. Times were hard and the farm's livelihood was not dependable enough to support a family of five, so they moved to Denver, with high hopes that an invention of my grandfather's would open the door to new prosperity and financial security. Yet in leaving Kit Carson, they left behind something which became to them a symbol of childhood, a place where innocence was not outdated, where the pace of life still permitted one time to be alone and to dream, and where one could go to escape when the pressures of job and existence became too over-bearing. Even now, the mention of Kit Carson evokes nostalgic memories and a burning, longing homesickness among my mother and her brother and sister. The three have all instilled in their children the same sacred image of the town, the same craving to go home, to return to times less strenuous and demanding. It is a different sort of world—although not untouched by the insensitive and often callous times we live in, it remains still a sanctuary, where one can walk out onto the prairie, breathe as deeply as possible, and feel a rare sense of complete inner peace, as if even miracles are possible and God not far away. **(3)**

There are those who cling yet to the town, like children clutching at their mother's skirts, certain that life elsewhere would be only a tarnished replica of life in Kit Carson. My great-grandparents are among these, their beings intricately woven within the fibers of the town's foundation. My great-grandfather will brook no criticism, disapproval, or even hinted dissatisfaction with his town, for it is "God's country" and "those big cities simply aren't fit for even animals to make their home." Outwardly, we scoff at Kit Carson's backwardness; inwardly we all feel its pull, yet we long for an actual confirmation of its magic, to prove to ourselves that it is not simply a land of dreams never realized. Easter brought us closer to this wish. **(4)**

We left early that Sunday morning, being unable to afford the time to go for the entire weekend. There was just the slightest hint of winter's last lingering sighs, as we sleepily crawled into our car. The sun seemed indecisive, resolving first to stretch its healing arms out toward the dormant earth, but then withdrawing its offer, as if uncertain that the spring had truly yet arrived. **(5)**

We spoke little on the trip, all caught up, I think, in our own thoughts and early morning sleepiness. We were restless, anticipating the celebration which lay ahead of us, as over fifty relatives gathered to mark my great-grandparents' sixtieth wedding anniversary. I stared lazily out the window, fixing my gaze on the telephone poles careening down the road, and struggling desperately against the fuzzy blanket of sleep which kept falling over my head. **(6)**

We were met in Kit Carson with a warm and loving welcome, immediately swallowed up in the overflowing concern oozing from each corner of the crowded house. The house was afire with conversation, exclamations, greetings issued to new arrivals, fantastic smells drifting out from the kitchen, and love tumbling from and between every person. Naturally, the occasion centered on my great-grandparents, who beamed proudly at the house filled with their family and loved ones. Both were beautifully dressed for the day. My great-grandmother resembled a velvet, pale pink rose, fragile and perhaps a little faded, yet with pride's stiff spine keeping her ever strong. Great-grandpa was filled with nervous energy, rushing from one group to another and beaming so joyously that an ache rose inside of me at the thought that perhaps soon a photograph would be our only tangible recollection of that grin. **(7)**

The day passed quickly in a blur of flashcubes, singing around the piano, and endless hugs, some from people I couldn't place. The afternoon was winding down, and many were beginning to talk of starting the drives back to their respective homes, when a young cousin ran into the house, shouting to my great-uncle that he should come outside immediately. He disappeared into the back, but shortly, two more young cousins came racing in, both eager to be the first to shout the news. My great-uncle, another romanticist, had several years earlier purchased ten buffalo and set them to graze upon his land, in an attempt to return that which rightfully belonged to the earth. Now one of the buffalo was having a baby and the young cousins were impatient that everyone should come to see. **(8)**

Although a couple of the adults were skeptical at first, the house grew quiet as everyone streamed into the back. My uncle confirmed that one of the buffalo was indeed calving and that the wait would not be long. At first, we all stood, gazing out over the fence into the pasture, laughing and joking about the coincidence of the birth on Easter. Soon, however, we were all caught up in the drama unfolding in front of us. It was a loud silence, so full was it of anticipation and unspoken thought. **(9)**

When a buffalo is in labor, it is on its own. As in the days of the early West, no veterinarian can make its task easier. To come near the animal would be to invite death for oneself or the newborn. It was soon apparent, however, that the mother buffalo was in serious trouble, and we stood in somber silence, voicing whispered prayers for the animals. It was as though a physical bond had those of us on the hillside tightly glued together, for we were straining as one, with frustration at our inability to aid the animals. My uncle paced nervously, almost certain that the birth was to be breech, for it appeared that the small calf's legs were emerging first. We waited what seemed an eon, squinting against the descending sun, and shivering from the slight breeze. **(10)**

It was hard to distinguish calf from mother when it began to appear, for from the distance it looked almost as one. Suddenly, though, my uncle gave a shout, and we could see the tiny calf was born and was standing, leaning its weight against its mother. As one, we all began to cheer and shout and talk in hushed voices about the miracle we had just witnessed. We began to vie with one another for the selection of an appropriate name, and dozens of suggestions were tossed out. Finally, one aunt cried that we should christen it "Resurrection," in light of the occasion and its close brush with death. **(11)**

Again quieted, we straggled back into the house and the prairie once more grew silent. I was the last to return inside and turned for one last glimpse of the newborn creature. In the twilight, the little calf was outlined against the prairie sky, still standing wobbly-kneed and shaky against the big mother buffalo. As I turned back around to return to the house, I saw spring's first flower, poking its head through the earth at the side of the building, and I was overwhelmed with the magnitude of what had just occurred. Kit Carson had confirmed its holiness, its magical potential as a place where miracles do not cease with growing up. I swallowed the lump in my throat and went inside. **(12)**

Questions for Writing and Discussion

1. Selby's essay is very much about human feelings and emotions. Stop and think for a moment. What specific feelings did you have as you read the essay?

2. Reread paragraphs 1 and 2. In terms of the rest of the essay, why does Selby spend so much time describing the *town* of Kit Carson? Is it necessary, or could it be deleted? Explain.

3. In writing about remembered people, places, or events, writers should make main ideas obvious without overstating them. What sentences contain the main point that Selby wants to make? (How does paragraph 5, for example, contribute to that thesis?) In your opinion, is Selby's thesis stated too obviously, not stated clearly enough, or given just the proper emphasis?

4. Good writers do not rush a story. They carefully set up the scene, let events develop, and take the time to recount the most important events. Reread this essay. Where do you notice Selby keeping a steady pace by refusing to rush her story?

5. Choose the best paragraph in this essay and copy it into your journal. When you have finished copying the paragraph, reread it. What is it about the sentences that makes them effective?

Resource Note

Question 5 may lead students to discover that Selby likes to write cumulative sentences (see paragraph 2, for example). For additional information about writing the cumulative sentence, see Christensen and Christensen, *Notes Toward a New Rhetoric*. After discussing Selby's and the Christensens' sentences, ask students to look at their own drafts and try working cumulative sentences into their own prose.

FIVE/READING

If we think of it, all that a University, or final highest School can do for us, is still but what the first School began doing—teach us to read.

—THOMAS CARLYLE, ON HEROES AND HERO WORSHIP

Reading involves a fair measure of push and shove. You make your mark on a book and it makes its mark on you. Reading is not simply a matter of hanging back and waiting for a piece, or its author, to tell you what the writing has to say.

—DAVID BARTHOLOMAE AND ANTHONY PETROSKY, AUTHORS OF WAYS OF READING

AS AN ASSIGNMENT IN CLASS, YOU ARE READING AND CRITIQUING AN ARTICLE BY DEBORAH TANNEN ON HOW MEN AND WOMEN RESPOND DIFFERENTLY DURING CLASS CONVERSATIONS. As you read the article, you like the thought-provoking examples, but soon you find yourself becoming frustrated. First, you have trouble locating the main focus of the article, and then you are disturbed by some unsupported assertions that she makes about typical behavior of men and women. Do men really like to argue and dominate class discussions? Do women always benefit from smaller, more intimate group discussions? You reread the article and make notes in the margin. After discussing your reactions with other readers, you write the draft of your summary and response. You argue that readers should expect clearer organization and fewer unsupported assertions about the gender-based differences between men and women.

AFTER DISCUSSING STEREOTYPED AND SEXIST IMAGES IN ADVERTISING, YOU LEAF THROUGH A COPY OF A POPULAR MAGAZINE. A two-page advertisement for Fila jeans catches your attention. The first page shows a man in jeans and a jeans jacket in the foreground with football players pictured in the background. The caption at the bottom of the page says, "SOME LIKE THEIR BLUES HARD." On the facing page is a woman curled up in a chair and wearing her blue jeans. Her background photograph shows a woman clad in a bikini. The caption says, "SOME LIKE THEIR BLUES SOFT." For your essay, you describe the features of the ad carefully and then offer your own analysis of the sexist features of the images and the language. The language and the imagery of the Fila jeans ad, you argue, stereotype and alienate the sexes by conveying the idea that men and women are not parallel in nature but are fundamentally separate and different.

AT FIRST GLANCE, A CHAPTER ON READING IN A TEXTBOOK ON WRITING MAY CATCH YOU BY SURPRISE. This chapter, however, is not about learning your ABC's or about reading *The Cat in the Hat.* It is about learning to read texts actively and critically. It is about learning how to summarize and respond to what you read. It is about using reading—along with observing and remembering—as a source for your writing.

At the beginning of this chapter, we need define two key terms: "texts" and "reading." Normally, when you think about a "text," you may think of a textbook. A "text," however, can be any graphic matter—a textbook, an essay, a poem, a story, a newspaper editorial, a graph, a design, or an advertisement. Some people expand the definition of "texts" to include anything or phenomenon in the world. In this widest sense, the layout of a restaurant, the behavior of children on a playground, or clouds in the sky could be "texts" that can be read.

Similarly, the term "reading" has both narrow and broad senses. In a narrow sense, reading is just understanding words on a page. But reading has a variety of wider meanings as well. Reading can mean analyzing, as when an architect "reads" blueprints and knows how to construct a roof. Reading can mean interpreting, as when a sailor "reads" the sky and knows that the day will bring winds and rough weather. Reading can mean making guesses about purpose or intention, as when a woman "reads" her boss's mind or a man "reads" between the lines of a friend's letter. All of these "readings" require close, repeated observation of the text and an ability to engage, respond to, analyze, and interpret the text.

In this chapter, you will practice a fairly specific kind of textual reading. Most of the texts will be essays on academic topics and your reading will be active, critical, and responsive. Implied in active, critical reading is writing. Reading and writing work together to make reading more active and writing more effective. Reading and writing are so inseparable that we sometimes use the phrase "reading/writing" to discuss any reading activity. In addition, there is an essential third dimension to critical reading: discussion. This third dimension can take a variety of forms—sharing ideas in small groups, engaging in a class conversation, or taking sides in a debate. Reading, writing, and discussing are all "reading" activities. We may be able to read the words on a page and write out our reactions, but we must also engage other readers' reactions and points of view in order to fully grasp the possible meanings of a text.

This chapter will show you how to use reading/writing/discussing strategies for three important tasks. First, you will learn how to write

BACKGROUND ON READING

This chapter gives students practice in a third strategy for rhetorical invention: reading. It focuses primarily on summarizing and responding to a text, but it also develops the reading/writing/dicussing skills that will be necessary to read and write the expository and argumentative essays in Chapters 6–12.

The *Video Guide* can help your students "read" television more critically, applying many of the same principles of analysis, interpretation, and evaluation of television texts as they apply to written texts.

Reading is not a passive process by which we soak up words and information from the page, but an active process by which we predict, sample, and confirm or correct our hypotheses about the written text.
—CONSTANCE WEAVER, AUTHOR OF READING PROCESS AND PRACTICE

short critiques or summary/response essays that are frequent college writing assignments. Second, you will practice reading your peers' drafts and essays actively and critically. Third, you will use critical reading to find information and generate ideas for expository or argumentative essays. Just as observing gives you descriptive strategies and remembering helps you to practice drawing on your personal experience, reading will help you critically analyze ideas, facts, statistics, and arguments—a skill that you will need for many college writing assignments.

■ **FREEWRITING: INVENTORY OF READING/WRITING STRATEGIES** Locate the textbook and class notes from a liberal arts course that you are currently taking. First, examine your textbook. What reading/writing strategies do you use as you study the text? Highlighting key passages? Underlining sentences? Writing notes and questions in the margins? Rereading key sections? Answering study questions? Writing out questions to ask in class? Now look at your class notes. Do you write down key ideas? Do you ask questions? Do you reread or review your notes after class? Do you reread your notes in a study group? List the reading/writing strategies that you use.

Reading . . . is a vital component of rhetorical invention, for it is an important way of participating in the conversation that gives us all of our meanings.
—DOUG BRENT, AUTHOR OF READING AS RHETORICAL INVENTION

TECHNIQUES FOR WRITING ABOUT READING

Writing about reading involves active and responsive reading as well as summarizing and responding to texts. Remember that reading, writing, and discussing are all interrelated and interactive strategies. Writing assists reading, discussing, and rereading. Reading and rereading helps you discuss and write. Conversations (written and oral) among readers and writers are integral to reading/writing. Focus on the techniques below as you write your summary/response or critique.

- **Using active and responsive reading/writing/discussing strategies.** Preview the author's background and the writing context. Prewrite about your own experiences with the subject. Read initially for information and enjoyment. As you reread, make annotations, write questions, or do a double-entry log. Discuss the text with other readers.
- **Summarizing the main ideas or features of the text**. A summary should *accurately and objectively* represent the key ideas. Summaries cite the author and title, accurately represent the main ideas, quote directly key phrases or sentences, and describe main features of the text.

- **Responding to or critiquing the ideas in the text.** Response should focus on your ideas and reactions—as distinguished from ideas set forth by the author/text. Types of responses include *analysis* of the argument, organization, or evidence in the text; *agreement or disagreement* with the author/text; or *interpretation* of the text.
- **Supporting the response with evidence.** As supporting evidence for the response, writers should analyze key features of the text, cite evidence from other relevant texts, and/or use examples from personal experience.
- **Combining summary and response into a coherent essay.** Usually, the summary appears first, followed by the reader's response, but be sure to *integrate* the two parts. Focus early on a main idea for your response. Use transitions between the summary and the response.

As you work on these techniques, don't simply read the text, discuss it in class, and then write out your critique. Instead, write notes as you read. Reread the text after class discussion. Reread and discuss the text after you have written your draft. Use the interactive powers of reading/writing/discussing to help you throughout your writing process.

Ask your students if they follow this three-step process when watching television shows. What prior experience, predictions, and testing of assumptions are they aware of during news broadcasts like those included in the *Video Library*?

How Readers Read

One of the purposes of this chapter is to show you how readers read. If you know how readers read and how they construct meaning from a text, you will become a more active reader and a more effective writer.

Reading, some theorists believe, involves a three-step process. First, readers bring their *prior experience* (about the subject, about language, and about culture) to their reading. Second, based on their prior experience, readers make *guesses* about how each passage relates to their prior experience and *predictions* about where the text is headed. Finally, as readers continue to read or reread, they *make meaning* or *comprehend* the text by testing (confirming or rejecting) the guesses and predictions that they have made. If readers have limited experiences with the subject or the language, making accurate predictions can be difficult. If readers have a good deal of prior experience, they are more likely to make accurate predictions. An oversimplified equation for this reading process is as follows.

Prior Experience +	Predictions	=	Comprehension
About the subject	Guesses about how the text relates to prior experience; predictions about the text's direction		Making meaning
About language			Understanding the text
About culture			

Reading depends upon prediction. . . . What I see is related to what I am looking for, not to all possible interpretations. . . . An important difference between a skilled driver and a learner is that the skilled driver is able to project the car into the future while the learner's mind is more closely anchored to where the car is now—when it is usually too late to avoid accidents.

—Frank Smith, author of Understanding Reading

As he engages with the text, the reader... entertains expectations as to what will follow, and uses these as guidelines for selecting out from alternative responses. As the text presents new elements, he may find it necessary to revise earlier syntheses or to develop new structuring principles.
—LOUISE ROSENBLATT, AUTHOR OF THE READER, THE TEXT, THE POEM

If this theory is true, it has three important lessons for any reader/writer:

First, prior knowledge about a text and its subject is extremely important. As a reader, you should activate your prior knowledge *before* reading the text. Doing a prereading journal exercise and discussing the subject with others are excellent strategies to activate and access what you already know.

Second, making guesses and predictions enables readers to make meaning. Making wrong guesses is just as important as making right guesses. Don't worry about making wrong guesses—they are a crucial part of the active reading process.

Third, learning to read actively will make you a better writer. Good writers know the problems that readers have making meaning. Good writers activate their reader's prior knowledge by using examples from their own experience. Good writers preview their main ideas so that their readers can make better guesses. Good writers use transitions or signals to help readers make meaning.

Summarizing and Responding to an Essay

Below is an essay by Barbara Ehrenreich, "Teach Diversity—with a Smile." First, write for five minutes on the suggested Prereading Journal Entry that precedes the essay. The purpose of the journal entry is to allow you to collect your thoughts about the subject *before* you read Ehrenreich's essay. You will be a much more responsive reader if you reflect on your experiences and articulate your opinions before you are influenced by the author and her text. If possible, discuss your experiences and opinions with your classmates after you write your entry but before you read the essay. Next, read the introductory note about Barbara Ehrenreich to understand her background and the context for the essay. Finally, practice active reading techniques as you read. Read first for information and enjoyment. Then, reread with a pen in your hand. Either write your comments and questions directly in the text or do a double-entry log, summarizing the main ideas on one side of a piece of paper and writing your questions and reactions on the other.

■ **Prereading Journal Entry** Describe the ethnic groups of people who live in your neighborhood or who attended your previous school. List all the groups you can recall. Then choose one of the following terms and briefly explain what it means: *Diversity*, *multiculturalism*, or *political correctness*. Finally, describe one personal experience that taught you something about diversity or political correctness. What was the experience and how did you react?

TEACH DIVERSITY—WITH A SMILE

BARBARA EHRENREICH

Barbara Ehrenreich was born in Butte, Montana, in 1941 and attended Reed College. She has been a health policy advisor and a professor of health sciences, but since 1974, she has spent most of her time writing books and articles about socialist and feminist issues. She has received a Ford Foundation award and a Guggenheim fellowship for her writings, which include The Hearts of Men: American Dreams and the Flight From Commitment *(1983),* Fear of Falling: The Inner Life of the Middle Class *(1989), and* The Worst Years of Our Lives: Irreverent Notes from a Decade of Greed *(1990). Her articles and essays have appeared in* Esquire, Mother Jones, Ms., New Republic, The New York Times Magazine, *and* Time. *The following essay on cultural diversity appeared April 8, 1991, in* Time *magazine.*

Something had to replace the threat of communism, and at last a workable substitute is at hand. "Multiculturalism," as the new menace is known, has been denounced in the media recently as the new McCarthyism, the new fundamentalism, even the new totalitarianism—take your choice. According to its critics, who include a flock of tenured conservative scholars, multiculturalism aims to toss out what it sees as the Eurocentric bias in education and replace Plato with Ntozake Shange and traditional math with the Yoruba number system. And that's just the beginning. The Jacobins of the multiculturalist movement, who are described derisively as P.C., or politically correct, are said to have launched a campus reign of terror against those who slip and innocently say "freshman" instead of "freshperson," "Indian" instead of "Native American" or, may the Goddess forgive them, "disabled" instead of "differently abled." **(1)**

So you can see what is at stake here: freedom of speech, freedom of thought, Western civilization and a great many professorial egos. But before we get carried away by the mounting backlash against multiculturalism, we ought to reflect for a moment on the system that the P.C. people aim to replace. I know all about it; in fact it's just about all I *do* know, since I—along with so many educated white people of my generation—was a victim of monoculturalism. **(2)**

American history, as it was taught to us, began with Columbus's "discovery" of an apparently unnamed, unpeopled America, and moved on to

TEACHING TIP

One effective way to use the "Prereading Journal Entry" is to have students write for 4–5 minutes in class just *before* you assign the Ehrenreich essay. After students write, have them share their responses. The point of this brief (10 minute) discussion is not to definitively define these terms but to elicit and record the *variety of prior experiences and attitudes* that your students are bringing to the text. Those experiences will prove to be important when students discuss their responses in the next day's class.

Watch the *Nightline* video on "Political Correctness" for another view of how multiculturalism has been "denounced in the media." See the video on "Teens Confront Prejudices" for one solution to the problem.

the Pilgrims serving pumpkin pie to a handful of grateful red-skinned folks. College expanded our horizons with courses called Humanities or sometimes Civ, which introduced us to a line of thought that started with Homer, worked its way through Rabelais and reached a poignant climax in the pensées of Matthew Arnold. Graduate students wrote dissertations on what long-dead men had thought of Chaucer's verse or Shakespeare's dramas; foreign languages meant French or German. If there had been high technology in ancient China, kingdoms in black Africa or women anywhere, at any time, doing anything worth noticing, we did not know it, nor did anyone think to tell us. **(3)**

Our families and neighborhoods reinforced the dogma of monoculturalism. In our heads, most of us '50s teenagers carried around a social map that was about as useful as the chart that guided Columbus to the "Indies." There were "Negroes," "whites" and "Orientals," the latter meaning Chinese and "Japs." Of religions, only three were known—Protestant, Catholic and Jewish—and not much was known about the last two types. The only remaining human categories were husbands and wives, and that was all the diversity the monocultural world could handle. Gays, lesbians, Buddhists, Muslims, Malaysians, Mormons, etc. were simply off the map. **(4)**

So I applaud—with one hand, anyway—the multiculturalist goal of preparing us all for a wider world. The other hand is tapping its fingers impatiently, because the critics are right about one thing: when advocates of multiculturalism adopt the haughty stance of political correctness, they quickly descend to silliness or worse. It's obnoxious, for example, to rely on university administrations to enforce P.C. standards of verbal inoffensiveness. Racist, sexist and homophobic thoughts cannot, alas, be abolished by fiat but only by the time-honored methods of persuasion, education and exposure to the other guy's—or, excuse me, woman's—point of view. **(5)**

And it's silly to mistake verbal purification for genuine social reform. Even after all women are "Ms." and all people are "he or she," women will still earn only 65¢ for every dollar earned by men. Minorities by any other name, such as "people of color," will still bear a hugely disproportionate burden of poverty and discrimination. Disabilities are not just "different abilities" when there are not enough ramps for wheelchairs, signers for the deaf or special classes for the "specially" endowed. With all due respect for the new politesse, actions still speak louder than fashionable phrases. **(6)**

But the worst thing about the P.C. people is that they are such poor advocates for the multicultural cause. No one was ever won over to a broader, more inclusive view of life by being bullied or relentlessly "corrected." Tell a 19-year-old white male that he can't say "girl" when he means "teen-age woman," and he will most likely snicker. This may be the reason why, despite the conservative alarms, P.C.-ness remains a relatively tiny trend. Most campuses have more serious and ancient problems: faculties still top-heavy with white males of the monocultural persuasion; fraternities that harass minorities and women; date rape; alcohol abuse; and tuition that excludes all but the upper fringe of the middle class. **(7)**

So both sides would be well advised to lighten up. The conservatives ought to realize that criticisms of the great books approach to learning do not amount to totalitarianism. And the advocates of multiculturalism need to regain the sense of humor that enabled their predecessors in the struggle to coin the term P.C. years ago—not in arrogance but in self-mockery. **(8)**

Beyond that, both sides should realize that the beneficiaries of multiculturalism are not only the "oppressed peoples" on the standard P.C. list (minorities, gays, etc.). The "unenlightened"—the victims of monoculturalism—are oppressed too, or at least deprived. Our educations, whether at Yale or at State U, were narrow and parochial and left us ill-equipped to navigate a society that truly is multicultural and is becoming more so every day. The culture that we studied was, in fact, *one* culture and, from a world perspective, all too limited and ingrown. Diversity is challenging, but those of us who have seen the alternative know it is also richer, livelier and ultimately more fun. **(9)**

SUMMARIZING

The purpose of a summary is to give a reader a condensed and objective account of the main ideas and features of a text. Usually, a summary has between one and three paragraphs or 100–300 words, depending on the length and complexity of the original essay and the intended audience and purpose. Typically, a summary will do the following:

- **Cite the author and title of the text.** In some cases, the place of publication or the context for the essay may also be included.
- **Indicate the main ideas of the text.** Accurately representing the main ideas (while omitting the less important details) is the major goal of a summary.
- **Use direct quotation of key words, phrases, or sentences.** *Quote* the text directly for a few key ideas; *paraphrase* the other important ideas (that is, express the ideas in your own words).

Inferences about the writer's intentions appear to be an essential building block—one that readers actively use to construct a meaningful text.
—LINDA FLOWER, AUTHOR OF "THE CONSTRUCTION OF PURPOSE"

- **Include author tags** ("according to Ehrenreich" or "as Ehrenreich says") to remind the reader that you are summarizing the author and the text, not giving your own ideas.
- **Avoid summarizing specific examples or data** unless they help illustrate the thesis or main idea of the text.
- **Report the main ideas as objectively as possible**. Represent the author and text as accurately and faithfully as possible. Do *not* include your reactions; save them for your response.

Summary of "Teach Diversity—with a Smile"

Below is a summary of Ehrenreich's essay. Do *not* read this summary, however, until you have tried to write your own. After you have made notes and written a draft for your own summary, you will more clearly understand the key features of a summary. Note: There are many ways to write a good summary. If your summary conveys the main ideas and has the features described above, it may be just as good as the following example. (Key features of a summary are annotated in the margin.)

Title and author
Main idea
Paraphrase
Context for essay
Author tag
Direct quotations
Main idea
Paraphrase
Author tag
Main idea
Paraphrase

In "Teach Diversity—with a Smile," journalist Barbara Ehrenreich explains the current conflict between people who would like to [replace our Eurocentric bias in education with a multicultural approach and those critics and conservative scholars who are leading the backlash against multiculturalism and "political correctness."] Writing for [readers of *Time* magazine,] Ehrenreich uses her own experience growing up in the 1950s to explain that her narrow education left her a "victim of monoculturalism," ill-equipped to cope with America's growing cultural diversity. [Ehrenreich applauds] multiculturalism's goal of preparing people for a culturally diverse world, but she is impatient at the "haughty stance" of the P.C. people because they mistake "verbal purification for genuine social reform" and they arrogantly bully people and "correct" their language. Since actions speak louder than words, Ehrenreich [says, the multiculturalists should focus more on genuine social reform—paying equal salaries for men and women, creating access for people with disabilities, and reducing date rape and alcohol abuse.] The solution to the problem, [according to Ehrenreich,] is for both sides to "lighten up." The conservatives should recognize that [criticizing the great books of Western civilization is not totalitarian, and the multiculturalists should be less arrogant and regain their sense of humor.]

Responding

A response requires your reaction and interpretation. Your own perspective—your experiences, beliefs, and attitudes—will guide your particular response. Your response may be totally different from another reader's response, but that does not necessarily make yours better or worse. Good responses say what you think, but then they *show why* you think so. They show the relationships between your opinions and the text, between the text and your experience, and between this text and other texts.

Depending on its purpose and intended audience, a response to a text can take several directions. Responses may focus on one or more of the following strategies. Consider your purpose and audience or check your assignment to see which type(s) you should emphasize.

Reading the world always precedes reading the word, and reading the word implies continually reading the world.

—PAULO FREIRE, AUTHOR OF <u>LITERACY: READING THE WORD AND THE WORLD</u>

- **Analyzing the effectiveness of the text.** In this case, the response analyzes key features such as the clarity of the main idea, the organization of the argument, the quality of the supporting evidence, and/or the effectiveness of the author's style, tone, and voice.
- **Agreeing and/or disagreeing with the ideas in the text.** Often, responders react to the ideas or the argument of the essay. In this case, the responders show why they agree and/or disagree with what the author/text says.
- **Interpreting and reflecting on the text.** The responder explains key passages or examines the underlying assumptions or the implications of the ideas. Often, the responder reflects on how his or her own experiences, attitudes, and observations relate to the text.

Analyzing, agreeing/disagreeing, and interpreting are all slightly different directions that a response may take. But regardless of the direction, responses must be supported by evidence, examples, facts, and details. A responder cannot simply offer an opinion or agree or disagree. Good responses draw on several kinds of supporting evidence:

TEACHING TIP

Written annotations of key features in summaries and responses help students see the formal features, but actually *writing* the annotations for a response integrates reading and writing more effectively. Bring sample summaries of and responses to Ehrenreich (drafts you have written or student samples) to class and have students practice doing annotations in small groups. On your master transparency or overhead copy, you can write out consensus annotations from the small groups.

- **Personal experience.** Responders may use *examples* from their personal experiences to show why they interpreted the text as they did, why they agreed or disagreed, or why they reacted to the ideas as they did.
- **Evidence from the text.** Responders should cite *specific phrases* or *sentences* from the text to support their explanation of a section, their analysis of the effectiveness of a passage, or their agreement or disagreement with a key point.
- **Evidence from other texts.** If appropriate, responders may bring in ideas and information from other relevant essays, articles, books, or graphic material.

Not all responses use all three kinds of supporting evidence, but all responses must have sufficient examples to support the responder's ideas, reactions, and opinions. Responders should not merely state their opinions. They must give evidence to *show* how and why they read the text as they did.

One final—and crucial—point about responses: A response should make a coherent, overall main point. It should not be just a laundry list of reactions, likes, and dislikes. Sometimes the main point is that the text is not convincing because it lacks evidence. Sometimes the overall point is that the text makes an original statement even though it is difficult to read. Perhaps the basic point is that the author/text stimulates the reader to reflect on his or her experience. Every response should focus on a coherent main idea.

Response to "Teach Diversity—with a Smile"

Below is one possible response to Ehrenreich's essay. There are, of course, many different but legitimate responses to any given essay. As you read Ehrenreich's essay, decide how your response would be similar to or different from this response. As you read, note the marginal annotations indicating the different types of responses and the different kinds of evidence this writer uses.

Analyzing effectiveness of text

What I like best about Barbara Ehrenreich's article is her effective use of personal experience to clarify the issues on both sides of the multiculturalism debate. However, her conclusion, that we should "lighten up" and accept diversity because it's "more fun," weakens her argument by ignoring the social inequalities at the heart of the debate. The issue in this debate, I believe, is not just enjoying diversity, which is easy to do, but changing cultural conditions, which is much more difficult.

Responder's main point

Ehrenreich effectively uses her own experiences—and her common sense—to let us see both the virtues and the excesses of multiculturalism. When she explains that her monocultural education gave her a social map that was "about as useful as the chart that guided Columbus to the 'Indies,'" she helps us understand how vital multicultural studies are in a society that is more like a glass mosaic than a melting pot. Interestingly, even her vocabulary reveals—perhaps unconsciously—her Western bias: "Jacobins," "pensees," "fiat," and "politesse" are all words that reveal her Eurocentric education. When Ehrenreich shifts to discussing the P. C. movement, her common-sense approach to the silliness of excessive social correctness ("the other guy's—or, excuse me, woman's—point of view") makes us as readers more willing to accept her compromise position.

Evidence from text

Evidence from text

Reflecting on the text

My own experience with multiculturalism certainly parallels Ehrenreich's impatience with the "haughty stance" of the P.C. people. Of course, we should avoid racist and sexist terms and use our increased sensitivity to language to reduce discrimination. But my own backlash began several years ago when a friend said I shouldn't use the word "girl." I said, "You mean, not ever? Not even for a ten-year-old female child?" She replied that the word had been so abused by people referring to a "woman" as a "girl" that the word "girl" now carried too many sexist connotations. Although I understand my friend's point, it seems that "girl" should still be a perfectly good word for a female child under the age of twelve. Which reminds me of a book I saw recently, *The Official Politically Correct Dictionary*. It is loaded with examples of political correctness out of control: Don't say "bald," say "hair disadvantaged." Don't use the

Personal experience

Evidence from other texts

word "pet," say "non-human companion." Don't call someone "old," say that they are "chronologically gifted." One humorous example even suggested that George Bush was "electorally slighted" when he was not re-elected.

Analyzing effectiveness of text

Ehrenreich does recommend keeping a sense of humor about the P. C. movement, but the conclusion to her essay weakens her argument. Instead of focusing on her earlier point that "it's silly to mistake verbal purification for genuine social reform," she advises both sides to lighten up and have fun with the diversity around us. Instead, I wanted her to conclude by reinforcing her point that "actions still speak louder than fashionable phrases." Changing the realities of illiteracy, poverty, alcohol abuse, and sexual harassment should be the focus of the multiculturalists. Of course, changing language is crucial to changing the world, but the language revolution has already happened—or at least begun. Ehrenreich's article would be more effective, I believe, if she concluded her essay with a call for both sides to help change cultural conditions rather than with a reference to the silly debate about what to call a teenage woman.

Responder's main point

Summarizing and Responding to an Advertisement

Summarizing and responding to graphic material, such as advertisements, is an excellent way to practice responding to texts. In this case, a summary must observe and describe the key features of the advertisement (layout, color, proportion, images, and copy). The response then "reads" the advertisement for the message, selling tactics, cultural stereotypes, or other implications. The focus of the response may be to analyze and explain the persuasive tactics, to interpret cultural values or stereotypes, to judge the effectiveness of the ad, and/or to reflect on assumptions and implications.

The following summary/response is to an advertisement for Fila jeans. Notice how the student writer, Karyn Lewis, carefully describes key features of the advertisement so her readers can clearly visualize it.

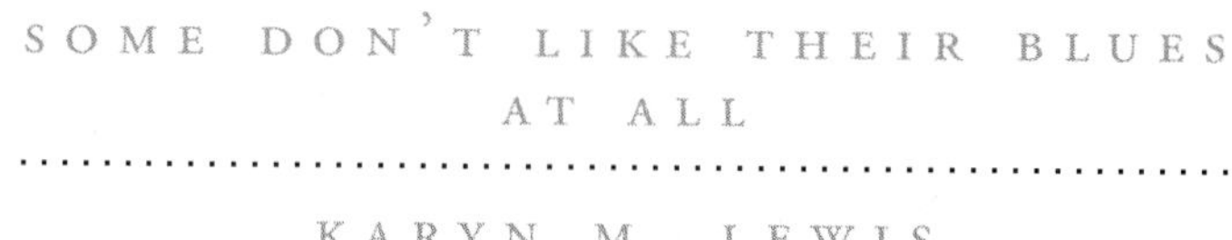

SOME DON'T LIKE THEIR BLUES AT ALL

KARYN M. LEWIS

He strides toward us in navy and white, his body muscled and heavyset, one arm holding his casually flung jeans jacket over his shoulder. A man in his prime, with just the right combination of macho and sartorial flair.

He is also black.

She is curled and giggling upon a chair, her hair loose and flowing around her shoulders, leaning forward innocently—the very picture of a blossoming, navy flower.

She is white.

They are each pictured on a magazine page of their own, situated opposite each other in a complementary two-page spread. They are stationed in front of a muted photograph which serves as a background for each one. They both merit their own captions: bold indigo letters presiding over them in the outer corners of each page.

His says: SOME LIKE THEIR BLUES HARD.

Hers says: SOME LIKE THEIR BLUES SOFT.

His background depicts a thrusting struggle between a quarterback and a leaping defender, a scene of arrested violence and high tension.

Her background is a lounging, bikini-clad goddess, who looks at the camera with intriguing, calm passion. She raises her hand to rest behind her head in a languid gesture as she tries to incite passion within the viewer.

At the bottom of the page blazes the proud emblem of the company who came up with this ad: FILA JEANS.

This advertisement blatantly uses stereotypes of men and women to sell its product. It caters to our need to fit into the roles that society has deemed for the individual sexes ever since patriarchal rule rose up and replaced the primitive worship of a mother goddess and the reverence of women. These stereotypes handed down to us throughout the centuries spell out to us that men are violence and power incarnate, and that the manly attitude brooks no room for weakness or softness of nature. And we find our role model of women in the compliant and eager female who obeys her man in all things, who must not say no to a male, and is not very bright—someone who flutters her eyelashes, giggles a lot, and uses tears to get her way.

This ad tells us, by offering the image of a hard, masculine male, who is deified in violence, that he is the role model men should aspire to, and that for women, their ideal is weak but sexual, innocent and at the same time, old enough to have sex. In viewing this ad, we see our aspirations clothed in FILA JEANS, and to be like them, we must buy the clothes pictured here. This ad also suggests that a man can become hard and powerful (or at least look it) dressed in these jeans; a woman can become sexually intense and desirable dressed in FILA's clothing

The words of the captions tantalize with their sexual innuendo. The phrase, "SOME LIKE THEIR BLUES HARD," hints at male sexual prowess. Most men and women in this country are obsessed with the male need to prove their virility, and FILA plays on this obsession. Females too have their own stereotype of what constitutes their sexuality.

"SOME LIKE THEIR BLUES SOFT" exemplifies this ideal: A woman should be soft and yielding. Her soft, sensuous body parts which so excite her partners have been transformed into her personal qualities. By using the term "soft," FILA immediately links the girl with her sexuality and sexual organs.

We are shown by the models' postures that men and women are (according to FILA) fundamentally different and total antonyms of one another. He is standing and walking with purpose; she sits, laughing trivially at the camera. Even the background hints at separation of the sexes.

The football players on the man's page are arranged in a diagonal line which starts at the upper left-hand corner and runs to the opposite corner, which is the center of the ad. On her page, the enchanting nymph in the bathing suit runs on a diagonal, beginning where his ends, and traveling up to the upper right-hand corner of her page. These two photos in effect create a "V" which both links the two models, and also suggests movement away from one another. Another good example of their autonomy from one another is their skin color. He is a black man, she's white. Black is the opposite color of white on an artist's color wheel and palette, and symbolizes dynamically opposed forces: good and evil, night and day, man and woman. This ad hits us with the idea that men and women are not parallel in nature to one another, but are fundamentally different in all things. It alienates the sexes from each other. Opposites may attract, but there is no room for understanding a nature completely alien to your own.

So in viewing this ad, and reading its captions, the consumer is left with the view that a woman must be "soft" and sensual, a male's sexual dream, and somehow still retain her innocence after having sex. She must be weak, the opposite of the violence which contrasts with her on the opposite page. The men looking at this ad read the message that they are supposed to be well-dressed, powerful, and possess a strength that borders on violent. As we are told by the caption, men should be "hard." Furthermore, men and women are opposite creatures, as different as two sides of a coin.

This ad is supposed to cause us to want to meet these requirements, but it fills me with a deep-rooted disgust that we still perpetrate the myth that men are unyielding creatures of iron and women are silly bits of fluff. The ad generates no good role models to aspire to where men and women are equal beings, and both can show compassion and still be strong. FILA may like their blues hard and soft, but I don't like their blues at all.

■ **Warming Up: Journal Exercises** The following topics will help you practice your reading and responding. Read all of the following exercises and then choose two or three for practice.

1. Because previewing material is an important part of active reading, most recent psychology or social science textbooks use previewing or prereading strategies at the beginning of each new chapter. Find one chapter in a textbook that uses these previewing techniques. How does the author preview the material? Does it help you understand the material in the chapter?

2. Practice your summarizing skills on the following two paragraphs from Peter Singer's book *Animal Liberation.* Begin by referring to the author and title. As you write your summary, remind your reader occasionally that these are the author's ideas by using "author tags," such as "according to Singer" or "as Singer says."

> If a being suffers there can be no moral justification for refusing to take that suffering into consideration. No matter what the nature of the being, the principle of equality requires that its suffering be counted equally with the like suffering—insofar as rough comparisons can be made—of any other being. If a being is not capable of suffering, or of experiencing enjoyment or happiness, there is nothing to be taken into account. . . . To mark this boundary by some other characteristic like intelligence or rationality would be to mark it in an arbitrary manner. Why not choose some other characteristic, like skin color?
>
> Racists violate the principle of equality by giving greater weight to the interests of members of their own race when there is a clash between their interests and the interests of those of another race. Sexists violate the principle of equality by favoring the interests of their own sex. Similarly, speciesists allow the interests of their own species to override the greater interests of members of other species. The pattern is identical in each case.

3. Reading the following paragraph illustrates how our prior experience can combine with our predictions to make meaning. The following passage describes a common procedure in our lives. Read the passage. Can you identify the procedure?

> The procedure is actually quite simple. First you arrange things into different groups. Of course, one pile may be sufficient depending on how much there is to do. If you have to go somewhere else due to lack of facilities, that is the next step; otherwise you are pretty well set. It is important not to overdo things. That is, it is better to do too few things at once than too many. In the short run this may not seem important but complications can easily arise. A mistake can be expensive as well. At first, the whole procedure will seem complicated. Soon, however, it will become just another facet of life. It is difficult to foresee any end

TEACHING TIP

Use journal exercise 2 as a prereading activity for Quammen's essay. Assign that journal entry and then discuss it in class on the day before you have students read it. Reviewing with students the basic issues of animal rights will make them more active readers and responders.

Also, Question 1, under "Questions for Writing and Discussion" that follow the Quammen essay, makes an excellent prereading activity.

to the necessity for this task in the immediate future, but then one can never tell. After the procedure is completed, one arranges the materials into different groups again. Then they can be put into their appropriate places. Eventually, they will be used once more and the whole cycle will then have to be repeated. However, that is part of life.

As you read, record your guesses. What words helped to orient you? Where did you make wrong guesses? Discuss your reactions in class.

4. The following reading exercise, reprinted by Diane L. Schallert in "Improving Memory for Prose," also illustrates how our prior experiences and predictions play a major role in understanding a text. In the following passage, the manager of a glassware factory describes a situation encountered during the summer. Read the passage quickly, spending no more than one minute. Then, without rereading any of the passage, write down what you remember about the passage.

> In the last days of August, we were all suffering from the unbearable heat. In a few short weeks, our daily job had turned from a game into hard labor. "All we need now," said the manager in one of his discouraged moods, "is a strike." I listened to him silently but I could not help him. I hit a fly. "I suppose things could get even worse," he continued. "Our most valuable pitchers may crack in this heat. If only we had more fans, we would all feel better, I'm sure. I wish our best man could come home. That certainly would improve everyone's morale, especially mine. Oh, well. I know a walk would cheer me up a little."

After you complete the summary, reread the passage. This time, assume that the passage is written by a manager of a baseball team. Describe how your understanding of the passage is changed from your first reading.

5. Study the print by Maurits Escher reproduced on the next page. How many different ways of perceiving this picture can you see? Describe each perspective. How is "reading" this picture similar to reading a printed text? How is it different?

6. Reading is a gradual process of making guesses and then confirming or rejecting those guesses. To dramatize how the process works, find an essay or a short story that you have not read before. (Either Edward Abbey's essay, "The Damnation of a Canyon," in Chapter 10 or Kate Chopin's short story, "The Story of an Hour," in Chapter 12 work well.) Read two paragraphs and then stop. Write down what has happened and what you predict

"Day and Night" (1938) by M.C. Escher.
© 1994 M.C. Escher. Cordon Art—Baarn, Holland

will happen next. Then read one more page and stop. Summarize in a sentence what has happened and predict what is coming. A third time, read one more page. Now stop and write. Then read the essay or the story through to the end. How accurately were you able to make predictions? Where did your guesses turn out to be wrong? If you read both the essay and the story, which was more predictable? Why?

7. One way to check whether writers are helping their readers make meaning is to scramble the original order of sentences in a paragraph and see if readers can reconstruct the original sequence. Below is a scrambled version of a paragraph from a review of a Stephen King novel. See if you can reconstruct the original order of the paragraph.

A. There is one survivor, however, who walks past the failed security apparatus, races home to his wife and child, bundles them into the car and speeds toward the Texas border.

B. A virus breaks through the isolation barrier and rapidly causes the death of nearly everyone working in the plant.

C. The general outline of the plot is fairly simple.

D. By the time they reach a gas station in Texas, he is very ill and his wife and daughter have died a horrible death that leaves their bodies bloated, blackened and stinking.

E. An accident occurs in an Army lab doing research on biological warfare.

TEACHING TIP

Prediction exercises, such as the one described in journal exercise 6, are an excellent way to dramatize for students how readers make meaning. (See Lynn Troyka's description of "prediction sessions" in her essay, "Closeness to Text: A Delineation of Reading Processes as They Affect Composing" in *Only Connect*, ed. T. Newkirk.) Prediction sessions work best *in class*, where students share their responses and predictions aloud after they read each paragraph, or each page.

What words or phrases in each of the above sentences helped you reconstruct the original order? (See paragraph 4 of Robert Keily's essay in Chapter 8 for the original order.)

READING: PROFESSIONAL WRITING

ANIMAL RIGHTS AND BEYOND

DAVID QUAMMEN

An award-winning writer of essays and fiction, David Quammen is best known for his regular column on nature in Outside *magazine. Essays originally published in his column appear in* Natural Acts: A Sidelong View of Science and Nature *(1985) and* The Flight of the Iguana: A Sidelong View of Science and Nature *(1988). Although Quammen often writes on the weird or offbeat curiosities of biology, such as the mating habits of the aphid (see "Is Sex Necessary?" in Chapter 7), he can tackle subjects requiring philosophical depth as well as biological learning. "Animal Rights and Beyond," which appears in* Natural Acts, *shows Quammen's talent for understanding the difficult moral problems behind the animal rights movement and responding in a sensible but humorous manner. Do animals have moral rights? Should we cease all scientific experiments with animals? Should we all become vegetarians? Here is Quammen's summary of two books by animal rights philosophers—Peter Singer and Tom Regan—and his own responses to the difficult questions they raise.*

WRITE TO LEARN

Be sure to have students practice their active reading strategies as they read this essay. You might assign students (singly or in small groups) to make written annotations in the margins of a photocopy of the text. Some students could do a double-entry reading log. Other students might do a small-group prediction exercise, summarizing each paragraph and making collaborative predictions before they read the next paragraph. After students discuss their various readings, ask them which reading strategies they personally find most effective.

Do non-human animals have rights? Should we humans feel morally bound to exercise consideration for the lives and well-being of individual members of other animal species? If so, how much consideration, and by what logic? Is it permissible to torture and kill? Is it permissible to kill cleanly, without prolonged pain? To abuse or exploit without killing? For a moment, don't think about whales or wolves or the California condor; don't think about the cat or the golden retriever with whom you share your house. Think about chickens. Think about laboratory monkeys and then think about lab rats and then also think about lab frogs. Think about scallops. Think about mosquitoes. **(1)**

It's a Gordian question, by my lights, but one not very well suited to Alexandrian answers. Some people would disagree, judging the matter simply enough settled, one way or the other. *Of course they have rights. Of course they don't.* I say beware any such snappy, steel-trap thinking. Some folk would even—this late in the evolution of human sensibility—call it a frivolous question, a time-filling diversion for emotional hemophiliacs and cranks. *Women's rights, gay rights, now for Christ sake they want ANIMAL rights.* Notwithstanding the ridicule, the strong biases toward each side, it is certainly a serious philosophical issue, important and tricky, with almost endless implications for the way we humans live and should live on this planet. (2)

Philosophers of earlier ages, if they touched the subject at all, were likely to be dismissive. Thomas Aquinas announced emphatically that animals "are intended for man's use in the natural order. Hence it is not wrong for man to make use of them, either by killing or in any other way whatever." Descartes held that animals are merely machines. As late as 1901, a moral logician named Joseph Rickaby (who happened to be a Jesuit, but don't necessarily hold that against him) declared: "Brute beasts, not having understanding and therefore not being persons, cannot have any rights. The conclusion is clear." Maybe not quite so clear. Recently, just during the past decade, professional academic philosophers have at last begun to address the matter more openmindedly. **(3)**

Two thinkers in particular have been influential: an Australian named Peter Singer, an American named Tom Regan. In 1975 Singer published a book titled *Animal Liberation*, which stirred up the debate among his colleagues and is still treated as a landmark. Eight years later Tom Regan published *The Case for Animal Rights*, a more thorough and ponderous opus that stands now as a sort of companion piece to the Singer book. In between there came a number of other discussions of animal rights—including a collection of essays edited jointly by Singer and Regan. Despite the one-time collaboration, Peter Singer and Tom Regan represent two distinct schools of thought: They reach similar conclusions about the obligations of humans to other animals, but the moral logic is very different, and possibly also the implications. Both men have produced some formidable work and both, to my simple mind, show some shocking limitations of vision. **(4)**

I've spent the past week amid these books, Singer's and Regan's and the rest. It has been an edifying experience, and now I'm more puzzled than ever. I keep thinking about monkeys and frogs and mosquitoes and—sorry, but I'm quite serious—carrots. **(5)**

* * *

Peter Singer's view is grounded upon the work of Jeremy Bentham, that eighteenth-century British philosopher generally known as the founder of utilitarianism. "The greatest good for the greatest number" is a familiar cartoon version of what, according to Bentham, should be achieved by the ethical ordering of society and behavior. A more precise summary is offered by Singer: "In other words, the interests of every being affected by an action are to be taken into account and given the same weight as the like interests of any other being." If this much is granted, the crucial next point is deciding what things constitute *interests* and who or what qualifies as a *being*. Evidently Bentham did not have just humans in mind. Back in 1789, optimistically and perhaps presciently, he wrote: "The day *may* come when the rest of the animal creation may acquire those rights which never could have been withholden from them but by the hand of tyranny." Most philosophers of his day were inclined (as most in our day are still inclined) to extend moral coverage only to humans, because only humans (supposedly) are rational and communicative. Jeremy Bentham took exception: "The question is not, 'Can they *reason*?' nor, 'Can they *talk*?' but, 'Can they *suffer*?'" On this crucial point, Peter Singer follows Bentham. **(6)**

The capacity to suffer, says Singer, is what separates a being with legitimate interests from an entity without interests. A stone has no interests that must be respected, because it cannot suffer. A mouse can suffer; therefore it has interests and those interests must be weighed in the moral balance. Fine, that much seems simple enough. Certain people of sophistic or Skinnerian bent would argue that there is no proof a mouse can in fact suffer, that it's merely an anthropomorphic assumption; but since each of us has no proof that *anyone* else actually suffers besides ourselves, we are willing, most of us, to grant the assumption. More problematic is that very large gray area between stones and mice. **(7)**

Peter Singer declares: "If a being suffers, there can be no moral justification for disregarding that suffering, or for refusing to count it equally with the like suffering of any other being. But the converse of this is also true. If a being is not capable of suffering, or of enjoyment, there is nothing to take into account." Where is the boundary? Where falls the line between creatures who suffer and those that are incapable? Singer's cold philosophic eye travels across the pageant of living species—chickens suffer, mice suffer, fish suffer, um, lobsters most likely suffer, *look alive, you other creatures!*—and his damning stare lands on the oyster. **(8)**

No I'm not making this up. The oyster, by Singer's best guess, doesn't suffer. Its nervous system lacks the requisite complexity. Therefore, while lobsters and crawfish and shrimp possess inviolable moral status, the oyster has none. It is a difficult judgment, Singer admits, by no means an infallible one, but "somewhere between a shrimp and an oyster seems as good a place to draw the line as any, and better than most." **(9)**

Moral philosophy, no one denies, is an imperfect science. **(10)**

Tom Regan takes exception with Singer on two important points.

First, he disavows the utilitarian framework, with its logic that abuse or killing of animals by humans is wrong because it yields a net *overall* decrease in welfare, among all beings who qualify for moral status. No, argues Regan, that logic is false and pernicious. The abuse or killing is wrong in its *essence*—however the balance comes out on overall welfare—because it violates the rights of those individual animals. Individual rights, in other words, take precedence over the maximizing of the common good. Second, in Regan's opinion the capacity to suffer is not what marks the elect. Mere suffering is not sufficient. Instead he posits the concept of *inherent value*, a complex and magical quality possessed by some living creatures but not others. **(11)**

A large portion of Regan's book is devoted to arguing toward this concept. He is more uncompromisingly protective of certain creatures—those with rights—than Singer, but he is also more selective; the hull of his ark is sturdier, but the gangplank is narrower. According to Regan, individual beings possess inherent value (and therefore inviolable rights) if they "are able to perceive and remember; if they have beliefs, desires, and preferences; if they are able to act intentionally in pursuit of their desires or goals; if they are sentient and have an emotional life; if they have a sense of the future, including a sense of their own future; if they have a psychophysical identity over time; and if they have an individual experiential welfare that is logically independent of their utility for, and the interests of, others." So Tom Regan is not handing rights around profligately, to every cute little beast that crawls over his foot. In fact we all probably know a few humans who, at least on a bad night, might have trouble meeting those standards. But how would Regan himself apply them? Where does he see the line falling? Who qualifies for inherent value, and what doesn't? **(12)**

Like Singer, Regan has thought this point through. Based on his grasp of biology and ethology, he is willing to grant rights to "mentally normal mammals of a year or more." **(13)**

Also like Singer, he admits that the judgment is not infallible: "Because we are uncertain where the boundaries of consciousness lie, it is not unreasonable to advocate a policy that bespeaks moral caution." So chickens and frogs should be given the benefit of the doubt, as should all other animals that bear a certain degree of anatomical and physiological resemblance to us mentally normal mammals. **(14)**

But Regan does not specify just what degree. **(15)**

The books by Singer and Regan leave me with two very separate reactions. The first combines admiration and gratitude. These men are applying the methods of systematic philosophy to an important and much-neglected question. Furthermore, they don't content themselves with just understanding and describing a pattern of gross injustice; they also emphatically say, "*Let's stop it!*" They are fighting a good fight. Peter Singer's book in particular has focused attention on the outrageous practices that are routine in American factory farms, in "psychological" experimentation, in research on the toxicity of cosmetics. Do you know how chickens are dealt with on the large poultry operations? How veal is produced? How the udders of dairy cows are kept flowing? Do you know the sorts of ingenious but pointless torment that thousands of monkeys and millions of rats endure, each year, to fill the time and the dissertations of uninspired graduate students? If you don't, by all means read Singer's *Animal Liberation.* **(16)**

The second reaction is negative. Peter Singer and Tom Regan, it seems to me, share a breathtaking smugness and myopia not too dissimilar to the brand they so forcefully condemn. Theirs is a righteous and vigorous smugness, not a passive and unreflective one. But still. **(17)**

Singer inveighs against a sin he labels *speciesism*—discrimination against certain creatures based solely upon the species to which they belong. Regan uses a slightly less confused and less clumsy phrase, *human chauvinism*, to indicate roughly the same thing. Both of them arrive (supposedly by sheer logic) at the position that vegetarianism is morally obligatory: To kill and eat a "higher" animal represents absolute violation of one being's rights; to kill and eat a plant evidently violates nothing at all. Both Singer and Regan claim to disparage the notion—pervasive in Western philosophy since Protagoras—that "Man is the measure of all things." Both argue elaborately against anthropocentrism, while creating new moral frameworks that are also decidedly anthropocentric. Make no mistake: Man is still the measure, for Singer and Regan. The test for inherent value has changed only slightly. Instead of asking, "*Is the creature a human?*," they simply ask, "*How similar to human is similar enough?*" **(18)**

Peter Singer explains that shrimp deserve brotherly treatment but oysters, so different from us, are fair game for the gumbo. In Tom Regan's vocabulary, the redwood tree is an "inanimate natural object," sharing that category with clouds and rocks. But some simple minds would say: Life is life. **(19)**

VOCABULARY

In your journal, write the meaning of each of the following words:

- A *Gordian* question (2)
- *Alexandrian* answers (2)
- perhaps *presciently* (6)

- people of *sophistic* or *Skinnerian* bent (7)
- *anthropomorphic* assumption (7)
- *inviolable* moral status (9)
- biology and *ethology* (13)

Questions for Writing and Discussion

1. Which of the following non-human species should or should not have rights protected by humans? Where you would draw the line, and on what basis? Use the following species—or make up your own list.

whales	snakes	fish	trees
wolves	scorpions	squid	orchids
cats and dogs	spiders	lobsters	cabbage
chickens	mosquitos	clams	carrots
mice and rats	chiggers	oysters	lichen

2. A good summary should mention the author and title, use direct quotation for key ideas, include author tags, and describe the main ideas objectively and fairly. Examine Quammen's summary of either Singer's or Regan's texts. Is his summary effective?

3. Responses can focus on analyzing the effectiveness of the text, agreeing or disagreeing with the ideas in the text, or reflecting on the meaning of the text. Does Quammen use all three of these kinds of responses? Which one does he emphasize?

4. Quammen focuses on a difficult philosophical problem, but he makes the organization of his essay easy to follow. Below is the basic outline.

I. Introduction to the question of animal rights
II. Review of early philosophers' views on animal rights
III. Summary and review of the books and philosophies of Singer and Regan

A. Singer's philosophy
B. Regan's philosophy

IV. Quammen's responses to Singer and Regan

A. Positive reactions
B. Negative reactions

For the above outline, indicate by numbers which paragraphs belong with each section. Then underline or write down the transitions or key words or phrases near the beginning of each section that *signal* for the reader the focus for that section. Where are his signals clear? Where should he use a better transition or more clearly state the focus?

5. A writer's tone and sense of humor can make a passage appealing to readers. Find three sentences where Quammen's sense of humor is apparent. In each instance, did Quammen's humor make the passage more interesting for you? Explain.

6. Reread Quammen's essay and write out your own responses to his essay. Then read Paula Fisher's essay on Quammen later in this chapter. Discuss your responses to both articles with your classmates. Then write your own summary and response to the conversation created by your classmates about these authors.

MASTERS OF DESIRE: THE CULTURE OF AMERICAN ADVERTISING

JACK SOLOMON

In this selection from The Signs of Our Time, *Solomon does a semiotic reading of several advertisements for automobiles and whisky. The term "semiotics" comes from the Greek word for "sign," and was used by seventeenth-century philosopher John Locke to describe a science of signs. More recently, European linguists and philosophers have applied this science of signs to literature and popular culture objects in order to "read" messages of power and culture that are "hidden" in language, symbols, and ordinary objects. Solomon's "reading" of automobile advertisements goes beyond describing typical Madison Avenue strategies to showing how the character of America is revealed in pictures, paper, and body language.*

Amongst democratic nations, men easily attain a certain equality of condition; but they can never attain as much as they desire.

ALEXIS DE TOCQUEVILLE

On May 10, 1831, a young French aristocrat named Alexis de Tocqueville arrived in New York City at the start of what would become one of the most famous visits to America in our history. He had come to observe firsthand the institutions of the freest, most egalitarian society of the age, but what he found was a paradox. For behind America's mythic promise of equal opportunity, Tocqueville discovered a desire for *unequal* social rewards, a ferocious competition for privilege and distinction. . . . We Americans dream of rising above the crowd, of attaining a social summit beyond the reach of ordinary citizens. And therein lies the paradox. **(1)**

The American dream, in other words, has two faces: the one communally egalitarian and the other competitively elitist. This contradiction is no accident; it is fundamental to the structure of American society. Even as America's great myth of equality celebrates the virtues of mom, apple pie, and the girl or boy next door, it also lures us to achieve social distinction, to rise above the crowd and bask alone in the glory. This land is your land and this land is my land, Woody Guthrie's populist anthem tells us, but we keep trying to increase the "my" at the expense of the "your." Rather than fostering contentment, the American dream breeds desire, a longing for a greater share of the pie. It is as if our society were a vast high-school football game, with the bulk of the participants noisily rooting in the stands while, deep down, each of them is wishing he or she could be the star quarterback or head cheerleader. **(2)**

For the semiotician, the contradictory nature of the American myth of equality is nowhere written so clearly as in the signs that American advertisers use to manipulate us into buying their wares. "Manipulate" is the word here, not "persuade"; for advertising campaigns are not sources of product information, they are exercises in behavior modification. Appealing to our subconscious emotions rather than to our conscious intellects, advertisements are designed to exploit the discontentments fostered by the American dream, the constant desire for social success and the material rewards that accompany it. America's consumer economy runs on desire, and advertising stokes the engines by transforming common objects—from peanut butter to political candidates—into signs of all the things that Americans covet most. **(3)**

In this [essay], we'll look at a representative sample of ads and what they say about the emotional climate of the country and the fast-changing trends of American life. Because ours is a highly diverse, pluralistic society, various advertisements may say different things depending on their intended audiences, but in every case they say something about America, about the status of our hopes, fears, desires, and beliefs. **(4)**

Let's begin with two ad campaigns conducted by the same company that bear out Alexis de Tocqueville's observations about the contradictory nature of American society: General Motors' campaigns for its Cadillac and Chevrolet lines. First, consider an early magazine ad for the Cadillac Allanté. Appearing as a full-color, four-page insert in *Time*, the ad seems to say "I'm special—and so is this car" even before we've begun to read it. Rather than being printed on the ordinary, flimsy pages of the magazine, the Allanté spread appears on glossy coated stock. The unwritten

TEACHING TIP

As a prereading activity for the Solomon essay, bring 5 or 6 advertisements to class and have students practice semiotic readings of the power and culture signs contained in the language, images, or graphics. After they practice with a few ads, they will have a practical understanding of semiotics, and they will be able to better understand and react to Solomon's essay.

message here is that an extraordinary car deserves an extraordinary advertisement, and that both car and ad are aimed at an extraordinary consumer, or at least one who wishes to appear extraordinary compared to his more ordinary fellow citizens. **(5)**

Ads of this kind work by creating symbolic associations between their product and what is most coveted by the consumers to whom they are addressed. It is significant, then, that this ad insists that the Allanté is virtually an Italian rather than an American car, an automobile, as its copy runs, "Conceived and Commissioned by America's Luxury Car Leader—Cadillac" but "Designed and Handcrafted by Europe's Renowned Design Leader—Pininfarina, SpA, of Turin, Italy." This is not simply a piece of product information, it's a sign of the prestige that European luxury cars enjoy in today's automotive marketplace. Once the luxury car of choice for America's status drivers, Cadillac has fallen far behind its European competitors in the race for the prestige market. So the Allanté essentially represents Cadillac's decision, after years of resisting the trend toward European cars, to introduce its own European import—whose high cost is clearly printed on the last page of the ad. Although $54,700 is a lot of money to pay for a Cadillac, it's about what you'd expect to pay for a top-of-the-line Mercedes-Benz. That's precisely the point the ad is trying to make: the Allanté is no mere car. It's a potent status symbol you can associate with the other major status symbols of the 1980s. **(6)**

Status symbols, then, are signs that identify their possessors' place in a social hierarchy, markers of rank and prestige. We can all think of any number of status symbols—Rolls-Royces, Beverly Hills mansions, even Shar Pei puppies (whose rareness and expense has rocketed them beyond Russian wolfhounds as status pets and has even inspired whole lines of wrinkle-faced stuffed toys)—but how do we know that something *is* a status symbol? The explanation is quite simple: when an object (or puppy!) either costs a lot of money or requires influential connections to possess, anyone who possesses it must also possess the necessary means and influence to acquire it. The object itself really doesn't matter, since it ultimately disappears behind the presumed social potency of its owner. Semiotically, what matters is the signal it sends, its value as a sign of power. One traditional sign of social distinction is owning a country estate and enjoying the peace and privacy that attend it. Advertisements for Mercedes-Benz, Jaguar, and Audi automobiles thus frequently feature drivers motoring quietly along a country road, presumably on their way to or from their country houses. **(7)**

Advertisers have been quick to exploit the status signals that belong to body language as well. As Hegel observed in the early nineteenth century, it is an ancient aristocratic prerogative to be seen by the lower orders without having to look at them in return. Tilting his chin high in the air and gazing down at the world under hooded eyelids, the aristocrat invites observation while refusing to look back. We can find such a pose exploited in an advertisement for Cadillac Seville in which we see an elegantly dressed woman out for a drive with her husband in their new Cadillac. If we look closely at the woman's body language, we can see her glance inwardly with a satisfied smile on her face but not outward toward the camera that represents our gaze. She is glad to be seen by us in her Seville, but she isn't interested in looking at *us*! **(8)**

Ads that are aimed at a broader market take the opposite approach. If the American dream encourages the desire to "arrive," to vault above the mass, it also fosters a desire to be popular, to "belong." Populist commercials accordingly transform products into signs of belonging, utilizing such common icons as country music, small-town life, family picnics, and farmyards. All of these icons are incorporated in GM's "Heartbeat of America" campaign for its Chevrolet line. Unlike the Seville commercial, the faces in the Chevy ads look straight at us and smile. Dress is casual; the mood upbeat. Quick camera cuts take us from rustic to suburban to urban scenes, creating an American montage filmed from sea to shining sea. We all "belong" in a Chevy. **(9)**

Where price alone doesn't determine the market for a product, advertisers can go either way. Both Johnnie Walker and Jack Daniel's are better-grade whiskies, but where a Johnnie Walker ad appeals to the buyer who wants a mark of aristocratic distinction in his liquor, a Jack Daniel's ad emphasizes the down-home, egalitarian folksiness of its product. Johnnie Walker associates itself with such conventional status symbols as sable coats, Rolls-Royces, and black gold; Jack Daniel's gives us a Good Ol' Boy in overalls. In fact, Jack Daniel's Good Ol'Boy is an icon of backwoods independence, recalling the days of the moonshiner and the Whisky Rebellion of 1794. Evoking emotions quite at odds with those stimulated in Johnnie Walker ads, the advertisers of Jack Daniel's have chosen to transform their product into a sign of America's populist tradition. The fact that both ads successfully sell whisky is itself a sign of the dual nature of the American dream. **(10)**

Vocabulary

In your journal, write the meaning of the following words:
most *egalitarian* society (1)

- competitively elitist (2)
- populist anthem (2)
- pluralistic society (4)
- social hierarchy (7)
- aristocratic prerogative (8)
- these icons (9)

Questions for Writing and Discussion

1. Look at the objects around you. Focus on one item. Design a full-page advertisement for this object to appear in one of the following magazines: *Time*, *Vogue*, or *Sports Illustrated.* Use appeals to social status to sell the object.

2. Explain the "paradox" referred to in the first paragraph of the essay.

3. In your own words, explain what Solomon means when he says, "The object itself really doesn't matter, since it ultimately disappears behind the presumed social potency of its owner." In particular, why does Solomon say that the object "disappears"?

4. Reread Solomon's article. Where does he help the reader by repeating main ideas, defining terms, or citing examples that trigger the reader's own experiences? Where could his explanations be clearer?

5. Find a full-page advertisement from a recent magazine. Write your own essay analyzing the signs in this ad. What is the written message or caption? What unwritten messages are conveyed by color, design, images, or body language? What does this ad say about American consumers?

Reading and Writing Processes

■ **Assignment for Reading/Writing** Write an essay that summarizes and then responds to one or more essays, articles, or advertisements. As you review your particular assignment, make sure you understand what text or texts you should respond to, how long your summary and response should be, and what type(s) of responses you should focus on.

Your purpose for this assignment is to represent the text(s) accurately and faithfully in your summary and to explain and support your response. Taken together, your summary and response should be a coherent essay, with a main idea and connections between summary and response. Assume that your audience is other members of the class, including the instructor, with whom you are sharing your reading.

Choosing a Subject

Suggested processes, activities, and strategies for reading and writing will be illustrated in response to the following essay by Dudley Erskine Devlin.

CHILDREN AND VIOLENCE IN AMERICA

DUDLEY ERSKINE DEVLIN

Dudley Erskine Devlin was born in Syracuse, New York, and attended the University of Kansas. Originally trained as a scientist, he currently teaches English at Colorado State University and writes columns and editorials on contemporary problems. The targets for his editorials are often the large and complicated issues of the day, such as education, violence, health care, and the media. "My first goal as a writer," Devlin said in a recent interview, "is to provoke response. If just one reader is angry enough to write me a letter of response, then my time is not wasted." As you read Devlin's essay, note places where you agree or disagree with his ideas. How would you reply to Devlin's argument?

Violence seems to be everywhere in America, but increasingly both the victims and the perpetrators are likely to be children and teenagers. According to a recent Department of Education study, 81 percent of the victims of violent crimes are now preteens and teenagers. Teenagers also lead adults in the number of serious crimes committed. As if to prove this point, recently a stray bullet from gang violence in Denver struck a 10-month-old child who was visiting the zoo. In another incident, a 13-year-old boy accidently shot his friend, and then in despair shot and killed himself. Even this morning's newspaper carries the story of a 15-year-old boy who accidently shot his 9-year-old sister while showing her how to load and unload his father's .22 semi-automatic handgun. The gun went off, and the bullet shattered her spine. The 9-year-old girl is now paralyzed. When people read these shocking and unbelievable stories, they begin to wonder about the causes of the problem. Why are children so frequently the victims or the perpetrators of violence? **(1)**

See the *Nightline* video on "Crime and Punishment" for another investigation of this topic.

The debate in America today is about the causes of violence involving children. But what exactly is the basic, underlying cause? Conventional explanations take an either/or approach: Either the cause lies in TV programs which promote violence or the cause is a society riddled with family instability, drugs, and poverty. It's a classic chicken-or-the-egg question: Does TV and movie violence promote social violence, or is social violence merely reflected in violent movies and television programs? **(2)**

I believe that we should not be fooled by this either/or logic. There is, after all, a third possible answer. Instead of the primary cause being TV violence or the decline in family values, I believe that the news media themselves are the underlying cause of our crisis. The truth is that the liberal media—particularly newspapers and network TV news—have cleverly staged this crisis of violence by hyping a few statistics and isolated cases of violence. To prove this claim, I need to review the conventional arguments. **(3)**

First, let's analyze the belief that violence on TV and in the movies is causing increased violence among children and teenagers. The self-appointed liberal reformers usually trot out a bunch of statistics and examples like the following:

- By the age of 18, the average American child will have seen 200,000 violent acts on television, including 40,000 murders. By the time an American child has left elementary school, he or she has witnessed 8,000 murders on TV.
- Today, television programs and films strive for high body counts, not high morals. *Terminator 2* seems like one long machine-gunning. In *RoboCop*, 32 people are killed. *Die Hard 2* may have the unofficial record with 264 people killed.
- In 1950, approximately 15 percent of America's homes had television; by 1990, 93 percent of America's homes had television. In that 40-year period, the murder rate per 100,000 people jumped from 5.3 to 10.2. That's almost a 100 percent increase in murders.

Using examples like these, the TV and media critics like Tipper Gore argue that children confuse images on TV with the real world, that they become desensitized to repeated acts of violence, and that they say that "it's fun" to do violence to others. Researchers like University of Illinois psychologists Leonard Eron and Rowell Huesmann argue that violence on TV does cause violent behavior: "Television violence affects youngsters of all ages, of both genders, at all socioeconomic levels. It cannot be denied or explained away." **(4)**

On the other side of this either/or argument are those who believe that social violence causes violent behavior in children and teenagers. Those who make this argument point to drug use, poverty, and the decline in family values. Their best evidence is that violence already exists in our children's public schools. They like to cite figures released by the National Education Association (NEA) that show that violence is an everyday part of every child's education. Every school day, the NEA claims, at least 100,000 students bring guns to school; 40 are hurt or killed by firearms; 6,250 teachers are threatened with bodily injury; and 260 teachers are physically assaulted. Everywhere, schools are installing metal detectors and police are stationed in the hallways. **(5)**

Obviously, each of these arguments represents a half-truth. Possibly there is some TV and movie violence that adds to the culture of violence in America. And yes, we can believe that there are a few, isolated pockets of violence in society and schools. But the real truth is that the newspaper media and the network news have actually invented this epidemic of violence in order to promote their product and frighten the public. Every day, reporters search for a few examples of violence to teens and children, plaster them on the front page, and blow the whole thing out of proportion. **(6)**

To be sure, there are violent TV shows and movies that a few people watch, but there are also family shows like *Home Improvement* and *Home Alone* that don't get the publicity of *RoboCop* or *Terminator 2*. There are, of course, one or two cities in America, like Los Angeles and Washington, D.C., where there is occasional violence on the streets and in children's schools. But the liberal establishment press has done its thing again, trying to scare the daylights out of the public in order to sell newspapers and raise their Neilsen ratings. **(7)**

So when you pick up your paper in the morning or turn on the TV news and see another story about teenage violence, take it with a big lump of salt and don't believe everything you read. As they say, one swallow doesn't make a summer, and one infant shot in the Denver Zoo does not mean that we have this huge crisis of violence. In terms of "telling it like it is," you'll find more truth if you turn to the comics and check out "Peanuts." When Lucy hits Charlie Brown, at least you know it's make-believe. **(8)**

Collecting

Once a text or texts has been selected or assigned for your summary and response, try the following reading/writing/discussing activities.

■ **Prereading Journal Entry** In your journal, write what you already know about the subject of the essay. For an essay about children and violence, for example, the following questions will help you to recall your prior experiences and think about your own opinions before you read the essay. The purpose of this entry is to think about your own experiences and opinions *before* you are influenced by the arguments of the essay.

What experiences have you had with guns and violence?
What acts of violence to or by children can you recall?
What seems to be the cause of these violent acts?
What would you do to solve the problem?

TEXT ANNOTATION Most experts on reading and writing agree that you will learn more and remember more if you actually write out your comments, questions, and reactions in the margins of the text you are reading. Writing your responses helps you begin a conversation with the text. Reproduced below are one reader's marginal responses to paragraphs 6 and 7 of Devlin's essay.

I think that both areas contribute to violence

Obviously, each of these arguments represents a half-truth. Possibly there is some TV and movie violence that adds to the culture of violence in America. And yes, we can believe that there are a few, isolated pockets of violence in society and schools. But the real truth is that the newspaper media and the network news have actually *invented* this epidemic of violence in order to promote their product and frighten the public. Every day, reporters search for a few examples of violence to teens and children, plaster them on the front page, and blow the whole thing out of proportion.

There's a lot of violence on TV and in society

? Network news didn't invent it, but they do hype it.

TV news does this every night

To be sure, there are violent TV shows and movies that a few people watch, but there are also family shows like *Home Improvement* and *Home Alone* that don't get the publicity of *RoboCop* or *Terminator 2*. There are, of course, *one or two cities in America*, like Los Angeles and Washington, D.C., where there is occasional violence on the streets and in children's schools. But the liberal establishment press has done its thing again, trying to scare the daylights out of the public in order to sell newspapers and raise their Neilsen ratings.

Home Alone was filled with violence

Huh? Violence exists in every city in America

Showing violence on TV does raise ratings

READING LOG A reading log, like text annotation, encourages you to interact with the author/text and write your comments and questions as you read. While text annotation helps you identify specific places in the text for commentary, a reading log encourages you to write out longer, more thoughtful responses. In a reading log, you can keep a record of your thoughts *while you read and reread* the text. Often, reading-log entries help you focus on a key idea to develop later in your response.

Below is one reader's response to Devlin's claim in paragraphs 6 and 7 that the violence is isolated in just a few cities.

> When Devlin says that violence happens in only a few cities like L.A. or D.C., I really disagree. One would never expect to hear of violence in a sparsely populated state like Montana, but it does happen there. Peers in my school bring weapons daily—guns, knives, and the like. So far, only threats have been made, but everyone lives in fear that one day someone will get hurt. Schools don't have to be in the slums to have violence. Three years ago, a boy walked into his classroom in Lewistown, Montana, and killed his teacher and wounded two others. This student went to a safe school, in a safe city, but somehow the violence found a way into this haven.

DOUBLE-ENTRY LOG One of the most effective strategies to promote active reading is a double-entry log. Draw a line down the middle of a page in your notebook. On the left-hand side, keep a running summary of the main ideas and features that you notice in the text. On the right hand side, write your questions and reactions. A double-entry log, especially if used with the *Rereading Guide* (below) can help you quickly organize your ideas for a summary/response essay.

Author and Title:

SUMMARY COMMENTS: MAIN IDEAS AND KEY FEATURES	RESPONSE: COMMENTS, REACTIONS, AND QUESTIONS

REREADING GUIDE After you've read an essay once, let the following set of questions guide your *rereadings* of the text. The questions on the left-hand side will help you summarize and analyze the text; the questions on the right-hand side will help focus your response.

Description	**Response**
I. Audience/Reader	
• Who is the *intended audience*?	• Are you part of the intended audience?
• What *assumptions* does the author make about the reader's knowledge orbeliefs?	• Does the author misjudge the reader's knowledge or beliefs? • Do you share the author's point of view on this subject?
• From what *point of view* is the author writing?	

Description	Response
II. Thesis and Main Ideas	
• What *questions* or *problems* does the author/text address? • What is the author's *thesis*?	• What assumptions does the essay make? • What are the implications or consequences of the essay's ideas?
• What *main ideas* are related to the thesis?	• Does the essay have contradictions or errors in logic?
• What are the *key moments* or *key passages* in the text?	• What ideas or arguments does the essay omit or ignore?
	• What experience or prior knowledge do you have about the topic?
	• Where do you agree or disagree?
III. Organization and Evidence	
• Where does the author *preview* the essay's organization?	• At what point could you accurately predict the organization of the essay?
• How does the author *signal* new sections of the essay?	• At what points were you confused about the organization?
• What *kinds of evidence* does the author use (personal experience, descriptions, statistics, other authorities, analytical reasoning, or other)?	• What evidence was most/least effective? • Where did the author rely on assertions rather than on evidence? • Which of your own personal experiences did you recall as you read the essay?
IV. Language and Style	
• What is the author's *tone* (casual, humorous, ironic, angry, preachy, academic, or other)?	• Did the tone support or distract from the author's purpose or meaning?
• Are *sentences* and *vocabulary* easy, average, or difficult?	• Did the sentences and vocabulary support or distract from the purpose or meaning?
• What key *words* or *images* recur throughout the text?	• Did recurring words or images relate to or support the purpose or meaning?

Description	Response
V. Purpose	
• Describe the author's overall *purpose* (to inform, explore, explain, evaluate, argue, entertain, or other purpose).	• Is the overall purpose clear or muddled? •Was the actual purpose different from the stated purpose?
•How does the author/text want to *affect* or *change* the reader?	• How did the text actually affect you?

Remember that not all these questions will be relevant to any given essay or text, but one or two of these questions may suggest a direction or give a *focus* to your overall response. When one of these questions suggests a focus for your response to the essay, *go back to the text, to other texts, and to your experience* to gather *evidence* and *examples* to support your response.

DISCUSSION AND REREADING After you have recorded your initial reactions in your reading log or double-entry log, discuss your reactions in small groups. Do a collaborative annotation of the text by recording your group's best responses in the margins of a photocopy of the text. Or perhaps your class or small group may want to debate the strengths and weaknesses of the text. After your class or small-group discussion activity, however, take time to enter your responses to the following questions:

What do you need to change in your summary?
What new responses did you hear?
Which of your original responses have you revised?
What will be the new focus or main emphasis of your response?

TEACHING TIP

It's important to have students suggest revisions to these discussion guidelines and then have them negotiate a satisfactory revision of them. This initial activity should itself model the processes of discussion, negotiation, and compromise.

GUIDELINES FOR CLASS DISCUSSION

Class discussions are an important part of the reading/writing/discussing process. Often, however, class discussions are not productive because not everyone knows the purpose of the discussion or how to discuss openly and fairly. Below is a suggested list of goals for class discussion. Read them carefully. *Make notes about any suggestions, revisions, or additions for your class.* Your class will then review these goals and agree to adopt, modify, or revise them for your own class discussions for the remainder of the semester.

Discussion Goals

1. To understand and *accurately represent* the views of the author(s) of the essays. The first discussion goal should be to summarize the author's views fairly.

2. To understand how the views and arguments of individual authors *relate* to each other. Comparing and contrasting different authors' views helps clarify each author's argument.

3. To encourage all members of the class to articulate their *understanding* of each essay and their *response* to the ideas in each essay. Class discussions should promote multiple responses rather than focus on a single "right" interpretation or response.

4. To hear class members' responses in an *open forum.* All points of view must be recognized. *Discussions in class should focus on ideas and arguments, not on individual class members.* Class members may attack ideas but not people.

5. To relate class discussions to the *assigned reading/writing task.* What effective writing strategies are illustrated in the essay the class is discussing? How can class members use any of these strategies in writing their own essays?

SHAPING

Summaries and responses have several possible shapes, depending on the writer's purpose and intended audience. Keep in mind, however, that in a summary/response essay or critique, *the summary and the response should be unified by the writer's overall response.* The summary and the response may be organized or drafted separately, but they are still parts of one essay, focused on the writer's most important or overall response.

SUMMARY SHAPING

Summaries should convey the main ideas, the essential argument, or the key features of a text. The purpose should be to represent the author's/text's ideas as accurately and as faithfully as possible. Summaries rely on description, paraphrase, and direct quotation. Below are definitions and examples for each of these terms.

DESCRIPTION The summary should describe the main features of an essay, including the author and title, the context or place of publication for the essay (if appropriate), the essay's thesis or main argument, and any key text features, such as sections, chapters, or important graphic material.

> In an editorial entitled "Children and Violence in America," Dudley Erskine Devlin documents the increasing violence in America done to children and by children. In addressing the question of why the violence has increased, he reports on the debate between those people who think that television violence is the main cause and those who think that the decline of social values is the cause. Devlin suggests that each of these arguments represents only a half-truth. In fact, Devlin argues, the news media have largely invented this crisis of violence.

PARAPHRASE A paraphrase restates a passage or text in different words. The purpose of a paraphrase is to recast the author's/text's words in your own language. A good paraphrase retains the original meaning without plagiarizing from the original text.

COMPUTER TIPS: COLLECTING AND SHAPING

1. If you like to do your prewriting at the computer, create a file for a reading log or a double-entry log. For a reading log, simply open a file and write your responses and reactions as you read. For a double-entry log, create a two-column page with your graphics program. (If you are in the computer lab, ask a monitor to help you.) Enter your summary notes in the left-hand column and your responses on the right. You can also do your Rereading Guide in a double-column format.

2. An important part of responding to texts is sharing and discussing your reactions with other readers. If you have an electronic bulletin board or e-mail program, write a one-paragraph response to the text you are reading and e-mail it to your classmates. Read the responses sent to you and respond in a short paragraph. An electronic mail program enables you to continue the conversation about the text outside of class.

Original: But the real truth is that the newspaper media and the network news have actually invented this epidemic of violence in order to promote their product and frighten the public.

Paraphrase: Television and print media have created an illusion that violence is widespread simply to attract anxious people to their programs and news stories.

As you can see, a paraphrase does not necessarily condense a passage. Actually, the paraphrase may be nearly as long as the original. A summary includes occasional paraphrasing of a few, selected, main ideas.

DIRECT QUOTATION Often, summaries directly quote a few key phrases or sentences from the source. *Remember: Any words or phrases within the quotation marks must be accurate, word-for-word transcriptions of the original.* Guidelines for direct quotation and examples are as follows. Use direct quotations sparingly to convey the key points in the essay:

> Devlin's essay addresses a simple but difficult question: "Why are children so frequently the victims or the perpetrators of violence?"

Use direct quotations when the author's phrasing is more memorable, more concise, or more accurate than your paraphrase might be:

> Devlin argues that media reporters are trying to "scare the daylights out of the public" in order to sell their stories.

Use direct quotations for key words or phrases that indicate the author's attitude, tone, or stance:

> Television and the news media, Devlin claims, have "invented" this crisis of violence.

Don't quote long sentences. Condense the original sentence to the most important phrases. Use just a short phrase from a sentence or use an ellipsis (three spaced periods . . .) to indicate words that you have left out.

> *Original*: But the real truth is that the newspaper media and the network news have actually invented this epidemic of violence in order to promote their product and frighten the public.
>
> *Condensed Quotation*: "The real truth," according to Devlin, is that the media "have actually invented this epidemic . . . to promote their product and frighten the public."

SAMPLE SUMMARIES Below are summaries of Devlin's essay written by two different readers. Notice that while both convey the main ideas of the essay by using description, paraphrase, and direct quotation, they are not identical. Check each summary to see how well it meets the following guidelines:

- Cite the author and title of the text.
- Indicate the main ideas of the text.
- Use direct quotation of key words, phrases, or sentences.
- Include author tags.
- Do not summarize most examples or data.
- Be as accurate, fair, and objective as possible.

SUMMARY NO. 1

In "Children and Violence in America," Dudley Erskine Devlin takes a different approach to explaining the apparent increase of violence involving children. Devlin begins by describing several cases of children and violence, and then he outlines the two major explanations for violence that most social analysts subscribe to. The first is that television promotes violence, and the second is that the decline in family values causes children to kill children. Devlin then offers his theory—that there is no real increase in child violence. The apparent increase is, in fact, caused by the liberal media "blowing the whole thing out of proportion." Devlin closes by urging the reader to think before jumping to conclusions about the causes of teenage violence.

SUMMARY NO. 2

Dudley Erskine Devlin's editorial, "Children and Violence in America," attempts to refute the claims of some people that violence on television and in movies leads to violence involving young people in real life. Devlin also argues against the idea that family instability, drugs, and poverty cause violence among young Americans. While Devlin agrees that "possibly there is some TV and movie violence that adds to the culture of violence in America," he argues that the media has "actually invented this epidemic of violence" to "frighten the public" and thus sell their stories. In actuality, Devlin claims, there is no problem with violence among young people in America. It is just something made up by the media to promote business.

Response Shaping

Strategies for organizing a response depend on the purpose for the response. Typically, responses combine several of the following three purposes:

- Analyzing the effectiveness of the text.
- Agreeing and/or disagreeing with the ideas in the text.
- Interpreting and reflecting on the text.

As the following explanations illustrate, each of these types of responses requires supporting evidence from the text, from other texts, and/or from the writer's own experience.

Analyzing Analysis requires dividing a whole into its parts in order to better understand the whole. In order to analyze a text for its effectiveness, start by examining key parts or features of the text, such as the purpose, the intended audience, the thesis and main ideas, the organization and evidence, and the language and style. Notice how the following paragraph analyzes Devlin's illogical use of *evidence.*

> Devlin's essay has some clear problems with supporting evidence. In one case, his evidence does not support his argument, and in another the evidence he gives refutes his main point. In Devlin's opening paragraph, two of his examples involve shooting *accidents*, not violent crimes. The boy who accidently shot his friend and the boy who accidentally shot his sister did not commit "violent crimes." To support his point in the first paragraph, Devlin needs examples showing children as victims and perpetrators of violent crime. Another obvious problem with supporting evidence occurs later in the essay. Devlin argues in paragraph 4 that TV and movie violence is *not* a major cause of teenage violence, but then he goes on to cite several convincing examples and statistics linking TV shows and movies with violence. In this case, Devlin gives plenty of evidence, but it supports the argument that he dismisses both in this paragraph and at the end of the essay.

Agreeing/Disagreeing Often, a response to a text focuses on agreeing and/or disagreeing with its major ideas. Responses may agree completely, disagree completely, or agree with some points but disagree with others. Responses that agree with some ideas but disagree with others are often more effective because they show that the responder sees both strengths and weaknesses in an argument. In the following paragraphs, notice how the responder agrees and disagrees and then supports each judgment with evidence.

> I agree with the author that the news media blow many stories out of proportion. It seems that every time I see a story about a child-related violent crime on the news, I am always told to stay tuned for more information. They keep going back to the same reporter, giving the same information. They usually have a special "follow-up report" on the next night. The more violent the crime, the more attention it gets. For example, if there is a high-speed chase involving a teenager, it will be mentioned on the news. If the chase ends in a crash, however, the story will be repeated in depth for several days. The media can stretch one incident into a crime story that lasts all week. The media always dwell on the bad. If news stories mention a teenager on a good note, it is shown just once, not shown or reprinted the rest of the week.
>
> I have to disagree with the author as well. Violent TV shows can lead to an increase in violent crimes. To see the effects of violent movies, you don't have to look any farther than the toy store at your local Wal-Mart. For every movie such as *RoboCop* or *Terminator 2*, there is a new line of violent toys. As children grow up playing with these toys, they begin associating violent objects with fun. As they grow older, they begin looking for more violent "toys." Pretty soon you have a 16-year-old kid holding a real 9-mm pistol to his best friend's head.

INTERPRETING AND REFLECTING Many responses contain interpretations of passages that might be read from different points of view or reflections on the assumptions or implications of an idea. An interpretation says, "Here is what the text says, but let me explain what it means, what assumptions the argument carries, or what the implications might be." Here is a paragraph from an interpretive response to Devlin's essay on children and violence:

> Finally, Devlin's closing line about Lucy hitting Charlie Brown really made me stop and think. Statistics show that 90 percent of domestic violence is perpetrated by men, not women. This example helped me realize that the real problem of violence goes deeper than the media. TV and movies only reflect a deeper culture of sexism in America. Movies constantly depict knifings and rapes and murders, most of them against women. Men will accept violence in the media as long as it's played out against women and children, but never, never against themselves. The movie "Thelma and Louise" created a firestorm of controversy simply because it showed a

woman shooting a rapist. Until the day comes when women and children are treated as equals to men, and not their property, there will be violence in this country.

Outlines for Summary/Response Essays

Three common outlines for summary/response essays are as follows. Select or modify one of these outlines to fit your audience, purpose, and kind of response. Typically, a summary/response will take the following form:

I. Introduction to text(s)

II. Summary of text (s)

III. Response(s)

- **A.** Point one
- **B.** Point two
- **C.** Point three, etc.

IV. Conclusion

A second kind of outline, illustrated by Quammen's essay in the chapter, focuses initially on key ideas or issues and then examines the text or texts for their contribution to these key ideas. This outline begins with the issues, then summarizes the text(s), and then moves to the reader's responses:

I. Introduction to key issues

II. Summary of relevant text(s)

III. Response(s)

- **A.** Point one
- **B.** Point two
- **C.** Point three, etc.

IV. Conclusion

A third outline integrates the summary and the response. It begins by introducing the issue and/or the text, gives a brief overall idea of the text, but then summarizes and responds point-by-point.

I. Introduction to issues and/or text(s)

II. Summary of text's point one/response to point one

III. Summary of text's point two/response to point two

IV. Summary of text's point three/response to point three, etc.

V. Conclusion.

Drafting

If you have been reading actively, you have been writing throughout the reading/writing/discussing process. At some point, however, you will gather your best ideas, have a rough direction or outline in mind, and begin writing a draft. Some writers like to have their examples and evidence ready when they begin drafting. Many writers have outlines in their heads or on paper. Perhaps you like to put your rough outline on the computer and then just expand each section as you write. Finally, most writers like to skim the text and *reread their notes* immediately before they start their drafts, just to make sure everything is fresh in their minds.

Once you start drafting, keep interruptions to a minimum. Because focus and concentration are important to good writing, try to keep writing as long as possible. If you come to a spot where you need an example that you don't have at your fingertips, just put a parentheses—(put the example about cosmetics and animal abuse here) and keep on writing. Concentrate on making all your separate responses add up to a focused, overall response.

Revising

Revision means, literally, *re-seeing*. Revising requires rereading the text and rewriting your summary and response. While revision begins as you read and reread the text, it continues until—and sometimes after—you turn in a paper or send it to its intended audience.

Guidelines for Revision

- **Review the purpose and audience for your assignment.** Is your draft addressed to the appropriate audience? Does it fulfill its intended purpose?
- **Continue to use your active reading/writing/discussing activities as you revise your draft.** If you are uncertain about parts of your summary or response, reread the text, check your notes, or discuss your draft with a classmate.

- **Reread your summary for key features.** Make sure your summary indicates author and title, cites main ideas, uses an occasional direct quotation, and includes author tags. Check your summary for accuracy and objectivity.
- **Check paraphrases and direct quotations.** If you are paraphrasing (without quotation marks) you should put the author's ideas into your own language. If you are quoting directly, make sure the words within the quotation marks are accurate, word-for-word transcriptions.
- **Review the purpose of your response.** Are you analyzing, agreeing/disagreeing, interpreting, or some combination of all three? Do your types of responses fit the assignment or address your intended audience and satisfy your purpose?
- **Amplify your supporting evidence.** Summary/response drafts often need additional, relevant evidence. Be sure you use sufficient personal experience, evidence from the text, or examples from other texts to support your response.
- **Focus on a clear, overall response.** Your responses should all add up to a focused, overall reaction. Delete or revise any passages that do not maintain your focus.
- **Revise sentences to improve clarity, conciseness, emphasis, and variety.** (See Handbook.)
- **Edit your final version.** Use the spell check on your computer. Have a friend help proofread. Check your Handbook for suspected problems in usage, grammar, and punctuation.

Postscript on the Writing Process

1. As you finish your essay, what questions do you still have about how to summarize? What questions do you have about writing a good response?

2. Which paragraphs in your response contain your most effective supporting evidence? What kind of evidence (analysis of the text, evidence from other texts, or personal experience) did you use?

3. What sentences in your response contain your overall reaction to the text?

4. If you had one more day to work on your essay, what would you change? Why?

5. What did you learn about reading that you applied to the writing of this essay? Where in your essay did you help your reader to make accurate predictions? Where did you use supporting evidence that might trigger your reader's prior knowledge?

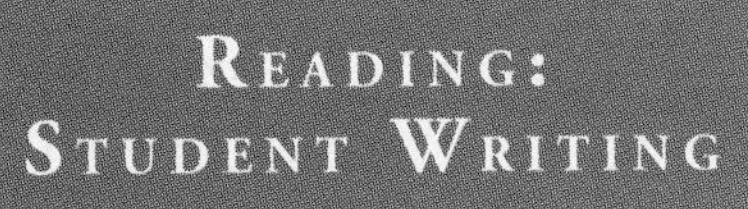

DRAWING THE LINE

PAULA FISHER

Paula Fisher, from Salt Lake City, Utah, wrote her essay while she was an occupational therapy major at Colorado State University. She chose to write a summary/response to David Quammen's essay, "Animal Rights and Beyond," because she could draw on her own personal experiences, both in an animal rights course and in cattle ranching. While reading the essay and making notes for her double-entry log (see below), Fisher says that she "specifically noticed that Quammen failed to present the anti-animal rights issue, a perspective I am familiar with, since all of my mother's side of the family are involved with cattle farming." As you read her essay, see if she clearly summarizes Quammen's essay and then supports her response with examples from her experience.

Fisher's writing process was to read the essay carefully and make notes on her copy of the essay. Then, working on her computer, she used the Rereading Guide to make a double-entry log. Once she completed the double-entry log, she completely drafted her essay. Reprinted below are her double-entry log and her final version.

Double-Entry Log: Notes from Rereading Guide

Description	Responses
I. Audience	
Begins with questions for the reader. Audience is readers of *Outside* magazine, so they're probably pro-animal rights.	Questions make beginning interesting.

DESCRIPTION	RESPONSES
II. Thesis and Main Ideas	
Thesis: Animal rights is a complex issue with no easy answers.	Difficult to pick out thesis—for me.
Talks about history of animal rights. Talks about Singer's and Regan's views. Singer: Greatest good for greatest number. Can animals suffer? Where is the boundary?	Where is the boundary between those who suffer and those who don't—oysters? Quammen's references to issues in animal rights are vague or missing.
Regan—Abuse wrong in essence. Argues for "inherent value" "mentally normal animals of 1 year or more"	My own experience—LD 50, humane society, cosmetics, animal testing, grad students, medical testing, farming
Quammen's responses positive and negative:	What about the mentally retarded?
Positive—they're fighting the good fight Negative—they're too smug. They think everyone should be vegetarians.	I had to read several times to grasp the references to "carrots," etc.
They are still chauvanistic—"How similar to human is similar enough?" Where do we draw the line? Doesn't everything have value?	I agree that issues are complex, but he ignores legitimate uses of farm animals and medical testing.
Quammen says man should not be the measure, since "Life is life."	No rebuttal at end?
III. Organization and Evidence	
No preview of ideas New sections signaled by extra space	What about anti-animal rights—he has no fair mention.
IV. Language and Style	
Tone is humorous, casual. Tad sarcastic, but well explained.	Gordian reference—didn't know Righteous gumbo—good metaphor
V. Purpose	
Purpose to explain Singer's and Regan's ideas and give his responses. He wants to make us see animal rights as a complex issue.	Succeeded in purpose.

Final Version

DRAWING THE LINE

In David Quammen's essay, "Animal Rights and Beyond," he discusses the issue of animal rights, taking the stance that it is a "serious philosophical issue" with no quick answers and serious implications for the way humans should live. Quammen, a nature column writer for Outside, briefly presents the historical anti-animal rights view, but quickly dismisses it. He goes on to discuss the writings of Peter Singer, an important animal rights advocate. Singer is willing to grant rights to animals that suffer, concluding that anything below an oyster doesn't. Quammen next discusses Tom Regan's philosophy. Regan asserts that animals have rights because they have inherent value, but is only willing to grant this value to mentally normal mammals. Quammen first commends these authors for their willingness to take a stance on this issue, but he also reprimands them for their lack of vision. According to Quammen, "man is still the measure" for these two authors. They simply changed the question from "Is the creature human?" to "How similar to human is enough?" **(1)**

I think that Quammen makes an excellent point in his essay: Animal rights is not an issue that has black or white answers. Gray areas exist everywhere. Quammen asserts that animal rights is an "important and tricky" issue that needs to be thought out carefully. His purpose seems to be to make his readers think. This particular essay was published in an environmental magazine that probably has many readers who advocate animal rights. Quammen seems to be challenging them to consider why they believe in animal rights. Is it because of complicated philosophical arguments or simply because "life is life"? Either way, he asserts, and I agree, that it is a difficult issue. **(2)**

When Quammen comments on Singer's and Regan's theories, he compliments them for "fighting a good fight." He asserts that they are focusing attention on "outrageous practices" that are commonplace throughout America. Not only are they writing about it, they are exclaiming, "Let's stop it!" I see this as an important distinction. Tests that blatantly mistreat animals, such as the LD-50 test, where a large number of animals are given a substance until 50 percent of them die, is cruel and wasteful. It often serves no other purpose than to be another figure in a scientist's logbook. Purposeless experiments by graduate students and brutal practices by some American farmers and cosmetic companies also need to be examined and controlled. **(3)**

On the other hand, issues from the anti-animal rights point of view also need to be carefully considered and weighed. This is an issue that Quammen fails to address fairly and realistically. One of the major issues involves the use of animals in medical research. Where does one draw the line between animal suffering and human suffering? The use of animals in medical research can and has helped scientists make breakthroughs that have saved human lives. I would have a hard time looking someone in the eye and saying, "You can't have a cure for cancer because some rats would have to die." It is not an issue that I can easily resolve for myself, and I contend it needs careful analysis and review. **(4)**

Another dilemma emerges when considering the rights of farmers versus the rights of farm animals. I come from a long line of cattle farmers, people whose livelihood revolves around raising animals. It's true, some practices are cruel and unnecessary and need to be regulated, but once again we need to consider where the farmers' rights end and the animals' rights begin. **(5)**

All things considered, I believe that Quammen makes a good claim. The issue of animal rights is truly a complex and complicated issue with no easy answers; if we carry animal rights too far, we won't be able to walk for fear of stepping on an ant, but if we don't consider animal rights we are blind and allowing cruel and inhumane practices to continue. **(6)**

Questions for Writing and Discussion

1. Reread David Quammen's article and make your own double-entry log. On the left-hand side of a piece of paper, record Quammen's main points; on the right-hand side, write your own questions and reactions. Compare your notes to Fisher's summary/response. How would you advise Fisher to revise her summary to make it more complete and accurate? What suggestions would you make about revising her response?

2. Supporting evidence in a summary/response may take the form of analysis of passages from the text, references to ideas or facts from outside texts, or specific examples from personal experience. Find examples of all three kinds of evidence in Fisher's essay. Which did she use most effectively?

3. Compare Fisher's notes in her double-entry log with her final essay. Which of those notes appears in her final version? Which do not? What ideas from her double-entry log would you suggest including or omitting in her final version? Explain your choices.

4. Using Quammen's article, Fisher's response, your class discussion, and your own ideas and experiences, write your own essay on the uses of animals in medical research. Should animals be used to develop cosmetics? To study neurotic behavior? To find a cure for cancer? Where would *you* draw the line—and why?

TWO RESPONSES TO DEBORAH TANNEN

JENNIFER KOESTER AND SONJA H. BROWE

The two essays reprinted here are written in response to an essay by Deborah Tannen, "How Male and Female Students Use Language Differently," which appears in Chapter 7, Explaining. Jennifer Koester and Sonja Browe have opposite responses to Tannen's essay. Jennifer Koester, a political science major at Colorado State University, argues that Tannen's essay is effective because she uses sufficient evidence and organizes her essay clearly. On the other hand, Sonja Browe, an English education major at the University of Wyoming, writes an essay that is critical of Deborah Tannen's focus and supporting evidence. Be sure to read Tannen's essay and decide for yourself before *you read the following essays.*

A RESPONSE TO DEBORAH TANNEN'S ESSAY

JENNIFER KOESTER

Deborah Tannen's "How Male and Female Students Use Language Differently" addresses how male and female conversational styles influence classroom discussions. Tannen asserts that women speak less than men in class because often the structure of discussion is more "congenial" to men's style of conversing. (1)

Tannen looks at three differences between the sexes that shape classroom interaction: classroom setting, debate format, and contrasting attitudes toward classroom discussion. First, Tannen says that during childhood, men "are expected to seize center stage: by exhibiting their skill, displaying their knowledge, and challenging and resisting challenge." Thus, as adults, men are more comfortable than women when speaking in front of a large group of strangers. On the other hand, women are more comfortable in small groups. (2)

Second, men are more comfortable with the debate format. Tannen asserts that many classrooms use the format of putting forth ideas followed by "argument and challenge." This too coincides with men's conversational experiences. However, Tannen asserts that women tend to "resist discussion they perceive as hostile." (3)

Third, men feel it is their duty to think of things to say and to voice them. On the other hand, women often regulate their participation and hold back to avoid dominating discussion. (4)

Tannen concludes that educators can no longer use just one format to facilitate classroom discussion. Tannen sees small groups as necessary for any "non-seminar" class along with discussion of differing styles of participation as solutions to the participation gap between the sexes. (5)

Three things work together to make Deborah Tannen's essay "How Male and Female Students Use Language Differently" effective: qualifications of her argument, evidence used, and the parallel format of comparison/contrast. (6)

First, Tannen's efforts to qualify her argument prevents her from committing logical errors. In the first paragraphs of her essay, she states, "This is not to say that all men talk in class, nor that no women do. It is simply that a greater percentage of discussion time is taken by men's voices." By acknowledging exceptions to her claim, Tannen avoids the mistake of oversimplification. She also strengthens her argument because this qualification tells the reader that she is aware of the complexity of this issue. (7)

Later, Tannen uses another qualification. She says, "No one's conversational style is absolute; everyone's style changes in response to the context and others' styles." Not only does this qualification avoid a logical fallacy, but it also strengthens Tannen's argument that classroom discussion must have several formats. By acknowledging that patterns of participation can change with the setting, Tannen avoids oversimplifying the issue and adds to her argument for classroom variety. (8)

Second, Tannen's evidence places a convincing argument before her reader. In the beginning of her essay, Tannen states that a greater percentage of discussion time in class is taken by men and that those women who attend single-sex schools tend to do better later in life. These two pieces of evidence present the reader with Tannen's jumping off point. These statistics are what Tannen wants to change. **(9)**

In addition, Tannen effectively uses anecdotal evidence. She presents the reader with stories from her colleagues and her own research. These stories are taken from the classroom, a place which her audience, as educators, are familiar with. Her anecdotal evidence is persuasive because it appeals to the common sense and personal experiences of the audience. While some might question the lack of hard statistics throughout the entire essay, the anecdotal evidence serves Tannen best because it reminds her audience of educators of their own experiences. When she reminds the audience of their experiences, she is able to make them see her logic. **(10)**

Third, the parallel format of comparison/contrast between the genders highlights for the reader Tannen's main points. Each time Tannen mentions the reactions of one gender she follows with the reaction of the other gender. For example, Tannen states, "So one reason men speak in class more than women is that many of them find the "public" classroom setting more conducive to speaking, whereas most women are more comfortable speaking in private to a small group of people they know well." Here, Tannen places the tendencies of men and of women together, thus preventing the reader from having to constantly refer back to another section of the essay. **(11)**

In an earlier example, Tannen discusses men's comfort with the debate format in class discussion. The majority of that paragraph relates why men feel comfortable with that format. After explaining this idea, Tannen then tells the reader how women feel about the debate structure. By placing how men and women feel about the debate format within a paragraph, the readers easily see the difference between the genders. Tannen's use of the parallel format in the above examples and the rest of the essay provides a clear explanation of the differences in men's and women's interactions in the classroom. **(12)**

Tannen writes her essay effectively. She makes the essay convincing by qualifying her claims about gender participation. This strengthens her argument that just as the classroom is diverse, so should the format be diverse. Her supporting evidence is convincing because it comes from Tannen's own experience, reminds the audience of its own experiences, and appeals to the audience's common sense. Finally, her parallel format for discussing the differences between men and women enhances the reader's understanding. Overall, Tannen's essay is effective because she qualifies her argument, uses convincing evidence, and makes clear how men and women use language differently through a parallel comparison/contrast format. **(13)**

IS DEBORAH TANNEN CONVINCING?

SONJA H. BROWE

In her article entitled "How Male and Female Students Use Language Differently," Deborah Tannen explores the issue of gender as it affects the way we use language to communicate. Specifically, she discusses how differences in the way males and females are socialized to use language affects their classroom interactions. She explains that as females are growing up, they learn to use language to talk to friends, and to tell secrets. She states that for females, it is the "telling of secrets, the fact and the way they talk to each other, that makes them best friends." Boys, on the other hand, are "expected to use language to seize center stage: by exhibiting their skill, displaying their knowledge, and challenging and resisting challenge." **(1)**

According to Tannen, these differences make classroom language use more conducive to the way males were taught to use language. Tannen suggests that speaking in front of groups and the debatelike formats used in many classrooms are more easily handled by male students. **(2)**

Finally, Tannen describes an experiment she conducted in her own classroom which allowed students to evaluate their own conversation transcripts. From this experience, she deduced that small-group interaction is essential in the classroom because it gives students who don't participate in whole class settings the opportunity for conversation and interaction. **(3)**

Though Tannen's research is a worthwhile consideration and provides information which could be of great interest to educators, this particular article lacks credibility and is unfocused. The points she is trying to make get lost in a world of unsupported assertions and she strays from her main focus, leaving the reader hanging and confused. **(4)**

Tannen does take some time at the beginning of her article to establish her authority on linguistic analysis, but we may still hold her accountable for supporting her assertions with evidence. However, Tannen makes sweeping declarations throughout the essay, expecting the reader to simply accept them as fact. For example, when discussing the practice of the teacher playing devil's advocate and debating with the students, she states that "many, if not most women would shrink from such a challenge, experiencing it as public humiliation." Following such an assertion, we expect to see some evidence. Who did Tannen talk to? What did they say? What percentage of women felt this way? This sort of evidence is completely lacking, making what Tannen states as fact to appear more like conjecture. **(5)**

Tannen makes another such unsupported pronouncement when she discusses the debatelike formats used in many classrooms. She explains that in contrast to males, this type of classroom interaction is in opposition to the way that females approach learning. She states that "it is not that females don't fight, but that they don't fight for fun. They don't ritualize opposition." Again, where is Tannen's evidence to support such a claim? **(6)**

When Tannen does bother to support her assertions, her evidence is trite and unconvincing. For example, she reviews Walter Ong's work on the pursuit of knowledge, in which he suggested that "ritual opposition . . . is fundamental to the way males approach almost any activity." Tannen supports this claim of Ong's in parentheses, saying, "Consider, for example, the little boy who shows he likes a little girl by pulling her braids and shoving her." This statement may serve as an example, but is not enough to convince the reader that ritual opposition is fundamental to the way males approach "almost any activity." **(7)**

Other evidence which Tannen uses to support her declarations comes in the form of conversations she has had with colleagues on these issues. Again, though these may provide examples, they do not represent a broad enough data base to support her claims. **(8)**

Finally, Tannen takes three pages of her article to describe in detail an experiment she conducted in her classroom. Though the information she collected from this experiment was interesting, it strayed from the main point of the essay. Originally, Tannen's article was directed specifically at gender differences in communication. In this classroom activity, she looks at language-use differences in general, including cultural differences. She states that some people may be more comfortable in classes where you are expected to raise your hand to speak, while others prefer to be able to talk freely. She makes no mention of gender in regard to this issue. **(9)**

Finally, at the close of her essay when we can expect to get the thrust of her argument or at least some sort of summary statement which ties into her main thesis, Tannen states that her experience in her classroom convinced her that "small-group interaction should be a part of any classroom" and that "having students become observers of their own interaction is a crucial part of their education." Again, these are interesting points, but they stray quite a bit from the original intention of the article. **(10)**

In this article, Tannen discusses important issues with which those of us who will be interacting with students in the classroom should be aware. However, her article loses a great deal of its impact because she does not stay focused on her original thesis and fails to support her ideas with convincing evidence. **(11)**

Questions for Writing and Discussion

1. Do your own double-entry log for Tannen's essay (see Chapter 7). On the left-hand side of a piece of paper, record Tannen's main points. On the right-hand side, write your own questions and reactions. Compare your notes to Koester's and Browe's responses. Whose response most closely matches your own? Where or how does your response differ from each?

2. Koester and Browe use different strategies for writing their summaries of Tannen's essay. Describe how the two summaries are different. Which summary is more accurate? Why?

3. Responses to texts may analyze the effectiveness of the text, agree or disagree with the ideas in the text, and/or interpret or reflect on the text. What kinds of responses do Koester and Browe give? Would a different kind of response work better for either writer? Why or why not?

4. Koester focuses on three writing strategies that Tannen uses to make her essay more effective. What are they? What weaknesses of Tannen's essay does Koester ignore or downplay?

5. Browe's response focuses on two criticisms of Tannen's essay. What are they? In which paragraphs does Browe develop each criticism? What strengths of Tannen's essay does Browe ignore or downplay?

6. Neither Browe nor Koester uses personal experience as supporting evidence. Think of one experience that you have had in a specific class illustrating the conversational preferences of men and women. Write out that specific example. Could either Browe or Koester use such a specific example? Where might each writer use it in her response?

7. Reread the essays by Tannen, Koester, and Browe. Review your reactions with your class members. Then write your own summary and response. In your response, mention both the strengths and weaknesses of Tannen's article. Then indicate whether or not you found Tannen's essay, in general, thought-provoking or convincing.

SIX / INVESTIGATING

When you stop learning, stop listening, stop looking and asking questions, always new questions, then it is time to die.

—LILLIAN SMITH, CIVIL RIGHTS ACTIVIST, JOURNALIST, AUTHOR OF KILLERS OF THE DREAM

As the free press develops, the paramount point is whether the journalist, like the scientist or scholar, puts truth in the first place or in the second.

—WALTER LIPPMANN, JOURNALIST AND AUTHOR

YOUR BOSS AT THE LOCAL SELF-SERVICE GAS STATION WANTS TO EXPAND THE STATION'S RANGE OF CONVENIENCE ITEMS. Currently, you sell only snacks, such as soda pop, candy, and ice cream. Your boss asks you to find out what is sold at other gas-station convenience stores. Next, she wants you to design a survey for your customers, asking which items they would like to have the station carry. After tabulating questionnaires from thirty-five customers, you write a short report for the boss outlining what the competition stocks, how you designed your questionnaire, and what the responses from your customers indicate.

WHILE WATCHING JOGGERS RUNNING IN THE PARK ONE DAY, YOU NOTICE THEIR STRAINING MUSCLES, THEIR LABORED BREATHING, AND THE GRIMACES ETCHED ON THEIR FACES. Why, you wonder, do people go through the pain of running? Does it have a physical or a psychological benefit? Or can it even become an addiction for those people who *have* to run every day? You decide to investigate this question in runners' magazines and professional journals and then interview a few serious runners to determine their motives and the effects that running has on them, both physically and psychologically. The results of your report, you hope, will prove interesting to those who run as well as to those who merely watch others run.

Vermeer, Jan, The Astronomer, 1668, Louvre, Paris, France

INVESTIGATING BEGINS WITH QUESTIONS. WHAT CAUSES THE GREENHOUSE EFFECT? How does illiteracy affect a person's life? How does rape affect the lives of women in America? How is AIDS transmitted? How do colleges recruit applicants? What can you find out about a famous person's personality, background, and achievements? At what age do children first acquire simple mathematical abilities? What kind of employee is most likely to be promoted? Why are sunsets yellow, then orange, red, and finally purple?

Investigating also carries an assumption that probing for answers to such questions—by observing and remembering, researching sources, interviewing key people, or conducting surveys—will uncover truths not generally known or accepted. As you dig for information, you learn *who, what, where*, and *when*. You may even learn *how* and *why*.

The purpose of investigating is to uncover or discover facts, opinions, and reactions for yourself and then to *report* that information to other people who want to know. A report strives to be as objective and informative as possible. It may summarize other people's judgments, but it does not editorialize. It may represent opposing viewpoints or arguments, but it does not argue for one side or the other. A report is a window on the world, allowing readers to see the information for themselves.

■ **FREEWRITING: INVESTIGATING YOUR OWN EXPERTISE** If you haven't done so already, write a personal "authority" list, naming subjects about which you have some expertise or information. Consider your hobbies, academic interests, occupational skills, friends and family members, social problems, community concerns, art, sports, travel, animals, films, TV shows, and so forth. Jot down a few words or phrases indicating what you know about each item on your list. Emphasize *what* or *who* it is, *how* it happens or *how* to do it, and *when* or *where* it happens. Because one of these topics may develop into an essay for this course, spend at least fifteen minutes on this exercise.

TECHNIQUES FOR INVESTIGATIVE WRITING

Investigative writing begins with asking questions and finding informed sources: published material, knowledgeable people, or both. In most cases, collecting information in an investigation requires the ability to use a library and then to summarize, paraphrase, and quote key ideas accurately from other people's writing. In addition, personal interviews

BACKGROUND ON INVESTIGATING

While this chapter builds on the reading and summarizing skills covered in Chapter 5, it adds basic library and field-research techniques. It focuses on *reporting* as a rhetorical purpose. In Chapters 7 to 11, investigating becomes an invention strategy that students use—along with their observing, remembering, and reading skills—to write expository, argumentative, or interpretive prose.

TEACHING TIP

The authority list that students generate in this freewriting exercise should become an important part of the students' journals. In this and in following chapters, encourage students to review, add to, and revise their authority lists as they think about potential subjects for their essays.

Curiosity is my natural state and has led me headlong into every worthwhile experience . . . I have ever had.

—ALICE WALKER, AUTHOR OF THE COLOR PURPLE

The *Video Library* is a rich source of investigative reporting. See Chapters 6 and 12 of the *Video Guide* for ways to analyze the news programs with a writer's eye.

RESOURCE NOTE

Although reporting strives for objectivity, Barzun and Graff, authors of *The Modern Researcher*, remind us that "the facts *never* speak for themselves. They must be selected, marshaled, linked together, and given a voice."

TEACHING TIP

Encourage students to use *graphics* with their reports, if appropriate. Some students may have access to excellent computer-graphics programs; others may want to hand-draw graphics to accompany their reports. *USA Today* is an easily accessible source for samples of graphics.

are often helpful or necessary. For an investigation, you might talk to an expert or an authority, an eyewitness or participant in an event, or even the subject of a personality profile. Finally, you may wish to survey the general public to determine opinions, trends, or reactions. Once you have collected your information, you must then present your findings in a written form suitable for your audience, with clear references in the text to your sources of information.

Investigative writing uses the following techniques:

- **Beginning with an interesting title and a catchy lead sentence or paragraph.** The first few sentences arouse your readers' *interest* and focus their attention on the subject.
- **Giving background information by answering relevant *who, what, when, where,* and *why* questions.** Answering the *reporter's "Wh" questions* ensures that readers have sufficient information to understand your report.
- **Stating the main idea, question, or focus of the investigation.** The purpose of a report is to convey information as *clearly* as possible. Readers shouldn't have to guess the main idea.
- **Summarizing or quoting information from written or oral sources; citing sources in the text.** Quote *accurately* any statistics, data, or sentences from your sources. Cite authors and titles.
- **Writing in a readable and interesting style appropriate for the intended audience.** Clear, direct, and readable language is essential in a report. Use graphs and charts as appropriate.

The following reports illustrate three common types of investigative writing: the *summary* of a single book or article, the *investigation* of a controversial issue (using multiple sources), and the *profile* of a person. The three types may overlap (the investigation of a controversial issue may contain a personality profile, for instance), and all three types may use summaries of written material, questionnaires, and interviews. While some investigative reports are brief, intended to be only short news items, others are full-length features.

The intended audience for each report is often determined by the publication in which the report appears: *Psychology Today* assumes that its readers are interested in personality and behavior; *Discover* magazine is for readers interested in popular science; readers of *Ms.* magazine expect coverage of contemporary issues concerning women.

SUMMARY OF A BOOK OR ARTICLE

The following report from *Psychology Today*, by journalist Jeff Meer, summarizes information taken from an article by Charlene L.

Muehlenhard and Melaney A. Linton that appeared in *Journal of Counseling Psychology*. Although the *Psychology Today* report summarizes only that one article, it demonstrates several key features of an investigative report.

Date Rape: Familiar Strangers

Attention-getting title

By now, everyone knows the scenario. Boy meets girl, they go to a party, get drunk, return to his apartment, and he forces her to have sex.

Lead-in paragraph

Most people assume that date rape occurs on a first or second date between relative strangers. But new research supports a different conclusion: The individuals involved generally know each other fairly well.

Focus of investigation or report

Psychologist Charlene L. Muehlenhard and undergraduate Melaney A. Linton asked more than 600 college men and women about their most recent dates, as well as their worst experience with "sexual aggression"—any time a woman was forced to participate in acts, ranging from kissing to intercourse, against her will. More than three quarters of the women and more than half of the men admitted to having an experience with sexual aggression on a date, either in high school or in college. And nearly 15 percent of the women and 7 percent of the men said they had intercourse against the woman's will.

Who, what, where questions answered

Summary of results

The researchers found that when a man initiated the date, drove to and from and paid for the date, sexual aggression was more likely. They also found that if both people got drunk (at a party, for example) and "parked," or found themselves in the man's dorm room or apartment, the date was more likely to end with the woman being forced to perform against her wishes. Men and women who thought of themselves as having traditional values and those who were more accepting of violence were also more likely to have been involved in date rape.

Summary of results

But contrary to what one might expect, date rape and sexual aggression were much more likely to happen between partners who knew each other. On average, students said they had known the partner almost a year before the incident. "If women were more aware of this, they might be less surprised and more prepared to deal with sexual aggression by someone they know well," Muehlenhard says.

Summary of results

quotation

She points out that communication is often a big problem on dates during which there is sexual aggression. Both men and women reported that the man had felt "led on" during such dates. Men said that women desired more sexual contact on these dates than had others on previous dates. Women said that they had desired less sexual contact than usual.

summary

quotation

Muehlenhard believes that a direct approach, such as a woman saying "I don't want to do anything more than kiss," might clear up confusion better than simply saying "No."

Investigation Using Multiple Sources

Most investigative reports draw on multiple sources—books and articles, research studies, and interviews. The following article, which appeared in *Psychology Today*, has all the key features of an interesting investigative report. The author, Anastasia Toufexis, focuses on the popular but controversial psychiatric drug Prozac. She catches our interest with personal case histories. She asks probing questions about the medical and psychological effects of the drug. She focuses her report on a bestselling book by Peter Kramer, but she also weaves in several interviews with other authorities on Prozac. Despite the controversial nature of her topic, however, Toufexis remains as neutral as possible. She presents the background information and lets the experts debate the issues so that her readers can judge for themselves.

Compare Toufexis's article to the *American Agenda* special entitled "Prozac" in the *Video Library*.

Critical Reading

Ask students to annotate the Toufexis article for key features of investigative writing. Students should annotate their own texts individually and then work in groups of three or four to collate their annotations on a photocopy of the essay that the instructor provides. This critical-reading strategy can then be the springboard for discussions about the article and/or can model a peer-revision workshop on the students' own drafts.

The Personality Pill

Susan Smith has everything going for her. A self-described workaholic, she runs a Cambridge, Massachusetts, real estate consulting company with her husband Charles and still finds time to cuddle and nurture their two young kids, David, 7, and Stacey, 6. What few people know is that Susan, 44, needs a little chemical help to be a supermom: she has been taking the antidepressant Prozac for five years.

Smith never had manic depression or any other severe form of mental illness. But before Prozac, she suffered from sharp mood swings, usually coinciding with her menstrual periods. "I would become highly emotional and sometimes very angry, and I really wasn't sure why I was angry," she recalls. Charles will never forget the time she threw her wedding band at him during a spat. Now, says Susan, "the lows aren't as low as they were. I'm more comfortable with myself." And she has no qualms about her long-term relationship with a psychoactive pill: "If there's a drug that makes you feel better, you use it."

Millions agree, making Prozac the hottest psychiatric drug in history. Since its introduction five years ago, 5 million Americans—and 10 million people worldwide—have used it. The drug is much more than a fad: it is a medical breakthrough that has brought unprecedented relief to many patients with severe depressions, phobias, obsessions and compulsions. But it is also increasingly used by people with milder problems, and its immense popularity is raising some unsettling questions. When should

Prozac be prescribed? How does a doctor draw the line between illness and normal behavior? If you feel better after taking Prozac, were you ill before? When does drug therapy become drug abuse? Will Prozac become the medically approved feel-good drug, a cocaine substitute without the dangerous highs and lows?

At medical meetings or dinner parties, the talk turns more and more often to Prozac, and what frequently sets off the discussion is a provocative book about the drug—*Listening to Prozac: A Psychiatrist Explores Antidepressant Drugs and the Remaking of the Self* by Dr. Peter Kramer of Brown University. Having quickly become a must-read, the book has perched near the top of the best-seller lists for three months.

The author, who uses Prozac in his private practice, is both impressed by the drug and uneasy about what its widespread use may portend for human society. In case after case, he contends, Prozac does more than treat disease; it has the power to transform personality, instill self-confidence and enhance a person's performance at work and play. One of the patients profiled in the book, an architect named Sam, claims that the drug made him "better than well." His depression lifted, and he became more poised and thoughtful, with keener concentration and a more reliable memory than ever before. Prozac, writes Kramer, seems "to give social confidence to the habitually timid, to make the sensitive brash, to lend the introvert the social skills of a salesman."

The psychiatrist maintains that the power of Prozac challenges basic assumptions about the origins and uniqueness of individual personalities. They may be less the result of experiences and more a matter of brain chemistry. If temperament lies in a tablet, is there an essential, immutable Self? Ultimately, Kramer muses, society could enter a new era of "cosmetic psychopharmacology," in which changing personality traits may be as simple as shampooing in a new hair color. "Since you only live once, why not do it as a blond?" he asks, and "why not as a peppy blond?" Already, pharmaceutical houses are churning out a whole new class of similar drugs, including Paxil and Zoloft, that mimic the effects of Prozac.

So what makes Prozac any different from all the other popular mood-altering potions down through history, from alcohol, opium and marijuana to widely prescribed "mother's little helpers" such as Librium and Valium? Unlike the typical street drug, which sends people soaring and then crashing, Prozac has an effect that is even and sustained. And it seems safer and has fewer bothersome side effects than previous medicines prescribed to lift people out of depression. Prozac is what scientists call a "clean" drug. Instead of playing havoc with much of the brain's chemistry, the medication has a very specific effect: it regulates the level of serotonin, a crucial compound that carries messages between nerve cells. "Prozac makes people feel different without making them feel drugged," notes Kramer.

Patients don't all react the same way, of course; some don't feel a bit better. And many psychiatrists and patients don't agree with Kramer about the drug's transformative powers. "I have my ability to not snap at people back, my energy back, notes a rabbi who recently started taking Prozac for mild depression. But, he adds, "I don't feel like Superman, and I still can't stand parties."

"There's a lot less than meets the eye with Prozac," says Dr. Daniel Auerbach of the Veterans Health Administration in Sepulveda, California. "Nothing changes personality. What gets changed is symptoms of a disease." In other words, Prozac enables a person's true personality, often imprisoned by illness, to come out. Contends Dr. Hyla Cass, a psychiatrist in Santa Monica, California: "I don't think Prozac is manipulating people, turning them into feel-goods. It is correcting an imbalance, allowing people to be who they can be."

But, counters Kramer, doesn't that broaden the boundaries of mental illness to include any condition that responds to Prozac? If a person responds to an antidepressant, does that necessarily mean that he or she is suffering from depression? Kramer questions whether the "imbalances" cured by the drug are always bad; maybe they are just frowned upon by current society. Are the vivacity and blithe spirits often produced by Prozac superior to shyness and a touch of melancholy? Do decisiveness and vigor have more merit than reticence and calmness? Should a business executive who lacks aggressiveness feel compelled to take a pill?

Just as ticklish is the question of when a doctor should stop prescribing Prozac. Satisfied customers don't want to abandon the drug even when their illness seems gone. Kramer's book tells the story of Tess, a businesswoman who became more assertive and outgoing after starting to take Prozac for depression. When Kramer took her off the drug, she complained that "I'm not myself." The psychiatrist renewed her prescription, but not without qualms. "You could say you're giving Prozac to her to prevent recurrence of depression," he observes, "but you could also say you're giving it to her to maintain her new personality."

Most psychiatrists argue that while Prozac may be abused, it is still a long way from being overused. A study by the National Institute of Mental Health shows that 40% to 50% of people with major depression are not receiving any kind of therapy.

With so many still going untreated, Kramer's book may do a service by alerting some of them to Prozac's potential benefits. But Kramer may also be raising expectations too high. Says Dr. Glen Gabbard, director of the Menninger Memorial Hospital in Topeka, Kansas: "We should not send patients rushing to their corner pharmacy in hopes of getting a magic chemical that will solve all their problems." For most people, happiness does not come packaged in a pill.

Profile of a Person

The following passage is a *profile* of a person—a biographical sketch intended to give a sense of the person's appearance, behavior, character, and accomplishments. These paragraphs are part of a profile of Oprah Winfrey written by journalist Joan Barthel for *Ms.* magazine.

Here Comes Oprah!

A profile of Oprah Winfrey is not just the story of a survivor, though she obviously is one: besides that bottom-line day five years ago [when she wrote a suicide note], she's survived early adolescent years so troubled that she became a runaway and was nearly placed in a juvenile detention home.

Nor is it just a success story of a black woman who's made it in the white man's world of network television, though she's done that, too. At 19, she was anchoring the news in Nashville—the first woman, the first black. She worked for seven years in Baltimore, first paying her dues as a TV street reporter, "hating every minute of it," especially when she was required to ask a woman who'd just lost her children and her house in a fire how she felt. (When she didn't have the heart to do that piece, her boss told her to get it or lose her job. She came back to the studio with the story and, on the air live, apologized for it.) She did everything she was told, including trying to remake herself. "They told me my nose was too wide, my hair too thick and long, and they sent me to a place in New York to get my first perm. I felt the lotion burning my skull, and I kept saying, 'Excuse me, this is beginning to burn a little.' They kept saying, 'Oh, just a few more minutes.'" Within a week all her hair had fallen out. "You learn a lot about yourself when you're bald," she says now.

Nor is it even a rags-to-riches tale, though her dazzling condominium apartment (marble floors, four baths, including one with a gold swan as the tub faucet and another with adjoining sauna) is a glamorous world apart from the Milwaukee housing project where she spent part of her childhood. "I don't think of myself as a poor deprived ghetto girl who made good," she declares. "I think of myself as somebody who from an early age knew I was responsible for myself, and I *had* to make good."

Knowing did not always mean doing, though. Which is why a profile of Oprah Winfrey is, mostly, a look at a woman in process.

■ **Warming Up: Journal Exercises** The following exercises will help you practice investigative writing. Read all of the following exercises and then, in your journal, write on the three that interest you most. One of these exercises may suggest an idea for your investigating essay.

1. Skim through your journal entries from the observing or remembering chapters. Is there some experience, memory, or observation that you could investigate by doing additional reading or interviewing? Choose one subject and list the *questions* that your investigation would answer.

2. Start a "curiosity" list. Make a list of subjects you are interested in and would like to know more about.

3. Page through the notebooks and texts from another course you are currently taking. What subjects mentioned in class or referred to in the text might you investigate? Make a list of topics for investigation that would help you in that course. During that class, jot down any other suggestions that occur to you. While the topics should not be topics for essays already assigned in that course, they could relate to relevant background reading.

4. An editor for the college newspaper has asked you to report on typical student activities on campus using your own activities during one calendar week from the school year. Select a recent week and write a summary of your activities.

5. Find a recent issue of a magazine you like to read—*Time, Science Digest, Ebony, Newsweek, Sports Illustrated, Ms., Rolling Stone, Playboy, Glamour, Jet, New Yorker*, and so forth. Your purpose is to determine current trends in magazine advertising. Using only the full-page ads as your subject, collect at least three ads and take notes on their important features: use of color, design, personalities, sex appeal, slogans, technology, or whatever else recurs frequently. What conclusions can you draw from your investigations?

6. Next semester, you will be taking a course in your major field, but you aren't sure which professor you should pick. To investigate the differences among the teachers, interview several students who have taken this course from different professors. Prepare questions that encourage factual responses: How many papers or tests does the teacher require? What is the grade distribution? What textbook was required? What was the reading or homework load? What were typical lecture topics? Was the teacher available outside of class?

7. As a member of the student governing board, your job is to solicit student opinions about some aspect of campus life that needs improving. Choose a subject such as dorms, classes, the library, parking, student clubs, the film or fine art series, or recreational opportunities. Then choose a question to focus your investigation and write a one-page questionnaire that you might distribute to students. (See the section on writing questionnaires in this chapter.)

8. Watch an investigative news show such as *60 Minutes* or *Nightline*, taking notes about the interviewer's techniques. Is there a sequence to the questions—say, from gentle and polite to critical or controversial? What information does the interviewer have *before* the interview? Can you tell which questions are planned or scripted and which are spontaneous? After taking notes on a show, explain what you think are the *three* most important tips for successful interviewing.

9. Interview a classmate for a 200- to 250-word "personality profile." Your object is to profile this person and *one* of his or her major interests. First, in your daybook, prepare questions you need to ask for biographical information. Then, in an eight- to ten-minute interview, ask questions about the person and about several topics from that person's "authority" list. After the interview, take two or three minutes to review your notes. At home, write up the results of your interview, which will appear in your local or campus newspaper.

The following programs from *Nightline* in the *Video Library* offer particularly good examples of interview techniques: "Lyme Disease," "Political Correctness," "Crime and Punishment."

Investigating: Professional Writing

The Triumph of the Wheel

LEWIS GROSSBERGER

In this excerpt from an investigative piece that appeared in a 1986 issue of Rolling Stone *magazine, freelance writer Lewis Grossberger focuses on one question: Why has* Wheel of Fortune, *a television game show, become so popular that it has achieved virtual cult status? In seeking an answer to this question, he considers several possibilities: Is it just an*

WRITE TO LEARN

Prereading journal assignments are effective write-to-learn activities. The day before assigning the Grossberger article, ask students to write for five minutes about their favorite television programs. Ask them to *explain why* they watch a given show—and why they think others like it. A brief discussion of why these shows are popular will set the stage for their own reading of the Grossberger essay.

entertaining family game? Is its popularity due to Vanna White's skill in turning letters? Is its popularity a reflection of American cultural values? In the process of his investigation, Grossberger researches articles about the show's popularity, observes how Wheel of Fortune *works, and interviews the show's key personalities.*

The first time I saw *Wheel of Fortune*, I thought it was a vapid piece of fluff that could appeal only to brain-dead TV zombies. Five minutes of this tedious dreck was all it took to waft me sleepward. **(1)**

But the second time my reaction was different. The second time I realized—having been assigned meantime to write an article on the show that would bring a much-needed fee—that *Wheel of Fortune* was, in fact, a fascinating, deeply significant national phenomenon, the comprehension of which was essential to any proper understanding of our era. **(2)**

Thank God I'm open-minded. **(3)**

Soon I was wafting westward on an urgent sociophilosophical inquiry, clutching an envelope fat with press clippings that further impressed upon me the importance of my subject. *The Washington Post's* TV critic said *Wheel* is watched by 42 million people a day. *Time* said *Wheel* is the highest-rated syndicated series in television history. *The New York Times* said *Wheel* is so popular it has become a dominant factor in TV scheduling, sometimes wreaking havoc with local and network news. *People* said that Vanna White has blond hair, weighs 107, measures 36-23-33 and adores greasy hamburgers from White Castle. **(4)**

Vanna White is the hostess on *Wheel of Fortune*, which should not be confused with the master of ceremonies, who is Pat Sajak, although he is not called the MC but the host. Despite the fact that Vanna's function is mainly decorative and that she is rarely permitted to utter more than a parting "bye," she has become, *People* assured me, a bigger cult sensation than Paul Shaffer, Max Headroom or even Willard Scott. **(5)**

The only thing the press failed to tell me was *why*. **(6)**

Why a silly game show based on a simple children's spelling game and a cheezy carnival wheel so captivates the mightiest nation on earth. Now here was a journalistic challenge worthy of Murrow, of Woodward and Bernstein, perhaps even of the great Geraldo Rivera. Immune to the show's mysterious allure, I could operate with scientific detachment. By God, I would take up the gauntlet. I would find out why—or doze off trying. **(7)**

"I swear on the grave of every game-show host who ever lived that I have no idea," said Pat Sajak. **(8)**

Pat Sajak is overqualified for his job in that he is capable of wit. A former TV weatherman, he sounds a little like Bob Newhart and looks like . . . well, if Dick Clark went through that teleportation gizmo from

The Fly and this time a chipmunk sneaked in, out would come Pat Sajak. **(9)**

I talked with Pat Sajak in his dressing room and found him a personable and modest man who readily admits that game-show hosting "is kind of a dopey way to make a living." I talked as rapidly as possible. When I arrived at the NBC studios in fabled Burbank, the publicity lady who collected me said that the staff would be taping five half-hour shows that night and that I could examine Pat and Vanna only during the fifteen-to-twenty minute breaks between shows. She was very apologetic, but, you know, everyone wants them, it's so exhausting, we have to protect them. I groused a bit—journalistic reflex—but, in truth, it didn't matter. Both host and hostess had been asked to explain the *why* before. They never could. **(10)**

"I mean, I know why it's successful," said Pat. "It's an easy game to play—you know, the people at home, unless you're a total moron, can generally solve the puzzles ahead of the people in the studio, so you feel kind of superior. It's a compelling game. You walk by the set and the puzzle's on and you tend to play along. But that just explains why it's a successful game show. Why it has gone beyond success to become—I don't know—part of the pop culture, I haven't the foggiest idea. I don't think anyone knows." **(11)**

I assured him that I would know. Soon. For that was my quest. My Grail. He responded politely enough, but I could see he was skeptical. It seemed like we'd been talking only a few minutes when a pounding on the door commenced, and a voice demanded Pat's presence, and he went forth to hostify. **(12)**

The *Wheel of Fortune* set looks like that of most Eighties game shows, decorated in feel-good Vegas Gaudy with bright splashes of color, flashing lights and revolving mounds of, as the announcer usually describes them, "fantastic prizes, fabulous and exciting merchandise." The studio audience of close to 200 well-behaved androids was stashed safely out of the way behind a sideline array of cameras, electronic gear, crew and staff. **(13)**

The actual gaming consists of a word puzzle and, naturally, a wheel. Large, multicolored, divided into slim wedges, each marked with a different dollar amount, the wheel is set horizontally in front of the three contestants, so they can lean forward and spin it. By doing so, they may accumulate a dollar account to be later spent on prizes. **(14)**

Between twirls, they take whacks at the word puzzle, which is basically that old childhood chestnut, hangman. The puzzle is mounted on a big vertical display board on a platform that's hauled on and off the set by crewmen at alarming speeds, usually with the courageous Vanna aboard. A display of blank tiles tells the contestants how many words and

CRITICAL READING

Connect critical-reading activities to the student's own writing. For example, ask groups of two or three students to answer Question 2 following this essay. At the board, summarize the groups' findings. Then have group members interview each other about their topics. What interviews, surveys, or articles from the library might each writer use for his or her own essay?

letters there are in a mystery phrase. As the contestants guess at the letters and Vanna rushes purposefully about, uncovering those correctly called out, the mystery phrase (usually something as banal as "walking on air" or "curiosity killed the cat") gradually emerges until someone identifies it. The winner then may go shopping among the pricetagged prizes until his or her account is exhausted. At the end of the proceedings, the champion tackles a bonus-round puzzle for a grand prize. **(15)**

During one break I was taken to meet the hostess. Vanna was in her dressing room, snacking from a take-out dish and wearing a snappy off-the-shoulder number. (She changes costume and hairdo for each show.) She was very energetic and cheerful and was able to maintain, under close interrogation, not only that Vanna White was her real name but also that she had known four other Vannas while growing up in South Carolina. **(16)**

A small-town girl, Vanna, who is not twenty-nine, drove to Hollywood in a U-Haul truck six years ago, because it was a childhood dream. Hollywood, not trucks. After landing some bit parts in movies, she heard that *Wheel of Fortune* needed a new hostess, and she beat out 200 other young women, even though in her final on-air audition she was so nervous her knees shook and she couldn't talk. Fortunately, speech was not a job qualification. **(17)**

Laboring under the cloud of bimbosity imposed by the alternately fawning and smirking media, Vanna told me what she always tells interviewers: "It's a lot harder than it looks. It really is." **(18)**

It seemed to me the wrong tactic. Were I her media adviser, I'd counsel this approach: "Hey, I look great, I walk sexy. For this they pay me a hundred big ones and put me on the cover of *People*. I should turn them down? Is it my fault I live in a society that accentuates superficial values? **(19)**

Too soon came the inevitable pounding, and Vanna vanished, leaving me back on the set, watching a woman named Ruth win a Toyota by guessing "League of Women Voters." I talked to a contestant from Fresno named Bill. Bill told me that his family watches *Wheel of Fortune* all the time and that he was so good at it his wife got after him to become a contestant. He did. But he hadn't won a Toyota, and he seemed a little tense. **(20)**

I was not to meet *Wheel*'s biggest winner. Who is that? Why, Merv Griffin. Yes, the same Merv Griffin who has spent the last twenty-three years demonstrating what Johnny Carson would be like without jokes. Merv always did seem a bit dazed, as though his mind were on something else. Now we know what. Puzzles. It was Merv who invented *Wheel of Fortune*, hired Pat Sajak and Vanna White and still approves every single puzzle. It was Merv who recently sold Merv Griffin Enterprises, which produces *Wheel* (not to mention *Jeopardy* and *Dance Fever*) to Coca-Cola for—my fingers go numb as I type this—a reported $250 million. According to Tom Shales, TV critic for *The Washington Post,* Merv was rumored to have run around his office waving his quarter-of-a-billion-dollar check in the air, joking that he couldn't find anyone to cash it. **(21)**

Puzzles. All this from puzzles. The man is a lifelong puzzle junkie. "You would think," said Sajak, "that a man who's worth $84 billion, or whatever he is, would have better things to do than make up puzzles—but he does. If you have lunch with Merv, the waiter comes over and says, 'May I take your order?' and Merv goes, 'Ooo! "May I take your order?" What a great puzzle!' and he writes it down." **(22)**

People, we underestimated Merv Griffin. We dismissed him as some kind of welfare agency for the Gabor sisters. But Merv figured out what America wanted, and he provided it. And became very, very rich. Much too rich to talk to the likes of me. But Nancy Jones, *Wheel's* producer, a woman who actually has puzzle meetings with Merv, did. Her take on *why* was family. "It's a show the whole family can enjoy. Anybody from six to a hundred can watch *Wheel of Fortune.* They're gonna understand what's going on. You know, there are kids in college now that learned their ABC's by watching *Wheel.*" Interesting, I thought, but not convincing. Not incisively all-encompassing. After all, there are plenty of family shows that don't have 42 million viewers. **(23)**

If stats like 42 million or quarter of a billion haven't sufficiently defined the scope of *Wheel's* triumph for you, surely Pat Sajak's parking spot will. It was one away from Johnny Carson's. Now *that's* success. I discovered this when Pat gave me a lift back to my hotel, a nice gesture. But he voiced a depressing vision. "This could literally be a show that is never canceled," he said. "You know, my grandkid will be up there, spinning the wheel, saying silly things and putting on hair spray." **(24)**

Considerably sobered, I retired and the next morning flew away. I'd already spent an evening on this investigation—in my view more than enough. Enroute to the airport, a chatty cabby pointed out an evocative sight: a new, exclusive real-estate development on a hill where, he said, the houses start at $1 million. The hill had previously served as a garbage dump, and the driver indicated a pumping station built to clear away the methane gas constantly seeping forth. So scarce is land in L.A. there had been no problem finding wealthy people to reside on top of Old Stinky. **(25)**

Soon afterward I was on the plane, thinking about *Wheel of Fortune,* which, as always, acted as a soporific. I dreamed of the lovely Vanna. She's in a terrific gold lamé jump suit, and she's starring in a big-budget disaster movie (a silent, oddly) about a gassy mountain threatening to explode and bury a nervous populace neck deep in putrid lava. Desperately trying to avert panic, Mayor Merv announces that the mountain, with its shining edifices concealing a rotten nether world, is merely a metaphor for an overly materialistic society, but then he whispers to me that only I can save the day—if I can complete this common, everyday phrase:

V__C__R__ __ __ S THR__LLS

Then Pat Sajak's grandkid spins the wheel. The pointer falls on BANKRUPT, and Swill Hill erupts, burying me neck deep in lethal sludge. I woke high over the Jersey swamps, and I had the answer. I knew *why*. **(26)**

Vicariousness. *Wheel of Fortune* creates the illusion for the hard-working, treadmill-trotting Middle American yearner that he or she is in the big game. Viewers don't exactly identify with the contestants; they *become* the contestants. **(27)**

Look at the elements of the show. **(28)**

The Players: *Wheel* contestants are ordinary folk who serve as the viewers' surrogates. In the whoopee-cushion Seventies, game-show contestants screamed, bounced and wet themselves, but in the we-mean-business Eighties, Americans are cooler and less likely to appear in public dressed as yams. *Wheel* subtly de-emphasizes its contestants, who seem interchangeable. Pat introduces these undemonstrative, low-profile types with the briefest possible questioning, then the camera quickly moves off them and zooms in on the game. With the contestants relegated to the background, the viewer can put himself in their place and play. In your fantasy, you are the star. **(29)**

The Game: Both games promise easy success, one through luck, the other skill. The wheel—hypnotic, alluring, symbolic of nearly everything—is luckier than a roulette wheel, since it can yield only two bad outcomes: BANKRUPT or LOSE A TURN. Any other spin wins. Nice odds. The word puzzle is simple but compelling—it gets easier as you play, because more letters fill in. As Pat Sajak noted, viewers often solve the puzzle before contestants. With the whole family watching, someone at home is almost bound to. The result: You feel happy, excited, superior. You're chalking up wins. You're on a roll. **(30)**

The Payoff: During play, the wheel-whirling contestants (and, by extension, the viewers) are given credit. A nice touch. Who doesn't love credit? It's like betting on someone else's tab. And when you win, you don't win mere cash or some preordained prize. You go *shopping*! A brilliant touch. Shopping may be the ultimate thrill in this commodity-crazed era, an actual addiction for some. And it doesn't hurt *Wheel* in the yuppie department, either. Merv himself once said, "It's like being let loose on Rodeo Drive." As the winner shops, the camera lovingly roves around the prize showcase, as though the viewers' own eyeballs have been let loose amid the VCRs, Isuzu pickups, Tahitian vacations and ceramic Dalmations. *Wheel*'s ambiance blends the organized excitement of the casino with the primal pull of the department store. **(31)**

The Cast: Game-show hosts are permitters and forgivers. Their benign presence signals that it's okay to indulge your greed, just in case some shred of conscience or old-fashioned values intrudes to make you feel guilty for craving wealth without work. Pat Sajak is today's kind of authority figure: casual, low-key, jocular, even a bit irreverent. Dignified and well dressed, he could be a yuppie cleric, lawyer or doctor. He could switch jobs with Ronald Reagan and little would change. **(32)**

And Vanna? Pat Sajak likes to say that Vanna's silence gives her a mysterious air. But there isn't any mystery. Her personality shines through without benefit of speech. She's a *cheerleader.* Your own personal cheerleader. Her most vital function is not really her letter turning (artistic though it is) but her clapping! She is forever clapping for the contestants (all of them—Vanna is impartial). When I asked if she'd been a cheerleader in high school, she said, "Of course. Who would have ever thought I'd still be a cheerleader?" **(33)**

And that's *why.* Now you know. Let me just add, before taking a well-deserved nap, that I doubt that Merv and his minions set out to design *Wheel of Fortune* around the Big V Principle or analyzed the economy. I think they just happened, by instinct, experience—and good luck—to hit on a formula that would make it the state-of-the-art Eighties game show. A formula that sucks the viewer through the screen and into that dazzling dreamscape—Vanna's Nirvana—where he is transformed from a nullity, a hapless anonymous bozo, a nobody from nowhere, to the only being now worth being: a Winner. Someone possessed of wealth, luck and, maybe more important, television exposure. Someone, in short, who finally exists. You know, a big wheel. **(34)**

Vocabulary

In your journal, write the meanings of the following words:

- *vapid* piece of fluff (1)
- tedious *dreck* (1)
- take up the *gauntlet* (7)
- My *Grail* (12)
- well-behaved *androids* (13)
- acted as a *soporific* (26)
- *putrid* lava (26)
- rotten *nether* world (26)
- *vicariousness* (27)

Teaching Tip

In addition to increasing students' "word power," vocabulary practice can help students learn to read critically. Students should see how Grossberger's wide-ranging vocabulary helps to create both his satiric tone ("vapid," "dreck," "soporific," "primal") and the mock-heroic dimensions of his investigation ("Grail," "gauntlet," "androids," "nether," "minions," "Nirvana").

- viewers' *surrogates* (29)
- *Wheel's ambiance* (31)
- *primal* pull (31)
- Merv and his *minions* (34)
- Vanna's *Nirvana* (34)

Questions for Writing and Discussion

1. Grossberg has several *purposes* in this article: *entertaining* readers; *informing* readers about Pat Sajak, Vanna White, the game show, and its reception in the media; and *explaining* why the show is so popular. Based on your own reading, which of these purposes did he accomplish most effectively? Least effectively? Explain.

2. In collecting the information for this article, Grossberger used several kinds of sources: summaries or quotations from written material, information and quotations from interviews, and observations of people, places, and events. Find one example of each kind of source.

3. Reread the article. Then give paragraph numbers identifying the following parts of the essay (each part may have several paragraph numbers):

Lead-in, catching the reader's interest	(______)
Main idea, thesis, or focus of the investigation	(______)
Narrative of writer's investigative steps	(______)
Profile of key people	(______)
Observation of the set and the game	(______)
Analysis of the elements of the show	(______)
Conclusion	(______)

4. As a freelance journalist, Grossberger creates a role, or persona, as he writes. Which specific passages most clearly reveal his real or assumed personality? Explain.

5. As the editor of *TV Guide*, you want to use an excerpt from Grossberger's article. To do so, you will need to cut this piece by two thirds and adapt it for the *TV Guide* audience. As you cut sections, consider your audience. How are readers of *TV Guide* likely to be different from the readers of *Rolling Stone*? (If you are not familiar with these magazines, look at current issues in your library.) What parts of this article will be most appealing to *TV Guide* readers?

THE HOMELESS AND THEIR CHILDREN

JONATHAN KOZOL

In his most famous book, Illiterate America *(1985), Jonathan Kozol says that because more than one-third of America's adults are at least partially illiterate, we should organize a massive government and volunteer army to liberate people imprisoned by illiteracy. In "The Homeless and Their Children," taken from* Rachel and Her Children *(1988), Kozol investigates individual cases of poverty in a New York City welfare hotel. He uses his own observations and interview transcripts to demonstrate vividly the connection between illiteracy and poverty. However, instead of arguing indignantly for literacy programs to save the lives of the poor and illiterate, Kozol simply reports the case of a single illiterate woman trying to raise her four children. The woman he calls Laura cannot decipher labels on products at the grocery store, cannot read notices from the welfare office, and cannot understand letters from the hospital warning of her children's lead poisoning.*

The Martinique Hotel, at Sixth Avenue and Thirty-second Street, is one of the largest hotels for homeless people in New York City. When I visited it, in December of 1985, nearly four hundred homeless families, including some twelve hundred children, were lodged in the hotel, by arrangement with the city's Human Resources Administration. One of the residents I spoke to at some length was an energetic, intelligent woman I'll call Kim. During one of our conversations, she mentioned a woman on the seventh floor who had seemingly begun to find her situation intolerable. Kim described this woman as "a broken stick," and offered to arrange for us to meet. **(1)**

The woman—I will call her Laura, but her name, certain other names, and certain details have been changed—is so fragile that I find it hard to start a conversation when we are introduced, a few nights later. Before I begin, she asks if I will read her a letter from the hospital. The oldest of her four children, a seven-year-old boy named Matthew, has been sick for several weeks. He was tested for lead poisoning in November, and the letter she hands me, from Roosevelt Hospital, says that the child has a dangerous lead level. She is told to bring him back for treatment. She received the letter some weeks ago. It has been buried in a pile of other documents that she cannot read. **(2)**

Although Laura cannot read, she knows enough about the dangers of lead to grasp the darker implications of this information. The crumbling plaster in the Martinique Hotel is covered with sweet-tasting paint, and children eat or chew chips of the paint as it flakes off the walls. Some of

WRITE TO LEARN

When you assign this essay (but before you discuss it), ask students to write a five-minute prereading journal entry describing an experience that they have had with a homeless person. Then have student volunteers read their journal entries. During the discussion, have students think about the predicament of the homeless, but also call attention to the tone of their accounts. Were students' entries objective reports or were they emotional? A brief discussion will orient students for their reading and discussion of Kozol's essay.

CRITICAL READING

An *ethnographer* is an investigator who explores and interprets a culture or community by observing and recording behavior in detail over an extended time. The ethnographer focuses more on presenting the complexity of culture and experience than on answering predetermined questions or proving hypotheses. Using this definition, ask students to compare the investigative styles of Kozol and Grossberger. Which essay is more ethnographic? Why? Compared to more formal research based on hypotheses, written research, data, and statistics, what are the advantages and/or disadvantages of an ethnographic method? If students have ideas or drafts for their own investigative essays, discuss which topics are best suited for an ethnographic approach.

the paint contains lead. Children with lead poisoning may suffer loss of coordination or undergo convulsions. The consequences of lead poisoning may be temporary or long-lasting. They may appear at once or not for several years. This final point is what instills so much uneasiness; even months of observation cannot calm a parent's fear. **(3)**

Lead poisoning, then, is Laura's first concern, but she has other problems. The bathroom plumbing has overflowed and left a pool of sewage on the floor. A radiator valve is broken, and every now and then releases a spray of scalding steam at the eye level of a child. A crib provided by the hotel appears to be unstable. A screw that holds two of its sides together is missing. When I test the crib with my hand, it starts to sway. There are four beds in the room, and they are dangerous, too. They have metal frames with unprotected corners, and the mattresses do not fit the frames; at one corner or another, metal is exposed. If a child has the energy or the playfulness to jump or turn a somersault or wrestle with a friend, and if he falls and strikes his head against the metal corner, the consequences can be serious. The week before, a child on the fourteenth floor fell in just this way, cut his forehead, and required stitches. Most of these matters have been brought to the attention of the hotel management; in Laura's case, complaints have brought no visible results. **(4)**

All of this would be enough to make life difficult for an illiterate young woman in New York, but Laura has one other urgent matter on her hands. It appears that she has failed to answer a request for information from her welfare office, and, for reasons that she doesn't understand, she did not receive her benefits this week. The timing is bad; it's a weekend. The city operates a crisis center in the Martinique, where residents can go for food and other help, but today the crisis center is not open, so there's nobody around to tide her over with emergency supplies. Laura's children have been eating cheese and bread and peanut butter for two days. "Those on welfare," the Community Service Society of New York said in a report published in 1984, may be suddenly removed from welfare rolls "for reasons unrelated to their actual need," or even to eligibility standards. Welfare workers in New York City call this practice "churning." Laura and her children are being churned. **(5)**

The room is lighted by fluorescent tubes in a ceiling fixture. They cast a stark light on four walls of greenish paint smeared over with sludge draining from someone's plumbing on the floor above. In the room are two boys with dark and hollowed eyes and an infant girl. A third boy is outside and joins us later. The children have the washed-out look of the children Walker Evans photographed for "Let Us Now Praise Famous Men." Besides the four beds and the crib, the room contains two chairs, a refrigerator, and a television set, which doesn't work. A metal hanger serves as an antenna, but there is no picture on the screen.

Instead, there is a storm of falling flakes and unclear lines. I wonder why Laura keeps it on. There are no table lamps to soften the fluorescent glare, no books, no decorations. Laura tells me that her father is of Panamanian birth but that she went to school in New York City. Spanish is her first language. I don't speak Spanish well. We talk in English. **(6)**

"I cannot read," Laura says. "I buy the New York *Post* to read the pictures. In the grocery, I know what to buy because I see the pictures." **(7)**

What of no-name products—generic brands, whose labels have no pictures but which could save her a great deal of money? **(8)**

"If there are no pictures, I don't buy it," she says. "I want to buy pancakes, I ask the lady, 'Where's the pancakes?' So they tell me." **(9)**

She points to the boys and says, "He's two. He's five. Matthew's seven. My daughter is four months. She has this rash." She shows me ugly skin eruptions on the baby's neck and jaw. "The carpets, they was filthy from the stuff, the leaks that come down on the wall. All my kids have rashes, but the worst she has it. There was pus all over. Somewhere here I have a letter from the nurse." She shuffles around but cannot find the letter. "She got something underneath the skin. Something that bites. The only way you can get rid of it is with a cream." **(10)**

She finds the letter. The little girl has scabies. **(11)**

Laura continues, "I have been living here two years. Before I came here, I was in a house we had to leave. There was rats. Big ones, they crawl on us. The rats, they come at night. They come into our house, run over my son's legs. The windows were broken. It was winter. Snow, it used to come inside. My mother lived with us before. Now she's staying at my grandma's house. My grandma's dying in the bed. She's sixty-five. My mother comes here once a week to do the groceries. Tomorrow she comes. Then she goes back to help my grandma. **(12)**

"I know my name, and I can write my name, my children's names. To read, I cannot do it. Medicines, I don't know the instructions. I was living here when I was pregnant with Corinne. No, I didn't see no doctor. I was hungry. What I ate was rice and beans, potato chips and soda. Up to now this week we don't have food. People ask me, 'Can you help? Do you got this? Do you got that?' I don't like to tell them no. If I have something, I give it. This week, I don't got. I can read baby books—like that, a little bit. If I could read, I would read newspapers. I would like to know what's going on. Matthew, he tells me I am stupid. 'You can't read.' You know, because he wants to read. He don't understand what something is. I tell him, 'I don't know it. I don't understand.' People laugh. You feel embarrassed. On the street. Or in the store." She weeps. "There's nothing here." **(13)**

Laura sweeps one hand in a wide arc, but I can't tell whether she means the gesture to take in the room or something more. Then she

DIVERSITY ISSUES

Kozol's report on Laura and her children dramatizes the lives of people on the margin. Several forces work to keep Laura powerless: She is illiterate; she is a woman; she is Hispanic; and she lives in the welfare underculture. To sensitize students to her problems, ask them to consider the sources of Laura's problems one at a time. If Laura were literate, how might she improve her siteuation? How would other people treat her differently? If she were a man, what options would open? If she were white? If she were not on welfare?

makes her meaning clear: "Everything I had, they put it on the sidewalk when I was evicted. I don't know if that's the law. Things like that—what is the law, what isn't? I can't read it, so I didn't understand. I lost everything I had. I sign papers. Somebody could come and take my children. They could come. 'Sign this. Sign that.' I don't know what it says. Adoption papers—I don't know. This here paper that I got I couldn't understand." **(14)**

She hands me another letter. This one is from the management of the hotel: "This notice is to inform you that your rent is due today. I would appreciate your cooperation in seeing to it that you go to your center today." Another form that she hands me asks her to fill out the names and the ages of her children. **(15)**

"Papers, documents—people give it to me. I don't know it: I don't understand." She pauses, and then says, "I'm a Catholic. Yes—I go two weeks ago to church. This lady say they have these little books that learn me how to spell. You see the letters. Put them together. I would like to read. I go to St. Francis' Church. Go inside and kneel—I pray. I don't talk to the priest. I done so many things—you know, bad things. I buy a bottle of wine. A bottle of beer. That costs a dollar. I don't want to say to God. I get a hundred and seventy-three dollars restaurant allowance. With that money I buy clothes. Food stamps, I get two hundred dollars. That's for groceries. Subway tokens I take out ten dollars. Washing machine, I do downstairs. Twenty-five dollars to dry and wash. Five dollars to buy soap. Thirty dollars twice a month." **(16)**

Another woman at the Martinique calculates her laundry costs at my request, and they come out to nearly the same figure. These may be the standard rates for a midtown site. The difficulty of getting out and traveling to find lower prices, whether for laundromats or for groceries, cannot be overstated. Families at the Martinique are trapped in a commercial district. **(17)**

I ask Laura who stays with the children when she does her chores. **(18)**

"My mother keeps the children when I do the wash," she replies. "If she can't, I ask somebody on the floor. 'Give me three dollars. I watch your kids.' For free? Nothing. Everything for money. Everybody's poor." **(19)**

Extending a hand, she says, "This is the radiator. Something's wrong." She shows me where the steam sprays out. I test it with my hand. "Sometimes it stops. The children get too close. Then it starts—like that! Leak is coming from upstairs down." I see the dark muck on the wall. "The window is broke. Lights broke." She points to the fluorescent tubes. They flicker on and off. "I ask them, 'Please, why don't you give me ordinary lights?' They don't do nothing. So it been two weeks. I go downstairs. They say they coming up. They never come. So I complain again. Mr. Tuccelli—Salvatore Tuccelli, the manager of the Martinique—said to come here to his office. Desks and decorations and a lot of pictures. It's above the lobby. So the manager was there. Mr. Tuccelli sat back in his chair. He had a gun. He had it here under his waist. You know, under his belt. I said, 'Don't show it to me if you isn't going to use it.' I can't tell what kind of gun it was. He had it in his waist. 'You are showing me the gun so I will be afraid.' If he was only going to show it, I would not be scared. If he's going to use it, I get scared. **(20)**

"So he says, 'You people bring us trouble.' I said, 'Why you give my son lead poison and you didn't care? My child is lead-poisoned.' He said, 'I don't want to hear of this again.' What I answer him is this: 'Listen. People like you live in nice apartments. You got a home. You got TV. You got a family. You got children in a school that learn them. They don't got lead poison.' **(21)**

"I don't know the reason for the guards. They let the junkies into the hotel. When my mother comes, I have to sign. If it's a family living good, they make it hard. If it's the drug dealers, they come in. Why they let the junkies in but keep away your mother? The guards, you see them taking women in the corner. You go down twelve-thirty in the night, they're in the corner with the girls. This is true. I seen it." **(22)**

She continues, "How I know about the lead is this: Matthew sits there and he reaches his fingers in the plaster and he put it in his mouth. So I ask him, 'Was you eating it?' He says, 'Don't hit me. Yes, I was.' So then I took him to the clinic and they took the blood. I don't know if something happen to him later on. I don't know if it affects him. When he's older . . . " **(23)**

I ask Laura why she goes to church. **(24)**

"I figure: Go to church. Pray God. Ask Him to help. I go on my knees. I ask Him from my heart. 'Jesus Christ, come help me, please. Why do you leave me here?' When I'm lying down at night, I ask, 'Why people got to live like this?' On the street, the people stare at you when you go out of the hotel. People look. They think, I wonder how they live in there. Sometimes I walk out this door. Garbage all over in the stairs. When it's hot, a lot of bugs around the trash. Sometimes there are fires in the trash. I got no fire escape. You have to get out through the hall. I got no sprinkler. Smoke detector doesn't work. When I cook and food is burning, it don't ring. If I smoke, it starts to ring. I look up. I say, 'Why you don't work? When I need you, you don't work. I'm gonna knock you down.' I did!" She laughs. **(25)**

There is a sprinkler system in the corridor. In 1987, the hotel management informed residents that the fire-alarm system was "inoperable." **(26)**

I ask Laura if the older children are enrolled in school. Nodding at Michael, her middle son, she says, "This one doesn't go to school. He's five. I need to call tomorrow. Get a quarter. Then you get some papers. Then you got to sign those papers. Then he can start school. **(27)**

"For this room I pay fifteen hundred dollars for two weeks. I don't pay. The welfare pays. I got to go and get it." The room, although it is undivided, was originally a two-room suite and is being rented at the two-room rate. "They send me this. I'm suppose to sign. I don't know what it is. Lots of things you suppose to sign. I sign it but I don't know what it is." **(28)**

While we are talking, Matthew comes in and sits beside his mother. He lowers his eyes when I shake his hand. **(29)**

Laura goes on, "Looking for a house, I got to do it." She explains that she's required to give evidence that she is searching for a place to live. "I can't read, so I can't use the paper. I get dressed. I put my makeup on. If I go like this, they look afraid. They say, 'They going to destroy the house!' You got to dress the children and look nice. Owners don't want homeless. Don't want welfare. Don't want kids. What I think? If they pay one thousand and five hundred dollars every two weeks, why not pay five hundred dollars for a good apartment?" **(30)**

She hands me another paper. "Can you tell me what is this?" **(31)**

It's a second letter from the hospital, telling her to bring her son for treatment. **(32)**

She says, "Every day, my son this week, last week was vomiting. Every time he eat his food, he throw it right back out. I got to take him to the clinic. **(33)**

"Christmas, they don't got. For my daughter I ask a Cabbage Patch. For my boys I ask for toys. I got them stockings." She shows me four cotton stockings tacked to the wall with nothing in them. "They say, 'Mommy, there's no toys.' I say not to worry. 'You are going to get something.' But they don't. They don't get nothing. I could not afford. No, this isn't my TV. Somebody lended it to me. Christmas tree I can't afford. Christmas I don't spend it happy. I am thinking of the kids. What we do on Christmas is we spend it laying on the bed. If I go outside, I feel a little better. When I'm here, I see those walls, the bed, and I feel sad. If I had my own apartment, maybe there would be another room. Somewhere to walk. Walk back and forth." **(34)**

I ask her, "How do you relax?" **(35)**

"If I want to rest, relax, I turn out the light and lie down on the bed," she says. "When I met his father, I was seventeen." She says she knew him before she was homeless, when she lived in Brooklyn with her mother. He was working at a pizza parlor near her mother's home. "One night, he bought me liquor. I had never tasted. So he took me to this hallway. Then my mother say that what I did is wrong. So I say that I already did it. So you have to live with what you did. I had the baby. No. I did not want to have abortion. The baby's father I still see. When he has a job, he brings me food. In the summer, he worked in a flower store. He would bring me flowers. Now he don't have any job. So he don't bring me flowers." **(36)**

She sweeps her hand in a broad arc and says again, "Nothing here. I feel embarrassed for the room. Flowers, things like that, you don't got. Pretty things you don't got. Nothing like that. No." **(37)**

In the window is a spindly geranium plant. It has no flowers, but some of the leaves are green. Before I go, we stand beside the window. Blowing snow hits the panes and blurs the dirt. **(38)**

"Some of the rooms high up, they got a view," Laura says. "You see the Empire State." **(39)**

I've noticed this—seen the building from a window. It towers high above the Martinique. **(40)**

"I talk to this plant. I tell him, 'Grow! Give me one flower!' He don't do it." Then, in an afterthought, "No pets. No. You don't got. Animals. They don't allow." **(41)**

It occurs to me that this is one of the few places I have been except a hospital or a reform school where there are hundreds of children and virtually no pets. A few people keep cats illegally. **(42)**

"I wish I had a dog," Laura says. "Brown dog. Something to hug." **(43)**

Vocabulary

In your journal, write the meanings of the following words:

- the darker *implications* (3)
- call this practice "*churning*" (5)
- ugly skin *eruptions* (10)
- girl has *scabies* (11)

Questions for Writing and Discussion

1. Describe your intellectual and emotional reaction to Kozol's article. What information about the lives of the poor and illiterate did you already know? What information surprised you? How did Kozol's essay make you feel about this problem?

2. The purpose of an investigative report is to give information without editorializing or arguing for or against a solution. In which paragraphs does Kozol remain most objective and unemotional? Which passages reveal Kozol's sympathy for Laura's situation? Does he avoid editorializing?

3. Reread the essay, marking those places where Laura's illiteracy causes her problems. Based on your notes, explain how her illiteracy (rather than her poverty) causes or magnifies her problems.

4. Describe the investigative techniques that Kozol probably used to write his essay. In addition to his interviews with Laura, what were his other probable sources of information?

5. According to the information provided by Kozol, what support does the welfare system provide Laura and her children? Howdoes the welfare system encourage Laura to improve her life? List three changes that you believe the welfare system should make to solve Laura's problems and make her more self-sufficient.

6. On your next trip to the grocery store, see which products would appeal to an illiterate person. List the items (and their prices) that you might buy based on the pictures on the labels. Write a paragraph describing your findings. Is Kozol correct in assuming that Laura pays too much for her groceries?

TEACHING TIP

This chapter introduces students to library and field-research skills that they can use later in Chapters 7 to 11. If students will be writing a longer research paper later in the term or year, the investigating paper can be a trial run for that more completely documented paper. If students are not writing a longer research paper, teachers may want to assign a paper focusing on summaries, interviews, personality profiles, or survey—approaches that require only minimal documentation. In either case, the assignment should clearly specify the amount and kind of documentation and research expected.

INVESTIGATING: THE WRITING PROCESS

■ **ASSIGNMENT FOR INVESTIGATING** Choose a subject to investigate: one aspect of a current social or political policy, a scientific discovery or principle, a historical event, a profile of a controversial public figure, or perhaps just an ordinary event, person, process, or place that you find interesting. Your initial purpose should be to discover or learn about your subject. Then, with a specific audience in mind, report your findings. A report presents the information that you find; it should not argue for or against any idea or plan. With the final copy of your investigative report, you must turn in photocopies of any sources you have summarized or cited, notes from your interview(s), and/or copies of questionnaires that you used.

Choosing a Subject

If one of your journal topics does not suggest a subject for your investigation, consider the following ideas. If you have a subject, go on to the collecting and shaping strategies.

- Choose some idea, principle, process, or theory discussed in a class that you are currently taking. Begin by interviewing classmates, graduate students, or a professor about how to investigate the history, development, or personalities behind this idea. With information from the interview, continue your investigation in the library, looking in appropriate magazines, books, or journals. As you read, focus your question on one *narrow* or *specific* area.
- Investigate and report on a campus or community service organization. Choose any academic, minority, cultural, or community organization. Visit the office. Interview an official. Read the organization's literature. Talk to students or community members who have used the service. Check the library for background information. Find people who are dissatisfied with or critical of the organization. Select an audience who might use this service or who might be interested in volunteering for the organization and report the relevant who, what, when, where, why and/or how information.
- At your workplace, investigate how something does or does not work, research how the business (or your part of the business) is organized, do a profile of a co-worker, or survey your customers to find out what they like best or least about your store or company.
- Write an investigation of some aspect of your favorite hobby. No matter what the subject is, you will find several magazines in the library devoted to it: fashion, cars, rock-climbing, music, cooking, fly fishing, photography, scuba diving, interior decorating, health foods, and so on. Find several magazines and browse through them. Based on what you find in the magazines, interview and/or survey other people interested in this subject. Focus your survey or interview on one specific aspect of this topic.
- Go back to your remembering essay. Do other people remember the person, place, or event? If so, interview one or more of them, either in person or on the phone. How do their recollections of the subject differ from yours? After investigating what happened from other points of view, rewrite your remembering essay to include the perspectives and memories of others.

Had I known the answer to any of these questions, I would never had needed to write.
—JOAN DIDION, ESSAYIST AND NOVELIST

Collecting

Analyze the heuristics in news reports like "Lyme Disease," "Smart Cars," or "Jack Smith's Vietnam Diary." How many of the "Wh" questions are asked and answered? How often are the classical "topics" covered?

RESOURCE NOTE

For additional ideas about rhetorical questioning, see Larson, "Discovery through Questioning: A Plan for Teaching Rhetorical Invention."

The collecting strategies discussed in Chapters 3, 4, and 5 (brainstorming, clustering, looping, mapping, sketching, reading, summarizing, taking double-entry notes) may be useful as you collect ideas. Other strategies particularly useful for investigating are suggested below. Try each of these collecting strategies for your subject.

ASKING QUESTIONS Asking the *right questions* is crucial to investigative writing. Sets of questions (often called *heuristics*) will help you narrow and focus your subject and tailor your approach to the expectations or needs of your audience. You don't know what information you need to collect until you know what questions your investigation needs to answer.

1. The "reporter's" or the familiar "Wh" questions are one basic heuristic:

Who? What? When? Where? Why?

Asking these questions of a topic ensures that you're not leaving out any crucial information. If, for example, you are investigating recreational opportunities in your city or on campus, you might ask the following questions to focus your investigation (remember to ask the *negative* version of each question, too):

- *Whom* is the recreation for?
- *Who* runs the programs?
- *Who* is excluded from the programs?
- *Who* pays for the programs?
- *What* is the program?
- *What* sports are included in the program?
- *What* sports are not included?
- *What* is the budget for these programs?
- *When* are these opportunities available or not available?
- *Where* do the activities take place?
- *Where* are they restricted?
- *Why* are these programs offered?
- *Why* are certain activities not offered?
- *Why* have activities been changed?

These questions might lead you to focus your investigation on the

Computer Tip: Collecting

Create a new file on the computer and enter the "Wh" questions or the questions derived from the classical topics. Then leave a few lines between each question so you have room to write and answer each question. Some of your answers may generate only a sentence or two, but others may lead to several sentences or paragraphs. Because these questions often relate to the shaping strategies discussed later in this chapter, you will be collecting ideas and at the same time shaping and drafting a trial version of part of your investigative essay.

scheduling, on why soccer has been excluded, or on why participants are charged a fee for one class or program but not for another.

2. The classical "topics" provide a second set of questions for an investigation.

Definition:	What is it?
Comparison:	What is it like or unlike?
Relationship:	What caused it? What are its consequences?
Testimony:	What has been said or written about it?

These questions can be used in conjunction with the reporter's questions to focus an investigation. Applied to the topic on recreational opportunities, the questions might be as follows:

Definition:	What activities exist? How can the activities be described, classified, or analyzed?
Comparison:	What are similarities to or differences from other programs?
Relationship:	What caused these programs to be offered? What causes people to use or avoid these activities? What are the consequences of these programs?
Testimony:	What do students think about these activities? What do administrators think? What have other schools done? What does research show? What proverbs or common sayings apply here?

Resource Note

For a discussion of Aristotle's *topoi*, or "topics," see Corbett, *Classical Rhetoric for the Modern Student*.

Teaching Tip

If you haven't done so already, plan a library tour to acquaint your students with their library resources. Make your tour relevant by asking students to have their topics in mind *before* going to the library. Ask each student to find and photocopy two or three sources for his or her topic. Encouraging students to work in pairs will help them find bibliographic sources and will reduce the inevitable frustration of learning a new library system.

COLLABORATIVE ACTIVITY

Investigative topics work well for collaborative writing projects. Below is one procedure for organizing collaboratively written essays. First, generate a list of investigative topics from students' brain storming or journal entries. Divide class members into groups of three according to topic interests. Each group should meet briefly during class an then again outside of class to draw up a writing plan: What is the investigative question and who will do the library research and interviews or surveys? After group members collect information and discuss the topic, each student should write his or her own draft based on the group's photocopies of sources and interview notes. The group then produces a collaboratively written final version of the essay. One grading scheme is as follows: plans for the project and photocopies of sources and notes (20 percent); each student's individual draft (50 percent); the collaboratively written final draft of the essay (30 percent).

These two sets of questions will *expand* your information, helping you collect facts, data, examples, and ideas—probably more than you can use in a short essay. Once you have all of this information, you can then *narrow* your topic.

USING THE LIBRARY Knowing how to use a library is crucial for most investigations. For this essay, you will not need to do exhaustive research on your topic, but you may need some background information, statistics, or information about current research, public opinion trends, or recent discoveries. Chapter 11, "Writing a Research Paper," will answer your research questions in more depth, but you can get information quickly in a library by using a few key sources.

- *Ask librarians for assistance.* Every library has librarians stationed at information desks, checkout counters, or reference desks whose job is to answer your questions. Be sure to ask for their advice when you need it. Because frustration is the number-one enemy of research projects, ask for assistance *early* in your investigation. The best procedure is simply to explain your project—what you intend to do and have done so far—and ask for advice or help. *There are no stupid questions in a library.*
- *Acquaint yourself with the basic sources of information in the library.* Most libraries offer group tours that familiarize their users with the location of the following:

The on-line catalogue or card catalogue
Basic references such as encyclopedias, almanacs, and dictionaries
Biographical reference sources:

Current Biography
Dictionary of American Biography
Notable American Women
Who's Who in America

Frequently used magazine or periodical indexes:

The Readers' Guide to Periodical Literature
Applied Science and Technology Index
Social Sciences and Humanities Index
The New York Times Index

Computer access systems:
Most traditional index searching can now be done on computer, whether in the main on-line computer system in the library, in the CD-ROM bases for ERIC, MLA, or DIALOGUE, or in popular newspaper and magazine systems such as INFOTRAK. Most of these systems will print out specific information about your source, give a brief abstract, or in some cases, print out the whole article. Be sure you acquaint yourself with your library computer systems.

Using Written Sources

- *Make photocopies of relevant articles.* The small amount of money you spend on copies will enable you to reread articles if necessary, quote or paraphrase from them accurately, and cite them accurately as references. (The money you spend is also excellent anti-frustration insurance, in case you return to the library stacks and discover that someone else has checked out your magazine or book.) On your photocopies, be sure to write source information: magazine or book title, author, publisher, date and place of publication, volume, and page numbers. For this investigative report, remember that you must turn in photocopies of any pages of articles or books you refer to or cite.
- *Make notes and summaries from your photocopied sources.* As you collect information from photocopied sources, jot down key facts, ideas, and direct quotations. For every note you take, record the author, title, publishing information, and page numbers. You may *paraphrase* another writer's ideas, examples, sentences, or short passages by writing them in your own words. Use *direct quotation* when words or phrases in a source are more striking than your paraphrase might be. You may edit a direct quotation by (1) deleting any irrelevant or unnecessary words or phrases by using ellipsis

TEACHING TIP

Summarizing looks easy, but many students find it difficult unless they practice. If students have not read Chapter 5, have them summarize short articles. In later classes, use their summarizing skills by having them summarize professional and student essays in this text and each other's drafts during workshops.

points (three spaced periods) to indicate the deleted words and by (2) inserting your own words in square brackets [ ] if you need to clarify a quoted passage. Otherwise, the words within the quotation marks must *accurately* reproduce the original: No altered spellings, changed words, or rephrasings are allowed.

- *Avoid plagiarism.* Use quotation marks whenever you quote more than a word or two from your source. Paraphrase in your own words rather than stringing together phrases and sentences written by someone else. Give credit for ideas, facts, and language by citing your sources. In informal investigative writing, you may simply mention the author and title of written sources, citing page numbers of direct quotations in parentheses. (All formal research papers and some investigative essays cite sources in full in a "Works Cited" section at the end. See Chapter 11, "Writing a Research Paper," for more details.)

SUMMARIZING As explained in Chapter 5, a *summary* is a concise explanation of the main and supporting ideas in a passage, report, essay, book, or speech. It is usually written in the present tense. It identifies the author and title of the source; it may refer to the context or the actual place where the study took place; it contains the passage's main ideas; and it may quote directly a few forceful or concise sentences or phrases. It will *not* usually cite the author's examples. A *paraphrase* usually expresses all the information in the passage—including examples—in your own words. Summary, paraphrase, and direct quotation often occur together as you use sources. (See Chapter 5 for more details.)

The following passage is a concise summary of Lewis Grossberger's article "The Triumph of the Wheel":

Source, author, title
Focus of article
Summary of article's main ideas

> In his *Rolling Stone* article, "The Triumph of the Wheel," Lewis Grossberger investigates why the television game show *Wheel of Fortune* has become so popular. Grossberger describes the workings of the game show, interviews the show's personalities (Pat Sajak and Vanna White) on location, describes Merv Griffin's role as producer and puzzle-maker for the show, and explains his own theory about why the show has reached the status of a "cult sensation."

Article's thesis
Summary of points that support the article's thesis

> *Wheel of Fortune* is popular, Grossberger contends, because it gives its viewers a vicarious sense of participating in the excitement of solving a puzzle and winning thousands of dollars' worth of merchandise. The show's contestants are not stars, so the viewers at home can imagine that they are the contestants. The game itself involves a simple roulette wheel and the puzzles are easy to solve, giving home viewers a sense of accomplishment and superiority.

> The selection of prizes after the contestant has solved the puzzle similarly allows viewers to shop, vicariously, with the winner. Finally the show's personalities are familiar, people-next-door types: Pat Sajak is low-key and occasionally humorous; Vanna White is the show's bouncy cheerleader. *Wheel of Fortune*, Grossberger concludes, is a state-of-the-art show that "sucks the viewer . . . into that dazzling dreamscape—Vanna's Nirvana—where he [or she] is transformed from a nullity, a hapless anonymous bozo . . . [into] the only being now worth being: a Winner."

Direct quotation from article

CITING SOURCES IN YOUR TEXT As you collect information, you should note authors, titles of books or magazines, dates of publication, publishers, and page numbers to give proper credit to your sources. For some journalistic writing, you may need to cite only the author, the title of your source, or both:

> *Time* said that *Wheel* is the highest-rated syndicated series in television history.
>
> According to Tom Shales, TV critic for *The Washington Post*, Merv was rumored to have run around his office waving his quarter-of-a-billion-dollar check in the air, joking that he couldn't find anyone to cash it.

According to the MLA (Modern Language Association) format, formal in-text citation requires that the author and page numbers be given, usually in parentheses, at the end of the sentence—for example, "(Grossberger 24–25)." If the author of the article you are citing is not known, use a shortened title—"(*Wheel* 27)."

If you refer to the author in the sentence introducing him or her, indicate just the page numbers in parentheses.

> Grossberger implies that, by and large, viewers of *Wheel of Fortune* are a bunch of bozos (28).

For additional information on formal, in-text citation, consult Chapter 11, "Writing a Research Paper."

TEACHING TIP

Ask students to examine how the authors in this chapter cite their sources. Meer refers to his authors in paragraph 3. Toufexis cites the author and title of her main source and then gives credentials for her experts. Grossberger describes several sources in paragraph 4. Kozol cites sources in paragraphs 1 and 5. Student writers Peterson and Stone refer to sources in their texts but do not cite page references (they did turn in photocopies of their sources). If you require MLA-style in-text citation, be sure to explain the requirements when you make the assignment.

INTERVIEWING After you have done some initial research, interviews are a logical next step. Remember that the more you know about the subject (and the person you're interviewing), the more productive the interview will be. In planning an interview, keep the following steps in mind.

1. Make an *appointment* with the person you wish to interview. Although you may feel hesitant or shy about calling someone for an interview, remember that most people are flattered that someone else is interested in them and wants to hear their opinions or learn about their areas of expertise.

2. Make a *list of questions*, in an appropriate *sequence*, that you can ask during the interview. The interview itself will generate additional topics, but your list will jog your memory if the interview gets off the track. Begin with relatively objective or factual questions and work your way, gradually, to the more subjective questions or controversial issues. Try to phrase your questions so that they require more than a yes or no answer.

3. Begin the interview by introducing yourself and describing your investigation. Keep *your* biases or opinions out of the questions. Be sure to *listen* carefully and ask follow-up questions: "What information do you have on that? What do the statistical studies suggest? In your opinion, do these data show any trends? What memorable experiences have you had relating to this topic?" Like a dog with a good bone, a reporter doesn't drop a topic until the meat's all gone.

4. During the interview, *take notes*, and, if appropriate, use a tape recorder to ensure accuracy. Don't hesitate to ask your interviewee to repeat or clarify a statement. Remember: People want you to get the facts right and quote them accurately. Especially if you're dong a personality profile, describe notable features of your interviewee: hair color, facial features, stature, dress, gestures, nervous habits, and details about the room or surroundings. Finally, don't forget to ask your interviewee for additional leads or sources. At the conclusion of the interview, express your thanks and ask if you can check with him or her later, if necessary, for additional details or facts.

5. Immediately after the interview, go over your notes. If you recorded the interview, listen to the tape and transcribe important responses. List other questions you may still have.

PEER RESPONSE

Before students actually give out their questionnaires or conduct their interviews, spend a few minutes in class—in small groups—having students test their interview or survey questions on each other. After group members have listened to interview questions or responded to drafts of questionnaires, ask them to give each writer some feedback: additional questions to use, questions to avoid, and clearer language for questions.

WRITING QUESTIONNAIRES Questionnaires are useful when you need to know the attitudes, preferences, or opinions of a large group of people. If you are surveying customers in your business, you may discover that 39 percent of those surveyed would prefer that your business stay open an additional hour, from 5 p.m. to 6 p.m. If you are surveying students to determine their knowledge of geography, you might discover that only 8 percent can correctly locate Beirut on a map of the Middle East. The accuracy and usefulness of a survey depend on the kinds of questions you ask, on the number of people you survey, and on the sample of people you select to respond to your questionnaire.

Open questions are easy to ask, but the answers can be difficult to interpret. For example, if you want to survey customers at a department store where you work, you might ask questions requiring a short written response:

- What is your opinion of the service provided by clerks at Macy's?
- What would make your shopping experience at Macy's more enjoyable?

While these questions may give you interesting—and often reliable—responses, the results may be difficult to tabulate. Open questions are often valuable in initial surveys because they can help you to determine specific areas or topics for further investigation.

Closed questions are more typical than open questions in surveys. They limit the responses so that you can focus on a particular topic and accurately tabulate the responses. Below are several types of closed questions:

- *Yes/No questions:* Have you shopped at Macy's in the last three months?

_____ Yes
_____ No

- *Multiple Choice*: How far did you travel to come to Macy's?

_____ 0–5 miles
_____ 5–10 miles
_____ 10–15 miles
_____ Over 15 miles

- How would you characterize the salespeople at Macy's?

_____ Exceptionally helpful
_____ Helpful
_____ Indifferent
_____ Occasionally rude
_____ Usually rude

- *Checklists*: Which departments at Macy's do you usually visit?

_____ Women's Wear
_____ Sporting Goods
_____ Children's Wear
_____ Lingerie
_____ Men's Wear
_____ Household Goods

- *Ranking Lists*: Rank the *times* you prefer to shop (1 indicates most convenient time, 2 indicates slightly less convenient, and so on).

Note how often television uses surveys. How appropriate and effective are the surveys in the *Video Library*?

______ 9 A.M. to 11 A.M.
______ 11 A.M. to 1 P.M.
______ 1 P.M. to 4 P.M.
______ 4 P.M. to 8 P.M.

As you design, administer, and use your questionnaire, keep the following tips in mind:

- Limit and focus your questions so that respondents can fill out the questionnaire quickly.
- Avoid loaded or biased questions. For example, don't ask, "How do you like the high-quality merchandise in Macy's sports department?"
- At the top of your questionnaire, write one or two sentences describing your study and thanking participants.
- Pretest your questionnaire by giving it to a few people. Based on their oral and written responses, focus and clarify your questions.
- Use a large sample group. Thirty responses will give you more accurate information about consumer attitudes than will three responses.
- Make your sample as *random* or as evenly representative as possible. Don't survey customers on only one floor, in only one department, or at only one time of day.
- Be sure to include a copy of your questionnaire with your article or essay.

But for whom have I tried so steadfastly to communicate? Who have I worried over in this writing? Who is my audience?
—CHERRIE MORAGA, SOCIAL CRITIC AND POET

Note: If you intend to do a formal study using questionnaires, check your library for additional sources to help you design and administer statistically reliable surveys.

SHAPING

As you begin shaping your material, reconsider your purpose and audience. Limit your subject to create a *narrowed* and *focused* topic. Don't try to cover everything; focus on the *most interesting questions and information.* Take the time to write out a statement of your topic, key questions, purpose, and audience. Then try the following strategies.

INVERTED PYRAMID A common form for reports, especially in journalism, is the *inverted pyramid.* The writer begins with a succinct but arresting title, opens the story with a sentence or short paragraph that answers the reporter's "Wh" questions, and then fills in the background information and details in order of importance, from the *most important* to the *least important.*

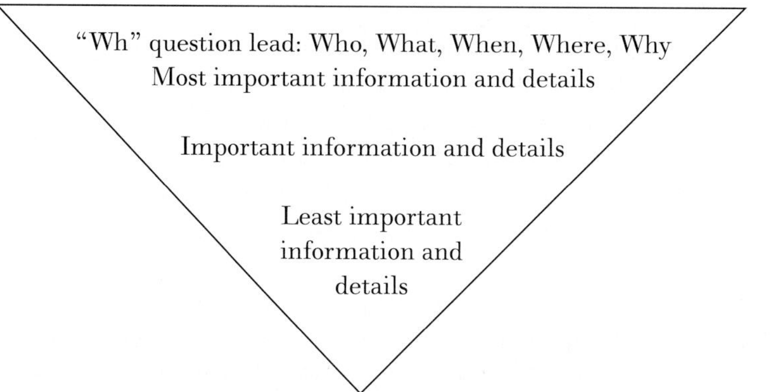

Writers use the inverted pyramid when concrete information and the convenience of the reader are most important. The advantage of the inverted pyramid is that a hurried reader can quickly gather the most important information and determine whether the rest of the story is worth reading. The disadvantage is that some details or information may be scattered or presented out of clear sequence. In investigative writing, therefore, writers often supplement the inverted pyramid with other forms of development: chronological order, definition, classification, or comparison/contrast.

TEACHING TIP

Some students may confuse the inverted pyramid with the background-to-thesis "funnel" introduction popularized by Baker in *The Practical Stylist.* Baker's funnel, however, is intended only for introductory paragraphs, not for entire reports.

CHRONOLOGICAL ORDER Often, writers present their information in the order in which they discovered it, enabling the reader to follow the research as though it were a "whodunit." In this format, you set forth the key questions for the investigation and then describe the steps in *your* investigation, from your earliest questions or clues to your final explanation or resolution.

Lewis Grossberger, for example, uses the chronology of his own investigation to shape his article about "Wheel of Fortune." The following sentences—most of them appearing at the beginning of paragraphs—illustrate how he uses chronological order to shape his account:

> The first time I saw *Wheel of Fortune*, I thought it was a vapid piece of fluff. . . .
>
> But the second time my reaction was different.
>
> Soon I was wafting westward on an urgent sociophilosophical inquiry. . . .
>
> Now here was a journalistic challenge. . . . By God, I would take up the gauntlet. I would find out why—or doze off trying.
>
> When I arrived at the NBC studios in fabled Burbank, the publicity lady who collected me said. . . .
>
> During one break I was taken to meet the hostess. Vanna was in her

TEACHING TIP

Students should test these shaping strategies against their topics by actually *writing* for five minutes and using at least three appropriate shaping strategies. Unless they actually do the writing, they may not see how one of these shapes can organize their essays. Answer students' questions about chronological order, comparison/contrast, definition, and analysis in the *context* of their own topics.

> dressing room. . . .
>
> Too soon came the inevitable pounding, and Vanna vanished. . . .
>
> Considerably sobered, I retired and the next morning flew away.
>
> Soon afterward I was on the plane, thinking about *Wheel of Fortune*, which, as always, acted as a soporific.
>
> I woke high over the Jersey swamps, and I had the answer. I knew *why*.

DEFINITION Definitions are central to investigating and reporting, whether they shape only a sentence or two or several paragraphs. Grossberger uses informal definition to shape one paragraph in his article that explains the meaning of the word "vicariousness," the condition of imagined participation in another person's experience or emotions:

> Vicariousness. *Wheel of Fortune* creates the illusion for the hard-working, treadmill-trotting Middle American yearner that he or she is in the big game. Viewers don't exactly identify with the contestants; they *become* the contestants.

COMPARISON AND CONTRAST Comparison and contrast are as essential to investigating and reporting as they are to observing and remembering. Consider how Lance Morrow uses comparison to shape the opening paragraphs of a *Time* magazine essay on AIDS. In this essay, entitled "The Start of a Plague Mentality," Morrow notes the similarities between attitudes created by a plague 200 years ago and contemporary attitudes toward AIDS.

> An epidemic of yellow fever struck Philadelphia in August 1793. Eyes glazed, flesh yellowed, minds went delirious. People died, not individually, here and there, but in clusters, in alarming patterns. A plague mentality set in. Friends recoiled from one another. If they met by chance, they did not shake hands but nodded distantly and hurried on. The very air felt diseased. People dodged to the windward of those they passed. They sealed themselves in their houses. The deaths went on, great ugly scythings. . . .
>
> In the past four years, some 6,000 people have died of AIDS in the U.S. From a statistical point of view, AIDS is not a major plague. Still, one begins to detect a plague mentality regarding the disease and those who carry it.

ANALYSIS In the process of investigating any subject, writers frequently use analysis to organize or shape their writing. Analysis simply involves dividing a whole into its parts. In the process of analyzing *why* "Wheel of

Fortune" is successful, for example, Grossberger devotes one paragraph to each of the four main elements of the show: the players, the game itself, the payoff, and the cast. Ask yourself, "What are the major components of my subject?" The answer may not only lead to some new ideas about your subject but may create a shape to help organize your material.

ADDITIONAL SHAPING STRATEGIES Other shaping strategies, discussed in previous chapters, may be useful for your investigation, too. *Classifying people, places, or things* may help organize your investigation. *Simile, metaphor, or analogy* may develop and shape parts of your article. Even in investigative reporting, writers may create an identifiable *persona* or adopt a humorous *tone*. In the examples of reports given earlier in this chapter, Anastasia Toufexis, Jeff Meer, and Joan Barthel assume a reporter's objective persona and use a serious, straightforward tone. In contrast, Lewis Grossberger establishes a humorous persona and tone. He admits that "Wheel" is "tedious dreck" and is "soporific," he makes fun of Vanna when she says that turning the letters is a "lot harder than it looks," and he even recounts his own weird dream about Old Stinky.

TITLE, INTRODUCTION, AND CONCLUSION Especially in an investigative report, a catchy title is important to help get your reader's interest and attention. Jot down several ideas for titles now and add to that list *after* you've drafted your essay.

In your introductory paragraph(s), answering the "Wh" questions will help focus your investigation. Or you may wish to use a short *narrative*. Grossberger, for example, begins his article by describing how he became interested in his investigation: "The first time I saw *Wheel of Fortune*, I thought it was a vapid piece of fluff. . . ." Joan Barthel begins her article with stories from Oprah Winfrey's life, pointing out that her profile "is not just the story of a survivor, though she obviously is one. . . ." Other types of lead-ins, such as a short *description*, a *question*, a *statement of a problem*, a *startling fact* or *statistic*, or an arresting *quotation*, may get the reader's interest and focus on the main idea you wish to investigate.

The conclusion should resolve the question or questions posed in the investigation, summarize the most important information (useful primarily for long or complicated reports), and give the reader a sense of completion, often by picking up an idea, fact, quotation, narrative, or bit of description used in the introduction. Grossberger's conclusion, for example, mentions the formula used in "Wheel of Fortune," reiterates the idea that viewers of "Wheel" want to be winners, and puns on the title of the show: "You know, a big wheel."

TEACHING TIP

When students are working on their own titles and leads, ask them to bring samples of popular magazines to class. In small groups, have them write down titles and describe effective lead-ins that they find. These examples will illustrate a range of strategies and prompt discussion about which titles and leads are effective for which subjects and audiences. After the students have worked with these examples, have them work on their own titles and leads.

All good writing is swimming under water and holding your breath.

—F. SCOTT FITZGERALD, AUTHOR OF THE GREAT GATSBY

TEACHING TIP

After students have drafts but before they begin revising is an excellent time to respond, orally or through written comment, to their writing. Once the paper is revised and the writer is finished with the essay, a teacher's extensive comments may be wasted. But if students are encouraged to articulate questions about their drafts and suggest their plans for revisions, a teacher's reactions and suggestions can be especially effective. Teachers can talk to students during class, schedule short conferences, or review photocopies of drafts.

Some writers like to have a title and know how they're going to start a piece of writing before they begin drafting. However, if you can't think of the perfect title or introduction, begin drafting and continue working on the title, introduction, and the conclusion after the first draft.

DRAFTING

Before you begin a first draft, reconsider your purpose in writing and further focus your questions, sense of audience, and shaping strategies.

The actual drafting of an investigative essay requires that you have all your facts, statistics, quotations, summaries, notes from interviews, or results of surveys ready to use. Organize your notes, decide on an overall shaping strategy, or write a sketch outline. In investigative writing, a primary danger is postponing writing too long in the mistaken belief that if you read just one more article or interview just one more person, you'll get the information you need. At some point, usually *before* you feel ready, you must begin writing. (Professional writers rarely feel they know enough about their subject, but deadlines require them to begin.) Your main problem, you'll quickly discover, will be having too much to say rather than not enough. If you have too much, go back to your focusing questions and see whether you can narrow your topic further.

COMPUTER TIP: TITLES, INTRODUCTIONS, AND CONCLUSIONS

Often your best ideas for snappy titles, good lead-ins, or smooth conclusions will come while you're working on something else—collecting material, practicing shaping strategies, or even drafting a trial version. If your computer can copy materials from one file and place it in another file (or even transfer it to the end of your file), try making copies of interesting examples, quotations, facts, and bits of narrative or description. You may use these in the body of your essay, or you might want to use them in an introduction or conclusion. After you draft your essay, you can then see which examples, facts, and so forth you want for the main part of your essay and which might make a good title, lead-in, or conclusion.

REVISING

Guidelines for Revision

As you add, delete, substitute, or rearrange materials, keep the following tips in mind:

- **Re-examine your purpose and audience:** Are you doing what you intended? You should be *reporting* your findings; you should *not* be arguing for or against any idea.
- **Is the form of your essay or report responsive to audience needs and expectations?** Use samples of other writing for your audience (from newspapers, magazines, or journals) as models.
- **Can you add any of your own observations or experiences to the investigation?** Remember that your own perceptions and experiences as a reporter are also relevant data.
- **Review the reporter's "Wh" questions.** Are you providing your readers with relevant information *early* in the report and also catching their interest with a key statistic, fact, quotation, example, question, description, or short narrative?
- **Recheck your summaries, paraphrases, or direct quotations.** Are they accurate, and have you cited these sources in your text?
- **Use signals, cues, and transitions to indicate your shaping strategies:**
  Chronological Order: before, then, afterward, next, soon, later, finally, at last
  Comparison/Contrast: likewise, similarly, however, yet, even so, in contrast
  Analysis: first, next, third, fourth, finally
- **Revise sentences for directness, clarity, and conciseness.** Avoid unnecessary passive voice.
- **Edit your report for appropriate word choice, usage, and grammar.** Check your writing for problems in spelling and punctuation.

■ **POSTSCRIPT ON THE WRITING PROCESS** While the process of writing an investigative essay is still fresh in your mind, answer the following questions in your journal.

1. What sources of information (articles, books, interviews, surveys) were most helpful in your investigation? Explain.

PEER RESPONSE

Because investigative reports are often directed to clearly defined audiences, conduct a peer workshop on audience response. Ask students, as homework, to write out audience analyses for their essays and bring copies of magazines, journals, or newspapers that might publish their essays. In class, after modeling how to revise a draft for a specific audience, have students work in groups of two to four, revising their essays to meet the individual audience and format requirements.

We are all apprentices at a craft where no one ever becomes a master.

—ERNEST HEMINGWAY, NOVELIST

TEACHING TIP

In addition to these questions, many teachers ask students to respond to an open question, such as "One question I wanted to ask when I was writing this paper was ___________." This feedback enables teachers to troubleshoot their own classes, the assignment, or a student's particular writing process.

2. Most researchers discover that the more they learn, the more they still need to know about their subjects. If you had more time to work on this essay, which sources would you investigate further?

3. What was the most difficult problem you had to solve during your collecting, shaping, drafting, and revising? What helped you most as you tried to solve this problem (further reading, additional writing, advice from peers)? Explain.

4. What was the single most important thing you learned about investigating as you wrote this paper?

5. What do you like best about the final version of your investigative report?

INVESTIGATING: STUDENT WRITING

SEE DICK RUN, RUN DICK RUN, WHY, WHY, WHY?

JAN PETERSON

Jan Peterson, a jogger herself, decided to investigate why jogging is so popular. She read several articles from popular magazines, such as Runner's World, *and also found a relevant article in a technical journal,* Research Quarterly for Exercise and Sport. *Then she interviewed several joggers to profile their jogging behavior and attitudes. Shown below are notes from one of the articles she read, questions and notes from one interview, her first rough draft, and the revised version.*

NOTES FROM AN ARTICLE

Notes from a photocopy of Albert Mehrabian and Marijke Lynne Bekken, "Temperament Characteristics of Individuals Who Participate in Strenuous Sports," Research Quarterly for Exercise and Sport, 1986, Vol. 57, No.2, pp 160-166.

In their article, Mehrabian and Bekken found that "those who participate in strenuous sports regularly and intensively are healthier psychologically than the general population" (160). Psychological health in this case was composed of dominance, pleasantness and a relaxed attitude. The authors also addressed the question of whether certain personality types gravitate towards certain types of sports, or whether certain sports activities seem to create certain temperament characteristics. They concluded that certain people gravitate towards certain types of sports (164). (Some of the language here was too technical-PFQ scales and formulas.) Also important: "Relaxed temperament is thus associated with low fear and low anxiety levels and high tolerance for discomfort and pain. Further, it is associated with the ability to delay gratification; to endure discomfort, stress, and pain to achieve desired results; and to cope with stressful situations or activities" (164). The most important conclusion of the paper appeared to be "that athletes are healthier psychologically than the general population" (165).

Questions for an Interview

1. How long have you been running?
2. Why did you start running?
3. Is running a personal thing - do you run alone or in a group?
4. Have your reasons for running changed over the years?
5. Do you experience a "runner's high"?
6. How do you feel after you run?
7. How do you feel when you don't run?
8. What do you think about when you run?
9. Do you compete at running?

Critical Reading

Ask students to describe Peterson's research process. Whom did she interview? What articles did she use from the library? Which of her own observations and remembered experiences did she use? After discussing Peterson's use of sources, ask students to read each other's drafts. What additional sources might each writer use to gather relevant information? Which sources or notes are *not* relevant to the focus of their essays?

Notes from an Interview

This runner started running in high school on cross country team – took up running again in 1979. Started running because he liked it and wanted to be on the track team – but wasn't fast enough to compete in shorter distances. He now runs to stay in shape, relax and relieve stress. However, he is unusual in that he enjoys several types of exercise – social forms – such as basketball where there is much more interaction between team members. Running relaxes him while he runs and those feelings of relaxation last long after the run ends. Not a "runner's high," as such. Things don't seem to bother him as much. He isn't extremely competitive – except with himself – he keeps track of his timed distances and tries to improve. He says he might have been an addicted runner had he started earlier.

First Draft

Question: Why do people run? **Audience:** General, readers of a local newspaper possibly **Purpose:** To report psychological effects of running

SEE JANE RUN—RUN, JANE, RUN—RUN, RUN, RUN

Why have so many thousands of people taken up a pastime lately which so closely resembles torture? You don't see runners or joggers smiling as they dash by you. What you see instead are painful grimaces etched into tight faces, and intense looks of concentration. What exactly is it that motivates these fanatics devoted to misery and self-abuse? **(1)**

According to Bruce Tuckman, author for *Runner's World* magazine, running can be "good medicine for bad moods." Tuckman says running has often been used as a treatment for clinical depression because "it incubates feelings of control, discipline, and self-worth in people who may have been feeling ineffectual." However, he also points out the possible dangers of developing a running addiction. This condition occurs in someone who depends too much on the good feelings provided by running, and is manifested in a person who can't and won't quit running. **(2)**

I interviewed one such person, who wishes to remain anonymous. Although he claims he is not addicted to running, I have suspicions to the contrary. Two days after a serious accident with a chainsaw in which he received 20 stitches in the middle of his shin, he attempted to hobble through his usual 6 mile course. The pain admittedly got to him, so he decided to wait 2 more days to try again. His repeated stressing of the injured leg resulted in a lump the size of a walnut on his shin bone. Perhaps he is not a total addict, as he did give up his passion for a few days, but I would surmise that addiction is just a matter of degree. Why is this person so dedicated to this form of self-abuse? **(3)**

It has been demonstrated that running causes biochemical as well as physiological changes in the body. In the past, endorphins, which are the body's naturally occurring opiates, were suspected to be at high levels in runners. But researchers were unable to detect a correlation between endorphins and runner's feelings of euphoria often known as a "runner's high." However, recently another drug has gained attention as a mood enhancer—the hormone noradrenaline. Tuckman claims that runners have higher levels of noradrenaline than do nonrunners. **(4)**

However, the editors of *The Complete Runner* claim that the calming effect produced from running has its roots in our heredity. Our ancestors had only two options in how to react to threats: fight—that is stand their ground and club each other (or that growling saber-toothed tiger), or flight—that is, run away from the apparent danger. Options for dealing with stress today are no longer so clear-cut. If our boss threatens us, we can't very well punch him or her, or run away. Instead we are forced to stand there and just take the verbal abuse—somehow internalizing the stress. But, we still must deal with the stress. Some of us deal with stress by numbing the effects with drugs or alcohol. Others have come to depend upon strenuous exercise, such as running, for our tension releaser. This perhaps sounds strange—because when you run you tense your muscles and it would appear that the very act of tensing muscles would inhibit tension release. However, recent research reported by the editors of *The Complete Runner* has revealed that "relaxation is most pronounced after muscular work." **(5)**

Revised Version

SEE DICK RUN. RUN, DICK, RUN. WHY, WHY, WHY?

Why have so many thousands of people taken up a pastime lately that so closely resembles self-abuse? You don't often see runners or joggers smiling as they trot past you—what you see instead are painful grimaces etched into tight faces and intense looks of concentration. What motivates these fanatics? What sort of satisfaction could they possibly be deriving from such agony? Or are they perhaps all just a bunch of masochists? **(1)**

People of all ages, shapes, and sizes have started running by the droves. You see them everywhere—at the park, downtown, on college campuses, at the beach, and in the mountains. Even more strange is the fact that once they start running, many of them won't, or *can't* quit. Now, I can understand the reasons why most people start a program of running—reasons such as wanting to lose weight or wanting to get into shape. What I fail to comprehend is why people continue to run after they find out what kind of pain is involved in the sport. **(2)**

Reasons for running are as varied and diverse as people are. One runner interviewed for this article claimed to have started running in high school. He said he joined the cross-country track team because he wanted to be a runner, but he was unable to compete effectively in shorter distance events. Now, however, he runs to stay in shape, relax, and relieve stress. A second interviewed runner began running in high school as well—also on the cross-country team. However, he ran only to be in better shape for his true love, wrestling. He says he runs now to stay in shape and keep his sanity. **(3)**

Runners may claim that running promotes sanity, but in fact there are both positive and negative psychological effects of running. In a recent *Runner's World* article entitled "Brighter Days," Bruce Tuckman explains that running can be "good medicine for bad moods." Tuckman says running has often been used as a treatment for clinical depression because "it incubates feelings of control, discipline, and self-worth in people who may have been feeling ineffectual." However, he also points out the possible dangers of developing a running addiction. This condition occurs in someone who depends too much on the good feelings provided by running and is manifested by a person who can't and won't quit running. **(4)**

One of the runners I interviewed provided a vivid example of the negative effects of running addiction. This person had an unfortunate encounter with a chain saw while cutting firewood. As a result of their rather abrupt meeting, he ended up with approximately twenty stitches in the middle of his shin. Two days after the accident occurred, he attempted to hobble through his usual six mile course. Crazy, you say? Not according to his philosophy—the more you use your body, the faster it heals! The result of this madness is a lump the size of a walnut in the middle of his shin, and a leg that still gives him problems. And he claims he runs just to stay in shape and keep his sanity—what sanity? (5)

Recent research has suggested that addiction to running may be caused, at least in part, by certain physiological or biochemical changes in the body. In the past, endorphins (the body's naturally occurring opiates) were suspected to be at high levels in runners. Researchers, however, were unable to detect a correlation between endorphins and runners' feelings of euphoria (often known as "runner's high"). Another mood-enhancing drug has gained attention more recently—the hormone noradrenaline. Tuckman claims runners have higher levels of noradrenaline than nonrunners. **(6)**

However, the editors of *The Complete Runner* argue that the calming effect produced by running has its roots in our heredity. Our ancestors had only two options for handling threats: fight (stand your ground and club each other) or flight (run away from that saber-toothed tiger that thinks you might make a scrumptious meal). Options for dealing with stress today are no longer so clear-cut. If your boss threatens you, you can't very well retaliate with a club. It probably wouldn't look too good if you ran away, either. So what are your choices? Stand there and internalize the stress, go home later and throw down a couple of martinis, yell at the wife and kids, and fall asleep watching television. This behavior, however, seems only to dull the tension rather than relieve it. The urges to fight or flee remain bottled up inside, and the stress is not alleviated. The only way we can release our stress and really relax is by voluntary muscular work. As the editors of *The Complete Runner* say, "Running offers one of the few chances left to get our feet on the ground—for the sake of our heads." **(7)**

Runners may be addicted psychologically or physiologically, but the result, some experts think, is positive. Albert Mehrabian and Marijke Bekken, writing in the *Research Quarterly for Exercise and Sport*, conclude that "those who participate in [running] regularly and intensively are healthier psychologically than the general population." These authors found that athletes in general have more dominant and pleasant temperaments than nonathletes. They also equated a relaxed temperament with those who run or exercise regularly. They defined "relaxed temperament" to be associated with "low fear and low anxiety levels and high tolerance for discomfort and pain. Further, it is associated with the ability to delay gratification; to endure discomfort, stress, and pain to achieve desired results; and to cope with stressful situations or activities." Do you suppose that the "chain-saw jogger" I interviewed may have a little more sanity than I previously gave him credit for? Maybe I'd better go put on my running shoes! **(8)**

Questions for Writing and Discussion

1. One purpose of an investigative report is to give readers information. Without looking back at Peterson's revised article, recall the information you got from it. Were you confused at some points in the article? Explain.

2. What information, ideas, or quotations does Peterson pick up from her article notes and interview to use in her revised version? Was there anything else she should have used but didn't?

3. Which shaping strategies discussed in this chapter does Peterson use to organize the revised version of her article? Referring to paragraph numbers, identify two important shaping strategies.

4. Compare Peterson's first draft with her revised version. Find one change in content (added or deleted facts, examples, quotations). Is the change an improvement over the first draft? Find one change in shaping or organization (look particularly at transitions in the opening sentences of paragraphs). Is the revision an improvement? Finally, find one change in wording in a sentence. Does the rewording improve the clarity or appropriateness of the sentence? Explain.

MY FRIEND MICHELLE, AN ALCOHOLIC

BRIDGID STONE

Bridgid Stone, a student at Southeast Missouri State University, decided to write her investigative essay on alcoholism. In the library, she was able to find quite a lot of information and statistics about alcohol. In her friend, Michelle, she had a living example of the consequences of alcohol abuse. The question, however, was how to combine the two. As you read her essay, notice how she interweaves description and dialogue with facts and statistics.

Five million teenagers are problem drinkers, according to *Group* magazine's article, "Sex, Drugs, and Alcohol." One of these five million teenagers is my friend, Michelle.

"I can't wait to go out tonight and get drunk," Michelle announces as she walks into my dorm room. I just sigh and shake my head. Michelle has been drunk every night since Wednesday. In the last three days, she has been to more fraternity parties than classes.

We leave a few hours later for a Sig Tau party. Even though I have been attending these parties for weeks now, the amount of alcohol present still amazes me. Almost everyone is walking around with a twelve-pack of beer. Others are carrying fifths of vodka or Jack Daniel's whiskey. As cited in *Fraternities and Sororities on the Contemporary College Campus*, seventy-three percent of fraternity advisors believe that alcohol is a problem in fraternities. I wish the other twenty-seven percent could be here now. Fraternities are synonymous with drinking.

Michelle and I both have innocent-looking squeeze bottles, but inside are very stiff screwdrivers. They probably have more vodka than orange juice. Michelle finishes her drink before I am halfway through with mine. So she finishes off mine too before disappearing into the throng of people at the party. The next time I see her, she is holding a beer in each hand. Her speech is slurred, and she can barely stand up on her own.

We head back to the dorm when Michelle starts vomiting. Once we are in her room, I help her undress and put her to bed.

"Bridgid, I am so sorry," Michelle cries," I promise never to drink again."

"Okay, just get some sleep," I tell her as I leave.

It's Thursday night and Michelle is ready to party again.

"I haven't been to my Friday 8:00 class in a month. Do you think I should just stay up all night after the party and go to class drunk? Or should I just not go to class and sleep in?" Michelle asks.

"Don't go out and get drunk. Stay home tonight and get up and go to your classes tomorrow," I advise.

"I am just going to sleep in," Michelle informs me as she leaves for the party.

Like Michelle, an estimated 4.6 million adolescents experience negative consequences of alcohol abuse, such as poor school performance. This was reported in a survey conducted by NIAAA for a United States Congressional report.

Early Friday morning, I get a phone call from the on-duty resident advisor. Michelle has passed out in the lobby of the Towers Complex. She couldn't remember her phone number or even what floor she lived on, but I had written my phone number on Michelle's hand, so she could call me if she got into any trouble. The R. A. had seen my number and decided to call, since Michelle was too drunk to dial the four digits.

"Could you please escort your friend up to your room," the R. A. asks. She doesn't sound very happy.

"Sure, I will be down in a few minutes," I promise. It takes me and another girl from our floor to get Michelle onto the elevator. She keeps lying down or passing out. Thirty minutes later, we get Michelle into bed. She is mumbling incoherently, and she reeks of alcohol. Needless to say, Michelle doesn't make it to her 8:00 a.m. class, again.

Saturday afternoon, I confront Michelle about the Thursday night incident. This is rather hard to do, since she doesn't remember any of it.

"I just drink to loosen up. I'm much more fun if I've been drinking," Michelle tells me.

"You are not much fun when you are puking or passing out," I reply. A desire to loosen up is one of the main reasons that teenagers drink, reports *Group* magazine. Other reasons include a need to escape and to rebel.

"I have to release steam every once in awhile," she argues. "School is really stressing me out."

"Michelle, you don't even go to class," I tell her.

"Everyone else drinks!" she says. "Why are you picking on me?" She stomps out of my room.

Michelle was partially correct, though, when she stated, "Everybody else drinks." As reported in *Alcohol and Youth*, more than eighty percent of all college students surveyed had been drinking in the previous month. But this doesn't mean that what Michelle is doing is any less serious. In all probability, Michelle is an alcoholic.

A test that is often used to determine if someone has a drinking problem can be found in *Getting Them Sober*, by Toby Rice Andrews. There are twenty questions on the test. A "yes" answer to two of the questions indicates a possible drinking problem. Questions include: "Do you miss time from school or work due to drinking?" "Do you drink to escape from worries or troubles?" "Do you drink because you are shy?" "Have you ever had a memory loss due to drinking?" Michelle would probably have answered "yes" to all of the above questions.

I moved out of the dorm at the beginning of the second semester, so I haven't seen much of Michelle. The last time I saw her was about three weeks ago. She had gotten arrested while in New Orleans for spring break. Apparently, Michelle had been out drinking and eventually had been arrested for public drunkenness.

"It wasn't that bad," she told me. "I don't even remember being in the jail cell. I was pretty trashed."

Works Cited

Barnes, Grace. *Alcohol and Youth*. Westport, Conneticut: Greenwood Press, 1982.

Andrews, Toby Rice. *Getting Them Sober*. South Plainfield, New Jersey: Bridge Publishing, 1980.

Pruett, Harold, and Vivian Brown. *Crisis Intervention and Prevention*. San Francisco: Jossey-Bass Inc., 1987.

"Sex, Drugs, and Alcohol." *Group*, February 1992: 17–20.

Van Pelt, Rich. *Intensive Care*. Grand Rapids, Michigan: Zondervan Publishing House, 1988.

Winston, Roger, William Nettles III, and John Opper, Jr. *Fraternities and Sororities on Contemporary College Campuses*. San Francisco: Jossey-Bass Inc., 1987.

Questions for Writing and Discussion

1. Investigative reports should remain as objective as possible. Describe how Stone's essay affected you. Does Stone remain objective or does she become emotionally involved? Where is she most objective? Where does her point of view color her report? How successfully does Stone maintain her reportorial stance?

2. Who is Stone's audience for her essay? Where would you recommend that Stone send her essay for possible publication? List two possible publication sources (magazines or newspapers) and explain your choices.

3. If Stone were revising her essay, what advice would you give her about balancing statistics and personal experience? Should she have more statistics? Should she have more narrative? Refer to specific paragraphs and examples in your response.

4. Stone's use of present tense adds dramatic impact to her essay. Reread her essay, noticing where she uses present tense and where she shifts to past tense. Where was the use of present tense most effective? Did her tense shifting confuse you at any point? Where?

5. Compare Stone's essay with Kozol's essay earlier in this chapter. What reporting strategies does Stone adapt from Kozol? How are their reporting strategies different? Explain your response by referring to specific passages from each author.

SEVEN / EXPLAINING

Become aware of the two-sided nature of your mental make-up: one thinks in terms of the connectedness of things, the other thinks in terms of parts and sequences.

GABRIELE LUSSER RICO,
AUTHOR OF WRITING THE NATURAL WAY

What [a writer] knows is almost always a matter of the relationships he establishes, between example and generalization, between one part of a narrative and the next, between the idea and the counteridea that the writer sees is also relevant.

ROGER SALE,
AUTHOR OF ON WRITING

YOU HAVE DECIDED TO QUIT YOUR PRESENT JOB, SO YOU WRITE A NOTE TO YOUR BOSS GIVING THIRTY DAYS' NOTICE. During your last few weeks at work, your boss asks you to write a three-page job description to help orient the person who will replace you. The job description should include a list of your current duties as well as advice to your replacement on how to execute them most efficiently. To write the description, you record your daily activities, look back through your calendar, comb through your records, and brainstorm a list of everything you do. As you write up the description, you include specific examples and illustrations of your typical responsibilities.

AS A GYMNAST AND DANCER, YOU GRADUALLY BECOME OBSESSED WITH LOSING WEIGHT. You start skipping meals, purging the little food you do eat, and lying about your eating habits to your parents. Before too long, you weigh less than seventy pounds, and your physician diagnoses your condition: *anorexia nervosa*. With advice from your physician and counseling from a psychologist, you gradually begin to control your disorder. To explain to others what anorexia is, how it is caused, and what its effects are, you write an essay in which you explain your ordeal, alerting other readers to the potential dangers of uncontrolled dieting.

Sandstone Hieroglyphics (Isao Inai/Photonica)

EXPLAINING AND DEMONSTRATING RELATIONSHIPS IS A FREQUENT PURPOSE FOR WRITING. Explaining goes beyond investigating the facts and reporting information; it analyzes the component parts of a subject and then shows how the parts fit in relation to one another. Its goal is to clarify for a particular group of readers *what* something is, *how* it happened or should happen, and/or *why* it happens.

Explaining begins with *analysis*: You divide a thing or phenomenon (object, person, place, feeling, belief, event, process, or cause) into its various parts. Explaining how to learn to play the piano, for example, begins with an analysis of the parts of the learning process: playing scales, learning chords, getting instruction from a teacher, sight reading, and performing in recitals. Explaining why two automobiles collided at an intersection begins with an analysis of the contributing factors: the nature of the intersection, the number of cars involved, the condition of the drivers, and the condition of each vehicle. Then you bring the parts together and show their *relationships*: You show how practicing scales on the piano fits into the process of learning to play the piano; you demonstrate why one small factor—such as a faulty turn signal—combined with other factors to cause an automobile accident.

The emphasis you give to the *analysis* of the object or phenomenon and the time you spend explaining *relationships* of the parts depends on your purpose, subject, and audience. If you want to explain how a flower reproduces, for example, you may begin by identifying the important parts, such as the pistil and stamen, that most readers need to know about before they can understand the reproductive process. However, if you are explaining the process to a botany major who already knows the parts of a flower, you might spend more time discussing the key operations in pollination or the reasons why some flowers cross-pollinate and others do not. In any effective explanation, analyzing parts and showing relationships must work together for that particular group of readers.

Because its purpose is to teach the reader, *expository writing*, or writing to explain, should be as clear as possible. Explanations, however, are more than organized pieces of information. Expository writing contains information that is focused by your point of view, by your experience, and by your reasoning powers. Thus, your explanation of a thing or phenomenon makes a point or has a thesis: This is the *right* way to define "happiness." This is how one *should* bake lasagne or do a calculus problem. These are the *most important* reasons why the senator from New York was elected. To make your explanation clear, you show what you mean by using specific support—facts, data, examples, illustrations, statistics, comparisons, analogies, and images. Your thesis is a *general* assertion about the relationships of the *specific* parts; the support helps

BACKGROUND ON EXPLAINING

This chapter assumes that expository writing often includes some mixture of definition, process analysis, and causal analysis. Although a completed essay may use just one of these as a primary strategy, a writer needs a *choice* of expository strategies for the thinking, learning, and composing process.

your reader identify the parts and see the relationships. Expository writing teaches the reader by alternating between generalizations and specific examples.

TEACHING TIP

As in previous chapters, this freewriting exercise should help students read and understand this chapter in light of their own writing. Draw on this exercise in workshops or class discussion of explaining techniques.

■ **FREEWRITING: EXPLAINING A TERM OR CONCEPT** Before you read further in this chapter, write a one-paragraph explanation of an idea, term, or concept that you have discussed in a class that you are currently taking. From biology, for example, you might define photosynthesis or gene splicing. From psychology, you might define psychosis or projection. From computer studies, you might define virtual reality or morphing. First identify someone who might need to know about this subject. Then give a definition and an illustration. Finally, describe how the term was discovered or invented, what its effects or applications are, and/or how it works.

The main thing I try to do is write as clearly as I can.
—E. B. WHITE, JOURNALIST AND CO-AUTHOR OF ELEMENTS OF STYLE

TECHNIQUES FOR EXPLAINING

Explaining requires first that you assess your subject and your audience. Although you will need to draw on your own observations and memories about this subject, you may also need to do some reading or perhaps interview an expert. As you consider your subject, keep in mind that while an explanation (involving both analysis and showing relationships) focuses on *what, how*, or *why*, it may involve all three. Below are five important techniques for writing clear explanations.

- **Getting the reader's attention and stating the thesis.** Devise an accurate but interesting *title*. Use an attention-getting *lead-in*. State the *thesis* clearly.
- **Defining key terms and describing *what* something is.** Analyze and *define* by describing, comparing, classifying, and giving examples.
- **Identifying the steps in a process and showing *how* each step relates to the overall process.** Describe how something should be done or how something typically happens.
- **Describing causes and effects and showing *why* certain causes lead to specific effects.** Analyze how several causes lead to a single effect or show how a single cause leads to multiple effects.
- **Supporting explanations with specific evidence.** Use descriptions, examples, comparisons, analogies, images, facts, data, or statistics to *show* what, how, or why.

In *Spirit of the Valley: Androgyny and Chinese Thought*, psychologist Sukie Colgrave illustrates many of these techniques as she explains an important concept from psychology: the phenomenon of "projection." Colgrave explains how we "project" attributes missing in our own personality onto another person—especially someone we love:

> A one-sided development of either the masculine or feminine principles has [an] unfortunate consequence for our psychological and intellectual health: it encourages the phenomenon termed "projection." This is the process by which we project onto other people, things, or ideologies, those aspects of ourselves which we have not, for whatever reason, acknowledged or developed. The most familiar example of this is the obsession which usually accompanies being "in love." A person whose feminine side is unrealised will often "fall in love" with the feminine which she or he "sees" in another person, and similarly with the masculine. The experience of being "in love" is one of powerful dependency. As long as the projection appears to fit its object nothing awakens the person to the reality of the projection. But sooner or later the lover usually becomes aware of certain discrepancies between her or his desires and the person chosen to satisfy them. Resentment, disappointment, anger and rejection rapidly follow, and often the relationship disintegrates . . . . But if we can explore our own psyches we may discover what it is we were demanding from our lover and start to develop it in ourselves. The moment this happens we begin to see other people a little more clearly. We are freed from some of our needs to make others what we want them to be, and can begin to love them more for what they are.

Explaining what: definition example

Explaining why: effects of projection

Explaining how: the process of freeing ourselves from dependency

EXPLAINING *WHAT*

Explaining *what* something is or means requires showing the relationship between it and the *class* of beings, objects, or concepts to which it belongs. *Formal definition*, which is often essential in explaining, has three parts: the thing or term to be defined, the class, and the distinguishing characteristics of the thing or term. The thing being defined can be concrete, such as a turkey, or abstract, such as democracy.

THING OR TERM		CLASS	DISTINGUISHING CHARACTERISTICS
A turkey	is a	bird	that has brownish plumage and a bare, wattled head and neck; it is widely domesticated for food.

Thing or Term		Class	Distinguishing Characteristics
Democracy	is	government	by the people, exercised directly or through elected representatives.

TEACHING TIP

Ask student to annotate the various techniques for extended definition illustrated in this paragraph on democracy. Their marginal notes might be as follows:

Frequently, writers use *extended definitions* when they need to give more than a mere formal definition. An extended definition may explain the word's etymology or historical roots, describe sensory characteristics of the term (how it looks, feels, sounds, tastes, smells), identify its parts, indicate how something is used, explain what it is not, provide an example of it, and/or note similarities or differences between this term and other words or things. The following extended definition of "democracy" begins with the etymology and then explains—using analysis, comparison, example, and description—what democracy is and what it is not:

Formal definition

Description: what democracy is

Etymology: analysis of the word's roots

Comparison: what democracy is not

Example

Formal definition

> Since democracy is government of the people, by the people, and for the people, a democratic form of government is not fixed or static. Democracy is dynamic; it adapts to the wishes and needs of the people. The term "democracy" derives from the Greek word *demos*, meaning "the common people," and *-kratia*, meaning "strength or power" used to govern or rule. Democracy is based on the notion that a majority of people creates laws and then everyone agrees to abide by those laws in the interest of the common good. In a democracy, people are not ruled by a king, a dictator, or a small group of powerful individuals. Instead, people elect officials who use the power temporarily granted to them to govern the society. For example, the people may agree that their government should raise money for defense, so the officials levy taxes to support an army. If enough people decide, however, that taxes for defense are too high, then they request that their elected officials change the laws or they elect new officials. The essence of democracy lies in its responsiveness: Democracy is a form of government in which laws and lawmakers change as the will of the majority changes.

Figurative expressions—vivid word pictures using similes, metaphors, or analogies—can also explain what something is. During World War II, for example, the Writer's War Board asked E. B. White (author of *Charlotte's Web* and many *New Yorker* magazine essays) to provide an explanation of democracy. Instead of giving a formal definition or etymology, White responded with a series of imaginative comparisons showing the *relationship* between various parts of American culture and the concept of democracy:

> Surely the Board knows what democracy is. It is the line that forms on the right. It is the don't in Don't Shove. It is the hole in the stuffed shirt through which the sawdust slowly trickles; it is the dent in the high hat. Democracy is the recurrent suspicion that more than half of the people are right more than half of the time. It is the feeling of privacy in the voting booths, the feeling of communion in the libraries, the feeling of vitality everywhere. Democracy is the score at the beginning of the ninth. It is an idea which hasn't been disproved yet, a song the words of which have not gone bad. It's the mustard on the hot dog and the cream in the rationed coffee. Democracy is a request from a War Board, in the middle of a morning in the middle of a war, wanting to know what democracy is.

Explaining *How*

Explaining *how* something should be done or how something happens is usually called *process analysis.* One kind of process analysis is the "how-to" explanation: how to cook a turkey, how to tune an engine, how to get a job. Such recipes or directions are *prescriptive*: You typically explain how something *should* be done. In a second kind of process analysis, you explain how something happens or is typically done—without being directive or prescriptive. In a *descriptive* process analysis, you explain how some natural or social process typically happens: how cells split during mitosis, how hailstones form in a cloud, how students react to the pressure of examinations, or how political candidates create their public images. In both prescriptive and descriptive explanations, however, you are analyzing a *process*—dividing the sequence into its parts or steps—and then showing how the parts contribute to the whole process.

Cookbooks, automobile-repair manuals, instructions for assembling toys or appliances, and self-improvement books are all examples of *prescriptive* process analysis. Writers of recipes, for example, begin with analyses of the ingredients and the steps in preparing the food. Then they carefully explain how the steps are related, how to avoid problems, and how to serve mouth-watering concoctions. Farley Mowat, naturalist and author of *Never Cry Wolf*, gives his readers the following detailed—and humorous—recipe for creamed mouse. Mowat became interested in this recipe when he decided to test the nutritional content of the wolf's diet. "In the event that any of my readers may be interested in personally exploiting this hitherto overlooked source of excellent animal protein," Mowat writes, "I give the recipe in full":

Souris á la Créme	**Ingredients:**	
One dozen fat mice	Salt and pepper	One cup white flour
Cloves	One piece sowbelly	Ethyl alcohol

TEACHING TIP

Explain that process analysis often contains two kinds of analyses: analysis of the ingredients, parts, or items used in the process and analysis of the chronology. In a recipe, for example, the analysis of parts occurs in the list of ingredients; the chronology is the instructions. Ask students to read the Mowat and Thomas excerpts for both kinds of analyses. Then ask them to apply both kinds of analyses, if appropriate, to their own topics or drafts.

For video examples of process analysis see "Smart Cars," "Lyme Disease," and "Teaching Values" in the Video Guide.

> Skin and gut the mice, but do not remove the heads; wash, then place in a pot with enough alcohol to cover the carcasses. Allow to marinate for about two hours. Cut sowbelly into small cubes and fry slowly until most of the fat has been rendered. Now remove the carcasses from the alcohol and roll them in a mixture of salt, pepper and flour; then place in frying pan and sauté for about five minutes (being careful not to allow the pan to get too hot, or the delicate meat will dry out and become tough and stringy). Now add a cup of alcohol and six or eight cloves. Cover the pan and allow to simmer slowly for fifteen minutes. The cream sauce can be made according to any standard recipe. When the sauce is ready, drench the carcasses with it, cover and allow to rest in a warm place for ten minutes before serving.

CRITICAL READING

Show students how writers use multiple strategies by asking them to identify rhetorical strategies that Thomas uses in this excerpt. In the margins, have students identify at least one example to illustrate definition, process, and causal strategies. If possible, connect this exercise to the students' own writing. Model identification of strategies with your own draft or with a sample piece of student writing. Then have students trade drafts or notes and have peer readers suggest how the writer may combine several explaining strategies.

Explaining "how" something happens or is typically done involves a *descriptive* process analysis. It requires showing the chronological relationship between one idea, event, or phenomenon and the next—and it depends on close observation. In *Lives of the Cell*, biologist and physician Lewis Thomas explains that ants are like humans: While they are individuals, they can also act together to create a social organism. Although exactly how ants communicate remains a mystery, Thomas explains how they combine to form a thinking, working organism:

> [Ants] seem to live two kinds of lives: they are individuals, going about the day's business without much evidence of thought for tomorrow, and they are at the same time component parts, cellular elements, in the huge, writhing, ruminating organism of the Hill, the nest, the hive....
>
> A Solitary ant, afield, cannot be considered to have much of anything on his mind; indeed, with only a few neurons strung together by fibers, he can't be imagined to have a mind at all, much less a thought. He is more like a ganglion on legs. Four ants together, or ten, encircling a dead moth on a path, begin to look more like an idea. They fumble and shove, gradually moving the food toward the Hill, but as though by blind chance. It is only when you watch the dense mass of thousands of ants, crowded together around the Hill, blackening the ground, that you begin to see the whole beast, and now you observe it thinking, planning, calculating. It is an intelligence, a kind of live computer, with crawling bits for its wits.
>
> At a stage in the construction, twigs of a certain size are needed, and all the members forage obsessively for twigs of just this size. Later, when outer walls are to be finished, thatched, the size must change, and as though given new orders by telephone, all the workers shift

the search to the new twigs. If you disturb the arrangement of a part of the Hill, hundreds of ants will set it vibrating, shifting, until it is put right again. Distant sources of food are somehow sensed, and long lines, like tentacles, reach out over the ground, up over walls, behind boulders, to fetch it in.

EXPLAINING *WHY*

"Why?" may be the question most commonly asked by human beings. We are fascinated by the reasons for everything that we experience in life. We ask questions about natural phenomena: Why is the sky blue? Why does a teakettle whistle? Why do some materials act as superconductors? We also find human attitudes and behavior intriguing: Why is chocolate so popular? Why do some people hit small leather balls with big sticks and then run around a field stomping on little white pillows? Why are America's farms economically depressed? Why did the United States go to war in Vietnam?

Explaining *why* something occurs can be the most fascinating—and difficult—kind of expository writing. Answering the question "why" usually requires analyzing *cause-and-effect relationships.* The causes, however, may be too complex or intangible to identify precisely. We are on comparatively secure ground when we ask *why* about physical phenomena that can be weighed, measured, and replicated under laboratory conditions. Under those conditions, we can determine cause and effect with precision. Fire, for example, has three *necessary* and *sufficient* causes: combustible material, oxygen, and ignition temperature. Without *each* of these causes, fire will not occur (each cause is "necessary"); taken together, these three causes are *enough* to cause fire (all three are "sufficient"). In this case, the cause-and-effect relationship can be illustrated by an equation:

CAUSE 1	+	CAUSE 2	+	CAUSE 3	=	EFFECT
(combustible material)		(oxygen)		(ignition temperature)		(fire)

Analyzing both necessary and sufficient causes is essential to explaining an effect. You may say, for example, that wind shear (an abrupt downdraft in a storm) "caused" an airplane crash. In fact, wind shear may have *helped* cause the crash (been necessary) but was not by itself the total (sufficient) cause of the crash: An airplane with enough power may be able to overcome wind-shear forces in certain circumstances. An explanation of the crash is not complete until you analyze the full range

WRITE TO LEARN

Write-to-learn activities don't have to be connected to a specific reading or text assignment. Any time you are giving instructions or discussing a point and hear yourself saying, "Does everyone understand that?" or "Does anyone have a question?" stop and give students one or two minutes to write down the main point of the discussion or to write down two questions about it. Such write-to-learn activities give every student a chance to respond actively and inform the teacher about students' questions and ideas.

of necessary *and* sufficient causes, which may include wind shear, lack of power, mechanical failure, and even pilot error.

Sometimes, explanations for physical phenomena are beyond our analytical powers. Astrophysicists, for example, have good theoretical reasons for believing that black holes cause gigantic gravitational whirlpools in outer space, but they have difficulty explaining why black holes exist—or whether they exist at all.

In the realm of human cause and effect, determining causes and effects can be as tricky as explaining why black holes exist. Why, for example, do some children learn math easily, while others fail? What effect does failing at math have on a child? What are necessary and sufficient causes for divorce? What are the effects of divorce on parents and children? Although you may not be able to explain all the causes or effects of something, you should not be satisfied until you have considered a wide range of possible causes and effects. Even then, you need to qualify or modify your statements, using such words as "might," "usually," "often," "seldom," "many," or "most," and then giving as much support and evidence as you can.

In the following paragraphs, Jonathan Kozol, a critic of America's educational system and author of *Illiterate America*, explains the multiple effects of a single cause: illiteracy. Kozol supports his explanation by citing specific ways that illiteracy affects the lives of people:

> Illiterates cannot read the menu in a restaurant.
>
> They cannot read the cost of items on the menu in the *window* of the restaurant before they enter.
>
> Illiterates cannot read the letters that their children bring home from their teachers. They cannot study school department circulars that tell them of the courses that their children must be taking if they hope to pass the SAT exams. They cannot help with homework. They cannot write a letter to the teacher. They are afraid to visit in the classroom. They do not want to humiliate their child or themselves....
>
> Many illiterates cannot read the admonition on a pack of cigarettes. Neither the Surgeon General's warning nor its reproduction on the package can alert them to the risks. Although most people learn by word of mouth that smoking is related to a number of grave physical disorders, they do not get the chance to read the detailed stories which can document this danger with the vividness that turns concern into determination to resist. They can see the handsome cowboy or the slim Virginia lady lighting up a filter cigarette; they cannot heed the words that tell them that this product is (not "may

be") dangerous to their health. Sixty million men and women are condemned to be the unalerted, high-risk candidates for cancer....

Illiterates cannot travel freely. When they attempt to do so, they encounter risks that few of us can dream of. They cannot read traffic signs and, while they often learn to recognize and to decipher symbols, they cannot manage street names which they haven't seen before. The same is true for bus and subway stops. While ingenuity can sometimes help a man or woman to discern directions from familiar landmarks, buildings, cemeteries, churches, and the like, most illiterates are virtually immobilized. They seldom wander past the streets and neighborhoods they know. Geographical paralysis becomes a bitter metaphor for their entire existence. They are immobilized in almost every sense we can imagine. They can't move up. They can't move out. They cannot see beyond.

■ **WARMING UP: JOURNAL EXERCISES** The following exercises will help you practice writing explanations. Read all of the following exercises and then write on the three that interest you most. If another idea occurs to you, write about it.

1. Reread your explanation of a term or concept from your Freewriting assignment at the beginning of this chapter. Based on what you have read in this chapter, revise your explanation to make it more specific and clearer for your reader.

2. Imitating E. B. White's short "definition" of democracy, use imaginative comparisons to write a short definition—serious or humorous—of one of the following words: "freedom," "adolescence," "mathematics," "politicians," "parents," "misery," "higher education," "luck," or a word of your own choice.

3. Novelist Ernest Hemingway once defined courage as "grace under pressure." Using this definition, explain how you or someone you know showed this kind of courage in a difficult situation.

4. When asked what jazz is, Louis Armstrong replied: "Man, if you gotta ask you'll never know." If you know quite a bit about jazz, explain what Armstrong meant. Or choose a familiar subject to which the same remark might apply. What can be "explained" about that subject and what cannot?

5. Choose a skill that you've acquired (for example, playing a musical instrument, operating a machine, playing a sport, drawing, counseling others, driving in rush-hour traffic, dieting) and explain to a novice how he or she can acquire that skill. Reread what you've written. Then write another version addressed to an expert. What parts can you leave out? What must you add?

6. At your place of work, you've just hired a substitute to fill in for you for one day. Write a note to that person explaining what he or she should do and how to do it.

7. Three-year-old children are insatiably curious. They ask older people a never-ending series of "why" questions. Imagine you are going for a walk in a familiar place with a three-year-old. What questions might the child ask you about either strange or commonplace things or occurrences? Select one "why" question. First write out an explanation of that question for another adult. Then write your explanation for the three-year-old.

EXPLAINING: PROFESSIONAL WRITING

IS SEX NECESSARY? VIRGIN BIRTH AND OPPORTUNISM IN THE GARDEN

DAVID QUAMMEN

In this selection from Natural Acts: A Sidelong View of Science and Nature *(1985), David Quammen uses his skills as a novelist and biology watcher to describe the mysterious sex life of the aphid. In the process of explaining how and why aphids reproduce, he humorously informs his readers about cloning and genetic evolution. Beginning with his catchy title—a reference to James Thurber and E. B. White's satire* Is Sex Necessary?*—Quammen teases his readers into the private world of those "little nebbishy sap-sucking insects." As Quammen admits, he is not a scientist but someone who haunts libraries and tags along on other people's field trips, "asking too many foolish questions and occasionally scribbling notes." Quammen's conversational tone, witty style, and natural curiosity immediately engage readers who might fall asleep over a biology textbook. Quammen is a versatile writer who has also written a spy thriller,* The Zolta Configuration *(1983); published a second collection of essays on science,* The Flight of the Iguana *(1988); and written a regular column for* Outside *magazine.*

Birds do it, bees do it, goes the tune. But the songsters, as usual, would mislead us with drastic oversimplifications. The full truth happens to be more eccentrically nonlibidinous: Sometimes they don't do it, those very creatures, and get the same results anyway. Bees of all species, for instance, are notable to geneticists precisely for their ability to produce offspring while doing without. Likewise at least one variety of bird—the Beltsville Small White turkey, a domestic dinner-table model out of Beltsville, Maryland—has achieved scientific renown for a similar feat. What we are talking about here is celibate motherhood, procreation without copulation, a phenomenon that goes by the technical name parthenogenesis. Translated from the Greek roots: virgin birth. **(1)**

And you don't have to be Catholic to believe in this one. **(2)**

Miraculous as it may seem, parthenogenesis is actually rather common throughout nature, practiced regularly or intermittently by at least some species within almost every group of animals except (for reasons still unknown) dragonflies and mammals. Reproduction by virgin females has been discovered among reptiles, birds, fishes, amphibians, crustaceans, mollusks, ticks, the jellyfish clan, flatworms, roundworms, segmented worms; and among insects (notwithstanding those unrelentingly sexy dragonflies) it is especially favored. The order Hymenoptera, including all bees and wasps, is uniformly parthenogenetic in the manner by which males are produced: Every male honeybee is born without any genetic contribution from a father. Among the beetles, there are thirty-five different forms of parthenogenetic weevil. The African weaver ant employs parthenogenesis, as do twenty-three species of fruit fly and at least one kind of roach. The gall midge *Miastor* is notorious for the exceptionally bizarre and grisly scenario that allows its fatherless young to see daylight: *Miastor* daughters cannibalize the mother from inside, with ruthless impatience, until her hollowed-out skin splits open like the door of an overcrowded nursery. But the foremost practitioners of virgin birth—their elaborate and versatile proficiency unmatched in the animal kingdom—are undoubtedly the aphids. **(3)**

Now no sensible reader of even this book can be expected, I realize, to care faintly about aphid biology *qua* aphid biology. That's just asking too much. But there's a larger rationale for dragging you aphid-ward. The life cycle of these little nebbishy sap-sucking insects, the very same that infest rose bushes and house plants, not only exemplifies *how* parthenogenetic reproduction is done; it also very clearly shows *why*. **(4)**

First the biographical facts. A typical aphid, which feeds entirely on plant juices tapped off from the vascular system of young leaves, spends winter dormant and protected, as an egg. The egg is attached near a bud site on the new growth of a poplar tree. In March, when the tree sap has begun to rise and the buds have begun to burgeon, an aphid hatchling

Critical Reading

The Quammen essay provides students with many examples of how an author connects with his readers. First, ask students to describe the intended audience. Then ask them to annotate the essay, noting *audience cues* that guide readers, such as his lead-in, map, paragraph hooks, and transitions between paragraphs. In addition, have students note devices that help Quammen *connect* with his readers: his tone and voice; his use of first, second, and third person; and even his anthropomorphism. (See Questions 3, 4, and 7 following the essay.) Students should then annotate the essay and collate their notes in small groups. After listing and discussing Quammen's methods at the board, give students a few minutes to try some of this author's strategies in their own essay drafts.

appears, plugging its sharp snout (like a mosquito's) into the tree's tenderest plumbing. This solitary individual aphid will be, necessarily, a wingless female. If she is lucky, she will become sole founder of a vast aphid population. Having sucked enough poplar sap to reach maturity, she produces—by *live birth* now, and without benefit of a mate—daughters identical to herself. These wingless daughters also plug into the tree's flow of sap, and they also produce further wingless daughters, until sometime in late May, when that particular branch of that particular tree can support no more thirsty aphids. Suddenly there is a change: The next generation of daughters are born with wings. They fly off in search of a better situation. **(5)**

One such aviatrix lands on an herbaceous plant—say a young climbing bean in some human's garden—and the pattern repeats. She plugs into the sap ducts on the underside of a new leaf, commences feasting destructively, and delivers by parthenogenesis a great brood of wingless daughters. The daughters beget more daughters, those daughters beget still more, and so on, until the poor bean plant is encrusted with a solid mob of these fat little elbowing greedy sisters. Then again, neatly triggered by the crowded conditions, a generation of daughters are born with wings. Away they fly, looking for prospects, and one of them lights on, say, a sugar beet. (The switch from bean to beet is fine, because our species of typical aphid is not inordinately choosy.) The sugar beet before long is covered, sucked upon mercilessly, victimized by a horde of mothers and nieces and granddaughters. Still not a single male aphid has appeared anywhere in the chain. **(6)**

The lurching from one plant to another continues; the alternation between wingless and winged daughters continues. But in September, with fresh tender plant growth increasingly hard to find, there is another change. **(7)**

Flying daughters are born who have a different destiny: They wing back to the poplar tree, where they give birth to a crop of wingless females that are unlike any so far. These latest girls know the meaning of sex! Meanwhile, at long last, the starving survivors back on that final bedraggled sugar beet have brought forth a generation of males. The males have wings. They take to the air in quest of poplar trees and first love. *Et violà.* The mated females lay eggs that will wait out the winter near bud sites on that poplar tree, and the circle is thus completed. One single aphid hatchling—call her the *fundatrix*—in this way can give rise in the course of a year, from her own ovaries exclusively, to roughly a zillion aphids. **(8)**

This is all well and good, you say. A zillion aphids. But what is the point of it? **(9)**

The point, for aphids as for most other parthenogenetic animals, is

Reader Response Activity

Chapter 5 explained that readers comprehend by testing predictions as they read. Quammen's essay works well for a prediction exercise. If students have not yet read the essay, ask them to read the title and the opening paragraph. Then ask them to summarize what they have just read and to predict what they expect Quammen to discuss next. Talk about their predictions. Then have them read the next two paragraphs, summarize what Quammen says, and predict what he will discuss next. Do this process one more time. The point of this exercise is to dramatize for students how readers bring their prior knowledge to a text, make predictions as they read, confirm or reject those predictions, and continue reading. Dramatizing this activity in class makes the point that writers need to help their readers by using examples that will trigger the readers' prior knowledge, by showing relationships, by using transitions, and by giving directional cues.

(1) exceptionally fast reproduction that allows (2) maximal exploitation of temporary resource abundance and unstable environmental conditions, while (3) facilitating the successful colonization of unfamiliar habitats. In other words the aphid, like the gall midge and the weaver ant and the rest of their fellow parthenogens, is by its evolved character a galloping opportunist. **(10)**

This is a term of science, not of abuse. Population ecologists make an illuminating distinction between what they label *equilibrium* and *opportunistic* species. According to William Birky and John Gilbert, from a paper in the journal *American Zoologist*: "Equilibrium species, exemplified by many vertebrates, maintain relatively constant population sizes, in part by being adapted to reproduce, at least slowly, in most of the environmental conditions which they meet. Opportunistic species, on the other hand, show extreme population fluctuations; they are adapted to reproduce only in a relatively narrow range of conditions, but make up for this by reproducing extremely rapidly in favorable circumstances. At least in some cases, opportunistic organisms can also be categorized as colonizing organisms." Birky and Gilbert also emphasize that "The potential for rapid reproduction is the essential evolutionary ticket for entry into the opportunistic life style." **(11)**

And parthenogenesis, in turn, is the greatest time-saving gimmick in the history of animal reproduction. No hours or days are wasted while a female looks for a mate; no minutes lost to the act of mating itself. The female aphid attains sexual maturity and, bang, she becomes automatically pregnant. No waiting, no courtship, no fooling around. She delivers her brood of daughters, they grow to puberty and, zap, another generation immediately. If humans worked as fast, Jane Fonda today would be a great-grandmother. The time saved to parthenogenetic species may seem trivial, but it is not. It adds up dizzyingly: In the same time taken by a sexually reproducing insect to complete three generations for a total of 1,200 offspring, an aphid (assuming the *same* time required for each female to mature, and the *same* number of progeny in each litter), squandering no time on courtship or sex, will progress through six generations for an extended family of 318,000,000. **(12)**

Even this isn't speedy enough for some restless opportunists. That matricidal gall midge *Miastor*, whose larvae feed on fleeting eruptions of fungus under the bark of trees, has developed a startling way to cut further time from the cycle of procreation. Far from waiting for a mate, *Miastor* does not even wait for maturity. When food is abundant, it is the *larva*, not the adult female fly, who is eaten alive from inside by her own daughters. And as those voracious daughters burst free of the husk that was their mother, each of them already contains further larval daughters taking shape ominously within its own ovaries. While the food lasts, while opportunity endures, no *Miastor* female can live to adulthood without dying of motherhood. **(13)**

The implicit principle behind all this nonsexual reproduction, all this hurry, is simple: Don't argue with success. Don't tamper with a genetic blueprint that works. Unmated female aphids, and gall midges, pass on their own gene patterns virtually unaltered (except for the occasional mutation) to their daughters. Sexual reproduction, on the other hand, constitutes, by its essence, genetic tampering. The whole purpose of joining sperm with egg is to shuffle the genes of both parents and come up with a new combination that might perhaps be more advantageous. Give the kid something neither Mom nor Pop ever had. Parthenogenetic species, during their hurried phases at least, dispense with this genetic shuffle. They stick stubbornly to the gene pattern that seems to be working. They produce (with certain complicated exceptions) natural clones of themselves. **(14)**

But what they gain thereby in reproductive rate, in great explosions of population, they give up in flexibility. They minimize their genetic options. They lessen their chances of adapting to unforeseen changes of circumstance. **(15)**

Which is why more than one biologist has drawn the same conclusion as M. J. D. White: "Parthenogenetic forms seem to be frequently successful in the particular ecological niche which they occupy, but sooner or later the inherent disadvantages of their genetic system must be expected to lead to a lack of adaptability, followed by eventual extinction, or perhaps in some cases by a return to sexuality." **(16)**

So it *is* necessary, at least intermittently (once a year, for the aphids, whether they need it or not), this thing called sex. As of course you and I knew it must be. Otherwise surely, by now, we mammals and dragonflies would have come up with something more dignified. **(17)**

VOCABULARY

In your journal, write the meanings of the following words:

- more eccentrically *nonlibidinous* (1)
- *celibate* motherhood (1)
- the technical name *parthenogenesis* (1)
- *qua* aphid biology (4)
- the *vascular* system (5)
- begun to *burgeon* (5)
- One such *aviatrix* (6)
- an *herbaceous* plant (6)

- That *matricidal* gall midge (13)
- natural *clones* of themselves (14)
- particular ecological *niche* (16)

Questions for Writing and Discussion

1. Write for five minutes describing your response to Quammen's essay. Did you enjoy reading it? Did you think Quammen was being too cute? Describe what you learned from the essay. Which biological terms or concepts were difficult or unfamiliar?

2. According to Quammen, what are the genetic advantages and disadvantages of parthenogenesis in the animal kingdom?

3. Quammen's essay illustrates how writers typically combine definition, process analysis, and causal analysis in a single essay. Identify paragraphs in which he *defines* key terms. Which paragraphs explain the stages in the *process* of parthenogenesis? (What are the major stages?) Which paragraphs explain the positive and negative *effects* of parthenogenesis?

4. Describe the intended audience for Quammen's essay. Where does he directly address his readers? Where does he cue his readers about what he intends to discuss? Find examples of the following audience cues: thesis sentence, essay map, paragraph hooks, transition words, and summaries of major points.

5. Describe Quammen's tone (his attitude toward his subject). Cite two passages that illustrate this tone. Describe Quammen's voice (his personality as projected in the essay). Cite two passages that reveal his voice. Based on your description, are his tone and voice appropriate for his subject and audience?

6. In paragraph 3, Quammen says that the gall midge's skin "splits open like the door of an overcrowded nursery." Find two other similes or images in his essay. Are his images vivid? Are they appropriate?

7. *Anthropomorphism* is the attribution of human motivation and behavior to nonhuman objects or species. Where is Quammen anthropomorphic in his essay? Is his humanizing of aphids entertaining or effective? Explain your answer, based on your perception of his intended purpose and audience.

TO DISPEL FEARS OF LIVE BURIAL

JESSICA MITFORD

In this selection from The American Way of Death, *Jessica Mitford illustrates the kind of investigative journalism (some call it "muckraking") that she has perfected. Other works by Mitford include* The Trial of Dr. Spock *(1969),* Kind and Unusual Punishment: The Prison Business *(1973), and* Poison Penmanship *(1979), a collection of articles. In "To Dispel Fears of Live Burial," Mitford explains what embalming is, shows how the process works, and suggests why funeral directors and the public agree to the whole affair. If writing exposition means the "act of exposing" as well as offering explanation, then Mitford is definitely writing "expository" prose. In fact, the exposure is so revealing that we are shocked by what we learn. As we read her essay, we begin to wonder about causes. Why doesn't the public know more about the funeral industry? Why are we so ignorant in these matters? Are we, as consumers, getting what we really want—and deserve?*

Embalming is indeed a most extraordinary procedure, and one must wonder at the docility of Americans who each year pay hundreds of millions of dollars for its perpetuation, blissfully ignorant of what it is all about, what is done, how it is done. Not one in ten thousand has any idea of what actually takes place. Books on the subject are extremely hard to come by. They are not to be found in most libraries or bookshops. **(1)**

In an era when huge television audiences watch surgical operations in the comfort of their living rooms, when, thanks to the animated cartoon, the geography of the digestive system has become familiar territory even to the nursery school set, in a land where the satisfaction of curiosity about almost all matters is a national pastime, the secrecy surrounding embalming can, surely, hardly be attributed to the inherent gruesomeness of the subject. Custom in this regard has within this century suffered a complete reversal. In the early days of American embalming, when it was performed in the home of the deceased, it was almost mandatory for some relative to stay by the embalmer's side and witness the procedure. Today, family members who might wish to be in attendance would certainly be dissuaded by the funeral director. All others, except apprentices, are excluded by law from the preparation room. **(2)**

A close look at what does actually take place may explain in large measure the undertaker's intractable reticence concerning a procedure that has become his major *raison d'être*. Is it possible he fears that public information about embalming might lead patrons to wonder if they really want this service? If the funeral men are loath to discuss the subject outside the trade, the reader may, understandably, be equally loath to go on reading at this point. For those who have the stomach for it, let us part the formaldehyde curtain.... **(3)**

The body is first laid out in the undertaker's morgue—or rather, Mr. Jones is reposing in the preparation room—to be readied to bid the world farewell. **(4)**

The preparation room in any of the better funeral establishments has the tiled and sterile look of a surgery, and indeed the embalmer-restorative artist who does his chores there is beginning to adopt the term "dermasurgeon" (appropriately corrupted by some mortician-writers as "demi-surgeon") to describe his calling. His equipment, consisting of scalpels, scissors, augers, forceps, clamps, needles, pumps, tubes, bowls and basins, is crudely imitative of the surgeon's, as is his technique, acquired in a nine- or twelve-month post-high-school course in an embalming school. He is supplied by an advanced chemical industry with a bewildering array of fluids, sprays, pastes, oils, powders, creams, to fix or soften tissue, shrink or distend it as needed, dry it here, restore the moisture there. There are cosmetics, waxes and paints to fill and cover features, even plaster of Paris to replace entire limbs. There are ingenious aids to prop and stabilize the cadaver: a Vari-Pose Head Rest, the Edwards Arm and Hand Positioner, the Repose Block (to support the shoulders during the embalming), and the Throop Foot Positioner, which resembles an old-fashioned stocks. **(5)**

Mr. John H. Eckels, president of the Eckels College of Mortuary Science, thus describes the first part of the embalming procedure. "In the hands of a skilled practitioner, this work may be done in a comparatively short time and without mutilating the body other than by slight incision—so slight that it scarcely would cause serious inconvenience if made upon a living person. It is necessary to remove the blood, and doing this not only helps in the disinfecting, but removes the principal cause of disfigurements due to discoloration." **(6)**

Another textbook discusses the all-important time element: "The earlier this is done, the better, for every hour that elapses between death and embalming will add to the problems and complications encountered...." Just how soon should one get going on the embalming? The author tells us, "On the basis of such scanty information made available to this profession through its rudimentary and haphazard system of technical research, we must conclude that the best results are to be obtained if the subject is embalmed before life is completely extinct—that is, before cellular death has occurred. In the average case, this would mean within an hour after somatic death." For those who feel that there is something a little rudimentary, not to say haphazard, about this advice, a comforting thought is offered by another writer. Speaking of fears enter-

CRITICAL READING

Understanding Mitford's diction and use of irony are essential to a critical reading of this essay. Ask students to find *euphemistic* words such as "restorative artist," "preparation room," "reposing," "cavity fluid," and "slumber room." Why does the funeral industry use euphemisms? Why does Mitford echo that language? As an exercise, ask students to substitute synonyms for such language (that is, "embalmer" for "restorative artist"). What effect do such substitutions have on the tone or meaning of the passage? Also have students identify and discuss Mitford's highly *ironic* language ("comforting thought," "dispel fears of live burial," "healthy glow") and language that contains outright puns ("intestinal fortitude").

tained in early days of premature burial, he points out, "One of the effects of embalming by chemical injection, however, has been to dispel fears of live burial." How true; once the blood is removed, chances of live burial are indeed remote. **(7)**

To return to Mr. Jones, the blood is drained out through the veins and replaced by embalming fluid pumped in through the arteries. As noted in *The Principles and Practices of Embalming*, "every operator has a favorite injection and drainage point—a fact which becomes a handicap only if he fails or refuses to forsake his favorites when conditions demand it." Typical favorites are the carotid artery, femoral artery, jugular vein, subclavian vein. There are various choices of embalming fluid. If Flextone is used, it will produce a "mild flexible rigidity. The skin retains a velvety softness, the tissues are rubbery and pliable. Ideal for women and children." It may be blended with B. and G. Products Company's Lyf-Lyk tint, which is guaranteed to reproduce "nature's own skin texture . . . the velvety appearance of living tissue." Suntone comes in three separate tints: Suntan; Special Cosmetic Tint, a pink shade "especially indicated for female subjects"; and Regular Cosmetic Tint, moderately pink. **(8)**

About three to six gallons of dyed and perfumed solution of formaldehyde, glycerin, borax, phenol, alcohol and water is soon circulating through Mr. Jones, whose mouth has been sewn together with a "needle directed upward between the upper lip and gum and brought out through the left nostril," with the corners raised slightly "for a more pleasant expression." If he should be bucktoothed, his teeth are cleaned with Bon Ami and coated with colorless nail polish. His eyes, meanwhile, are closed with flesh-tinted eye caps and eye cement. **(9)**

The next step is to have at Mr. Jones with a thing called a trocar. This is a long, hollow needle attached to a tube. It is jabbed into the abdomen, poked around the entrails and chest cavity, the contents of which are pumped out and replaced with "cavity fluid." This done, and the hole in the abdomen sewn up, Mr. Jones' face is heavily creamed (to protect the skin from burns which may be caused by leakage of the chemicals), and he is covered with a sheet and left unmolested for a while. But not for long—there is more, much more, in store for him. He has been embalmed, but not yet restored, and the best time to start the restorative work is eight to ten hours after embalming, when the tissues have become firm and dry. **(10)**

The object of all this attention to the corpse, it must be remembered, is to make it presentable for viewing in an attitude of healthy repose. "Our customs require the presentation of our dead in the semblance of normality ... unmarred by the ravages of illness, disease or mutilation," says Mr. J. Sheridan Mayer in his *Restorative Art*. This is rather a large order since few people die in the full bloom of health, unravaged by illness and unmarked by some disfigurement. The funeral industry is equal to the challenge: "In some cases, the gruesome appearance of a mutilated or disease-ridden subject may be quite discouraging. The task of restoration may seem impossible and shake the confidence of the embalmer. This is the time for intestinal fortitude and determination. Once the formative work is begun and affected tissues are cleaned or removed, all doubts of success vanish. It is surprising and gratifying to discover the results which may be obtained." **(11)**

The embalmer, having allowed an appropriate interval to elapse, returns to the attack, but now he brings into play the skill and equipment of sculptor and cosmetician. Is a hand missing? Casting one in plaster of Paris is a simple matter. "For replacement purposes, only a cast of the back of the hand is necessary; this is within the ability of the average operator and is quite adequate." If a lip or two, a nose or an ear should be missing, the embalmer has at hand a variety of restorative waxes with which to model replacements. Pores and skin texture are simulated by stippling with a little brush, and over this cosmetics are laid on. Head off? Decapitation cases are rather routinely handled. Ragged edges are trimmed, and head joined to torso with a series of splints, wires and sutures. It is a good idea to have a little something at the neck—a scarf or a high collar—when time for viewing comes. Swollen mouth? Cut out tissue as needed from inside the lips. If too much is removed, the surface contour can easily be restored by padding with cotton. Swollen necks and cheeks are reduced by removing tissue through vertical incisions made down each side of the neck. "When the deceased is casketed, the pillow will hide the suture incisions ... as an extra precaution against leakage, the suture may be painted with liquid sealer." **(12)**

The opposite condition is more likely to present itself—that of emaciation. His hypodermic syringe now loaded with massage cream, the embalmer seeks out and fills the hollowed and sunken areas by injection. In this procedure the backs of the hands and fingers and the under-chin area should not be neglected. **(13)**

Positioning the lips is a problem that recurrently challenges the ingenuity of the embalmer. Closed too tightly, they tend to give a stern, even disapproving expression. Ideally, embalmers feel, the lips should give the impression of being ever so slightly parted, the upper lip protruding slightly for a more youthful appearance. This takes some engineering, however, as the lips tend to drift apart. Lip drift can sometimes be remedied by pushing one or two straight pins through the inner margin of the lower lip and then inserting them between the two front upper teeth. If Mr. Jones happens to have no teeth, the pins can just as easily be anchored in his Armstrong Face Former and Denture Replacer. Another method to maintain lip closure is to dislocate the lower jaw, which is then held in its new position by a wire run through holes which have been drilled through the upper and lower jaws at the midline. As the French are fond of saying, *il faut souffrir pour être belle.* **(14)**

If Mr. Jones has died of jaundice, the embalming fluid will very likely turn him green. Does this deter the embalmer? Not if he has intestinal fortitude. Masking pastes and cosmetics are heavily laid on, burial garments and casket interiors are color-correlated with particular care, and Jones is displayed beneath rose-colored lights. Friends will say "How well he looks." Death by carbon monoxide, on the other hand, can be rather a good thing from the embalmer's viewpoint: "One advantage is the fact that this type of discoloration is an exaggerated form of a natural pink coloration." This is nice because the healthy glow is already present and needs but little attention. **(15)**

The patching and filling completed, Mr. Jones is now shaved, washed and dressed. Cream-based cosmetic, available in pink, flesh, suntan, brunette and blond, is applied to his hands and face, his hair is shampooed and combed (and, in the case of Mrs. Jones, set), his hands manicured. For the horny-handed son of toil special care must be taken; cream should be applied to remove ingrained grime, and the nails cleaned. "If he were not in the habit of having them manicured in life, trimming and shaping is advised for better appearance—never questioned by kin." **(16)**

Jones is now ready for casketing (this is the present participle of the verb "to casket"). In this operation his right shoulder should be depressed slightly "to turn the body a bit to the right and soften the appearance of lying flat on the back." Positioning the hands is a matter of importance, and special rubber positioning blocks may be used. The hands should be cupped slightly for a more lifelike, relaxed appearance. Proper placement of the body requires a delicate sense of balance. It should lie as high as possible in the casket, yet not so high that the lid, when lowered, will hit the nose. On the other hand, we are cautioned, placing the body too low "creates the impression that the body is in a box." **(17)**

Jones is next wheeled into the appointed slumber room where a few last touches may be added—his favorite pipe placed in his hand or, if he was a great reader, a book propped into position. (In the case of little Master Jones a Teddy bear may be clutched.) Here he will hold open house for a few days, visiting hours 10 a.m. to 9 p.m. **(18)**

Vocabulary

In your journal, write the meaning of the following words:

- *docility* of Americans (1)
- *intractable reticence* concerning a procedure (3)

- *raison d'être* [reason for being] (3)
- *loath* to discuss the subject (3)
- *rudimentary* and haphazard system (7)
- *somatic* death (7)
- splints, wires and *sutures* (12)
- that of *emaciation* (13)
- *il faut souffrir pour être belle* [one must suffer in order to be beautiful] (14)
- died of *jaundice* (15)

Questions for Writing and Discussion

1. What word best describes your initial reaction to this article: disgust, nausea, confusion, anger, surprise, amazement, disbelief, or some other word? Explain your reaction.

2. Funeral directors all over the country were outraged when *The American Way of Death* appeared. What passages from this selection would most likely anger them—and why?

3. Do you believe Mitford's *purpose* in this essay was just to *inform* us about the embalming procedure? To *explain* how and why it happens? To *persuade* us to adopt some belief or take action? What parts of the essay illustrate her purpose(s) most clearly? (Refer to paragraph numbers.)

4. The contrast between appearance and reality is a recurring theme in this essay—for instance, the lifelike appearance of the embalmed and prepared body versus the reality of death. Where in the essay is this contrast most obvious?

5. Mitford's essay illustrates organization by process analysis—her explanation of *how* the embalming process occurs. List the major steps in the embalming process. (Refer to paragraph numbers for each step.) What references to time or sequence does she use for transitions at the beginning of the paragraphs?

6. Without conducting a thorough investigation, Mitford could not have learned enough to write this explanation of embalming. What books, journals, or interviews does she refer to in her essay? What direct quotations does she use?

7. Describe the *persona* that Mitford projects in this essay. What is her *tone* or attitude toward her subject? Is she writing from the perspective of a sympathetic observer of the funeral industry or of one hostile to its pretensions? Where in the essay is her tone most obvious?

HOW MALE AND FEMALE STUDENTS USE LANGUAGE DIFFERENTLY

DEBORAH TANNEN

Everyone knows that men and women communicate differently, but Deborah Tannen, a linguist at Georgetown University, has spent her career studying how *and* why *their conversational styles are different. Tannen's books include* Conversational Style: Analyzing Talk among Friends *(1984) and her best-selling* You Just Don't Understand: Women and Men in Conversation *(1990). In the following article from* The Chronicle of Higher Education, *Tannen applies her knowledge of conversational styles to the classroom. How do men and women communicate differently in the classroom? What teaching styles best promote open communication and learning for both sexes? As you read her essay, think about your own classes. Do the men in your classes talk more than the women? Do men like to argue in large groups, while women prefer conversations in small groups? How clearly—and convincingly—does Tannen explain discussion preferences and their effects in the classroom?*

When I researched and wrote my latest book, *You Just Don't Understand: Women and Men in Conversation*, the furthest thing from my mind was reevaluating my teaching strategies. But that has been one of the direct benefits of having written the book. **(1)**

The primary focus of my linguistic research always has been the language of everyday conversation. One facet of this is conversational style: how different regional, ethnic, and class backgrounds, as well as age and gender, result in different ways of using language to communicate. *You Just Don't Understand* is about the conversational styles of women and men. As I gained more insight into typically male and female ways of using language, I began to suspect some of the causes of the troubling facts that women who go to single-sex schools do better in later life, and that when young women sit next to young men in classrooms, the males talk more. This is not to say that all men talk in class, nor that no women do. It is simply that a greater percentage of discussion time is taken by men's voices. **(2)**

The research of sociologists and anthropologists such as Janet Lever, Marjorie Harness Goodwin, and Donna Eder has shown that girls and boys learn to use language differently in their sex-separate peer groups.

Typically, a girl has a best friend with whom she sits and talks, frequently telling secrets. It's the telling of secrets, the fact and the way that they talk to each other, that makes them best friends. For boys, activities are central: their best friends are the ones they do things with. Boys also tend to play in larger groups that are hierarchical. High-status boys give orders and push low-status boys around. So boys are expected to use language to seize center stage: by exhibiting their skill, displaying their knowledge, and challenging and resisting challenges. **(3)**

These patterns have stunning implications for classroom interaction. Most faculty members assume that participating in class discussion is a necessary part of successful performance. Yet speaking in a classroom is more congenial to boys' language experience than to girls', since it entails putting oneself forward in front of a large group of people, many of whom are strangers and at least one of whom is sure to judge speakers' knowledge and intelligence by their verbal display. **(4)**

Another aspect of many classrooms that makes them more hospitable to most men than to most women is the use of debate-like formats as a learning tool. Our educational system, as Walter Ong argues persuasively in his book *Fighting for Life* (Cornell University Press, 1981), is fundamentally male in that the pursuit of knowledge is believed to be achieved by ritual opposition: public display followed by argument and challenge. Father Ong demonstrates that ritual opposition—what he calls "adversativeness" or "agonism"—is fundamental to the way most males approach almost any activity. (Consider, for example, the little boy who shows he likes a little girl by pulling her braids and shoving her.) But ritual opposition is antithetical to the way most females learn and like to interact. It is not that females don't fight, but that they don't fight for fun. They don't *ritualize* opposition. **(5)**

Anthropologists working in widely disparate parts of the world have found contrasting verbal rituals for women and men. Women in completely unrelated cultures (for example, Greece and Bali) engage in ritual laments: spontaneously produced rhyming couplets that express their pain, for example, over the loss of loved ones. Men do not take part in laments. They have their own, very different verbal ritual: a contest, a war of words in which they vie with each other to devise clever insults. **(6)**

When discussing these phenomena with a colleague, I commented that I see these two styles in American conversation: many women bond by talking about troubles, and many men bond by exchanging playful insults and put-downs, and other sorts of verbal sparring. He exclaimed: "I never thought of this, but that's the way I teach: I have students read an article, and then I invite them to tear it apart. After we've torn it to shreds, we talk about how to build a better model." **(7)**

This contrasts sharply with the way I teach: I open the discussion of

CRITICAL READING

In Chapter 5, Sonja Browe argues in her summary/response essay that Tannen's description of her own classroom research widens the focus of the essay from gender differences to cultural differences. Therefore, Browe claims, Tannen does not "stay focused on her original thesis." Ask students to review Tannen's essay, focusing on paragraphs 15–24. Does their analysis confirm or refute Browe's claim?

readings by asking, "What did you find useful in this? What can we use in our own theory building and our own methods?" I note what I see as weaknesses in the author's approach, but I also point out that the writer's discipline and purposes might be different from ours. Finally, I offer personal anecdotes illustrating the phenomena under discussion and praise students' anecdotes as well as their critical acumen. **(8)**

These different teaching styles must make our classrooms wildly different places and hospitable to different students. Male students are more likely to be comfortable attacking the readings and might find the inclusion of personal anecdotes irrelevant and "soft." Women are more likely to resist discussion they perceive as hostile, and, indeed, it is women in my classes who are most likely to offer personal anecdotes. **(9)**

A colleague who read my book commented that he had always taken for granted that the best way to deal with students' comments is to challenge them; this, he felt it was self-evident, sharpens their minds and helps them develop debating skills. But he had noticed that women were relatively silent in his classes, so he decided to try beginning discussion with relatively open-ended questions and letting comments go unchallenged. He found, to his amazement and satisfaction, that more women began to speak up. **(10)**

Though some of the women in his class clearly liked this better, perhaps some of the men liked it less. One young man in my class wrote in a questionnaire about a history professor who gave students questions to think about and called on people to answer them: "He would then play devil's advocate ... *i.e.*, he debated us.... That class *really* sharpened me intellectually.... We as students do need to know how to defend ourselves." This young man valued the experience of being attacked and challenged publicly. Many, if not most, women would shrink from such "challenge," experiencing it as public humiliation. **(11)**

A professor at Hamilton College told me of a young man who was upset because he felt his class presentation had been a failure. The professor was puzzled because he had observed that class members had listened attentively and agreed with the student's observations. It turned out that it was this very agreement that the student interpreted as failure: since no one had engaged his ideas by arguing with him, he felt they had found them unworthy of attention. **(12)**

So one reason men speak in class more than women is that many of them find the "public" classroom setting more conducive to speaking, whereas most women are more comfortable speaking in private to a small group of people they know well. A second reason is that men are more likely to be comfortable with the debate-like form that discussion may take. Yet another reason is the different attitudes toward speaking in class that typify women and men. **(13)**

CRITICAL READING

In a response to Tannen's essay, one student wrote that his participation in class depended more on the subject than on either classroom environment or gender. He noted that in his economics class, he was usually silent, but when the subject shifted one day to World Cup soccer, he found himself eagerly participating—even leading the conversation. Ask students to consider what factors—other than discussion environment and gender—might affect participation in class discussions.

Students who speak frequently in class, many of whom are men, assume that it is their job to think of contributions and try to get the floor to express them. But many women monitor their participation not only to get the floor but to avoid getting it. Women students in my class tell me that if they have spoken up once or twice, they hold back for the rest of the class because they don't want to dominate. If they have spoken a lot one week, they will remain silent the next. These different ethics of participation are, of course, unstated, so those who speak freely assume that those who remain silent have nothing to say, and those who are reining themselves in assume that the big talkers are selfish and hoggish. **(14)**

When I looked around my classes, I could see these differing ethics and habits at work. For example, my graduate class in analyzing conversation had twenty students, eleven women and nine men. Of the men, four were foreign students: two Japanese, one Chinese, and one Syrian. With the exception of the three Asian men, all the men spoke in class at least occasionally. The biggest talker in the class was a woman, but there were also five women who never spoke at all, only one of whom was Japanese. I decided to try something different. **(15)**

I broke the class into small groups to discuss the issues raised in the readings and to analyze their own conversational transcripts. I devised three ways of dividing the students into groups: one by the degree program they were in, one by gender, and one by conversational style, as closely as I could guess it. This meant that when the class was grouped according to conversational style, I put Asian students together, fast talkers together, and quiet students together. The class split into groups six times during the semester, so they met in each grouping twice. I told students to regard the groups as examples of interactional data and to note the different ways they participated in the different groups. Toward the end of the term, I gave them a questionnaire asking about their class and group participation. **(16)**

I could see plainly from my observation of the groups at work that women who never opened their mouths in class were talking away in the small groups. In fact, the Japanese woman commented that she found it particularly hard to contribute to the all-woman group she was in because "I was overwhelmed by how talkative the female students were in the female-only group." This is particularly revealing because it highlights that the same person who can be "oppressed" into silence in one context can become the talkative "oppressor" in another. No one's conversational style is absolute; everyone's style changes in response to the context and others' styles. **(17)**

Some of the students (seven) said they preferred the same-gender groups; others preferred the same-style groups. In answer to the question "Would you have liked to speak in class more than you did?" six of the

CRITICAL READING

In the second sentence in paragraph 2, Tannen suggests that conversational style is determined by "different regional, ethnic, and class backgrounds, as well as age and gender." In paragraph 17, however, she says, "No one's conversational style is absolute: everyone's style changes in response to the context and others' styles." Ask students to discuss the tension or possible contradiction in these statements.

seven who said yes were women; the one man was Japanese. Most startlingly, this response did not come only from quiet women; it came from women who had indicated they had spoken in class never, rarely, sometimes, and often. Of the eleven students who said the amount they had spoken was fine, seven were men. Of the four women who checked "fine," two added qualifications indicating it wasn't completely fine: One wrote in "maybe more," and one wrote, "I have an urge to participate but often feel I should have something more interesting/relevant/wonderful/intelligent to say!!" **(18)**

I counted my experiment a success. Everyone in the class found the small groups interesting, and no one indicated he or she would have preferred that the class not break into groups. Perhaps most instructive, however, was the fact that the experience of breaking into groups, and of talking about participation in class, raised everyone's awareness about classroom participation. After we had talked about it, some of the quietest women in the class made a few voluntary contributions, though sometimes I had to ensure their participation by interrupting the students who were exuberantly speaking out. **(19)**

Americans are often proud that they discount the significance of cultural differences: "We are all individuals," many people boast. Ignoring such issues as gender and ethnicity becomes a source of pride: "I treat everyone the same." But treating people the same is not equal treatment if they are not the same. **(20)**

The classroom is a different environment for those who feel comfortable putting themselves forward in a group than it is for those who find the prospect of doing so chastening, or even terrifying. When a professor asks, "Are there any questions?" students who can formulate statements the fastest have the greatest opportunity to respond. Those who need significant time to do so have not really been given a chance at all, since by the time they are ready to speak, someone else has the floor. **(21)**

In a class where some students speak out without raising hands, those who feel they must raise their hands and wait to be recognized do not have equal opportunity to speak. Telling them to feel free to jump in will not make them feel free; one's sense of timing, of one's rights and obligations in a classroom, are automatic, learned over years of interaction. They may be changed over time, with motivation and effort, but they cannot be changed on the spot. And everyone assumes his or her own way is best. When I asked my students how the class could be changed to make it easier for them to speak more, the most talkative woman said she would prefer it if no one had to raise hands, and a foreign student said he wished people would raise their hands and wait to be recognized. **(22)**

My experience in this class has convinced me that small-group interaction should be part of any class that is not a small seminar. I also am convinced that having the students become observers of their own interaction is a crucial part of their education. Talking about ways of talking in class makes students aware that their ways of talking affect other students, that the motivations they impute to others may not truly reflect others' motives, and that the behaviors they assume to be self-evidently right are not universal norms. **(23)**

The goal of complete equal opportunity in class may not be attainable, but realizing that one monolithic classroom-participation structure is not equal opportunity is itself a powerful motivation to find more-diverse methods to serve diverse students—and every classroom is diverse. **(24)**

VOCABULARY

In your journal, write the meanings of the following words:

- ritual opposition is *antithetical* (5)
- personal *anecdotes* (8)
- *conducive* to speaking (13)
- *ethics* of participation (14)
- *monolithic* classroom-participation structure (24)

QUESTIONS FOR WRITING AND DISCUSSION

1. Reread Tannen's essay, noting places where your experiences as a student match or do not match her observations. In what contexts were your experiences similar to or different from Tannen's? Explain what might account for the different observations.

2. In her essay, Tannen states and then continues to restate her thesis. Reread her essay, underlining all the sentences that seem to state or rephrase her main idea. Do her restatements of the main idea make her essay clearer? Explain.

3. Explaining essays may explain *what* (describe and define), explain *how* (process analysis), and/or explain *why* (causal analysis). Find one example of each of these strategies in Tannen's essay. Which of these three is the dominant shaping strategy? Support your answer with references to specific sentences or paragraphs.

4. Effective explaining essays must have supporting evidence—specific examples, facts, quotations, testimony from experts, statistics, and so on. Choose four consecutive paragraphs from Tannen's essay and list the kinds of supporting evidence she uses. Based on your inventory, rate her supporting evidence as weak, average, or strong. Explain your choice.

5. Does the style of Tannen's essay support her thesis that men and women have different ways of communicating? Does Tannen, in fact, use a "woman's style" of writing that is similar to women's conversational style? Examine Tannen's tone (her attitude toward her subject and audience), her voice (the projection of her personality in her language), and her supporting evidence (her use of facts and statistics or anecdotal, contextual evidence). Cite specific passages to support your analysis.

6. In another class where students discuss frequently, sit in the back row where you can observe the participation of men and women. First, record the number of men and the number of women in the class. Then, during one class period, record the following: (1) When the teacher calls on a student, record whether the student is male or female. (2) When students talk without raising their hands, record whether the student is male or female. (3) When students speak in class, record how long they talk and whether they are male or female. Once you have collected and analyzed your data, explain whether they seem to support or refute Tannen's claims.

TEACHING TIP

In most writing, definition *(what)*, process analysis *(how)*, and causal analysis *(why)* occur together as writers explain their subjects. Because definition and causal analysis can be difficult for many writers, however, teachers may prefer to give short journal assignments focusing on each of the separate strategies before assigning an integrated expository essay.

EXPLAINING: THE WRITING PROCESS

■ **ASSIGNMENT FOR EXPLAINING** Explain *what* something means or is, *how* it should be done or how it occurs, and/or *why* something occurs. Choose from your personal experiences, talents, or interests or choose from ideas, concepts, theories, or strategies that you are learning in other courses. Your purpose is to explain something as clearly as possible for your audience by analyzing, showing relationships, and demonstrating with examples, facts, illustrations, data, or other information.

You can write about anything, *and if you write well enough, even the reader with no intrinsic interest in the subject will become involved.*
—TRACY KIDDER
NOVELIST

CHOOSING A SUBJECT

If one of your journal entries suggested a possible subject, go on to the collecting and shaping strategies. If you still need an interesting subject, consider the following suggestions:

- Reread your authority list or the most interesting journal entries from previous chapters. Do they contain ideas that you might define or explain, processes suitable for how-to explanations, or causes or effects that you could analyze and explain for a certain audience?

- Brainstorm a list of the five most important things that you've done in the last three years. Focus on one thing, event, or idea. Now imagine that your audience is someone like you, only three years younger. Explain this topic.
- Reread your notes from another class in which you have an upcoming examination. Select some topic, idea, principle, process, famous person, or event from the text or your notes. Investigate other texts, popular magazines, or journals for information on that topic. If appropriate, interview someone or conduct a survey. Explain this principle or process to a member of your writing class.

COLLECTING

QUESTIONS Once you have a tentative subject and audience in mind, consider which of the following will be your *primary* focus (all three may be relevant):

- *What* something means or is
- *How* something occurs or is done (or should be done)
- *Why* something occurs or what its effects are.

To explain *what* something is, jot down answers to each of the following questions. The more you can write on each question, the more details you'll have for your topic.

- What are its class and distinguishing characteristics?
- What is its etymology?
- How can you describe it?
- What examples can you give?
- What are its parts or its functions?
- What is it similar to? What is it *not*?
- What figurative comparisons apply?
- How can it be classified?
- Which of the above is most useful to your audience?

To explain *how* something occurs or is done, answer the following questions:

- What are the component parts or steps in the whole process?
- What is the exact sequence of steps or events?
- Are several of the steps or events related?

RESOURCE NOTE

As D'Angelo explains in *A Conceptual Theory of Rhetoric*, rhetorical strategies—such as definition, process analysis, comparison, and causal analysis—are, simultaneously, modes of thinking, invention strategies, and patterns for arrangement. Invention (collecting) exercises anticipate arrangement (shaping) patterns, just as shapes are invitations for collecting and inventing. See also Coe, "An Apology for Form."

- If steps or events were omitted, would the outcome change?
- Which steps or events are most crucial?
- Which steps or events does your audience most need to know?

To explain *why* something occurs or what its effects are, consider the following issues:

- Which are the necessary or sufficient causes?
- Which causes are remote in time and which are immediate?
- What is the order or sequence of the causes? Do the causes occur simultaneously?
- What are the effects? Do they occur in a sequence or simultaneously?
- Do the causes and effects occur in a "chain reaction"?
- Is there an action or situation that would have prevented the effect?
- Are there comparable things or events that have similar causes or effects?
- Which causes or effects need special clarification for your audience?

BRANCHING Often, *branching* can help you visually analyze your subject. Start with your topic and then subdivide each idea into its component parts. The resulting analysis will not only help generate ideas but may also suggest ways to shape an essay:

Branching can also take the form of a tree, with a main trunk for the subject and separate branches for each subtopic. For an essay on effective job hunting, information might be diagrammed like this:

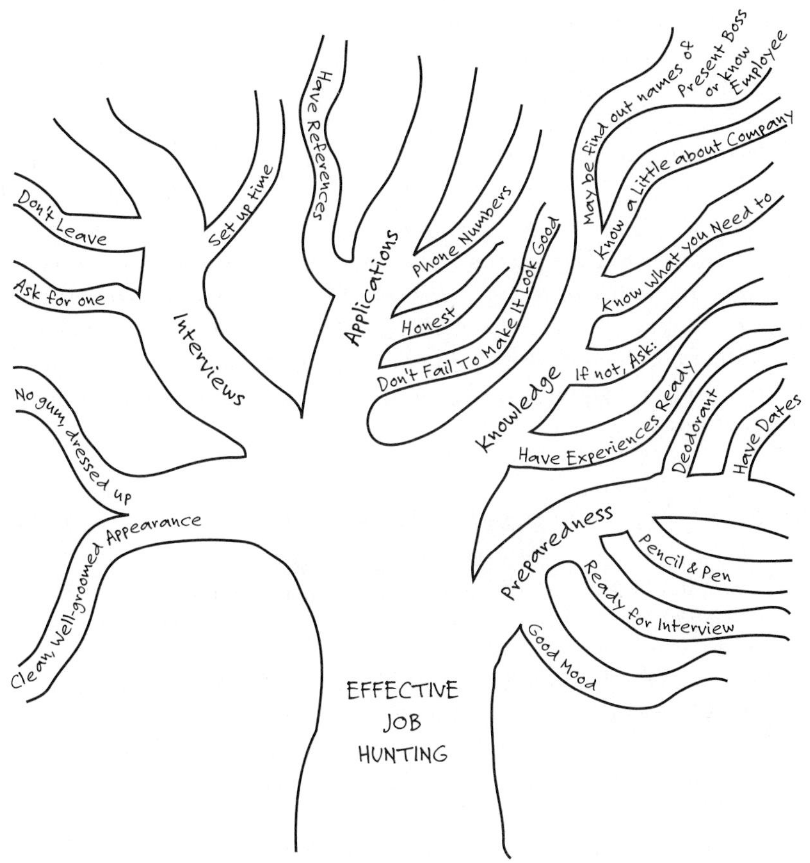

OBSERVING If you can observe your subject, try drawing it, describing it, or taking careful notes. Which senses can you use to describe it—sight, sound, touch, smell, taste? If it is a scientific experiment that you can reproduce or a social situation you can reconstruct, go through it again and observe carefully. As you observe it, put yourself in your readers' shoes: What do you need to explain it to them?

REMEMBERING Your own experience and memory are essential for explaining. *Freewriting*, *looping*, and *clustering* may all generate detailed information, good examples, and interesting perspectives that will make your explanation clearer and more vivid. (See Chapter 4 for an explanation of looping and clustering.)

COLLABORATIVE ACTIVITY

Group students in pairs and have them interview each other about their prospective papers: What is the probable focus of the paper? Why are they writing it? What sources do they still need? What have they written so far?

READING When you find written texts about your subject, be sure to use your active reading strategies. You may need only a few sources if you reread them carefully. Write out a short summary for each source. Respond to each source by analyzing its effectiveness, agreeing or disagreeing with its ideas, or interpreting the text. The quality of your understanding is more important than the sheer number of sources you cite.

INVESTIGATING Use sources available in the library, textbooks containing relevant information, or interviews with teachers, participants, or experts. Interview your classmates about their own subjects for this assignment: Someone else's subject may trigger an idea that you can write about or suggest a fresh approach to the subject that you have already chosen.

TEACHING TIP

The best approach to teaching research is to keep practicing and reinforcing research strategies, such as gathering, citing, and documenting sources. If you are teaching a more extensive research paper later in the term, you may also wish to require students to practice keeping a research log (see Chapter 11).

RESEARCH TIPS

Review your topic for research possibilities. Four research strategies are direct *observation*, use of *memories* and personal experience, *field research* (including interviews and surveys), and *library research.* (See Chapter 6 for interview and survey techniques. See Chapter 11 on Using and Documenting Sources.) Tips to remember: Make *photocopies* of all the sources that you plan to cite in your essay. When you make copies, be sure to *write all relevant information* on the photocopies, such as author, date, publisher, place of publication, journal title, and volume numbers. When you cite sources in the text, be sure to *introduce* your sources. Make sure your direct quotations are *accurate* word-for-word transcriptions.

RESOURCE NOTE

For an effective focusing strategy, see Coe, "If Not to Narrow, Then How to Focus: Two Techniques for Focusing."

SHAPING

As you collect information and generate ideas from your collecting activities, be sure to *narrow* and *focus* your subject into a topic suitable for a short essay. You will not be able to cover everything you've read, thought, or experienced about your subject. Choose the most interesting ideas—for you and for your audience—and shape, order, and clarify those ideas. In addition to *spatial order* and *comparison/contrast*, which are discussed in Chapters 3 and 4, one of the following shaping strategies may help you organize your essay.

Definition and Classification An essay explaining *what* something means or is can be shaped by using a variety of definition strategies or by classifying the subject.

Definition itself is not a single organizing strategy; it supports a variety of strategies that may be useful in shaping your essay: description, analysis of parts or function, comparison/contrast, development by examples, or figures of speech such as simile, metaphor, and analogy.

Classification, on the other hand, is a single strategy that can organize a paragraph or even a whole essay quickly. Observers of human behavior, for example, love to use classification. Grocery shoppers might be classified by types: racers (the ones who seem to have just won forty-five seconds of free shopping and run down the aisles filling their carts as fast as possible), talkers (the ones whose phone must be out of order because they stand in the aisles gossiping forever), penny-pinchers (who always have their calculators out and read the unit-price labels for everything), party shoppers (who camp out in the junk-food aisles, filling their carts with potato chips, dip, candy, peanuts, and drink mixers), and dawdlers (who leave their carts crosswise in the aisles while they read twenty-nine different soup-can labels). You can write a sentence or two about each type or devote a whole paragraph to explaining a single type.

Readers may be strangers who have no immediate reason to care about your writing. They want order, clarity, and stimulation....
—Elizabeth Cowan Neeld,
teacher and author

Example Development by example can effectively illustrate what something is or means, but it can also help explain how or why something happens. Usually, an example describes a specific incident, located at a certain place and occurring at a particular time, that *shows* or *demonstrates* the main idea. In the following paragraph from *Mediaspeak*, Donna Woolfolk Cross explains what effects soap operas can have on addicted viewers. This paragraph is developed by several examples—some described in detail, others referred to briefly:

> Dedicated watchers of soap operas often confuse fact with fiction.... Stars of soap operas tell hair-raising stories of their encounters with fans suffering from this affliction. Susan Lucci, who plays the promiscuous Erica Kane on "All My Children," tells of a time she was riding in a parade: "We were in a crowd of about 250,000 traveling in an antique open car moving ver-r-ry slowly. At that time in the series I was involved with a character named Nick. Some man broke through, came right up to the car and said to me, 'Why don't you give *me* a little bit of what you've been giving Nick?'" The man hung onto the car, menacingly, until she was rescued by the police. Another time, when she was in church, the reverent silence was broken by a woman's astonished remark, "Oh, my god, Erica prays!" Margaret Mason, who plays the villainous Lisa Anderson in "Days of Our Lives," was accosted by a woman who poured a carton of

Teaching Tip

Students often describe habitual actions for examples: "I used to watch soap operas a lot to help me relax." Encouraging them to focus on one *specific time* will help generate a more vivid, specific example: "To break the tension before my organic chemistry final, I reviewed equations for four hours in the morning and then relaxed after lunch with 'All My Children.' In effect, this more specific example *illustrates* how television relaxed the writer on all those other occasions.

> milk all over her in the supermarket. And once a woman actually tried to force her car off the Ventura Freeway.

Voice and Tone Writers also use voice and tone to shape and control whole passages, often in combination with other shaping strategies. In the following paragraph, Toni Bambara, author of *The Salt Eaters* and numerous short stories, explains *what* being a writer is all about. This paragraph is shaped both by a single extended example and by Bambara's voice talking directly to the reader:

> When I replay the tapes on file in my head, tapes of speeches I've given at writing conferences over the years, I invariably hear myself saying—"A writer, like any other cultural worker, like any other member of the community, ought to try to put her/his skills in the service of the community." Some years ago when I returned south, my picture in the paper prompted several neighbors to come visit. "You a writer? What all you write?" Before I could begin the catalogue, one old gent interrupted with—"Ya know Miz Mary down the block? She need a writer to help her send off a letter to her grandson overseas." So I began a career as the neighborhood scribe—letters to relatives, snarling letters to the traffic chief about the promised stop sign, nasty letters to the utilities, angry letters to the principal about that confederate flag hanging in front of the school, contracts to transfer a truck from seller to buyer, etc. While my efforts have been graciously appreciated in the form of sweet potato dumplings, herb teas, hair braiding, and the like, there is still much room for improvement—"For a writer, honey, you've got a mighty bad hand. Didn't they teach penmanship at that college?" Another example, I guess of words setting things in motion. What goes around, comes around, as the elders say.

Chronological Order and Process Analysis Using chronological order for a *how* explanation creates a process analysis. For example, Jessica Mitford's explanation of embalming illustrates how chronological order or process analysis can shape a whole essay. Notice how the beginnings of several body paragraphs use transitions that *signal* to the reader the chronological order of the embalming process:

> The body is *first* laid out in the undertaker's morgue.... (4)
>
> Mr. John H. Eckels ... describes the *first part* of the embalming procedure.... (6)
>
> *To return* to Mr. Jones, the blood is drained out through the veins... (8)

The *next step* is to have at Mr. Jones with a thing called a trocar. (10)

The embalmer, *having allowed an appropriate interval to elapse, returns* to the attack.... (12)

The patching and filling *completed*, Mr. Jones is *now* shaved, washed and dressed. (16)

Jones is *now* ready for casketing.... (17)

Jones is *next* wheeled into the appointed slumber room.... (18)

CAUSAL ANALYSIS In order to explain *why* something happens or what the effects of something are, writers often use one of the following three patterns of cause and effect to shape their material:

Cause 1 + Cause 2 + Cause 3 ... + Cause $n \longrightarrow$ Effect

In the case of fire, for example, we know that three causes lead to a single effect. These causes do not occur in any special sequence; they must all be present at the same time. For historical events, however, we usually list causes in chronological order.

Sometimes one cause has several effects. In that case, we reverse the pattern:

Cause$\longrightarrow$ Effect 1 + Effect 2 + Effect 3 ... + Effect n

For example, an explanation of the collapse of the economy following the stock market crash of 1929 might follow this pattern. The crash (itself a symptom of other causes) led to a depreciated economy, widespread unemployment, bankruptcy for thousands of businesses, foreclosures on farms, and so forth. An essay on the effects of the crash might devote one or two paragraphs to each effect.

In the third pattern, causes and effects form a pattern of chain reactions. One cause leads to an effect that then becomes the cause of another effect, and so on:

Cause 1$\longrightarrow$ Effect 1 (Cause 2)$\longrightarrow$ Effect 2 (Cause 3)$\longrightarrow$ Effect 3

We could analyze events in the Middle East prior to the Persian Gulf War as a series of actions and reactions in which each effect becomes the cause of the next effect in the chain of skirmishes, car bombings, air raids, terrorist hijackings, and kidnappings. An essay on the chain reaction of events in the Middle East might have a paragraph or two on each of the links in this chain.

TEACHING TIP

Teachers may usefully distinguish between the *writer's* thesis sentence and map (a working version intended to help the writer focus on a subject and start a draft) and a *reader's* thesis and map (a revised version intended to help the reader construct meaning). The distinction helps some writers as they compose and revise.

INTRODUCTION, PARAGRAPH TRANSITIONS AND HOOKS, AND BODY PARAGRAPHS The *introduction* to an explaining essay—whether one paragraph or several—usually contains the following features:

- *Lead-in*: Some example, description, statistic, startling statement, short narrative, or quotation to get the reader's interest *and* focus on the topic you will explain.
- *Thesis*: Statement of main idea; a "promise" to the reader that the essay fulfills.
- *Essay Map*: A sentence, or part of a sentence, that *lists* (in the order in which the essay discusses them) the main subtopics for the essay.

In her essay on *anorexia nervosa* at the end of this chapter, Nancie Brosseau's introductory paragraph has all three features:

Lead-in: startling statement

Description

Statistics

Thesis

Essay map

> I knew my dieting had gotten out of hand, but when I could actually see the movement of my heart beating beneath my clothes I knew I was in trouble. At first, the family doctor reassured my parents that my rapid weight loss was a "temporary phase among teenage girls." However, when I, at 14 years old and 5′0″ tall, weighed in at 63 pounds, my doctor changed his diagnosis from "temporary phase" to "anorexia nervosa." Anorexia nervosa is the process of self-starvation that affects over one hundred thousand young girls each year. Almost six thousand of these girls die every year. Anorexia nervosa is a self-mutilating disease that affects its victim both physically and emotionally. (1)

COLLABORATIVE ACTIVITY

For additional practice in identifying paragraph hooks and transitions, have students annotate Quammen's essay (which has excellent audience cues) or Brosseau's essay, "Anorexia Nervosa," reprinted at the end of this chapter. Then ask students to work on audience cues (maps, hooks, transitions) in their own drafts.

The *essay map* is contained in the phrase "both physically and emotionally": The first half of the essay discusses the *physical* effects of anorexia nervosa; the second half explains the *emotional* effects. Like a road map, the essay map helps the reader anticipate what topics the writer will explain.

Transition words and *paragraph hooks* are audience cues that help the reader shift from one paragraph to the next. These connections between paragraphs help the reader see the relationships of the various parts. *Transition words*—"first," "second," "next," "another," "last," "finally," and so forth—signal your reader that a new idea or a new part of the idea is coming up. In addition to transition words, writers often tie paragraphs together by using a key *word* or *idea* from a previous paragraph in the opening sentence of the following paragraph to "hook" the paragraphs together. The following paragraphs from Mitford's essay on embalming illustrate how transition words and paragraph hooks work together to create smooth connections between paragraphs:

About three to six gallons of a dyed and perfumed solution of formaldehyde, glycerin, borax, phenol, alcohol and water is soon circulating through Mr. Jones.... If he should be bucktoothed, his teeth are cleaned with Bon Ami and coated with colorless nail polish. His eyes, meanwhile, are closed with flesh-tinted eye caps and eye cement. (9)

The *next step* is to have at Mr. Jones with a thing called a trocar.... This done, and the hole in the abdomen sewn up, Mr. Jone's face is heavily creamed ... and he is covered with a sheet and left unmolested for a while. But not for long—there is more, much more, in store for him. He has embalmed, but not yet restored, and the best time to start the restorative work is eight to ten hours after embalming, when the tissues have become firm and dry. (10)

Transition: "next step"

The object of all this attention to the corpse, it must be remembered, is to make it presentable for viewing in an attitude of healthy repose.... The funeral industry is equal to the challenge: "In some cases, the gruesome appearance of a mutilated or disease-ridden subject may be quite discouraging. The task of restoration may seem impossible and shake the confidence of the embalmer.... It is surprising and gratifying to discover the results which may be obtained." (11)

Hook: "Mr. Jones"
Hooks: "this attention," "corpse"

The embalmer, having allowed an appropriate interval to elapse, returns to the attack, *but now* he brings into play the skill and equipment of sculptor and cosmetician. Is a hand missing? Casting one in plaster of Paris is a simple matter....

Hooks: "embalmer," "attack"
Transition: "but now"

Body paragraphs in expository writing are the main paragraphs in an essay, excluding any introductory, concluding, or transition paragraphs. They often contain the following features:

- *Topic sentence:* To promote clarity and precision, writers often use topic sentences to announce the main ideas of paragraphs. The main idea should be clearly related to the writer's thesis. A topic sentence usually occurs early in the paragraph (first or second sentence) or at the end of the paragraph.
- *Unity:* To avoid confusing readers, writers focus on a single idea for each paragraph. Writing unified paragraphs helps writers—and their readers—concentrate on one point at a time.
- *Coherence:* To make their writing flow smoothly from one sentence to the next, writers supplement their shaping strategies with coherence devices: repeated key words, pronouns referring to key nouns, and transition words.

The following body paragraph from Mitford's essay illustrates these features. The paragraph begins with a topic sentence; it has unity because it focuses on a single idea (positioning the lips) and it uses transitions, pronouns, and repeated key words to promote coherence:

Topic sentence
Pronoun: "They"
Repeated key words: "lips," "embalmer"
Transition: "however"
Repeated key word: "lip"
Transition: "Another"

> *Positioning the lips is a problem that recurrently challenges the ingenuity of the embalmer.* Closed too tightly, they tend to give a stern, even disapproving expression. Ideally, embalmers feel, the lips should give the impression of being ever so slightly parted, the upper lip protruding slightly for a more youthful appearance. This takes some engineering, *however*, as the lips tend to drift apart. Lip drift can sometimes be remedied by pushing one or two straight pins through the inner margin of the lower lip and then inserting them between the two front upper teeth. If Mr. Jones happens to have no teeth, the pins can just as easily be anchored in his Armstrong Face Former and Denture Replacer. *Another* method to maintain lip closure is to dislocate the lower jaw, which is then held in its new position by a wire run through holes which have been drilled through the upper and lower jaws at the midline. As the French are fond of saying, *il faut souffrir pour être belle.*

RESOURCE NOTE

See Lindemann's chapter, "Teaching Paragraphing," in *A Rhetoric for Writing Teachers.* She suggests that teachers avoid teaching the paragraph as product, noting that, as writers, "we don't begin with form, pouring content into paragraph molds; rather we begin with content, and in the act of drafting discover form." See Braddock, "The Frequency and Placement of Topic Sentences in Expository Prose," but also D'Angelo, "The Topic Sentence Revisited," and Eden and Mitchell, "Paragraphing for the Reader."

DRAFTING

Before you begin drafting, reconsider your purpose and audience. What you explain depends on what your audience needs to know or what would demonstrate or show your point most effectively.

As you work from an outline or from an organizing strategy, remember that all three questions—*what, how,* and *why*—are interrelated. If you are writing about causes, for example, an explanation of *what* the topic is and *how* the causes function may also be necessary to explain your subject clearly. As you write, balance your sense of plan and organization with a willingness to pursue ideas that you discover as you write. While you need to have a plan, you should be ready to change course if you discover a more interesting idea or angle.

PEER RESPONSE

The instructions below will help you give and receive constructive advice about the rough draft of your explaining essay. You may use these guidelines for an in-class workshop, a take-home review, or a computer e-mail response.

WRITER: Before you exchange drafts with another reader, write out the following on your essay draft:

1. Purpose Briefly, describe your purpose and intended audience.

2. Revision Plans What do you still intend to work on as you revise your draft?

3. Questions Write out one or two questions that you still have about your draft. What questions would you like your reader to answer?

READER: First, read the entire draft from start to finish. As you *reread* the draft, answer the following questions:

1. Clarity What passages were clearest? Where were you most confused? Refer to specific sentences or passages to support your response. How and where could the writer make the draft clearer?

2. Evidence Where does the writer have good supporting evidence (specific examples, facts, analysis, statistics, interview results, or citations from sources)? Where does the writer need additional evidence? Refer to specific sentences or passages to support your response.

3. Organization Summarize or briefly outline the main ideas of the essay. Where was the organization most clear? Where were you confused? Refer to specific passages as you suggest ways to improve the draft.

4. Purpose Underline sentences that express the purpose or contain the thesis of the essay. Does your understanding of the essay's purpose match the writer's statement about purpose? Explain. How might the writer clarify the thesis?

5. Reader's Response Overall, describe what you liked best about the draft. Then identify one major area that the writer should focus on during the revision. Does your suggestion match the writer's revision plans? Explain. Answer the writer's own question or questions about the draft.

REVISING

Because clarity is the primary goal in explaining, concentrate on making yourself perfectly clear, on illustrating with examples where your reader might be confused, and on signaling the relationship of the parts of your essay to your reader.

PEER RESPONSE

If your students complain that their peers do not give good advice during revision workshops, two activities may help. First, *model* the workshop process on your own draft. (Make sure your draft is really rough and has clear problems.) If students are comfortable critiquing your draft, they will be more effective in reviewing each other's drafts. Second, have students practice *identifying* key features (thesis, map, specific examples, paragraph hooks, definition, and so on) in a draft. Often, students give poor advice because they cannot yet identify rhetorical features in writing. A further benefit of this exercise is that *identifying features* (rather than *evaluating*) does not require students to give negative criticism and thus makes them more comfortable in peer groups. Once students can correctly identify features, then return to a regular revision workshop.

I wish he would explain his explanation.
—LORD BYRON,
POET

Guidelines For Revision

- **Compare your thesis sentence with what you say in your conclusion.** You may have a clearer statement of your thesis near the end of your paper. Revise your original thesis sentence to make it clearer, more focused, or more in line with what your essay actually says.
- **Explaining means *showing* and *demonstrating* relationships.** Be sure to follow general statements with *specific examples, details, facts, statistics, memories, dialogues*, or other *illustrations*.
- **In a formal definition, be sure to include the class of objects or concepts to which the term belongs.** Avoid ungrammatical writing, such as "Photosynthesis is *when* plants absorb oxygen" or "The lymphatic system is *where* the body removes bacteria and transports fatty cells."
- **Avoid introducing definitions with "Webster says. . . ."** Instead, read definitions from several dictionaries and give the best or most appropriate definition.
- **Remember that you can modify the dictionary definition of a term or concept to fit your particular context.** For example, to you, "heroism" may mean having the courage to *say* what you believe, not just to endanger your life through selfless actions.
- **Don't mix categories when you are classifying objects or ideas.** If you are classifying houses *by floor design* (ranch, bilevel, split-level, two-story), don't bring in other categories, such as passive-solar, which could be incorporated into any of those designs.
- **In explaining *how* something occurs or should be done, be sure to indicate to your audience which steps are *most important*.**
- **In cause-and-effect explanations, avoid *post hoc* fallacies**. This term comes from the Latin phrase *post hoc, ergo propter hoc*: "after this, therefore because of this." For example, just because Event B occurred after Event A, it does not follow necessarily, that A caused B. If, for example, statistics show that traffic fatalities in your state actually declined after the speed limit on interstate highways was increased, you should not conclude that higher speeds actually caused the reduction in fatalities. Other causes—increased radar patrols, stiffer drunk-driving penalties, or more rigorous vehicle-maintenance laws—may have been responsible for the reduction.

Computer Tips: Editing

Most word-processing programs have built-in dictionaries or spell checkers to catch spelling errors and typos. Too often, however, writers rely on spell checkers to catch all their errors. While spell checks are useful editing aids, don't rely on them to proofread.

As you proofread, check for words that are spelled correctly but used incorrectly, such as affect/effect or principal/principle. Look for "computos"—errors that frequently occur while drafting and revising on a computer. Check for *omissions*, for words or phrases mistakenly deleted. Similarly, look for *word doubles*, or repetitions created by failing to delete a word or phrase. Finally, check for *shifts* in sentence construction or phrasing. Don't expect spell checkers to catch these problems.

One effective proofreading strategy is to reduce the margins on your text and display it in narrow columns. Often, errors that you may have overlooked will suddenly pop out at you. See, for example, if you can find the errors in the following text display:

> Most word-processing programs have a dictionary to check for catch your spelling errors and typos. Although a spell-checking program may site obvious spelling errors but then miss an embarrassing error. The program cannot advice you to fix a word a word that is spelled correctly. You have to except responsibility for it's limitations. Reformatting your text in narrow columns may enable you to see problems see problems the spell checker misses.

- **As you revise to sharpen your meaning or make your organization clearer, use appropriate transitional words and phrases to signal the *relationships among the various parts of your subject.***

TEACHING TIP

This journal entry should be central to a teacher's response to and evaluation of students' writing. Teachers should respond to students' intentions ("Does the essay achieve the writer's purpose?"), to students' evaluations of their own writing ("Does the writer accurately perceive strengths and weaknesses?"), and to students' descriptions of their own writing processes ("Would a modified writing process improve weaknesses in the final product?"). As necessary, the teacher should tailor these postscript questions to the specific assignment.

To signal relation in time: before, meanwhile, later, soon, at last, earlier, thereafter, afterward, by that time, from then on, first, next, now, presently, shortly, immediately, finally

To signal similarity: likewise, similarly, once again, once more

To signal difference: but, yet, however, although, whereas, though, even so, nonetheless, still, on the other hand, on the contrary

To signal consequences: as a result, consequently, therefore, hence, for this reason

■ **POSTSCRIPT ON THE WRITING PROCESS** Before you hand in your essay, reflect on your writing and learning process. In your journal, spend a few minutes answering each of the following questions:

1. Describe the purpose and intended audience for your essay.

2. What was the best workshop advice that you received? What did you revise in your draft because of that advice? What piece of advice did you ignore? Why?

3. What caused you the most difficulty with this essay? How did you solve the problem—or attempt to solve it? With what parts are you still least satisfied?

4. What are the best parts of your paper? Refer to specific paragraphs—what do you like most about them?

5. What was the most important thing you learned about writing or your writing process as you wrote this paper?

EXPLAINING: STUDENT WRITING

"THE POLICE WERE CALLING ME NAMES": AN EXPLANATION OF HARD-CORE PUNK ROCK

DENNIS ALEXANDER

Dennis Alexander's essay on hard-core punk rock explains what punk rock is, but he uses definition and analysis to make his own point: Punk rock, despite the charges of its detractors, is a legitimate form of music.

Alexander's Postscript on His Writing Process

When I was thinking about this paper, I wanted to write a cause-and-effect type of paper, but I couldn't seem to come up with any ideas I wanted to write on. Then one night I ordered a pizza and a really punked-out guy delivered it. I was playing some hard core and he said something about how few people understand it. This gave me my idea for the paper. I wanted to express the idea that punk was a real and legitimate form of music, so I spent some time looking up words in the dictionary, defining terms and finding the right words. I listened to a lot of music. This was harder than it sounds, going verse by verse to figure out the lyrics. I also listened to 180 minutes of interview tape from a radio interview with various hard-core artists. Then, after some brainstorming and outlining, I finally came up with a good thesis. When I had enough evidence to give good support to my thesis and also explain about punk, I wrote my essay and revised it.

Notes for Outline

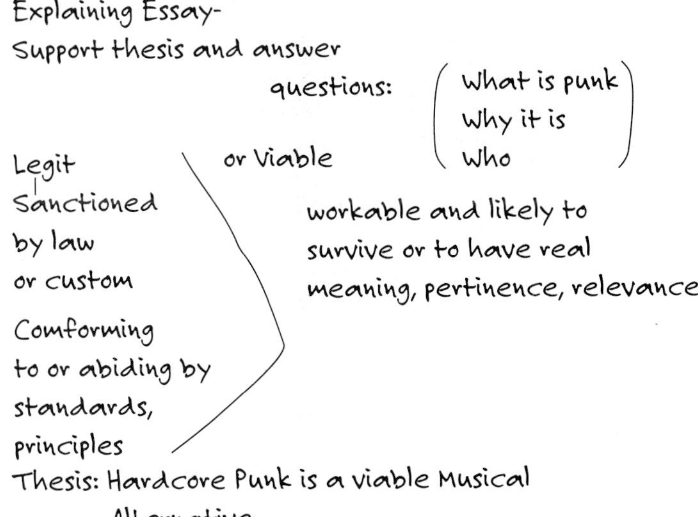

Explaining Essay-
Support thesis and answer
questions:
What is punk
Why it is
Who
Legit
or Viable
Sanctioned
by law
or custom
workable and likely to
survive or to have real
meaning, pertinence, relevance
Comforming
to or abiding by
standards,
principles
Thesis: Hardcore Punk is a viable Musical
Alternative

* It is alternative music
~~Just Beat~~
Revival of Old Rock
New Raw Rock & Roll
Not New Wave
Fast Beat
or satiric of other music

It is music
It is alternative
It is viable

Fits definition: Combination of vocal and instrumental sounds or tones in varying melody, harmony, rhythm, and timbre so as to form structurally complete and emotionally expressive compositions.
Fast Beat, Back Beat, 180 Beats/Min
Not as many chords, melody

* It is alternative
  - Revival of Old Rock
  - New Rock & Roll, Fun
  - Satirical of other music/lifestyles
  - Not New Wave

* It is viable
  - it is workable
    - provides for change
    - doesn't later to like
  - Likely to survive
    - survived since origin in early 70's in England
    - Brought to USA
  - Has meaning, pertinence, relevance
    - commentary on war
    - political statement
    - social statement
    - draws attention to community problems (landlords/police or social issues, war, politics, religion, poverty, social welfare, police)

First Draft

Purpose: To explain that hardcore is a viable musical alternative

Audience: General, but especially young people who like music but may not like hard core—probably because they don't understand it.

Hard Core

What you need boy is a holiday in Cambodia
Where you'll kiss ass or crack.
Sweat for the price of your life
With a bowl of rice as a snack.
—The Dead Kennedys
"Fresh Fruit for Rotting Vegetables"

Musical tastes vary as much as the people who like music. In any record store in America, it is not uncommon to find rock, country, and classical albums for sale. It is uncommon for a typical record store to have a variety of hard-core punk rock records for sale. This is unusual considering that hard core is a viable musical alternative. **(1)**

Some people think that punk is not music. Webster's dictionary defines music as combinations of vocal and instrumental sounds or tones in varying melody, harmony, rhythm and timbre so as to form structurally complete and emotionally expressive compositions. Hard-core punk fits this definition. Having developed from rock music in the early 70's punk inherited its rhythm and beat. The melody and harmony in rock and punk are also similar although punk has a much harsher, distorted sound. It is structurally complete and expresses a variety of emotions. Hard core may or may not sound as pleasant to the ear as other socially accepted forms of music. But this does not disqualify it as music. **(2)**

Most of all the other forms of music are accepted as legitimate. They conform and abide by socially accepted standards and customs. Because punk does not, it provides an alternative. It does not fit into other categories, it is non-conformist music. The names of common groups express this: The Germs, The Dead Kennedys, The Suicidal Tendencies, Two Sounds of Liberty (T.S.O.L.). In some ways, punk tries to revive old rock and roll into new raw rock. In other ways, punk music attempts to satirize other musical forms and the lifestyles they represent. Most importantly, punk is not new wave music. In the words of a singer from The Germs: "There was never any such thing as new wave. New wave was the polite thing to say when you were trying to explain you were not into the boring old rock but you didn't dare say punk because you were afraid to get kicked out of the f——— party." Because of the large difference between musical styles, punk is an excellent alternative. **(3)**

Despite its differences, hard-core is a viable form of music. It is workable. It can evolve and change. Because of its base on nonconformity, it easily provides for change and does not cater to sentiment. Punk is likely to survive. From its roots in the late 60's it has prospered,

TEACHING TIP

Perhaps the most exciting new teaching tool in the classroom combines the computer screen with the overhead projector. Many schools now have portable computers that can project computer screens overhead so that the whole class can observe one student in the actual process of revising. You do not have to be in a computer lab to use this technology. You just need the portable equipment and students who are drafting their essays on a compatible program. Ask a student to sit at the computer and actually make changes in his or her draft as suggested by the class.

spread and is stronger than ever. Hard-core punk also has meaning, pertinence, and relevance. It often provides a satirical social comment. **(4)**

Punk highlights social problems by advocating crude solutions. Such satirically oriented songs are: "Kill the Poor," and "Lets Lynch a Landlord" by ____________. Punk music is not afraid to hide opinion, in fact it is made blatantly clear. This opinion can be on such issues as war, religion and politics. Opinion is expressed in lyrics like "Army, Navy, Airforce, or Jail" and "President Reagan can shove it" by T.S.O.L. In these ways, punk draws attention to community and social problems and reaffirms Americans' right to free speech. It is, therefore, viable. **(5)**

Because hard-core punk is a viable musical alternative there is no reason that it should be subject to undue discrimination or censorship. Just because it does not fit some people's idea of "good taste," it should not be cleared from the shelves. Hard-core punk is legitimate music that belongs on the shelves of music stores. **(6)**

REVISED VERSION

"THE POLICE WERE CALLING ME NAMES": AN EXPLANATION OF HARD-CORE PUNK ROCK"

I sat in my dorm room waiting for a pizza to be delivered. The Dead Kennedys blasted out through my stereo speakers. "What is that shit?" someone asked as he walked by with his fingers in his ears. The pizza guy finally arrived and walked into my room wearing combat boots, chains, spiked leather and a black and blonde mohawk. His foot tapped to the beat as I paid for the pie. He looked me over from my Levis jacket to my cowboy boots and said, "You listen to the D.K.? Way cool man!" Looking back on this incident, I think that the reaction of the pizza guy was normal while the attitudes of the dorm residents were narrow-minded. Hard-core punk rock is, in fact, a viable musical alternative. **(1)**

Is hard-core punk really music or is it just so much loud noise? Perhaps we need to define what music is. Music is a combination of vocal and instrumental sounds or tones that vary in melody, harmony, rhythm and timbre. The sounds should form a structurally complete and emotionally expressive composition. Hard-core punk fits this definition. Having developed from rock in the late 60s, punk inherited its rhythm and beat. The melody and harmony in rock and punk are also similar, although punk has a much harsher, distorted sound. It is also structurally complete and expresses a variety of emotions. Hard-core may or may not sound as pleasing to the ear as other socially accepted forms of music, but this does not disqualify it as music. **(2)**

Almost all of the other forms of music, such as country, rock, and classical, are accepted as legitimate. They conform to and abide by socially accepted standards and customs. Because punk does not, it provides an alternative. It does not fit into other categories; it is non-conformist music. The names of common groups express their nonconformity; "The Germs," "The Dead Kennedys," the "Suicidal Tendencies," "Religious Vomit," and "Two Sounds of Liberty." In some ways, punk tries to revive old music into new raw rock (Dead Kennedys, "Rawhide"). In other ways, punk attempts to satirize other musical forms and the lifestyles they represent. The Dead Milkmen do this in "Bitching Camaro" when they say, "Don't forget to buy your Motley Crue T-shirts, all proceeds go to get their lead singer out of jail." Most importantly punk is not new wave music. In the words of a singer for The Germs, "There was never any such thing as new wave. It was the polite thing to say when you were trying to explain that you were not into the boring old rock, but you did not dare say punk because you were afraid to get kicked out of the f——— party." Because of the noticeable difference in musical styles, punk is an excellent musical alternative. **(3)**

Despite its difference from rock, hard-core is a viable form of music. Let us consider some of the terms related to viability: ability to evolve, survivability, and relevance. Punk can evolve and change. Because of its basis in nonconformity, it easily provides for change and does not cater to fixed norms or sentiments. Punk is likely to survive. From its roots in the late 60s it has prospered and is stronger than ever. Hard-core punk also has meaning and relevance. It often provides a satirical social comment. Punk highlights social problems by advocating crude solutions. Such satirically oriented songs are "Kill the Poor" and "Let's Lynch a Landlord" by the Dead Kennedys. Punk music is not afraid to hide its opinion on relevant matters such as politics, war, religion, and human rights. Opinion is expressed in lyrics such as "Army, Navy, Air Force or jail" and "President Reagan can shove it." In these ways punk draws attention to community and social problems and reaffirms the right to free speech. It is, therefore, viable. **(4)**

Whether people like hard-core rock or not, it is a viable musical alternative. It is a musical version of the freedom of speech guaranteed by our constitution. Punk music is an expression of feelings just like the pizza deliveryman expresses his feelings through his mohawk and chains. So the next time you hear some punk music, don't plug your ears or slam the door. Listen to it as though it were real music: it is. **(5)**

TEACHING TIP

This student essay (as well as other student and professional writing in this text) could be improved. In workshop groups, have students find possible revisions to all three areas in Question 3.

Questions for Writing and Discussion

1. Compare Alexander's first and revised drafts. Cite two specific changes that improved his revised version.

2. Alexander explains what punk music is, but he also takes a stand: He wants to convince his readers that it is a legitimate form of music. Where in his essay does he explain most clearly what punk music is? Where does he try to convince you that it is legitimate?

3. Assume that Alexander wants your advice before writing a third draft of this essay. What part of the writing process should he concentrate on: (1) collecting additional information and examples to clarify his explanation or make his thesis more convincing; (2) improving the organization, transitions, and coherence; or (3) editing sentences for grammar, punctuation, and clarity? Support your choice by citing a specific passage that needs improvement.

ANOREXIA NERVOSA

NANCIE BROSSEAU

In her essay on anorexia nervosa, Nancie Brosseau writes from her own experience, explaining what anorexia nervosa is and what its effects are. Her essay succeeds not only because it is organized clearly, but also because it is so vivid and memorable. Relying on specific details, her explanation shows the effects of anorexia on her life.

I knew my dieting had gotten out of hand, but when I could actually see the movement of my heart beating beneath my clothes I knew I was in trouble. At first, the family doctor reassured my parents that my rapid weight loss was a "temporary phase among teenage girls." However, when I, at 14 years old and 5′ 0″ tall, weighed in at 63 pounds, my doctor changed his diagnosis from "temporary phase" to "anorexia nervosa." Anorexia nervosa is the process of self-starvation that affects over one hundred thousand young girls each year. Almost six thousand of these girls die every year. Anorexia nervosa is a self-mutilating disease that affects its victim both physically and emotionally. **(1)**

As both a gymnast and a dancer, I was constantly surrounded by lithe, muscular people, all of them extremely conscious about their weight. Although I wasn't overweight to begin with, I thought that if I lost five to ten pounds I would look, feel, dance, and tumble better. I figured the quickest way to accomplish this was by drastically limiting my intake of food. By doing this, I lost ten pounds in one week and gained the approval of my peers. Soon, I could no longer control myself and ten pounds turned into twenty, twenty into forty, and so on, until I finally ended up weighing 58 pounds. **(2)**

Several serious health problems bombarded me, and it's a wonder I'm still alive. Because my body was receiving no nourishment at all, my muscles and essential organs, including my heart, liver, kidneys, and intestines, started to compensate by slowly disintegrating. My body was feeding on itself! As my weight plummeted, my circulation grew increasingly worse. My hands, feet, lips and ears took on a bluish-purple tint, and I was constantly freezing cold. My hair started to fall out and my whole body took on a very skeletal appearance. My eyes appeared to have sunken into my face, and my forehead, cheekbones, and chin protruded sharply. My wrists were the largest part of my entire arm, as were my knees the widest part of my legs. My pants rubbed my hips raw because I had to wear my belts at their tightest notch to keep them up. I would force myself to vomit as soon as possible if I was forced to eat. The enamel on my teeth started to be eaten away by the acid in the vomit, and my lips cracked and bled regularly. I stopped menstruating completely because I was not producing enough estrogen. Instead of improving my skills as a dancer and a gymnast, I drastically reduced them because I was so weak. One time, while executing a chain of back handsprings, I broke all five fingers on one hand and three on the other because my bones had become so brittle. My doctor realized the serious danger I was in and told me I either had to see a psychologist or be put in the hospital. I chose to see a psychologist, and she helped me sort out the emotional aspects of anorexia which in turn solved the physical problems. **(3)**

The emotional problems associated with anorexia nervosa are equally disastrous to the victim's health. Self-deception, lying, and depression are three examples of the emotions and actions an anorexic often experiences. During my entire bout with anorexia, I deceived myself into thinking I had complete control over my body. Hunger pains became a pleasant feeling, and sore muscles from over-exercising just proved to me that I still needed to lose more weight. When my psychologist showed me pictures of girls that were of normal weight for my age group, they honestly looked obese to me. I truly believed that even the smallest amount of food would make me extremely fat. **(4)**

Another problem, lying, occurred most often when my parents tried to force me to eat. Because I was at the gym until around eight o'clock every night, I told my mother not to save me dinner. I would come home and make a sandwich and feed it to my dog. I lied to my parents every day about eating lunch at school. For example, I would bring a sack lunch and sell it to someone and use the money to buy diet pills. I always told my parents that I ate my own lunch. I lied to my doctor when he asked if I was taking an appetite suppressant. I had to cover one lie with another to keep from being found out, although it was obvious that I was not eating by looking at me. **(5)**

Still another emotion I felt, as a result of my anorexia, was severe depression. It seemed that, no matter how hard I tried, I kept growing fatter. Of course, I was getting thinner all the time, but I couldn't see that. One time, I licked a postage stamp to put on a letter and immediately remembered that there was 1/4 of a calorie in the glue on the stamp. I punished myself by doing 100 extra situps every night for one week. I pinched my skin until it bruised as I lay awake at night because I was so ashamed of the way I thought I looked. I doomed myself to a life of obesity. I would often slip into a mood my psychologist described as a "blue funk." That is, I would become so depressed, I seriously considered committing suicide. The emotional instabilities associated with anorexia nervosa can be fatal. **(6)**

Through psychological and physical treatment, I was able to overcome anorexia nervosa. I still have a few complications today due to anorexia, such as dysmenorrhea (severe menstrual cramps), and the tendency to fast. However, these problems are minute compared to the problems I would have had if I hadn't received immediate help. Separately, the physical and emotional problems that anorexia nervosa create can greatly harm its victim. However, when the two are teamed together, the results are deadly. **(7)**

Questions for Writing and Discussion

1. Without looking back at this essay, jot down the specific examples that you found most memorable. How would you describe these examples: tedious and commonplace, eye-opening, shocking, upsetting, persuasive? Explain.

2. Identify the thesis statement and essay map. Referring to paragraph numbers, show how the essay map sets up the organization of the essay.

3. Reread the opening sentences of each body paragraph.

Identify one opening sentence that creates a smooth transition from the previous paragraph. Identify one opening sentence in which the transition could be smoother. Revise this sentence to improve the transition with a paragraph hook.

4. In this essay, Brosseau defines anorexia nervosa, explains its physical and emotional effects (and hints as its causes), and analyzes the process of the disorder, from its inception to its cure. Identify passages that illustrate each of these strategies: definition, cause-and-effect analysis, process analysis.

EIGHT / EVALUATING

When we evaluate, we have in mind... an ideal of what a good thing—pianist, painting, or professor—should be and do, and we apply that ideal to the individual instance before us.

—JEANNE FAHNESTOCK AND MARIE SECOR, AUTHORS OF A RHETORIC OF ARGUMENT

Purpose and craftsmanship—ends and means—these are the keys to your judgment.

—MARYA MANNES, JOURNALIST AND SOCIAL COMMENTATOR

IN A LETTER TO YOUR PARENTS, YOU EXPLAIN THAT YOU ARE CONSIDERING TRANSFERRING TO A DIFFERENT SCHOOL FOR THE FOLLOWING YEAR. You have some misgivings about your decision to change, but after listing your criteria and ranking them in order from most to least important, you are convinced that you're making the right choice. In the letter, you explain your decision, based on your criteria, and ask that your parents continue to support your education.

DURING YOUR FALL SEMESTER LIBRARY-ORIENTATION TOUR, YOU DISCOVER A SMALL OFFICE TUCKED AWAY IN THE CORNER OF THE LIBRARY BUILDING: THE INTERLIBRARY LOAN OFFICE. Because you occasionally need to see articles and books that your library does not have, you decide to investigate the interlibrary-loan service and evaluate the helpfulness of the staff as well as the convenience, speed, and cost of obtaining materials. As part of your evaluation, you interview the office coordinator as well as several teachers and students who have used the service. Their responses—combined with your own observations—indicate that although an interlibrary loan can sometimes take a couple of weeks, the loan office gets high marks for its service. The staff is always helpful and patient, the service is easily accessible through electronic mail, and the cost of books and articles is surprisingly low.

Jacob Lawrence, "The Curator," 1937. Gouavhe on paper. 11 x 8½ inches. Photo: Manu Sassoonian. Schomburg Center for Research in Black Culture, Art and Artifact Division, The New York Public LIbrary. Astor Lenox and Tilden Foundations.

HARDLY A DAY PASSES WHEN WE DO NOT EXPRESS OUR LIKES OR DISLIKES. We constantly pass judgment on people, places, objects, events, ideas, and policies in the world around us. "Sue is a wonderful person." "The food in this cafeteria is horrible." "That movie we saw Saturday night ought to get an Oscar nomination for best picture." "The Brady gun law is a good piece of legislation." "The Vietnam War was a national tragedy." At the same time, we are constantly exposed to the opinions of our friends, family members, teachers, and business associates. And, of course, the media barrages us with claims about products, famous personalities, and candidates for public office.

A claim or opinion, however, is not an *evaluation.* Your reaction to a person, a sports event, a meal, a movie, or a public policy becomes an evaluation *only* when you support your value judgment with clear standards and specific evidence. Your goal in evaluating something is not only to express your viewpoint, but also to *persuade others* to accept your judgment. You convince your readers by indicating the standards for your judgment and then supporting it with evidence: "The food in this cafeteria is horrible [your claim]. I know that not all cafeteria food tastes great, but it should at least be sanitary [one standard of judgment]. Yesterday, I had to dig a piece of green mold out of the meatloaf, and just as I stuck my fork into the green salad, a large black roach ran out [evidence]."

Most people interested in a subject agree that certain standards are important—for example, that a cafeteria be clean and pest-free. The standards that you share with your audience are the *criteria* for your evaluation. You convince your readers that something is good or bad, ugly or beautiful, tasty or nauseating by analyzing your subject in terms of your criteria. For each separate criterion, you support your judgment with specific *evidence*: descriptions, statistics, testimony, or examples from your personal experience. If your readers agree that your standards or criteria are appropriate, and if you supply detailed evidence, your readers should be convinced. They will take your evaluation seriously—and think twice about eating at that roach-infested cafeteria.

■ **FREEWRITING: EVALUATING** Choose one of the following subjects: an art object, painting, or poster in your room; a book, sports performance, or television program you have seen within the last twenty-four hours; a brand-name product that you have used today; or the actions of a friend, family member, or teacher whom you observed today. Timing yourself for fifteen minutes, write an evaluation of your subject for an audience consisting of several close acquaintances.

BACKGROUND ON EVALUATING

Chapter 8, "Evaluating," is the first of three chapters on writing argumentative essays. Chapter 9 focuses on solving problems and writing proposals, and Chapter 10 introduces students to handling opposing arguments—whether the writer makes a claim of fact, cause and effect, value, or policy. Although these chapters constitute a sequential unit, teachers may skip a chapter or combine chapters according to their students' needs.

RESOURCE NOTE

Chapters 8, 9, and 10 are informed by a theory of argument based on the classical *stases.* For an explanation of this scheme for argument, see Jeanne Fahnestock and Marie Secor, "Teaching Argument: A Theory of Types," or *A Rhetoric of Argument.*

It is as hard to find a neutral critic as it is a neutral country in a time of war.
—KATHERINE ANNE PORTER, NOVELIST AND SHORT STORY WRITER

RESOURCE NOTE

The terms *claim* and *data* are based on Toulmin's approach to informal logic in *The Uses of Argument.* Although this text does not use Toulmin's term "warrant," a warrant states the assumptions that show how the data are relevant to the writer's claim.

TECHNIQUES FOR WRITING EVALUATIONS

Any writing that requires a *value judgment* uses the techniques of evaluating—whether you're writing about consumer products or services, works of art, or performances by people. Effective evaluations use the following techniques:

- **Stating an *overall claim* about your subject.** This statement serves as the *thesis* for your evaluation.
- **Describing the person, place, object, event, service, or performance being evaluated.** Readers need basic information—*who, what, when*, and *where*—to form a clear judgment.
- **Clarifying the *criteria* for your evaluation**. A criterion is a standard of judgment that most people interested in your subject agree is important. A criterion serves as a yardstick against which you measure your subject.
- **Stating a *judgment* for each criterion.** The overall claim is based on your judgment of each separate criterion. Include both positive *and* negative judgments.
- **Supporting each judgment with *evidence*.** Support can include detailed description, facts, examples, testimony, or statistics.

In the following evaluation of a Chinese restaurant in Washington, DC, journalist and critic Phyllis C. Richman illustrates the main features of an evaluation:

Hunan Dynasty

Information & description

215 Pennsylvania Ave. SE. 546-6161
Open daily 11 A.M. to 3 P.M. for lunch, 3 P.M. to 10 P.M. for dinner, until 11 P.M. on Friday and Saturday.
Reservations suggested for large parties.
Prices for lunch: appetizers $2 to $4.50, entrees $4.75 to $6.50; for dinner, appetizers $1 to $13.95 (combination platter), entrees $6.75 to $18.
Complete dinner with wine or beer, tax and tip about $20 a person.

Description

Chinese restaurants in America were once places one went just to eat. Now one goes to dine. There are now waiters in black tie, cloths on the tables and space between those tables, art on the walls and decoratively carved vegetables on the plate—elegance has become routine in Chinese restaurants. What's more, in Chinese restaurants the ingredients are fresh (have you ever found frozen broccoli in a Chinese kitchen?), and the cooking almost never sinks below decent. . . . And it is usually moderately priced. In other words, if you're among unfamiliar restaurants and looking for good value, Chinese restaurants now are routinely better than ever.

The Hunan Dynasty is an example of what makes Chinese restaurants such reliable choices. A great restaurant? It is not. A good value? Definitely. A restaurant to fit nearly any diner's need? Probably.

Overall claim

First, it is attractive. There are no silk tassels, blaring red lacquer or Formica tables; instead there are white tablecloths and subtle glass etchings. It is a dining room—or dining rooms, for the vastness has been carved into smaller spaces—of gracefulness and lavish space.

Criterion #1: nice setting
Judgment: attractive
Evidence

Second, service is a strong priority. The waiters look and act polished, and serve with flourishes from the carving of a Peking duck to the portioning of dishes among the diners. I have found some glitches—a forgotten appetizer, a recommendation of two dishes that turned out nearly identical—but most often the service has been expert. . . .

Criterion #2: good service

Judgment: often expert
Evidence

As for the main dishes, don't take the "hot and spicy" asterisks too seriously, for this kitchen is not out to offer you a test of fire. The peppers are there, but not in great number. And, like the appetizers, the main dishes are generally good but not often memorable. Fried dishes—and an inordinate number of them seem to be fried—are crunchy and not greasy. Vegetables are bright and crisp. Eggplant with hot garlic sauce is properly unctuous; Peking duck is as fat-free and crackly-skinned as you could hope (though pancakes were rubbery). And seafoods—shrimp, scallops, lobster—are tenderly cooked, though they are not the most full-flavored examples of those ingredients.

Criterion #3: good main dishes

Judgment: good but not memorable

Evidence

I have found only one dismal main dish in a fairly broad sampling: lemon chicken had no redeeming feature in its doughy, greasy, overcooked and underseasoned presentation. Otherwise, not much goes wrong. Crispy shrimp with walnuts might be preferable stir-fried rather than batter-fried, but the tomato-red sauce and crunchy walnuts made a good dish. Orange beef could use more seasoning but the coating was nicely crusty and the meat tender. . . .

Criterion #3 cont'd
Judgment: sometimes bad
Evidence

So with the opening of the Hunan Dynasty, Washington did not add a stellar Chinese restaurant to its repertoire, but that is not necessarily what the city needed anyway. Hunan Dynasty is a top-flight neighborhood restaurant—with good food, caring service and very fair prices—that is attractive enough to set a mood for celebration and easygoing enough for an uncomplicated dinner with the family after work.

Overall claim restated

TEACHING TIP

Advertising language contrasts sharply with the language of objective evaluation. Have students bring to class advertisements for products that they have tried. In small groups, students can then write more objective evaluations of the items (see journal entry 2), using their collective experiences to support their judgments. Ask each group to analyze the differences between the language of advertising and the language of evaluation.

CRITICAL READING

Have students do marginal annotations on the Yugo and the Goya excerpts, noting the overall claims, specific criteria, judgments, and evidence. Then have them select a possible topic for their evaluations and practice a three-column log (see the "Collecting" section of this chapter).

EVALUATING COMMERCIAL PRODUCTS OR SERVICES

Writers frequently evaluate commercial products or services. Consumer magazines test and rate every imaginable product or service—from cars and dishwashers to peanut butter and brokerage houses. Guidebooks evaluate tourist spots, restaurants, colleges, and hunting lodges. Specialty magazines, such as *Modern Photography*, *Road and Track*, *Skiing*, and *Byte*, often rate products and services of interest to their readers. To qualify as evaluation—and not just advertising—the authors and the publishers must maintain an independent status, uninfluenced by the manufacturers of the products or services they are judging.

Consider, first, the following "evaluation" of a wine, found on a bottle of Cabernet Sauvignon:

> "This Cabernet Sauvignon is a dry, robust, and complex wine whose hearty character is balanced by an unusual softness."

This "evaluative" language is so vague and esoteric that it may mean very little to the average consumer who just wants some wine with dinner. *Dry*: How can a liquid be dry? *Robust*: Does this refer to physique? *Soft*: Wine is not a pillow, though it might put you to sleep. *Complex*: Are they describing a wine or conducting a psychological analysis? While an independent evaluator may legitimately use these terms for knowledgeable wine drinkers, this particular description suggests that the wine is absolutely everything the buyer would like it to be—dry yet robust, hearty but at the same time soft. Apparently, the writer's purpose here is not to evaluate a product but to flatter readers who imagine themselves connoisseurs of wine.

Now consider the following report on the Yugo, in which *Consumer Reports* illustrates a more objective evaluation of a consumer product. In this brief excerpt, the editors present the criteria, the evidence, and their judgments. Clearly, this is not the language of advertising or uncritical promotion:

How Much Car for $3990?

> An unusual new import, the *Yugo GV*, arrived in the U.S. last August. It's a tiny car—a couple of feet shorter than the *Chevrolet Chevette*—made in Yugoslavia by Zavodi Crvena Zastava (Red Flag Works). But the most unusual thing about it is the advertised price—$3990. The price quickens the pulse at a time when the average car sells for nearly $12,000 and a similar-sized car, the Japanese-made *Chevrolet Sprint*, sells for about $5570.

Can you really buy a *Yugo* for $3990?

No. Dealer preparation, included in the base price of most other cars, is $90 extra, and the destination charge is $299. If you add the official *Yugo* stereo radio with two speakers and a cassette player for $265, you have a $4644 automobile.

Well, what's wrong with a *Yugo* for $4644? We'll let our test results speak for themselves.

Engine and Transmission

Acceleration. All-out acceleration from a standstill was adequate, but the *Yugo* struggled and strained to climb highway grades in high gear. Our 0-60 mph run took 18.5 seconds.

Transmission. Easily the worst we've encountered in years. The shifter was very imprecise and often balky. The sloppy shift linkage made it hard to tell which gear you were in.

Economy. Well below what you'd expect from a small car with such a small engine. Figure on averaging about 32 mpg. (The *Chevrolet Sprint*, a Japanese minicar, averages about 50 mpg). Cruising range is only about 250 miles.

Ride and Noise

Ride. Snappy and jerky on back roads, and harsh and busy even on expressways. But the *Yugo* took large bumps in stride. When the car carried its full recommended load—770 pounds—its ride softened just a bit.

Noise. Tiring. The small engine churned and buzzed on the highway. Coarse pavement increased the noise considerably. Wind noise, especially from the closed front vent windows, was also obtrusive.

Seating Accommodations

Driving position. Extremely awkward. The non-tilt steering wheel is too high, too far away, and too horizontal, and the steering column is angled toward the right. The pedals are too close to one another, and the intrusive wheel housing makes a very poor foot rest.

Rear seating. Unsuitable for adults. Six footers have to bow their head penitently and wrap their knees around the front seat back. The overly erect seatback forces passengers to slouch forward in a fetal tuck with all their weight on the base of their spine.

Our *Yugo* was a sorry sample indeed. We noted 21 defects attributable to sloppy assembly or incomplete dealer preparation. Oil dripped

Ask your students to compare the standards of evaluating in writing and in television. Check the *Video Library* and transcripts for examples of value judgments, claims, criteria, evidence, and reasoning. The programs on "Teaching Values" and "Political Correctness" are good places to begin.

> from the engine and coated the underbody as we drove. When it contacted the hot exhaust system, the car filled with acrid smoke. . . . The brakes squealed, and every so often they dragged so badly that we could barely coax the car to 45 mph on level pavement.

Recommendations

> Is low price sufficient justification for buying the Yugo? We don't think so. Overall, the *Yugo* scored below every other small car we've tested in recent years. It's heavy for its size, and though its tiny engine revs willingly enough, it delivers weak performance and unimpressive fuel economy. Handling was competent and braking was very effective, but comfort, ride, shifting, heating, and the design of the controls were below par.

Evaluating Works of Art

TEACHING TIP

Throughout, this text encourages students to write about what they are learning in their other classes. Writing teachers often assign topics in literature, hoping that their students will share their interest—and expertise. The next two models, however, encourage students to select subjects in sculpture, art, theater, film, music, or dance, thus allowing them a chance to be an "expert" on their own topics.

Evaluations of commercial products and services tend to emphasize usefulness, practicality, convenience, and cost. Evaluations of works of art, on the other hand, focus on form, color, texture, design, balance, image, or theme. Even the phrase "appreciating a work of art" suggests that we are making a value judgment, though usually not one based on money. Through evaluation, writers teach us to appreciate all kinds of art: paintings, sculpture, photographs, buildings, antique cars or furniture, novels, short stories, essays, poems, and tapestries. A Dior fashion, a quilt, a silverware pattern, even an old pair of jeans might be evaluated primarily on aesthetic rather than practical grounds.

In the following selection, art critic Mark Stevens evaluates Francisco Goya's painting "Tre Maggio," which is reprinted here. This painting depicts the execution of Spanish hostages by Napoleon's forces, in retaliation for an attack by a mob on the previous day. As Stevens explains, Goya does not portray the doomed hostages as heroic martyrs; instead, he tries to show the horrors of war and death. In doing that, Stevens believes, Goya "told the truth: what happened on the third of May was a butchering."

> The iconography, the color and light, the composition—all contribute to the power of this picture. Its most impressive aspect, in my view, is that Goya . . . transformed the conventions of hope into those of despair. This makes the horror all the greater, for we can see what we have lost, in addition to what we have. In the background, for example, the spire of the church is a dark, dim reminder, certainly not a cause for hope. The cruelty of the execu-

Goya: *Tre Maggio* (Scala/Art Resources)

Goya: *Tre Maggio* (detail) (Scala/Art Resources)

tion, which takes place in a melodramatic light, reminds us of acts of martyrdom—but without the traditional promise of heavenly reward.

Of course, the outstretched arms of the central figure also recall the Crucifixion, and the man's hands bear stigmata. However, the traditional religious gesture of acceptance—the outstretched arms of Christ—has here been turned into an expression of outrage, terror and meaninglessness. What is the victim saying? There is nothing he can say, for his situation is one in which neither faith nor reason matter. His outflung arms are mirrored by those of the corpse in the foreground: such is the promise of resurrection. The corpse itself is perhaps the most truthful ever painted, for it exhibits the unbearable banality, the crumpled emptiness of death.

The men around the central victim display a variety of other reactions to their fate, none noble. One looks heavenward, but his expression is groveling. The praying man cannot raise his eyes. A third hides his face, as do the victims who await execution. Goya's use of light enhances their horror. The light contains no spiritual overtone, but rather emanates from a common lantern; an intense glow is cast on the small, grisly scene, but it cannot pierce the dark reaches. This light—glaring, without delicacy, lurid, almost artificial—seems peculiarly modern. . . .

In addition to his brilliant use of light and shade, which isolates the central figure, Goya used several other formal devices to make his point. He employed sweeping diagonal lines to scissor the picture into sharp, claustrophobic spaces. He foreshortened the corpse, so that the body seems to draw toward the viewer. (It almost looks as though the dead man is bidding the viewer welcome.) Otherwise, Goya has positioned the figures so that the viewer, curiously, is placed on the side of the executioners. You and I, observing, are implicated in mankind's folly.

Evaluating Performances

Evaluating live, recorded, or filmed performances of people in sports, dance, drama, debate, public meetings or lectures, and music may involve practical criteria, such as the prices of tickets to sports events or rock concerts. However, there are also aesthetic criteria that apply to people and their performances. In film evaluations, for example, the usual criteria are good acting and directing, entertaining or believable story or plot, memorable characters, dramatic special effects, and so forth.

In the following review of *Malcolm X*, critic Peter Travers evaluates the film itself, the script and directing by Spike Lee, and the performances of the main actors and actresses. As you read this review, notice how Travers interweaves both positive and negative judgments as he describes the film.

CRITICAL READING

Ask students to make three-column logs for Travers's review of *Malcolm X*, noting specific criteria, judgments, and evidence. After students work on this exercise, either singly or in groups, they should see that distinct criteria, which were obvious in the Yugo evaluation, are less distinct here. Then, make the point that some film or art reviews heavily emphasize description and minimize evaluative judgments. (For comparison, have students read Kiely's review of *The Stand* or Y'Blood's review of *The Big Chill* at the end of this chapter.) Those essays make clear evaluative judgments, but not as explicitly as the *Consumer Reports* article. Students need to see that each essay's balance abetween description and evaluation helps to define its purpose and audience.

THE YEAR OF MALCOLM X

IN SPIKE LEE'S STRIVING, UNEVEN but finally triumphant *Malcolm X*, Denzel Washington gives the performance of the year as the militant champion of black self-determination. Once a thief, an addict and a zoot-suited pimp, the Nebraska-born Malcolm Little experienced a spiritual enlightenment in prison during the fifties, joined the Nation of Islam (NOI) and preached the pursuit of black liberation "by any means necessary" until a 1964 pilgrimage to Mecca convinced him that racial harmony was possible, though never at the price of black subservience.

Gunned down in 1965 at thirty-nine, Malcolm X remains a focal point of the black struggle. And Washington brings it all home—the intelligence, the humor, the sexuality, the shame, the pride, the raised-fist indignation and, most of all, the stinging eloquence that continues to inspire and provoke any reader of the autobiography Malcolm wrote with Alex Haley, which Lee and co-writer Arnold Perl have adapted for the screen.

Though the sprawling, $35 million, three-and-a-half-hour film tries to touch all the bases, Lee's accommodations sometimes clash with his ambitions. He has toned down Malcolm's life to a PG-13 level to open the film to the widest possible audience. A compromise? You bet, but not a fatal one. Telling details emerge: Malcolm conks his hair with scalding lye to look more white; Malcolm learns the ropes from Harlem gangster West Indian Archie (a superb Delroy Lindo); Malcolm demands that his white mistress (Kate Vernon) kiss his feet and spoon-feed him in bed—an act of self-loathing masked as her subjugation.

Inexplicably, Lee squanders time on atmospherics like a jitterbug number; his own performance as Shorty, Malcolm's pimp pal, is vivid but extraneous. Flashbacks rush us through such vital events as the murder of Malcolm's father (Tommy Hollis) and the breakdown of his mother (Lonette McKee). Few links are made between his preacher father's activism and Malcolm's conversion. An exception is the KKK's torching of the Little home—camera wiz Ernest Dickerson realizes a *coup de cinéma* as white-sheeted horsemen ride off into a poisonously full moon.

Lee shows a surer hand when Malcolm emerges from prison in 1952 to begin his mission. Washington delivers Malcolm's words with a spellbinding urgency, revealing the brother-minister's growing confidence and ambition under the American leader of the NOI, Elijah Muhammad (a mesmerizing turn from Al Freeman Jr.).

In a searingly powerful reenactment, Malcolm leads a march on a Harlem police precinct, demanding that a Muslim victim of police brutality be given medical attention. Given the context of the fifties—exemplified by the insufferably banal sound of Perry Como's "Round and Round" on the radio—Malcolm is a storm unleashed. His victory in facing down the police builds Malcolm into an international figure that some saw as a protector and others as a threat.

Washington's fusion with the role is uncanny. He alone fills in some of the emotional and ideological transitions that the script misses as it moves in lock step through Malcolm's marriage to a nurse, Betty X (the very fine but underused Angela Bassett), the birth of their four daughters, the resentment his outspokenness engenders in his fellow ministers, his split from the NOI when Elijah Muhammad's sexual misconduct is revealed, his pilgrimage to Mecca, the firebombing of his house in Queens and the growing political fervor that made him a threat to the government as well as the NOI and led to his murder.

Lee's *Malcolm X* is far from the last word. It's more like a primer that illuminates its subject in brisk, broad strokes. But those who deride Lee as a self-promoter merely out to sell X hats and T-shirts and turn Malcolm into another manageable martyr for the white Hollywood Establishment just aren't paying attention. From the opening image of an American flag burning over the infamous video of the Rodney King beating in L.A. to Nelson Mandela's final eulogy, the film is a tribute to Malcolm's living, fighting spirit. Spike Lee has accomplished something historic in movies: a rousing, full-sized epic about a defiantly idealistic black hero whose humanism never extends to turning the other cheek.

■ **Warming Up: Journal Exercises** The following exercises will help you practice writing evaluations. Read all of the following exercises and then write on the three that interest you most. If another idea occurs to you, write about it:

1. Choose the best of the courses that you are currently taking. To persuade a friend to take it, evaluate the course, the teacher, or both. What criteria and evidence would you select to persuade your friend?

2. Evaluate an object related to one of your hobbies or special interests—stereo or video equipment, water or snow skiis, a cooking appliance or utensil, diving or hiking equipment, photography or art equipment, ranching or farming apparatus, fishing rods or reels, some part of a car, or computers. Write an evaluation of that object following the format used by *Consumer Reports.*

3. Listen carefully in several classes for your teachers' evaluations of ideas, historical or contemporary events, famous people, or important policies or laws. Take notes and then write a short analysis of one teacher's evaluation: What were the instructor's criteria and evidence?

4. Evaluate a TV show that you find particularly irritating, boring, or insipid, but which you find yourself watching occasionally anyway. Watch the show, taking notes about scenes, characters, dialogue, and plot. Write a critique of the show for other students in this class.

5. To gather some information for yourself about a possible job or career, interview a person in your prospective field about his or her job or profession. Focus your questions on the person's opinions and judgments about this career. What criteria does this person use to judge it? What other jobs serve as a good basis for comparison? What details from this person's daily routine support his or her judgments?

6. At your place of work, evaluate one of your products or services. Write down the criteria and evidence that your business might use to determine whether it is a "good" product or service. Then list the criteria and evidence that your customers or patrons probably use. Are these two sets of criteria and evidence identical? Explain.

7. Choose a piece of modern art (painting, drawing, poster, sculpture, ceramics, and so forth). Describe and evaluate it for an audience that is indifferent or possibly even hostile toward contemporary art. Explain why your readers should appreciate this particular art object.

8. Read James Gorman's essay "Man, Bytes, Dog." Imitating Gorman's essay, write a comparative evaluation of two dissimilar things.

MAN, BYTES, DOG

JAMES GORMAN

Many people have asked me about the Cairn Terrier. How about memory, they want to know. Is it I.B.M.-compatible? Why didn't I get the I.B.M. itself, or a Kaypro, Compaq, or Macintosh? I think the best way to answer these questions is to look at the Macintosh and the Cairn head on. I almost did buy the Macintosh. It has terrific graphics, good word-processing capabilities, and the mouse. But in the end I decided on the Cairn, and I think I made the right decision.

Let's start out with the basics:

MACINTOSH:
Weight (without printer): 20 lbs.
Memory (RAM): 128 K
Price (with printer): $3,090
CAIRN TERRIER:
Weight (without printer): 14 lbs.
Memory (RAM): Some
Price (without printer): $250

Just on the basis of price and weight, the choice is obvious. Another plus is that the Cairn Terrier comes in one unit. No printer is necessary, or useful. And—this was a big attraction to me—there is no user's manual.

Here are some of the other qualities I found put the Cairn out ahead of the Macintosh:

PORTABILITY: To give you a better idea of size, Toto in "The Wizard of Oz" was a Cairn Terrier. So you can see that if the young Judy Garland was able to carry Toto around in that little picnic basket, you will have no trouble at all moving your Cairn from place to place. For short trips it will move under its own power. The Macintosh will not.

RELIABILITY: In five to ten years, I am sure, the Macintosh will be superseded by a new model, like the Delicious or the Granny Smith. The Cairn Terrier, on the other hand, has held its share of the market with only minor modifications for hundreds of years. In the short term, Cairns seldom need servicing, apart from shots and the odd worming, and most function without interruption during electrical storms.

COMPATIBILITY: Cairn Terriers get along with everyone. And for communications with any other dog, of any breed, within a radius of three miles, no additional hardware is necessary. All dogs share a common operating system.

SOFTWARE: The Cairn will run three standard programs, SIT, COME, and NO, and whatever else you create. It is true that, being microcanine, the Cairn is limited here, but it does load the programs instantaneously. No disk drives. No tapes.

Admittedly, these are peripheral advantages. The real comparison has to be on the basis of capabilities. What can the Macintosh and the Cairn do? Let's start on the Macintosh's turf—income-tax preparation, recipe storage, graphics, and astrophysics problems:

	Taxes	Recipes	Graphics	Astrophysics
Macintosh	yes	yes	yes	yes
Cairn	no	no	no	no

At first glance it looks bad for the Cairn. But it's important to look beneath the surface with this kind of chart. If you yourself are leaning toward the Macintosh, ask yourself these questions: Do you want to do your own income taxes? Do you want to type all your recipes into a computer? In your graph, what would you put on the x axis? The y axis? Do you have any astrophysics problems you want solved?

Then consider the Cairn's specialties: playing fetch and tug-of-war, licking your face, and chasing foxes out of rock cairns (eponymously). Note that no software is necessary. All these functions are part of the operating system:

	Fetch	Tug-of-War	Face	Foxes
Cairn	yes	yes	yes	yes
Macintosh	no	no	no	no

Another point to keep in mind is that computers, even the Macintosh, only do what you tell them to do. Cairns perform their functions all on their own. Here are some of the additional capabilities that I discovered once I got the Cairn home and housebroken:

Word Processing: Remarkably, the Cairn seems to understand every word I say. He has a nice way of pricking up his ears at words like "out" or "ball." He also has highly tuned voice-recognition.

Education: The Cairn provides children with hands-on experience at an early age, contributing to social interaction, crawling ability, and language skills. At age one, my daughter could say "Sit," "Come," and "No."

Cleaning: This function was a pleasant surprise. But of course cleaning up around the cave is one of the reasons dogs were developed in the first place. Users with young (below age two) children will still find this function useful. The Cairn Terrier cleans the floor, spoons, bib, and baby, and has an unerring ability to distinguish strained peas from ears, nose, and fingers.

Psychotherapy: Here the Cairn really shines. And remember, therapy is something that computers have tried. There is a program that makes the computer ask you questions when you tell it your problems. You say, "I'm afraid of foxes." The computer says, "You're afraid of foxes?"

The Cairn won't give you that kind of echo. Like Freudian analysts, Cairns are mercifully silent; unlike Freudians, they are infinitely sympathetic. I've found that the Cairn will share, in a nonjudgmental fashion, disappointments, joys, and frustrations. And you don't have to know BASIC.

This last capability is related to the Cairn's strongest point, which was the final deciding factor in my decision against the Macintosh—user-friendliness. On this criterion, there is simply no comparison. The Cairn Terrier is the essence of user-friendliness. It has fur, it doesn't flicker when you look at it, and it wags its tail.

Evaluating: Professional Writing

The Gettysburg Address

Abraham Lincoln

Abraham Lincoln's Gettysburg Address, delivered as part of a memorial ceremony at the Gettysburg, Pennsylvania, battlefield in 1863, is a classic speech in American history. Brevity is surely one of its virtues—it is only 268 words long—but it is an excellent speech for other reasons as well. Gilbert Highet, a scholar and teacher of Latin and Greek for many years at Columbia University, describes the events leading up to the speech, the speech itself, and its reception by the audience and in the nation's leading newspapers. Highet claims that the Gettysburg Address is "one of the greatest speeches in all history." Read Lincoln's Gettysburg Address—aloud if possible—and then read Highet's evaluation. Do you agree with Highet's judgment?

Fourscore and seven years ago our fathers brought forth upon this continent a new nation, conceived in liberty, and dedicated to the proposition that all men are created equal.

Now we are engaged in a great civil war, testing whether that nation, or any nation so conceived and so dedicated, can long endure. We are met on a great battlefield of that war. We have come to dedicate a portion of that field as a final resting place for those who here gave their lives that that nation might live. It is altogether fitting and proper that we should do this.

But in a larger sense we cannot dedicate, we cannot consecrate, we cannot hallow this ground. The brave men, living and dead, who struggled here, have consecrated it far above our poor power to add or detract. The world will little note, nor long remember, what we say here, but it can never forget what they did here. It is for us the living, rather, to be dedicated here to the unfinished work which they who fought here have thus far so nobly advanced. It is rather for us to be here dedicated to the great task remaining before us, that from these honored dead we take increased devotion to that cause for which they gave the last full measure of devotion; that we here highly resolve that these dead shall not have died in vain; that this nation, under God, shall have a new birth of freedom; and that government of the people, by the people, and for the people, shall not perish from the earth.

THE GETTYSBURG ADDRESS

GILBERT HIGHET

Fourscore and seven years ago. . . . **(1)**

These five words stand at the entrance to the best-known monument of American prose, one of the finest utterances in the entire language, and surely one of the greatest speeches in all history. Greatness is like granite; it is molded in fire, and it lasts for many centuries. . . . **(2)**

The dedication of the graveyard at Gettysburg was one of the supreme moments of American history. The battle itself had been a turning point of the war. On the 4th of July 1863, General Meade repelled Lee's invasion of Pennsylvania. Although he did not follow up his victory, he had broken one of the most formidable aggressive enterprises of the Confederate armies. Losses were heavy on both sides. Thousands of dead were left on the field, and thousands of wounded died in the hot days following the battle. At first, their burial was more or less haphazard; but thoughtful men gradually came to feel that an adequate burying place and memorial were required. These were established by an interstate commission that autumn, and the finest speaker in the North was invited to dedicate them. This was the scholar and statesman Edward Everett of Harvard. He made a good speech—which is still extant: not at all academic, it is full of close strategic analysis and deep historical understanding. **(3)**

Lincoln was not invited to speak, at first. Although people knew him as an effective debater, they were not sure whether he was capable of making a serious speech on such a solemn occasion. But one of the impressive things about Lincoln's career is that he constantly strove to *grow*. He was anxious to appear on that occasion and to say something worthy of it. (Also, it has been suggested, he was anxious to remove the impression that he did not know how to behave properly—an impression which had been strengthened by a shocking story about his clowning on the battlefield of Antietam the previous year.) Therefore when he was invited he took considerable care with his speech. He drafted rather more than half of it in the White House before leaving, finished it in the

COLLABORATIVE ACTIVITY

Whenever possible, connect critical-reading activities to the students' writing. Have students do a critical-reading exercise of a student or professional essay (for example, collaboratively annotating Highet's text for criteria, evidence, and judgments). Then have students apply the *same* critical-reading activity to their own essay drafts. Following their critical reading of each other's drafts (in groups of two or three), give students a chance to ask questions about their own drafts. Finally, have students write for five minutes, outlining their *revision plans* for their essays.

hotel at Gettysburg the night before the ceremony (not in the train, as sometimes reported), and wrote a fair copy next morning. **(4)**

There are many accounts of the day itself, 19 November 1863. There are many descriptions of Lincoln, all showing the same curious blend of grandeur and awkwardness, or lack of dignity, or—it would be best to call it humility. In the procession he rode horseback: a tall lean man in a high plug hat, straddling a short horse, with his feet too near the ground. He arrived before the chief speaker, and had to wait patiently for half an hour or more. His own speech came right at the end of a long and exhausting ceremony, lasted less than three minutes, and made little impression on the audience. In part this was because they were tired, in part because (as eyewitnesses said) he ended almost before they knew he had begun, and in part because he did not speak the Address, but read it, very slowly, in a thin high voice, with a marked Kentucky accent, pronouncing "to" as "toe" and dropping his final R's. **(5)**

Some people of course were alert enough to be impressed. Everett congratulated him at once. But most of the newspapers paid little attention to the speech, and some sneered at it. The *Patriot and Union* of Harrisburg wrote, "We pass over the silly remarks of the President; for the credit of the nation we are willing . . . that they shall no more be repeated or thought of"; and the London *Times* said, "The ceremony was rendered ludicrous by some of the sallies of that poor President Lincoln," calling his remarks "dull and commonplace." The first commendation of the Address came in a single sentence of the Chicago *Tribune*, and the first discriminating and detailed praise of it appeared in the Springfield *Republican*, the Providence *Journal*, and the Philadelphia *Bulletin*. However, three weeks after the ceremony and then again the following spring, the editor of *Harper's Weekly* published a sincere and thorough eulogy of the Address, and soon it was attaining recognition as a masterpiece. **(6)**

At the time, Lincoln could not care much about the reception of his words. He was exhausted and ill. In the train back to Washington, he lay down with a wet towel on his head. He had caught smallpox. At that moment he was incubating it, and he was stricken down soon after he reentered the White House. Fortunately it was a mild attack, and it evoked one of his best jokes: he told his visitors, "At last I have something I can give to everybody." **(7)**

He had more than that to give to everybody. He was a unique person, far greater than most people realize until they read his life with care. The wisdom of his policy, the sources of his statesmanship—these were things too complex to be discussed in a brief essay. But we can say something about the Gettysburg Address as a work of art. **(8)**

A work of art. Yes: for Lincoln was a literary artist, trained both by others and by himself. The textbooks he used as a boy were full of difficult exercises and skillful devices in formal rhetoric, stressing the qualities he practiced in his own speaking: antithesis, parallelism, and verbal harmony. Then he read and reread many admirable models of thought and expression: the King James Bible, the essays of Bacon, the best plays of Shakespeare. His favorites were *Hamlet, Lear, Macbeth, Richard III,* and *Henry VIII,* which he had read dozens of times. He loved reading aloud, too, and spent hours reading poetry to his friends. (He told his partner Herndon that he preferred getting the sense of any document by reading it aloud.) Therefore his serious speeches are important parts of the long and noble classical tradition of oratory which begins in Greece, runs through Rome to the modern world, and is still capable (if we do not neglect it) of producing masterpieces. **(9)**

The first proof of this is that the Gettysburg Address is full of quotations—or rather of adaptations—which give it strength. It is partly religious, partly (in the highest sense) political: therefore it is interwoven with memories of the Bible and memories of American history. The first and the last words are Biblical cadences. Normally Lincoln did not say "fourscore" when he meant eighty; but on this solemn occasion he recalled the important dates in the Bible—such as the age of Abraham when his first son was born to him, and he was "fourscore and six years old." Similarly he did not say there was a chance that democracy might die out: he recalled the somber phrasing in the Book of Job—where Bildad speaks of the destruction of one who shall vanish without a trace, and says that "his branch shall be cut off; his remembrance shall perish from the earth." Then again, the famous description of our State as "government of the people, by the people, for the people" was adumbrated by Daniel Webster in 1830 (he spoke of "the people's government, made for the people, made by the people, and answerable to the people") and then elaborated in 1854 by the abolitionist Theodore Parker (as "government of all the people, by all the people, for all the people"). **(10)**

Analyzing the Address further, we find that it is based on a highly imaginative theme, or group of themes. The subject is—how can we put it so as not to disfigure it?—the subject is the kinship of life and death, that mysterious linkage which we see sometimes as the physical succession of birth and death in our world, sometimes as the contrast, which is perhaps a unity, between death and immortality. The first sentence is concerned with birth:

> Our *fathers brought forth* a *new* nation, *conceived* in liberty.

The final phrase but one expresses the hope that

> this nation, under God, shall have a *new birth* of freedom.

And the last phrase of all speaks of continuing life as the triumph over death. Again and again throughout the speech, this mystical contrast and kinship reappear: "those who *gave their lives* that that nation might *live*," "the brave men *living* and *dead*," and so in the central assertion that the dead have already consecrated their own burial place, while "it is for us, the *living*, rather to be dedicated . . . to the great task remaining." The Gettysburg Address is a prose poem; it belongs to the same world as the great elegies, and the adagios of Beethoven. **(11)**

Its structure, however, is that of a skillfully contrived speech. The oratorical pattern is perfectly clear. Lincoln describes the occasion, dedicates the ground, and then draws a larger conclusion by calling on his hearers to dedicate themselves to the preservation of the Union. But within that, we can trace his constant use of at least two important rhetorical devices. **(12)**

The first of these is *antithesis*: opposition, contrast. The speech is full of it. Listen:

The world will little	*note*		
nor long	*remember*	what *we say*	here
but it can never	*forget*	what *they did*	here

And so in nearly every sentence: "brave men, *living* and *dead*"; "to *add* or *detract*." There is the antithesis of the Founding Fathers and men of Lincoln's own time:

> Our *fathers brought forth* a new nation . . .
> now *we* are testing whether that nation . . . can *long endure*.

And there is the more terrible antithesis of those who have already died and those who still live to do their duty. Now, antithesis is the figure of contrast and conflict. Lincoln was speaking in the midst of a great civil war. **(13)**

The other important pattern is different. It is technically called *tricolon*—the division of an idea into three harmonious parts, usually of increasing power. The most famous phrase of the Address is a tricolon:

> government of the people
> by the people
> for the people

The most solemn sentence is a tricolon:

> we cannot dedicate
> we cannot consecrate
> we cannot hallow this ground.

And above all, the last sentence (which has sometimes been criticized as too complex) is essentially two parallel phrases, with a tricolon growing out of the second and then producing another tricolon: a trunk, three branches, and a cluster of flowers. Lincoln says that it is for his hearers to be dedicated to the great task remaining before them. Then he goes on,

> that from these honored dead

—apparently he means "in such a way that from these honored dead"—

> we take increased devotion to that cause.

Next, he restates this more briefly:

> that we here highly resolve. . . .

And now the actual resolution follows, in three parts of growing intensity:

> that these dead shall not have died in vain
> that this nation, under God, shall have a new birth of freedom

and that (one more tricolon)

> government of the people
> by the people
> for the people
> shall not perish from the earth.

Now, the tricolon is the figure which, through division, emphasizes basic harmony and unity. Lincoln used antithesis because he was speaking to a people at war. He used the tricolon because he was hoping, planning, praying for peace. **(14)**

No one thinks that when he was drafting the Gettysburg Address, Lincoln deliberately looked up these quotations and consciously chose these particular patterns of thought. No, he chose the theme. From its development and from the emotional tone of the entire occasion, all the rest followed, or grew—by that marvelous process of choice and rejection which is essential to artistic creation. It does not spoil such a work of art to analyze it as closely as we have done; it is altogether fitting and proper that we do this: for it helps us to penetrate more deeply into the rich meaning of the Gettysburg Address, and it allows us the very rare privilege of watching the workings of a great man's mind. **(15)**

VOCABULARY

In your journal, write down the meanings of the following words:

- *fourscore* and seven **(1)**
- is still *extant* **(3)**
- wrote a *fair* copy **(4)**
- a sincere and thorough *eulogy* **(6)**
- formal *rhetoric* **(9)**

- Biblical *cadences* (10)
- was *adumbrated* by Daniel Webster (10)
- the *abolitionist* Theodore Parker (10)
- *consecrated* their own burial place (11)
- the great *elegies* (11)
- the *adagios* of Beethoven (11)
- the tricolon is the *figure* (14)

Questions for Writing and Discussion

1. Imagine that you are the mother of a soldier—actually just a fifteen-year-old boy—who died in battle at Gettysburg. You have been against the war from the start. You stand patiently throughout the long ceremony, but after listening to Lincoln's comments, you still believe your son died in vain. Write a short letter to Lincoln, responding to his address.

2. Read Lincoln's Gettysburg Address aloud. From your own point of view, do you agree with the original newspaper reports that found the speech "dull and commonplace"? Do you agree with Highet's high praise, or are your judgments mixed? Brainstorm a list of *your* positive and negative reactions to this speech. Then write one sentence expressing your overall impression.

3. List the *criteria* that Highet uses to evaluate the Gettysburg Address. Then, following each criterion, jot down examples of the support or evidence that he gives. Which criteria and supporting examples do you find *least* convincing? Which are *most* convincing? Explain.

4. Highet evaluates not only Lincoln's speech but Lincoln himself. List the criteria that he uses and cite the support he gives for his judgments.

5. Identify the following structural elements in Highet's essay. For each item, indicate the appropriate paragraph number or numbers:

- Lead-in:
- Thesis or overall claim:
- Background description, information about Lincoln and Gettysburg:

- Criterion #1: judgment and evidence:
- Criterion #2: judgment and evidence:
- Criterion #3: judgment and evidence:
- Conclusion:

ARMAGEDDON, COMPLETE AND UNCUT

ROBERT KIELY

In his article on Stephen King's The Stand, *Robert Kiely follows a book-review format. Kiely's purpose, therefore, is partly to assess the novel's strengths and weaknesses, but partly to describe the novel in detail for his readers. Just as Gilbert Highet includes several paragraphs describing Lincoln's delivery of the Gettysburg Address, so Kiely devotes over half of his review to summarizing (and interpreting) King's novel. Readers of* The New York Times Book Review, *where Kiely's article appeared, certainly expect in-depth information about characters, plot, and themes in the unabridged version of* The Stand. *Kiely's overall judgment—that the novel's immensity is a source of both strengths and weaknesses—is stated directly and illustrated in the plot summary. An English professor at Harvard University, Kiely has published dozens of books and articles on a variety of the best 19th- and 20th-century novelists.*

The Stand
The Complete and Uncut Edition.
By Stephen King.
Illustrated. 1,153 pp. New York:
Doubleday. $24.95.

What is longer than "Moby-Dick," "War and Peace" or "Ulysses"? If you guessed the Bible or the Manhattan telephone book, you would not be wrong (though there are small-print Bibles that are under a thousand pages). There are, of course, other longer books, but not many are novels and few of those have been able to sustain a hold on the popular imagination. "The Stand," unabridged and 1,153 pages long, may prove the exception. **(1)**

In 1978, Stephen King, the author of "Carrie" and "The Shining," published "The Stand" and almost immediately added thousands of new readers to his already huge following. At that time, Mr. King's publishers thought the book would be better and certainly more salable if it were cut—in fact, cut by 500 pages, nearly half of its original length. Now the

Collaborative Activity

At the board, list possible criteria for an effective book review. Then, in groups of three or four, ask your students to select from that list a few appropriate criteria to evaluate Kiely's article. Once groups have agreed on criteria, give them ten minutes to reread and annotate the essay, based on their criteria. Following the annotation, groups should reach consensus about the strengths and weaknesses of the article (a recorder should note consensus points). Reconvene the class and ask for reports from each recorder. During the discussion, be sure to *relate* the groups' criteria and judgments to their own essay assignment. To what extent is each student's projected essay like or unlike the book review format?

TEACHING TIP

Kiely's review cites Stephen King's many allusions to literary figures and cultural icons (see paragraph 7). Ask the class to reread the article, underlining all the references. Then discuss these references and allusions. Collectively, the class should be able to identify most of them, though some (Norman Rockwell, Melville, Dos Passos, Gary Cooper) may need your clarification. Ask the class to respond to Kiely's references (and speculate on King's allusions). Are they effective?

novel has been reissued with the missing 150,000 words reinstated, plus a preface by the author and 12 black-and-white illustrations by Bernie Wrightson. **(2)**

It might seem unfair or irrelevant to dwell on size when assessing a novel, yet in this case it is impossible to do otherwise. One simply cannot ignore the bulk of this volume. Besides, a preoccupation with size and weight, particularly an American preoccupation with size and weight, is, as Mr. King insists, central to "The Stand." As it is linked with images of the land, of the spaciousness and diversity and opportunity of the nation, this is a familiar American theme. Mr. King has not only read his Melville but also his Whitman and Dos Passos. Like his predecessors, Mr. King is aware that there is menace as well as promise in the immensity of the United States. What appears modern (or postmodern) in Mr. King is that both the menace and the promise have been tainted by a cheap tedium, a repetition of bravado and monotony of violence. This is not another book about a still raw, untried, half-hidden America, but a nation exposed over and over to itself, as in an enormous mirror, part trite situation comedy, part science fiction, part cop show. In "The Stand," Mr. King comes across as the people's Thomas Pynchon. His characters are "toilers in the vinyl vineyards," just plain folks who drink Gatorade and V8 but who also may happen to have jobs on top secret Government installations in the barren recesses of Nevada. **(3)**

The general outline of the plot is fairly simple. An accident occurs in an Army lab doing research on biological warfare. A virus breaks through the isolation barrier and rapidly causes the death of nearly everyone working in the plant. There is one survivor, however, who walks past the failed security apparatus, races home to his wife and child, bundles them into the car and speeds toward the Texas border. By the time they reach a gas station in Texas, he is very ill and his wife and daughter have died a horrible death that leaves their bodies bloated, blackened and stinking. **(4)**

Of course, the handful of people at the gas station are also contaminated and they, in turn, pass on the virus to others in a macabre chain of association that is described in loving detail, like a parody of the circulation of money (the perennial bad penny) or a mammoth game of pin the tail on the donkey. From Texas to Maine, Los Angeles to New York, in a gruesome variation on the refrain of "This Land Is Your Land," the superflu spreads, causing its victims at first merely to sniffle and sneeze but soon after to expire in paroxysms of pain and burning fever. (The AIDS epidemic had not been identified when Mr. King originally wrote this book. What in 1978 might have looked like a fantastic exaggeration, in 1990 still appears statistically exaggerated but, sadly, not so fantastic). **(5)**

Hundreds of pages of text are devoted to vignettes—some poignant, nearly all disgusting—of Americans in all regions and walks of life being stopped in the tracks of their ordinary existence by the dread and incurable disease. Two things make Mr. King's rendering of this phenomenon peculiar, one might almost say original. The first is the sheer number of cases reported and described. At first, you read along expecting things to change, a cure to be found, an escape to be discovered, but after 300 or more pages it becomes clear that variations on one theme—not progress—are the novelist's plan. **(6)**

The second thing that makes these vignettes, and indeed the entire novel, peculiar is that the characters and situations are virtually all reproductions of American cultural icons. "L.A. Law" meets "The Wizard of Oz"; "On the Road" meets "The Grapes of Wrath"; "Rebel Without a Cause" meets "Walden"; Li'l Abner gets lost in the House of Usher; Huck Finn finds Rambo. The New England we see is Norman Rockwell's; the West is John Wayne's. They are often pointed out, lest the reader miss them. "She looked like a woman from an Irwin Shaw novel" or "It's like Bonnie and Clyde" are common interjections from the narrator and the characters. At the same time, neither comic parody nor a Joycean complexity is at work here. The reproduction of the familiar seems instead a kind of corporate raid, a literary equivalent of a megamonopoly in which the new owner parades brand names to show off the extent and importance of the newly purchased domain. **(7)**

Everything is processed through a gigantic American meat grinder. Just as foreign monuments become a "Leaning Tower of Pizza" or "the Forbidden City Cafe," so the names and words of writers from other parts of the world are reproduced, respelled and repronounced. An admiring general turns Yeats into Yeets: "He said that things fall apart. He said the center doesn't hold. I believe he meant that things get flaky. . . . That's what I believe he meant. Yeets knew that sooner or later things get . . . flaky around the edges even if he didn't know anything else." **(8)**

The few healthy characters seem not just to have survived the plague; they have also survived a rough-and-tumble translation from another medium. There is a Woody Allen look- and sound-alike: a New York songwriter with a sassy mother, who nags and pampers her successful and neurotic son during one of his rare visits home. There is a Jane Fonda character from Maine who is gutsy, beautiful, bursting with aerobic energy and slightly pregnant. And there is the hero, a strong, silent Texan, an amalgam of Gary Cooper and Kevin Costner. When the virus eventually peters out, after having done away with what appears to be most of the population, these and a few others gradually converge on the road, with their battered motorcycles, jalopies, slick sports cars and stolen bicycles, or just tramp exhaustedly from empty town to empty town in search of life and some place to start over. **(9)**

Boulder, Colo., turns out to be the point of convergence for these friendly and cinematically familiar survivors and some dozens of others like them. No sooner do they find one another than they begin planning a government. Someone suggests a meeting in which they all ratify the Declaration of Independence, the United States Constitution and the Bill of Rights. Another objects that this is unnecessary since "we're all Americans." But, it is quickly explained, government is really an "*idea*," and the reality of a democracy no longer exists: "The President is dead, the Pentagon is for rent, nobody is debating anything in the House or the Senate except maybe for the termites and the cockroaches." **(10)**

It is all too shockingly and heavy-handedly clear that such statements—literally accurate within the plot of the novel—could (like the deadly virus) serve as metaphors for the dangerous and deplorable state of things in this country. However, rather than analysis or narrative development, there is a prophetic and programmatic explanation: a satanic figure, who has gathered his evil forces in Las Vegas, Nev. (where else?), has been haunting the American dream with fearful nightmares. He must be stopped. A few hand-picked heroes, macho males from "Butch Cassidy and the Sundance Kid" or "The Longest Day," scramble over dangerous, desolate terrain to get him, but are saved the trouble when he and his minions melt, like the Wicked Witch of the West, in a nuclear accident. **(11)**

In short (well, not so short), this is the book that has everything—adventure, romance, prophecy, allegory, satire, fantasy, realism, apocalypse, etc., etc. Even Roger Rabbit gets mentioned. "The Stand" does have some great moments and some great lines. A desperate character trying to save his mother reaches an answering machine: "This is a recording made at Mercy General Hospital. Right now all of our circuits are busy." And there is a wonderful description of "mankind's final traffic jam." But the overall effect is more oppressive than imposing. **(12)**

In many ways, this is a book for the 1990's, when America is beginning to see itself less and less in the tall image of Lincoln or even the robust one of Johnny Appleseed and more and more as a dazed behemoth with padded shoulders. Americans seemed delighted but in an odd way humiliated when Vaclav Havel, a tiny man from a small country, entered the great halls of Congress and delivered an uninflated Jeffersonian address. "The Stand," complete and uncut, is about the padded shoulders and the behemoth and the humiliation. Unfortunately, it also reproduces at length all the empty excesses that it appears to deplore. **(13)**

Vocabulary

In your journal, write the meanings of the following words:

- a *preoccupation* with size (3)
- a cheap *tedium* (3)
- *macabre* chain (5)
- *paroxysms* of pain (5)
- cultural *icons* (7)
- comic *parody* (7)
- an *amalgam* (9)
- point of *convergence* (10)
- *allegory*, *satire*, fantasy, realism, *apocalypse* (12)
- appears to *deplore* (13)

Questions for Writing and Discussion

1. If you have read a novel by Stephen King, write a one-paragraph review of that work. Refer to the major characters, outline the plot, and support one or two judgments about the novel's strengths and weaknesses.

2. Kiely says his purpose is to "assess" the novel. Reread his article, noting words or phrases that indicate his evaluation of the strengths and weaknesses of *The Stand.* List Kiely's positive and negative judgments.

3. Locate a copy of a recent *New York Times Book Review.* First, list at least five books reviewed in that issue. Then photocopy and read one book review. Based on your inspection of that issue and your reading of one article, profile the *audience* for that periodical. Bring your photocopy and notes to class for discussion.

4. Identify and list Kiely's cues about the organization of his review. What words and phrases signal or promise the reader that a new idea or section is coming?

5. Many of Stephen King's fans are younger people who are not readers of *The New York Times Book Review.* Select three or four paragraphs from Kiely's article and rewrite them for a high school or college audience. Assume that this revision will appear in a campus newspaper.

I love criticism so long as it's unqualified praise.
—NOEL COWARD, PLAYWRIGHT AND SONGWRITER

Evaluating: The Writing Process

■ **Assignment for Evaluating** With a specific audience in mind, evaluate a product or service, a work of art, or a performance. Choose a subject that is **reobservable**—that you can revisit or review as you write your essay. Select criteria appropriate for your subject and audience. Collect evidence to support or determine a judgment for each criterion.

Choosing a Subject

If you have already settled on a possible subject, try the collecting and shaping strategies below. If you have not found a subject, consider the following ideas:

- Evaluating requires some expertise about a particular person, performance, place, object, or service. You generate expertise not only through experience but also through writing, reading, and rewriting. Review your authority list from Chapter 6. Which of those subjects could you evaluate? Reread your journal entries on observing and investigating. Did you observe or investigate some person, place, or thing that you could write about again, this time for the purpose of evaluating it?
- Comparing and contrasting leads naturally to evaluation. For example, compare two places you've lived, two friends, or two jobs. Compare two newspapers for their coverage of international news, local features, sports, or business. Compare two famous people from the same profession. Compare your expectations about a person, place, or event with the reality. The purpose of your comparison is to determine, for a specific audience, which is "better," based on the criteria you select and the evidence you find.

Teaching Tip

One focused evaluative assignment is as follows: Ask students to evaluate a campus or community organization or service. Students should begin their research by looking through the college directory for advocacy or support groups or by calling a community information or hot line. They can then interview the organization's administrators and the students or local citizens who have used the service. They should determine appropriate criteria as they collect evidence. This assignment avoids the sometimes trivial evaluations of commercial products or the excessively difficult art evaluations. In addition, it gives students valuable practice in using observation, field research, and personal experience.

Collecting

Once you have a tentative subject and audience in mind, ask the following questions to focus your collecting activities:

- Can you narrow, restrict, or define your subject to focus your paper?
- What *criteria* will you use to evaluate your subject?
- What *evidence* might you gather? As you collect evidence, focus on three questions:

- What *comparisons* can you make between your subject and similar subjects?
- What are the *uses* or *consequences* of this subject?
- What *experiments* or *authorities* might you cite for support?
- What initial *judgments* are you going to make?

OBSERVING Observation and description of your subject are crucial to a clear evaluation. In most cases, your audience will need to know *what* your subject is before they can understand your evaluation.

- Examine a place or object repeatedly, looking at it from different points of view. Take notes. Describe it. Draw it, if appropriate. Analyze its component parts. List its uses. To which senses does it appeal—sight, sound, touch, smell, taste? If you are comparing your subject to other similar subjects, observe them carefully. Remember: The second or third time you observe your subject, you will see even more key details.
- If you are evaluating a person, collect information about this person's life, interests, abilities, accomplishments, and plans for the future. If you are able to observe the person directly, describe his or her physical features, write down what he or she says, and describe the person's environment.
- If you are evaluating a performance or an event, a tape recording or videotape can be extremely useful. If possible, choose a concert, film, or play on tape so that you can stop and review it if and when necessary. If a tape recording or videotape is not available, attend the performance or event twice.

Making notes in a *three-column log* is an excellent collecting strategy for evaluations. Using the following example from Phyllis Richman's evaluation of the Hunan Dynasty restaurant, list the criteria, evidence, and judgments for your subject:

Subject: Hunan Dynasty Restaurant

CRITERIA	EVIDENCE	JUDGMENT
Attractive setting	No blaring red-lacquer tables White tablecloths Subtle glass etchings	Graceful
Good service	Waiters serve with flourishes Some glitches, such as a forgotten appetizer	Often expert

TEACHING TIP

One way to explain the key elements of the three-column log is to tell students the following: Criteria describe how the subject *should be* (the ideal), the evidence shows the way it *is* (the real), and the judgment is based on the *difference* between the two (between the ideal and the real). If there is no difference, the judgment is positive, but if the discrepancy is significant, the judgment is negative.

COLLABORATIVE ACTIVITY

Sometimes particular *sequences* of invention strategies can be effective. Have students cluster on a potential topic for their essays, then in groups of two or three, exchange their clusters and interview each other about the experiences, ideas, or possible criteria and judgments. After the interviews, students then freewrite for ten minutes on their own clusters.

REMEMBERING You are already an authority on many subjects, and your personal experiences may help you evaluate your subject. Try *freewriting, looping, branching*, or *clustering* your subject to help you remember relevant events, impressions, and information. In evaluating appliances for consumer magazines, for example, reporters often use products over a period of months, recording data, impressions, and experiences. Those experiences and memories are then used to support criteria and judgments. Evaluating a film often requires remembering similar films that you have liked or disliked. An evaluation of a great athlete may include your memories of previous performances. A vivid narrative of those memories can help convince an audience that a performance is good or bad.

READING Some of the ideas and evidence for your evaluation may come from reading descriptions of your subject, other evaluations of your subject, or the testimony of experts. Be sure you read these texts critically: Who is the intended audience for the text? What evidence does the text give? What is the author's bias? What are other points of view? Read your potential sources critically.

INVESTIGATING All evaluations involve some degree of formal or informal investigation as you probe the characteristics of your subject and seek evidence to support your judgments.

Using the Library

Check the library for information on your subject, for ideas about how to design and conduct an evaluation of that subject, for possible criteria, for data in evaluations already performed, and for a sense of different possible audiences. In its evaluation of chocolate-chip cookies, for example, *Consumer Reports* magazine suggests criteria and outlines procedures. The magazine rated some two-dozen popular store-bought brands, as well as four "boutique" or freshly baked varieties, on "strength of chocolate flavor and aroma, cookie and chip texture, and freedom from sensory defects." When the magazine's evaluators faced a problem sampling the fresh cookies in the lab, they decided to move the lab: "We ended up loading a station wagon with scoresheet, pencils, clipboards, water containers, cups, napkins . . . and setting off on a tasting safari to shopping malls."

Gathering Field Data

You may want to supplement your personal evaluation with a sample of other people's opinions by using *questionnaires* or *interviews*. (See Chapter 6.) If you are rating a film, for example, you might give people leaving the theater a very brief *questionnaire*, asking for their responses on key criteria relating to the movie that they just saw. If you are rating a class, you might want to *interview* several students in the class to support your claim that the class was either effective or ineffective. The interviews might also give you some specific examples—descriptions of their experiences that you can then use as evidence to support your own judgments.

Shaping

While the shaping strategies that you have used in previous essays may be helpful, the strategies that follow are particularly appropriate for shaping evaluations.

Analysis by Criteria Often, evaluations are organized by criteria. You decide which criteria are appropriate for the subject and audience, and then you use those criteria to outline the essay. Your first few paragraphs of introduction establish your thesis or overall claim and then give background information: what the subject is, why you are evaluating it, what the competition is, and how you gathered your data. Then you order the criteria according to some plan: chronological order, spatial order, order of importance, or another logical sequence. Phyllis Richman's evaluation of the Hunan Dynasty restaurant follows the criteria pattern:

- Introductory paragraphs: *information* about the restaurant (location, hours, prices), general *description* of Chinese restaurants today, and *overall claim*: The Hunan Dynasty is reliable, a good value, and versatile.
- Criterion #1/Judgment: Good restaurants should have an attractive setting and atmosphere / Hunan Dynasty is attractive.
- Criterion #2/Judgment: Good restaurants should give strong priority to service / Hunan Dynasty has, despite an occasional glitch, expert service.
- Criterion #3/Judgment: Restaurants that serve moderately priced food should have quality main dishes / Main dishes at Hunan Dynasty are generally good but not often memorable. (Note: The most important criterion—the quality of the main dishes—is saved for last.)
- Concluding paragraphs: Hunan Dynasty is a top-flight neighborhood restaurant.

Comparison and Contrast Many evaluations compare two subjects in order to demonstrate why one is preferable to another. Books, films, restaurants, courses, music, writers, scientists, historical events, sports—all can be evaluated using comparison and contrast. In evaluating

Teaching Tip

As usual, while the shaping strategies offer a range of choices, students may need to see the teacher model for the class a systematic testing of each shape for a specific subject. Students should see which shapes work best for a given subject, purpose, and audience.

Computer Tip: Collecting And Shaping

Open a file for your evaluating essay and write a list of possible criteria for your subject. Select the most important criteria for your audience and leave some space between each category. Background information or description:

Criteria #1:
Judgment:
Evidence:
Criteria #2:
Judgment:
Evidence:
Criteria #3:
(continue)

Then *freewrite* for five minutes on the background information and on each criterion, putting down all the data or evidence you have read, observed, or can remember about your subject. As you accumulate evidence, state your judgment for each criterion. When you have a judgment and evidence for each criteria, try *ranking* your criteria. Which of these criteria is most or least important for your audience? Try arranging them in various orders. The word processor will help you "see" how the different orders will look to your readers.

two oriental restaurants, for example, student writer Chris Cameron uses a comparison-and-contrast structure to shape her essay. In the following body paragraph from her essay, Cameron compares two restaurants, the Unicorn and the Yakitori, on the basis of her first criterion—an atmosphere that seemed authentically Asian:

> Of the two restaurants, we preferred the authentic atmosphere of the Unicorn to the cultural confusion at the Yakitori. At first impression, the Yakitori looked like a converted truck-stop, sparsely decorated with a few bamboo slats and Japanese print fabric hanging in slices as Bruce Springsteen wailed loudly in the ears of the customers. The feeling at the Unicorn was quite the opposite as we entered a room that seemed transported from Chinatown. The whole room had a red tint from the light shining through the flowered curtains, and the place looked truly authentic from the Chinese patterned rug on the wall to the elaborate dragon on the ceiling. Soft oriental music played as the customers sipped tea from small porcelain cups and ate fortune cookies.

Cameron used the following *alternating* comparison-and-contrast shape for her whole essay:

- Introductory paragraph(s)

  Thesis: Although several friends recommended the Yakitori, we preferred the Unicorn for its more authentic atmosphere, courteous service, and well-prepared food.
- Authentic atmosphere: Yakitori vs. Unicorn
- Courteous service: Yakitori vs. Unicorn
- Well-prepared food: Yakitori vs. Unicorn
- Concluding paragraph(s)

On the other hand, Cameron might have used a *block* comparison-and-contrast structure. In this organizational pattern, the outline would be as follows:

- Introductory paragraph(s)

  Thesis: Although several friends recommended the Yakitori, we preferred the Unicorn for its more authentic atmosphere, courteous service, and well-prepared food.
- **The Yakitori**: atmosphere, service, and food
- **The Unicorn:** atmosphere, service, and food as compared to the Yakitori
- Concluding paragraph(s)

CHRONOLOGICAL ORDER Writers often use chronological order to shape parts of their evaluations. In his essay on Lincoln's Gettysburg Address, for example, Gilbert Highet organizes his first seven paragraphs around the historical sequence of events. First, Highet describes the background to the dedication at Gettysburg. Then, he describes in order Lincoln's earlier talk at Antietam, Lincoln's riding on horseback in the procession, and the delivery of the speech itself. Finally, Highet narrates the early reactions to the speech and Lincoln's exhausting train trip back to Washington.

Film reviewers often rely on chronological order to sketch the main outlines of the plot as they comment on the quality of the acting, directing, or cinematography. At the end of this chapter, for example, Kent Y'Blood's review of the film *The Big Chill* uses chronological order to organize the middle paragraphs of his essay.

CAUSAL ANALYSIS Analyzing the *causes or effects* of a place, object, event, or policy can shape an entire evaluation. Works of art or performances, for example, often measure the *effect* on the viewers or audience. Mark Stevens, for example, claims that Goya's painting has several definite effects on the viewer; those specific effects become the evidence that supports the claim:

- Criterion #1/Judgment: The iconography, or use of symbols, contributes to the powerful effect of this picture on the viewer.

  Evidence: The church as a symbol of hopefulness contrasts with the cruelty of the execution. The spire on the church emphasizes for the viewer how powerless the Church is to save the victims.

- Criterion #2/Judgment: The use of light contributes to the powerful effect of the picture on the viewer.

  Evidence: The light casts an intense glow on the scene, and its glaring, lurid, and artificial qualities create the same effect on the viewer that modern art sometimes does.

- Criterion #3/Judgment: The composition or use of formal devices contributes to the powerful effect of the picture on the viewer.

  Evidence: The diagonal lines scissor the picture into spaces that give the viewer a claustrophobic feeling. The corpse is foreshortened, so that it looks as though the dead man is bidding the viewer welcome.

Research Tip

Before you draft your evaluating essay, stop for a moment and *evaluate your sources* of information and opinion. If you are citing ideas or information from library articles, be skeptical. How reliable is your source? What do you know about the periodical's editorial slant or audience? Does the author have a particular bias? Be sure to *qualify* any biased or absolute statements you use from your sources. (See Chapter 11 for additional ideas on evaluating written sources.)

If you cite observations or field sources (interviews, surveys), evaluate the information you collected. Does it reflect only one point of view? How is it biased? Are your responses in surveys limited in number or point of view? Remember: You may use sources that reflect a limited perspective, but *be sure to alert your readers to those limitations*. For example, you might say, "Obviously, these reactions represent only four viewers who saw this film, but . . . " or "Of course, the administrator wanted to defend this student program when he said . . . "

TITLE, INTRODUCTION, AND CONCLUSION Titles of evaluative writing tend to be short and succinct, stating what product, service, wor of art, or performance you are evaluating ("The Gettysburg Address," Goya's *Tre Maggio*) or suggesting a key question or conclusion in the evaluation ("How Much Car for $3990?").

Introductory paragraphs provide background information and description and usually give an overall claim or thesis. In some cases, however, the overall claim comes last, in a concluding "Recommendations" section or in a final summary paragraph. If the overall claim appears in the opening paragraphs, the concluding paragraph may simply review the strengths or weaknesses, or just advise the reader: This *is* or *is not* worth seeing, reading, watching, doing, or buying.

I have to stop being afraid of being wrong; I can't wait until everything is perfect before the work comes out. I don't have that kind of time.
—SHERLEY ANNE WILLIAMS, NOVELIST AND CRITIC

DRAFTING

With your criteria in front of you, your data or evidence at hand, and a general plan or sketch outline in mind, begin writing your draft. As you write, focus on your audience. If your evaluation needs to be short, you may have to use only those criteria that will appeal most effectively to your audience. As you write, check occasionally to be sure that you are including your key criteria. While some parts of the essay may seem forced or awkward as you write, other parts will grow and expand as you get your thoughts on paper. As in other papers, don't stop to check spelling or worry about an occasional awkward sentence. If you stop and can't get going, reread what you have written, look over your notes or sketch outline, and pick up the thread again.

PEER RESPONSE

The guidelines below will help you give and receive constructive advice about the rough draft of your evaluating essay.

READER: Before you answer the questions below, read the entire draft from start to finish. As you *reread* the draft, do the following:

1. Underline the sentence(s) that state the writer's ***overall claim*** about the subject.

TEACHING TIP

These peer-response guidelines should be revised and adapted to the needs of your own class. For a more effective peer workshop, have students spend a few minutes in class the day *before* the workshop revising these guidelines. If students help to revise the guidelines, they will better understand the purpose of the workshop and will be more invested in giving constructive advice. (Workshop guidelines should, of course, reflect your grading guidelines.)

2. In the margin, put large brackets [] around paragraphs that ***describe*** what the writer is evaluating.

3. On a separate piece of paper or at the end of the writer's essay, make a ***three-column log*** indicating the writer's criteria, evidence, and judgments. (Does the log include both positive and negative judgments?)

4. Identify with an asterisk (*) any passages in which the writer needs more ***evidence*** to support the judgments.

5. Write out one ***criterion*** that is missing or that is not appropriate or necessary for the given subject.

6. If possible, describe one of ***your experiences*** with this subject that the writer might find interesting or relevant.

WRITER: As you read your peer reviewer's notes and comments, do the following:

1. Consider your peer reviewer's comments and notes. Has your reviewer correctly identified your overall claim? Do you need to add more description of your subject? Does the reviewer's three column log look like yours? Do you need to revise your criteria or add additional evidence? Do you balance positive and negative judgments?

2. Based on your review, draw up a ***revision plan.*** Write out the three most important things you need to do as you revise your essay.

I have rewritten—often several times—every word I have ever published. My pencils outlast their erasers.

—VLADIMIR NABOKOV, NOVELIST

REVISING

Remember that revision is not just changing a word here and there or correcting occasional spelling errors. Make your evaluation more effective for your reader by including more specific evidence, changing the order of your paragraphs to make them clearer, cutting out an unimportant point, or adding a point that one of your readers suggests.

Guidelines for Revision

During your revision, keep the following tips in mind:

- **Criteria are *standards of value*.** They contain categories *and* judgments, as in "good fuel economy," "good reliability," or "powerful use of light and shade in a painting." Some categories, such as "price," have clearly implied judgments ("low price"), but make sure that your criteria refer implicitly or explicitly to a standard of value.
- **Examine your criteria from your audience's point of view.** Which criteria are most important in evaluating your subject? Will your readers agree that the criteria you select are indeed the most important ones? Will changing the order in which you present your criteria make your evaluation more convincing?
- **Include both positive and negative evaluations of your subject.** If all of your judgments are positive, your evaluation will sound like an advertisement. If all of your judgments are negative, your readers may think you are too critical.
- **Be sure to include supporting evidence for each criterion.** Without any data or support, your evaluation will be just an opinion that will not persuade your reader.
- **Avoid overgeneralizing in your claims.** If you are evaluating only three software programs, you cannot say that Lotus 1-2-3 is the best business program around. You can say only that it is the best among the group or the best in the particular class that you measured.
- **Unless your goal is humor or irony, compare subjects that belong in the same class.** Comparing a Yugo to a BMW is absurd because they are not similar cars in terms of cost, design, or purpose.
- **If you need additional evidence to persuade your readers, review the questions at the beginning of the "Collecting" section of this chapter.** Have you addressed all the key questions listed there?
- **If you are citing other people's data or quoting sources, check to make sure your summaries and data are accurate.**
- ***Signal* the major divisions in your evaluation to your reader using clear transitions, key words, and paragraph hooks.** At the beginning of new paragraphs or sections in your essay, let your reader know where you are going.
- **Revise sentences for directness and clarity.**
- **Edit your evaluation for correct spelling, appropriate word choice, punctuation, usage, and grammar.**

PEER RESPONSE

To ensure that revision workshops focus on more than mere editing, write questions for your group sessions that encourage students to "read against the text"—to challenge assumptions made and assertions that do not have supporting evidence. For example, ask students to find one criterion that is *not* appropriate for the subject or the audience, or one criterion that the writer does *not* consider—but should for that particular audience. Next, ask each student to find two places in the draft where the writer does *not* provide accurate or sufficient evidence. Model this activity using a sample draft before you divide into peer groups.

TEACHING TIP

During this assignment, students often connect the evaluations *in* their essays to your evaluations *of* their essays. Use the language of this chapter to discuss your evaluation process: how you determine and rank criteria, how you judge on evidence, and how you reach an overall evaluation. Your purpose is not just to explain your grading but to make students themselves more adept at responding to and evaluating written discourse.

■ **POSTSCRIPT ON THE WRITING PROCESS** When you finish writing your essay, answer the following questions:

1. Who is the intended audience for your evaluation? Write out one sentence from your essay in which you appeal to or address this audience.

2. Describe the main problem that you had writing this essay, such as finding a topic, collecting evidence, or writing or revising the draft.

3. Describe the parts or paragraphs of your essay that you like best. What do you like about them?

4. Explain what helped you most with your revision: advice from your peers, conference with the teacher, advice from a writing center tutor, rereading your draft several times, or some other source.

5. Write out one question that you still have about the assignment or about your writing and revising process.

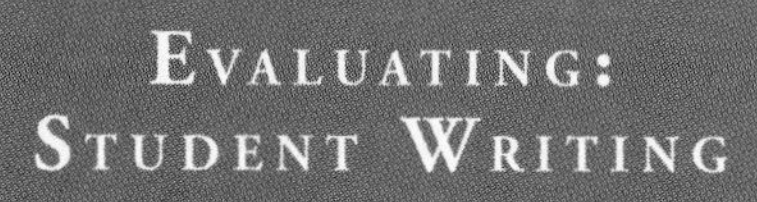

BORROWERS CAN BE CHOOSY

LINDA MEININGER

Linda Meininger wrote her evaluation essay on the Interlibrary Loan Office at her campus library. Her purpose was to advise her readers—other students—about the usefulness of the interlibrary loan service. In order to gather information about her essay, she visited the office, learned how to access an interlibrary loan with her computer, interviewed the coordinator of the office, and surveyed nine people who had used the library service. Overall, she discovered that the interlibrary loan office provided a surprisingly convenient, helpful, and inexpensive service. Included on the next page are the following writing-process materials: a draft of her interview and survey questions; a three-column log; her first rough draft; questions for a conference with her instructor; and her final draft.

Draft of Interview and Survey Questions

Interview Questions for Interlibrary Loan Office (ILL) Coordinator:

1. Have you surveyed your clients to get their impressions about the service? Results? Favorable—why? Unfavorable—why? Valid or not—why?
2. How do you and your employees rate your service?
3. Do you offer any special services for your clients?
4. Have you received any recognition for your work in The ILL?
5. What institutions lend documents to our library?
6. How convenient do you make it for clients to use your services?

Survey Questions

1. Were you satisfied with the interlibrary loan service you received? Why? Why not?
2. How often do you use the service?
3. How much lead time did you allow for your request?
4. What is your area of research?
5. What type of materials did you request? Periodicals? Books? Documents? Theses?
6. What was the cost of using the service?

Draft of Three-Column Log

Claim: The Interlibrary Loan Office runs a well organized and efficient operation

Audience: Students

Purpose: To evaluate the service and encourage students to use it.

Criteria	Evidence	Judgment
1. Timely delivery of materials	Survey results	Mixed
2. Helpful service 3. Convenience for users	Personal experience and survey	Positive Positive
4. Scope of libraries available	Interview and brochure	Positive
5. Reasonable cost	Survey and interview	Positive

Teaching Tip

Before students do a peer-response workshop on each other's drafts, have them practice on Meininger's rough draft. If time permits, students might examine key sections of Meininger's final draft to see how she solved the problems that students identified in the draft.

First Rough Draft

Are you someone who has searched endlessly through the library's computer database or the card catalog only to have that elusive title never appear? Go directly to Room 210, Morgan Library and collect an Interlibrary Loan request card, or if that's too far to walk, place your order via e-mail from your PC. **(1)**

How useful can this service be to you? Stay tuned and I'll show you everything you need to know about Morgan Library Interlibrary Loan (ILL). In evaluating this service, available to all who are affiliated with CSU as a student or employee, I will be looking at the following criteria: convenience and ease of use; timely arrival of materials requested; cooperation and assistance from the ILL staff; and reasonable fees for use of loaned materials. **(2)**

Jane Smith of the ILL department informed me that request cards can be found in many locations in the library. These color-coded cards are used to request documents, periodicals, theses, or books. The color of the card corresponds to the type of material. Requests may be left at any of the reference desks or you may drop off your request in person in Room 210 of the library, Monday through Friday. **(3)**

Students and employees with a PC and a modem may request materials from their office or home. According to Jane Smith, electronic access was developed in-house by the ILL department. A new service has also been established, called the Library Retrieval and Delivery Service (LRDS). This is available to disabled students on campus. Requests may be made by the computer or manually. **(4)**

Jane Smith of the ILL office informed me that normal turnaround for requests is 24 hours. That translates to one day from the time the requests leave the ILL office for another lending institution. Unless . . . it's spring semester. Then, look out! Deadlines for theses and research are closing in and everyone is in need of the materials yesterday. Then the turnaround time is a week. Most likely materials will not arrive until the end of the school year. Requests at spring semester jump to 300–400 per day as compared to a normal of approximately 200 daily. **(5)**

I would say that being able to fill 300 requests for material is efficient by my standards. Jane was delighted to inform me that Morgan Library was chosen most efficient in the state by other ILL's in Colorado. I think that could be comparable to a Good Housekeeping Seal of Approval or a five-star rating by AAA. **(6)**

When I visited the ILL office I discovered a staff willing to answer my questions and with a sense of humor. They made me feel comfortable and at ease. One of the brochures I picked up was a pamphlet with their job descriptions: Queen of the World, Resident Geek, ILL's Mouthpiece, Double Agent, ILL's Movie Star and answer to Greta Garbo, and Leading (Lending) Lady. The pamphlet shows me that these people like what they do and can laugh at themselves and their idiosyncrasies. I believe this impression is relayed to their patrons. **(7)**

Conference Questions

1. Are the criteria I have sufficient? Should I have chosen more of the criteria from my log? Or other criteria from my list?

2. My development needs improvement. I need more evidence to substantiate my criteria. What if I didn't secure the surveys necessary (ten) to be fairly objective?

3. Should I introduce my criteria in a subtle manner, or just come right out and state them?

4. After class today, I felt that I needed to state judgments for each of my criteria, although they could change after the survey results.

5. Does it sound like I'm writing to a student audience?

REVISED VERSION

BORROWERS CAN BE CHOOSY

Are you someone who has searched endlessly through the library's computer listing, the card catalog, or even the stacks, only to have that elusive title never appear? Don't give up. Go directly to Room 210, Morgan Library, and collect an Interlibrary Loan request card. If that's too far to walk, just place your order via e-Mail with your PC, a modem, and some communications software. **(1)**

This service can be useful to you during your four-year educational experience at Colorado State University. So stay tuned, and I'll review four characteristics of Morgan Library Interlibrary Loan (ILL). In evaluating this service, which is available to all CSU students, faculty, or staff, I will be looking at the following criteria: convenience and ease of use, timely arrival of materials requested, reasonable fees for materials, and cooperation and assistance from the ILL staff. To gain evidence about the performance of this department, I interviewed the staff, observed their operation, and conducted a survey of CSU students, faculty and employees (see Appendix for results of survey). Out of nine survey respondents, the level of usage varied from four one-time users to two weekly users. **(2)**

The convenience and ease of using the interlibrary loan service was definitely a high point. Jane Smith of the ILL department informed me that request cards have been placed in many locations in the library for convenient access. These color-coded cards are used to request documents, periodicals, theses, or books. The color of the card corresponds to the type of material requested. Cards may be left at any of the reference desks, or you may drop off your request in person in Room 210 of the library, just off to your left at the top of the stairs, Monday through Friday, 8:00 a.m.–5:00 p.m. **(3)**

The addition of computer access to interlibrary loan also adds to the ease of requesting materials. At the present time, students, faculty, and employees with a PC and a modem may request materials from their office or home. According to Ms. Smith, electronic access was developed in-house by the ILL department, making their service available 24 hours per day. Julie Wessling, coordinator of the Interlibrary Loan Department, said, "About one-third of our users request their specific information via our electronic service." **(4)**

The ILL has also established another convenient new service, called Library Retrieval and Delivery Service (LRDS). This is available to disabled students on campus and other off-campus users. Requests may be made by computer or by using the request cards. Delivery or notice of non-availability of materials will be made within 48 hours to three sites on campus: Braiden Hall, the RDS Office in 116 Student Services Building, and the ILL office. There is also dial-up access to the library's computer listings. This service is especially valuable to off-campus users or students with mobility problems. The ILL staff retrieves requests, most of which—according to Ms. Wessling—are in the CSU stacks, and then delivers them to one of the collection sites for pickup by the patron. **(5)**

Overall, I found the request forms and located the ILL office without any problem, and according to nine out of the nine people surveyed, the ILL service was "easy to use and locate." Judy Lira, a Rocky Mountain High School Media Specialist, FAXes her requests and feels that the technology is a service to the staff and students at her school. Bonnie Mueller, a Morgan Library cataloguing employee, uses LAN to order materials, and she states, "It's wonderful!" While I was in the ILL office, a student was filling out request cards. I tried to enlist her aid for my survey, but she declined, saying that this was her first time using the interlibrary loan service. However, she did have one comment for me: "They [the ILL office] need to make us [students] more aware of this." It appears that the convenient access to the ILL system makes it an asset to CSU students and to the local schools. **(6)**

I wished to experiment personally with the ILL to evaluate the timely arrival of requests, but Ms. Smith explained to me that it would be impossible to receive anything within the time frame I was allotted to finish this essay. Therefore, I will be relying on the experiences and testimony of others. **(7)**

The normal processing turnaround time for requests, Ms. Smith informed me, is 24 hours. That means that it takes one day from the time the request is made by the borrower to the time it leaves the ILL office for another lending institution. Unless . . . it's spring semester. Then look out! Deadlines for theses and research papers are closing in, and students and faculty need their materials yesterday. Ms. Smith related the story of a student who recently came in on a Wednesday and wanted the item by Monday. She had to tell him, "Sorry, it's not possible, especially now." She said at this time of the year—spring semester—the processing time is approximately one week, and that's just until the request leaves the CSU ILL office. Most likely, materials will not arrive until April or the end of the school year. Normal arrival time seems to vary between ten days to two weeks, according to survey results. Requests at spring semester jump to 300–400 per day, and these requests include not only the CSU customers, but the borrowers from other institutions who are requesting materials from Morgan Library, reported Ms. Wessling. **(8)**

The normal processing time can be speeded up, however, in some cases. Ms. Wessling explained that "the use of e-Mail allows us to locate and help process customers' requests faster. This allows the student or professor to receive the information more quickly. The only thing holding the process back is the time it takes to get the specific request in the mail." Also, articles from periodicals or a document can be sent electronically or by FAX. When materials are needed in a hurry, a RUSH may be affixed to the card and a last usable date recorded. This will bring the request to the attention of the office, and they will give it priority to try to locate a copy at a nearby library for pickup by the client. Of the nine people I surveyed, six reported that their materials arrived within 24 hours to two weeks, but one person reported that it took eight weeks and didn't arrive in time to be of use. He allowed two weeks of lead time, but he ordered the material in April. Another person stated that she had to wait over six weeks for materials to arrive. Her materials were "very difficult to locate." My accounting professor, Dr. Middlemist, usually allows a two-week lead time when ordering and said that the "time taken to arrive depended on where the materials were coming from." Dr. Middlemist stated that she uses the service 10-12 times per year, maybe more, depending on what her needs are. **(9)**

By my standards, being able to fill 300 requests for materials is efficient. In addition, Ms. Smith was delighted to inform me that Morgan Library was chosen most efficient by other ILL's in Colorado and will be "looked over" by a team from the state so that their efficient and innovative ideas may be used in other libraries. I think that could be comparable to a Good Housekeeping Seal of Approval or a four-star rating by AAA. **(10)**

While the timely arrival of materials was a problem, especially in the spring semester, the cost of materials received was very reasonable. For most requests, there is no charge for the service. I found that only on the journal request card was there a line item for maximum cost. This is in the event that there could be photocopying charges. Eight of my nine respondents said they received their materials (books, theses, and journals) free of charge, and the other paid a reasonable fee for xeroxing one time. It is through the lending and borrowing reciprocal agreement between libraries that the ILL service can be offered at no cost or low cost to the user. **(11)**

Perhaps the strongest feature of the ILL service was the willingness of the staff to help patrons, answer questions, and keep their sense of humor. They made me feel comfortable and at ease. One of the brochures I picked up was a pamphlet with their job descriptions: Queen of the World, resident Geek, ILL's Mouthpiece, Double Agent, ILL's

Movie Star and Answer to Greta Garbo, and Leading (Lending) Lady. This pamphlet shows that these people like what they do and can laugh at themselves and their idiosyncrasies. Something else Ms. Smith said really sticks in my mind. She said, "I think we're the only department in the whole library where everyone really likes what they do." I believe this impression is relayed to their patrons. My survey results concurred with this, as seven respondents felt that the staff was friendly and helpful. One dissenting student felt that the office could have presented the information she needed over the phone, saving her a trip to the library. The other person felt there wasn't any follow-up on a trace request to see if a book had been lost. Morgan Library has lost this patron to another library. Some of the positive comments received were as follows: "The ILL personnel went out of their way to help me." "What I needed was extremely obscure, and they got most of it." "They found a German book in Berlin, and they xeroxed it and sent the whole thing FREE!" **(12)**

As a result of my investigation and evaluation of the ILL office, I hope I have occasion to use their service in the future. I know from my conversations with the staff and other users of ILL that the service and staff are reliable and willing to assist at any time (during office hours, of course). The cost is well within the reach of all patrons, and we have two methods of booking our requests, manually on cards and electronically by computer. So the next time you need an item that the CSU library doesn't own, remember that you do have another resource available at your fingertips: Morgan Library's Interlibrary Loan. **(13)**

Works Cited

Interlibrary Loan. Fort Collins: Colorado State University, 1992.

It's Here! Fort Collins: Colorado State University, 1992.

Libraries Retrieval and Delivery Service. Fort Collins: Colorado State University, 1992.

Morgan Library Interlibrary Loan Survey. Personal Survey. 2 March 1992.

Self-Guided Tour of Morgan Library. Fort Collins: Colorado State University, 1992.

Smith, Jane. Personal Interview. 27 February and 2 March 1992.

Wessling, Julie. Personal Interview. 2 March 1992.

Appendix

Morgan Library Interlibrary Loan Survey

The following survey was completed by nine students and faculty members. Responses follow each question.

1. What was the subject area of the materials requested?

Accounting-1	Ben Jonson-17th C writer & critic-1
Agriculture-1	Cognitive Development-1
Ancient Roman Art-1	Popular Fiction-1
Anthropology-1	Travelogues-1800's -1
Archaeology-1	Various Subjects-1

2. What type of material did you request?

Book______7______ Journal______6______
Thesis______1______ Documents______0______

3. How much lead time did you allow the interlibrary loan office to secure your materials?

No deadline - 5
24 hours - 1
1 week - 1
2 weeks - 2

4. What time of the year did you request materials?

Fall semester	Specify month	3 in Oct, Nov and Dec
Spring semester	Specify month	1-Jan, 4-Feb & Mar, 2-April, 1-May

5. Did your materials arrive in a timely manner? How much time did it take?

24 hours-1	Very quickly-1
1 week-1	Not more than 1 1/2 -2 months -1
8 weeks-1	Over 3 weeks-1
Typically timely-1	10 days-1

6. Were you satisfied with the service you received? Why? Why not?

No, not friendly, no follow-up if lost -1
Yes, friendly and helpful -1
Yes -2
Yes, very satisfied -1

Very, needed extremely obscure stuff-got most of it -1
Extremely satisfied, wonderful to have access to otherwise unreachable materials -1
No problem with service or individuals, satisfied -1
Friendly -1

7. How often do you use the service?
1 time -3
Weekly -1
2 times/year -1
One semester a lot of times -1
10–12 times/year -1
Goes to Boulder-CU library -1
2–3 times/week ave., usually turns in requests in batches -1

8. Was there a charge for your requested materials? If so did you feel the charge was reasonable or not? How much was it?
No charge -8
Xeroxing charge, reasonable -1

9. Was the staff of the inter-library loan office helpful? Friendly? Gave out of the ordinary service?
Not friendly, not helpful, no out of ordinary service -1
Could have presented info over phone, save trip to library -1
Staff went out of their way to help -1
Worked hard on obscure stuff -1
Always do their best -1
Very friendly -3
Friendly & helpful -3
Regular service -1
FAX requests -1

10. Did you feel that the service was convenient to use (i.e., easy to order materials and pick them up, forms to be filled out, the open hours of the office, etc.)?
Easy to use -2 Very -2 Yes -2
Used LAN -1
Yes, feels guilty about amt. of paper involved in all of the requests -1
FAX technology availability real service to students & staff -1

11. From which institution did you receive your materials?
Northwestern -1
Dartmouth -1
Berlin -1
Denver Public Library -1
Oklahoma State University -1
CU-Boulder -1
Don't know -2

Questions for Writing and Discussion

1. Evaluate Meininger's final draft, using the Peer Response guidelines in this chapter. What are the strengths and weaknesses of her essay? Now read Meininger's first rough draft. Which areas did she improve most in her revision?

2. Based on her final draft, make a revised version of Meininger's three-column log. Write out each criterion, the main supporting evidence for that criterion, and the judgment. Indicate the paragraphs (by number) that Meininger devotes to each of her criteria.

3. In her Postscript, Meininger wrote, "I revised my criteria and rearranged them in a different order after we talked in class. I didn't want to have my weakest criteria last." Compare her criteria (see her three-column log) with her revised draft. Explain how her additions, deletions, and reordering improved her criteria—and her essay.

4. Reread the questionnaire in Meininger's Appendix. How might she improve that questionnaire? What questions might she add or delete? How might she rephrase the questions?

5. Brainstorm a list of other campus services or organizations that you could evaluate. Choose one of those services or organizations and write a three-column log, indicating the subject, the audience, the criteria, and the possible kinds of evidence that you might collect for your essay.

"THE BIG CHILL"

KENT Y'BLOOD

In his review of The Big Chill, *Kent Y'Blood writes a compact evaluation of the film for a campus newspaper audience. Film-review writers often need to walk a tightrope: They should give the basic information about key characters and plot—without revealing too much about the story;*

they should analyze and evaluate the film—without so much analysis that the reader is bored. As you read the essay, decide how successful Y'Blood is at both informing yet entertaining the reader.

"The Big Chill" is an actor's film in the very best sense. It's no easy task to create eight major characters we can care about immediately without resorting to some form of cinematic stereotyping, but director Lawrence Kasdan does it. We meet eight individuals whose stories of fading youthful optimism are familiar in many ways. These characters are not mere representatives of those stories but living, breathing people in a psychological comedy. **(1)**

And what a dark comedy it is. Death pervades every scene, and not just the death of The Movement, or the death of Revolutionary Ideals, or the death of The Spirit of a Generation. Those generalizations have little place here. "The Big Chill" is about a real, particular death: that of Alex Marshall, permanent dropout, college friend of Sam, Sarah, Michael, Nick, Harold, Meg and Karen. He committed suicide in Harold's and Sarah's house where he was staying with his young girlfriend Chloe. The old friends, who haven't seen much of each other in years, regroup for his funeral and all decide to spend a weekend at Harold's and Sarah's house in Georgia to try to sort out their confusion over Alex's act. **(2)**

At the beginning of the film, Kasdan packs plenty of character information into a relatively short space so that we get to know the people well. As they make their various ways to the funeral, spread out across the country as they are, we begin to learn about them. Sam (Tom Berenger) lines up four miniature vodka bottles on his airplane tray and charms the stewardess out of just one more. Nick (William Hurt) empties out a collection of pills on the seat of his Porsche, downs a couple, and the car roars out ahead of the camera. We get glimpses of the other characters intercut with shots of a man dressing in a pinstripe suit and white shirt, all to the tune of Marvin Gaye's "I Heard It Through the Grapevine." Kasdan ends this scene with a shocker. As a sewn-up wrist is slipped beneath a white cuff, we realize it was Alex's corpse we saw being dressed. This combination of expository information with emotionally powerful action is superb movie making, and Kasdan does not let down after the promise of this opening sequence. **(3)**

At the funeral itself, we learn more about the principals. Michael (Jeff Goldblum) obviously wants more than comfort from Chloe (Meg Tilly). Harold (Kevin Kline) intones a eulogy and breaks down as he remembers "there was something about Alex that was too good for this world." His wife Sarah (Glen Close) weeps but holds together admirably. Throughout the film, all the characters are true to our first impressions

CRITICAL READING

As part of a prereading assignment for this essay, choose a popular film and make copies of two or three reviews. If possible, find reviews from sources aimed at different audiences (your local or campus paper, *Time*, *The New Yorker*, and so on). Hand out copies of the reviews and discuss the different criteria, judgments, and evidence used by each critic. A variant of this assignment is to have the class select one or two popular films and then ask each student to bring a review to class. After discussing these reviews (and their intended purposes and audiences), ask students to read Y'Blood's essay. With a clearer notion of the variations of the film-review genre, students can better respond to this essay.

of them, but are not mechanically programmed to act predictably. They can still surprise us, and they all do. Later, when the characters get assigned their bedrooms, we get a glimpse of their luggage. Knowing who brings the economy-size bottle of Maalox, who the TV script and a volume of Kafka, and who has many pairs of designer men's underwear just adds that much more to our sense of who each of these people is. It is a weekend of talk, but the talk is supplemented by what we've observed about these people, so the dialogue doesn't have to carry all the weight in the film. **(4)**

When they do talk, the chat is brilliant. Their sentiment is constantly undercut by jokes that don't weaken their emotions, just complicate them. When Beth rises to play Alex's favorite song on the organ at the funeral (Rolling Stones' "You Can't Always Get What You Want"), it is simultaneously funny and heartbreaking. The friends collectively try to work out how they failed Alex, how they failed their younger selves by becoming successful and rich, and how the people they were became the people they are. **(5)**

"The Big Chill" is beautifully edited, masterfully acted, and has a script that has more depth than anything I've seen in a long time. The film directly confronts such tough themes as the endurance of friendship, the question of suicide, isolation, meaninglessness—and all to the '60s music of the Temptations, Smokey Robinson, and the Rascals. That's what I call a good movie. **(6)**

Questions for Writing and Discussion

1. Profile yourself as a typical reader for this review: Give your age, note whether you frequently go to movies, describe the kinds of films you enjoy, describe your attitude toward music or events from the sixties, and indicate whether or not you have seen *The Big Chill.* With these notes, come to class prepared to discuss whether or not Y'Blood's review succeeded. Did it make you want to see the movie? If you've seen the film already, was his evaluation convincing? Was it entertaining?

2. Y'Blood's writing-process materials are not reproduced here, but how do you suppose that he collected all the information and supporting evidence for his review? Describe a plausible sequence for his collecting activities.

3. In his review, Y'Blood emphasized Lawrence Kasdan's skills in directing this film. However, if he had chosen to focus on one particular actor's performance (for example, William Hurt's performance as Nick) or on the relationship of the songs to the story, how would that have changed the review? For practice, rewrite the opening paragraph of this review, focusing either on one principal actor or on the sixties songs.

NINE/PROBLEM SOLVING

This country has more problems than it should tolerate and more solutions than it uses.

—RALPH NADER, CONSUMER-RIGHTS ADVOCATE

Whenever life doesn't seem to give an answer, we create one.

—LORRAINE HANSBERRY, AUTHOR OF A RAISIN IN THE SUN

TRYING TO TAKE NOTES IN YOUR PSYCH I LECTURE CLASS—ALONG WITH 250 OTHER STUDENTS—YOU REALIZE THAT YOU ARE COMPLETELY LOST AND CONFUSED. So you raise your hand to ask a question, but the professor keeps on talking, throwing out more new terms and examples. You look at your neighbor, who just shrugs and keeps on writing. After class, when you think about how hard you've worked to pay your tuition, you realize that you deserve better classes for your money. The problem, you decide, is in the large lecture format—there are just too many students for the teacher to answer questions and explain difficult concepts. So you decide to write a letter to the head of the psychology department (with a copy for the dean of Arts and Sciences) outlining the problems with this class and proposing that Psychology I be taught in classes no larger than fifty. Where the administrators get additional teachers, you decide, is their responsibility. You argue that, as administrators, it is their duty to give quality education the highest priority.

IN YOUR WRITING CLASS, YOU READ A CONVERSATION BETWEEN TWO MINORITY WOMEN ABOUT RACIAL TENSIONS IN AFRICAN-AMERICAN AND ASIAN-AMERICAN COMMUNITIES. The problems, you realize, are continuing and widespread. Publicized instances include a boycott by blacks on Korean shops in New York City and the looting of Korean stores during the Los Angeles riots. As a member of the American-Korean community, you decide to propose three solutions to promote education and understanding. First, encourage the American-Korean media to educate Koreans about cultural differences. Next, ask Korean-American churches to cooperate with churches in African-American communities. Finally, appeal to Korean businesspeople to invest in the black communities where they work. Communities, you argue, cannot wait for local or federal governments to solve these problems. They must take the initiative and work cooperatively to solve their problems.

Miriam Schapiro, Night Shade, 1986. Acrylic and fabric collage on canvas, 48'' x 96", Private Collection, NY.

WE DON'T HAVE TO LOOK DILIGENTLY TO LOCATE PROBLEMS IN OUR LIVES. They have a habit of seeking us out. It seems that if something can go wrong, it will. Countries are fighting each other, the environment is polluted, unemployment is too high, prejudice is still rampant, television shows are too violent, sports are corrupted by drugs and money, education is too impersonal, and people drive so recklessly that you take your life in your hands every time you go across town. Everywhere we look, someone else creates problems for us—from minor bureaucratic hassles to serious or life-threatening situations. (On rare occasions, of course, we're part of the problem ourselves.)

If you write in order *to propose a solution* to some problem, you have no lack of subjects. First, however, you may well ask whether your problem is one that *can* be solved. As journalist Charles Dudley Warner once observed, "Everybody talks about the weather, but nobody does anything about it." For the short term, the weather is not a problem that has a solution. Although we can predict the weather (sometimes), experiment with cloud seeding, or prepare for the effects of hurricanes or blizzards, wisdom dictates that we accept the weather that comes. For the long term, however, we know that ozone depletion and greenhouse warming are serious weather-related problems that need worldwide planning and cooperation.

If the problem can be solved, the difficult part is to propose a solution and then persuade others that your solution will in fact solve the problem—without creating new problems and without costing too much. Because your proposal may ask readers to take some action, vote in a certain way, or actually work to implement your proposal, you must make sure that your readers vividly perceive the problem and agree that your plan outlines the most logical and feasible solution.

■ **FREEWRITING: PROBLEM SOLVING** Wishful-Thinking Department: Assume that as a member of the student government, your organization has been given $10,000 to spend on a campus-improvement project. Think of some campus problem that needs solving. Describe why it is a problem. Then outline your plan for a solution, indicating how you would spend the money to help solve the problem.

BACKGROUND ON PROBLEM SOLVING

Chapter 9, "Problem Solving," shows how to write papers that identify problems and propose solutions. It builds on Chapter 8, "Evaluating," because writers must evaluate problems before proposing solutions. Writers can then draw on their evaluations and problem-solving skills in Chapter 10, "Arguing," as they practice arguing for claims and responding to opposing arguments.

Most television programming involves some kind of problem solving, from soap operas and game shows to talk shows and news reports. Consult the *Video Guide* for some lively examples, especially "Teens Consult Prejudices" and "Crime and Punishment."

You see things; and you say, "Why?" But I dream things that never were; and I say, "Why not?"
—GEORGE BERNARD SHAW, DRAMATIST

TECHNIQUES FOR PROBLEM SOLVING

Problem solving requires all your skills as a writer. You need to observe carefully to see if a problem exists. You may need to remember experiences that illustrate the seriousness of the problem. You need to investigate which solutions have worked or have not worked. You often have to explain what the problem is and why or how your proposal would remedy the situation. You may need to evaluate both the problem and alternative solutions. To help you identify the problem and convince your readers of the soundness of your proposal, keep the following techniques in mind:

- **Identifying and understanding your *audience*.** If you want something done, fixed, changed, improved, subsidized, banned, reorganized, or made legal or illegal, make sure that you are writing to the appropriate audience.

- **Demonstrating that a *problem exists*.** Some problems are so obvious that your readers will readily acknowledge them: nuclear weapons, conflict in the Middle East, acid rain in industrialized nations, and drug and alcohol abuse. Often, however, you must first convince your audience that a problem exists: Are food preservatives really a serious problem, or would eliminating them cause even more problems?

- **Proposing a *solution*** that will solve the problem. After convincing your readers that a serious problem exists, you must then propose a remedy, plan, or course of action that will eliminate or reduce the problem.

- **Convincing your readers that your *proposal will work*,** that it is *feasible*, or that it is better than the *alternative solutions*. You convince your readers by supporting your proposal with *reasons* and *evidence*.

TEACHING TIP

Most college writers eagerly approach a problem-solving assignment. The audience is often specific and local, the purpose is immediately relevant, and the logic and structure are readily apparent. As these techniques illustrate, however, a proposal is an ambitious project. To compensate for these difficulties, teachers may have students write on topics they have already explored in previous essays, write papers in groups of two or three, and/or narrow the scope of essays to limited problems.

DEMONSTRATING THAT A PROBLEM EXISTS

A proposal begins with a description of a problem. Demonstrating that the problem exists (and is serious) will make your readers more receptive to your plan for a solution. The following selection from Frank Trippett's *Time* magazine essay "A Red Light for Scofflaws" identifies a problem and provides sufficient examples to demonstrate that scofflawry is pervasive and serious enough to warrant attention. Even if we haven't been personally attacked while driving the Houston or Miami or Los Angeles freeways, Trippett convinces us that *scofflawry*—deliberately disobeying ("scoffing at") laws—is serious. His vivid description makes us aware of the problem:

Demonstrating that a problem exists

> Law and order is the longest-running and probably the best-loved political issue in U.S. history. Yet it is painfully apparent that millions of Americans who would never think of themselves as lawbreakers, let alone criminals, are taking increasing liberties with the legal codes that are designed to protect and nourish their society. Indeed, there are moments today—amid outlaw litter, tax cheating, illicit noise, and motorized anarchy—when it seems as though the scofflaw represents the wave of the future. Harvard sociologist David Riesman suspects that a majority of Americans have blithely taken to committing supposedly minor derelictions as a matter of course. Already, Riesman says, the ethic of U.S. society is in danger of becoming this: "You're a fool if you obey the rules."

Evidence: authority

> The dangers of scofflawry vary wildly. The person who illegally spits on the sidewalk remains disgusting, but clearly poses less risk to others than the company that illegally buries hazardous chemical waste in an unauthorized location. The fare beater on the subway presents less threat to life than the landlord who ignores fire safety statutes. The most immediately and measurably dangerous scofflawry, however, also happens to be the most visible. The culprit is the American driver, whose lawless activities today add up to a colossal public nuisance. The hazards range from routine double parking that jams city streets to the drunk driving that kills some 25,000 people and injures at least 650,000 others yearly.

Evidence: examples

Evidence: statistics

> The most flagrant scofflaw of them all is the red-light runner. The flouting of stop signals has got so bad in Boston that residents tell an anecdote about a cabby who insists that red lights are "just for decoration." The power of the stoplight to control traffic seems to be waning everywhere. In Los Angeles, red-light running has become perhaps the city's most common traffic violation. In New York City, going through an intersection is like Russian roulette. Admits Police Commissioner Robert J. McGuire: "Today it's a 50-50 toss-up as to whether people will stop for a red light." Meanwhile, his own police largely ignore the lawbreaking.

Evidence: authority

> The prospect of the collapse of public manners is not merely a matter of etiquette. Society's first concern will remain major crime, but a foretaste of the seriousness of incivility is suggested by what has been happening in Houston. Drivers on Houston freeways have been showing an increasing tendency to replace the rules of the road with violent outbreaks. Items from the Houston police department's new statistical category—freeway traffic violence: (1) Driver

Evidence: examples

flashes high-beam lights at car that cut in front of him, whose occupants then hurl a beer can at his windshield, kick out his tail lights, slug him eight stitches worth. (2) Dump-truck driver annoyed by delay batters trunk of stalled car ahead and its driver with steel bolt. (3) Hurrying driver of 18-wheel truck deliberately rear-ends car whose driver was trying to stay within 55 m.p.h. limit.

Proposing a Solution and Convincing Your Readers

Once you have vividly described the problem, you are ready to propose a solution and convince your readers. In "Making the Case for Full Employment," an article that appeared in *The Christian Century*, Marjorie Hope and James Young propose a solution to a problem that everyone recognizes: high unemployment. In the following excerpt from their proposal, the authors move quickly from the problem to their specific proposals—and the supporting evidence. Notice that the audience requires the authors to focus on how churches and church organizers can become part of the solution:

Proposal

> Following the U.S. Catholic bishops' call for full employment in their pastoral letter, "Economic Justice for All," they were often criticized as utopian. However, more recently there has been a flurry of interest in full employment on the part of economists, church leaders, sociologists, community organizers and others who see it as an achievable goal.

Demonstrating that a problem exists

Evidence: list of examples

> Clergy, union organizers and ordinary citizens have witnessed the suffering and disorientation caused by changes in the world of work: the decline of unions, the migration of American industry to countries where labor costs are cheaper, the replacement of workers by technology, the influx of undocumented foreign workers willing to take jobs that pay below minimum wage, persistently high unemployment among blacks and Hispanics, and the growing numbers of women who labor for low pay. Around the world the gap between rich and poor is widening. Unemployment has reached crisis proportions in many countries that enjoyed prosperity and low unemployment in the '60s and early '70s. The need for concerted action is urgent.

Proposal

> Current advocates of full employment are calling not only for jobs for those people able to work but for jobs with decent pay and working conditions, for equal access to jobs and training opportunities, for improved education for the employed and the underemployed, and for jobs that respect the environment.

Proposal specifics

> Some of the specific proposals being advanced include the following:

- *Raising the minimum wage.* Michael Harrington suggests that the minimum wage be set somewhere around $5.00 an hour, and that the government guarantee a useful job to everyone who wants to work.
- *Shortening the work week.* Frank Riessman, co-editor of the journal *Social Policy*, points out that in 1938, "revolutionary" legislation cut the work week to 40 hours. A new revolution is long overdue. A four-day work week would spread jobs around, give people time to learn skills needed to keep up with rapidly changing technology, and lessen tensions experienced by working parents who want to spend more time with their children.

Advantages of proposal

- *Special efforts to reach minorities.* Economist John Jeffries points out that although all workers are threatened by the labor crisis, reform efforts should emphasize narrowing the most glaring income gaps—those between males and females and between whites and people of color. The unemployment rate for blacks is well over twice that for whites; the rate for black youth generally exceeds 40 per cent.

Reason + evidence

- *Government support for a radical extension of quality daycare and related family support services, with fees based on ability to pay.* Such action is necessary for improving the status of women, whose mean earnings when they work full-time come to only 63 percent of full-time earnings for men. Providing daycare, preschool and other social services would both lessen the psychological and economic burden of parents, and would create more jobs.

Reason + evidence

- *A balance between public- and private-sector involvement.* In the past, say Frank Reissman and Sheila Collins, full employment initiatives have relied too heavily on direct job programs, inviting the criticism that they were just "make work" affairs and were pervaded by political favoritism. We could instead, like some European countries, subsidize hiring efforts by voluntary associations and private firms. Other approaches would include job vouchers for the unemployed and tax subsidies for corporations that create jobs in areas of high unemployment.

Feasibility: how to make proposal work

Who would benefit from a coordinated full employment policy? Virtually all Americans. More jobs mean more tax dollars collected and fewer funds paid out in unemployment insurance and welfare. Studies show that an increase of 1 million jobs would reduce the federal deficit by $40 billion. Thus a national health plan and daycare program could be paid for with the revenue created by full employment.

Advantages of proposal

Evidence

Forging the political will to achieve full employment is an enormous task. Church groups that recognize full employment as a cornerstone of a just social order have limited resources. Hence mainline Protestant denominations have generally chosen to play the catalytic role of supporting local and regional coalitions of religious, labor and community groups. Through these alliances, and directly from the pulpit, they have attempted to educate their constituencies about the human damage wrought by joblessness and about the possibilities for a new policy, and they have provided financial support for community organizing.

Call to action

The question confronting all of us is: do we have the political will to make full employment a reality?

■ **Warming Up: Journal Exercises** The following exercises will help you practice problem solving. Read all of the following exercises and then write on the three that interest you most. If another idea occurs to you, write about it.

1. As a student assistant for a campus residence hall, you have just listened to the twenty-third student this week complain about noise in the hall. You decide to formulate a policy that will solve the problem, but before you can implement it, you must present your idea at a student resident-assistant meeting. Write out the proposal that you will present at that meeting.

A good solution solves more than one problem, and it does not make new problems. I am talking about health as opposed to almost any cure, coherence of pattern as opposed to almost any solution produced piecemeal or in isolation.
—WENDELL BERRY, AUTHOR OF THE GIFT OF THE GOOD LAND

2. Reread Frank Trippett's analysis of the scofflaw problem. Write a letter to the city council recommending a solution to *one* of the problems that Trippett identifies—a solution that the city council has the power to implement.

3. Eldridge Cleaver once said, "You're either part of the solution or part of the problem." Examine one of your activities or pastimes—sports, shopping, cruising, eating, drinking, or even studying. How does what you do possibly create a problem, from someone else's point of view? Explain.

4. After being away from your high school for a while, you can see more clearly its specific problems. Brainstorm or freewrite about the most important problems that students faced in your high school. Write a letter to the school principal, explaining one specific problem that could and should be solved. Then propose your solution.

5. "Let the buyer beware" is a time-honored maxim for all consumers. Unless you are vigilant, you can easily be ripped off. Write a letter to the Better Business Bureau explaining some consumer problem or rip-off that you've recently experienced and suggest a solution that will prevent others from being exploited.

6. Changing the rules of some sports might make them more enjoyable, less violent, or fairer: introducing the 30-second clock in NCAA basketball, using TV instant replays in professional and college football and basketball, imposing stiffer fines for brawls in hockey games, requiring boxers to wear padded helmets, giving equal pay and media coverage to women's sports. Choose a sport you enjoy as a participant or observer, identify and explain the problem you want to solve, and justify your solution in a letter to the editors of *Sports Illustrated.*

God, give us grace to accept with serenity the things that cannot be changed, courage to change the things which should be changed, and the wisdom to distinguish the one from the other.
—REINHOLD NIEBUHR, AUTHOR AND THEOLOGIAN

PROBLEM SOLVING: PROFESSIONAL WRITING

SOLVING FOR PATTERN

WENDELL BERRY

A native of Kentucky and professor of English at the University of Kentucky, Wendell Berry is a prolific writer of poetry, fiction, and nonfiction. He is most noted for his essays and books on agricultural and ecological topics, including The Unforeseen Wilderness: An Essay on Kentucky's Red River Gorge *(1971),* The Unsettling of America: Culture and Agriculture *(1977),* The Gift of Good Land *(1981),* Home Economics *(1987), and* What Are People For? *(1990). In this selection from "Solving for Pattern," which appears in* The Gift of the Good Land, *while Berry talks about solving specific problems in farming and agriculture, he focuses on the nature of problem solving itself. Although too many farm "solutions" (larger tractors, feed lots, overuse of fertilizers and pesticides) solve one problem, they create a host of destructive side effects. Good solutions, Berry argues, do not address problems in isolation. Good solutions must promote the harmony, health, and quality of the whole system.*

Our dilemma in agriculture now is that the industrial methods that have so spectacularly solved some of the problems of food production have been accompanied by "side effects" so damaging as to threaten the survival of farming. Perhaps the best clue to the nature and the gravity

CRITICAL READING

Encourage students to challenge Berry's statements or his logic in this essay. Are there more than just "three types" of solutions? Is it true, as Berry states at the end of paragraph 6, that "no one prospers by them but the suppliers of fuel and equipment"? And in paragraph 9, are air conditioners really trying to solve air pollution problems? Is the analogy between farming and organic health valid or useful? Encourage students to identify and analyze other possible problems or contradictions in Berry's text.

of this dilemma is that it is not limited to agriculture. My immediate concern here is with the irony of agricultural methods that destroy, first, the health of the soil and, finally, the health of human communities. But I could just as easily be talking about sanitation systems that pollute, school systems that graduate illiterate students, medical cures that cause disease, or nuclear armaments that explode in the midst of the people they are meant to protect. This is a kind of surprise that is characteristic of our time: The cure proves incurable; security results in the evacuation of a neighborhood or a town. It is only when it is understood that our agricultural dilemma is characteristic not of our agriculture but of our time that we can begin to understand why these surprises happen, and to work out standards of judgment that may prevent them. **(1)**

To the problems of farming, then, as to other problems of our time, there appear to be three kinds of solutions: **(2)**

There is, first, the solution that causes a ramifying series of new problems, the only limiting criterion being, apparently, that the new problems should arise beyond the purview of the expertise that produced the solution—as, in agriculture, industrial solutions to the problem of production have invariably caused problems of maintenance, conservation, economics, community health, etc., etc. **(3)**

If, for example, beef cattle are fed in large feed lots, within the boundaries of the feeding operation itself a certain factorylike order and efficiency can be achieved. But even within those boundaries that mechanical order immediately produces biological disorder, for we know that health problems and dependence on drugs will be greater among cattle so confined than among cattle on pasture. **(4)**

And beyond those boundaries, the problems multiply. Pen feeding of cattle in large numbers involves, first, a manure-removal problem, which becomes at some point a health problem for the animals themselves, for the local watershed, and for the adjoining ecosystems and human communities. If the manure is disposed of without returning it to the soil that produced the feed, a serious problem of soil fertility is involved. But we know too that large concentrations of animals in feed lots in one place tend to be associated with, and to promote, large cash-grain monocultures in other places. These monocultures tend to be accompanied by a whole set of specifically agricultural problems: soil erosion, soil compaction, epidemic infestations of pests, weeds, and disease. But they are also accompanied by a set of agricultural-economic problems (dependence on purchased technology; dependence on purchased fuels, fertilizers, and poisons; dependence on credit)—and by a set of community problems, beginning with depopulation and the removal of sources, services, and markets to more and more distant towns. And these are, so to speak, only the first circle of the bad effects of a bad solution. With a little care, their branchings can be traced on into nature, into the life of the cities, and into the cultural and economic life of the nation. **(5)**

The second kind of solution is that which immediately worsens the problem it is intended to solve, causing a hellish symbiosis in which problem and solution reciprocally enlarge one another in a sequence that, so far as its own logic is concerned, is limitless—as when the problem of soil compaction is "solved" by a bigger tractor, which further compacts the soil, which makes a need for a still bigger tractor, and so on and on. There is an identical symbiosis between coal-fired power plants and air conditioners. It is characteristic of such solutions that no one prospers by them but the suppliers of fuel and equipment. **(6)**

These two kinds of solutions are obviously bad. They always serve one good at the expense of another or of several others, and I believe that if all their effects were ever to be accounted for they would be seen to involve, too frequently if not invariably, a net loss to nature, agriculture, and the human commonwealth. **(7)**

Such solutions always involve a definition of the problem that is either false or so narrow as to be virtually false. To define an agricultural problem as if it were solely a problem of agriculture—or solely a problem of production or technology or economics—is simply to misunderstand the problem, either inadvertently or deliberately, either for profit or because of a prevalent fashion of thought. The whole problem must be solved, not just some handily identifiable and simplifiable aspect of it. **(8)**

Both kinds of bad solutions leave their problems unsolved. Bigger tractors do not solve the problem of soil compaction any more than air conditioners solve the problem of air pollution. Nor does the large confinement-feeding operation solve the problem of food production; it is, rather, a way calculated to allow large-scale ambition and greed to profit from food production.

The real problem of food production occurs within a complex, mutually influential relationship of soil, plants, animals, and people. A real solution to that problem will therefore be ecologically, agriculturally, and culturally healthful. **(9)**

Perhaps it is not until health is set down as the aim that we come in sight of the third kind of solution: that which causes a ramifying series of solutions—as when meat animals are fed on the farm where the feed is raised, and where the feed is raised to be fed to the animals that are on the farm. Even so rudimentary a description implies a concern for pattern, for quality, which necessarily complicates the concern for production. The farmer has put plants and animals into a relationship of mutual dependence, and must perforce be concerned for balance or symmetry, a reciprocating connection in the pattern of the farm that is biological, not industrial, and that involves solutions to problems of fertility, soil husbandry, economics, sanitation—the whole complex of problems whose proper solutions add up to *health*: the health of the soil, of plants and animals, of farm and farmer, of farm family and farm community, all involved in the same internested, interlocking pattern—or pattern of patterns. **(10)**

A bad solution is bad, then, because it acts destructively upon the larger patterns in which it is contained. It acts destructively upon those patterns, most likely, because it is formed in ignorance or disregard of them. A bad solution solves for a single purpose or goal, such as increased production. And it is typical of such solutions that they achieve stupendous increases in production at exorbitant biological and social costs. **(11)**

A good solution is good because it is in harmony with those larger patterns—and this harmony will, I think, be found to have the nature of analogy. A bad solution acts within the larger pattern the way a disease or addiction acts within the body. A good solution acts within the larger pattern the way a healthy organ acts within the body. But it must at once be understood that a healthy organ does not—as the mechanistic or industrial mind would like to say—"give" health to the body, is not exploited for the body's health, but is *a part* of its health. The health of organ and organism is the same, just as the health of organism and ecosystem is the same. And these structures of organ, organism, and ecosystem belong to a series of analogical integrities that begins with the organelle and ends with the biosphere. **(12)**

TEACHING TIP

Let students see how learning new vocabulary words is part of active, critical reading. Berry uses the word "ramifying" several times in his essay. The word comes from the Latin *ramus* meaning "branch." The idea of the branching relationships of all things is central to Berry's ecological and organic analogies. Also, show students how the words "husbandry," "symbiosis," and "analogical" are central to Berry's argument.

VOCABULARY

In your journal, write the meanings of the following words:

ramifying series of new problems (3)
purview of the expertise (3)
hellish *symbiosis* (6)
soil *husbandry* (10)
analogical integrities (12)
begins with the *organelle* (12)

QUESTIONS FOR WRITING AND DISCUSSION

1. Reread your response to the freewriting exercise at the beginning of this chapter. What campus problem did you describe and what was your solution? Now, assume that you are Wendell Berry. Write one paragraph of Berry's response to your solution. Specifically, consider how well your solution meets

Berry's goal of solving for the harmony, health, and quality of the whole college or university system.

2. Berry's essay explains three kinds of solutions. What are these three types of solutions and what makes the third kind the best?

3. In paragraph 1, Berry says that he "could just as easily be talking about sanitation systems that pollute, school systems that graduate illiterate students, [or] medical cures that cause disease." Choose one of these problems (or another common problem) and explain how Berry would analyze the problem.

4. Berry clarifies his explanation for his reader by using audience cues (transitions, paragraph hooks, and topic sentences) at the beginning of paragraphs. Choose any three successive paragraphs (for example, paragraphs 3, 4, and 5) and identify any words or phrases that (a) make a transition from the previous paragraph or idea and (b) announce or preview the subject of the new paragraph. Make a sketch outline of Berry's essay.

5. An *analogy* is a comparison between two things or processes in which a simple or familiar thing helps to explain a complex or unfamiliar thing. Thus, we can explain how the human heart works by drawing an analogy with a simple mechanical pump. In paragraph 12, Berry says that a "bad solution acts within the larger pattern the way a disease or addiction acts within the body." Explain Berry's analogy. Then apply this analogy to one specific problem that you have discussed in class. Does Berry's organic analogy make sense in that particular case? Why or why not?

6. Apply Berry's ideas about "solving for pattern" to either the following essay by Gloria Steinem or the subsequent essay by Paul Zimmerman. How well do their arguments and solutions address the overall harmony, health, and quality of the system?

SEX, LIES, AND ADVERTISING

GLORIA STEINEM

Does America have complete freedom of the press? Do advertisers control the editorial policies of magazines? Most readers assume that magazines are free to print any article of interest to their readers. As Gloria Steinem's essay illustrates, however, advertisers can and do influence editorial pol-

icy by refusing to run ads without accompanying articles supporting their industries and products. Steinem cites examples of specific companies—Philip Morris, Clairol, Pillsbury, American Express, Estée Lauder—who refused to advertise in Ms. *magazine without editorial changes in the magazine. Although* Ms. *eventually sidestepped the problem by going to an ad-free format, Steinem proposes changes that pressure advertisers, readers, and magazine editors to reduce advertisers' control over the content of articles. A longtime editor of* Ms. *magazine, Steinem has written numerous articles on feminist issues and has published several books, including* Outrageous Acts and Everyday Rebellions *(1983),* Marilyn: Norma Jeane *(1986), and* Bedside Book of Self-Esteem *(1989).*

COLLABORATIVE ACTIVITY

As a prereading exercise, ask students to bring in copies of popular magazine. In class, ask each student to inventory his or her magazine for the following: total number of pages, number of pages of ads, types of products being advertised, subjects of feature articles, and subjects in the magazine's regular "departments." Then, in groups of three or four, have students review their findings and discuss the relationship between the subjects of the articles and the products advertised. Do the magazine articles support the advertisers' products?

About three years ago, as *glasnost* was beginning and *Ms.* seemed to be ending, I was invited to a press lunch for a Soviet official. He entertained us with anecdotes about new problems of democracy in his country. Local Communist leaders were being criticized in their media for the first time, he explained, and they were angry. **(1)**

"So I'll have to ask my American friends," he finished pointedly, "how more *subtly* to control the press." In the silence that followed, I said, "Advertising." **(2)**

The reporters laughed, but later, one of them took me aside: How *dare* I suggest that freedom of the press was limited? How dare I imply that his newsweekly could be influenced by ads? **(3)**

I explained that I was thinking of advertising's media-wide influence on most of what we read. Even newsmagazines use "soft" cover stories to sell ads, confuse readers with "advertorials," and occasionally self-censor on subjects known to be a problem with big advertisers. **(4)**

But, I also explained, I was thinking especially of women's magazines. There, it isn't just a little content that's devoted to attracting ads, it's almost all of it. That's why advertisers—not readers—have always been the problem for *Ms.* As the only women's magazine that didn't supply what the ad world euphemistically describes as "supportive editorial atmosphere" or "complementary copy" (for instance, articles that praise food/fashion/beauty subjects to "support" and "complement" food/fashion/beauty ads), *Ms.* could never attract enough advertising to break even. **(5)**

"Oh, *women's* magazines," the journalist said with contempt. "Everybody knows they're catalogs—but who cares? They have nothing to do with journalism." **(6)**

I can't tell you how many times I've had this argument in 25 years of working for many kinds of publications. Except as money-making machines—"cash cows" as they are so elegantly called in the trade—women's magazines are rarely taken seriously. Though changes being made by women have been called more far-reaching than the industrial revolution—and though many editors try hard to reflect some of them in the few pages left to them after all the ad-related subjects have been covered—the magazines serving the female half of this country are still far below the journalistic and ethical standards of news and general interest publications. Most depressing of all, this doesn't even rate an exposé. **(7)**

If *Time* and *Newsweek* had to lavish praise on cars in general and credit General Motors in particular to get GM ads, there would be a scandal—maybe a criminal investigation. When women's magazines from *Seventeen* to *Lear's* praise beauty products in general and credit Revlon in particular to get ads, it's just business as usual. **(8)**

When *Ms.* began, we didn't consider *not* taking ads. The most important reason was keeping the price of a feminist magazine low enough for most women to afford. But the second and almost equal reason was providing a forum where women and advertisers could talk to each other and improve advertising itself. After all, it was (and still is) as potent a source of information in this country as news or TV and movie dramas. **(9)**

We decided to proceed in two stages. First, we would convince makers of "people products" used by both men and women but advertised mostly to men—cars, credit cards, insurance, sound equipment, financial services, and the like—that their ads should be placed in a women's magazine. Since they were accustomed to the division between editorial and advertising in news and general interest magazines, this would allow our editorial content to be free and diverse. Second, we would add the best ads for whatever traditional "women's products" (clothes, shampoo, fragrance, food, and so on) that surveys showed *Ms.* readers used. But we would ask them to come in *without* the usual quid pro quo of "complementary copy." **(10)**

We knew the second step might be harder. Food advertisers have always demanded that women's magazines publish recipes and articles on entertaining (preferably ones that name their products) in return for their ads; clothing advertisers expect to be surrounded by fashion spreads (especially ones that credit their designers); and shampoo, fragrance, and beauty products in general usually insist on positive editorial coverage of beauty subjects, plus photo credits besides. That's why women's magazines look the way they do. But if we could break this link between ads and editorial content, then we wanted good ads for "women's products," too. **(11)**

By playing their part in this unprecedented mix of *all* the things our readers need and use, advertisers also would be rewarded: ads for products like cars and mutual funds would find a new growth market; the best ads for women's products would no longer be lost in oceans of ads for the same category; and both would have access to a laboratory of smart and caring readers whose response would help create effective ads for other media as well. **(12)**

CRITICAL READING

Steinem's excellent specific examples can be the focus for "reading against the text" (challenging the writer's arguments and assumptions) and for "reading with a writer's eye" (seeing how good writers construct well-developed, specific examples). For the former, ask students to reread Steinem's examples or scenarios (paragraphs 18–45) to determine whether the advertisers were actually blackmailing *Ms.* into changing editorial policies or whether they were simply exercising their right to refuse to run a specific ad. For the latter, show how Steinem's examples are located in time and place and are amply developed with specific details. Then ask students to read their own drafts and revise to make their examples fuller and more specific.

I thought then that our main problem would be the imagery in ads themselves. Carmakers were still draping blondes in evening gowns over the hoods like ornaments. Authority figures were almost always male, even in ads for products that only women used. Sadistic, he-man campaigns even won industry praise. (For instance, *Advertising Age* had hailed the infamous Silva Thin cigarette theme, "How to Get a Woman's Attention: Ignore Her," as "brilliant.") Even in medical journals, tranquilizer ads showed depressed housewives standing beside piles of dirty dishes and promised to get them back to work. **(13)**

Obviously, *Ms.* would have to avoid such ads and seek out the best ones—but this didn't seem impossible. *The New Yorker* had been selecting ads for aesthetic reasons for years, a practice that only seemed to make advertisers more eager to be in its pages. *Ebony* and *Essence* were asking for ads with positive black images, and though their struggle was hard, they weren't being called unreasonable. **(14)**

Clearly, what *Ms.* needed was a very special publisher and ad sales staff. I could think of only one woman with experience on the business side of magazines—Patricia Carbine, who recently had become a vice president of *McCall's* as well as its editor in chief—and the reason I knew her name was a good omen. She had been managing editor at *Look* (really *the* editor, but its owner refused to put a female name at the top of his masthead) when I was writing a column there. After I did an early interview with Cesar Chavez, then just emerging as a leader of migrant labor, and the publisher turned it down because he was worried about ads from Sunkist, Pat was the one who intervened. As I learned later, she had told the publisher she would resign if the interview wasn't published. Mainly because *Look* couldn't afford to lose Pat, it *was* published (and the ads from Sunkist never arrived). **(15)**

Though I barely knew this woman, she had done two things I always remembered: put her job on the line in a way that editors often talk about but rarely do, and been so loyal to her colleagues that she never told me or anyone outside *Look* that she had done so. **(16)**

Fortunately, Pat did agree to leave *McCall's* and take a huge cut in salary to become publisher of *Ms.* She became responsible for training and inspiring generations of young women who joined the *Ms.* ad sales force, many of whom went on to become "firsts" at the top of publishing. When *Ms.* first started, however, there were so few women with experience selling space that Pat and I made the rounds of ad agencies ourselves. Later, the fact that *Ms.* was asking companies to do business in a different way meant our saleswomen had to make many times the usual number of calls—first to convince agencies and then client companies besides—and to present endless amounts of research. I was often asked to do a final ad presentation, or see some higher decision-maker, or speak to women employees so executives could see the interest of women they worked with. That's why I spent more time persuading advertisers than editing or writing for *Ms.* and why I ended up with an unsentimental education in the seamy underside of publishing that few writers see (and even fewer magazines can publish). **(17)**

Let me take you with us through some experiences, just as they happened:

• Cheered on by early support from Volkswagen and one or two other car companies, we scrape together time and money to put on a major reception in Detroit. We know U.S. carmakers firmly believe that women choose the upholstery, not the car, but we are armed with statistics and reader mail to prove the contrary: a car is an important purchase for women, one that symbolizes mobility and freedom. **(18)**

But almost nobody comes. We are left with many pounds of shrimp on the table, and quite a lot of egg on our face. We blame ourselves for not guessing that there would be a baseball pennant play-off on the same day, but executives go out of their way to explain they wouldn't have come anyway. Thus begins ten years of knocking on hostile doors, presenting endless documentation, and hiring a full-time saleswoman in Detroit; all necessary before *Ms.* gets any real results. **(19)**

This long saga has a semihappy ending: foreign and, later, domestic carmakers eventually provided *Ms.* with enough advertising to make cars one of our top sources of ad revenue. Slowly, Detroit began to take the women's market seriously enough to put car ads in other women's magazines, too, thus freeing a few pages from the hothouse of fashion-beauty-food ads. **(20)**

But long after figures showed a third, even a half, of many car models being bought by women, U.S. makers continued to be uncomfortable addressing women. Unlike foreign carmakers, Detroit never quite learned the secret of creating intelligent ads that exclude no one, and then placing them in women's magazines to overcome past exclusion. (*Ms.* readers were so grateful for a routine Honda ad featuring rack and pinion steering, for instance, that they sent fan mail.) Even now, Detroit continues to ask, "Should we make special ads for women?" Perhaps that's why some foreign cars still have a disproportionate share of the U.S. women's market. **(21)**

• In the *Ms.* Gazette, we do a brief report on a congressional hearing into chemicals used in hair dyes that are absorbed through the skin and may be carcinogenic. Newspapers report this too, but Clairol, a Bristol-Myers subsidiary that makes dozens of products—a few of which have just begun to advertise in *Ms.*—is outraged. Not at newspapers or newsmagazines, just at us. It's bad enough that *Ms.* is the only women's magazine refusing to provide the usual "complementary" articles and beauty photos, but to criticize one of their categories—*that* is going too far. **(22)**

We offer to publish a letter from Clairol telling its side of the story. In an excess of solicitousness, we even put this letter in the Gazette, not in Letters to the Editors where it belongs. Nonetheless—and in spite of surveys that show *Ms.* readers are active women who use more of almost everything Clairol makes than do the readers of any other women's magazine—*Ms.* gets almost none of these ads for the rest of its natural life. **(23)**

Meanwhile, Clairol changes its hair coloring formula, apparently in response to the hearings we reported. **(24)**

• Our saleswomen set out early to attract ads for consumer electronics: sound equipment, calculators, computers, VCRs, and the like. We know that our readers are determined to be included in the technological revolution. We know from reader surveys that *Ms.* readers are buying this stuff in numbers as high as those of magazines like *Playboy*; or "men 18 to 34," the prime targets of the consumer electronics industry. Moreover, unlike traditional women's products that our readers buy but don't need to read articles about, these are subjects they want covered in our pages. There actually *is* a supportive editorial atmosphere. **(25)**

"But women don't understand technology," say executives at the end of ad presentations. "Maybe not," we respond, "but neither do men—and we all buy it." **(26)**

"If women *do* buy it," say the decision-makers, "they're asking their husbands and boyfriends what to buy first." We produce letters from *Ms.* readers saying how turned off they are when salesmen say things like "Let me know when your husband can come in." **(27)**

After several years of this, we get a few ads for compact sound systems. Some of them come from JVC, whose vice president, Harry Elias, is trying to convince his Japanese bosses that there is something called a women's market. At his invitation, I find myself speaking at huge trade shows in Chicago and Las Vegas, trying to persuade JVC dealers that showrooms don't have to be locker rooms where women are made to feel unwelcome. But as it turns out, the shows themselves are part of the problem. In Las Vegas, the only women around the technology displays are seminude models serving champagne. In Chicago, the big attraction is Marilyn Chambers, who followed Linda Lovelace of *Deep Throat* fame as Chuck Traynor's captive and/or employee. VCRs are being demonstrated with her porn videos. **(28)**

In the end, we get ads for a car stereo now and then, but no VCRs; some IBM personal computers, but no Apple or Japanese ones. We notice that office magazines like *Working Woman* and *Savvy* don't benefit as much as they should from office equipment ads either. In the electronics world, women and technology seem mutually exclusive. It remains a decade behind even Detroit. . . . **(29)**

- When *Ms.* begins, the staff decides not to accept ads for feminine hygiene sprays or cigarettes: they are damaging and carry no appropriate health warnings. Though we don't think we should tell our readers what to do, we do think we should provide facts so they can decide for themselves. Since the antismoking lobby has been pressing for health warnings on cigarette ads, we decide to take them only as they comply. **(30)**

Philip Morris is among the first to do so. One of its brands, Virginia Slims, is also sponsoring women's tennis and the first national polls of women's opinions. On the other hand, the Virginia Slims theme, "You've come a long way, baby," has more than a "baby" problem. It makes smoking a symbol of progress for women. **(31)**

We explain to Philip Morris that this slogan won't do well in our pages, but they are convinced its success with some women means it will work with *all* women. Finally, we agree to publish an ad for a Virginia Slims calendar as a test. The letters from readers are critical—and smart. For instance: Would you show a black man picking cotton, the same man in a Cardin suit, and symbolize the antislavery and civil rights movements by smoking? Of course not. But instead of honoring the test results, the Philip Morris people seem angry to be proven wrong. They take away ads for *all* their many brands. **(32)**

This costs *Ms.* about $250,000 the first year. After five years, we can no longer keep track. Occasionally, a new set of executives listens to *Ms.* saleswomen, but because we won't take Virginia Slims, not one Philip Morris product returns to our pages for the next 16 years. **(33)**

Gradually, we also realize our naiveté in thinking we *could* decide against taking cigarette ads. They became a disproportionate support of magazines the moment they were banned on television, and few magazines could compete and survive without them; certainly not *Ms.*, which lacks so many other categories. By the time statistics in the 1980s showed that women's rate of lung cancer was approaching men's, the necessity of taking cigarette ads has become a kind of prison. **(34)**

- General Mills, Pillsbury, Carnation, DelMonte, Dole, Kraft, Stouffer, Hormel, Nabisco: you name the food giant, we try it. But no matter how desirable the *Ms.* readership, our lack of recipes is lethal. **(35)**

We explain to them that placing food ads *only* next to recipes associates food with work. For many women, it is a negative that works *against* the ads. Why not place food ads in diverse media without recipes (thus reaching more men, who are now a third of the shoppers in supermarkets anyway), and leave the recipes to specialty magazines like *Gourmet* (a third of whose readers are also men)? **(36)**

These arguments elicit interest, but except for an occasional ad for a convenience food, instant coffee, diet drinks, yogurt, or such extras as avocados and almonds, this mainstay of the publishing industry stays closed to us. Period. **(37)**

• Traditionally, wines and liquors didn't advertise to women: men were thought to make the brand decisions, even if women did the buying. But after endless presentations, we begin to make a dent in this category. Thanks to the unconventional Michael Roux of Carillon Importers (distributors of Grand Marnier, Absolut Vodka, and others), who assumes that food and drink have no gender, some ads are leaving their men's club. **(38)**

Beermakers are still selling masculinity. It takes *Ms.* fully eight years to get its first beer ad (Michelob). In general, however, liquor ads are less stereotyped in their imagery—and far less controlling of the editorial content around them—than are women's products. But given the underrepresentation of other categories, these very facts tend to create a disproportionate number of alcohol ads in the pages of *Ms.* This in turn dismays readers worried about women and alcoholism. . . . **(39)**

• Women's access to insurance and credit is vital, but with the exception of Equitable and a few other ad pioneers, such financial services address men. For almost a decade after the Equal Credit Opportunity Act passes in 1974, we try to convince American Express that women are a growth market—but nothing works. **(40)**

Finally, a former professor of Russian named Jerry Welsh becomes head of marketing. He assumes that women should be card-holders, and persuades his colleagues to feature women in a campaign. Thanks to this 1980s series, the growth rate for female card-holders surpasses that for men. **(41)**

For this article, I asked Jerry Welsh if he would explain why American Express waited so long. "Sure," he said, "they were afraid of having a 'pink' card." **(42)**

• Women of color read *Ms.* in disproportionate numbers. This is a source of pride to *Ms.* staffers, who are also more racially representative than the editors of other women's magazines. But this reality is obscured by ads filled with enough white women to make a reader snowblind. **(43)**

Pat Carbine remembers mostly "astonishment" when she requested African American, Hispanic, Asian, and other diverse images. Marcia Ann Gillespie, a *Ms.* editor who was previously the editor in chief of *Essence*, witnesses ad bias a second time: having tried for *Essence* to get white advertisers to use black images (Revlon did so eventually, but L'Oréal, Lauder, Chanel, and other companies never did), she sees similar problems getting integrated ads for an integrated magazine. Indeed, the ad world often creates black and Hispanic ads only for black and Hispanic media. In an exact parallel of the fear that marketing a product to women will endanger its appeal to men, the response is usually, "But your [white] readers won't identify." **(44)**

In fact, those we are able to get—for instance, a Max Factor ad made for *Essence* that Linda Wachner gives us after she becomes president—are praised by white readers, too. But there are pathetically few such images. **(45)**

- By the end of 1986, production and mailing costs have risen astronomically, ad income is flat, and competition for ads is stiffer than ever. The 60/40 preponderance of edit over ads that we promised to readers becomes 50/50; children's stories, most poetry, and some fiction are casualties of less space; in order to get variety into limited pages, the length (and sometimes the depth) of articles suffers; and, though we do refuse most of the ads that would look like a parody in our pages, we get so worn down that some slip through. (See this issue's No Comment.) Still, readers perform miracles. Though we haven't been able to afford a subscription mailing in two years, they maintain our guaranteed circulation of 450,000. **(46)**

Nonetheless, media reports on *Ms.* often insist that our unprofitability must be due to reader disinterest. The myth that advertisers simply follow readers is very strong. Not one reporter notes that other comparable magazines our size (say, *Vanity Fair* or *The Atlantic*) have been losing more money in one year than *Ms.* has lost in 16 years. No matter how much never-to-be-recovered cash is poured into starting a magazine or keeping one going, appearances seem to be all that matter. (Which is why we haven't been able to explain our fragile state in public. Nothing causes ad-flight like the smell of nonsuccess.) **(47)**

My healthy response is anger. My not-so-healthy response is constant worry. Also an obsession with finding one more rescue. There is hardly a night when I don't wake up with sweaty palms and pounding heart, scared that we won't be able to pay the printer or the post office; scared most of all that closing our doors will hurt the women's movement. **(48)**

Out of chutzpah and desperation, I arrange a lunch with Leonard Lauder, president of Estée Lauder. With the exception of Clinique (the brainchild of Carol Phillips), none of Lauder's hundreds of products has been advertised in *Ms.* A year's schedule of ads for just three or four of them could save us. Indeed, as the scion of a family-owned company whose ad practices are followed by the beauty industry, he is one of the few men who could liberate many pages in all women's magazines just by changing his mind about "complementary copy." **(49)**

Over a lunch that costs more than we can pay for some articles, I explain the need for his leadership. I also lay out the record of *Ms.*: more literary and journalistic prizes won, more new issues introduced into the mainstream, new writers discovered, and impact on society than any other magazine; more articles that became books, stories that became movies, ideas that became television series, and newly advertised products that became profitable; and, most important for him, a place for his ads to reach women who aren't reachable through any other women's magazine. Indeed, if there is one constant characteristic of the ever-changing *Ms.* readership, it is their impact as leaders. Whether it's waiting until later to have first babies, or pioneering PABA as sun protection in cosmetics, *whatever* they are doing today, a third to a half of American women will be doing three to five years from now. It's never failed. **(50)**

But, he says, *Ms.* readers are not *our* women. They're not interested in things like fragrance and blush-on. If they were, *Ms.* would write articles about them. **(51)**

On the contrary, I explain, surveys show they are more likely to buy such things than the readers of, say, *Cosmopolitan* or *Vogue*. They're good customers because they're out in the world enough to need several sets of everything: home, work, purse, travel, gym, and so on. They just don't need to read articles about these things. Would he ask a men's magazine to publish monthly columns on how to shave before he advertised Aramis products (his line for men)? **(52)**

He concedes that beauty features are often concocted more for advertisers than readers. But *Ms.* isn't appropriate for his ads anyway, he explains. Why? Because Estée Lauder is selling "a kept-woman mentality." **(53)**

I can't quite believe this. Sixty percent of the users of his products are salaried, and generally resemble *Ms.* readers. Besides, his company has the appeal of having been started by a creative and hardworking woman, his mother, Estée Lauder. **(54)**

That doesn't matter, he says. He knows his customers, and they would *like* to be kept women. That's why he will never advertise in *Ms.* . . . **(55)**

What could women's magazines be like if they were as free as books? as realistic as newspapers? as creative as films? as diverse as women's lives? We don't know. **(56)**

But we'll only find out if we take women's magazines seriously. If readers were to act in a concerted way to change traditional practices of *all* women's magazines and the marketing of *all* women's products, we could do it. After all, they are operating on our consumer dollars; money that we now control. You and I could:

- write to editors and publishers (with copies to advertisers) that we're willing to pay *more* for magazines with editorial independence, but will *not* continue to pay for those that are just editorial extensions of ads;
- write to advertisers (with copies to editors and publishers) that we want fiction, political reporting, consumer reporting—whatever is, or is not, supported by their ads;

- put as much energy into breaking advertising's control over content as into changing the images in ads, or protesting ads for harmful products like cigarettes;
- support only those women's magazines and products that take *us* seriously as readers and consumers. **(57)**

Those of us in the magazine world can also use the carrot-and-stick technique. For instance: pointing out that, if magazines were a regulated medium like television, the demands of advertisers would be against FCC rules. Payola and extortion could be punished. As it is, there are probably illegalities. A magazine's postal rates are determined by the ratio of ad to edit pages, and the former costs more than the latter. So much for the stick. **(58)**

The carrot means appealing to enlightened self-interest. For instance: there are many studies showing that the greatest factor in determining an ad's effectiveness is the credibility of its surroundings. The "higher the rating of editorial believability," concluded a 1987 survey by the *Journal of Advertising Research*, "the higher the rating of the advertising." Thus, an impenetrable wall between edit and ads would also be in the best interest of advertisers. **(59)**

Unfortunately, few agencies or clients hear such arguments. Editors often maintain the false purity of refusing to talk to them at all. Instead, they see ad salespeople who know little about editorial, are trained in business as usual, and are usually paid by commission. Editors might also band together to take on controversy. That happened once when all the major women's magazines did articles in the same month on the Equal Rights Amendment. It could happen again. **(60)**

It's almost three years away from life between the grindstones of advertising pressures and readers' needs. I'm just beginning to realize how edges got smoothed down—in spite of all our resistance. **(61)**

I remember feeling put upon when I changed "Porsche" to "car" in a piece about Nazi imagery in German pornography by Andrea Dworkin—feeling sure Andrea would understand that Volkswagen, the distributor of Porsche and one of our few supportive advertisers, asked only to be far away from Nazi subjects. It's taken me all this time to realize that Andrea was the one with a right to feel put upon. **(62)**

Even as I write this, I get a call from a writer for *Elle*, who is doing a whole article on where women part their hair. Why, she wants to know, do I part mine in the middle? **(63)**

It's all so familiar. A writer trying to make something of a nothing assignment; an editor laboring to think of new ways to attract ads; readers assuming that other women must want this ridiculous stuff; more women suffering for lack of information, insight, creativity, and laughter that could be on these same pages. **(64)**

I ask you: Can't we do better than this? **(65)**

VOCABULARY

In your journal, write the meanings of the following words:

- *euphemistically* describes (5)
- the usual *quid pro quo* (10)
- *disproportionate* share (21)
- may be *carcinogenic* (22)
- an excess of *solicitousness* (23)
- seem *mutually exclusive* (29)
- realize our *naiveté* (34)
- *preponderance* of edit over ads (46)
- as the *scion* (49)

QUESTIONS FOR WRITING AND DISCUSSION

1. Explain your response to Steinem's article. What problem does she describe? Do you agree that the problem is serious? What solutions does she offer? Do you believe that her solutions will help solve the problem?

2. In context, explain what Steinem means by the italicized words or phrases in the following sentences. "On the other hand, the Virginia Slims theme, 'You've come a long way, *baby*,' has more than a 'baby' problem" (paragraph 31). "By the time statistics in the 1980s showed that women's rate of lung cancer was approaching men's, the necessity of taking cigarette ads *has become a kind of prison*" (paragraph 34). "'Sure,' he said, 'they were afraid of having a "pink" card'" (paragraph 42). "The myth that *advertisers simply follow readers* is very strong" (paragraph 47).

3. Profile the intended audience for Steinem's article. To support your profile, find at least three specific examples, references, or sentences in the essay which are explicitly directed toward that audience.

4.. Beginning with paragraph 18, Steinem cites specific examples from her own experience to illustrate the problem. How many such examples or scenarios does she give? Which of these examples are most effective? Why are they effective?

5. In a sidebar to her article, Steinem says that magazines often have "editorial pages devoted to 'complementary copy'; to text or photos that praise advertised categories, instruct in their use, or generally act as extensions of ads." Her own survey reports the following statistics: *Glamour*, April 1990, contains 339 pages total but only 65 non-ad or ad-related pages. (The remaining 274 pages are ads or "complementary copy.") *Vogue*, May 1990, has 319 pages total with just 38 non-ad or ad-related pages. *Family Circle*, March 13, 1990, has a total of 180 pages, of which only 33 are non-ad or ad-related. Survey a popular magazine: What is the ratio of pages of ads to pages of copy not ad-related? What conclusions can you draw from your survey?

THE AGONY MUST END

PAUL ZIMMERMAN

In a proposal written for Sports Illustrated, *sportswriter Paul Zimmerman describes the problems of injuries in the National Football League and then proposes his solutions. In his article, Zimmerman documents the seriousness of the problem by referring to actual players injured, interviewing NFL players, and citing information and statistics provided by the NFL, team trainers, and the Players Association. Then he proposes several major changes, discusses the costs, and examines the feasibility of his changes. Read his essay and see if you agree with his proposals. Notice that although Zimmerman is writing for a general audience of readers interested in football, he clearly hopes that the people responsible for making a decision will also read his proposal.*

They are the assassins waiting behind the door in a dark room. They are pro football's unpredictable—yet only too predictable—curse. Injuries. As the fractures, concussions and bruises that play havoc with America's No. 1 sport struck down 183 NFL starters in the first half of the season, medical reports like these became commonplace:

> Two defensive backs, Anthony Young of Indianapolis and Tim Lewis of Green Bay, damaged nerves in their necks while making fairly routine tackles. They will never make any more. To do so would be to risk paralysis.
>
> On Oct. 26 the San Francisco 49ers fielded only 37 healthy players out of a possible 45 for their game with Green Bay.
>
> Dallas running back Tony Dorsett, after nine relatively injury-free years, missed three of his first eight games this season and hobbled through three more on an ailing knee.

CRITICAL READING

Encourage students to read with a writer's eye by noting Zimmerman's sources. What are his probable sources of information? Ask students to identify places in the essay where Zimmerman draws on observation, personal experience, interviews, and statistics or comments from written sources. Then have students, individually or in groups, reexamine the collecting strategies for their own essays. Which of Zimmerman's strategies or kinds of sources might work for them?

CRITICAL VIEWING. Encourage your students to view television with a "producer's eye." Foster the habit of noticing how news reports draw on observation, interviews, statistics, and other information sources to explore a problem or support a thesis.

Two Kansas City Chiefs, linebacker Ken McAlister and wide receiver Anthony Hancock, underwent surgery after their knees buckled on artificial turf without having been hit. **(1)**

"Injuries," says Philip Rosenthal, the assistant director of New York's Nicholas Institute of Sports Medicine and Athletic Trauma, "are inherent to football. It's the nature of the beast." **(2)**

O.K., but where does it stop? When do we make the breakthrough and start reducing injuries? The average playing career, 4.6 years in 1983, is now 3.6 years. Speed has increased through natural selection and lighter equipment. Size has shown a natural gain, too, but it also has an unnatural side because of the anabolic steroids that are such a major part of the weight-training programs favored by a number of players. **(3)**

Artificial turf abounds, and it's still as hated by the players as it was 21 years ago when the Houston Astrodome opened. Where's the end of it? Today's 240-pounder is a pumped-up 280, thanks to the steroids. In five years maybe he'll be 300, moving even faster, inflicting greater damage. Can medical science keep up with that? Or will the incidence of injury be even higher? It's time that the NFL takes a long look at the problem and steps in, before football becomes Rollerball. **(4)**

Questionable and conflicting data from the league, the Players Association and the trainers make it hard to determine exact percentages on injuries and whether they're up a great deal, up only slightly or staying more or less level. One thing that's certain is that they're not declining, and this in itself is frightening. Modern equipment is supposedly safer, and rule changes meant to protect players from injuries have been adopted. Then why, in a world in which modern medicine has discovered how to transplant organs, are pro football players still getting hurt at the same rate as they were in the old days? **(5)**

The medical breakthroughs in football have been curative, not preventive. For example, arthroscopic surgery can mend a wounded knee and have a player who once would have been out for the season back on the field in three weeks. Arthroscopy can diagnose a minute fracture that used to be called water on the knee. Medical science and the equipment people are in a race against the changing physics of pro football, and they're not winning. They can't gain any ground on the steroid labs, which are turning out bigger, artificially built-up athletes, who move at higher speeds on faster tracks, thanks to synthetic turf. The result is higher-speed collisions by larger people, a ferocity of hitting never before seen in football or any other sport. **(6)**

Injuries are publicized most heavily when quarterbacks are hurt. The quarterback thrashing is a constant. NFL figures show that after eight weeks of the '84 season there had been 41 different starting quarterbacks,

12 getting the call because of injury. Last year the midseason numbers were 40 and 11; this year they are 44 and 14. **(7)**

So the damage goes on, week after week, year after year. What should be done? Steroids are a good place to start. Everybody hates them, everybody knows the long-range damage they can cause, and lots of players in the NFL use them—and don't admit it. **(8)**

"That's about right," Los Angeles Raider defensive end Howie Long says. "At least 50 percent of the big guys. The offensive line—75 percent. Defensive line—40 percent, plus 35 percent of the linebackers. I don't know about the speed positions, but I've heard they're used there, too." **(9)**

The dangers are threefold: No. 1, the long-range risks—cancers, urinary tract problems and other perils. No. 2, turning pro football games into a game for artificially created giants, able to inflict great damage by their sheer mass. Danger No. 3 is that the artificial bulk causes more insidious injuries—muscle pulls and tendon strains that won't go away. **(10)**

"Eighty percent of the time when a big guy tears a muscle, steroids are probably the reason why," Long says. "You put 50 pounds of muscle on a player, and he goes from a baggage carrier in the jungle to Tarzan, and he says, 'Wow, this is great!' But something has to give. You're putting too much muscle fiber on a body not designed for it." **(11)**

Trainers around the league are slowly starting to realize he might be right. "I look with suspicion on some of those injuries when you can't determine how they happened," Saints trainer Dean Kleinschmidt says. "Steroids do strange things to your body. When a guy is pumped up on steroids, there's always a weak link, maybe an Achilles, maybe a patellar tendon." **(12)**

Solution: Attack anabolic steroids at the league level. A tough project. There hasn't been much concern about the question until recently. Steroids are not illegal unless they are obtained without a prescription. Testing is expensive. Each test costs about $100. O.K., it's worth it. Two spot checks for each player, every year, will cost a club about $10,000. **(13)**

Any effective antisteroid effort must become part of the new Players Association contract. The program will certainly have more bite and greater impact if the NFLPA enters into a joint endorsement with the league. **(14)**

The Players Association has another duty to perform, if it wishes to do something about the injury problem. It has to take a serious position on artificial turf. Both the NFL-sponsored Stanford Research Institute International's 1974 study and the NCAA's 1982 study showed that the incidence of injury on synthetic turf was significantly higher than on grass. Since then, the NFL has offered no research to the contrary. Two weeks ago in Giants Stadium, the Jets lost two Pro Bowlers, noseguard

Joe Klecko for a game and linebacker Lance Mehl for the season, because of noncontact injuries attributable to the artificial turf. **(15)**

New, softer carpets, with better cushions, are more comfortable to fall on, but according to some people they also increase traction so that the cleats catch, causing knee injuries. "When the nap of the turf is new there's just too much traction," Cincinnati trainer Paul Sparling says. "Archie Griffin tried to cut once on new turf and his foot stuck so firmly that he tore up his abdominal muscles in addition to his leg. He was out for the year." **(16)**

The players' general hatred of artificial turf is well documented. Very few of them like fake grass, but in the last two contract sessions, while elimination of synthetics was a blanket demand, it quickly became a throwaway issue in former executive director Ed Garvey's negotiating strategy when the heavy matters came up—like money. Note to current association director Gene Upshaw: Worker safety is a top priority for a responsible union. It's not a throwaway. **(17)**

San Francisco coach Bill Walsh's idea of a joint player-management committee to examine the carpets every year and replace them when necessary, or at least to eliminate the more unsafe aspects, is a good one. If a particular field proves to be unsafe no matter what is done, then bring back the grass in that particular stadium—assuming it's outdoors (sad to say, grass won't grow properly in the domes). Make that a keynote demand at the contract talks. **(18)**

Cheap shots cause injuries, too. It's a fact of life in football—always was, always will be. The problem is that the people responsible for the cheap shots are now so much better equipped to deliver the crippling blow—again, the size and speed factors. The NFL takes a curious approach to cheap shots—protect the quarterback, protect the head. The cosmetic approach. Granted, quarterbacks must be protected from late hits, out-of-bounds hits and general mayhem. **(19)**

Consistency in officiating is the key. But why protect only the quarterback? How about the running back who gets teed up by two tacklers and finished off by a third one as Bengal fullback Bill Johnson was against the Steelers (he missed one game with a neck injury). That's the play that really needs the quick whistle. **(20)**

The NFL's interpretation of anatomy is strange. Head shots are severely penalized, but the crippling blindsider to the knee is O.K., especially when linemen do it to each other. It's time to take intent into account. Deliberate attempts to maim must be punished, even in cases in which a blow to the head is not involved. **(21)**

Solution: Pass a rule that says no cut-blocking unless you're face-up with a man. Clipping is illegal everywhere else on the field. It should be on the line, too. **(22)**

But how about the illegal, career-ending type of injury? New Orleans safety Antonio Gibson put the Giants' Lionel Manuel out six weeks ago with a vicious knee shot in the end zone after a pass had sailed out of reach. No flag. No nothing. The intent? Well, you don't go to break up a pass at knee level, and there's nothing to be gained by a low tackle in the end zone. Instead of worrying about hands-to-the-face calls, this is the type of thing the NFL should go after. **(23)**

Solution: Biblical justice. An eye-for-an-eye penalty. If a player puts someone out for a week with a blatantly illegal blow, suspend *him* for a week. If the other guy is out for a month, suspend the culprit for a month, a year for a year, a career for a career. Think about it. If you want to eliminate the really bad cheap shots, then hand out really tough punishment. **(24)**:

Drastic problems need bold solutions. I have this to say:

- To Gene Upshaw—get your union members a safe surface to play on. The owners won't do it; it's up to you. The membership deserves it.
- To [NFL Commissioner] Pete Rozelle—begin steroid testing right now. Get rid of the freak show in the NFL.
- To Art McNally—make sure your refs are working on the same page. Get them to recognize intent to maim and punish it accordingly.
- To the Competition Committee—no more clipping. Don't build up the passing stats at the sake of people's knees.
- To the owners—spend some dough to preserve careers. Too many are being cut short. Just ask all those guys with casts on their knees and arms. **(25)**

Vocabulary

In your journal, write the meanings of the following words:

- are *inherent* to football (2)
- *anabolic steroids* (3)
- the *incidence* of injury (4)
- *arthroscopic* surgery (6)
- more *insidious* injuries (10)
- a *patellar* tendon (12)
- *clipping* is illegal (22)
- *blatantly* illegal blow (24)

Critical Reading

Reviewing vocabulary can lead naturally to a discussion of audience. In addition to medical terms such as "arthroscopic" and "patellar," ask students to find other words that define (and thus limit) the audience: references to the Players Association, kinds of illegal blocks, and names of players, trainers, coaches, and administrators.

Questions for Writing and Discussion

1. To convince their readers, proposal writers usually explain or document problems, suggest solutions, examine the feasibility of their plans, and answer objections. Referring to paragraph numbers, indicate where Zimmerman uses each strategy to help convince his readers.

2. Explain your reaction to Zimmerman's proposal by answering the following questions: Which of Zimmerman's proposals is most realistic? Which changes have already taken place? What alternatives for reducing injuries in football does he ignore? What is most unrealistic about his proposal?

3. Assume that you are one of the following: a football player, a fan, a referee, or an owner. Which of Zimmerman's proposals would you agree with? What objections would you raise about Zimmerman's proposals? Explain.

4. Writers of proposals usually adopt a reasonable tone. What sentences in this essay most clearly illustrate Zimmerman's tone? What word would you use to describe the tone in those sentences: *reasonable*, *angry*, *humorous*, *impatient*, *confident*, *demanding*? Would you use another word? Explain.

Problem Solving: The Writing Process

■ **Assignment for Problem Solving** Select a problem that you believe needs a solution. Narrow and focus the problem and choose an appropriate audience. Describe the problem and, if necessary, demonstrate for your audience that it needs a solution. State your solution and justify it with reasons and evidence. Where appropriate, weigh alternative solutions, examine the feasibility of your own solution, and answer objections to your solution.

Teaching Tip

This assignment calls for writers to "answer objections to your solution" where appropriate. Because responding to opposing arguments is covered in Chapter 10, teachers should not unduly emphasize this part of the proposal.

Choosing a Subject

If one of your journal entries suggests a possible subject, try the collecting and shaping strategies below. If none of these leads to a workable subject, consider the following suggestions:

- Evaluating leads naturally into problem solving. Reread your journal entries and topic ideas for "evaluating." If your evaluation of your subject was negative, consider what would make your evaluation more positive. Based on your evaluation, write a proposal, addressed to the proper audience, explaining the problem and offering your solution.

- Organized groups are already trying to solve a number of national and international problems: homelessness, illegal aliens, the slaughter of whales, acid rain, abuse of animals in scientific experiments, drug and alcohol abuse, toxic-waste disposal, and so forth. Read several current articles on one of these topics. Then narrow the problem to one aspect that students or residents of your town could help to resolve. Write an essay outlining the problem and proposing some *specific and limited* actions that citizens could take.

- Employers are always looking for workers with initiative and good ideas. At your place of work, take ten minutes during a break and *observe* what's going on around you. Take notes over a span of several days. Even though people may be getting the job done, would different procedures or policies improve efficiency, safety, quality, or personal relations? Write a letter to your boss identifying the problem that you've noticed and justifying your solution.

"I can't think of anything I have no problem with."

COLLABORATIVE ACTIVITY

Collaborative-writing projects work especially well with problem-solving essays. If you wish to have students collaborate on a single essay, have groups of two or three students draw up a plan, assign collecting duties, draft separate parts of the essay, and collaboratively revise a final draft. (See the student essay by Busch, Krause, and Wright at the end of the chapter.) You may, however, simply have volunteer groups of three or four students choose a single topic; share collecting notes, photocopies, notes from interviews, and so on; discuss their findings; and then have each student write his or her own essay from the notes and discussion. Students should be encouraged to add additional sources or choose slightly different angles or focal points for their own essays.

- Take an inventory of the personal problems that you regularly face, day to day. List the things that cost unnecessary amounts of time or money, that cause fear in your life, that increase your frustration level, or that simply make you less happy or productive than you could be. Then compare your inventory with a classmate's or friend's list. If there are common problems, discuss whether or how these problems might be solved.

Collecting

With a possible subject and audience in mind, write out answers for each of the following topics. Remember that not all of these approaches will apply to your subject; some topics will suggest very little, while others may prompt you to generate ideas or specific examples appropriate for your problem and solution. A hypothetical problem—large classes that hinder learning—illustrates how these topics may help you focus on your subject and collect relevant ideas and information.

- *Identify and focus on the specific problem.* Answer the first four "Wh" questions:

  Who: A Psychology I professor; the Psychology Department

  What: Psychology I class

  When: Spring semester (the structure of this class may be slightly different from previous semesters)

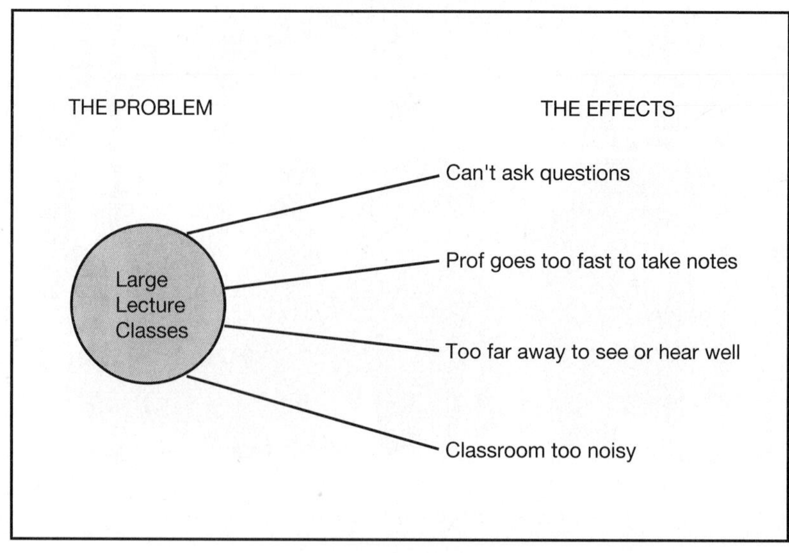

Where: University of Michigan (large lecture classes at one school may be different from those at another)

You may want to generalize about large lecture classes everywhere, but begin by identifying the specific problem at hand.

- *Demonstrate that the problem needs a solution.* Map out the *effects* of a problem. (See the diagram on page 390.)

You may want to map out both *short-term effects* and *long-term effects.* Over the short term, large lecture classes prevent you from asking questions; over the long term, you may do poorly on examinations, get a lower grade in the class, lose interest in the subject, be unable to cope with your own and others' psychological problems, or end up in a different career or job.

- *Discover possible solutions.* One strategy is to map out the *history* or the *causes* of the problem. If you can discover what caused the problem in the first place, you may have a possible solution. (See the diagram below.)

A second strategy takes the imaginative approach. Brainstorm hypothetical cases by asking, "What if . . . "

> "What if students petitioned the president of the university to abolish all lecture classes with enrollments over 100 students?" Would that work?
>
> "What if students invited the professor to answer questions at a weekly study session?" Would the professor attend? Would students attend?

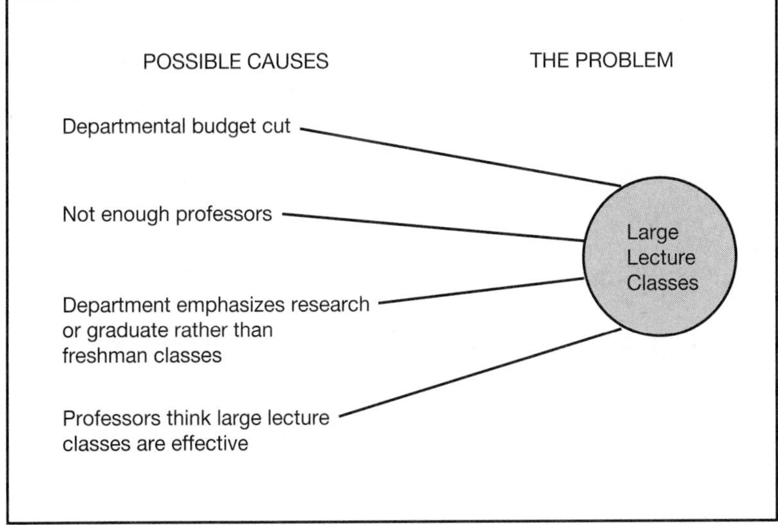

"What if students taught each other in a psychology class?" How would that work?

- *Evaluate possible solutions.* Apply the "If . . . then . . ." test on each possible solution: Consider whether each proposal would:

A. actually solve the problem;

B. meet certain criteria, such as cost-effectiveness, practicality, ethicality, legality;

C. not create new problems.

"*If* classes were smaller, *then* students would learn more":

If classes were smaller, students might learn more, but a small class size does not necessarily guarantee greater learning.

Although students might learn more, do smaller classes meet other criteria? While they are legal and ethical, are they practical and cost-effective?

Would smaller classes create new problems? Smaller classes might mean fewer upper-level course offerings. Is that a serious new problem?

Convince your readers. Support your proposed solutions by stating *reasons* and finding supporting *evidence*:

Reason: Smaller classes are worth the additional expense because students actually engage the material rather than just memorizing for exams.

Evidence: data from studies comparing large and small classes; personal testimony by students, interviews, or questionnaires; testimony or evidence from authorities on teaching.

- *Answer possible objections to your proposal.* Every solution has a down side or possible drawbacks. You need to respond to the most important objections.

List Drawbacks

Small classes cost more.

Small classes might reduce course offerings.

Small classes might mean less money for research.

List Your Responses

Good education does cost more. The University of Michigan has a reputation as an excellent undergraduate institution, and small classes would help it maintain quality education.

Perhaps some classes with low demand could be cut, but the necessary funds should not be taken out of upper-division classes for psychology majors or research projects.

- *List possible steps for implementation.* If appropriate, indicate the key steps or chronological sequence of your proposal:

1. Poll students and teachers of large lecture classes to confirm that the problem warrants attention.

2. Gather evidence from other colleges or universities to show how they reduced class sizes.

3. Present results of polls and other evidence to the state legislature to request more funds.

OBSERVING As you gather evidence and examples, use your observation skills. If the problem is large lecture classes, attend classes and *observe* the behavior of students and professors. Are students distracted by noise? Can they ask questions? Does the professor talk too softly to be heard in the back row? Remember that *repeated* observation is essential. If necessary, observe your subject over a period of several days or weeks.

REMEMBERING Use *freewriting, looping*, or *clustering* to help you

RESEARCH TIP

As you begin researching your problem, *don't* rush off to the library and start collecting articles. *Do* start by interviewing people who may know about your problem. Use your investigating skills to locate authorities and interview them. (See Chapter 6) Find out what other people have already done to solve the problem—or why current solutions are not working. Interview a teacher who knows about the problem, a student who has firsthand experience with the problem, an owner of a local business, or the coordinator of a community service. Save your library research until you know what the problem really is and what is currently being done to correct it.

The best time for planning . . . is when you're doing the dishes.
—AGATHA CHRISTIE, MYSTERY WRITER

remember examples from your experience of the problem or of possible solutions. Brainstorm or freewrite about previous class sessions in Psychology I. Do looping or mapping on other small-enrollment classes: What made these classes effective or ineffective? What teaching strategies, projects, or small-group activities were possible in these classes that would not be possible in a class of 250 students?

Reading and Investigating *Use the library* to find books or articles about the particular problem. Other writers have no doubt offered solutions to your problem that you could consider. Articles may even suggest objections to your proposed solution that you need to answer.

Interview participants or authorities on the problem. The professor who is teaching your Psychology I class may have some ideas about a solution. Administrations—department chairs, deans, even the president—may agree to answer your questions and react to your possible solutions; schedule interviews.

Design a questionnaire that addresses aspects of your problem. Responses to questionnaires provide evidence that a problem is serious, immediate, and in need of a solution. If the results of a questionnaire show that 175 of the 200 people in Psychology I who returned it favor smaller sections, you can include that data in your letter to the head of the department and the dean of the college.

Shaping

Teaching Tip

Although students should *consider* all five of these elements, not all proposals actually include all five. Students may need to hear you say that they don't have to include all of these areas mechanically. As the outlines or templates indicate, some essays emphasize two or three elements and ignore others. The student's decision should be based on the subject, the audience, and the purpose of the proposal.

Writers of proposals often do the following:

- Identify and demonstrate problems
- Evaluate alternative solutions
- Make proposals
- Give reasons and evidence to support their proposals; answer objections, discuss feasibility and costs
- Indicate implementation or call for action

Of course not all problem-solving essays have all five elements. Some do not discuss feasibility or do not evaluate alternative solutions. Zimmerman's proposal, for example, suggests only four important ways to solve the problem—without considering alternative solutions.

Outlines for Problem Solving The following patterns indicate four possible ways to organize a problem-solving essay. One of these patterns may help you organize your proposal:

Problem-solving Pattern

I. Introduction

II. The problem: identify and demonstrate

III. The solution(s)

IV. Answering possible objections, costs, drawbacks

V. Conclusion: implementation plan; call to action

Point-by-Point Pattern

I. Introduction

II. The overall problem: identify and demonstrate

III. One part of the problem, solution, evidence, answers to possible objections, feasibility

IV. Second part of the problem, solution, evidence, answers to objections, feasibility

V. Third part of the problem, solution, evidence, and so on

VI. Conclusion: implementation; call to action

Alternative Pattern

I. Introduction

II. The problem: identify and demonstrate

III. Alternative solution 1; why it's not satisfactory

IV. Alternative solution 2; why it's not satisfactory

V. Alternative solution 3; why it works best: evidence, objections, feasibility

VI. Conclusion: implementation; call to action

Step-by-Step Pattern

I. Introduction

II. The problem: identify and demonstrate

Don't miss opportunities to point out shaping strategies in television news programs. Scanning the *Video Guide* transcripts with a writer's eye can reinforce a student's understanding of these problem-solving patterns and their general serviceability.

III. Plan for implementing the solution or how solution has worked in the past:

A. Step one: reasons and evidence showing why this step is necessary and feasible

B. Step two: reasons and evidence showing why this step is necessary and feasible

C. Step three: reasons and evidence showing why this step is necessary and feasible

IV. Conclusion

CAUSAL ANALYSIS Causal analysis can be used to organize some paragraphs of a proposal. In arguing the benefits or advantages of a proposed solution, you are actually explaining the *effects* of your solution.

- The effects or advantages of smaller class sections in Psychology I would be greater student participation, fewer distractions, more discussion during lectures, and more individual or small-group learning.
- Shortening the work week to thirty-two hours would increase the number of jobs, reduce tensions for working parents, and give employees time to learn new skills.
- Eliminating steroid use among NFL athletes would reduce the impact of collisions and enable players to recover from injuries faster. Long-term effects of eliminating steroids would be to reduce incidence of cancers and urinary-tract problems.

In each of these cases, each effect or advantage can become a separate point and, sometimes, a separate body paragraph.

WRITE TO LEARN

Use write-to-learn strategies to help your students *listen actively* whenever you or your students read aloud excerpts from professional articles or essay drafts. Before the oral reading begins, ask students to listen for key elements and jot them down as they listen. If you're focusing on shaping strategies, for example, ask students to note thesis statements, essay maps, transitions, or other audience cues that signal organization to the reader. If you're focusing on voice or tone, ask students to write down specific phrases that illustrate the writer's voice or tone. Whenever appropriate, set up specific note-taking directions to help students listen actively.

CRITERIA ANALYSIS In some cases, the *criteria* for a good solution are quite clear. For example, cost-effectiveness, feasibility, and worker morale might be important criteria for a business-related proposal. If you work in a fast-food restaurant and are concerned about the increasing number of crimes, for example, you might propose that your manager add a video surveillance system. In order to overcome the manager's resistance to spending the needed funds, you could defend your proposal (and answer possible objections) by discussing relevant criteria:

Proposal: To reduce theft and protect the employees of the restaurant by installing a video surveillance system.

- *Cost effectiveness.* Citing evidence from other stores that have video cameras, you could prove that the equipment would pay for itself in less than a year. In addition, you could argue that if the life of just one employee—or possibly one manager—were saved, the cost would be worth it.

Computer Tip: Collecting and Shaping

Choose one of the four outlines or patterns for problem solving presented in the *shaping* section that might work for your essay. Enter that pattern in your computer file, open up space between each heading, and type in ideas and information that you've collected. For example, if you choose pattern 1, enter the outline, and then add notes and information under the appropriate heading: Problem-Solution Pattern

I. Introduction

II. The problem: identify and demonstrate [Enter your ideas, information, statistics, and examples here.]

III. The solution(s) [Enter your ideas, information, statistics, and examples here.]

IV. Answering possible objections, costs, drawbacks [Enter your ideas, information, statistics, and examples here.]

V. Conclusion: implementation plan; call to action

This process will give you a rough idea of a plan to use during drafting. After you have entered some information, however, you may decide to organize your essay using another pattern. If so, save the information that you've entered and try another organizational pattern.

- *Feasibility.* Installing a security system would not require any extensive remodeling nor any significant training time for employees to learn how to operate the system.
- *Employee morale.* The benefits to employee morale would be significant: Workers would feel more secure, they would feel that the management cares about them, and they would work more productively.

Chronological Order If your proposal stresses the means of imple-

Peer Response

Writer: Provide the following information about your essay before you exchange drafts with a peer reader.

1. (a) audience
   (b) statement of problem
   (c) possible or alternative solutions
   (d) your recommended solution(s)
2. Write out one or two questions about your draft that you want your reader to answer.

Reader: Read the writer's entire draft. As you *reread* the draft, do the following:

1. Without looking at the writer's responses, above, describe the essay's (a) intended audience, (b) the main problem that it identifies, (c) the possible or alternative solutions, and (d) the writer's recommended solution. What feasibility problems or additional solutions should the writer consider? Why?
2. Indicate one paragraph in which the writer's evidence is strong. Then find one paragraph in which the writer needs more evidence. What additional *kinds* of evidence (personal experience, testimony from authorities, statistics, specific examples, etc.) might the writer use in this paragraph? Explain.
3. Number the paragraphs in the writer's essay and then describe, briefly, the purpose or main idea of each paragraph. For example, paragraph 1 introduces the problem, paragraph 2 gives the writer's personal experience with the problem, etc. When you finish, explain how the writer might improve the organization of the essay.
4. List the three most important things that the writer should focus on during revision.
5. Respond to the writer's questions in number 2, above.

Writer: When your essay is returned, read the comments by your peer reader(s) and do the following:

1. Compare your description of the audience, the problem, and the solutions with your reader's description. Where there are differences, try to clarify your essay.

2. Reconsider and revise your recommended solution(s).

3. What additional kinds of evidence will make your recommendations stronger?

4. Make a revision plan. List, in order, the three most important things that you need to do as you revise your essay.

menting your solution to a problem, you may organize several paragraphs or even an entire essay using a chronological order or step-by-step pattern.

A proposal to reduce boating accidents on a lake, for example, might involve a plan for educating boaters and enforcing regulations over a three-year period. During the first year, notices about dangers might be posted at key docks. During the second year, the county could pass a law requiring marinas to give a short instruction course for renters and set up voluntary classes on the lake for boat owners. Offenders might be given warnings and required to take classes. In the third year, offenders might face stiff fines.

A proposal to improve the reading skills of children might be justified by a series of coordinated steps, beginning by organizing seminars for teachers and PTA meetings to discuss possible solutions; establishing minimal reading requirements in grades K-6 that teachers and parents agree on; offering reading prizes; and organizing media coverage of students who participate in reading programs.

Vigorous writing is concise.
—WILLIAM STRUNK, JR., AUTHOR AND TEACHER

DRAFTING

Using your examples, recorded observations, reading, interviews, results from questionnaires, or your own experience, make a sketch outline and begin writing. As you write, let your own proposal and your intended audience guide you. In your first draft, get as much as possible on paper. Don't worry about spelling or awkward sentences. If you hit a snag, stop and read what you have written so far or reread your collecting-and-shaping notes.

RESOURCE NOTE

Because problem-solving essays can become complex, short teacher-student conferences can effectively supplement small-group responses to drafts. For a brief but informative article on conferences, see Madigan, "Applying Donald Murray's 'Responsive Teaching.'"

REVISING

Use the following revising guidelines to identify areas for improving your draft. Even at this point, don't hesitate to collect additional information, if necessary, or reorganize your material. If a reader makes suggestions, reread your draft to see if those changes will improve your essay.

Guidelines for Revision

- **Have a classmate or someone who might understand your audience read your draft and play devil's advocate.** Have your reader pretend to be hostile to your solution and ask questions about alternative solutions or weaknesses in your own solution. Revise your proposal so that it answers any important objections.

- **Review your proposal for key elements.** If you are missing one of the following, would adding it make your proposal more effective for your audience? Remember: Proposals do not necessarily have to have all of these elements. Develop the items that are most applicable to your proposal.
  Show that a problem exists and needs attention
  Evaluate alternative solutions
  Propose your solution
  Show that your solution meets certain criteria: feasibility, cost-effectiveness, legality
  Answer possible objections
  Suggest implementation or call for action

- **Be sure that you *show*** what you mean, using specific examples, facts, details, statistics, quotations from interviews or articles. Don't rely on general assertions.

- **Signal the major parts of your proposal with key words and transitions.**

- **Avoid the following errors in logic and generalization**.

  Don't commit an "either-or" fallacy. For example, don't say that "*either* we reduce class sizes or students will drop out of the university." There are more than two possible alternatives.

  Don't commit an "***ad hominem***" fallacy by arguing "to the man" rather than to the issue. Don't say, for example, that Paul Zimmerman's proposal would never work because he's never been a player and doesn't understand the issues.

  Test your proposal for "If . . . then . . ." statements. Does it really follow that "If we introduce tokens for grocery carts, then carts will never be stolen again?"

  Avoid overgeneralizing your solution. If all your research applies to solving problems in large lecture classes in psychology, don't

TEACHING TIP

Because students have just written essays attempting to solve particular problems, they should be ready to apply what they have learned to their own problems in writing. Students' responses to Question 2 may prompt a useful discussion about the problem-solving tactics they use during their own writing.

assume that your solution will apply to, say, classes in physics or physical education.

- **If you are citing data or quoting sources, check to be sure that your material is accurately cited.**

- **Read your proposal aloud for flabby, wordy, or awkward sentences.** Revise your sentences for clarity, precision, and forcefulness.

- **Edit your proposal for spelling, appropriate word choice, punctuation, usage, mechanics, and grammar.** Remember that, in part, your form and audience help determine what is appropriate usage and mechanics.

■ **Postscript on the Writing Process** Before you turn in your essay, answer the following questions in your journal.

1. List the skills you used in writing this paper: observing people, places, or events; remembering personal experience; using questionnaires and interviews; reading written material; explaining ideas; evaluating solutions. Which of these skills was most useful to you in writing this essay?

2. What was your most difficult problem to solve while writing this paper? Were you able to solve it yourself, or did your readers suggest a solution?

3. In one sentence, describe the most important thing you learned about writing while working on this essay.

4. What were the most successful parts of your essay?

Problem Solving: Student Writing

NO PARKING

KRISTY BUSCH, STEVE KRAUSE, AND KEITH WRIGHT

Kristy Busch, Steve Krause, and Keith Wright worked together on a proposal to solve the parking problem at their university. They met several times to discuss the topic, select questions for the survey and interview, divide the research responsibilities, and determine who was going to draft

Teaching Tip

The problem-solving assignment adapts easily to a collaborative-writing project. As this description indicates, groups need to plan their tactics carefully and agree about responsibilities before undertaking their projects. Students and the teacher also need to agree on an evaluation procedure.

each section. They agreed that Keith Wright would interview the director of parking management, and Kristy Busch and Steve Krause would survey students about the parking problem. After they collected their information, Wright drafted a first version of the section on the multilevel garage, Busch worked on the shuttle-bus proposal, and Krause wrote out the introduction and the rezoning proposal. Then they worked together to combine and revise their drafts, adding new information, reorganizing the paragraphs, and editing the final draft. Shown below are the questions for the interview, the results of the survey, the first draft of the introduction and rezoning proposal, and the revised draft of the entire proposal.

Interview Questions for Wes Westfall,
Director of Parking Management

1. Do you perceive a serious parking problem at CSU?
2. Do you think that students' arguments about lack of "X" parking spaces along the dorms on the north side of the campus are valid?
3. How many stickers for each zone are issued each year? Do these numbers fluctuate?
4. Are you in favor of building a multi-level parking facility?
   Where would you build such a structure?
   What would it cost? Is it feasible?
   How long would it take to build?
5. Have you considered a shuttle-bus system between Moby Gym and the central campus?
   What would it cost? Is it feasible?
6. Is rezoning possible? Is it currently under consideration? Would it solve the problem?
   Is it feasible? What would it cost?

INTERVIEW

PARKING SURVEY RESULTS

1. Do you drive to CSU?

Yes: 36

Occasionally: 53

No: 11

2. Does CSU need more parking for students?

Yes: 62

No: 38

3. Would rezoning close-in lots to eliminate dorm parking help?

Yes: 78

No: 22

4. Class (Fr., Soph., Jr., Sr., Other)

Fr: 33

Soph: 20

Jr: 22

Sr: 13

Other: 12

First Draft

If you drive to CSU, you may already know how hard it can be to find a parking place. If not then now would be a good time to make the changes necessary to accommodate more cars (before you start driving). Not only is the parking inadequate for the number of cars, but it is also poorly organized and poorly distributed among the groups who use it. A very common occurrence is being forced to park very far from the building where you need to go. Not only students are affected; faculty, staff, and visitors also have problems finding somewhere to park. For a visitor this is very distressing and certainly doesn't present an attractive first impression of CSU. It is clear that something will have to be done; what is unclear is exactly what would be the most practical and cost effective solution. First, and probably the most effective for the immediate future would be to rezone the existing parking to better accommodate the users. A shuttle-bus system could also be used; however this could be costly and would have to be used a lot to make it a practical investment. The ominous "multilevel parking facility" is a drastic last measure that we would have a lot of trouble paying for. [add closing sentence]

The most cost-effective and probably the most immediately effective would be a partial rezoning of existing parking. This year, the office of parking management sold 7,641 parking stickers for an available 6,238 spaces, a difference of 1,703. This means that there are a lot more stickers than places to park. Granted, all these people do not drive at the same time, but enough do to cause a problem. In poll taken this March, 78 percent of the people said that they would like to see the parking rezoned. In rezoning we should first look at the parking areas which are not full and determine why and then shift the zones in a way in which they will help. For example, the western sections of the "Z" lot at Moby Gym could be changed to "X" for those dorm dwellers. Then the close-in lots could be changed to "Z" for the commuting students. Or we could eliminate the metered parking and put "Z" parking in its place. Rezoning the lots would seem to be the easiest solution to the problem, but it cannot be permanent, since if this school survives it will inevitably grow.

This student essay opens with an engaging individual instance of a general problem, a strategy that should be familiar from print and television journalism. See "Prozac" and "Teens Confront Prejudices" in the *Video Library*. For a related topic, see the video on "Smart Cars."

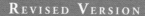

Revised Version

NO PARKING

On Monday morning, Jennifer Martin left her apartment at 8:30 to drive to the Colorado State University campus, hoping to arrive on time for a test in her 9 A.M. sociology class. When she arrived at the student parking lot west of Aylesworth hall, there were no parking spots. So she began cruising up and down the lot, hoping that someone would soon pull out. As she drove slowly up and down the lanes, she muttered to herself and clenched her hands on the steering wheel. She did have a permit to park in the lot, but there were obviously more permits than spaces. About five minutes before class, a car pulled out of a place at the far end of the lot. She accelerated down the next lane, driving as fast as she could without running over other students, but just as she arrived, a green Ford Pinto cut in front of her and darted into the vacant space. She honked her horn and waved her fist, but the person got quickly out of the car and walked away. At this point, she realized that she had no choice. She wheeled into the area marked for motorcycles, parked her car, and raced for class. She was angry because she knew she was going to get a ticket even though she had a legal permit. **(1)**

If you drive to the CSU campus for classes, you have probably had a similar experience. But students are not the only ones who have parking problems on campus: faculty, staff, and visitors also have problems finding places to park. Especially for visitors, the overcrowded conditions don't present an attractive first impression of the campus. Clearly, something has to be done to improve parking facilities. After studying the problem, interviewing the director of parking management and polling one hundred students, we believe that there are three alternatives which the CSU administration should consider: building a multilevel parking facility, starting a shuttle-bus from remote lots, and rezoning the existing parking lots to better serve the users. **(2)**

A first possible solution to CSU's parking problem would be to build a multilevel parking facility. This sounds like a promising idea because it would allow more students, faculty, and staff to park over the same amount of ground space. CSU could build this facility at any of several locations. One place is on the west side of the Morgan Library, where the "A" parking zone—for faculty—is now. This location would provide parking convenient to classes, faculty offices, and the library. A second site would be the open parking lot west of Moby Gym. Although this location is further from classes, it would also be used during basketball games and concerts. A third location might be the large parking lot north of the Student Center. This too, like the library lot, would be close to classrooms and faculty offices. **(3)**

While these sites are all promising, we discovered that a multilevel parking facility has some serious drawbacks. Wes Westfall, manager of CSU parking, explained that there are several problems with these garages that most people don't consider. A first drawback to the parking garage is the expense. Westfall said that a multilevel garage would cost a minimum of $6,000 per parking space, raising the price of a parking permit from $30 to over $300. And that would be for a sticky piece of paper that still wouldn't guarantee a parking space for every car. Perhaps the president of the university could pay $300 a year, but most students can barely afford $30. **(4)**

A second drawback to a parking garage is that it doesn't last forever, and the maintenance costs can be considerable. Mr. Westfall has some frightening photographs of sections of strong, stable-looking concrete that has collapsed for no visible reason at all. One picture shows a whole garage leveled as though a good-sized bomb had hit it—nothing was left standing except for an occasional pillar here and there. Unless garages are carefully maintained, Westfall stated, they may not last over 20 years. The problem, he explained, lies in the rebarb (steel rods inside the concrete) that reinforces the concrete. Gas, oil, and anti-freeze from cars are gradually absorbed into the concrete, causing the rebarb to deteriorate and weaken the whole structure. The only way to check for this kind of damage, Westfall noted, is to use an expensive concrete X-ray machine. So even the maintenance for a garage can be an expensive proposition. **(5)**

The third and most serious problem, Westfall claims, is security. Parking garages can become just another place for sexual assault, drug trafficking, vandalism, and theft. Westfall commented that most garages have a monitor system and guards, but those precautions are not totally effective. By the time the guard detects a theft over the security system and arrives at the location, the thief has usually fled. In addition, any security system adds to the already high costs of a parking facility. Clearly, the problems connected with a multilevel garage make it a last resort for solving the parking problems on campus. **(6)**

A second alternative for solving the parking problems on the CSU campus is to use a bus shuttle service from the outlying "Z" lot at Moby Gym to the central campus. Students who responded to our survey frequently said that the lots on the perimeter of the campus were nearly empty, but they were too far away from the library and the classrooms. The shuttle would solve this problem by taking the following route: beginning at the Lory Student Center, the bus would head west down North Drive (along the residence halls) to the Moby Gym lot, and then stop and pick up drivers at both the north and south ends of the lot. It would then turn south onto Shields at the stoplight and turn east on South Drive, returning to central campus. This system would allow easier access to the core of the campus and, in return, put to full use the 539 parking spaces available in the Moby Gym parking lot. Of course, the shuttle, driver, and maintenance would cost money, so this solution would require a commitment from the university administration. **(7)**

The most cost-effective solution would be a partial rezoning of the parking lots. This past year, the office of parking management sold 7,461 parking stickers for an available 6,238 spaces, a difference of 1,403. This means that they sold 1,403 more stickers than there are places to park. Not all people need to park at the same time, but enough do to cause a problem. Of the 100 students that we polled, 78 percent said that they would like to see the central campus lots rezoned. In this scheme, students parking their cars for long periods of time would use the outlying lots and commuting students, faculty, and staff would use the closer lots. For example, if we changed the western section of the outlying "Z" lot to "X" for those students living in the dorms, the parking spaces near the dorms along South Drive could be made available to those who have to drive every day to campus to attend classes. Such rezoning seems to be the easiest and least expensive solution. **(8)**

One main problem to overcoming CSU's parking problem is money. A multilevel parking facility would accommodate more cars per acre of ground space, yet it is the most expensive solution. The shuttle-bus system—which could still be implemented—is more economical, but it would require raising additional revenue, most likely by raising the price of parking stickers. We certainly recommend that the university try a shuttle system on an experimental basis to determine the exact costs and see whether the number of riders justifies the expense. Rezoning the lots, however, is clearly the least complicated and most economical solution. Signs could be changed during the summer months, and new maps and brochures printed in time for the beginning of fall semester. Our group proposes that the university rezone the lots at the end of this academic year and start planning for a shuttle bus and a garage to meet the need in future years. With more careful management of the close-in lots, the new parking stickers might be more than just a hunting license. A person with a permit might actually be able to arrive at a lot at 8:45 and still make that nine o'clock class. **(9)**

Questions for Writing and Discussion

1. After reading the revised version, look again at the questions for the interview and the survey. How would you advise the authors to modify either set of questions? What questions would you add? What questions would you change or delete? Explain.

2.. Compare the introduction in the first draft with the introduction in the revised version. Which is more effective? Jot down an idea for a third introduction which the authors might consider.

3. Reread the revised version and *outline* the major parts of the proposal. Then compare that outline with the authors' initial outline, given below:

- **I.** Introduction
- **II.** Rezoning proposal
- **III.** Shuttle-bus proposal
- **IV.** Multilevel garage proposal
- **V.** Conclusion

Do you think that their revised plan for organizing the paper was an improvement? Explain.

4. Who is the intended audience for this proposal? What revisions would make this proposal appeal even more strongly to that audience? (During the planning stages of this essay, the authors decided to send this proposal to Wes Westfall, director of parking management. How do you think Westfall would react to this proposal, as it stands?)

WHO SHOULD TAKE CHARGE?

EUI YOUNG HWANG

Eui Young Hwang, a student at the University of Illinois, wrote his problem-solving paper on the issue of Black/Asian conflicts. After reading a conversation published in Ms. *magazine between Vicki Alexander, an African-American civil and medical rights activist, and Grace Lyu-Volckhausen, the Asian-American founder of the Korean YWCA, Hwang decided to enter their conversation by offering his own solutions to the racial tensions between the two communities. Hwang's solutions are to use the Korean-American media to help educate the community about cultural differences, to ask Korean-American Churches to create religious and social opportunities for interaction, and to ask Korean-American businesses to return some profits to the African-American communities. Reprinted below is an excerpt from the* Ms. *conversation, followed by Hwang's own essay.*

BLACK/ASIAN CONFLICT: WHERE DO WE BEGIN?

VICKI ALEXANDER AND GRACE LYU-VOLCKHAUSEN

Grace Lyu-Volckhausen: For me, being a feminist is in my genes. My grandmother was one of the earliest Korean feminists; my mom was one of the founders of the Korean Women's Association, and my father was one of the few Korean legislators who sponsored a women's rights bill. So when I came here in 1960 and women were fighting for their rights, I asked, "What is this? We have always been fighting."

I got involved with the women's movement here as a student in the 1960s. At that time, there were about 80 Koreans in New York, mostly students. Within five years, Koreans started to come in. I realized that Korean women were getting jobs in all kinds of labor markets and were getting taken advantage of. So we started the Korean YWCA; I worked with women's groups like Asian Women United. Now I spend most of my time and energy with immigrant women.

Vicki Alexander: I grew up in Los Angeles. My father was U.S. black, Blackfoot Indian, and Irish. Indians often allowed blacks or people escaping disasters like the Irish potato famine to stay on the reservation. We were welcomed there. My mother was a Polish-Russian Jew. My father was a union organizer, and from a very early age I was involved in progressive activities. In the early 1960s I married a college classmate—he was from Korea, a mathematician; he died in 1974 from a brain tumor.

I first was in the movement to free South Africa in the early 1960s, and then the movement for civil rights in this country. I had always wanted to be a doctor, but when I graduated from college I was not accepted by any medical school; after the civil rights movement, I reapplied and was accepted everywhere, with scholarships, and with no change in my record. So the civil rights movement was very important in my becoming a doctor. I decided to become an ob-gyn because the ones I saw didn't help women. . . .

Grace: The yearlong boycott of two Korean grocery stores by people in the African American community [on Church Avenue in the Flatbush section of Brooklyn] really soured a lot of things. I think it has soured New York as a whole. During the crisis I was behind the scenes trying to work things out. It was very frustrating.

Vicki: Well, everybody was talking about it. In the group I was in at the time, we were trying to analyze it and ask ourselves, "What's going on here? Should we take a side? Is there a side to take? Is there a middle road?" We tried to understand Korean immigration, because none of the people in the group were Korean.

Grace: So they just studied the situation.

Vicki: Right. We didn't engage in it. It was so nasty; it was terrible. All these guys, the black leaders, who have become discredited—the Sharptons and the Carsons—really discredited us.

Grace: I think Koreans wondered, why didn't David Dinkins [New York City's African American mayor] come down to the store? It took him eight months. When the crisis started, we asked him to come out right away—but he vacillated.

Our children remember these things. When they see their parents getting hurt, they remember it. And they have long memories.

Vicki: I think that among U.S. blacks there is a real hatred of people coming into our community and ripping us off. Once again getting ripped off by people who aren't us. Nationalism in the black community is very high, so blacks can come in and rip us off really badly, and they don't get chastised. The feeling gets fueled by racial incidents. And it's certainly been fueled on a national level by Reagan and Bush.

I feel that there is a long-standing kind of negativism that stems from nationalism; it says if it isn't black, it isn't good. No matter what. I think that's where a lot of the community is coming from. When you look historically at where black people have lived, we have not owned the stores. And on the whole, the money generated through the stores does not get reinvested in the community. So historically, you have a level of oppression not only based on class, but, in the eyes of those blacks and in reality, based on race.

Then come Koreans. Koreans—and Arabs—own stores. But still, they are not black. There is that resentment, but what is clear about Arabs is that they are coming from a poor section of the world. So that's not as antagonistic as the white Jewish store owner. But then, in come Koreans, and nobody knows nothing about Koreans or the struggle in Korea—that's that world over there, Korea, China. The U.S. population is so ignorant, purposely so. But in the eyes of U.S. blacks, that is another body of folks coming over, taking over, and we don't know where they are from. So we must assume there is some money behind them. Maybe they don't have money, but we are assuming that they must have some money to come into our community and build whatever.

When it was just white-black, it wasn't as hard to understand. But when it is black-Asian-Arab, it starts to get very confusing, the class and race stuff starts to overlap. Because of the lack of education in the U.S., it's really a problem. What people need to start is a major education campaign.

Grace: From the Korean point of view, it doesn't matter what community we come into—black or white. The Koreans come in with a small amount of capital that they borrowed from their friends. They have trouble getting jobs because of discrimination, so they try to make a living by starting businesses that use the least amount of capital; they expend whatever amount of labor is necessary. Where do they go? The places with lowest rents, where there are not that many stores. So they end up going to black neighborhoods, where rent is cheap, where, if you work long hours, you can make profits—they all end up going there. But they don't know who these people are in the communities they go into.

Let me tell you an interesting story, an incredible misunderstanding between blacks and Koreans. Once a former black co-worker of mine was furious. He said, "You see that Korean woman there. I am so angry. She is insulting us." I asked, "What did she do?" He said, "Whenever I go there, the woman never puts the change in my hand, she always puts it on the counter." And I said, "Richard, this is because in Korea, a woman does not touch a man's hand. Except her own husband's—in private." He didn't know. It's just a little thing that becomes a big problem. I hear such comments all the time: "That Korean woman never smiles. They are so unfriendly." But in Korea, if you smile that much, they think you are stupid.

Vicki: Also, if you smile at men, it has a prostitution connotation.

Grace: Absolutely. This cultural gap is so great. Of course, Koreans will say, "These black people, they are always dancing, they are always loud."

Vicki: Or, "They're lazy. They don't work very hard."

Grace: My only regret in the Church Avenue crisis was that women were not able to get together. Korean women couldn't get together with African American women because we were just so engrossed in our own problems. We were all wringing our hands, "What do we do? What do we do?" And then all these politicians were running away from us. I felt like a pariah when I went to community meetings. People would see me and would not see me. They didn't want to deal with the Koreans because we were a time bomb.

I agonized that we could not pull our women together. Maybe next time there is a crisis we should bring our women together and tell these guys to shut up.

If I called you because of a black-Korean crisis, would you come out with your friends?

Vicki: Sure. You have to start building toward it now, at a time of no crisis. You have to establish a relationship with people. And one of the best places to do that is the Medgar Evers College women's center, a black women's center. I think it would be good if the overture came from Korean women, as people who come from an oppressed state. You were born in South Korea, an oppressed state, and I was born in the U.S., an oppressed state. We're both women oppressed within the oppressed state. There is a real commonality. We are struggling and fighting for our people, but to bridge some of those gaps, we have to start educating now.

WHO SHOULD TAKE CHARGE?

EUI YOUNG HWANG

A boycott by blacks on a Korean grocery store in New York and lootings primarily on Korean-owned stores during the L.A. riots have focussed Americans' attentions on racial conflicts between blacks and Koreans.

Most Koreans are immigrants, not familiar to the American culture yet, and do business in poor black communities in the inner city. Vicki Alexander and Grace Lyu-Volckhausen, in "Black/Asian Conflict: Where Do We Begin?" assert that education on cultural differences and interactions is needed to reduce tension between blacks and Koreans. However, the authors fail to specify how to implement their solutions. Intervention by Korean American media, churches, and business organizations is needed in order to reduce racial conflict between blacks and Koreans caused by a lack of knowledge, few interactions, and Koreans' dominant business in black inner-city communities. **(1)**

Korean-American media can help to avoid misunderstandings between Koreans and blacks by educating Koreans about cultural differences. Korean merchants are often accused of insulting customers by not smiling and not putting change into a customer's hand. Lyu-Volckhausen explains that in Korean culture, a person smiling too often is considered stupid, and a woman does not touch a man's hand. Koreans, unaware of the cultural differences in America, often behave "rudely" to their black customers. Such little misunderstandings due to cultural differences often create an unfriendly relationship between blacks and Koreans. Korean-American media can readily educate Koreans about cultural differences. An organization might try to hold a program to educate Koreans on cultural sensitivities. Many Koreans are, however, too busy to attend any educational programs. The easiest way to get the attention of Koreans would be to use media in Korean communities. In big cities like New York, Los Angeles, and Chicago, where most Koreans live, there are a number of Korean-American television stations, radio channels, and newspapers. Korean-American media have large Korean audiences. With such big influences on Koreans, Korean-American media can easily get Koreans' attention in order to teach them about the cultural differences between Koreans and blacks. When compared to other organizations, Korean media provides the easiest method to reach and educate Koreans on cultural sensitivities. **(2)**

Korean-American churches can also increase cultural sensitivity and generate interactions between blacks and Koreans. Many Koreans think that blacks are lazy, untrustworthy, and violent. Blacks may perceive that Koreans have racism against blacks. On the other hand, Koreans may build bad images about blacks, since they often hear about blacks having no jobs, stealing, and murdering. To make matters worse, Koreans have too few contacts with blacks to overcome their stereotypical images about blacks. Therefore, frequent interactions between Koreans and blacks are necessary. Korean-American churches have the most potential in terms of promoting interactions between Koreans and blacks. One may argue that churches are too limited because they appeal to only Christians. On the contrary, churches include more Koreans than any other Korean-American organization, since many Koreans go to churches. Lyu-Volckhausen talks about blacks and Koreans singing together in church choirs and the opportunity it gives the two groups to get to know each other. Korean churches could cooperate with churches in black communities to hold religious activities and thus give both Koreans and blacks chances to establish friendly relationships. Korean-American churches can help Koreans to overcome stereotypical images of blacks by promoting interactions between blacks and Koreans and by holding religious activities with black churches. **(3)**

Finally, Korean-American business organizations need to reduce blacks' anger toward Korean businesses in black communities. They could begin by contributing some of their profits to black communities and helping blacks economically. Alexander points out that historically, blacks have not owned stores in their own communities, and the profit generated through stores does not get reinvested in black communities. Blacks often assume that Koreans take over black communities with money and that Koreans have an advantage over black businesses because they get money from secret financial sources, or were wealthy in Korea. Lyu-Volckhausen explains that Koreans with a small amount of capital often go to the poor black community because the rent is cheap and then make profits by working hard. There are several Korean-American business organizations which lead many Korean businesses. These Korean-American business organizations can reduce hatred among blacks toward Koreans by contributing some of the profits of Korean businesses to black communities and helping blacks economically. In fact, some business organizations in Chicago have been trying to reduce tension between blacks and Koreans by donating scholarships to local black students, helping the homeless in black communities, encouraging Koreans to hire black employees, and helping local blacks' businesses by using their products. Some Koreans may say they should use their money however they want to. However, it may be more logical to contribute some of the profit to the community where they made the profit. By contributing a part of the profit to the black community, Korean business organizations can reduce not only the hatred among blacks toward Koreans but also the racial incidents like boycotts and lootings that have greatly hurt Koreans' businesses. **(4)**

Korean-American media, churches, and business organizations can greatly help to clear up misunderstandings and reduce tension between blacks and Koreans. Black organizations also need to cooperate with

Korean-American organizations in order to establish friendly relationships between blacks and Koreans. Korean and black communities are too involved with each other to ignore the conflicts between them. That is, they need each other. First, Koreans and blacks need to show their willingness to listen to each other. Then, both Koreans and blacks should volunteer their efforts to reduce tension. Koreans and blacks cannot wait for the government to intervene to solve the conflicts between two communities. Conflicts between them hurt both Koreans and blacks too much to wait, and Koreans and blacks themselves are the only ones who can solve the problems. **(5)**

Questions for Writing and Discussion

1. Before you read Hwang's essay, read the *Ms.* conversation and write your own response. Explain which of their ideas might work and which might not work. Then brainstorm a list of other actions that might reduce the racial tensions that Alexander and Lyu-Volckhausen describe.

2. Read Hwang's essay. In which paragraphs does he refer to ideas that Alexander and Lyu-Volckhausen discuss? Explain how his solutions further develop the ideas in their conversation.

3. Describe Hwang's three solutions. Which has the greatest promise for solving the problem? Which solution might not work or might cause other problems? What other solutions from your list might Hwang consider? Explain your responses.

4. In "Solving for Pattern," Wendell Berry argues that good solutions must consider the harmony, health, and quality of the overall system. How well does Hwang meet Berry's criterion for a good solution? Explain.

5. In which paragraphs does Hwang anticipate possible objections, analyze feasibility problems, or provide effective supporting evidence for his solutions? In which paragraphs should Hwang provide more analysis or more specific examples? Citing specific passages, point out strengths and suggest possible revisions for Hwang.

6. Use the excerpts from the *Ms.* conversation and Hwang's essay as starting points for your own essay on solving some aspect

of interracial or intercultural tension. You may focus on conflicts between or among any racial or cultural groups. Draw on your own experience. Describe the problems and offer your solution(s).

TEN/ARGUING

Give me liberty to know, to utter, and to argue freely according to conscience, above all liberties.

—JOHN MILTON, POET

❦

Freedom of speech is established to achieve its essential purpose only when different opinions are expounded in the same hall to the same audience. . . . The opposition is indispensable.

—WALTER LIPPMANN, JOURNALIST

AFTER BEING CITED FOR NOT WEARING A SEAT BELT WHILE OPERATING A MOTOR VEHICLE, YOU DECIDE THAT YOUR RIGHTS HAVE BEEN VIOLATED. In order to write a convincing argument to your representative that seat-belt laws are unfair, you research current articles about the law and interview a law professor on the issue. You decide to claim that the seat-belt laws should be repealed because they are a fundamental violation of individual liberty. You believe that the opposing argument—that seat belts save lives and reduce insurance rates for everyone—is not relevant to the issue of individual liberty. Because your representative has supported seat-belt laws, you present both sides of the issue but stress the arguments supporting your viewpoint.

❦

AFTER READING SEVERAL ACCOUNTS OF NEWS-MEDIA CENSORSHIP DURING THE PERSIAN GULF WAR, YOU DECIDE TO WRITE AN ESSAY ARGUING THAT CENSORSHIP IN THE NAME OF MILITARY SECURITY SHOULD NOT BE TOLERATED. As you read about U.S. military censorship, you find other examples of censorship from World Wars I and II, from the Korean conflict and the Vietnam War, and from the operations in Grenada and Panama. Rather than putting soldiers' lives at risk, you believe, open coverage by the news media might actually reduce the death toll by shortening conflicts. Ultimately, you argue that a free society cannot tolerate any form of censorship that undermines its principles of freedom.

Purple Gallinule (Eliot Porter/Amon Carter Museum)

WHEN PEOPLE ARGUE WITH EACH OTHER, THEY OFTEN BECOME HIGHLY EMOTIONAL OR CONFRONTATIONAL. Remember the last heated argument you had with a friend or family member—at the end of the argument, one person stomped out of the room, slammed the door, and didn't speak to the other for days. In the aftermath of such a scene, you felt angry with the other person and angry with yourself. Nothing was accomplished. Neither of you came close to achieving what you wanted when you began the argument. Rather than understanding each other's point of view and working out your differences, you effectively closed the lines of communication.

When writers construct arguments, however, they try, through reason and use of evidence, to avoid the emotional outbursts that often turn verbal arguments into displays of temper. Strong feelings may energize an argument—few of us make the effort to argue without emotional investment in the subject—but written argument stresses a fair weighing of pros and cons. While you advocate one position, you keep the lines of communication open by acknowledging and evaluating opposing arguments. Because written arguments are public, they take on a civilized manner. They implicitly say, "Let's be reasonable about this. Let's look at the evidence for *both* sides. Let's not shout or fight; let's be as objective as we can."

As writers construct written arguments, they carefully consider their audiences. Does the audience know about this controversy, or do they need background information? Do the readers hold the opposing viewpoint, or are they likely to listen to both sides and decide what to believe? What arguments will they find most persuasive? A written argument creates an atmosphere of reason, which encourages readers to examine their own views clearly and dispassionately. When successful, such argument convinces rather than alienates an audience. It changes people's minds or persuades them to adopt a recommended course of action.

■ **FREEWRITING: ARGUING** Time yourself for fifteen minutes. Argue either for or against the following claim: "In college, all elective courses should be graded pass-fail." Brainstorm a list of reasons for and against your claim. Decide on an audience. Then choose the *two* best reasons for your claim and list evidence or describe specific examples from your personal experience that you could use to support each reason.

BACKGROUND ON ARGUING

This chapter defines argument as a specific kind of persuasion, characterized by logical use of evidence to support a claim and a fair and reasonable countering of opposing arguments. Arguments may be based on claims of fact, cause and effect, value, policy, or some combination. Claims of value and policy are treated in Chapters 8 and 9.

WRITE TO LEARN

As in earlier chapters, students' freewriting can prompt class discussion on the chapter. Following a discussion of their freewriting and the elements of argument, have students write a second entry—based on what they learned in class.

All writing . . . is propaganda for something.
—ELIZABETH DREW, WRITER AND CRITIC.

Since television news programs and talk shows thrive on controversy, they offer instructive, spirited lessons in the art of argument. Watch how debatable claims and opposing viewpoints are represented in "Lyme Disease," "Prozac," "Crime and Punishment," and "Political Correctness."

Techniques for Writing Argument

A written argument is similar to a public debate—between attorneys in a court of law or members of Congress who represent different political parties. It begins with a *debatable* issue: Is this a good bill? Should we vote for it? In such debates, one person argues *for* a position or proposal, while the other argues *against* it. The onlookers (the members of Congress, the jury, or the public) then decide what to believe or what to do. *Written argument imitates this situation by examining the opinions both for and against a position and then advocating one of the positions or proposing a solution.* Written argument *evaluates* the conflicting positions and then uses reasons and evidence to support the writer's claim. The writer represents the opposing arguments, refutes them (if possible), and advocates his or her own position. A sound written argument uses the following techniques:

- **Focusing on a *debatable proposition or claim*.** This claim becomes your thesis.
- ***Analyzing the audience* to determine what they already believe and how to convince them to believe or act on your thesis.**
- **Representing and evaluating the *opposing points of view*** on the issue fairly and accurately.
- **Arguing reasonably *against the opposition and for your claim.*** State and refute opposing arguments. State the best arguments supporting your claim.
- **Supporting your claims with *sufficient evidence*.** Use first-hand observations; examples from personal experience; statistics, facts, and quotations from your reading; and results from surveys and interviews.

In an article entitled "Active and Passive Euthanasia," James Rachels claims that active euthanasia may be defensible for patients with incurable and painful diseases. The following paragraphs from that article illustrate the key features of argument:

Opposing position

> The distinction between active and passive euthanasia is thought to be crucial for medical ethics. The idea is that it is permissible, at least in some cases, to withhold treatment and allow a patient to die, but it is never permissible to take any direct action designed to kill the patient. This doctrine seems to be accepted by most doctors. . . .

Claim

> However, a strong case can be made against this doctrine. In what

follows I will set out some of the relevant arguments, and urge doctors to reconsider their views on this matter.

Audience

To begin with a familiar type of situation, a patient who is dying of incurable cancer of the throat is in terrible pain, which can no longer be satisfactorily alleviated. He is certain to die within a few days, even if present treatment is continued, but he does not want to go on living for those days, since the pain is unbearable. So he asks the doctor for an end to it, and his family joins in the request.

Argument for claim
Example

Suppose the doctor agrees to withhold treatment, as the conventional doctrine says he may. The justification for his doing so is that the patient is in terrible agony, and since he is going to die anyway, it would be wrong to prolong his suffering needlessly. But now notice this. If one simply withholds treatment, it may take the patient longer to die, and so he may suffer more than he would if more direct action were taken and a lethal injection given. This fact provides strong reason for thinking that, once the initial decision not to prolong his agony has been made, active euthanasia is actually preferable to passive euthanasia, rather than the reverse. To say otherwise is to endorse the option that leads to more suffering rather than less, and is contrary to the humanitarian impulse that prompts the decision not to prolong his life in the first place.

Example

Argument against opposition

Claims for Written Argument

The thesis of your argument is a claim that must be debatable. Opinions on both sides of the issue must have some merit. Claims for a written argument usually fall into one of four categories: claims of fact, claims about cause and effect, claims about value, and claims about solutions and policies. A claim may occasionally fall into several categories or even overlap categories.

RESOURCE NOTE

For background on the use of these claims, see Fahnestock and Secor, "Teaching Argument: A Theory of Types," and Kneupper, "Teaching Argument: An Introduction to the Toulmin Model."

Claims of Fact

- Grades do not measure intelligence or achievement.
- Polygraph tests do not accurately detect lies.
- Women face serious discrimination in the job market.

These claims are about matters of "fact" that are not easily measured or agreed upon. If I claimed that a Lhasa apso was an ancient Chinese ruler, you could check a dictionary and find out that I was wrong. A Lhasa apso is, in fact, a small Tibetan dog. There is no argument. But people do disagree about some *supposed* "facts": Do grades measure achievement? Are polygraph tests accurate? They also disagree about

TEACHING TIP

For practice, have students generate two or three claims from the topics suggested in journal exercise 1. Then, at the board or in small groups, test to see (1) if claims are debatable; (2) whether the claims are of fact, cause and effect, value, policy, or some combination; and (3) if claims are sufficiently focused for the essay's intended audience and length. Once students have tentative subjects for their essays, have them write trial claims and apply the same three tests.

matters of "degree": Sexual discrimination exists in the marketplace, but is it "serious"? How prevalent and extreme are the economic inequities? What is "discrimination" anyway? *Definition* is a key to claims of fact: What do we mean by "detect lies"? Does "accurate" mean one hundred percent of the time? Ninety percent? Eighty percent? What does "serious discrimination" mean? Does the fact that female workers currently earn only sixty-seven cents for every dollar that male workers earn qualify as "serious discrimination"?

In an excerpt from a *Newsweek* column entitled "A Case of Severe Bias," Patricia Raybon makes a claim of fact when she argues that the news media's portrayal of black America is inaccurate, biased, and stereotyped:

> This is who I am not. I am not a crack addict. I am not a welfare mother. I am not illiterate. I am not a prostitute. I have never been in jail. My children are not in gangs. My husband doesn't beat me. My home is not a tenement. None of these things defines who I am, nor do they describe the other black people I've known and worked with and loved and befriended over these 40 years of my life.
>
> Nor does it describe most of black America, period.
>
> Yet in the eyes of the American news media, this is what black America is: poor, criminal, addicted and dysfunctional. Indeed, media coverage of black America is so one-sided, so imbalanced that the most victimized and hurting segment of the black community—a small segment, at best—is presented not as the exception but as the norm. It is an insidious practice, all the uglier for its blatancy.
>
> In recent months, oftentimes in this very magazine, I have observed a steady offering of media reports on crack babies, gang warfare, violent youth, poverty and homelessness—and in most cases, the people featured in the photos and stories were black. At the same time, articles that discuss other aspects of American life—from home buying to medicine to technology to nutrition—rarely, if ever, show blacks playing a positive role, or for that matter, any role at all.
>
> Day after day, week after week, this message—that black America is dysfunctional and unwhole—gets transmitted across the American landscape. Sadly, as a result, America never learns the truth about what is actually a wonderful, vibrant, creative community of people.

Claims about Cause and Effect

- Cigarettes cause lung cancer.
- Capital punishment does not deter violent crime.
- Rock music weakens the moral fiber of America's youth.

Unlike the claim "Grades affect admission to college," these claims about cause and effect are debatable. The claim that cigarettes cause lung cancer is, of course, less debatable than it was twenty years ago, before the evidence demonstrating the link became overwhelming. The deterring effect of capital punishment is still an arguable proposition with reasonable arguments on both sides. The argument that rock music weakens the moral fiber of youth is certainly debatable; the writer would have to counter the argument that rock music sometimes raises social consciousness and fights world hunger.

In a selection from her book, *The Plug-In Drug: Television, Children, and the Family*, Marie Winn argues that television has a negative effect on family life. In her opening paragraphs, she sets forth both sides of the controversy and then argues that the overall effect is negative:

> Television's contribution to family life has been an equivocal one. For while it has, indeed, kept the members of the family from dispersing, it has not served to bring them *together*. By its domination of the time families spend together, it destroys the special quality that depends to a great extent on what a family *does*, what special rituals, games, recurrent jokes, familiar songs, and shared activities it accumulates.
>
> "Like the sorcerer of old," writes Urie Bronfenbrenner, "the television set casts its magic spell, freezing speech and action, turning the living into silent statues so long as the enchantment lasts. The primary danger of the television screen lies not so much in the behavior it produces—although there is danger there—as in the behavior it prevents: the talks, the games, the family festivities and arguments through which much of the child's learning takes place and through which his character is formed. Turning on the television set can turn off the process that transforms children into people."
>
> Yet parents have accepted a television-dominated family life so completely that they cannot see how the medium is involved in whatever problems they might be having. . . .

Claims about Value

- Boxing is a dehumanizing sport.
- The Ford Edsel is the ugliest automobile ever built in America.
- Toni Morrison is a great American novelist.

Claims about value lead to evaluative essays. All the strategies discussed in Chapter 8 apply here, with the additional requirement that you must counter opposing arguments. The argumentative essay that attempts to prove that boxing is dehumanizing must refute the argument that boxing is merely another form of competition that promotes athletic excellence. Arguing that Morrison is a great American novelist requires setting criteria for great American novels and then refuting critics who argue that Morrison's talent does not reach those standards.

In "College Is a Waste of Time and Money," teacher and journalist Caroline Bird argues that many students go to college simply because it is the "thing to do." For those students, Bird claims, college is not a good idea:

> Nowadays, says one sociologist, you don't have to have a reason for going to college; it's an institution. His definition of an institution is an arrangement everyone accepts without question; the burden of proof is not on why you go, but why anyone thinks there might be a reason for not going. The implication is that an 18-year-old . . . should listen to those who know best and go to college.
>
> I don't agree. I believe that college has to be judged not on what other people think is good for students, but on how good it feels to the students themselves.
>
> I believe that people have an inside view of what's good for them. If a child doesn't want to go to school some morning, better let him stay at home, at least until you find out why. Maybe he knows something you don't. It's the same with college. If high-school graduates don't want to go, or if they don't want to go right away, they may perceive more clearly than their elders that college is not for them. It is no longer obvious that adolescents are best off studying a core curriculum that was constructed when all educated men could agree on what made them educated, or that professors, advisors, or parents can be of any particular help to young people in choosing a major or a career. High-school graduates see college graduates driving cabs and decide it's not worth going. College students find no intellectual stimulation in their studies and drop out.

Claims about Solutions or Policies

- Students with AIDS should be allowed to attend classes.
- The penalty for drunk driving should be a mandatory jail sentence and loss of driver's license.
- To reduce exploitation and sensationalism, the news media should not be allowed to interview victims of crime or disaster.

Claims about solutions or policies sometimes occur *along with* claims of fact, cause and effect, or value. Because grades do not measure achievement (argue that this is a fact), they should be abolished (argue for this policy). Boxing is a dehumanizing sport (argue this claim of value); therefore, boxing should be banned (argue for this solution). Claims about solutions or policies involve all the strategies used for problem solving (see Chapter 8), but with special emphasis on countering opposing arguments: "Students with AIDS should be allowed to attend classes because attending school is their constitutional right and because AIDS is not transmitted by the kind of casual contact that occurs among schoolchildren."

In *When Society Becomes an Addict*, psychotherapist Anne Wilson Schaef argues that our society has become an "Addictive System" that has many characteristics in common with alcoholism and other addictions. Advertising becomes addictive, causing us to behave dishonestly; the social pressure to be "nice" can become addictive, causing us to lie to ourselves. Schaef argues that the solution for our social addictions begins when we face the reality of our dependency:

> We cannot recover from an addiction unless we first admit that we have it. Naming our reality is essential to recovery. Unless we admit that we are indeed functioning in an addictive process in an Addictive System, we shall never have the option of recovery. Once we name something, we own it . . . . Remember, to name the system as addict is not to condemn it: it is to offer it the possibility of recovery.
>
> Paradoxically, the only way to reclaim our personal power is by admitting our powerlessness. The first part of Step One of the AA [Alcoholics Anonymous] Twelve-Step Program reads, "We admitted we were powerless over alcohol." It is important to recognize that admitting to powerlessness over an addiction is not the same as admitting powerlessness as a person. In fact, it can be very powerfull to recognize the futility of the illusion of control.

Teaching Tip

In the sequence of claims (fact, cause and effect, value, policy), later claims often contain earlier claims, like Chinese boxes. Proposing a solution may contain value judgments, cause-and-effect analysis, and assumptions about the facts. Arguing a value judgment may require proving that certain causes lead to negative effects and that certain facts are true.

Appeals for Written Argument

To support claims and refute opposing arguments, writers use *appeals* to the audience. Argument uses three important types of appeals: to *reason* (logic and evidence support the claim), to *character* (the writer's good character itself supports the claim), and to *emotion* (the writer's expression of feelings about the issue may support the claim). Effective arguments emphasize the appeal to reason but may also appeal to character or emotion.

Mere knowledge of the truth will not give you the art of persuasion.

PLATO, PHAEDRUS

Appeal to reason, character, or emotion can vary with a writer's sense of audience. Ask your students to compare the use of these appeals in different kinds of argument—written and televised—paying particular attention to the subject, purpose, and intended audience of each.

APPEAL TO REASON An appeal to reason depends most frequently on *inductive logic*, which is sometimes called the "scientific method." Inductive logic draws a general conclusion from personal observation or experience, specific facts, reports, statistics, testimony of authorities, and other bits of data.

Experience is the best teacher, we always say, and experience teaches inductively. Suppose, using biologist Thomas Huxley's famous example, you pick a green apple from a tree and take a bite. Halfway through the bite you discover that the apple is sour and quickly spit it out. But, you think, perhaps the next green apple will be ripe and will taste better. You pick a second green apple, take a bite, and realize that it is just as sour as the first. However, you know that some apples—like the Granny Smith—look green even when they're ripe, so you take a bite out of a third apple. It is also sour. You're beginning to draw a conclusion. In fact, if you taste a fourth or fifth apple, other people may begin to question your intelligence. How many green apples from this tree must you taste before you get the idea that all of these green apples are sour?

Experience, however, may lead to wrong conclusions. You've tasted enough of these apples to convince *you* that all these apples are sour, but will others think that these apples are sour? Perhaps you have funny taste buds. You may need to ask several friends to taste the apples. Or perhaps you are dealing with a slightly weird tree—in fact, some apple trees are hybrids, with several different kinds of apples grafted onto one tree. Before you draw a conclusion, you may need to consult an expert in order to be certain that your tree is a standard, single-variety apple tree. If your friends and the expert also agree that all of these green apples are sour, you may use your experience *and* their testimony to reach a conclusion—and to provide evidence to make your argument more convincing to others.

In inductive logic, a reasonable conclusion is based on a *sufficient* quantity of accurate and reliable evidence that is selected in a *random* manner to reduce human bias or to take into account variation in the sample. The definition of "sufficient" varies, but generally the number must be large enough to convince your audience that your sample fairly represents the whole subject.

Let's take an example to illustrate inductive reasoning. Suppose you ask a student, one of fifty in a Psychology I class, a question of value: "Is Professor X a good teacher?" If this student says, "Professor X is the worst teacher I've ever had!" what conclusion can you draw? If you avoid taking the class based on a sample of one, you may miss an excellent class. So you decide to gather a *sufficient sample* by polling twenty of the fifty students in the class. But which twenty do you interview? If you ask the first student for a list of students, you may receive the names of twenty other students who also hate the professor. To reduce human or accidental bias, then, you choose a *random* method for collecting your evidence: As the students leave the class, you give a questionnaire to two out of every five students. If they all fill out the questionnaires, you probably have a *sufficient* and *random* sample.

Finally, if the responses to your questionnaire show that fifteen out of twenty students rate Professor X as an excellent teacher, what *valid conclusion* should you draw? You should not say, categorically, "X is an excellent teacher." Your conclusion must be restricted by your evidence and the method of gathering it: "Seventy-five percent of the students polled in Psychology I believe that Professor X is an excellent teacher."

Most arguments use a shorthand version of the inductive method of reasoning. A writer makes a *claim* and then supports it with *reasons* and representative *examples* or *data:*

Claim:	Professor X is an excellent psychology teacher.
Reason #1:	Professor X is an excellent teacher because she gives stimulating lectures that students rarely miss.
	Evidence: Sixty percent of the students polled said that they rarely missed a lecture. Three students cited Professor X's lecture on "assertiveness" as the best lecture they'd ever heard.
Reason #2:	Professor X is an excellent teacher because she gives tests that encourage learning rather than sheer memorization.
	Evidence: Seventy percent of the students polled said that Professor X's essay tests required thinking and learning rather than memorization. One student said that Professor X's tests always made her think about what she'd read. Another student said she always liked to discuss Professor X's test questions with her classmates and friends.

APPEAL TO CHARACTER An appeal to your good character as a writer can also be important in argument. (The appeal to character is frequently called the "ethical" appeal because readers make a value judgment about the writer's character.) In a written argument, you show your audience—through your reasonable persona, voice, and tone—that you are a person who abides by moral standards that your audience shares: You have a good reputation, you are honest and trustworthy, and you argue "fairly."

A person's reputation often affects how we react to a claim, but also the *argument itself* should establish the writer's trustworthiness. You don't have to be a Mahatma Gandhi or a Mother Teresa to generate a strong ethical appeal for your claim. Even if your readers have never heard your name before, they will feel confident about your character if you are knowledgeable about your subject, present the pros and cons fairly, and support your own claim with sufficient, reliable evidence.

If your readers have reason to suspect your motives or think that you may have something personal to gain from your argument, you may need to bend over backward to be fair. If you do have something to gain, lay your cards on the table. Declare your vested interest but explain, for example, how your solution would benefit everyone equally. Similarly, don't try to cover up or distort the opponents' arguments; acknowledge the opposition's strong arguments and refute the weak ones.

APPEAL TO EMOTION Appeals to emotion can be tricky because, as we have seen, when emotions come in through the door, reasonableness may fly out the window. Argument emphasizes reason, not emotion. We know, for example, how advertising plays on emotions, by means of loaded or exaggerated language or through images of famous or sexy people. Emotional appeals designed to *deceive* or *frighten* people or to *misrepresent* the virtues of a person, place, or object have no place in rational argument. But emotional appeals that illustrate a truth or movingly depict a reality are legitimate and effective means of convincing readers.

COMBINED APPEALS Appeals may be used in combination. Writers may appeal to reason and, at the same time, establish trustworthy characters and use legitimate emotional appeals. The following excerpt from Martin Luther King's "Letter from Birmingham Jail—April 16, 1963" illustrates all three appeals. He appeals to reason, arguing that, historically, civil rights reforms are rarely made without political pressure. He establishes his integrity and good character by treating the opposition (in this case, the Birmingham clergy) with respect and by showing moderation and restraint. Finally, he uses emotional appeals, describing his six-year-old daughter in tears and recalling his own humiliation at being refused a place to sleep. King uses these emotional appeals legitimately; he is not misrepresenting reality or trying to deceive his readers.

Appeal to character and appeal to reason

> One of the basic points in [the statement by the Birmingham clergy] is that the action that I and my associates have taken in Birmingham is untimely. Some have asked: "Why didn't you give the new city administration time to act?" The only answer that I can give to this query is that the new Birmingham administration must be prodded about as much as the outgoing one, before it will act. We are sadly mistaken if we feel that the election of Albert

Boutwell as mayor will bring the millennium to Birmingham. While Mr. Boutwell is a much more gentle person than Mr. Connor, they are both segregationists, dedicated to the maintenance of the status quo. I have hoped that Mr. Boutwell will be reasonable enough to see the futility of massive resistance to desegregation. But he will not see this without pressure from devotees of civil rights. My friends, I must say to you that we have not made a single gain in civil rights without determined legal and nonviolent pressure. Lamentably, it is an historical fact that privileged groups seldom give up their privileges voluntarily. Individuals may see the moral light and voluntarily give up their unjust posture; but, as Reinhold Niebuhr has reminded us, groups tend to be more immoral than individuals.

Appeal to reason

Evidence

We know through painful experience that freedom is never voluntarily given by the oppressor; it must be demanded by the oppressed. Frankly, I have yet to engage in a direct-action campaign that was "well timed" in the view of those who have not suffered unduly from the disease of segregation. For years now I have heard the word "Wait!" It rings in the ear of every Negro with piercing familiarity. This "Wait" has almost always meant "Never." We must come to see, with one of our distinguished jurists, that "justice too long delayed is justice denied."

Appeal to character and reason

We have waited for more than 340 years for our constitutional and God-given rights. . . . Perhaps it is easy for those who have never felt the stinging darts of segregation to say, "Wait." But when you have seen vicious mobs lynch your mothers and fathers at will and drown your sisters and brothers at whim; when you have seen hate-filled policemen curse, kick, and even kill your black brothers and sisters; when you see the vast majority of your twenty million Negro brothers smothering in an airtight cage of poverty in the midst of an affluent society; when you suddenly find your tongue twisted and your speech stammering as you seek to explain to your six-year-old daughter why she can't go to the public amusement park that has just been advertised on television, and see tears welling up in her eyes when she is told that Funtown is closed to colored children . . . when you take a cross-country drive and find it necessary to sleep night after night in the uncomfortable corners of your automobile because no motel will accept you; when you are humiliated day in and day out by nagging signs reading "white" and "colored"; when your first name becomes "nigger," your middle name becomes "boy" (however old you are) and your last name becomes "John" . . . —then you will understand why we find it difficult to wait. There comes a time when the cup of endurance runs over, and men are no longer willing to be plunged into the abyss of despair. I hope, sirs, you can understand our legitimate and unavoidable impatience.

Appeal to emotion

Evidence

Appeal to emotion

Evidence

Appeal to emotion

Evidence

Appeal to character

RESOURCE NOTE

See Young, Becker, and Pike, *Rhetoric: Discovery and Change* for the original adaptation of Carl Rogers's communication strategies to written argument. For application, of Rogers's theories to the teaching of writing, see Hairston, "Using Carl Rogers's Communication Theories in the Composition Classroom."

See the *ABC News Nightline* interviews for examples of Rogerian argument. The general purpose of this show is to open lines of communication and exchange information, not necessarily to seek a winner.

ROGERIAN ARGUMENT

Traditional argument presumes that the audience is not the opposition but a group of people who are relatively uninformed or undecided about the issue. Those with definite opposing views are a separate group of people, the writer's *adversaries.* The writer argues reasonably and fairly, but traditional argument becomes a kind of struggle or war as the writer attempts to "defeat" the arguments of the opposition. The purpose of the argument is to convince the undecided audience that the writer has "won a fight" and emerged "victorious" over the opposition.

In some arguments, however, the issues are particularly sensitive and the audience that we are trying to persuade is, in fact, the opposition. In such cases, *Rogerian argument*—named after psychologist Carl Rogers—may be more effective than the traditional approach. Rogerian, or *nonthreatening* argument, opens the lines of communication by reducing conflict. When people's beliefs are attacked, they instinctively become defensive and strike back. As a result, the argument becomes polarized: The writer argues for a claim, the reader digs in to defend his or her position, and no one budges.

Crucial to Rogerian argument is the fact that convictions and beliefs are not abstract but reside in *people.* If people are to agree, they must be sensitive to each other's beliefs. Rogerian argument, therefore, contains a clear appeal to character. While Rogerian argument uses reason and logic, its primary goal is not to "win" the argument but to open the lines of communication. To do that, the writer must be sympathetic to different points of view and willing to modify his or her claims in response to opposing arguments. Once the reader sees that the writer is open to change, the reader may become more flexible.

Once both sides are more flexible, a compromise position or solution becomes possible. As Rogers says, "This procedure gradually achieves a mutual communication. Mutual communication tends to be pointed toward solving a problem rather than toward attacking a person or group." Rogerian argument, then, imitates not a courtroom debate but the mutual communication that may take place between two people. Whereas traditional argument intends to change the actions or the beliefs of the opposition, Rogerian argument works toward changes *in both sides* as a means of establishing common ground and reaching a solution.

If you choose Rogerian argument, remember that you must actually be willing to change your beliefs. Often, in fact, when you need to use Rogerian argument most, you may be least inclined to use it—simply because you are inflexible on an issue. If you are unwilling to modify your own position, your reader will probably sense your basic insincerity and realize that you are just playing a trick of rhetoric.

Rogerian argument is appropriate in a variety of sensitive or highly controversial situations. You may want to choose Rogerian argument if you are an employer requesting union members to accept a pay cut in order to help the company avoid bankruptcy. Similarly, if you argue to husbands that they should assume responsibility for half of the housework, or if you argue to Anglo-Americans that Spanish language and culture should play a larger role in public education, you may want to use a Rogerian strategy. By showing that you empathize with the opposition's position and are willing to compromise, you create a climate for mutual communication.

Rogerian argument makes a claim, considers the opposition, and presents evidence to support your claim, but in addition it avoids threatening or adversarial language and promotes mutual communication and learning. A Rogerian argument uses the following strategies:

- **Avoiding a** *confrontational stance.* Confrontation threatens your audience and increases their defensiveness. Threat hinders communication.
- **Presenting your** *character* as someone who understands and can empathize with the opposition. Show that you understand by restating the opposing position accurately.
- **Establishing** *common ground* with the opposition. Indicate the beliefs and values that you share.
- **Being willing to** *change your views.* Show where your position is not reasonable and could be modified.
- **Directing your argument toward a** *compromise or workable solution.*

Note: An argument does not have to be either entirely adversarial or entirely Rogerian. You may use Rogerian techniques for the most sensitive points in an argument that is otherwise traditional or confrontational.

In his essay "Animal Rights versus Human Health," biology professor Albert Rosenfeld illustrates several features of Rogerian argument. Rosenfeld argues that animals should be used for medical experiments, but he is aware that the issues are emotional and that his audience is likely to be antagonistic. In these paragraphs, Rosenfeld avoids threatening language, represents the opposition fairly, grants that he is guilty of *specieism*, and says that he sympathizes with the demand to look for alternatives. He indicates that his position is flexible: Most researchers, he says, are delighted when they can use alternatives. He grants that there is some room for compromise, but he is firm in his position that some animal experimentation is necessary for advancements in medicine.

States opposing position fairly and sympathetically

It is fair to say that millions of animals—probably more rats and mice than any other species—are subjected to experiments that cause them pain, discomfort, and distress, sometimes lots of it over long periods of time. . . . All new forms of medication or surgery are tried out on animals first. Every new substance that is released into the environment, or put on the market, is tested on animals. . . .

States opposing position fairly

In 1975, Australian philosopher Peter Singer wrote his influential book called *Animal Liberation*, in which he accuses us all of "speciesism"—as reprehensible, to him, as racism or sexism. He freely describes the "pain and suffering" inflicted in the "tyranny of human over nonhuman animals" and sharply challenges our biblical license to exercise "dominion over the fish of the sea, and over the fowl of the air, and over every living thing that moveth upon the Earth."

Acknowledges common ground

Sympathetic to opposing position

Well, certainly we are guilty of speciesism. We do act as if we had dominion over other living creatures. But domination also entails some custodial responsibility. And the questions continue to be raised: Do we have the right to abuse animals? To eat them? To hunt them for sport? To keep them imprisoned in zoos—or, for that matter, in our households? Especially to do experiments on these creatures who can't fight back?

Suggests compromise position

Hardly any advance in either human or veterinary medicine—cure, vaccine, operation, drug, therapy—has come about without experiments on animals. . . . I certainly sympathize with the demand that we look for ways to get the information we want without using animals. Most investigators are delighted when they can get their data by means of tissue cultures or computer simulations. But as we look for alternative ways to get information, do we meanwhile just do without?

Warming Up: Journal Exercises

1. From the following list of "should" statements, choose *one* that relates to your experience and freewrite for ten minutes. When you finish your freewriting, state a *claim* and list arguments on both sides of the issue.

- Tuition should be free at state universities.
- Bicyclists should be subject to regular traffic laws, including DWI.
- The sale of all handguns should be illegal.
- Unions should be abolished.
- NCAA football should have playoffs.
- High-quality child care should be available to all working parents at public expense.

- Computer literacy courses should be required at the college level.
- Police should live in the neighborhoods they serve.
- Fraternities and sororities should be forbidden to serve alcoholic beverages during rush.
- Students should work for one year between high school and college.
- Businesses should be required to provide free health insurance for all employees.
- Rock music should be rated and labeled, from "PG" to "X," as films are.
- Unsportsmanlike behavior in tennis should result in a match forfeit.
- Drug tests should be required for your job or at your school.
- Nonmajor courses should be graded pass/fail.
- After committing three felonies, criminals should receive mandatory life sentences.

A society which is clamoring for choice . . . [is] filled with many articulate groups, each arguing its own brand of salvation. . . .
—MARGARET MEAD, ANTHROPOLOGIST

2. Controversial subjects depend as much on the audience as they do on the issue itself. Make a quick list of things you do every day—the kind of clothes you wear, the food you eat, the books you read, the friends you have, the ideas you discuss. For *one* of these activities, imagine a person who might find what you do immoral, illogical, unjust, or unhealthy. What claim might they make about your activity? What reasons or evidence might they use to argue that your activity should be abolished, outlawed, or changed? Write for five minutes arguing *their* point of view.

3. Television and television advertising are often the subject of much criticism, such as in Marie Winn's excerpt from "The Effects of Television on Family Life." Write a letter to Marie Winn, to your local or college newspaper, or to members of the PTA in your city defending the *positive* effects or value of television. Cite *one* particular program or commercial as an example.

4. Grades are important, but in some courses they get in the way of learning. Choose an actual course that you have taken and write an open letter to the school administration, arguing for Credit/No Credit grading in that particular course. Assume that you intend to submit your letter to the campus newspaper.

5. News items often contain incidents that spark arguments about morality or justice. Choose a recent controversial news

story and write out the arguments for or against the action taken in the case.

6. Does the cartoon above from Gary Larson's "The Far Side" make a statement? Citing specific details from the cartoon, write a paragraph that explains the "point" of the cartoon. (If "The Far Side" is not one of your favorites, choose another cartoon that makes a controversial point and explain the "claim" it makes.)

DARWIN'S MIDDLE ROAD

STEPHEN JAY GOULD

In his distinguished career as a spokesperson for the wonders of biology and the theory of evolution, Harvard professor Stephen Jay Gould has written dozens of scientific and popular articles and has published several collections of essays and award-winning books, including Ever Since Darwin *(1977),* The Panda's Thumb *(1980),* Hen's Teeth and Horse's Toes *(1983),* The Flamingo's Smile *(1985), and* Time's Arrow, Time's

Cycle *(1987). "Science is not a heartless pursuit of objective information," Gould has said, "it is a creative human activity." That idea is clearly illustrated in "Darwin's Middle Road." Gould opens the essay with an episode from Homer's epic poem* The Odyssey. *At one point during his adventures, Odysseus must sail between the horrible six-headed monster Scylla and the giant ocean whirlpool created by Charybdis. Odysseus's predicament dramatizes the focus of Gould's essay. Gould's subject is the nature of scientific creativity and his central question is whether great scientific theories are based on purely inductive, data-driven research or whether they arise primarily from intuition, hunches, and flashes of genius. Gould's claim is that the theory of natural selection sprang from Darwin's unique blending of careful, inductive observation with reflection, intuition, and synthesis.*

"We began to sail up the narrow strait lamenting," narrates Odysseus. "For on the one hand lay Scylla, with twelve feet all dangling down; and six necks exceeding long, and on each a hideous head, and therein three rows of teeth set thick and close, full of black death. And on the other mighty Charybdis sucked down the salt sea water. As often as she belched it forth, like a cauldron on a great fire she would seethe up through all her troubled deeps." Odysseus managed to swerve around Charybdis, but Scylla grabbed six of his finest men and devoured them in his sight—"the most pitiful thing mine eyes have seen of all my travail in searching out the paths of the sea." **(1)**

False lures and dangers often come in pairs in our legends and metaphors—consider the frying pan and the fire, or the devil and the deep blue sea. Prescriptions for avoidance either emphasize a dogged steadiness—the straight and narrow of Christian evangelists—or an averaging between unpleasant alternatives—the golden mean of Aristotle. The idea of steering a course between undesirable extremes emerges as a central prescription for a sensible life. **(2)**

The nature of scientific creativity is both a perennial topic of discussion and a prime candidate for seeking a golden mean. The two extreme positions have not been directly competing for allegiance of the unwary. They have, rather, replaced each other sequentially, with one now in the ascendency, the other eclipsed. **(3)**

The first—inductivism—held that great scientists are primarily great observers and patient accumulators of information. For new and significant theory, the inductivists claimed, can only arise from a firm foundation of facts. In this architectural view, each fact is a brick in a structure built without blueprints. Any talk or thought about theory (the completed building) is fatuous and premature before the bricks are set. Inductivism once commanded great prestige within science, and even represented an "official" position of sorts, for it touted, however falsely,

CRITICAL READING

Much academic writing, like Gould's essay, is dense and difficult. When you assign this essay, stress three important critical-reading strategies. First, students must *reread* difficult essays at least twice. Second, they must read *actively*, annotating their own reactions and highlighting key ideas. Third, they must look up *unfamiliar words* as they reread. As the vocabulary list suggests, students will not understand this essay unless they look up key words, such as "marsupial fauna," "speciation," "archetype," "serendipitous," "laissez faire," and "oligopoly."

the utter honesty, complete objectivity, and almost automatic nature of scientific progress towards final and incontrovertible truth. (4)

Yet, as its critics so rightly claimed, inductivism also depicted science as a heartless, almost inhuman discipline offering no legitimate place to quirkiness, intuition, and all the other subjective attributes adhering to our vernacular notion of genius. Great scientists, the critics claimed, are distinguished more by their powers of hunch and synthesis, than their skill in experiment or observation. The criticisms of inductivism are certainly valid and I welcome its dethroning during the past thirty years as a necessary prelude to better understanding. Yet, in attacking it so strongly, some critics have tried to substitute an alternative equally extreme and unproductive in its emphasis on the essential subjectivity of creative thought. In this, "eureka" view, creativity is an ineffable something, accessible only to persons of genius. It arises like a bolt of lightning, unanticipated, unpredictable and unanalyzable—but the bolts strike only a few special people. We ordinary mortals must stand in awe and thanks. (The name refers, of course, to the legendary story of Archimedes running naked through the streets of Syracuse shouting eureka [I have discovered it] when water displaced by his bathing body washed the scales abruptly from his eyes and suggested a method for measuring volumes.) (5)

I am equally disenchanted by both these opposing extremes. Inductivism reduces genius to dull, rote operations; eurekaism grants it an inaccessible status more in the domain of intrinsic mystery than in a realm where we might understand and learn from it. Might we not marry the good features of each view, and abandon both the elitism of eurekaism and the pedestrian qualities of inductivism. May we not acknowledge the personal and subjective character of creativity, but still comprehend it as a mode of thinking that emphasizes or exaggerates capacities sufficiently common to all of us that we may at least understand if not hope to imitate. (6)

In the hagiography of science, a few men hold such high positions that all arguments must apply to them if they are to have any validity. Charles Darwin, as the principal saint of evolutionary biology, has therefore been presented both as an inductivist and as a primary example of eurekaism. I will attempt to show that these interpretations are equally inadequate, and that recent scholarship on Darwin's own odyssey towards the theory of natural selection supports an intermediate position. (7)

So great was the prestige of inductivism in his own day, that Darwin himself fell under its sway and, as an old man, falsely depicted his youthful accomplishments in its light. In an autobiography, written as a lesson in morality for his children and not intended for publication, he penned some famous lines that misled historians for nearly a hundred years. Describing his path to the theory of natural selection, he claimed: "I

Collaborative Activity

Divide the class into groups of two or three students. Assign each group three or four paragraphs from the essay. Each group should appoint a recorder. Groups should write out the rhetorical *purpose* of each paragraph. For example, the purpose of paragraph 1 is to provide a lead-in for the readers and introduce the ideas of the journey and the perilous extremes. The purpose of paragraph 2 is to connect Odysseus's adventures to the idea of the golden mean, and so on. Each group should spend ten minutes on this activity. Recorders should then report to the class. The resulting discussion should reveal how Gould shapes his essay and how he cues his readers during the course of the essay. If time permits, have groups try the same annotating tactic with their own essay drafts.

worked on true Baconian principles, and without any theory collected facts on a wholesale scale." **(8)**

The inductivist interpretation focuses on Darwin's five years aboard the *Beagle* and explains his transition from a student for the ministry to the nemesis of preachers as the result of his keen powers of observation applied to the whole world. Thus, the traditional story goes, Darwin's eyes opened wider and wider as he saw, in sequence, the bones of giant South American fossil mammals, the turtles and finches of the Galapagos, and the marsupial fauna of Australia. The truth of evolution and its mechanism of natural selection crept up gradually upon him as he sifted facts in a sieve of utter objectivity. **(9)**

The inadequacies of this tale are best illustrated by the falsity of its conventional premier example—the so-called Darwin's finches of the Galapagos. We now know that although these birds share a recent and common ancestry on the South American mainland, they have radiated into an impressive array of species on the outlying Galapagos. Few terrestrial species manage to cross the wide oceanic barrier between South America and the Galapagos. But the fortunate migrants often find a sparsely inhabited world devoid of the competitors that limit their opportunities on the crowded mainland. Hence, the finches evolved into roles normally occupied by other birds and developed their famous set of adaptations for feeding—seed crushing, insect eating, even grasping and manipulating a cactus needle to dislodge insects from plants. Isolation—both of the islands from the mainland and among the islands themselves—provided an opportunity for separation, independent adaptation, and speciation. **(10)**

According to the traditional view, Darwin discovered these finches, correctly inferred their history, and wrote the famous lines in his notebook: "If there is the slightest foundation for these remarks the zoology of Archipelagoes will be worth examining; for such facts would undermine the stability of Species." But, as with so many heroic tales from Washington's cherry tree to the piety of Crusaders, hope rather than truth motivates the common reading. Darwin found the finches to be sure. But he didn't recognize them as variants of a common stock. In fact, he didn't even record the island of discovery for many of them—some of his labels just read "Galapagos Islands." So much for his immediate recognition of the role of isolation in the formation of new species. He reconstructed the evolutionary tale only after his return to London, when a British Museum ornithologist correctly identified all the birds as finches. **(11)**

The famous quotation from his notebook refers to Galapagos tortoises and to the claim of native inhabitants that they can "at once pronounce from which Island any Tortoise may have been brought" from subtle differences in size and shape of body and scales. This is a statement of different, and much reduced, order from the traditional tale of finches. For the finches are true and separate species—a living example of evolution. The subtle differences among tortoises represent minor geographic variation within a species. It is a jump in reasoning, albeit a valid one as we now know, to argue that such small differences can be amplified to produce a new species. All creationists, after all, acknowledged geographic variation (consider human races), but argued that it could not proceed beyond the rigid limits of a created archetype. **(12)**

I don't wish to downplay the pivotal influence of the *Beagle* voyage on Darwin's career. It gave him space, freedom and endless time to think in his favored mode of independent self-stimulation. (His ambivalence towards university life, and his middling performance there by conventional standards, reflected his unhappiness with a curriculum of received wisdom.) He writes from South America in 1834: "I have not one clear idea about cleavage, stratification, lines of upheaval. I have no books, which tell me much and what they do I cannot apply to what I see. In consequence I draw my own conclusions, and most gloriously ridiculous ones they are." The rocks and plants and animals that he saw did provoke him to the crucial attitude of doubt—midwife of all creativity. Sydney, Australia—1836. Darwin wonders why a rational God would create so many marsupials on Australia since nothing about its climate or geography suggests any superiority for pouches: "I had been lying on a sunny bank and was reflecting on the strange character of the animals of this country as compared to the rest of the World. An unbeliever in everything beyond his own reason might exclaim, 'Surely two distinct Creators must have been at work.'" **(13)**

Nonetheless, Darwin returned to London without an evolutionary theory. He suspected the truth of evolution, but had no mechanism to explain it. Natural selection did not arise from any direct reading of the *Beagle's* facts, but from two subsequent years of thought and struggle as reflected in a series of remarkable notebooks that have been unearthed and published during the past twenty years. In these notebooks, we see Darwin testing and abandoning a number of theories and pursuing a multitude of false leads—so much for his later claim about recording facts with an empty mind. He read philosophers, poets, and economists, always searching for meaning and insight—so much for the notion that natural selection arose inductively from the *Beagle's* facts. Later, he labelled one notebook as "full of metaphysics on morals." **(14)**

Yet if this tortuous path belies the Scylla of inductivism, it has engendered an equally simplistic myth—the Charybdis of eurekaism. In his maddeningly misleading autobiography, Darwin does record a eureka and suggests that natural selection struck him as a sudden, serendipitous flash after more than a year of groping frustration:

> In October 1838, that is, fifteen months after I had begun my systematic inquiry, I happened to read for amusement Malthus on Population, and being well prepared to appreciate the struggle for existence which everywhere goes on from long-continued observation of the habits of animals and plants, it at once struck me that under these circumstances favorable variations would tend to be preserved, and unfavorable ones to be destroyed. The result of this would be the formation of new species. Here, then, I had at last got a theory by which to work. **(15)**

Yet, again, the notebooks belie Darwin's later recollections—in this case by their utter failure to record, at the time it happened, any special exultation over his Malthusian insight. He inscribes it as a fairly short and sober entry without a single exclamation point, though he habitually used two or three in moments of excitement. He did not drop everything and reinterpret a confusing world in its light. On the very next day, he wrote an even longer passage on the sexual curiosity of primates. **(16)**

The theory of natural selection arose neither as a workmanlike induction from nature's facts, nor as a mysterious bolt from Darwin's subconscious, triggered by an accidental reading of Malthus. It emerged instead as the result of a conscious and productive search, proceeding in a ramifying but ordered manner, and utilizing both the facts of natural history and an astonishingly broad range of insights from disparate disciplines far from his own. Darwin trod the middle path between inductivism and eurekaism. His genius is neither pedestrian nor inaccessible. **(17)**

Darwinian scholarship has exploded since the centennial of the *Origin* in 1959. The publication of Darwin's notebooks and the attention devoted by several scholars to the two crucial years between the *Beagle's* docking and the demoted Malthusian insight has clinched the argument for a "middle path" theory of Darwin's creativity. Two particularly important works focus on the broadest and narrowest scales. Howard E. Gruber's masterful intellectual and psychological biography of this phase in Darwin's life, *Darwin on Man*, traces all the false leads and turning points in Darwin's search. Gruber shows that Darwin was continually proposing, testing, and abandoning hypotheses, and that he never simply collected facts in a blind way. He began with a fanciful theory involving the idea that new species arise with a prefixed life span, and worked his way gradually, if fitfully, towards an idea of extinction by competition in a world of struggle. He recorded no exultation upon reading Malthus, because the jigsaw puzzle was only missing a piece or two at the time. **(18)**

Silvan S. Schweber has reconstructed, in detail as minute as the record will allow, Darwin's activities during the few weeks before Malthus (The Origin of the *Origin* Revisited, *Journal of the History of*

Biology, 1977). He argues that the final pieces arose not from new facts in natural history, but from Darwin's intellectual wanderings in distant fields. In particular, he read a long review of social scientist and philosopher Auguste Comte's most famous work, the *Cours de philosophie positive*. He was particularly struck by Comte's insistence that a proper theory be predictive and at least potentially quantitative. He then turned to Dugald Stewart's *On the Life and Writing of Adam Smith*, and imbibed the basic belief of the Scottish economists that theories of overall social structure must begin by analyzing the unconstrained actions of individuals. (Natural selection is, above all, a theory about the struggle of individual organisms for success in reproduction.) Then, searching for quantification, he read a lengthy analysis of work by the most famous statistician of his time—the Belgian Adolphe Quetelet. In the review of Quetelet, he found, among other things, a forceful statement of Malthus's quantitative claim—that population would grow geometrically and food supplies only arithmetically, thus guaranteeing an intense struggle for existence. In fact, Darwin had read the Malthusian statement several times before; but only now was he prepared to appreciate its significance. Thus, he did not turn to Malthus by accident, and he already knew what it contained. His "amusement," we must assume, consisted only in a desire to read in its original formulation the familiar statement that had so impressed him in Quetelet's secondary account. **(19)**

In reading Schweber's detailed account of the moments preceding Darwin's formulation of natural selection, I was particularly struck by the absence of deciding influence from his own field of biology. The immediate precipitators were a social scientist, an economist, and a statistician. If genius has any common denominator, I would propose breadth of interest and the ability to construct fruitful analogies between fields. **(20)**

In fact, I believe that the theory of natural selection should be viewed as an extended analogy—whether conscious or unconscious on Darwin's part I do not know—to the laissez faire economics of Adam Smith. The essence of Smith's argument is a paradox of sorts: if you want an ordered economy providing maximal benefits to all, then let individuals compete and struggle for their own advantages. The result, after appropriate sorting and elimination of the inefficient, will be a stable and harmonious polity. Apparent order arises naturally from the struggle among individuals, not from predestined principles or higher control. Dugald Stewart epitomized Smith's system in the book Darwin read:

> The most effective plan for advancing a people . . . is by allowing every man, as long as he observes the rules of justice, to pursue his own interest in his own way, and to bring both his industry and his capital into the freest competition with those of his fellow citizens. Every system of policy which endeavors . . . to draw towards a par-

> ticular species of industry a greater share of the capital of the society than would naturally go to it . . . is, in reality, subversive of the great purpose which it means to promote.

As Schweber states: "The Scottish analysis of society contends that the combined effect of individual actions results in the institutions upon which society is based, and that such a society is a stable and evolving one and functions without a designing and directing mind." **(21)**

We know that Darwin's uniqueness does not reside in his support for the idea of evolution—scores of scientists had preceded him in this. His special contribution rests upon his documentation and upon the novel character of his theory about how evolution operates. Previous evolutionists had proposed unworkable schemes based on internal perfecting tendencies and inherent directions. Darwin advocated a natural and testable theory based on immediate interaction among individuals (his opponents considered it heartlessly mechanistic). The theory of natural selection is a creative transfer to biology of Adam Smith's basic argument for a rational economy: the balance and order of nature does not arise from a higher, external (divine) control, or from the existence of laws operating directly upon the whole, but from struggle among individuals for their own benefits (in modern terms, for the transmission of their genes to future generations through differential success in reproduction). **(22)**

Many people are distressed to hear such an argument. Does it not compromise the integrity of science if some of its primary conclusions originate by analogy from contemporary politics and culture rather than from data of the discipline itself? In a famous letter to Engels, Karl Marx identified the similarities between natural selection and the English social scene:

> It is remarkable how Darwin recognizes among beasts and plants his English society with its division of labor, competition, opening up of new markets, 'invention,' and the Malthusian 'struggle for existence.' It is Hobbes' *bellum omnium contra omnes* (the war of all against all).

Yet Marx was a great admirer of Darwin—and in this apparent paradox lies resolution. For reasons involving all the themes I have emphasized here—that inductivism is inadequate, that creativity demands breadth, and that analogy is a profound source of insight—great thinkers cannot be divorced from their social background. But the source of an idea is one thing; its truth or fruitfulness is another. The psychology and utility of discovery are very different subjects indeed. Darwin may have cribbed the idea of natural selection from economics, but it may still be right. As the German socialist Karl Kautsky wrote in 1902: "The fact that an idea emanates from a particular class, or accords with their interests, of course proves nothing as to its truth or falsity." In this case, it is ironic that Adam Smith's system of laissez faire does not work in his own domain of economics, for it leads to oligopoly and revolution, rather than to order and harmony. Struggle among individuals does, however, seem to be the law of nature. **(23)**

Many people use such arguments about social context to ascribe great insights primarily to the indefinable phenomenon of good luck. Thus, Darwin was lucky to be born rich, lucky to be on the *Beagle*, lucky to live amidst the ideas of his age, lucky to trip over Parson Malthus—essentially little more than a man in the right place at the right time. Yet, when we read of his personal struggle to understand, the breadth of his concerns and study, and the directedness of his search for a mechanism of evolution, we understand why Pasteur made his famous quip that fortune favors the prepared mind. **(24)**

Vocabulary

In your journal, write the meanings of the following words:

- is *fatuous* (4)
- an *ineffable* something (5)
- the *hagiography* of science (7)
- the *nemesis* of preachers (9)
- the *marsupial fauna* of Australia (9)
- *speciation* (10)
- British Museum *ornithologist* (11)
- a created *archetype* (12)
- *metaphysics* on morals (14)
- *serendipitous* flash (15)
- the immediate *precipitators* (20)
- an extended *analogy* (21)
- *laissez faire* economics (21)
- harmonious *polity* (21)
- leads to *oligopoly* (23)

Questions for Writing and Discussion

1. In your own words, explain the two "extremes" of inductivism and eurekaism. Describe Darwin's middle path through these extremes.

2. In the course of his essay, Gould defines both "genius" and "natural selection." Identify sentences from the essay that describe or define these terms.

3. Argument begins with a debatable proposition or question. In your own words, state the question that Gould addresses. Identify the "pro" side of this argument (Gould's position) and the "con" side (the position that Gould argues against).

4. In argument, refutations of opposing positions must be supported by evidence, testimony, facts, statistics, or other data. Find two paragraphs in which Gould refutes an opposing argument. List the evidence that Gould provides in that paragraph. Which evidence best supports Gould's argument?

5. Gould has written a monthly column, "This View of Life," for *Natural History* magazine. Review a copy of *Natural History* and then profile Gould's intended audience. Where in "Darwin's Middle Road" does Gould appeal to this audience?

6. Gould popularizes his subjects without trivializing them. Compare Gould's essay with David Quammen's essay in Chapter 7. Assuming that your class is the target audience, which essay does the best job of informing this audience about the subject? Cite examples from each essay of vocabulary, sentence length, tone, organization, and content to support your evaluation.

ARGUING: PROFESSIONAL WRITING

THE DAMNATION OF A CANYON

EDWARD ABBEY

"In wildness is the preservation of the world." Henry David Thoreau's words serve to introduce Edward Abbey's own nature ethic. Beginning with the classic Desert Solitaire *(1968) and including* The Monkey Wrench Gang *(1975),* Abbey's Road *(1979), and* Down the River *(1982), Abbey's writings celebrate the American West, its deserts, canyons, mountains, and rivers. But always in full view are Abbey's villains in the black hats: Industrialists, Bureaucrats, and Developers. And Dammers. In this selection, taken from* Beyond the Wall *(1984), Abbey*

contrasts the Eden that was Glen Canyon with the stagnant, lifeless waters of Lake Powell. Abbey's argument is shaped by a clear outline—his claim, his refutation of the opposing view, his analysis of consequences, and his solution—but also by Abbey's insistent, cranky, and passionate voice that echoes throughout the essay.

CRITICAL READING

In class, students may comment that Abbey "breaks the rules" of argument. He does not follow the guidelines outlined in the first three paragraphs of this chapter. Instead of fairly countering opposing arguments with evidence, he occasionally resorts to exaggeration and ridicule. Ask students to decide whether Abbey's essay is, in fact, a good model of argumentation. Which of Abbey's tactics should they use in their own essays? The resulting discussion should illustrate the difference between "rational" argument (see Gould's essay) and other, more emotional forms of *persuasion*. Let the class determine the guidelines for their particular assignments.

There was a time when, in my search for essences, I concluded that the canyonland country has no heart. I was wrong. The canyonlands did have a heart, a living heart, and that heart was Glen Canyon and the golden, flowing Colorado River. **(1)**

In the summer of 1959 a friend and I made a float trip in little rubber rafts down through the length of Glen Canyon, starting at Hite and getting off the river near Gunsight Butte—The Crossing of the Fathers. In this voyage of some 150 miles and ten days our only motive power, and all that we needed, was the current of the Colorado River. **(2)**

In the summer and fall of 1967 I worked as a seasonal park ranger at the new Glen Canyon National Recreation Area. During my five-month tour of duty I worked at the main marina and headquarters area called Wahweap, at Bullfrog Basin toward the upper end of the reservoir, and finally at Lee's Ferry downriver from Glen Canyon Dam. In a number of powerboat tours I was privileged to see almost all of our nation's newest, biggest and most impressive "recreational facility." **(3)**

Having thus seen Glen Canyon both before and after what we may fairly call its damnation, I feel that I am in a position to evaluate the transformation of the region caused by construction of the dam. I have had the unique opportunity to observe firsthand some of the differences between the environment of a free river and a powerplant reservoir. **(4)**

One should admit at the outset to a certain bias. Indeed I am a "butterfly chaser, googly eyed bleeding heart and wild conservative." I take a dim view of dams; I find it hard to learn to love cement; I am poorly impressed by concrete aggregates and statistics in the cubic tons. But in this weakness I am not alone, for I belong to that ever-growing number of Americans, probably a good majority now, who have become aware that a fully industrialized, thoroughly urbanized, elegantly computerized social system is not suitable for human habitation. Great for machines, yes: But unfit for people. **(5)**

Lake Powell, formed by Glen Canyon Dam, is not a lake. It is a reservoir, with a constantly fluctuating water level—more like a bathtub that is never drained than a true lake. As at Hoover (or Boulder) Dam, the sole practical function of this impounded water is to drive the turbines that generate electricity in the powerhouse at the base of the dam. Recreational benefits were of secondary importance in the minds of those who conceived and built this dam. As a result the volume of water in the reservoir is continually being increased or decreased according to the requirements of the Basin States Compact and the power-grid system of which Glen Canyon Dam is a component. **(6)**

The rising and falling water level entails various consequences. One of the most obvious, well known to all who have seen Lake Mead, is the "bathtub ring" left on the canyon walls after each drawdown of water, or what rangers at Glen Canyon call the Bathtub Foundation. This phenomenon is perhaps of no more than aesthetic importance; yet it is sufficient to dispel any illusion one might have, in contemplating the scene, that you are looking upon a natural lake. **(7)**

The utter barrenness of the reservoir shoreline recalls by contrast the aspect of things before the dam, when Glen Canyon formed the course of the untamed Colorado. Then we had a wild and flowing river lined by boulder-strewn shores, sandy beaches, thickets of tamarisk and willow, and glades of cottonwoods. **(8)**

The thickets teemed with songbirds: vireos, warblers, mockingbirds and thrushes. On the open beaches were killdeer, sandpipers, herons, ibises, egrets. Living in grottoes in the canyon walls were swallows, swifts, hawks, wrens and owls. Beaver were common if not abundant: not an evening would pass, in drifting down the river, that we did not see them or at least hear the whack of their flat tails on the water. Above the river shores were the great recessed alcoves where water seeped from the sandstone, nourishing the semitropical hanging gardens of orchid, ivy and columbine, with their associated swarms of insects and birdlife. **(9)**

Up most of the side canyon, before damnation, there were springs, sometimes flowing streams, waterfalls and plunge pools—the kind of marvels you can now find only in such small scale remnants of Glen Canyon as the Escalante area. In the rich flora of these laterals the larger mammals—mule deer, coyote, bobcat, ring-tailed cat, gray fox, kit fox, skunk, badger and others—found a home. When the river was dammed almost all of these things were lost. Crowded out—or drowned and buried under mud. **(10)**

The difference between the present reservoir, with its silent sterile shores and debris choked side canyons, and the original Glen Canyon, is the difference between death and life. Glen Canyon was alive. Lake Powell is a graveyard. **(11)**

For those who may think I exaggerate the contrast between the former river canyon and the present man-made impoundment, I suggest a trip on Lake Powell followed immediately by another boat trip on the river below the dam. Take a boat from Lee's Ferry up the river to within sight of the dam, then shut off the motor and allow yourself the rare delight of a quiet, effortless drifting down the stream. In that twelve-mile stretch of living green, singing birds, flowing water and untarnished canyon walls—sights and sounds a million years older and infinitely lovelier than the roar of motorboats—you will rediscover a small and imperfect sampling of the kind of experience that was taken away from everybody when the oligarchs and politicians condemned our river for purposes of their own. **(12)**

Lake Powell, though not a lake, may well be as its defenders assert the most beautiful reservoir in the world. Certainly it has a photogenic backdrop of buttes and mesas projecting above the expansive surface of stagnant waters where the speedboats, houseboats and cabin cruisers play. But it is no longer a wilderness. It is no longer a place of natural life. It is no longer Glen Canyon. **(13)**

The defenders of the dam argue that the recreational benefits available on the surface of the reservoir outweigh the loss of Indian ruins, historical sites, wildlife and wilderness adventure. Relying on the familiar quantitative logic of business and bureaucracy, they assert that whereas only a few thousand citizens even ventured down the river through Glen Canyon, now millions can—or will—enjoy the motorized boating and hatchery fishing available on the reservoir. They will also argue that the rising waters behind the dam have made such places as Rainbow Bridge accessible by powerboat. Formerly you could get there only by walking (six miles). **(14)**

This argument appeals to the wheelchair ethos of the wealthy, upper-middle-class American slob. If Rainbow Bridge is worth seeing at all, then by God it should be easily, readily, immediately available to everybody with the money to buy a big powerboat. Why should a trip to such a place be the privilege only of those who are willing to walk six miles? Or if Pikes Peak is worth getting to, then why not build a highway to the top of it so that anyone can get there? Anytime? Without effort? Or as my old man would say, "By Christ, one man's just as good as another—if not a damn sight better." **(15)**

It is quite true that the flooding of Glen Canyon has opened up to the motorboat explorer parts of side canyons that formerly could be reached only by people able to walk. But the sum total of terrain visible to the eye and touchable by hand and foot has been greatly diminished, not increased. Because of the dam the river is gone, the inner canyon is gone, the best parts of the numerous side canyons are gone—all hidden beneath hundreds of feet of polluted water, accumulating silt, and mounting tons of trash. This portion of Glen Canyon—and who can estimate how many cubic miles were lost?—*is no longer accessible to anybody*. (Except scuba divers.) And this, do not forget, was the most valuable part of Glen Canyon, richest in scenery, archaeology, history, flora and fauna. **(16)**

Not only has the heart of Glen Canyon been buried, but many of the side canyons above the fluctuating waterline are now rendered more difficult, not easier, to get into. This because the debris brought down into them by desert storms, no longer carried away by the river, must unavoidably build up in the area where flood meets reservoir. Narrow Canyon, for example, at the head of the impounded waters, is already beginning to silt up and to amass huge quantities of driftwood, some of it floating on the surface, some of it half afloat beneath the surface. Anyone who has tried to pilot a motorboat through a raft of half-sunken logs and bloated dead cows will have his own thoughts on the accessibility of these waters. **(17)**

Second, the question of costs. It is often stated that the dam and its reservoir have opened up to the many what was formerly restricted to the few, implying in this case that what was once expensive has now been made cheap. Exactly the opposite is true. **(18)**

Before the dam, a float trip down the river through Glen Canyon would cost you a minimum of seven days' time, well within anyone's vacation allotment, and a capital outlay of about forty dollars—the prevailing price of a two-man rubber boat with oars, available at any army-navy surplus store. A life jacket might be useful but not required, for there were no dangerous rapids in the 150 miles of Glen Canyon. As the name implies, this stretch of the river was in fact so easy and gentle that the trip could be and was made by all sorts of amateurs: by Boy Scouts, Camp Fire Girls, stenographers, schoolteachers, students, little old ladies in inner tubes. Guides, professional boatmen, giant pontoons, outboard motors, radios, rescue equipment were not needed. The Glen Canyon float trip was an adventure anyone could enjoy, on his own, for a cost less than that of spending two days and nights in a Page motel. Even food was there, in the water: the channel catfish were easier to catch and a lot better eating than the striped bass and rainbow trout dumped by the ton into the reservoir these days. And one other thing: at the end of the float trip you still owned your boat, usable for many more such casual and carefree expeditions. **(19)**

What is the situation now? Float trips are no longer possible. The only way left for the exploration of the reservoir and what remains of Glen Canyon demands the use of a powerboat. Here you have three options: (1) buy your own boat and engine, the necessary auxiliary equipment, the fuel to keep it moving, the parts and repairs to keep it running, the permits and licenses required for legal operation, the trailer to transport it; (2) rent a boat; or (3) go on a commercial excursion boat, packed in with other sightseers, following a preplanned itinerary. This kind of play is only for the affluent. **(20)**

The inescapable conclusion is that no matter how one attempts to calculate the cost in dollars and cents, a float trip down Glen Canyon was much cheaper than a powerboat tour of the reservoir. Being less expensive, as well as safer and easier, the float trip was an adventure open to far more people than will ever be able to afford motorboat excursions in the area now. **(21)**

All of the foregoing would be nothing but a futile exercise in nostalgia (so much water over the dam) if I had nothing constructive and concrete to offer. But I do. As alternate methods of power generation are developed, such as solar, and as the nation establishes a way of life adapted to actual resources and basic needs, so that the demand for electrical power begins to diminish, we can shut down the Glen Canyon power plant, open the diversion tunnels, and drain the reservoir. **(22)**

This will no doubt expose a drear and hideous scene: immense mud flats and whole plateaus of sodden garbage strewn with dead trees, sunken boats, the skeletons of long-forgotten, decomposing water-skiers. But to those who find the prospect too appalling, I say give nature a little time. In five years, at most in ten, the sun and wind and storms will cleanse and sterilize the repellent mess. The inevitable floods will soon remove all that does not belong within the canyons. Fresh green willow, box elder and redbud will reappear; and the ancient drowned cottonwoods (noble monuments to themselves) will be replaced by young of their own kind. With the renewal of plant life will come the insects, the birds, the lizards and snakes, the mammals. Within a generation—thirty years—I predict the river and canyons will bear a decent resemblance to their former selves. Within the lifetime of our children Glen Canyon and the living river, heart of the canyonlands, will be restored to us. The wilderness will again belong to God, the people and the wild things that call it home. **(23)**

Vocabulary

Look up the meanings of the following words:

- concrete *aggregates* (5)
- *aesthetic* importance (7)
- recessed *alcoves* (9)
- *oligarchs* and politicians (12)
- the wheelchair *ethos* (15)
- richest in . . . *archaeology* (16)
- preplanned *itinerary* (20)
- a *drear* and hideous scene (23)

Questions for Writing and Discussion

1. Do you consider yourself an "environmentalist"—someone who is in favor of preserving wild rivers, designating wilderness areas, and forbidding mining, grazing, or the use of motorized vehicles in national parks? Or do you believe that federal lands, parks, and rivers should serve multiple uses? Explain, using a state or national park you have visited to give specific examples.

2. Which of Abbey's arguments did you find most persuasive? Which were least persuasive? Are there opposing arguments that Abbey does not answer? Explain, *referring to your own beliefs* outlined above.

3. An argument contains a *claim, reasons* that support the claim or refute the opposition, and *evidence.*

- What sentence or sentences best illustrate Abbey's overall claim or thesis for this essay? Does he make a claim of fact, value, cause, or solution—or some combination of these? Explain.
- List the *reasons* Abbey gives to support his claim and refute the opposing arguments.
- For *one* of his reasons, list the evidence, facts, examples, or testimony that Abbey gives.

4. Note passages in which Abbey's *appeal to character* is evident. Where is he most reasonable? Where is he most cantankerous or even misanthropic? Are these facets of his character consistent with the persona portrayed in paragraph 5? In your judgment, does his appeal to character help or hurt his argument? Explain.

5. Cite one sentence in which Abbey uses an *emotional appeal.* Does this sentence make his argument more effective?

6. Assume you are the controller of the Glen Canyon dam. Write a short response to Abbey explaining why his solution—to "open the diversion tunnels, and drain the reservoir"—is absurd. Choose either an adversarial or a Rogerian strategy, whichever would work best for Abbey.

ARGUING: THE WRITING PROCESS

■ **ASSIGNMENT FOR ARGUING** For this assignment, choose a subject that interests *you* or relates to *your own* experience. You may even choose a subject that you have already written about for this class. Then examine the subject for a debatable claim of fact, value, cause and effect, or policy that you could make about it. If the claim is arguable, you have a focus for your arguing paper. Analyze your probable audience to guide your argumentative strategy. (Avoid ready-made pro/con subjects such as abortion, drinking age, drugs, and euthanasia *unless* you have clear beliefs based on your own experience.)

TEACHING TIP

Advise students to be prepared to reverse their claims if they find the evidence on the opposing side more compelling. Some teachers require students to write short papers or briefs defending the *opposing positions* before they draft their own.

Choosing a Subject

If a journal entry suggested a possible subject, do the collecting-and-shaping strategies. Otherwise, consider the following ideas:

- Review your journal entries from previous chapters and the papers that you have already written for this class. Test these subjects for an arguable claim that you could make, opposing arguments you could consider, and an appropriate audience for an argumentative piece of writing.
- Brainstorm possible ideas for argumentative subjects from the other courses you are currently taking or have taken. What controversial issues in psychology, art, philosophy, journalism, biology, nutrition, engineering, physical education, or literature have you discussed in your classes? Ask current or past instructors for possible controversial topics relating to their courses.
- Newspapers and magazines are full of controversial subjects in sports, medicine, law, business, and family. Browse through current issues looking for possible subjects. Check news items, editorials, and cartoons. Look for subjects related to your own interests, your job, your leisure activities, or your experiences.
- Interview your friends, family, or classmates. What controversial issues are affecting their lives most directly? What would they most like to change about their lives? What has irritated or angered them most in the recent past?

You can write about anything, and if you write well enough, even the reader with no intrinsic interest in the subject will become involved.
—TRACY KIDDER, NOVELIST

Collecting

NARROWING AND FOCUSING YOUR CLAIM Narrow your subject to a specific topic and sharpen your focus by applying the "Wh" questions. If your subject is "grades" your responses might be as follows:

Subject: Grades

- *Who:* College students
- *What:* Letter grades
- *When:* In freshman and sophomore years
- *Where:* Especially in nonmajor courses
- *Why:* What purpose do grades serve in nonmajor courses?

Determine what claim or claims you want to make. Make sure that your claim is *arguable*. (Remember that claims can overlap; an argument may combine several related claims.)

Claim of Fact:

- Letter grades exist. (not arguable)
- Employers consider grades when hiring. (slightly more arguable, but not very controversial)
- Grades do not measure learning. (very arguable)

Claim about Cause or Effect:

- Grades create anxiety for students. (not very arguable)
- Grades actually prevent discovery and learning. (arguable)

Claim about Value:

- Grades are not fair. (not very arguable: "fairness" can usually be determined)
- Grades are bad because they discourage individual initiative. (arguable)
- Grades are good because they give students an incentive to learn. (arguable)

Claim about a Solution or Policy:

- Grades should be eliminated altogether. (arguable—but difficult)
- Grades should be eliminated in humanities courses. (arguable)
- Grades should change to pass/fail in nonmajor courses. (arguable—and more practical)

Focusing and narrowing your *claim* helps determine what evidence you need to collect. Use your observing, remembering, and investigative skills to gather the evidence. *Note:* An argumentative essay should not be a mathematical equation that uses only abstract and impersonal evidence. *Your experience* can be crucial to a successful argumentative essay. Start by doing the *remembering* exercises. Your audience wants to know not only why you are writing on this particular *topic*, but also why the subject is of interest to *you*.

REMEMBERING Use *freewriting, looping, branching,* or *clustering* to recall experiences, ideas, events, and people who are relevant to your claim. If you are writing about grades, brainstorm about how *your* teachers used grades, how you reacted to specific grades in one specific class, how your friends or parents reacted, and what you felt or thought. These prewriting exercises will help you understand your claim and give you specific examples that you can use for evidence.

OBSERVING If possible for your topic, collect data and evidence by observing, firsthand, the facts, values, effects, or possible solutions related to your claim. *Repeated* observation will give you good inductive evidence to support your argument.

INVESTIGATING For most argumentative essays, some research or investigation is essential. Because it is difficult to imagine all the valid counterarguments, interview friends, classmates, family, co-workers, and authorities on your topic. From the library, gather books and articles that contain arguments in support of your claim. *Note:* As you do research in the library, make photocopies of key passages from relevant sources to hand in with your essay. If you cite sources from your research, list them on a "Work Cited" page following your essay. (See Chapter 12 for the proper format.)

TEACHING TIP

To reduce the number of "canned" argumentative essays, emphasize these remembering activities. Even if students decide not to use examples from their own lives, understanding their experiences in light of the public controversy will help them sharpen their stances.

TEACHING TIP

Allow students sufficient time to gather information. To avoid having research overwhelm students, remind them that this paper is not a contest to see who can find the most sources. They should read until they learn about the major arguments on both sides. Four to eight written sources should be sufficient.

SHAPING

As you begin your shaping activities, reconsider your audience. Imagine one real person who might be among your readers. Is this person open-minded and likely to be convinced by your evidence? Does this person represent the opposing position? Would a Rogerian strategy be effective in this case? Reread your collecting notes and *underline* the reasons and evidence that would be most effective for this reader. After reconsidering your audience and rereading your collecting notes, try the shaping strategies below.

No one can write decently who is distrustful of the reader's intelligence, or whose attitude is patronizing.
—E.B. WHITE, ESSAYIST

LIST OF "PRO" AND "CON" ARGUMENTS Either on paper or in a computer file, write out your *claim* and then list the arguments for your position ("Pro") and the arguments for the opposing position ("Con"). After you have made the list, match up arguments by drawing lines, as indicated below. (On the computer file, move "Con" arguments so they appear directly opposite the corresponding "Pro" arguments.)

Claim: Grades should be changed to pass/fail in nonmajor courses.

PRO	CON
Grades inhibit learning by putting too much emphasis on competition.	Grades actually promote learning by getting students to study as hard as possible.
Pass/fail grading encourages students to explore nonmajor fields.	Students should be encouraged to compete with majors. They may want to change majors and need to know if they can compete.
Grade competition with majors in the field can be discouraging.	If students don't have traditional grading, they won't take nonmajor courses seriously.
Some students do better without the pressure of grades; they need to find out if they can motivate themselves without grades, but they shouldn't have to risk grades in their major field to discover that.	

If some pro and con arguments "match," you will be able to argue against the con and for your claim at the same time. If some arguments do not "match," you will need to consider them separately. The outlines below suggest ways of organizing your pro and con arguments.

OUTLINES FOR ARGUMENTS For more than two thousand years, writers and speakers have been trying to determine the most effective means to persuade audiences. One of the oldest outlines for a successful argument comes from classical rhetoric. The following six-part outline is intended as a guideline rather than a rigid list. Test this outline; see if it will work for *your* argument.

Introduction:	Announces subject; *gets audience's interest and attention;* establishes a trustworthy character for the writer
Narration:	Gives *background,* context, statement of problem, or definition
Partition:	States thesis or *claim,* outlines or *maps* arguments

Argument:	Makes *arguments* and gives *evidence* for the claim or thesis
Refutation:	Shows why *opposing arguments* are not true or valid
Conclusion:	Summarizes arguments, suggests solution, *ties into the introduction or background*

Most arguments have these features, but not necessarily in this order. Some writers prefer to refute opposing arguments *before* giving the arguments in support of their claims. When con and pro arguments match, refuting an argument followed by the argument for your claim may work best. As you organize your own arguments, put your *strongest* argument last and your *weakest* argument either first or in the middle.

Because most short argumentative essays contain the introduction, narration, and partition all in a few introductory paragraphs, you may use the following abbreviated outlines for argument:

Outline #1	Introduction (attention getter, background, claim or thesis, map)
	Your arguments
	Refutation of opposing arguments
	Conclusion
Outline #2	Introduction
	Refutation of opposing arguments
	Your arguments
	Conclusion
Outline #3	Introduction
	Refutation of first opposing argument that matches your first argument
	Refutation of second opposing argument that matches your second argument, and so on
	Additional arguments
	Conclusion

For Rogerian arguments, you can follow one of the above outlines, but the emphasis, tone, and attitude are different:

Introduction:	Attention getter, background
	Claim (often downplayed to reduce threat)
	Map (often omitted)
	Appeal to character (crucial to Rogerian argument)
Opposing Arguments:	State opposing arguments fairly

	Show where, how, or when those arguments may be valid; establish common ground
Your Arguments:	State your position fairly
	Show where, how, or when your arguments are valid
Resolution:	Present compromise position
	State your solution to the problem and show its advantages to both sides

Computer Tip: Shaping and Drafting

If you already have your draft on a computer file, you can quickly move paragraphs around to change your outline. First, print a copy of your current draft. If, for example, you are using *Outline #1* (above), shift your paragraphs around to fit *Outline #2*. Your arguments will now come last. Print a copy of this reorganized version. Read both versions, or have a reader compare both versions. Which is more effective?

Similarly, the computer will allow you to *reorder* your arguments. If you put your weakest argument first and your strongest last, perhaps you would like to see how the argument would read if you hid your weakest argument in the middle. Print a copy of your current draft, rearrange the paragraphs, and print a second copy for comparison.

In both cases, you will need to rewrite connections and transitions, but the computer can let you see how another sequence or organization might work. If you like your first version best, you can switch back in just a few seconds.

Developing Arguments Think of your argument as a series of *because* statements, each supported by evidence, statistics, testimony, expert opinion, data, specific examples from your experience, or a combination of these.

THESIS OR CLAIM: Grades should be abolished in nonmajor courses

Reason #1 Because they may keep a student from attempting a difficult nonmajor course

Statistics, testimony, data, and examples

TEACHING TIP

As beginning writers attempt to incorporate research in arguing essays, they frequently allow their research materials to dominate their arguments. Typically, they resort to the "quotation quilt"—colorful patches of quotations that lack focus and coherence. Equally common is the "one-legged" essay whose argument and evidence rely excessively on one source. To reduce these problems, schedule an *in-class essay* a week before the final draft is due. Students should write out their arguments, using their own words, as fully as possible. Once writers have articulated their positions, it is easier to subordinate evidence to the writer's argument.

Reason #2 Because competition with majors in the field can be discouraging

Statistics, testimony, data, and examples

Reason #3 Because grades inhibit students learning in nonmajor fields

Statistics, testimony, data, and examples

You can develop each reason using a variety of strategies. The following strategies may help you generate additional reasons and examples.

Definition: Define the crucial terms or ideas. (What do you mean by "learning"?)

Comparison: Compare the background, situation, context with another similar context. (What other schools have tried pass/fail grading for nonmajor courses? How has it worked?)

Process: How does or should a change occur? (How do nonmajors become discouraged? How should a school implement pass/fail in grading?)

These strategies may help you develop an argument coherently and effectively. If several strategies are possible, consider which would be most effective for your *audience*.

RESEARCH TIP

When you draft your arguing essay, don't let your citations or direct quotations overpower your own argument. Two tactics will keep you in control of your argument:

First, "sandwich" your quotations. *Introduce* quotations by referring to the author, the source, and/or the author's study. *Follow* quotations with a sentence or two explaining how the author's evidence supports your argument. For examples, see paragraphs 8 and 9 in the essay by student writer Jim Haas.

Second, keep your direct quotations *short.* If possible, reduce a long passage to one sentence and incorporate the quoted material in the flow of your own language. For example, in his essay at the end of the chapter, Haas writes,

> In fact, twenty-nine other countries have mandatory seat belt laws. "Where statistics are available," Transportation Secretary Dole says, "they show that highway deaths have declined by an average of 25 percent." (34)

DRAFTING You will never really know "enough" about your subject or have "enough" evidence. At some point, however, you must stop collecting and start your draft. The most frequent problem with drafting an argumentative essay is delaying the actual writing too long, until the deadline is too close.

For argumentative essays, start with a working order or sequence and sketch an outline on paper or in your head. Additional examples and appeals to reason, character, or emotion may occur to you as you develop your argument or refute opposing arguments. In addition, if you have done some research, have your notes, photocopies of key data, statistics, quotations, and citations of authorities close at hand. As you write, you will discover that some information or arguments simply don't fit into the flow of your essay. Don't force arguments into your draft if they no longer seem to belong.

PEER RESPONSE

Writer: Before you exchange drafts with a peer reader, provide the following information about your essay:

1. (a) intended audience

(b) primary claim or thesis

(c) opposing arguments that you refute

(d) arguments supporting your claim

2. Write out one or two questions about your draft that you want your reader to answer.

Reader: Read the writer's entire draft. As you *reread*, answer the following questions:

1. *Arguments.* Without looking at the writer's responses above, describe the essay's (a) target audience, (b) primary claim, (c) opposing arguments that are refuted, (d) arguments supporting the claim. Which of these did you have trouble identifying? What additional pro or con arguments should the writer consider?

2. *Organization.* Identify the following parts of the writer's draft: introduction, narration, partition, argument, refutation, and conclusion. Does the writer need all of these for his or her particular subject and audience? Why or why not? Where could the writer clarify transitions between sections? Explain.

3. *Appeals.* Identify places where the writer appeals to reason, to character, and to emotion. Where could these appeals be stronger? Identify sentences where the writer is overly emotional or illogical (see the section on "Revising Fallacies in Logic").

4. *Evidence.* Identify at least one paragraph in which the supporting evidence is strong. Then identify at least one paragraph in which the writer makes assertions without sufficient supporting evidence. What kind of evidence might the writer use—firsthand observation, personal examples, testimony from experts, interviews, statistics, or other? Explain.

5. *Revision Plan.* List three key changes that the writer should make during the revision.

6. Answer the writer's questions above.

Writer: When your essay is returned, read the comments by your peer reader(s) and do the following:

1. Compare your descriptions of the audience, claim, and pro and con arguments with your reader's descriptions. Where there are differences, clarify your essay.

2. Read all of your peer reader's responses. List revisions that you intend to make in each of the following areas: *arguments, organization, appeals,* and *supporting evidence.*

REVISING

Argumentation is the most public of the purposes for writing. It requires that you become aware of many different points of view. You must counter the arguments of others and recognize the flaws in your own logic. Test your argument by having friends or classmates read it. Explain your claim, your focus, and your intended audience. Ask your readers to look for possible opposing arguments that you need to counter or weaknesses in your own argument or evidence. Were your appeals effective? Ask them if your argument should be more adversarial or more Rogerian.

Guidelines for Revision

- **When you finish your draft, reconsider your *audience.*** Persuading your audience requires that you tailor your reasons and evidence to your audience and situation. Do an audience analysis, and then reread your draft and make appropriate changes.
- **Ask a class member or friend to read your draft to determine the intended audience for your argument.** See which arguments your reader thinks would not be effective for your audience.
- **Ask your reader to tell you what kind of *claim* you are making, whether your arguments or counterarguments are logical, and whether your ethical or emotional appeals are effective for your audience.**
- **Which of your *because* arguments are most effective?** Least effective? Should you change the outline or structure that you initially chose?
- **Revise your draft to avoid fallacies or errors in reasoning.** Errors in logic create two problems: They can destroy your rational appeal and open your argument to a logical rebuttal, and they lessen your credibility—and thus reduce your appeal to your character. (Review the list below.)
- **Support your reasons with evidence: *data, facts, statistics, quotations, observations, testimony, statistics, or specific examples from your experience.*** Check your collecting notes once again for additional evidence to add to your weakest argument. Is there a weak or unsupported argument that you should simply omit?
- **Signal the major arguments and counterarguments in your partition or map.** Between paragraphs, use clear transitions and paragraph hooks.
- **If you cite sources in your essay, check the *accuracy* of statistics, quotations, and source references.** (See Chapter 12 for the proper format of in-text documentation and "Works Cited" page.)
- **Revise sentences to improve conciseness and clarity.**
- **Edit sentences for grammar, punctuation, and spelling.**

Revising Fallacies in Logic

Listed below are common fallacies in logic. Reread your draft or your peer's draft and revise as appropriate to avoid these logical errors.

- *Hasty Generalization:* Conclusion not logically justified by sufficient or unbiased evidence. If your friend Mary tells you that Professor Paramecium is a hard grader because he gave her a 36

Collaborative Activity

To encourage students to revise rather than merely edit argumentative drafts, have students trade essay drafts. Each student should then write for fifteen minutes, *defending the position that the writer is trying to refute.* What important opposing arguments does the writer not consider? How could the writer's position be attacked? What assertions are not supported by evidence? What is logically faulty in the writer's argument? (See "Fallacies in Logic.") Then have students return essays and their responses to the writers. Writers should use the responses to help revise their essays.

TEACHING TIP

Review these fallacies *after* the students have drafted first versions. Teachers or students in small groups should be able to find other examples of faulty logic from the students' own drafts. Because problems in reasoning can undermine a whole essay, students should receive feedback from teachers or peer reviewers before the essay is evaluated.

In television, anchors, moderators, or talk show hosts sometimes serve as critical voices. Note how Ted Koppel or Barbara Walters point out weaknesses or fallacies in opposing arguments.

percent on the first biology test, she is making a hasty generalization. It may be *true*—Prof P. may *be* a difficult grader—but Mary's logic is not valid. She cannot logically draw that conclusion from a sample of one; the rest of the class may have received grades of between 80 and 100.

- *Post Hoc Ergo Propter Hoc:* Literally, "after this, therefore because of this." Just because event B *occurred after* event A, it does not mean that A *necessarily caused* B. You washed your car in the morning, and it rained in the afternoon. Though we joke about how it always rains after we wash the car, there is, of course, no causal relationship between the two events. "I forgot to leave the porch light on when I went out last night, and someone robbed my house." Without further evidence, we cannot assume that the lack of light contributed to the robbery. A more obvious cause might be the back door you left unlocked.
- *Genetic Fallacy:* Arguing that the *origins* of a person, object, or institution determine its character, nature, or worth. Like the "post hoc" fallacy, the genetic fallacy is an error in causal relationships.

  This automobile was made in Detroit. It'll probably fall apart after 10,000 miles.

  He speaks with a funny oriental accent. He's really stupid, you know.

  He started Celestial Seasonings Herb Teas just to make a quick buck; it's just another phony yuppie product.

The second half of each statement *may* or *may not* be true; the logical error is in assuming that the origin of something will necessarily determine its worth or quality. Stereotyping is frequently caused by a genetic fallacy.

- *Begging the Question:* Loading the conclusion in the claim. Arguing that "pornography should be banned because it corrupts our youth" is a logical claim. However, saying that "filthy and corrupting pornography should be banned" is begging the question: the conclusion that the writer should *prove* (that pornography corrupts) is *assumed* in the claim. Other examples: "Those useless psychology classes should be dropped from the curriculum"; "Senator Swingle's sexist behavior should be censured by Congress"; "Everyone knows that our ineffective drug control program is a miserable failure." The writers must *prove* that the psychology classes are useless, that Senator Swingle is sexist, and that the drug program is a failure.
- *Circular Argument:* A sentence or argument that restates rather than proves. Thus, it goes in a circle: "President Reagan was a

great communicator because he had that knack of talking effectively to the people." The terms in the beginning of the sentence ("great communicator") and the end of the sentence ("talking effectively") are interchangeable. The sentence ends where it started.

- *Either/Or:* An oversimplification that reduces alternatives to only two choices, thereby creating a false dilemma. Statements such as "love it or leave it" attempt to reduce the alternatives to two. If you don't love your school, your town, or your country, you don't have to leave: A third choice is to change it and make it better. Proposed solutions frequently have an "either/or" fallacy: "Either we ban boxing or hundreds of young men will be senselessly killed." A third alternative is to change boxing's rules or equipment. "If we don't provide farmers with low-interest loans, they will go bankrupt." Increasing prices for farm products might be a better alternative.
- *Faulty Comparison or Analogy:* Basing an argument on a comparison of two things, ideas, events, or situations that are similar but not identical. Although comparisons or analogies are often effective in argument, they can hide logical problems. "We can solve the cocaine problem the same way we reduced the DWI problem: Attack it with increased enforcement and mandatory jail sentences." Although the situations are similar, they are not identical. The DWI solution will not necessarily work on drugs. An analogy is an extended comparison that uses something simple or familiar to explain something complex or less familiar. "Solving a mathematics problem is like baking a cake: You have to take it one step at a time. First you assemble your ingredients or your known data. . . ." Like baking, solving a problem does involve a process; unlike baking, however, mathematics is more exact. Changing the amount of flour in a recipe by 1 percent will not make the cake fall; changing a numeric value by 1 percent, however, may ruin the whole problem. The point, however, is *not* to avoid comparisons or analogies. Simply make sure that your conclusions are qualified; acknowledge the *differences* between the two things compared as well as the similarities.
- *Ad Hominem (literally, "to the man"):* An attack on the character of the individual or the opponent rather than his or her actual opinions, arguments, or qualifications. "Susan Davidson, the prosecuting attorney, drinks heavily. There's no way she can present an effective case." This is an attack on Ms. Davidson's character rather than an analysis of her legal talents. Her record in court may be excellent.

- *Ad Populum (literally, "to the people"):* An emotional appeal to positive concepts (God, mother, country, liberty, democracy, apple pie) or negative concepts (fascism, atheism) rather than a direct discussion of the real issue: "Those senators voting to increase the defense budget are really warmongers at heart." "If you are a true American, you should be for tariffs to protect the garment industry."
- *Red Herring and Straw Man:* Diversionary tactics designed to avoid confronting the key issue. *Red herring* refers to the practice of dragging a smelly fish across the trail to divert tracking dogs away from the real quarry. A "red herring" occurs when writers avoid countering an opposing argument directly: "Of course equal pay for women is an important issue, but I wonder whether women really want to take the responsibility that comes with higher paying jobs? Do they really want the additional stress?" This writer diverts attention away from the argument about equal pay to another issue, stress—thus, a "red herring." In the *straw man* diversion, the writer sets up an artificially easy argument to refute in place of the real issue. Former President Richard Nixon's famous "Checkers" speech is a good example. Accused of spending $18,000 in campaign gifts for personal use, Nixon described how he received Checkers, a little black-and-white spotted cocker spaniel dog. Because his daughter Tricia loved this dog, Nixon decided to keep it. Surely, there's nothing wrong with that, is there? The "Checkers" argument is a "straw man" diversion: justifying his personal use of this gift is much easier than explaining how and why he spent the $18,000. Avoid "red herring" and "straw man" by either refuting an argument directly or acknowledging that it has some merit. Don't just change the subject.

■ **POSTSCRIPT ON THE WRITING PROCESS** In your journal, answer the following questions.

1. Describe how your beliefs about your subject changed from the time you decided on your claim until you revised your essay. What caused the change in your views?

2. What opposing argument was most difficult to counter? Explain how you handled it.

3. Which was your strongest argument? Did you use logical appeals and evidence, or did you rely more on appeals to character or emotion? Explain.

4. How did your writing process for the argumentative essay change from previous essays? What steps or stages took longer? What stages did you have to go back and rework?

ARGUMENT: STUDENT WRITING

PROTECT YOURSELF—BUCKLE UP!

JIM HAAS

Jim Haas decided to write his arguing paper about seat-belt laws, primarily because he had been in several accidents and had failed to fasten his own seat belt. He began collecting for this paper by writing a narrative of his own experience. Then, once he realized that he had a good subject, he read some articles in the library and clipped some stories from his home-town newspaper. Reproduced below are the narrative from his remembering exercise, a list of pro and con arguments, and the final draft.

REMEMBERING EXERCISE

Nick, Milo, D.J. and I were on our way back from a bar in Mondamin, Iowa, where we had spent the previous six hours drinking brandy and beer. We were all riding in the cab of Nick's pickup and we were almost to Nick's house where our girlfriends were making dinner. Nick turned off the road and drove down by the irrigation canal adjacent to his farm. He thought it would be fun to turn off his lights and drive around in the darkness. We were driving in the blackness when we told him to turn his lights back on and he did so just in time for us to see the ground go out from underneath us. We had just driven off a twenty-five foot cliff. We hit nose first, then flipped over the top. We all escaped serious injury. Milo and D.J. were not injured at all, Nick had to have his thumb sewn back on because the roof smashed down on the steering wheel where he was holding on, and I hit the dashboard and the roof with my face and forehead. I had two black eyes and had to eat soup for the next week because I ripped apart the inside of my mouth.

I have been in two other automobile accidents and in all of them, the vehicle I was riding in was totalled, but I escaped serious injury. I consider myself lucky, because many people have died in lesser accidents. I was not wearing a seat belt when any of the accidents occurred. I think if I had been wearing a seat belt, I might have been saved the pain of injury and the bother of filling out insurance forms.

List of Pro and Con Arguments

Claim: A mandatory seat belt law would save lives.

Pro	Con
Saves lives	Restricts freedom
Cut down on medical bills	Opens door for other laws which may restrict freedom
Will reduce insurance costs	Cannot be fairly enforced
Saves money - will prevent manufacturers from using airbags, which will raise cost of automobiles	Costs money for inspecting seat belts to make sure they are working
Reduce taxes spent on government subsidized medical care	Seat belts will trap people in burning vehicles
	People can avoid injury by bracing themselves before a crash

Revised Version

PROTECT YOURSELF—BUCKLE UP!

> Two men were killed early Sunday morning in separate car accidents in El Paso County. Steven D. Carmichael, 29, of Palmer Lake was pronounced dead at 12:45 a.m. Sunday after a pickup he was driving went off the road. Carmichael, who was alone in the truck, was not wearing a seat belt. In the second accident . . . Joseph David Vasquez, 21, of 22105 Farmer Road, died of massive head and chest injuries after he was thrown from a pickup truck just east of Enoch Road. . . . Vasquez wasn't wearing a seat belt. (Hill 3)

All too often, unfortunately, articles like this one appear in newspapers across the country. Even more unfortunate is the fact that many of these traffic-related deaths could be prevented if more people in the United States would use their seat belts. This has prompted fourteen states, so far, to pass mandatory seat belt laws, requiring all persons in automobiles to use safety belts, or risk paying fines if they're caught not using them (Sundstrom 16). Mandatory seat belt laws are opposed in some states, but the law is a good idea to immediately reduce deaths on our highways and cut the social costs that accompany them. **(1)**

U. S. Secretary of Transportation, Elizabeth Dole, states that "every year more than 40,000 persons are killed in auto accidents on our highways. . . . Car crashes are the leading cause of death of people up to [age] 34. For teenagers, car crash fatalities outnumber the next five causes of death combined" (33). These are sobering statistics, yet 85% of Americans still don't use the single most preventative measure to insure their survival in a car crash: seat belts (Horton 22). **(2)**

Seat belts save lives. The Highway Users Federation says that because 15% of Americans use seat belts, 1,800 lives are saved each year. They estimate that if 25% of all Americans used seat belts, 3,000 lives would be saved, and if 85% of Americans used seat belts, 9,600 human lives would be spared on our nation's highways each year (145). Philip Caldwell, Chairman of the Board at Ford Motor Company, explains: "Statistics show that in a typical auto accident, occupants restrained by standard safety belts have at least a 50% better chance of avoiding death or serious injury than those who are unrestrained" (38). **(3)**

Many opponents of seat belt usage believe it is safer to be thrown from a car than to be trapped in it, but according to Virginia Tech behavioral psychologist E. Scott Geller, who has been studying the use of seat belts for over six years, "being thrown from a car is twenty-five times more lethal than being 'trapped.' The exceptions are widely publicized, and that perpetuates the myth" (Horton 22). A friend of mine who works on an ambulance and who has helped many victims of automobile crashes reminded me of the value of seat belts when he said that he had never unbuckled a dead body from a seat belt. **(4)**

Other opponents are afraid that their car will end up underwater or on fire, and that they won't be able to escape. Actually the reverse is true. B. J. Campbell, director of Highway Safety Research Center at the University of North Carolina, tells us, "If you're wearing a [safety] belt, you've got a better chance of being conscious and not having your legs broken—distinct advantages in getting out of a dangerous situation" (Horton 22). **(5)**

Another myth about auto accidents is addressed by Roslyn Kaiser of the National Highway Traffic Safety Administration (NHTSA). She points out that most people don't understand the dynamics of crashes: "They think they can save themselves by bracing with their arms. But a ten-mile-an-hour collision is equivalent to catching a two-hundred-pound bag of cement dropped from a second-story window" (Horton 22). I can attest to that. I've been in three automobile accidents in my lifetime, and all three were potentially life-threatening, but two of them really proved Kaiser's point. The first accident happened when a pickup truck I was riding in went over a twenty-five foot cliff. I was not wearing a seat belt, but I had braced myself against the seat by placing my hands against the dashboard. The moment before we hit (we hit front-end first, then flipped over), I had my arms locked straight against the dashboard, but when we hit, I don't remember my arms giving way. I don't even remember hitting the dashboard because it happened so quickly, but I did hit it, receiving two black eyes and two gashes inside my mouth. **(6)**

My second accident also illustrated how helpless people are in an accident. I was a passenger in a 12-ton mobile drilling rig that rolled over while going about 50 miles per hour. I wasn't wearing a seat belt, and as the rig rolled over one and one-half times, I was thrown around like a rag doll. I received only minor injuries and was absent from work for only one week, but that accident impressed upon me how little control I had on the outcome of my life in such accidents. I definitely agree with Roger B. Smith, Chairman of General Motors, when he says, "The one sure way to achieve an immediate and dramatic reduction in accident injuries and fatalities is to get significantly more people to use the belt systems that are already in their cars" (35). **(7)**

If one proves that seat belt usage saves lives, the next step is to find out how to increase their use. I think the mandatory seat belt law is the answer. The United States is not the first country to implement such a law. In fact, twenty-nine other countries have mandatory seat belt laws. "Where statistics are available," Transportation Secretary Dole says, "they show that highway deaths have declined by an average of 25 percent" (34). Lee Iacocca of Chrysler agrees:

> In France, the automobile accident death rate has dropped 25 percent after their belt law was passed. In Australia, nearly 90 percent of the people are buckling up. Right across the river from Detroit, the Province of Ontario has enjoyed similar success. Not one nation, state or territory has repealed a belt use law once they've adopted it—because the laws work. (36)

Passing any kind of law is difficult, but the declining death rates indicate that the benefits from a mandatory seat belt law will be worth the effort. **(8)**

Some people are against mandatory seat belt laws because they believe passive restraints and automatic seat belts would be more effective. Those people need to realize that passive restraints, alone, are not as effective. Anyone who does not want seat belts would just disconnect the automatic seat belt, and they would be left with very little protection. In addition, air bags are effective only in front-end collisions. Writing in the *National Safety News*, Philip Caldwell says that "the air bag offers [only] supplemental protection. . . . The air bag offers added protection in frontal collisions at speeds greater than 12 to 15 miles per hour, but it does not provide protection, as safety belts do, in other kinds of accidents—like secondary collisions (after air bag deployment) and rollovers, or rear-end or side-impact collisions" (74). Dole, Iacocca, and Smith agree with Caldwell that safety belts are still the single most effective safety feature in the automotive industry, and they should not be substituted for, but supplemented with, air bags and other passive restraints. **(9)**

The most serious argument against the mandatory seat belt law is that it infringes on an individual's freedom to choose whether or not he or she wishes to use the safety belt. People who take this position believe seat belt use should be a private, personal choice, since it affects only the person who wears it. I once agreed with this view until I discovered that my choice affects all people in society. As Iacocca explains, "People who get injured because they don't use belts raise our taxes, increase our medical and hospitalization insurance, clog our courts, soak up social services for accident victims and survivors, and cause grief for friends and family. So the people who don't use belts because it hampers their freedom are already intruding on our freedom" (74). **(10)**

Of course wearing seat belts would not eliminate these effects, but it would reduce them. A Michigan state legislator notes, "It is estimated that each traffic fatality costs the state and family about $333,000. Injuries and lost wages, caused by the nonuse of belts, cost society $2,500 per accident" (Goodman 12). There is overwhelming evidence that the nonuse of safety belts has a significant effect on most people in society who have to give up part of their earned wage to pay for other people's failure to protect themselves. **(11)**

I think the heavy monetary cost that has to be absorbed by society as a result of death and injuries caused by the nonuse of seat belts, the loss of life itself, and the evidence that mandatory seat belt laws do reduce automobile fatalities are arguments that far outweigh any of the opposing arguments. Perhaps if our state had a seat belt law, I might have worn one and avoided the hospital costs and the days missed from work. More importantly, if Steven Carmichael and Joseph Vasquez had been required by law to wear seat belts, they might be alive today. Let's work together in an effort to reduce these tragic deaths on our nation's highways. Support the mandatory seat belt law, and in the meantime, protect your loved ones and protect yourself. Buckle up. **(12)**

Works Cited

Caldwell, Philip. "A Rational Approach to Car-Occupant Protection." *National Safety News* Feb. 1985: 38, 74–75.

Goodman, Walter. "Fair Game—Reflections on Forced Buckling." *New Leader* 26 Nov. 1985: 12.

Highway Users Federation. "Buckle Up." *Reader's Digest* Dec. 1985: 145.

Hill, David. "Two Men Killed in Separate Accidents." *Colorado Springs Sun* 9 Dec. 1985: 3.

Horton, Elizabeth. "Why Don't We Buckle Up?" *Science Digest* Feb. 1985: 22.

Iacocca, Lee A. "Grass-Roots Pressure Can Make Restraints Mandatory." *National Safety News* Feb. 1985: 36, 74.

Smith, Roger B. "Built-in Protection Complements Passenger Restraints." *National Safety News* Feb. 1985: 35, 74.

Sundstrom, Geoff. "40 Percent Now Covered by Belt Laws." *Automotive News* 5 Aug. 1985: 16.

Questions for Writing and Discussion

1. Does Haas make a claim of fact, value, cause and effect, policy, or some combination? Explain.

2. Were you convinced when you finished this essay? What evidence convinced you most? The personal experience? The statistics? The quotations from authorities? Explain.

3. Compare the version of Haas's personal experience in the remembering exercise with the account in the final version. What specific details were omitted in the final version? Would you recommend including them, leaving the final version the way it is, or condensing it even more? Explain.

4. Read the list of pro and con arguments. Which arguments were omitted from the essay? Were any added that were not on that original list? If you were writing the essay, which points would you include?

GAMES THE MILITARY PLAY

DAVID THOMAS

Should the U. S. military be permitted to control or censor news stories related to combat operations? David Thomas, a student majoring in business at Southeast Missouri State University, addresses a question with legitimate claims on both sides. The military believes that the security of war operations and the safety of individual soldiers requires some censorship of the news media. Private citizens, however, may argue that censorship violates their First Amendment rights and conceals vital information about the goals and conduct of a war. Citing examples from World War I to the Persian Gulf War, Thomas argues that censorship should not be tolerated—especially during times of war. As you read his essay, notice how Thomas counters opposing arguments. Are you persuaded by his reasons and examples?

Your students may want to compare the media coverage of the Gulf War to the coverage of Vietnam. See the video on "Jack Smith's Vietnam Diary."

The young lieutenant lay on a hospital bed, his face flushed with fever. Reporter Marguerite Higgens of the *New York Herald Tribune* leaned closer to hear, careful not to touch the bandages covering his shattered arm. The soldier looked up at her and asked, "Are you correspondents telling people back home the truth? Are you telling them that out of one platoon of twenty men we have three left? Are you telling them that we have nothing to fight with, and that this is an utterly useless war?" (Lubow 24). **(1)**

Yes, they did tell the people back home, at least until General Douglas MacArthur imposed formal censorship on all material concerning the Korean War. Do you remember reading or hearing a soldier making negative comments like that during the recent Persian Gulf War? In fact, can you remember hearing, reading, or seeing anything negative? Perhaps this is because the Pentagon imposed the strictest set of guidelines to control the media since the Revolutionary War. Citing "military security" or "compromising operations," the military infringed on our right to know during the Gulf War. In reality, protecting the image of the military and controlling public opinion are the real reasons our government tramples on our First Amendment rights. Censorship should not be tolerated in a democracy under any circumstances, least of all in times of war. **(2)**

Throughout our history, censorship in various forms has been used in times of war. In 1798, only seven years after passing the First Amendment guaranteeing our freedom of speech, Congress passed the Alien and Sedition Acts. These acts made it possible for people to be fined and jailed for speaking or writing against the government (Zinn 15). This was followed in 1917 with the passing of the Espionage Act. The government used this act to prosecute anyone who criticized the U.S. involvement in WW I (Zinn 17). Under the direction of the Office of Censorship and the Office of War Information, censorship was widely imposed during WW II (Lubow 24). During the Korean Conflict, censorship was imposed but not strictly enforced. In Vietnam, there was no formal declaration of war, therefore, censorship could not be enforced (Lubow 25). The startling footage of casualties, which contradicted the propaganda the government was feeding the public, finally began to erode public support for the Vietnam War. The myth that the press cost the United States victory in Vietnam is precisely why the military drafted a new set of rules concerning censorship, starting with Grenada in 1983. Very few members of the press were allowed on the island, and no reporters were allowed at the scene of battle. According to the belief that censorship worked so well, it was formally adopted in Panama, where the U.S. public has only a dim memory of what happened (Galloway 49). In the Gulf War, censorship received an official name: Operation Annex Foxtrot. Its unstated purpose was to control the information and public opinion concerning the Gulf War. **(3)**

Officially, the reasons for censorship of news from the Gulf War were that operations, troop movements, and battle plans could be accidentally betrayed. While this is a valid concern, it is not justified. All members of the media are willing to hold back information that might jeopardize security. According to David Broder of the *The Washington Post*, members of the media found out about General Schwarzkopf's deceptive flanking maneuver in the Persian Gulf Sea and did not release the information until after the enemy had realized it (A2). As Henry Kissinger admitted after the Vietnam Conflict, the only stories released during Vietnam that had the potential to be security risks were leaked from the State Department in Washington D.C. In fact, out of hundreds of correspondents who wrote thousands of stories during Vietnam, only two reporters had their privileges revoked (Shanberg 23). **(4)**

Another reason frequently cited was that large numbers of reporters roaming around the desert would be dangerous because they could be captured and held as hostages. In fact, censorship was the reason many journalists ventured out on their own. Perhaps if they could have gotten all the information they needed, they would have stayed under the protection of the troops. One example of this is when Bob Simon, reporter for CBS News, frustrated by the censorship, struck out on his own and was captured by the Iraqis (Browne 45). **(5)**

A third reason the Pentagon decided to censor war news was the theory held by many people, including Saddam Hussein, that a prolonged war with heavy casualties would erode public support for the war (Schanberg 23). This may be true, but isn't that precisely why we need to know what is happening? Perhaps there is a good reason why a long war with heavy casualties would not be popular. Perhaps the people know how many soldiers are worth sacrificing to protect another country. How would we feel if the Gulf War were still going on today? And what if our death toll had reached two thousand? **(6)**

This is precisely why we should not have censorship. The public has a right to know. The Gulf War could easily have become another Vietnam, with a tremendous cost in human life. Fifty years ago there was another government that had complete censorship. The leader filled his people with propaganda and told them the war was a "just" war. After the war, many citizens of his country claimed they were kept in the dark and didn't know of the horrors he had committed. His name was Adolph Hitler. **(7)**

Keeping war news from the public will eventually raise suspicion from the public. At first, the public will accept token bits of information, but soon they will be asking, "What is the government hiding?" As Walter Cronkite said, "Hiding information will eventually lead to a breakdown in home-front confidence, just like Vietnam, which is precisely what the Pentagon fears the most" (43). The massive propaganda campaign the Johnson administration used during the Vietnam campaign conflicted with the truth. Eventually, the public realized this, and it wasn't long before public protests started. This loss of trust is what eventually undermined the war effort and ended the Johnson administration at the same time. **(8)**

The Gulf War has been over for several years now. According to our government it was an unequaled victory for the United States. Or was it? Thanks to military censorship we do not have enough information to give an intelligent answer. For example, we have no idea how many innocent Iraqi lives were lost. One hundred, a thousand, ten thousand? Censorship has not only denied us the right to decide if this was a "just" war, it also prevents us from using it as a guideline to decide whether or not to involve ourselves in the defense of another country. **(9)**

Our huge budget deficit is threatening the very economic security of our nation. One way to help the deficit is to cut unnecessary military spending. There is good reason to believe that the military consistently misleads us about the need of certain weapons systems. One specific example is the B-2 bomber. There has always been controversy about whether we actually need this plane. Of course, the military insists it is vital for our defense to maintain production, and they took measures in the Gulf War to protect its role as our primary bomber. One such measure is illustrated in a story by Malcolm W. Browne, a reporter for *The New York Times Magazine*. He filed a story about an air-raid attack on Baghdad, describing the F117-A as a fighter-bomber. Indeed, it had carried a heavy payload of bombs in the air attack. His story was censored, however, changing "fighter-bomber" to just "fighter." Apparently, the military is concerned that the public will wonder why we need the B-2 bomber if the F117-A can do the job (29). **(10)**

Military censorship has many forms. It could be outright censorship of a story, propaganda about our reasons for being in a war, misinformation about results of battles, or attempts to control public opinion by manipulating the media, which is illustrated in a story by Jason De Parle in the May 4 edition of *The New York Times*. During the buildup of troops in the Gulf War, correspondents from many large papers and magazines were denied access to the troops. However, reporters from small-town newspapers were not only allowed access, the military—in a program called Hometown News Program—provided free transportation and any equipment they might need to spend four days with troops from their hometowns. Why were those reporters allowed and not others? As the administrator of the program, Lieutenant Colonel Michael Cox of the Air Force admitted, "If they know they are getting a free ride, and they can't afford the $2,000 ticket, there is going to be a tendency to be sympathetic to our side" (A20). **(11)**

Whatever the disguise, censorship must not be allowed to interfere with our right to know. In the future, it is our duty to demand full disclosure about any military operations. After all, we are free people, governed by free people, and protected by an army of free people. And isn't that what the Gulf War was about, trying to keep the people of Kuwait free? **(12)**

Works Cited

Broder, David S. "The War Story," *The Washington Post* 11 Feb. 1991: A2.

Browne, Malcolm. "The Military vs. the Press." *The New York Times Magazine* 3 March 1991: 26–30, 44–45.

Cronkite, Walter. "What is There to Hide?" *Newsweek* 25 Feb. 1991: 43.

DeParle, Jason. "Long Series of Military Decisions Led to Gulf War News Censorship." *The New York Times* 4 May 1991: A1, A20.

Galloway, Joseph. "Who's Afraid of the Truth?" *U.S. News and World Report* 4 Feb. 1991: 49.

Lubow, Arthur. "Read Some About It: A Short History of Wartime Censorship." *New Republic* 18 March 1991: 23–25.

Schanberg, Sydney. "Censoring for Political Security." *Washington Journalism Review* March 1991: 23–25.

Zinn, Howard. "Second Thoughts on the First Amendment." *The Humanist* Nov.–Dec. 1991: 15–24, 42.

Questions for Writing and Discussion

1. Assume that you were a soldier in the Persian Gulf War who believes that his or her safety would have been compromised by unlimited media coverage. Write a letter of response to Thomas.

Explain when and how the military should restrict the media's access to news.

2. The "Shaping" section of this chapter identifies the six parts of a classical argument: introduction, narration, partition, argument, refutation, and conclusion. Identify by paragraph numbers the points at which Thomas uses each of these parts of a classical argument. Where does he alter the order? Should he reorganize his essay to follow the order indicated above? Explain why or why not.

3. Imitating the "pro" and "con" shaping strategy on page 453, make a list of the pro and con arguments that Thomas uses in his essay. (The pro arguments will be arguments in favor of eliminating military censorship; the con arguments are those supporting military censorship.) Which opposing arguments does he refute? What additional arguments does he give in favor of complete freedom of the press?

4. List one piece of *evidence* that Thomas gives to support each of the following claims. (1) There was censorship during the Gulf War (claim of fact). (2) Censorship by the military is not good (claim of value). (3) Censorship may increase our budget deficit (claim of cause and effect). Citizens should demand full disclosure about any military operations (claim of policy). Which claims and pieces of evidence were most persuasive? Where does Thomas need additional evidence?

5. One reader of this essay has charged that Thomas uses emotional appeals too strongly when he refers to the bandages covering the soldier's "shattered arm" in paragraph 1, when he uses loaded language in paragraph 3, and when he cites Adolph Hitler in paragraph 7. Assume that you are helping Thomas revise his essay. Should Thomas change these passages? Write a note explaining specifically how and why each passage should (or should not) be changed.

6. In a letter to Thomas Jefferson in 1798, James Madison wrote: "Perhaps it is a universal truth that the loss of liberty at home is to be charged to provisions against danger real or pretended from abroad." Explain what Madison meant and how this statement relates to Thomas's essay.

ELEVEN / RESPONDING TO LITERATURE

I hungered for new books, new ways of looking and seeing. It was not a matter of believing or disbelieving what I read, but of feeling something new, of being affected by something that made the look of the world different.

—RICHARD WRIGHT, AUTHOR OF BLACK BOY

No one else can read a literary work for us. The benefits of literature can emerge only from creative activity on the part of the reader.

—LOUISE ROSENBLATT, AUTHOR OF LITERATURE AS EXPLORATION

IN A FILM CLASS, YOU WATCH ROMAN POLANSKI'S *TESS*, AN ADAPTATION OF THOMAS HARDY'S NOVEL *TESS OF THE D'URBERVILLES.* You decide to compare the film with the novel, focusing on four key episodes: the "strawberry scene," in which Tess meets Alec; the rape scene at night; the harvesting scene; and the final scene at Stonehenge. On the basis of your comparison, you argue that Polanski's interpretation (and the acting of Nastassia Kinski) retains Hardy's view of Tess as a victim of social and sexist repression.

IN AN INTRODUCTION TO LITERATURE CLASS, YOU AND A FRIEND ARE ASSIGNED TO WORK COLLABORATIVELY ON AN ESSAY ABOUT EUDORA WELTY'S "A WORN PATH." You are both interested in how Phoenix Jackson's journey contains images of the phoenix: a mythological bird said to live for five hundred years, after which it burns itself to death and then rises from its ashes to become youthful and beautiful again. You draft your essays separately and then read each other's drafts. At that point, you collaborate on a single essay, combining the best ideas and evidence from your separate drafts. Your collaborative essay shows how Phoenix Jackson is characterized by birdlike images, how she calmly faces images of fire and death on her journey, and how her grandson represents her rebirth.

Morisot, Berthe, French, 1841–1895, La Lecture (Reading), 1888, oil on canvas, 29.25" x 36.5"

RESPONDING TO LITERATURE REQUIRES THAT READERS PARTICIPATE *IMAGINATIVELY* WHILE THEY READ A LITERARY WORK, *REREAD* TO SEE HOW THE PARTS OF THE WORK RELATE TO THE WHOLE, AND *SHARE* THEIR INTERPRETATIONS OF A PIECE OF LITERATURE WITH OTHER READERS.

First, readers must *imagine* and re-create that special world described by the writer. The first sentences of a short story, for example, throw open a door to a world that—attractive or repulsive—tempts our curiosity and imagination. Like Alice in *Alice in Wonderland*, we cannot resist following a white rabbit with pink eyes who mutters to himself, checks his watch, and then zips down a rabbit hole and into an imaginary world.

Here are three opening sentences to three very different short stories:

> Young Goodman Brown came forth at sunset into the street at Salem village; but put his head back, after crossing the threshold, to exchange a parting kiss with his young wife.
>
> —Nathaniel Hawthorne, "Young Goodman Brown"

> As Gregor Samsa awoke one morning from uneasy dreams he found himself transformed in his bed into a gigantic insect.
>
> —Franz Kafka, "The Metamorphosis"

> The morning of June 27th was clear and sunny, with the fresh warmth of a full-summer day; the flowers were blossoming profusely and the grass was green.
>
> —Shirley Jackson, "The Lottery"

Whether our imaginations construct the disturbing image of a "gigantic insect" or the seemingly peaceful picture of a perfect summer day, we actively create each story. Responding to literature does not mean passively reacting to the writer's story. As readers, we should anticipate, imagine, feel, worry, and question. A story is like an empty balloon that we must inflate with the warm breath of our imagination and experience. Our participation makes us partners with the author in the artistic creation.

Responding to literature also requires that readers *reread*. If we read a story or a poem only once, we have misunderstood the whole point of literature. Great literature is worthy of study because the more we reread, the more we learn and discover. If we assume that the purpose of a story is merely to entertain us or to provide a moment's diversion, then we should stick to television sitcoms written for an audience of couch potatoes who want only predictable, unimaginative plots and canned studio laughter.

Since much of the literature available to students is now on film or video, you may want to compare the experience of watching a story to the experience of reading one. What is lost or gained in the translation of a story to the screen? Can original screenplays or docudramas be considered literature? What kind of imagination, rereading, and sharing are involved in the act of viewing stories?

Rereading requires two distinct but related operations. First, you should *reread for yourself*—that is, reread to write down your ideas, questions, feelings, and reactions. To heighten your role in creating a story, you should note, in the margins, your questions and responses to important events, main characters, bits of description, and images that catch your attention: "What about the names Hawthorne uses? Is Young Goodman Brown really good? Is his wife, Faith, really faithful?" "I don't understand why Kafka's narrator thinks he is a gigantic insect. Is this happening, or is he dreaming?" "Why does Shirley Jackson's lottery happen on such a beautiful summer day?" Don't just underline or highlight passages. Actually *write* your responses in the margin.

Second, you should *reread with a writer's eye*. In fiction, identify the main and minor characters. Look for and note the conflicts between characters. Mark passages that contain *foreshadowing*—that urge you to think ahead imaginatively. Pinpoint sentences that reveal the narrative point of view. Use the appropriate critical terms *(character, plot, conflict, point of view, setting, style,* and *theme)* to help you reread with a writer's eye and to see how the parts of a story relate to the whole. Each critical term is a tool—a magnifying glass that helps you understand and interpret the story more clearly.

In addition to rereading, responding to literature requires that readers *share* ideas, reactions, and interpretations. Sharing usually begins in small-group or class discussions, but it continues as you explain your interpretation in writing. A work of literature is not a mathematical equation with a single answer. Great literature is worth interpreting precisely because each reader responds differently. The purpose of literature is to encourage you to reflect on your life and the lives of others—to look for new ways of seeing and understanding your world—and ultimately to expand your world. Sharing is crucial to appreciating literature.

> Hawthorne doesn't come right out and say that people become disillusioned by experiencing evil. He shows how it actually happens in the life of young Goodman Brown.
>
> Shirley Jackson's "The Lottery" helps me see that the notion of human sacrifice and the idea of the human scapegoat still exist in our culture today.

Invite your students to share their responses to the profile of "Maya Angelou" in the *Video Library*, which includes excerpts of her lyrical performance at President Clinton's inauguration.

Writing about your responses and sharing them with other readers helps you "reread" your own ideas in order to explain them fully and clearly to other readers.

■ **FREEWRITING: RESPONDING TO A SHORT STORY** Read and respond to Kate Chopin's "The Story of an Hour." Use your imagination to help create the story as you read. Then *reread* the story, noting in the margin your questions and responses. When you finish rereading and annotating your reactions, write your interpretation of the *last line* of the story.

THE STORY OF AN HOUR

KATE CHOPIN

Kate O'Flaherty Chopin (1851–1904) was an American writer whose mother was French and Creole and whose father was Irish. In 1870, she moved from St. Louis to New Orleans with her husband, Oscar Chopin, and over the next ten years she gave birth to five sons. After her husband died in 1882, Chopin returned to St. Louis to begin a new life as a writer. Many of her best stories are about Louisiana people and places, and her most famous novel, The Awakening, *tells the story of Edna, a woman who leaves her marriage and her children to fulfill herself through an artistic career.*

Knowing that Mrs. Mallard was afflicted with a heart trouble, great care was taken to break to her as gently as possible the news of her husband's death. **(1)**

It was her sister Josephine who told her, in broken sentences, veiled hints that revealed in half concealing. Her husband's friend Richards was there, too, near her. It was he who had been in the newspaper office when intelligence of the railroad disaster was received, with Brently Mallard's name leading the list of "killed." He had only taken the time to assure himself of its truth by a second telegram, and had hastened to forestall any less careful, less tender friend in bearing the sad message. **(2)**

She did not hear the story as many women have heard the same, with a paralyzed inability to accept its significance. She wept at once, with sudden, wild abandonment, in her sister's arms. When the storm of grief had spent itself she went away to her room alone. She would have no one follow her. **(3)**

There stood, facing the open window, a comfortable, roomy armchair. Into this she sank, pressed down by a physical exhaustion that haunted her body and seemed to reach into her soul. **(4)**

She could see in the open square before her house the tops of trees that were all aquiver with the new spring life. The delicious breath of rain was in the air. In the street below a peddler was crying his wares. The notes of a distant song which someone was singing reached her faintly, and countless sparrows were twittering in the eaves. **(5)**

There were patches of blue sky showing here and there through the clouds that had met and piled above the other in the west facing her window. **(6)**

She sat with her head thrown back upon the cushion of the chair quite motionless, except when a sob came up into her throat and shook her, as a child who has cried itself to sleep continues to sob in its dreams. **(7)**

She was young, with a fair, calm face, whose lines bespoke repression and even a certain strength. But now there was a dull stare in her eyes, whose gaze was fixed away off yonder on one of those patches of blue sky. It was not a glance of reflection, but rather indicated a suspension of intelligent thought. **(8)**

There was something coming to her and she was waiting for it, fearfully. What was it? She did not know; it was too subtle and elusive to name. But she felt it, creeping out of the sky, reaching toward her through the sounds, the scents, the color that filled the air. **(9)**

Now her bosom rose and fell tumultuously. She was beginning to recognize this thing that was approaching to possess her, and she was striving to beat it back with her will—as powerless as her two white slender hands would have been. **(10)**

When she abandoned herself a little whispered word escaped her slightly parted lips. She said it over and over under her breath: "Free, free, free!" The vacant stare and the look of terror that had followed it went from her eyes. They stayed keen and bright. Her pulses beat fast, and the coursing blood warmed and relaxed every inch of her body. **(11)**

She did not stop to ask if it were not a monstrous joy that held her. A clear and exalted perception enabled her to dismiss the suggestion as trivial. **(12)**

She knew that she would weep again when she saw the kind, tender hands folded in death; the face that had never looked save with love upon her, fixed and gray and dead. But she saw beyond that bitter moment a long procession of years to come that would belong to her absolutely. And she opened and spread her arms out to them in welcome. **(13)**

There would be no one to live for during those coming years; she would live for herself. There would be no powerful will bending her in that blind persistence with which men and women believe they have a right to impose a private will upon a fellow creature. A kind intention or a cruel intention made the act seem no less a crime as she looked upon it in that brief moment of illumination. **(14)**

And yet she had loved him—sometimes. Often she had not. What did it matter! What could love, the unsolved mystery, count for in face of this possession of self-assertion which she suddenly recognized as the strongest impulse of her being. **(15)**

"Free! Body and soul free!" she kept whispering. **(16)**

Josephine was kneeling before the closed door with her lips to the keyhole, imploring for admission. "Louise, open the door! I beg; open the door—you will make yourself ill. What are you doing, Louise? For heaven's sake open the door." **(17)**

"Go away. I am not making myself ill." No; she was drinking in a very elixir of life through that open window. **(18)**

Her fancy was running riot along those days ahead of her. Spring days, and summer days, and all sorts of days that would be her own. She breathed a quick prayer that life might be long. It was only yesterday she had thought with a shudder that life might be long. **(19)**

She arose at length and opened the door to her sister's importunities. There was a feverish triumph in her eyes, and she carried herself unwittingly like a goddess of Victory. She clasped her sister's waist, and together they descended the stairs. Richards stood waiting for them at the bottom. **(20)**

Someone was opening the front door with a latchkey. It was Brently Mallard who entered, a little travel-stained, composedly carrying his grip-sack and umbrella. He had been far from the scene of accident, and did not even know there had been one. He stood amazed at Josephine's piercing cry; at Richards's quick motion to screen him from the view of his wife. **(21)**

But Richards was too late. **(22)**

When the doctors came they said she had died of heart disease—of joy that kills. **(23)**

TECHNIQUES FOR RESPONDING TO LITERATURE

As you read and respond to a work of literature, keep the following techniques in mind.

- **Understanding the assignment and selecting a possible purpose and audience.** Unless stated otherwise in your assignment, your purpose is to *interpret* a work of literature. Your audience will be other members of your class, including the teacher.

- **Actively reading, annotating, and discussing the literary work.** Remember that literature often contains *highly condensed experiences.* In order to give imaginative life to literature, you need to reread patiently both the major events and the seemingly insignificant passages. In discussions, look for the differences between your responses and other readers' ideas.

- **Focusing your essay on a single, clearly defined interpretation.** In your essay, clearly state your main idea or thesis, focusing on a single idea or aspect of the piece of literature. Your thesis should *not be a statement of fact.* Whether you are explaining, evaluating, or arguing, your interpretation must be clearly stated.
- **Supporting your interpretation with evidence.** Because your readers will probably have different interpretations, you must show which specific characters, events, conflicts, images, or themes prompted your response, and you must support your interpretation. *Do not merely retell the major events of the story—your readers have already read it.*

■ WARMING UP: JOURNAL EXERCISES Read all of the following questions and then write for five minutes on two or three. These questions should clarify your perceptions about literature and develop your specific responses to "The Story of an Hour."

Don't overlook the video store or television as sources of good stories for this warm-up exercise.

1. Describe a work of literature (a poem, short story, novel, or play) that you have read recently. Why did you read it? What did you like best about it? What did you not like about it?

2. On your bookshelves or in the library, find a short story or poem that you read at least six months ago. Before you reread it, write down the name of the author and the title of the work. Note when you read it last and describe what you remember about it. Then reread the story or poem. When you finish, write for five minutes, describing what you noticed that you did not notice the last time you read it.

3. Find a popular song whose lyrics describe a character and tell a story about that person. Listen to the record and copy down the words. Compare it to Kate Chopin's "The Story of an Hour." Do the lyrics have the basic ingredients of short fiction (character, plot, point of view, setting, style, and theme)? Is it a miniature story? What elements does it lack?

4. Write out the *question* that "The Story of an Hour" seems to ask. What is your answer to this question? What might have been Kate Chopin's answer?

5. Read the Responding to Short Fiction section in this chapter. Review the descriptions of character, plot, point of view, setting, and style. Explain which of these terms and definitions best helps you find *evidence* in "The Story of an Hour" to answer the question that you identified in Question 4, above.

6. The words "heart," "joy," "free," "life," and "death" appear several times in "The Story of an Hour." Underline these words (or synonyms) each time they appear. Explain how the meaning of each of these words seems to *change* during the story. Is each word used ironically?

7. Write out a dictionary definition of word "feminism." Then write out your own definition. Is Mrs. Mallard a feminist? Is Kate Chopin a feminist? What evidence in the story supports your answers?

8. Kate Chopin's biographer, Per Seyersted, says that Chopin saw that "truth is manifold" and thus preferred not to "take sides or point a moral." Explain how "The Story of an Hour" does or does not illustrate Seyersted's observations.

9. Literature often expresses common themes or tensions, such as the individual versus society, appearance versus reality, self-knowledge versus self-deception, or civilization versus nature. Which of these themes are most apparent in "The Story of an Hour"? Explain your choices.

Purposes for Responding to Literature

In responding to literature, you should be guided by the purposes that you have already practiced in previous chapters. As you read a piece of literature and respond in the margin, begin by writing *for yourself*. Your purposes are to observe, feel, remember, understand, and relate the work of literature to your own life: What is happening? What memories does it trigger? How does it make you feel? Why is this passage confusing? Why do you like or dislike this character? Literature has special, personal value. You should write about literature initially in order to discover and understand its importance in your life.

When you write an interpretative essay, however, you are writing *for others*. You are sharing your experience in working with the author as imaginative partners in re-creating the work. Your purposes will often be mixed, but an interpretative essay often contains elements of *explaining, evaluating, problem solving*, and *arguing*.

- **Explaining.** Interpretative essays about literature explain the *what, why*, and *how* of a piece of literature. What is the key subject? What is the most important event or character? What are the major conflicts or the key images? What motivates a character? How does a character's world build or unravel? How does a story meet or fail to meet our expectations? How did our interpretations develop? Each of these questions might lead to an interpretative essay that explains the *what, why*, and *how* of your response.
- **Evaluating.** Readers and writers often talk about "appreciating" a work of literature. *Appreciating* means establishing its value or worth. It may mean praising the work's literary virtues; it may mean finding faults or weaknesses. Usually, evaluating essays measure *both strengths and weaknesses*, according to specific criteria. What important standards for literature do you wish to apply? How does the work in question measure up? What kinds of readers might find this story worth reading? An evaluative essay cites evidence to show why a story is exciting, boring, dramatic, puzzling, vivid, relevant, or memorable.
- **Problem Solving.** Writers of interpretative essays occasionally take a problem-solving approach, focusing on how the reader overcomes obstacles in understanding the story or how the author of a story solved problems in writing key scenes, creating characters, setting a plot in motion, and creating and resolving conflicts. Particularly if you like to write fiction yourself, you may wish to take the writer's point of view: How did the writer solve (or fail to solve) problems of setting, character, plot, or theme?
- **Arguing.** As readers share responses, they may discover that their interpretations diverge sharply from the ideas of other readers. Does "The Story of an Hour" have a "feminist" theme? Is it about women or about human nature in general? Is the main character admirable, or is she selfish? In interpretative essays, writers sometimes argue for their beliefs. They present evidence that refutes an opposing interpretation and supports their own reading.

Most interpretative essays about literature will be focused by these purposes, whether used singly or in combination. Writers should *select* the purpose(s) that are most appropriate for the work of literature and their own responses.

Responding to Short Fiction

Responding as a Reader

Begin by noting in the margins your reactions at key points. *Summarize* in your own words what is happening in the story. Write down your *observations* or *reactions* to striking or surprising passages. Ask yourself *questions* about ambiguous or confusing passages. Below are examples written by students that illustrate all three kinds of responses.

Summary Comments

Mrs. Mallard is initially paralyzed by the news.

Mrs. Mallard feels her sister will protect her. She weeps in her sister's arms.

From the security of her chair, she stares at life outside her window.

Mrs. Mallard is young, but the lines on her face reveal repression.

Mrs. Mallard now feels "free, free, free" of the bonds of marriage.

News of her husband's death does not kill her, but news of his life does.

Observations and Reactions

Mrs. Mallard has "heart trouble"—possible double meaning.

Although Mrs. Mallard is experiencing shock and grief, outside her window the world is full of life.

The mistaken belief that men and women have a right to impose their will on others—this may be the point of the story.

Joy that kills = monstrous joy.

She does not die of the joy that kills—she dies of killed joy.

Questions

Why does the "storm" of grief come so quickly and then disappear?

She would live for herself: Is this selfishness or just a desire to be free?

Why does Chopin make Mrs. Mallard seem powerless, as though she was overcome by a fever?

Should we admire Mrs. Mallard for wanting her freedom?

Is this the story of an hour or the story of her life?

The elements of fiction sometimes are easier to see in fiction films. Consider how an actor's voice and gestures contribute to characterization, for example, or how the camera's position supports a narrative point of view.

Reading with a Writer's Eye

After you respond initially and make your marginal annotations, use the following basic elements of fiction to help you *analyze how the parts of a short story relate to the whole.* Pay attention to how setting or plot affects the character, or how style and setting affect the theme. Because analysis artificially separates plot, character, and theme, look for ways to *synthesize* the parts: Seeing how these parts *relate* to each other should suggest an idea, focus, or angle to use in your interpretation.

CHARACTER A short story usually focuses on a *major character*—particularly on how that character faces conflicts, undergoes changes, or reveals himself or herself. *Minor characters* may be flat (one-dimensional), static (unchanging), or stereotyped. To get a start on analyzing character, diagram the *conflicts* between or among characters. Examine characters for *motivation:* What causes them to behave as they do? Is their behavior affected by *internal* or *external* forces? Do the major characters reveal themselves *directly* (through their thoughts, dialogue, and actions) or indirectly (through what other people say, think, or do)?

PLOT *Plot* is the sequence of events in a story, but it is also the cause-and-effect relationship of one event to another. As you study a story's plot, pay attention to *exposition, foreshadowing, conflict, climax,* and *denouement.* To clarify elements of the plot, draw a time line for the story, listing in chronological order every event—including events that occur before the story opens. *Exposition* describes the initial circumstances and reveals what has happened before the story opens. *Foreshadowing* is an author's hint of what will occur before it happens. *Conflicts* within characters, between characters, and between characters and their environment may explain why one event leads to the next. The *climax* is the high point, the point of no return, or the most dramatic moment in a story. At the climax of a story, readers discover something important about the main character(s). *Denouement* literally means the "unraveling" of the complications and conflicts at the end of the story. In "The Story of an Hour," climax and denouement occur almost at the same time, in the last lines of the story.

NARRATIVE POINT OF VIEW Fiction is usually narrated from either the first-person or the third-person point of view.

A *first-person narrator* is a character who tells the story from his or her point of view. A first-person narrator may be a minor or a major character. This character may be relatively *reliable* (trustworthy) or *unre-*

liable (naive or misleading). Although reliable first-person narrators may invite the reader to identify with their perspectives or predicaments, unreliable narrators may cause readers to be wary of their naive judgments or unbalanced states of mind.

A *third-person omniscient* narrator is not a character or participant in the story. Omniscient narrators are assumed to know everything about the characters and events. They move through space and time, giving readers necessary information at any point in the story. A *selective omniscient* narrator usually limits his or her focus to a single character's experiences and thoughts, as Kate Chopin focuses on Mrs. Mallard in "The Story of an Hour." One kind of selective omniscient point of view is *stream-of-consciousness* narration, in which the author presents the thoughts, memories, and associations of one character in the story. Omniscient narrators may be *intrusive*, jumping into the story to give their editorial judgments, or they may be *objective*, removing themselves from the action and the minds of the characters. Objective point of view creates the impression that events are being recorded by a camera or acted on a stage.

Reminder: As you reread a story, do not stop with analysis. Do not quit, for example, after you have identified and labeled the point of view. Determine how the point of view *affects* your reaction to the central character or to your understanding of the theme. How would a different narrative point of view change the story? If a different character told the story, how would that affect the theme?

SETTING *Setting* is the physical place, scene, and time of the story. It also includes the social or historical context of the story. The setting in "The Story of an Hour" is the house and the room in which Mrs. Mallard waits, but it is also the social and historical time frame. *Setting is usually important for what it reveals about the characters, the plot, or the theme of the story*. Does the setting reflect a character's state of mind? Is the environment a source of tension or conflict in the story? Do changes in setting reflect changes in key characters? Do sensory details of sight, touch, smell, hearing, or taste affect or reflect the characters or events? Does the author's portrait of the setting contain images and symbols that help you interpret the story?

STYLE *Style* is a general term that may refer to sentence structure, figurative language and symbols, as well as to the author's tone or use of irony. *Sentence structure* may be long and complicated or relatively short and simple. Authors may use *figurative language* (Mrs. Mallard is described in "The Story of an Hour" as sobbing, "as a child who has cried itself to sleep continues to sob in its dreams"). A *symbol* is a person, place, thing, or event that suggests or signifies something beyond itself. In "The Story of an Hour," the open window and the new spring life suggest or represent Mrs. Mallard's new freedom. *Tone* is the author's attitude toward the characters, setting, or plot. Tone may be sympathetic, humorous, serious, detached, or critical. *Irony* suggests a double meaning. It occurs when the author or a character says or does one thing but means the opposite or something altogether different. The ending of "A Story of an Hour" is ironic: The doctors say Mrs. Mallard dies "of joy that kills." In fact, she dies of killed joy.

THEME The focus of an interpretative essay is often on the theme of a story. In arriving at a theme, ask how the characters, plot, point of view, setting, and style *contribute to* the main ideas or point of the story. The theme of a story depends, within limits, upon your reactions as a reader. "The Story of an Hour" is *not* about relationships between sisters, nor is it about medical malpractice. It *is* an ironic story about love, personal freedom, and death, but what precisely is the *theme*? Does "The Story of an Hour" carry a feminist message, or is it more universally about the repressive power of love? Is Mrs. Mallard to be admired or criticized for her impulse to free herself? The theme of a story should not be trivialized by looking for some simple "moral." In describing the theme, you should deal with the complexity of life re-created in the story.

SHORT FICTION: PROFESSIONAL WRITING

A WORN PATH

EUDORA WELTY

Eudora Welty was born in Jackson, Mississippi in 1909 and earned degrees from Mississippi State College, the University of Wisconsin, and Columbia University. While she was writing short stories during the early 1930s, Welty held jobs with the Works Progress Authority, a Jackson radio station, and local newspapers. Like Flannery O'Connor and William Faulkner, Eudora Welty wrote stories and novels set in the South. Her first major publication, A Curtain of Green, and Other Stories *appeared in 1941 and was followed by three more collections of short stories. Her novels include* Delta Wedding *(1946) and* The Optimist's Daughter *(1972), which won a Pulitzer Prize. Welty's collection of reviews and essays,* The Eye of the Story *(1978), and her brief autobiography,* One Writer's Beginnings *(1984), provide insight into her fiction and her life.*

It was December—a bright frozen day in the early morning. Far out in the country there was an old Negro woman with her head tied in a red rag, coming along a path through the pinewoods. Her name was Phoenix Jackson. She was very old and small and she walked slowly in the dark pine shadows, moving a little from side to side in her steps, with the balanced heaviness and lightness of a pendulum in a grandfather clock. She carried a thin, small cane made from an umbrella, and with this she kept tapping the frozen earth in front of her. This made a grave and persistent noise in the still air, that seemed meditative like the chirping of a solitary little bird. **(1)**

She wore a dark striped dress reaching down to her shoe tops, and an equally long apron of bleached sugar sacks, with a full pocket: all neat and tidy, but every time she took a step she might have fallen over her shoe-laces, which dragged from her unlaced shoes. She looked straight ahead. Her eyes were blue with age. Her skin had a pattern all its own of numberless branching wrinkles and as though a whole little tree stood in the middle of her forehead, but a golden color ran underneath, and the two knobs of her cheeks were illuminated by a yellow burning under the dark. Under the red rag her hair came down on her neck in the frailest of ringlets, still black, and with an odor like copper. **(2)**

Now and then there was a quivering in the thicket. Old Phoenix said, "Out of my way, all you foxes, owls, beetles, jack rabbits, coons, and wild animals! . . . Keep out from under these feet, little bob-whites. . . . Keep the big wild hogs out of my path. Don't let none of those come running my direction. I got a long way." Under her small black-freckled hand her cane, limber as a buggy whip, would switch at the brush as if to rouse up any hiding things. **(3)**

On she went. The woods were deep and still. The sun made the pine needles almost too bright to look at, up where the wind rocked. The cones dropped as light as feathers. Down in the hollow was the mourning dove—it was not too late for him. **(4)**

The path ran up a hill. "Seem like there is chains about my feet, time I get this far," she said, in the voice of argument old people keep to use with themselves. "Something always take a hold of me on this hill—pleads I should stay." **(5)**

After she got to the top she turned and gave a full, severe look behind her where she had come. "Up through pines," she said at length. "Now down through oaks." **(6)**

Her eyes opened their widest, and she started down gently. But before she got to the bottom of the hill a bush caught her dress. **(7)**

Her fingers were busy and intent, but her skirts were full and long, so that before she could pull them free in one place they were caught in another. It was not possible to allow the dress to tear. "I in the thorny bush," she said. "Thorns, you doing your appointed work. Never want to let folks pass—no sir. Old eyes thought you was a pretty little *green* bush." **(8)**

Finally, trembling all over, she stood free, and after a moment dared to stoop for her cane. **(9)**

"Sun so high!" she cried, leaning back and looking, while the thick tears went over her eyes. "The time getting all gone here." **(10)**

At the foot of this hill was a place where a log was laid across the creek. **(11)**

"Now comes the trial," said Phoenix. **(12)**

Putting her right foot out, she mounted the log and shut her eyes. Lifting her skirt, leveling her cane fiercely before her, like a festival figure in some parade, she began to march across. Then she opened her eyes and she was safe on the other side. **(13)**

"I wasn't as old as I thought," she said. **(14)**

But she sat down to rest. She spread her skirts on the bank around her and folded her hands over her knees. Up above her was a tree in a pearly cloud of mistletoe. She did not dare to close her eyes, and when a little boy brought her a little plate with a slice of marble-cake on it she spoke to him. "That would be acceptable," she said. But when she went to take it there was just her own hand in the air. **(15)**

So she left that tree, and had to go through a barbed-wire fence. There she had to creep and crawl, spreading her knees and stretching her fingers like a baby trying to climb the steps. But she talked loudly to herself: she could not let her dress be torn now, so late in the day, and she could not pay for having her arm or her leg sawed off if she got caught fast where she was. **(16)**

At last she was safe through the fence and risen up out in the clearing. Big dead trees, like black men with one arm, were standing in the purple stalks of the withered cotton field. There sat a buzzard. **(17)**

"Who you watching?" **(18)**

In the furrow she made her way along. **(19)**

"Glad this not the season for bulls," she said, looking sideways, "and the good Lord made his snakes to curl up and sleep in the winter. A pleasure I don't see no two-headed snake coming around that tree, where it come once. It took a while to get by him, back in the summer." **(20)**

She passed through the old cotton and went into a field of dead corn. It whispered and shook and was taller than her head. "Through the maze now," she said, for there was no path. **(21)**

Then there was something tall, black, and skinny there, moving before her. **(22)**

At first she took it for a man. It could have been a man dancing in the field. But she stood still and listened, and it did not make a sound. It was as silent as a ghost. **(23)**

"Ghost," she said sharply, "who be you the ghost of? For I have heard of nary death close by." **(24)**

But there was no answer—only the ragged dancing in the wind. **(25)**

She shut her eyes, reached out her hand, and touched a sleeve. She found a coat and inside that an emptiness, cold as ice. **(26)**

"You scarecrow," she said. Her face lighted. "I ought to be shut up for good," she said with laughter. "My senses is gone, I too old. I the oldest people I ever know. Dance, old scarecrow," she said, "while I dancing with you." She kicked her foot over the furrow, and with mouth drawn down, shook her head once or twice in a little strutting way. Some husks blew down and whirled in streamers about her skirts. **(27)**

Then she went on, parting her way from side to side with the cane, through the whispering field. At last she came to the end, to a wagon track where the silver grass blew between the red ruts. The quail were walking around like pullets, seeming all dainty and unseen. **(28)**

"Walk pretty," she said. "This the easy place. This the easy going." **(29)**

She followed the track, swaying through the quiet bare fields, through the little strings of trees silver in their dead leaves, pass cabins silver from weather, with the doors and windows boarded shut, all like old women under a spell sitting there. "I walking in their sleep," she said, nodding her head vigorously. **(30)**

In a ravine she went where a spring was silently flowing through a hollow log. Old Phoenix bent and drank. "Sweet-gum makes the water sweet," she said, and drank more. "Nobody know who made this well, for it was here when I was born." **(31)**

The track crossed a swampy part where the moss hung as white as lace from every limb. "Sleep on, alligators, and blow your bubbles." Then the track went into the road. **(32)**

Deep, deep the road went down between the high green-colored banks. Overhead the live-oaks met, and it was as dark as a cave. **(33)**

A black dog with a lolling tongue came up out of the weeds by the ditch. She was meditating, and not ready, and when he came at her she only hit him a little with her cane. Over she went in the ditch, like a little puff of milk-weed. **(34)**

Down there, her senses drifted away. A dream visited her, and she reached her hand up, but nothing reached down and gave her a pull. So she lay there and presently went to talking. "Old woman," she said to herself, "that black dog come up out of the weeds to stall you off, and now there he sitting on his fine tail, smiling at you." **(35)**

A white man finally came along and found her—a hunter, a young man, with his dog on a chain. **(36)**

"Well, Granny!" he laughed, "what are you doing there?" **(37)**

"Lying on my back like a June-bug waiting to be turned over, mister," she said, reaching up her hand. **(38)**

He lifted her up, gave her a swing in the air, and set her down. "Anything broken, Granny?" **(39)**

"No sir, them old dead weeds is springy enough," said Phoenix, when she had got her breath. "I thank you for your trouble." **(40)**

"Where do you live, Granny?" he asked, while the two dogs were growling at each other. **(41)**

"Away back yonder, sir, behind the ridge. You can't even see it from here." **(42)**

"On your way home?" **(43)**

"No, sir, I going to town." **(44)**

"Why, that's too far! That's as far as I walk when I come out myself, and I get something for my trouble." He patted the stuffed bag he carried, and there hung down a little closed claw. It was one of the bob-whites, with its beak hooked bitterly to show it was dead. "Now you go on home, Granny!" **(45)**

"I bound to go to town, mister," said Phoenix. "The time come around." **(46)**

He gave another laugh, filling the whole landscape. "I know you old colored people! Wouldn't miss going to town to see Santa Claus!" **(47)**

But something held Old Phoenix very still. The deep lines in her face went into a fierce and different radiation. Without warning, she had seen with her own eyes a flashing nickel fall out of the man's pocket onto the ground. **(48)**

"How old are you, Granny?" he was saying. **(49)**

"There is no telling, mister," she said, "no telling." **(50)**

Then she gave a little cry and clapped her hands and said, "Git on away from here, dog! Look! Look at that dog!" She laughed as if in admiration. "He ain't scared of nobody. He a big black dog." She whispered, "Sic him!" **(51)**

"Watch me get rid of that cur," said the man. "Sic him, Pete! Sic him!" **(52)**

Phoenix heard the dogs fighting, and heard the man running and throwing sticks. She even heard a gunshot. But she was slowly bending forward by that time, further and further forward, the lids stretched down over her eyes, as if she were doing this in her sleep. Her chin was lowered almost to her knees. The yellow palm of her hand came out from the fold of her apron. Her fingers slid down and along the ground under the piece of money with the grace and care they would have in lifting an egg from under a sitting hen. Then she slowly straightened up, she stood erect, and the nickel was in her apron pocket. A bird flew by. Her lips moved. "God watching me the whole time, I come to stealing." **(53)**

The man came back, and his own dog panted about them. "Well, I scared him off that time," he said, and then he laughed and lifted his gun and pointed it at Phoenix. **(54)**

She stood straight and faced him. **(55)**

"Doesn't the gun scare you?" he said, still pointing it. **(56)**

"No, sir, I seen plenty go off closer by, in my day, and for less than what I done," she said, holding utterly still. **(57)**

He smiled, and shouldered the gun. "Well, Granny," he said, "You must be a hundred years old, and scared of nothing. I'd give you a dime if I had any money with me. But you take my advice and stay home, and nothing will happen to you." **(58)**

"I bound to go on my way, mister," said Phoenix. She inclined her head in the red rag. Then they went in different directions, but she could hear the gun shooting again and again over the hill. **(59)**

She walked on. The shadows hung from the oak trees to the road like curtains. Then she smelled wood-smoke, and smelled the river, and she saw a steeple and the cabins on their steep steps. Dozens of little black children whirled around her. There ahead was Natchez shining. Bells were ringing. She walked on. **(60)**

In the paved city it was Christmas time. There were red and green electric lights strung and crisscrossed everywhere, and all turned on in the daytime. Old Phoenix would have been lost if she had not distrusted her eyesight and depended on her feet to know where to take her. **(61)**

She paused quietly on the sidewalk where people were passing by. A lady came along in the crowd, carrying an armful of red-, green-, and silver-wrapped presents; she gave off perfume like the red roses in hot summer, and Phoenix stopped her. **(62)**

"Please, missy, will you lace up my shoe?" She held up her foot. **(63)**

"What do you want, Grandma?" **(64)**

"See my shoe," said Phoenix. "Do all right for out in the country, but wouldn't look right to go in a big building." **(65)**

"Stand still then, Grandma," said the lady. She put her packages down on the sidewalk beside her and laced and tied both shoes tightly. **(66)**

"Can't lace 'em with a cane," said Phoenix. "Thank you, missy. I doesn't mind asking a nice lady to tie up my shoe, when I gets out on the street." **(67)**

Moving slowly and from side to side, she went into the big building and into a tower of steps, where she walked up and around and around until her feet knew to stop. **(68)**

She entered a door, and there she saw nailed up on the wall the document that had been stamped with the gold seal and framed in the gold frame, which matched the dream that was hung up in her head. **(69)**

"Here I be." she said. There was a fixed and ceremonial stiffness over her body. **(70)**

"A charity case, I suppose," said an attendant who sat at the desk before her. **(71)**

But Phoenix only looked above her head. There was sweat on her face, the wrinkles in her skin shone like a bright net. **(72)**

"Speak up, Grandma," the woman said: "What's your name? We must have your history, you know. Have you been here before? What seems to be the trouble with you?" **(73)**

Old Phoenix only gave a twitch to her face as if a fly were bothering her. **(74)**

"Are you deaf?" cried the attendant. **(75)**

But then the nurse came in. **(76)**

"Oh, that's just old Aunt Phoenix," she said. "She doesn't come for herself—she has a little grandson. She makes these trips just as regular as clockwork. She lives away back off the old Natchez Trace." She bent down. "Well, Aunt Phoenix, why don't you just take a seat? We won't keep you standing after your long trip." She pointed. **(77)**

The old woman sat down, bolt upright in the chair. **(78)**

"Now, how is the boy?" asked the nurse. **(79)**

Old Phoenix did not speak. **(80)**

"I said, how is the boy?" **(81)**

But Phoenix only waited and stared straight ahead, her face very solemn and withdrawn into rigidity. **(82)**

"Is his throat any better?" asked the nurse. "Aunt Phoenix, don't you hear me? Is your grandson's throat any better since the last time you came for the medicine?" **(83)**

With her hands on her knees, the old woman waited, silent, erect and motionless, just as if she were in armor. **(84)**

"You mustn't take up our time this way, Aunt Phoenix," the nurse said. "Tell us quickly about your grandson, and get it over. He isn't dead, is he?" **(85)**

At last there came a flicker and then a flame of comprehension across her face, and she spoke. **(86)**

"My grandson. It was my memory had left me. There I sat and forgot why I made my long trip." **(87)**

"Forgot?" The nurse frowned. "After you came so far?" **(88)**

Then Phoenix was like an old woman begging a dignified forgiveness for waking up frightened in the night. "I never did go to school, I was too old at the Surrender," she said in a soft voice. "I'm an old woman without an education. It was my memory fail me. My little grandson, he is just the same, and I forgot it in the coming." **(89)**

"Throat never heals, does it?" said the nurse, speaking in a loud, sure voice to Old Phoenix. By now she had a card with something written on it, a little list. "Yes. Swallowed lye. When was it—January—two-three years ago—" **(90)**

Phoenix spoke unasked now. "No, missy, he not dead, he just the same. Every little while his throat begin to close up again, and he not able to swallow. He not get his breath. He not able to help himself. So the time come around, and I go on another trip for the soothing medicine." **(91)**

"All right. The doctor said as long as you came to get it, you could have it," said the nurse. "But it's an obstinate case." **(92)**

"My little grandson, he sit up there in the house all wrapped up, waiting by himself," Phoenix went on. "We is the only two left in the world. He suffer and it don't seem to put him back at all. He got a sweet look. He going to last. He wear a little patch quilt and peep out holding his mouth open like a little bird. I remembers so plain now. I not going to forget him again, no, the whole enduring time. I could tell him from all the others in creation." **(93)**

"All right." The nurse was trying to hush her now. She brought her a bottle of medicine. "Charity," she said, making a check mark in a book. **(94)**

Old Phoenix held the bottle close to her eyes and then carefully put it into her pocket. **(95)**

"I thank you," she said. **(96)**

"It's Christmas time, Grandma," said the attendant. "Could I give you a few pennies out of my purse?" **(97)**

"Five pennies is a nickel," said Phoenix stiffly. **(98)**

"Here's a nickel," said the attendant. **(99)**

Phoenix rose carefully and held out her hand. She received the nickel and then fished the other nickel out of her pocket and laid it beside the new one. She stared at her palm closely, with her head on one side. **(100)**

Then she gave a tap with her cane on the floor. **(101)**

"This is what come to me to do," she said. "I going to the store and buy my child a little windmill they sells, made out of paper. He going to find it hard to believe there such a thing in the world. I'll march myself back where he waiting, holding it straight up in this hand." **(102)**

She lifted her free hand, gave a little nod, turned round, and walked out of the doctor's office. Then her slow step began on the stairs, going down. **(103)**

Questions for Writing and Discussion

1. Which of the following approximates your response(s) to the character of Phoenix Jackson: Surprise that she should be the subject of a story? Anger that no one helps her on her journey? Boredom that you just read a story in which nothing seems to happen? Puzzlement at her apparently senile behavior? Amazement at her determination and courage? Describe any other responses you may have.

2. According to legend, the Phoenix is a mythological bird that lives for five hundred years, burns itself to death, and then rises from its ashes in the freshness of youth to live through another life cycle. What *events*, *references*, and *images* in the story suggest that Welty's Phoenix Jackson is like the mythological bird?

3. One reader has suggested that during her journey, Phoenix encounters twelve obstacles (internal and external) that represent tests, or trials, of her faith and courage. How many of these tests can you find? Does she "pass" each test? What do these tests reveal about her character?

4. In an essay entitled "Is Phoenix Jackson's Grandson Really Dead?" Eudora Welty says, "The story is told through Phoenix's mind as she undertakes her errand. As the author at one with the character as I tell it, I must assume that the boy is alive. As the reader, you are free to think as you like, of course: the story invites you to believe that no matter what happens, Phoenix for as long as she is able to walk and can hold to her purpose will make her journey." Explain how the boy's actual condition might affect your interpretation of the story.

5. Kate Chopin's "The Story of an Hour" and Eudora Welty's "A Worn Path" are both stories about love. By way of contrast, what do the character and behavior of Mrs. Mallard tell you about Phoenix? What do the character and behavior of Phoenix reveal about Mrs. Mallard?

THE LESSON

TONI CADE BAMBARA

Toni Cade Bambara is an activist for the African-American community on many fronts—political, cultural, and literary. She has worked for political and social causes in urban communities, taught African-American Studies at a half a dozen different colleges and universities, and is the author of several collections of short stories and novels, including Gorilla, My Love *(1972),* The Sea Birds Are Still Alive *(1977),* The Salt Eaters *(1980), and* If Blessing Comes *(1987). "The Lesson," which appears in* Gorilla, My Love, *dramatizes the gradual awakening of several children to the political and economic realities of contemporary urban life. As you read the story, pay attention to the narrator, Sylvia. What is the lesson and what does Sylvia learn?*

Back in the days when everyone was old and stupid or young and foolish and me and Sugar were the only ones just right, this lady moved on our block with nappy hair and proper speech and no makeup. And quite naturally we laughed at her, laughed the way we did at the junk man who went about his business like he was some big-time president and his sorry-ass horse his secretary. And we kinda hated her too, hated the way we did the winos who cluttered up our parks and pissed on our handball walls and stank up our hallways and stairs so you couldn't halfway play hide-and-seek without a goddamn gas mask. Miss Moore was her name. The only woman on the block with no first name. And she was black as hell, cept for her feet, which were fish-white and spooky. And she was always planning these boring-ass things for us to do, us being my cousins, mostly, who lived on the block cause we all moved North the same time and to the same apartment then spread out gradual to breathe. And our parents would yank our heads into some kinda shape and crisp up our clothes so we'd be presentable for travel with Miss Moore, who always looked like she was going to church, though she never did. Which is just one of the things the grownups talked about when they talked behind her back like a dog. But when she came calling with some sachet she'd sewed up or some gingerbread she'd made or some book, why then they'd all be too embarrassed to turn her down and we'd get handed over all spruced up. She'd been to college and said it was only right that she should take responsibility for the young ones' education, and she not even related by marriage or blood. So they'd go for it. Specially Aunt Gretchen. She was the main gofer in the family. You got some ole dumb shit foolishness you want somebody to go for, you send for Aunt Gretchen. She been screwed into the go-along for so long, it's a blood-deep natural thing with her. Which is how she got saddled with me and Sugar and Junior in the first place while our mothers were in a la-de-da apartment up the block having a good ole time. **(1)**

So this one day Miss Moore rounds us all up at the mailbox and it's puredee hot and she's knockin herself out about arithmetic. And school suppose to let up in summer I heard, but she don't never let up. And the starch in my pinafore scratching the shit outta me and I'm really hating this nappy-head bitch and her goddamn college degree. I'd much rather go to the pool or to the show where it's cool. So me and Sugar leaning on the mailbox being surly, which is a Miss Moore word. And Flyboy checking out what everybody brought for lunch. And Fat Butt already wasting his peanut-butter-and-jelly sandwich like the pig he is. And Junebug punchin on Q.T.'s arm for potato chips. And Rosie Giraffe shifting from one hip to the other waiting for somebody to step on her foot or ask her if she from Georgia so she can kick ass, preferably Mercedes's. And Miss Moore asking us do we know what money is, like we a bunch of retards. I mean real money, she say, like it's only poker chips or monopoly papers we lay on the grocer. So right away I'm tired of this and say so. And would much rather snatch Sugar and go to the Sunset and terrorize the West Indian kids and take their hair ribbons and their money too. And Miss Moore files that remark away for next week's lesson on brotherhood, I can tell. And finally I say we oughta get to the subway cause it's cooler and besides we might meet some cute boys. Sugar done swiped her mama's lipstick, so we ready. **(2)**

So we heading down the street and she's boring us silly about what things cost and what our parents make and how much goes for rent and how money ain't divided up right in this country. And then she gets to the part about we all poor and live in the slums, which I don't feature. And I'm ready to speak on that, but she steps out in the street and hails two cabs just like that. Then she hustles half the crew in with her and hands me a five-dollar bill and tells me to calculate 10 percent tip for the driver. And we're off. Me and Sugar and Junebug and Flyboy hangin out the window and hollering to everybody, putting lipstick on each other cause Flyboy a faggot anyway, and making farts with our sweaty armpits. But I'm mostly trying to figure how to spend this money. But they all fascinated with the meter ticking and Junebug starts laying bets as to how much it'll read when Flyboy can't hold his breath no more. Then Sugar lays bets as to how much it'll be when we get there. So I'm stuck. Don't nobody want to go for my plan, which is to jump out at the next light and run off to the first bar-b-que we can find. Then the driver tells us to get the hell out cause we there already. And the meter reads eighty-five cents. And I'm stalling to figure out the tip and Sugar say give him a dime. And I decide he don't need it bad as I do, so later for him. But then he tries to take off with Junebug foot still in the door so we talk about his mama something ferocious. Then we check out that we on Fifth Avenue and everybody dressed up in stockings. One lady in a fur coat, hot as it is. White folks crazy. **(3)**

"This is the place," Miss Moore say, presenting it to us in the voice she uses at the museum. "Let's look in the windows before we go in." **(4)**

"Can we steal?" Sugar asks very serious like she's getting the ground rules squared away before she plays. "I beg your pardon," say Miss Moore, and we fall out. So she leads us around the windows of the toy store and me and Sugar screamin, "This is mine, that's mine, I gotta have that, that was made for me, I was born for that," till Big Butt drowns us out. **(5)**

"Hey, I'm goin to buy that there." **(6)**

"That there? You don't even know what it is, stupid." **(7)**

"I do so," he say punchin on Rosie Giraffe. "It's a microscope." **(8)**

"Whatcha gonna do with a microscope, fool?" **(9)**

"Look at things." **(10)**

"Like what, Ronald?" ask Miss Moore. And Big Butt ain't got the first notion. So here go Miss Moore gabbing about the thousands of bacteria in a drop of water and the somethinorother in a speck of blood and the million and one living things in the air around us is invisible to the naked eye. And what she say that for? Junebug go to town on that "naked" and we rolling. Then Miss Moore ask what it cost. So we all jam into the window smudgin it up and the price tag say $300. So then she ask how long'd take for Big Butt and Junebug to save up their allowances. "Too long," I say. "Yeh," adds Sugar, "outgrown it by that time." And Miss Moore say no, you never outgrow learning instruments. "Why, even medical students and interns and," blah, blah, blah. And we ready to choke Big Butt for bringing it up in the first damn place. **(11)**

"This here costs four hundred eighty dollars," say Rosie Giraffe. So we pile up all over her to see what she pointin out. My eyes tell me it's a chunk of glass cracked with something heavy, and different-color inks dripped into the splits, then the whole thing put into a oven or something. But for $480 it don't make sense. **(12)**

"That's a paperweight made of semi-precious stones fused together under tremendous pressure," she explains slowly, with her hands doing the mining and all the factory work. **(13)**

"So what's a paperweight?" asks Rosie Giraffe. **(14)**

"To weigh paper with, dumbbell," say Flyboy, the wise man from the East. **(15)**

"Not exactly," say Miss Moore, which is what she say when you warm or way off too. "It's to weigh paper down so it won't scatter and make your desk untidy." So right away me and Sugar curtsy to each other and then to Mercedes who is more the tidy type. **(16)**

"We don't keep paper on top of the desk in my class," say Junebug, figuring Miss Moore crazy or lyin one. **(17)**

"At home, then," she say. "Don't you have a calendar and a pencil case and a blotter and a letter-opener on your desk at home where you do your homework?" And she know damn well what our homes look like cause she nosys around in them every chance she gets. **(18)**

"I don't even have a desk," say Junebug. "Do we?" **(19)**

"No. And I don't get no homework neither," says Big Butt. **(20)**

"And I don't even have a home," say Flyboy like he do at school to keep the white folks off his back and sorry for him. Send this poor kid to camp posters, is his specialty. **(21)**

"I do," says Mercedes. "I have a box of stationery on my desk and a picture of my cat. My godmother bought the stationery and the desk. There's a big rose on each sheet and the envelopes smell like roses." **(22)**

"Who wants to know about your smelly-ass stationery," say Rosie Giraffe fore I can get my two cents in. **(23)**

"It's important to have a work area all your own so that . . ." **(24)**

"Will you look at this sailboat, please," say Flyboy, cuttin her off and pointin to the thing like it was his. So once again we tumble all over each other to gaze at this magnificent thing in the toy store which is just big enough to maybe sail two kittens across the pond if you strap them to the posts tight. We all start reciting the price tag like we in assembly. "Handcrafted sailboat of fiberglass at one thousand one hundred ninety-five dollars." **(25)**

"Unbelievable," I hear myself say and am really stunned. I read it again for myself just in case the group recitation put me in a trance. Same thing. For some reason this pisses me off. We look at Miss Moore and she lookin at us, waiting for I dunno what. **(26)**

"Who'd pay all that when you can buy a sailboat set for a quarter at Pop's, a tube of glue for a dime, and a ball of string for eight cents? It must have a motor and a whole lot else besides," I say. "My sailboat cost me about fifty cents." **(27)**

"But will it take water?" say Mercedes with her smart ass. **(28)**

"Took mine to Alley Pond Park once," say Flyboy. "String broke. Lost it. Pity." **(29)**

"Sailed mine in Central Park and it keeled over and sank. Had to ask my father for another dollar." **(30)**

"And you got the strap," laugh Big Butt. "The jerk didn't even have a string on it. My old man wailed on his behind." **(31)**

Little Q.T. was staring hard at the sailboat and you could see he wanted it bad. But he too little and somebody'd just take it from him. So what the hell. "This boat for kids, Miss Moore?" **(32)**

"Parents silly to buy something like that just to get all broke up," say Rosie Giraffe. **(33)**

"That much money it should last forever," I figure. **(34)**

"My father'd buy it for me if I wanted it." **(35)**

"Your father, my ass," say Rosie Giraffe getting a chance to finally push Mercedes. **(36)**

"Must be rich people shop here," say Q.T. **(37)**

"You are a very bright boy," say Flyboy. "What was your first clue?" And he rap him on the head with the back of his knuckles, since Q.T. the only one he could get away with. Though Q.T. liable to come up behind you years later and get his licks in when you half expect it. **(38)**

"What I want to know is," I says to Miss Moore though I never talk to her, I wouldn't give the bitch that satisfaction, "is how much a real boat costs? I figure a thousand'd get you a yacht any day." **(39)**

"Why don't you check that out," she says, "and report back to the group?" Which really pains my ass. If you gonna mess up a perfectly good swim day least you could do is have some answers. "Let's go in," she say like she got something up her sleeve. Only she don't lead the way. So me and Sugar turn the corner to where the entrance is, but when we get there I kinda hang back. Not that I'm scared, what's there to be afraid of, just a toy store. But I feel funny, shame. But what I got to be shamed about? Got as much right to go in as anybody. But somehow I can't seem to get hold of the door, so I step away for Sugar to lead. But she hangs back too. And I look at her and she looks at me and this is ridiculous. I mean, damn, I have never ever been shy about doing nothing or going nowhere. But then Mercedes steps up and then Rosie Giraffe and Big Butt crowd in behind and shove, and next thing we all stuffed into the doorway with only Mercedes squeezing past us, smoothing out her jumper and walking right down the aisle. Then the rest of us tumble in like a glued-together jigsaw done all wrong. And people lookin at us. And it's like the time me and Sugar crashed into the Catholic church on a dare. But once we got in there and everything so hushed and holy and the candles and the bowin and the handkerchiefs on all the drooping heads, I just couldn't go through with the plan. Which was for me to run up to the altar and do a tap dance while Sugar played the nose flute and messed around in the holy water. And Sugar kept givin me the elbow. Then later teased me so bad I tied her up in the shower and turned it on and locked her in. And she'd be there till this day if Aunt Gretchen hadn't finally figured I was lyin about the boarder takin a shower. **(40)**

Same thing in the store. We all walkin on tiptoe and hardly touchin the games and puzzles and things. And I watched Miss Moore who is steady watchin us like she waitin for a sign. Like Mama Drewery watches the sky and sniffs the air and takes note of just how much slant is in the bird formation. Then me and Sugar bump smack into each other, so busy gazing at the toys, 'specially the sailboat. But we don't laugh and go into our fat-lady bump-stomach routine. We just stare at that price tag. Then Sugar run a finger over the whole boat. And I'm jealous and want to hit her. Maybe not her, but I sure want to punch somebody in the mouth. **(41)**

"Watcha bring us here for, Miss Moore?" **(42)**

"You sound angry, Sylvia. Are you mad about something?" Givin me one of them grins like she tellin a grown-up joke that never turns out to be funny. And she's lookin very closely at me like maybe she plannin to do my portrait from memory. I'm mad, but I won't give her that satisfaction. So I slouch around the store bein very bored and say, "Let's go." **(43)**

Me and Sugar at the back of the train watchin the tracks whizzin by large then small then gettin gobbled up in the dark. I'm thinkin about this tricky toy I saw in the store. A clown that somersaults on a bar then does chin-ups just cause you yank lightly at his leg. Cost $35. I could see me askin my mother for a $35 birthday clown. "You wanna who that costs what?" she'd say, cocking her head to the side to get a better view of the hole in my head. Thirty-five dollars could buy new bunk beds for Junior and Gretchen's boy. Thirty-five dollars and the whole household could go visit Granddaddy Nelson in the country. Thirty-five dollars would pay for the rent and the piano bill too. Who are these people that spend that much for performing clowns and $1,000 for toy sailboats? What kinda work they do and how they live and how come we ain't in on it? Where we are is who we are, Miss Moore always pointin out. But it don't necessarily have to be that way, she always adds then waits for somebody to say that poor people have to wake up and demand their share of the pie and don't none of us know what kind of pie she talkin about in the first damn place. But she ain't so smart cause I still got her four dollars from the taxi and she sure ain't gettin it. Messin up my day with this shit. Sugar nudges me in my pocket and winks. **(44)**

Miss Moore lines us up in front of the mailbox where we started from, seem like years ago, and I got a headache for thinkin so hard. And we lean all over each other so we can hold up under the draggy-ass lecture she always finishes us off with at the end before we thank her for borin us to tears. But she just looks at us like she readin tea leaves. Finally she say, "Well, what did you think of F. A. O. Schwarz?" **(45)**

Rosie Giraffe mumbles, "White folks crazy." **(46)**

"I'd like to go there again when I get my birthday money," says Mercedes, and we shove her out the pack so she has to lean on the mailbox by herself. **(47)**

"I'd like a shower. Tiring day," say Flyboy. **(48)**

Then Sugar surprises me by sayin, "You know, Miss Moore, I don't think all of us here put together eat in a year what that sailboat costs." And Miss Moore lights up like somebody goosed her. "And?" she say, urging Sugar on. Only I'm standin on her foot so she don't continue. **(49)**

"Imagine for a minute what kind of society it is in which some people can spend on a toy what it would cost to feed a family of six or seven. What do you think?" **(50)**

"I think," say Sugar pushing me off her feet like she never done before, cause I whip her ass in a minute, "that this is not much of a democracy if you ask me. Equal chance to pursue happiness means an equal crack at the dough, don't it?" Miss Moore is besides herself and I am disgusted with Sugar's treachery. So I stand on her foot one more time to see if she'll shove me. She shuts up, and Miss Moore looks at me, sorrowfully I'm thinkin. And somethin weird is goin on, I can feel it in my chest. **(51)**

"Anybody else learn anything today?" lookin dead at me. I walk away and Sugar has to run to catch up and don't even seem to notice when I shrug her arm off my shoulder. **(52)**

"Well, we got four dollars anyway," she says. **(53)**

"Uh hunh." **(54)**

"We could go to Hascombs and get half a chocolate layer and then go to the Sunset and still have plenty money for potato chips and ice cream sodas." **(55)**

"Uh hunh." **(56)**

"Race you to Hascombs," she say. **(57)**

We start down the block and she gets ahead which is O.K. by me cause I'm going to the West End and then over to the Drive to think this day through. She can run if she want to and even run faster. But ain't nobody gonna beat me at nuthin. **(58)**

Questions for Writing and Discussion

1. Describe one incident when a parent, friend, or family member tried to get you to do something that you didn't want to do. How did you react? How was your behavior similar to or different from the reaction of Sylvia, the narrator in "The Lesson"?

2. Reread the opening sentence of the story. What does the first half of that sentence reveal about the character of the narrator? Does the rest of the story confirm that initial impression? Explain.

3. Locate at least one sentence or passage describing the reactions of each of the following children to the merchandise at F.A.O. Schwartz: Sylvia (the narrator), Sugar, Flyboy, Mercedes,

Big Butt, Junebug, Rosie Giraffe, and Q.T. How do their reactions to the toys and their prices affect the narrator? Why does Bambara include all of these children in the story rather than tell it using just Miss Moore, Sylvia, and Sugar?

4. Miss Moore is the "teacher" for this "lesson," but what kind of teacher is she and how do her students react to her? What strategies does she use to help the children learn? Are her methods effective? How do the children react to each other's learning? Does Miss Moore make some mistakes?

5. What evidence (cite specific sentences) suggests that Sylvia is learning more from this lesson than she wants to? What exactly is she learning? Describe what she might do in the future as a result of what she learns.

6. Explain how each of the following quotations from Sylvia's thoughts relates to the theme or main idea of "The Lesson":

> "White folks crazy."
> "I mean, damn, I have never ever been shy about doing nothing or going nowhere."
> "If you gonna mess up a perfectly good swim day least you could do is have some answers."
> "But ain't nobody gonna beat me at nuthin."

7. Write two paragraphs comparing and contrasting the "awakenings" of Mrs. Mallard in "The Story of an Hour" and Sylvia in "The Lesson." What—and how—does each character learn? How do they react to what they learn? What do we, as readers, learn?

Responding to Literature: The Writing Process

■ **Assignment for Responding to Literature** Choose one of the short stories from this chapter (or a work of literature assigned in your class) and read it actively, reread and annotate the work, and share your responses with others in the class. Then write an interpretative essay. Assume that you are writing for other members of your class (including your instructor) who have read the work but who may not understand or agree with your interpretation.

COLLECTING

In addition to reading, rereading, annotating, and sharing your responses, try the following collecting strategies:

- **Collaborative Annotation.** In small groups, choose a work of literature or select a passage that you have already annotated. In the group, read each other's annotations. Then discuss each annotation. Which annotations does your group agree are the best? Have a group recorder record the best annotations.

- **Elements of Fiction Analysis.** Reread the paragraphs defining character, plot, point of view, setting, and style. Choose three of these elements that seem most important in the story that you are reading. Reread the story, annotating for these three elements. Then freewrite a paragraph explaining *how these three elements are interrelated* or *how they explain the theme.*

- **Time Line.** In your journal, draw a time line for the story. List above the line everything that happens in the story. Below the line, indicate where the story opens, when the major conflicts occur, and where the climax and the denouement occur. For "The Story of an Hour," student writer Karen Ehrhardt drew the following time line:

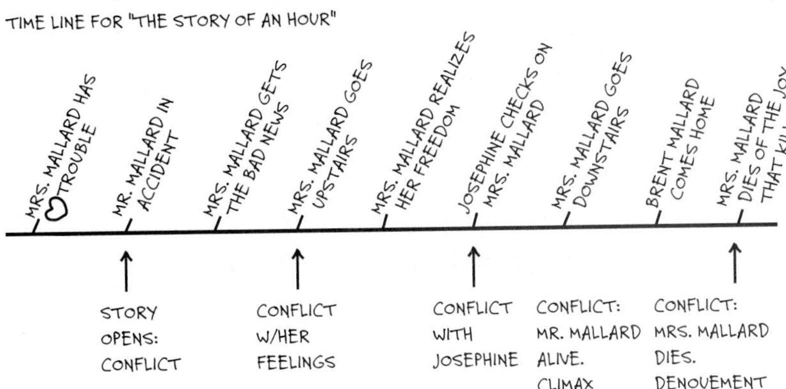

- **Character Conflict Map.** Start with a full page of paper. Draw a main character in the center of the page. Locate the other major characters, internal forces, and external forces (including social, economic, and environmental pressures) in a circle around the main character. Draw a line between each of these peripheral characters or forces and the main character. For his character conflict map for "The Story of an Hour," student writer Darren Marshall used images from his computer program to surround his picture of Mrs. Mallard:

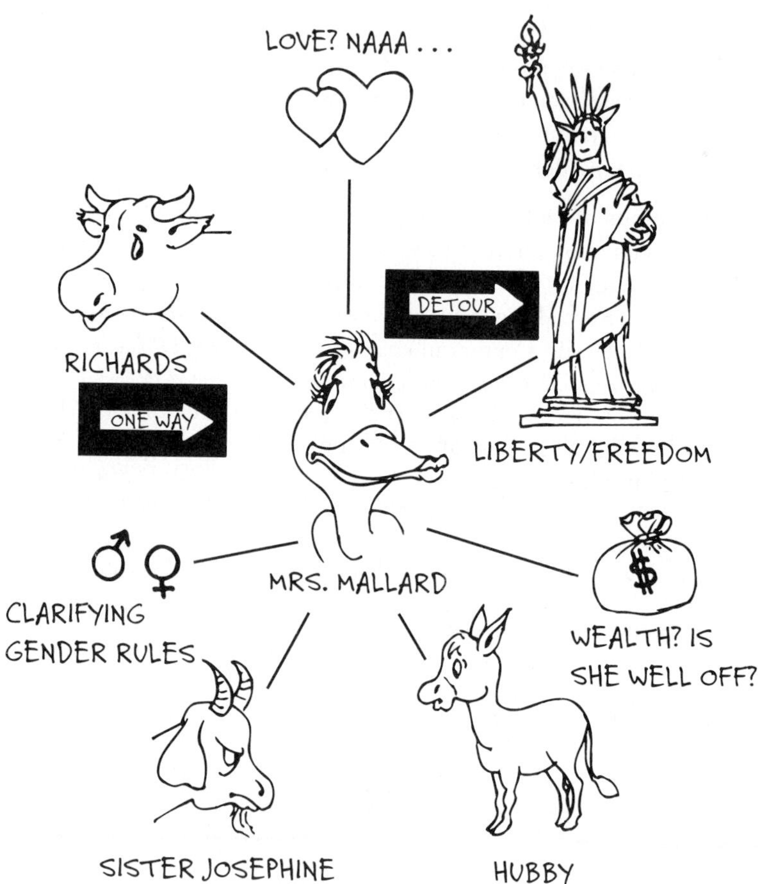

- **Story Picture.** Draw a picture of the story, based on the time line and conflict mapping, that represents the entire story. Use the information from your character analysis, time line, and character conflicts to help you draw a single picture of the complete story. Student writer Lori Van Skike drew a picture for "The Story of an Hour" that shows how the rising and falling action of the plot parallels Mrs. Mallard's ascent and descent of the stairs:

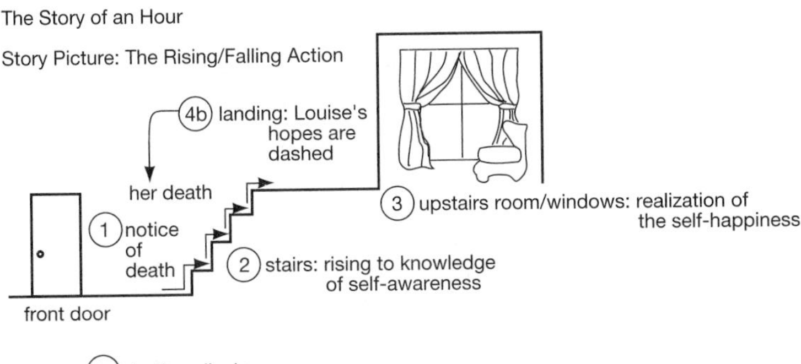

- **Feature List.** Choose a character trait, repeated image, or idea that you wish to investigate in the story. List, in order of appearance, every word, image, or reference that you find in the story.
- **Scene Vision or Revision.** Write a scene for this story in which you change some part of it. You may *add* a scene to the beginning, middle, or end of the story. You may *change* a scene in the story. You may write a scene in the story from a different character's point of view. You may change the style of the story for your scene. How, for example, might Eudora Welty have described the opening scene of "The Story of an Hour"?
- **Background Investigation.** Investigate the biographical, social, historical, or geographical context for the story. Locate a biography of the author. How are the major events of the author's life relevant to the story? Read about the historical or economic background of the story. Look at maps or descriptions of the setting for the story. How do these background sources increase your appreciation or widen your understanding of the story?
- **Reconsideration of Purposes.** What idea, theme, or approach most interests you? Will you be explaining, evaluating, problem solving, or arguing? Are you combining purposes? Do these purposes suggest what kinds of information you might collect?

SHAPING

Test each of the following possible shapes against your ideas for your essay. Use or adapt the shape or shapes that are most appropriate for your own interpretation.

EXPLAINING RELATIONSHIPS Often interpretative essays analyze how the parts of a story relate to the whole. As you explain these relationships, you should show how key lines or scenes contribute to the portrait of the major character or to the overall theme of the story. Your focus might be on how *plot* or *character conflicts* affect your understanding of the major character, on how the *setting* reflects the theme, or on how *images* reveal character and/or contribute to the theme.

Introduction and thesis:	The images in story "X" reveal that the theme is "Y."
First scene or part:	How key images contribute to theme
Second scene or part:	How key images contribute to theme
Third scene or part:	How key images contribute to theme
Conclusion:	

EVALUATING If your response suggests an evaluating purpose, you may wish to set up *criteria* for an effective short story and then provide evidence that shows how the particular story does or does not measure up to your standards. Your thesis might be "Story 'X' is highly dramatic because the main character undergoes emotional changes, the character conflicts heighten the tension, and the theme is controversial." A similar shaping strategy might be to set a *definition* of a "hero" or "heroine" and then analyze how the main character fits your definition.

Introduction and thesis:	Story "X" is highly dramatic.
Criteria #1:	A dramatic short story should focus on a character who changes his or her behavior or beliefs.
	Judgment and evidence for criteria #1:
Criteria #2:	A dramatic story must have striking conflicts that lead to a crisis or a predicament.
	Judgment and evidence for criteria #2:
Criteria #3:	A dramatic story should have a theme that makes a controversial point.
	Judgment and evidence for criteria #3:
Conclusion:	

ARGUING During class discussion, you may disagree with another person's response. Your thesis may then take the form, "Although some readers believe this story is about 'X,' the story is really about 'Y.'" In an argumentative structure, you counter opposing interpretations by first pointing to evidence in the story and then supporting your interpretation with evidence.

Introduction and thesis: Although some readers suggest that the story is about "X," it is really about "Y."

Body paragraphs: State the opposing interpretation and give evidence that this interpretation cites:

State your interpretation and give evidence (description, dialogue, images, points of conflict, incidents from the plot):

Conclusion:

INVESTIGATING CHANGES IN INTERPRETATION Often, readers *change* interpretations during the course of responding to a piece of literature. Thus, your main point might be, "Although I initially thought 'X' about the story, I gradually realized the theme of the story was 'Y.'" If that sentence expresses your main idea, you may wish to organize your essay following the *chronology* or the *steps* in the changes in your interpretation:

Introduction and thesis: "Although I initially thought "X," I now believe "Y."

Body paragraphs: First step (your original interpretation of the story and supporting evidence):

Second step (additional or contradictory ideas and evidence that forced you to reconsider your interpretation):

Third step (your final interpretation and supporting evidence):

Conclusion:

Note: One strategy you should *not* use is to simply retell the main events of the story. A review of the plot is not an acceptable interpretation. Your audience has already read the story. They want you to state your interpretation and then use details from the story to show how and why your interpretation is credible. *Although you will cite events from the plot, you must explain how or why these events support your interpretation.*

Computer Tip: Revising

When you have finished your draft, you need to revise your main idea or thesis. *The exact phrasing of your main idea or interpretation is crucial.* On the computer, use a block move to copy your conclusion and place it just above your introduction. (You can also use your split-screen function to compare the two paragraphs.)

Concluding paragraph(s):

Introductory paragraph(s):

With both your conclusion and introduction in front of you on the screen, reread them carefully. If you wrote your conclusion *after* you wrote the body of the essay, it probably contains a clearer statement of your main idea. Revise your introduction so that it includes the clearest and most concise statement of your interpretation. If you have to move a key sentence from the conclusion to the introduction, do so. You can then revise your conclusion as necessary..

Drafting

To prepare to draft your essay, read through your annotations and gather your collecting and shaping notes. Some writers prefer to write one-sentence statements of their main ideas at the top of the page to keep them focused as they write. Other writers prefer to make rough outlines to follow, based on their adaptations of one of the above shaping strategies. When you begin drafting, you may wish to skip your introduction and start with the body of your essay. You can fill in the introduction after you have written a draft.

Once you start writing, keep your momentum going. If you draw a blank, reread what you have already written or look at your notes. If you cannot think of a particular word or are unsure about a spelling, draw a line ___________ and keep on writing.

Revising

Use the following guidelines as you read your classmates' drafts and revise your own essay. Be prepared to make changes in your ideas, organization, and evidence, as well as to fix problems in sentences and word choice.

Guildelines for Revisions

- **Clarify your main idea or interpretation.** Ask your readers to write, in one sentence, the main point of your interpretation. If their statements do not exactly match your main point, clarify your thesis. Your interpretation (not a statement of fact) should be clearly stated early in your essay.
- **Do not give a plot summary.** Your readers have read the story, so do not simply retell the plot. Do, however, give ample evidence. You must also explain how that evidence supports your main point.
- **Support each part of your interpretation with references to specific passages from the text.** Do not be satisfied with one piece of evidence. Find as many bits of evidence as possible. The case for your interpretation grows stronger with each additional piece of evidence.
- **Explain how each piece of evidence supports your interpretation.** Do not just cite several pieces of evidence and go on to your next point. Explain for your readers *how* the evidence supports your interpretation.
- **Define key terms in your essay.** If you are writing about the *hero* in a story, define what you mean by "hero" or "heroine." If you are arguing that "The Story of an Hour" has a *feminist* theme, define "feminism."
- **Signal the major parts of your interpretation.** Let your readers know when you shift to a new point. Use transitions and paragraph hooks at the beginning of body paragraphs.
- **Use the present tense as you describe the events in the story.** If you are describing the end of "The Story of an Hour," write "Mrs. Mallard descends the stairs and learns the 'good news' about her husband."
- **Quote accurately and cite page numbers for each reference.** Double-check your quotations to make sure they are accurate, word-for-word transcriptions. Following each direct quotation, cite page references as follows: In the first sentence, Kate Chopin says, "Mrs. Mallard was afflicted with a heart trouble" **(479). Note:** The period goes outside the parentheses. See Chapter 12 for correct documentation style.
- **Revise your essay for sentence clarity and conciseness.** Read your essay aloud or have a classmate read it. Reduce unnecessary

repetition. Use active verbs. Rework awkward or confusing sentences.

- **Edit your essay.** Check your essay for correct spelling, word choice, punctuation, and grammar.

■ **Postscript on the Writing Process** Before you turn in your essay, answer the following questions in your journal.

1. Explain what part of this essay (collecting ideas and evidence, focusing on your interpretation, shaping your essay, drafting, or revising) was most difficult for you. How did you work around that problem?

2. What do you like best about your essay? Refer to specific places in the essay (lead-in, thesis, pieces of evidence, ideas, conclusion). Which specific paragraphs did you like best? Why?

3. What did you learn about the story by writing your interpretation? What do you realize now that you did not understand when you first read the story?

4. If you had two more hours to work on this essay, what would you change? Why?

Responding to Literature: Student Writing

A Worn Path

Julia MacMillan and Brett MacFadden

Julia MacMillan and Brett MacFadden collaboratively wrote their essay on the Phoenix imagery in Eudora Welty's "A Worn Path." They drafted their own essays separately and then collaborated on a revision that shared their interpretations and their best textual evidence. Included below are their original separate notes and drafts, their plans for their collaborative revision, and their final revised interpretation. Read their separate versions first, and then see how they collaborated to produce their revised essay.

ROUGH DRAFTS

JULIA MACMILLAN

The journey that Phoenix Jackson makes in Eudora Welty's "A Worn Path" is very similar to that made by the mythological phoenix on its way to rebirth. Much of the symbolism and figurative language throughout the story shows the succession of events that parallel a Phoenix-like ending to the old woman.

We can feel, almost from the beginning, that Phoenix's long life is coming to an end. She is described with "the two knots of her cheeks illuminated by a yellow burning under the dark" (289). In only a few more sentences, however, we hear the mourning dove, apparently mourning for Phoenix. The yellow burning under the dark is almost a desperate, final fiery burst in the face of oncoming death.

Her death is also foreshadowed in the mention of a buzzard, watching her from the tall, dead trees. She asks of him, "Who are you watching?" as if she knows it is herself. Further in her journey, upon meeting the white hunter, her impending death as well as her expectation of it are shown. The little bob-white, "its beak hooked bitterly to show it was dead" (262), that the hunter was carrying on his bag quite forcefully shows us her death. The fact that she does not fear, but expects this death is shown when the hunter points his gun at Phoenix, and she "stood straight and faced him" quite fearlessly (263). In not fearing this death and seeming to understand its nearness, Phoenix Jackson becomes more like the bird she is named for.

It is most clearly seen that the author intended her reader to see the Phoenix imagery when the grandson is introduced near the end of the story. On page 264, she "entered a door, and there she saw the document that had been stamped with the gold seal and framed in the gold frame, which matched the dream that was hung up in her head." The gold in this passage seems to represent flame—the flame of her funeral pyre and the dream in her head of perpetuation and reincarnation through her grandson's life. It is even more clearly stated when, once in the doctor's office, she goes into a strange trance, becoming unable to answer the agitated nurse's questions. When finally asked, "He isn't dead, is he?" a "flutter, then a flame of comprehension comes across her face" (265). These flames are symbolic of her death, yet they are caused by her remembering the importance of her grandson's life to her. This life is most precious to her, because it is through her grandson that Phoenix, like the mythological bird, will live again.

BRETT MACFADDEN

In many ways Phoenix Jackson is like the mythical bird she is named after; her physical characteristics, her purpose in life, and her extreme age and nearness to death all support her likeness to the mythological Phoenix.

The Phoenix is a bird of myth that lives for 500 years and then burns itself to death, rising from its ashes renewed and beautiful. Phoenix Jackson in the story "A Worn Path" by Eudora Welty is a very old black woman near the end of her life cycle who takes a long walk through the woods to town in order to get medicine for her ailing grandson. The core story is very simple, and it is because of this simplicity that the reader is forced to look beyond the core for a more complex tale. One of the first clues toward the inner story is the name of the main character, Phoenix. With the knowledge of what a Phoenix is, we can find many clues supporting the idea of the old woman living her life as a Phoenix.

Throughout the short story, words and phrases that describe the old woman might also describe the mythological bird. Her skin is black with a "golden color underneath" (259) and the "two knobs of her cheeks were illuminated by a yellow burning under the dark" (259). Both the golden color and especially the yellow burning are colors of fire, symbolizing the bird's fiery death. A red rag that she wears on top of her head is also another color of flame. Her black, wrinkled skin can be thought of as looking quite like ashes, and assuming that her grandson is a blood relative, his skin should also be the color of charred ash. She is like a fire that is almost out. It is mostly black, but there is the small flicker of flame to show you it is not yet extinguished.

Assuming the reader chooses to believe that Phoenix does in fact have a grandson and he is in fact sick, then the main purpose of her trip is to get the boy his medicine. This idea goes along nicely with the phoenix theme because she is giving everything she has left for the benefit of her grandson. She is essentially burning herself up so that the new person can exist. We can assume from the physical appearance and actions of Phoenix that she is pretty nearly burnt out. Phoenix knows her grandson is the one with the potential now, and so she gives all the effort she has to get him his medicine. Her only wish is to see him rise from his sick bed.

There are many hints to Phoenix's extreme age. At one time she tells herself, "I is the oldest person I ever know" (261), indicating that she has lived longer than most. Another time the hunter that she came across estimated that she was "a hundred years old" (263). Much of the imagery in the story symbolizes her oncoming death. The fact that it is winter can be seen as the winter of her life. Other death images include the big dead trees, the buzzard, the scarecrow she mistakes for a ghost, and the black dog that knocks her into the ditch.

A SINGULAR PERPETUATION

BRETT MACFADDEN
AND JULIA MACMILLAN

Phoenix Jackson, in the story "A Worn Path," by Eudora Welty, is in many ways like the mythological bird she is named after. Her purpose in life, birdlike characteristics, and nearness to death all support a clear parallel between the character and her namesake. The story is very simple, and because of this simplicity the reader is forced to search for a more meaningful tale. One of the first clues towards the inner story is the name of the main character, Phoenix. With the knowledge of what a Phoenix is, it is possible to find many clues supporting the idea of the old woman living her life as a Phoenix, burning herself out for the benefit of the new bird, her grandson. **(1)**

The Phoenix is a mythological bird who after living for 500 years, burns itself to ashes on a pyre, and rises renewed to live another cycle. Phoenix Jackson journeys through the woods to town to get medicine for her ailing grandson. This idea parallels the Phoenix theme, because she is making what appears to be her final journey, in order that her grandson may rise from his sickbed. The legend of the Phoenix is one of singular perpetuation; only one exists in the world. This is shown when she tells the nurses that "We is the only two left in the world" (255). Phoenix is concerned because if both of them were to die, then it would result in the extinction of the species. As much as she worries about him surviving, she is confident that he, like the immortal bird, will survive. Speaking to the nurses again, she says, "He suffer and it don't seem to put him back at all. . . . He going to last" (265–66). As well as his immortality, his birdlike characteristics and dependence on Phoenix for his perseverance are shown when he peeps out of his quilt "holding his mouth open like a little bird" (266). He is her reincarnation, and she is devoted to his successful ascension. **(2)**

Throughout the story many words and phrases that describe the old woman might also describe the mythological bird. Her skin is described as black with "a golden color underneath," and the "two knobs of her cheeks were illuminated by a yellow burning under the dark" (259). She wears on top of her head a red rag. Both the "golden color," and the "yellow burning," as well as the red of her rag are colors of fire, symbolizing her approaching death. As she walks, the tapping of her umbrella sounds like "the chirping of a solitary little bird" (259). Her likeness to a bird is evidenced when, in passing a scarecrow in a field, she is frightened, as a bird would be. When startled by a dog, she fell into a ditch "like a little puff of milk-weed" (262). This gives the appearance that she is a light creature, mostly flame and feather. These birdlike characteristics of Phoenix seem to imply that the author intended her to represent the mythical bird. **(3)**

The myth of the Phoenix holds that when ". . . its eyes begin to grow dim, it knows that the time of death has come" (Oswalt 239). When we are first introduced to the main character, as well as being old, she is described as having "eyes . . . blue with age" (259). Many images of death, some quite vivid, link Phoenix Jackson's impending death to that of the Phoenix of myth. At one point in her journey she stoops and looks upwards exclaiming, "Sun so high! Time getting all gone here" (260). This clearly indicates her knowledge of her approaching death. Her death is also foreshadowed by the mention of several images that bombard us from the dawn of the story. Early on she reflects on the call of a mourning dove—mourning being something done in the wake of death. Later she comes upon a buzzard sitting in a dead tree. She asks of him, "Who you watching?" (261), as if she knows it is herself. Her death is foreshadowed further when walking through a cornfield she happens upon what she perceives to be a ghost. Upon closer inspection, the ghost turned out to be a scarecrow. However, she shows no fear approaching what she thinks is a ghost, which demonstrates that she is comfortable with dying. The black dog that knocks her into a ditch is another vivid image of death. Further in her journey, upon meeting a white hunter, her impending death as well as her expectation of it are shown. The little bob-white, "its beak hooked bitterly to show that it was dead" (262) that the hunter was carrying on his bag quite forcefully shows us her anticipated death. The fact that she does not fear, but expects this death is shown when the hunter pointed his gun at Phoenix, and she "stood straight and faced him" quite fearlessly" (263). In not fearing this death and seeming to understand its nearness, Phoenix Jackson becomes more like the bird she is named for. **(4)**

A carefully wrought story, "A Worn Path" is more than a tale of an old woman's formidable journey. It is the rebirth of an age-old myth wrapped in the cloak of conventionality. In examining some of the symbols, allusions, and the underlying legend, we find a well hidden but evident parallel between the lives of the main character and her namesake, the Phoenix. **(5)**

Works Cited

Oswalt, Sabine G. *Concise Encyclopedia of Greek and Roman Mythology*. Chicago: Follett Publishing Co., 1969.

■ **Postscript on the Collaborative Revision** We began this collaboration by reading each other's papers and rereading our own in order to find the strengths and weaknesses of each paper. Then together we combed through each paper, pulling out what we both agreed were our strongest points and compiled these into a thesis. For our thesis, we used the second sentence in the first paragraph: "Her [Phoenix's] purpose in life, her birdlike characteristics, and her nearness to death support a clear parallel between the character and her namesake."

Having decided on a thesis and a rough plan of action, we then went to the computer lab and began writing. At this point, the paper became more difficult because we had to narrow two papers into one and decide what we should omit. For example, Julia's paper discussed the emblem on the doctor's office wall as another symbol of Phoenix's fiery death. After discussing this scene, we decided that the symbolism was not strong enough and should be left out. We both knew each other before deciding to write the collaborative essay, so we were both comfortable around each other and were able to say what we really thought about each other's writing. We knew also that our basic writing styles were opposing. Brett's was concise, while Julia's was more flowing. Our different writing styles had to be combined into one smooth style. We did this by having one person dictate and the other type, which caused an intertwining of our styles by the time the words hit the screen. We had fun working on this paper and learned quite a bit about collaboration in the process. For example, we found it challenging because we had to work on one sentence at a time, making sure each sentence was right before we went on to the next one. This process made the revision take far longer to complete than if it had been done by one person.

QUESTIONS FOR WRITING AND DISCUSSION

1. What are the best ideas or evidence in this essay? Explain the points at which you might disagree with the writers' interpretation.

2. Compare MacMillan's and MacFadden's drafts with the final version of their essay. Explain how their interpretation changed as they worked collaboratively on the final version. What did they add to their final version? What did they omit from the earlier drafts?

3. In the final version, MacMillan and MacFadden do not cite evidence from the final part of the story. Explain why the events in town support or do not support the Phoenix parallels.

4. Review the Guidelines for Revision. In the authors' essay, underline sentences that contain the *main idea*, that *define key* *terms*, that contain *evidence* or support, that *explain* how the evidence supports the thesis, that *signal* major parts of the interpretation, and that contain *accurate* quotations. Based on your annotations, what suggestions for further revision do you have for the authors?

DEATH: THE FINAL FREEDOM

PAT RUSSELL

Following a class discussion of the feminist theme in Kate Chopin's "The Story of an Hour," Pat Russell wrote in his journal, "Is the story a feminist one? No. It is not just about feminism but about how people stifle their own needs and desires to accommodate those of their mate." In his essay, Russell argues that the traditional feminist reading limits the universal theme of the story. As you read his essay, see if you are persuaded by his argument.

The poor treatment of women and their struggle for an individual identity is a major underlying theme of Kate Chopin's stories. Although many regard Chopin's "The Story of an Hour" as a feminist story, today a more universal interpretation is appropriate. This story is not about the oppression of a woman, but about how people strive to maintain the normalcy and security of their relationships by suppressing their own individual wants and needs. **(1)**

Evidence in favor of the feminist argument begins with the period the story was written in, sometime around the turn of the century. Society prevented women from coming out of the household. Most women weren't allowed to run a business, and for that matter, they couldn't even vote. Their most important jobs were wife and mother. This background sets the tone for the main character's life. In the beginning we are told Mrs. Mallard has a "fair, calm face whose lines bespoke repression" (414). There is also evidence that suggests her husband was ignorant of her ideas and forceful with his own. Chopin writes: "There would be no powerful will bending her in that blind persistence with which men and women believe they have a right to impose a private will upon a fellow creature" (415). In addition, Mrs. Mallard is described early on as fearful and powerless, and later as a triumphant "goddess of Victory," indicating her rebirth. These citations suggest that this is a feminist story, but this label limits the meaning behind the story. **(2)**

Many people who are unhappy with their marriages either fail to recognize their unhappiness or refuse to accept responsibility for it. I feel sorry for those who don't recognize their unhappiness. However, it is pathetic to see someone such as Mrs. Mallard hold onto a relationship simply because she doesn't know how to let go. "And yet she had loved him—sometimes. Often she had not" (415). She continuously fell in and out of love with her husband until he "died," at which point she told herself that love didn't matter compared to the self-assertion "which she suddenly recognized as the strongest impulse of her being" (415). It is as if she had waited for all of her life for this moment; she prayed for a long life, when only the day before she had dreaded it. She wept for him but at the same time compared her husband to a criminal, a man whom she had lived her life for, never once thinking of herself. But now "there would be no one to live for during those coming years; she would live for herself" (415). She was lucky in that she felt "free." Her emotional suppression was over, and she would no longer have anyone to blame for her unhappiness. **(3)**

It is important not only to try to interpret the author's intended meaning of the story, but also to think about what message. "The Story of an Hour" has for us today. As a feminist story, the lesson "The Story of an Hour" teaches is one dimensional. Interpreting it as a story about the struggle of all people opens up the possibility of teaching others that selfishness and selflessness are both good, when used in moderation. In Mrs. Mallard's case, correcting this balance became a matter of life and death. In the face of her suppressor, her desperation for freedom forced her to choose death. **(4)**

Questions for Writing and Discussion

1. With what parts of Russell's interpretation do you agree? What additional evidence from the story might Russell cite in support of his interpretation? What ideas or sentences might you challenge? What evidence from the story might refute those statements?

2. Write out your definition of *feminism*. Where does or should Russell explain his definition? How should Russell clarify his definition?

3. Write out Russell's main idea or thesis. Explain why his thesis is an interpretation and not just a statement of fact.

4. What shaping strategy does Russell use to organize his essay?

5. Write out two other possible titles for Russell's essay. Explain why your alternate titles are (or are not) better than Russell's title.

TWELVE / WRITING A RESEARCH PAPER

Research is formalized curiosity. It is poking and prying with a purpose.

—ZORA NEALE HURSTON, NOVELIST AND FOLKLORE RESEARCHER

You know when you think about writing a book, you think it is overwhelming. But, actually, you break it down into tiny little tasks any moron could do.

—ANNIE DILLARD, NATURALIST, AUTHOR OF PILGRIM AT TINKER CREEK

WHILE READING TONI MORRISON'S *SONG OF SOLOMON* AND TALKING WITH RELATIVES ABOUT YOUR OWN FAMILY TREE, YOU DECIDE TO LEARN MORE ABOUT YOUR ANCESTORS—WHERE THEY CAME FROM, WHAT JOBS THEY HELD, WHICH ONES WERE FAMOUS AND WHICH WERE NOT, AND WHY THESE PEOPLE LIVED THE LIVES THEY DID. In the process, you hope to learn more about yourself and your immediate family. During your research, you read family records and letters, interview your parents and grandparents, check county records, and research genealogies in the library. You intend to write an investigative paper documenting not only what you find but the process of your search and the discoveries that you make along the way.

AFTER SPENDING TWO MONTHS IN FRANCE LIVING WITH A FAMILY AND TRYING TO UNDERSTAND THEIR DINNER CONVERSATION, YOU WONDER WHY YOU—AND OTHER AMERICANS—KNOW SO LITTLE ABOUT FOREIGN LANGUAGES. After reflecting on your inadequate background in French language and culture, you decide to investigate the current state of foreign-language studies in the United States. During your research, you discover that Americans know very little about foreign languages and cultures simply because foreign languages are rarely required of students either in high school or in college. You decide to write a research paper that documents the current state of foreign-language studies and demonstrates a need for a mandatory foreign-language requirement for secondary schools. You hope that it will persuade more students to study foreign languages and encourage some schools to revise their requirements.

Raffaello, The School of Athens, (Erich Lessing/Art Resource)

ALTHOUGH THE WORDS "RESEARCH PAPER" SOUND IMPOSING TO MOST PEOPLE, RESEARCH IS REALLY A NATURAL AND ENJOYABLE PART OF OUR EVERYDAY EXPERIENCE, BOTH OUTSIDE AND INSIDE COLLEGE CLASSROOMS. We pride ourselves on being good detectives—whether it's window-shopping for a good bargain, finding the hottest used sports car, asking co-workers for tips on the best Mexican food in town, or just browsing in bookstores for something fun to read. Even in college classes, curiosity leads us to discover new ideas. Whenever we wonder about what causes ozone holes, why teenagers commit suicide, what makes computer programs work, how artists turn clay into beautiful pottery, or what the national debt means, the seed for a research idea drops into our minds. At some point, the idea becomes a question, takes root, and begins to grow. When that happens, we want to learn about something, to find out what others already know or don't know. Curiosity blooms into research when we'd rather discover the answers for ourselves instead of being handed an answer—an "answer" that may have the manufactured feel of a plastic flower.

Whether or not you called it by that name, the essays that you have already written in this course have involved research. The word "research" literally means "to seek out" or "to search again." All writing requires research. Your observing essay, for example, required you to "look again" at your subject in order to describe it well. For your remembering essay, you recalled special events from the past, researching your mind for memories. You have also investigated topics by searching in written documents and by doing surveys and interviews. You have explained, evaluated, argued, and even explored subjects using research. In short, you are already a researcher with considerable experience in presenting the results of your research to a chosen audience. A research paper—sometimes called a "term paper"—is simply a more thorough and systematic extension of skills that you have already practiced.

This chapter will show you how to write a research paper—preparing, locating sources, taking notes, collecting and shaping information, revising, and documenting your sources. As in other writing assignments, the process is recursive. Often, you will need to back up, collect new information, redraft parts of your paper, or refocus your subject during the writing process. At the end of this chapter, student writer Kate McNerny's paper, "Foreign Language Study: An American Necessity" illustrates the important features of a research paper. During the chapter, however, samples from her research log, bibliography, notes, drafts, and

Background on Writing a Research Paper

It may be useful to explode the myth that the research paper is entirely different from the writing that students have done in Chapters 3–11. A research paper merely requires systematic library or field research, is sometimes long, and documents its sources. The purposes for writing (reporting, explaining, evaluating, persuading, exploring) and the dimensions of the writing process (collecting, shaping, drafting, revising) still apply.

Resource Note

For additional information about the research process, see a guide such as Barzun and Graff, *The Modern Researcher*. For complete information about the MLA style, see Gibaldi and Achtert, eds., *MLA Handbook for Writers of Research Papers*, Third Edition (1988).

documentation illustrate various stages in one writer's process of writing a research paper.

■ FREEWRITING: RESEARCHING In the library, find an issue of a magazine or newspaper published on or near the date and year of your birth. The issue may be on microfilm. Record the date and title of the newspaper or magazine. Browse through the issue, looking at headlines, articles, advertisements, editorials, comics, weather, sports, local news, and so forth. As you look through the issue, *record* any items, facts, or historical incidents that interest you. Photocopy one page that you find especially interesting. Explain why that page captured your attention.

Criticism [is] a disinterested endeavor to learn and propagate the best that is known and thought in the world.
—MATTHEW ARNOLD, POET AND ESSAYIST

TECHNIQUES FOR WRITING A RESEARCH PAPER

Like other kinds of writing, a research paper requires that you focus on a particular subject, develop a claim or thesis, and support your position with convincing evidence: background information, facts, statistics, descriptions, and other people's evaluations and judgments. The evidence that you present in a research paper, however, is more detailed than that in an essay, and the sources must be cited in the text and documented at the end of the paper.

In a sense, a research paper is like a scientific experiment. **Your readers should be able to trace your whole experiment—to see what ideas and evidence you worked with, where you found them, and how you used them in your paper**. If readers have any questions about the information you've presented or the conclusions you've reached, they can start with your sources and re-create or check the "experiment" for themselves. If they want to investigate your subject further, your sources will guide their reading. As you write your research paper, keep the following techniques in mind:

See Chapter 12 of the *Video Guide* for a description of how news teams do research. Much of the process becomes visible to students once they are aware of it.

- **Using *purpose, audience, and form* as your guides for writing.** Research is just a method of collecting and documenting ideas and evidence. Purpose, audience, and form should still direct your writing.

- **Finding *the best that has been written or said* about your subject.** Instead of trying to reinvent the wheel, discover what other people or writers already know (or don't know) and then build on what they have learned.

- **Using sources to make *your* point.** As you gather information, you may revise your thesis in light of what you learn, but don't let the tail wag the dog. Don't allow raw information to control you or your paper.

- ***Documenting* your sources, both in the text and at the end of the paper.** (Using ideas, information, or actual language from your sources without proper documentation is *plagiarism.*)

USING PURPOSE, AUDIENCE, AND FORM AS GUIDES

Like any other kind of writing, research papers have a *purpose*. Reporting, explaining, evaluating, problem solving, and arguing are all purposes for research papers. Purposes may appear in combinations, as in a paper that summarizes current research and then proposes a solution to a problem. Research papers, however, are not just reports of other people's ideas or evidence. What you, the researcher, observe and remember and learn is important, too. Most subjects are not interesting until writers make them so. Your curiosity, your interests in the subject, your reason and intuition establish why the subject is worth researching in the first place—and why a reader would want to read the paper once it is finished.

Research papers have a defined *audience*, too. The subject you choose, the kind of research you do, the documentation format, the vocabulary and style you use—all should be appropriate for your selected audience. If you write a senior research paper in your major, you will write for a professor and for a community of people knowledgeable about your field. If you are a legal assistant or a junior attorney in a law firm, a superior may ask you to research a specific legal precedent. If you work for a manufacturer, a manager may assign you a research report on the sales and strategies of a competitor. Although your classmates and teacher will probably read the research paper that you write for this class, you will ask them to role-play your audience. They will try to read your paper from the point of view of a defined audience—an employer, a politician, a nutritionist, an artist, an astronomer, or a senior law partner. In fact, your instructor may ask you to send your paper to some person or persons who actually are part of your audience.

Television programming illustrates the rewards—and risks—of trying to make a subject interesting. Check the *Video Library* for examples.

Finally, your research paper will follow a *form* that fits your purpose and meets the expectations and needs of your audience. First, form is controlled by purpose. If you are writing a research paper evaluating some product or performance, it may look like an evaluating paper, organized around your claims, criteria, judgments, and evidence. If you are writing a problem-solving paper, you will demonstrate the problem, propose a solution, and convince your readers that your proposal is necessary or will work. If you are arguing for a position or claim, you will present research showing both sides of the controversy and then try to convince your reader to believe or act on your claim. In each case, however, you will cite your sources in the body or text of your paper and include a list of your sources (a *bibliography*) at the end.

The *form* for your research paper is also affected by your intended audience. If you are researching new advances in sports medicine for an audience of experts, you may choose an elaborate form, with an abstract or summary of your ideas at the beginning, a section reviewing and evaluating current research, subsections for each of your main points with diagrams and charts, and an appendix with supplementary materials. If, however, you are writing primarily for jogging enthusiasts, your research paper may look more like an informal essay. Magazines and journals in the field illustrate a variety of appropriate forms for research papers. The student essay by Kate McNerny at the end of this chapter illustrates one form.

Finding the Best Sources

Accessing information from both published and unpublished sources is central to all research. To find good sources, you need to hone your detective skills. Unfortunately, Hollywood has promoted the myth that good detectives follow their suspects in high-speed car chases or through glamorous affairs. Of course, that's just fantasy. Detectives must do actual research—paperwork and legwork—to track down leads. Writers are, in a real sense, also detectives, constantly researching their own experiences and the experiences of others. Journalists, lawyers, psychologists, doctors, businesspeople, coaches, scientists, novelists—all sorts of people practice their skills in locating key bits of information and tracking down good leads.

Research combines careful planning with good luck, mindless drudgery and moments of inspiration, many dead ends and a few rare discoveries. As coaches sometimes say, those who prepare and work hard make their own luck. The following excerpt from the introduction to Pauli Murray's *Proud Shoes: The Story of an American Family* recounts her research into her family genealogy, which included slaves, free blacks, some racially mixed family members, and other relatives who were white and socially prominent. Although her detective work took several years and involved both library and field research, her account reflects the problems and successes that all researchers experience.

> My field research had the thrill of detection when the clues panned out. Rigorous discipline was needed for the drudgery of sifting through masses of documentary material in search of one relevant

fact or one confirmation of a family legend. The trail of the Fitzgerald family led me into nearly a dozen localities in several states. It took me into musty basements of old courthouses to pore over dust-silted and sometimes indecipherable handwritten entries in old volumes. I found that each locality had its own captivating legends preserved in family papers; its traditions recorded in pamphlets and privately published little books; its stories printed in almanacs, newspapers, business directories. Almost every place had "the oldest living inhabitants" and their recollections. Most important, almost every locality had its own regional-history enthusiasts, who welcomed me into a fellowship of digging into the past. Some of them gave me expert guidance which improved the efficiency of my research and shortened my labors.

Using Sources to Make *Your* Point

When your hard work does yield a source that has good information and ideas on your exact subject, don't be tempted to let that source take over your paper. If you start stringing together passages from only one or two key sources, you'll be summarizing rather than doing research. You'll be letting the sources tell you what to think, what information is important, or what conclusions to reach. Use your sources, then, to support *your* point. Write your own paper; don't let your sources write it for you.

Documenting Your Sources

Documenting your sources is an important part of writing a research paper. Documentation takes place in two stages: first, in the body or text of your paper, you give credit to any material that you have taken from your sources. Then, at the end of the paper, you include a list of "Works Cited" or "Works Consulted" that gives fuller information about these sources for your readers. If your readers doubt a fact or statistic, they can check your sources for themselves. If your readers want more information, your documentation enables them to track down the sources.

Preparing Yourself for the Research Process

Writing a research paper involves the same process that you used in writing essays. The major difference is that each stage or dimension of the process takes longer. You may spend two weeks just collecting sources,

TEACHING TIP

Teachers need to readjust their inner clocks as well. Don't assume that your students can do a research paper in two or three weeks. If, students are to learn from the research process, four weeks is the minimum. If your syllabus is crowded, start the research project early and work in shorter assignments—critical reading or summary-response exercises—related to the research project. Respond to the research project in stages: prospectus, report on bibliographical findings, draft of ideas *without* research citations, and final project.

reading articles and books, jotting down ideas, testing your ideas on classmates and friends, and narrowing and focusing your subject. And because you gather so much material, the shaping and organizing processes are also more demanding. Sometimes you may feel as if you're trying to put forty frogs in a dishpan: By the time you arrange ten, the first four have already jumped out. The revising also takes longer, partly because you have to include your documentation, but partly because the pieces of the paper may not fit together as smoothly as you had hoped. There is really no way to rush research. If writing an ordinary paper is like fixing your lunch, then writing a research paper is like preparing Thanksgiving dinner. You can't microwave a research paper. Good things take time.

The first step in writing a research paper is to *readjust your inner clock*. Initially, you'll think that you're not making much progress. You'll think that you're in a slow-motion movie or that you're trying to jog through butter. However, once you readjust your inner clock, set more modest goals, and content yourself with a slower but more persistent pace, you've won half the battle. By reducing the pressure on yourself, you'll feel less frustrated when you reach a dead end but also readier to appreciate valuable information when you discover it.

To help you adjust mentally and physically to a new pace and an extended writing process, begin your preparation by making a research notebook, outlining a realistic timetable for the paper, and selecting a documentation format.

■ **WARMING UP: JOURNAL EXERCISES** Do at least one of the following journal exercises to help get yourself into a research frame of mind or to discover a possible research subject.

1. Sit down with a family member, friend, or classmate. On a sheet of paper, write down the subject of the most interesting course that you are currently taking. Hand the sheet of paper to that person and ask him or her to write down questions for an interview designed to find out *why* you like this course and *what* you like best about it. Then have that person interview you and record your responses. At the end of the interview, discuss your responses. What ideas could you research in order to explain to your interviewer what is interesting about this subject?

2. If you are *not* in the library, try this exercise. Reread your authority list from the journal entries in Chapter 6, Investigating. Choose one subject from that list. Assume that you are on a scavenger hunt, trying to track down bits of information about that subject *without leaving the building that you are cur-*

rently in. Anything is fair game: a dictionary, a textbook, a telephone directory, a telephone, a computer terminal, a friend or roommate, this textbook, your journal, or anything you can observe or remember. You have twenty-five minutes to complete the hunt. Write down all the sources you use and the information you discover from each source.

3. In the library, wander down the stacks, looking at titles of books that might interest you. Choose one volume from the shelf. In your journal, record the basic information about that book: author, title, place of publication, publisher, date. In that book, find *three* specific sources that the author refers to or used to write the book. (If the book does not cite sources, choose another volume.) Does your library have these sources? If so, determine where these sources are located. Ask the reference librarian for help if you need it.

RESEARCH NOTEBOOK

Although many researchers recommend using index cards for recording bibliographic entries and notes, for most shorter research projects (up to twenty pages), a loose-leaf notebook or a spiral notebook with pockets for additional papers and photocopies may be more functional. Divide your notebook into four sections: research log, bibliography, notes from sources (including photocopies), and drafts and ideas.

The *research log* section of your notebook serves as a scratch pad and log of your research progress. In it, you will record what you accomplish during that session, potential references you need to check, reminders to yourself, questions to ask a librarian or your instructor, and notes about your problems, progress, and intended next steps. As you work or when you finish each research session, jot down what you did or need to do. These notes about your problems, progress, questions, and next steps will help you maintain momentum and continuity on your research project. Each time you return to the library or to your research, you can check your notes to see what you need to do next.

Below is an excerpt from student writer Kate McNerny's research log:

4/26

4:30–6:00 p.m.

Still working on finding articles. Found the Delbert and Roberta Long article. It has some good stuff. Education is on microfilm, so I learned

TEACHING TIP

To reduce the chances of plagiarism and to increase the learning opportunities for students during their research, include the research notebook in your evaluation scheme for this paper. Whether you grade the notebooks or merely respond to students' problems and questions, you can justifiably make the notebook worth 30 percent of the final grade on the research paper. Set due dates for collection and review.

how to photocopy from microfilm. Of course, just when I had the machine turned to exactly the right page, I discovered I didn't have a nickel for the copy machine, so I had to leave the room (some guy waiting in line looked irritated as I explained I'd be back in a minute). I ran to the change machine, got my nickels and copied the article!

April issue of Parents magazine missing from the shelves. UGH – I hate that.

Question: Do I want to survey students to find out about typical attitudes toward taking foreign languages? What questions could I ask?

Another question: Is this going to be an arguing paper? Is there a controversy? Are there two sides??

Try to find tomorrow: three Education Digest articles on microfilm (L11/E3): Oct. 84, p. 32
Dec. 85, p. 36
Mar. 86, p. 24

Check Education Index.

Remember that 5 – 6 p.m. is a good time to work in the library. Everyone clears out, so I don't have to fight over the microfilm machines.

In the *bibliography* section of your notebook, keep a list of every source that you consult, with complete information about each source. Leave space between entries for additional information, such as call numbers. This list becomes your *working bibliography*. McNerny's bibliography included the following entries:

Long, Delbert H. and Roberta Long. "Toward the Promotion of Foreign Language Study and Global Understanding." Education Volume 105 Summer 1985: 366 - 368.

L11/ .E2 Periodical Microfilm Room

Mayor, Barbara and A.K. Pugh, editors. Language, Communication, and Education: A Reader. London: Croom Helm in association with the Open University, 1987.

P/ 106/ .L317/ 1987 East Wing stacks

In addition, include in the bibliography section any printouts from computer searches or photocopies of relevant pages from indexes or bibliographies.

In the *source notes* section, leave plenty of pages to record direct quotations, paraphrases of key ideas, and facts from the sources in your bibliography list. Introduce each section with a reference to the author and a short version of the title. After each note, indicate the page number or numbers. One page of McNerny's notes contained the following entries:

Long and Long, Promotion of Foreign Language Study

Study by the Longs - group of intellectually gifted 7th graders wrote stories about Soviet children. The 7th graders had acquired many "facts" regarding communism and the Soviet Union, but had many misconceptions, too.

"They expressed fear for the children and thought all schools were military schools with strict rules and harsh punishment. They believed that many Soviet children couldn't attend school because they had to work in the fields and ride horse-drawn wagons . . . . " p. 367

Ranwez and Rogers, Status of Foreign Languages

91% of Colorado secondary schools the 536 schools responding to the questionnaire offered foreign languages, but 91% of schools responding didn't require any foreign language credits for graduation. pp. 99-100

For your source notes section, make *photocopies* of any valuable source materials. Write author, title, and page numbers on each photocopied source.

TEACHING TIP

Although taking notes from sources sounds elementary, many novice writers either take too few notes or spend hours copying everything. To assist your students, try modeling note taking. Hand out photocopies of an article to each of several small groups. Then record bibliographic information, show how to skim the source by picking out key words and phrases, and write your notes at the board. After you model this process, have students work with sources that they have brought to class.

In the *drafts and ideas* section of the notebook, jot down brainstorms, looping or clustering exercises, sketch outlines, trial drafts, and examples from your own experience. During a research project, ideas can come to you at any time. When they do, take time to write them down. This section of your notebook serves as a journal devoted solely to your research paper. One example from McNerny's drafts and ideas section records her personal experience with foreign languages:

4/29

I can remember my mom always telling me, "Take French classes, learn how to speak French so that you can go visit your cousins in France some day." At the time (junior high school) though, learning a foreign language was low on my priority list. I did take French classes for two years – but dropped out after my sophomore year and immediately lost any basic competency I might have acquired.

In college, I'd like to take a language again, but it never seems to fit with my schedule. But last year, as my mom had promised, I got the opportunity to visit my cousins in France. For some reason, the fact that I couldn't speak French didn't seem to me like it would be a big problem. That was until I stepped off the train at Gare du Nord in Paris and couldn't find the relative who was supposed to meet me. After frantically searching the entire station several times, I had to break down and ask for help. At the information desk a few completely butchered French phrases escaped my lips – only to be received by an unimpressed, unresponsive station attendant. He muttered something about dumb Americans and then pointed me off towards some unknown destination. Well I survived that ordeal – but at the same time swore to myself that I would never make another trip to France until I could speak the language.

Computer Tip

If you prefer to write on a computer and have access to a battery-operated "notebook" or portable computer, use it as your research notebook. Create separate files for each section in the notebook and then take the computer with you when you do research. After each research session, save your notes on a disk and print them out on hard copy.

If you are accustomed to composing on a computer, the notebook computer makes it easier to take notes, draft ideas, and record information during your research. In addition, the final organizing and drafting will be quicker because your sources will already be on file or in the computer's memory.

Research Timetable

Before you begin your research, write out a tentative schedule. Your instructor may assign due dates for specific parts of the paper (invention exercises, topic selection, working bibliography, rough draft), but you should make a schedule that fits your work habits and your weekly schedule.

The following schedule assumes that you have at least a month to work on your research paper. The amount of time required by each part depends on the amount of time you can work each day. On some days, you may have only thirty minutes. On other days, you may have several hours. *The key is to do a little bit every day to keep your momentum going.*

Prepare for research. Buy and organize a research notebook; set up a time table; select documentation format.	1–2 days
Choose a subject. Begin the narrowing and focusing process.	2–3 days
Collect sources. Find library sources; identify and find unpublished sources; do interviews or surveys; record personal experiences. Evaluate source materials; take notes on selected sources; photocopy sources.	12–14 days
Shape and outline ideas; *reread* notes and photocopies; *draft* sections of essay. Continue to *focus* thesis while rereading, planning, and drafting.	6–10 days
Revise draft. Get peer response, collect additional information, sharpen thesis, reshape or revise outline, cite sources in the text and in the bibliographic list, and edit and proofread the paper.	6–8 days

Tailor your schedule to your own temperament and work habits. If you like to work exactly to a schedule or even finish early, design your schedule so you can finish a day or two before the due date. If you are like most writers—you love to procrastinate or you are often up all night just before an assignment is due—then use your schedule to set *early* target dates, to get your momentum going. When you finish drafting your schedule, put a copy in the *research log* section of your notebook, so that you can check your progress as you work.

Documentation Format: MLA and APA Styles

A final step in preparing for the research paper is to select a documentation style. This chapter illustrates both the MLA and APA styles. If you are writing a paper for the humanities, follow the Modern Language Association (MLA) style set forth in the *MLA Handbook for Writers of Research Papers* (1988). If you are writing a paper in the behavioral sciences, use the American Psychological Association (APA) style as described in the *Publication Manual of the American Psychological Association* (1984). For some scientific subjects, follow the Council of Biology Editors (CBE) format illustrated in the *CBE Style Manual* (1983). While this chapter illustrates only the MLA and APA styles, all three style manuals are available in most college bookstores.

Leading academic and professional journals also illustrate the documentation styles customary in specialized fields. You may want to consult issues of those journals to determine the exact format for footnotes or in-text citation of sources. *Before you begin doing research, however, select a documentation style* that is appropriate for your subject, purpose, and audience. Then practice that style as you compile your working bibliography.

Teaching Tip

Early in the research project, informal interviews between peers or between student and teacher can help students articulate and focus their topics. Often, teachers can spot problems—selection of overly broad topics or reliance on unreliable sources—before the writers get off track.

Research Paper: The Writing Process

■ **Assignment for the Research Paper** Choose a subject that strongly interests you and about which you would like to learn more. It may be a subject that you have already written about in this course. Research this subject in a library and, if appropriate, supplement your library research with questionnaires, interviews, or other unpublished sources of information. Check with your instructor for suggested length, appropriate number or kinds of sources, and additional format requirements. Use a documentation style appropriate for your subject, purpose, and audience.

Choosing a Subject

For this research paper, choose a subject in which you already have personal interest or experience. Start by rereading your journal entries for possible research subjects. Even a personal entry may suggest an idea. If you wrote about how you fainted in the gym during aerobics or weight training, you might research the potential dangers of exercising in high heat and humidity or sitting in a sauna after hard exercise. If you wrote a journal entry about a friend's drinking problem, you might like to read more about the causes and treatments for alcoholism.

In addition, reread the essays that you have written to see whether one of them refers to a possible research subject. If your observing essay, for example, was about a special place you visited, use that essay as the starting point for futher investigation and research. Who could you interview to find out more about the place? What is the history of that place? How is it being used? What controversies surround its use? What resources does your library have about this particular place—or similar places? You might also use a topic from your remembering, reading, or investigating essays as starting places for additional reading and research. *Build on what you already know and what already interests you rather than launch into an entirely unknown subject.*

Resource Note

Richard Coe's article, "If Not to Narrow, Then How to Focus" (*CCC*, Oct. 1981) suggests that narrowing a subject is just part of the battle; writers must find a key issue, angle, or focus for their research. Focusing on a key *problem* or *controversy* may be more useful than simply narrowing the subject to "alcohol abuse problems in middle-aged homeless men living in Denver's Capital Hill neighborhood."

Narrowing and Focusing Your Subject Once you have a tentative idea, remember that you'll need to narrow it, focus it, or otherwise limit the subject. The topic of alcoholism is too general. Focus your question: "Do beer commercials on television contribute to alcoholism?" "What methods does Alcoholics Anonymous use to help people?" "Has raising the drinking age to 21 reduced the incidence of alcoholism?" Only after you've started your research, however, will you know whether your question is still too broad (you can't begin to read everything about it in just two weeks) or too narrow (in two weeks, you can't find enough information about that question).

Two techniques may help narrow and focus your subject. *You may wish to try these now, wait until you have done some initial reading, or do them several times during your collecting and shaping.*

A *topic cross* uses lists of key terms to focus ideas. In a topic cross, you list, on the vertical axis, key terms related to your subject, from most general to most specific. Then, once you've focused on a level that you think might work for your research, list, on the horizontal axis, similar kinds or examples of topics. Assume, for example, that your general subject is nutrition or diets. Make the vertical axis first. Put the most general subjects or categories at the top, the most specific at the bottom:

Food
Nutrition
Menus
Diets
Vegetarianism
Reducing diets
Reducing diets for joggers
Reducing diets for marathon runners

Choose a topic midway down the list that might relate to your specific interests. Then, for that topic, list on the horizontal axis any examples or similar kinds of topics. If you focus on reducing diets, you might sketch in the horizontal axis as follows:

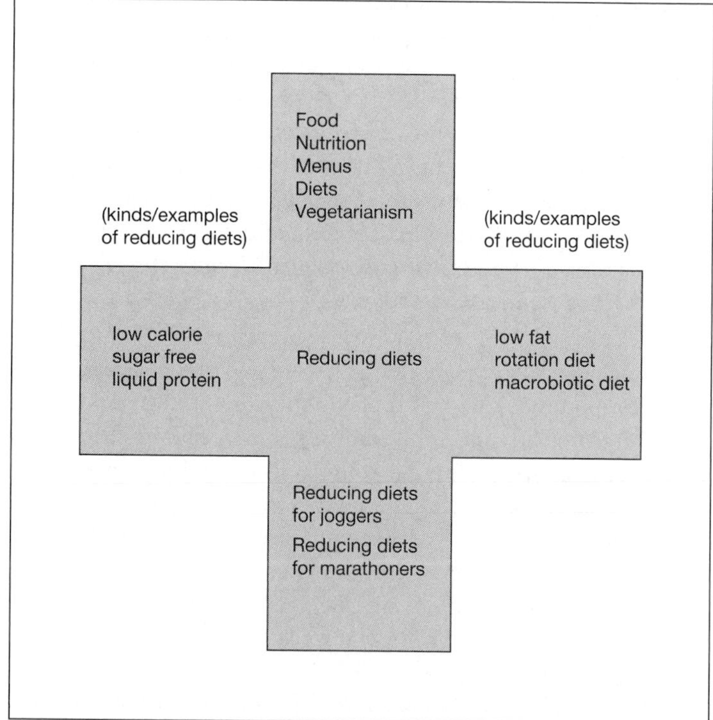

One of those diets—the low-fat diet—might become the focus of your research. The *topic cross* enables you to "sight in" on a topic as though you were adjusting the cross hairs in a microscope. If your topic is too general, move down the vertical axis. If you are on the right level, brainstorm for other examples you might focus on.

Question analysis is a second narrowing and focusing strategy. The *who, what, when, where* and *why* questions that you use to focus your topic are the same questions that reference librarians use to help you focus your research in the library.

Who: What group of people are interested or affected?
What: How are key terms defined? What academic discipline is involved?
When: What is the period or time span?
Where: What continent, country, state, or town is involved?
Why: What are possible effects or implications?

Answering these questions—by yourself, in a group, or with a reference librarian—may suggest new angles, new avenues for research, or subtopics that could lead to a focus for your research paper. As you narrow your topic, you are narrowing and focusing the range of your research in the library. Student writer Kate McNerny, brainstorming with another class member, applied these questions to her subject about foreign-language study and came up with the following possibilities:

Foreign Language Study

Who? Ans: I am interested in Americans. Specifically, I want to focus on why Americans should begin learning a foreign language early in school, in grade school, secondary school and college. Learning a foreign language would affect how foreigners see us.

What? Ans: Key terms defined - perhaps what "learning" means. Does it mean just basic speaking competency? Probably. If I could have asked a few simple questions in the Gare du Nord, I wouldn't have felt so stupid. Academic discipline - learning the foreign language is important, but culture is part of it, too. History should teach us about foreign cultures. So should psychology - do the Japanese think differently from the Spanish? Why did the French seem rude and Italians friendly? Do I want to research the psychology of languages? I don't think so.

When? Ans: I really want to know why foreign language studies are currently not emphasized. The 1980's. But what about trends - is it getting better or worse? Are more people learning foreign languages than a few years ago? I don't know.

Where? Ans: In the United States. In my home town. Why is it that in the French schools, children as a matter of course learn several languages while we aren't required to learn any? Supposedly, we are the "melting pot" for many different languages and cultures, but we don't know each other's languages.

Why? Ans. I can make a long list of the effects
- We can't communicate when we're tourists
- We can't read anything printed in their language.
- We don't understand their culture.
- We don't even understand the cultures of the millions of Americans from other cultures.
- We isolate ourselves in business, too.

To avoid these effects, I want to argue for stronger foreign language requirements in secondary schools and colleges.

As a result of her question analysis, McNerny decided to discuss both language and culture, to focus on the current conditions, and to recommend that secondary schools require foreign languages. *In any research, however, what you look for and what you find are always different. You will need to modify your focus as you read and learn.*

COLLECTING

With ideas for a tentative subject, a possible purpose, and an audience, you can focus on collecting information. Collecting data for your research paper will require identifying and locating published and unpublished sources, evaluating your sources and choosing those that are the most appropriate for your needs, and then taking notes on your selected sources. *Remember, however, that finding sources—like writing itself—is an ongoing and recursive process.* You often identify new sources after you have taken notes on others. Although you may begin your search in the on-line catalogue, the card catalogue, or the reference section, as you narrow and focus your topic or draft sections of your paper, you may come back and recheck the on-line catalogue, basic references, periodical indexes, or bibliographies.

Use *informal contacts* with friends or acquaintances as an integral part of your collecting process. Friends, family members, business associates, or teachers may be able to suggest key questions or give you some sources: relevant books and magazine articles, television programs that are available in transcript, or local experts on your subject. One student, for example, was doing research on successful techniques for job interviews. She mentioned her project during a telephone conversation with her father. As it turned out, he regularly interviewed job applicants at his company. The student was able to interview him for specific recommendations. Another student was doing biographical research on television reporter Charles Kuralt. He mentioned his project to his journalism professor who, as it turned out, knew Kuralt personally and gave the student both some personal anecdotes and the titles of several recent articles. Most teachers, in fact, are happy to talk about their fields and recommend key sources of information.

UNPUBLISHED SOURCES Although the library may be your main source of information, other sources can be important, too. You may *interview* authorities on your subject or design a *questionnaire* to measure people's responses. (Interviews and questionnaires are discussed in Chapter 6.) *Phone calls* and *letters* to experts, government agencies, or businesses may yield background information, statistics, or quotations. *Notes from classes, public lectures, or television programs* are useful sources. Use a tape recorder to ensure that you transcribe your information accurately. A *scientific experiment* may even be appropriate. *Unpublished public documents*, such as deeds, wills, surveyors' maps, and environmental impact statements, may contain gold mines of information. Finally, don't ignore the most obvious sources: Your room, the attic in your home, or your relatives may have repositories of valuable unpublished data—*private letters, diaries, old bills*, or *check stubs*.

For her research paper, Kate McNerny decided to conduct an informal survey of attitudes toward foreign languages. She recorded the responses in the "Drafts and Ideas" section of her research notebook. When she drafted her paper, she used some of these responses in the introduction to her paper:

Q: Should foreign languages be required in Junior and Senior High?

A: (Mindy, 21, student) Yes, I think its a good idea - It would have been more valuable to me than some of the other required classes I took - like P.E.

A: (Jodi, 22, student) No, I had a hard enough time with English. Besides, I don't think I'd ever need to use it.

A: (Roger, 23, carpenter) Yes, I was in Europe last year and missed out on a lot because I couldn't speak any other language. Europeans don't speak English as much as we hear they do, but most of the people I Met there spoke at least two languages.

A: (Jim, 49, contractor) No, I've never gone to Europe and never needed to speak another language for any other reason. I had enough trouble getting through other classes.

A: (Carolyn, 59, teacher) Yes, when I was teaching there were few language classes available. But as a reading teacher I can see many ways in which language studies would have enhanced our program.

PRIMARY AND SECONDARY SOURCES Some sources—accounts of scientific experiments, transcripts of speeches or lectures, questionnaires, interviews, private documents—are known as *primary sources.* They are original, firsthand information, "straight from the horse's mouth." Secondhand reports, analyses, and descriptions based on primary sources are known as *secondary sources.* Secondary sources may contain the same information, but they are once-removed. For example, a lecture or experiment by an expert in food irradiation is a primary source; the newspaper report of that lecture or experiment is a secondary source.

The distinction between primary and secondary sources is important for two related reasons. First, secondary sources may contain errors. The newspaper account, for example, may misquote the expert or misrepresent the experiment. If possible, therefore, find the primary source—a copy of the actual lecture or a published article about the experiment. Second, finding the primary sources may make your research document more persuasive through an appeal to character (see Chapter 10). If you can cite the original source—or even show how some secondary accounts distorted the original experiment—you will gain your readers' trust and faith. Uncovering the primary data not only makes your research more accurate, but your additional effort makes all your data and arguments appear more credible.

LIBRARY SOURCES Before you begin collecting information, acquaint yourself with the library itself. If you have not already done so, inquire at the information desk about library tours or walk through the library with a friend or classmate. Locate the *reference section*; the *on-line catalog* for books and articles; the *indexes* for newspapers, journals, and magazines; the *microfilm room*; the *stacks*; and the *government documents* section. Don't assume that because you've used one library, you can immediately start your research in a new library. Remember: Librarians themselves are valuable sources of information. Use their expertise early in your research.

TEACHING TIP

Although library tours are helpful, often the information quickly overloads students. It is often better, after a *short* introductory tour, to supply information gradually, as students encounter problems. If possible, schedule a class period when you are in the library while students are gathering sources. For questions you can't answer, direct students to the appropriate librarian.

BACKGROUND INFORMATION AND GENERAL REFERENCE Before you consult the on-line or card catalog or run to the *Readers' Guide to Periodical Literature*, you may need a general overview of your subject. Start with an encyclopedia, dictionary, almanac, or biography for background information. Many people associate encyclopedias with their grade-school "research"—when they copied passages out of *The World Book* or *Collier's Encyclopedia*. But encyclopedias are an excellent source of basic information and terminology that may help you focus, narrow, and define your subject. Use them as background reading, however, not as major sources.

In addition to the general encyclopedias, there are hundreds of references—one or two might just save you hours of research in the library and lead you directly to key facts or important information on your topic. (You may wish to begin your collecting in the reference room or check there only after you have collected information from other books and articles. Often these references are more valuable *after* you have done some reading on your subject.) Beyond the standard college dictionary or thesaurus, the *Oxford English Dictionary*, known as the *OED*, or *Webster's Third New International Dictionary of the English Language* may help you find key ideas or definitions.

There are also many specialized dictionaries for scientific terms, slang words, symbols, and a host of other specialized vocabularies. If you need facts, figures, or statistics, consult the *World Almanac* or the *Statistical Abstract of the United States*. If your subject is a person, check one of the references that indexes collections of biographies. *Biography and Genealogy Master Index* and *Biographical Dictionaries* reference more than three million biographical sketches.

The librarian is still the most valuable resource for your research. At some point during your research in the library, probably after you have a focused topic and have collected some sources, talk to a reference librarian. For many writers, asking for help can be really intimidating. To make the process of asking for help as painless—and productive—as possible, try saying something like the following: "Hi, I'm Kate McNerny. I'm doing a research project for my college writing course. My topic is foreign-language study in the United States. I'm trying to find information about the current state of foreign-language study in the United States and collect some arguments for increasing requirements in secondary schools and colleges. Here's what I've found so far [explain what you've done]. What additional reference books, indexes, dictionaries, or bibliographies might help me in my research?" The resulting conversation may be the most productive five minutes of your entire library research. After you've talked to the librarian once, it will be easier to return and ask a question when you hit a snag.

THE ON-LINE CATALOG The good news for researchers in the 1990s is that computerized databases have revolutionized the whole process of library research. In most university libraries, a computer terminal can, in a few seconds, give you information that used to require hours of searching card catalogs or printed indexes. You can easily locate books, articles, and government documents relevant to your topic. You can find the library call numbers and locations of sources. You can determine if a source is available or checked out. Often, you can get an abstract or a short description of a source. For some systems, you can print out the bibliographic information so that you don't have to take notes. Occasionally, you can print out whole articles right there. Often you can access most of this information from a personal computer at home.

Knowledge is of two kinds. We know a subject ourselves, or we know where we can find information upon it.
—SAMUEL JOHNSON, FROM BOSWELL'S LIFE OF JOHNSON

The only bad news is that nearly every on-line catalog system is different. Most colleges have OPAC's (On Line Public Access Catalogs) that allow you to access the library's holdings. Your college may use OCLC (On Line Computer Library System), which is the largest of the public-access catalogs, or you may use systems such as NOTIS, RLIN, MELVYL, or CARL. But whatever system your library uses, you need to spend time learning the tricks of that particular database. Don't try to learn the system by yourself. Take a library orientation tour. Collect the library's handouts about your computerized databases. Ask the librarians for help. And don't wait until your research paper is assigned to walk into the library. If you have to learn a new computer system *and* write your paper at the same time, you will be inviting massive frustration.

As you practice with your library's on-line or compact disk (CD-ROM) systems, you'll discover that the *search strategy* you use and the *key words* you enter become very critical. Should you use a *word* or a *name* search? Should you use *browse* or *express* to search your database? You need to practice with your system to see how it works. Next, you need to pay attention to the key words you enter. If you are writing an essay about teenagers' psychological problems, entering the word "teen" may get you nowhere, while entering the word "adolescent" or even "teenage" may hit the jackpot. To help with your key-word search, try the following. First, make a list in your research notebook of all the possible terms that may relate to your subject. When you do an express search, note the other possible terms or headings given on the computer terminal. Second, stop and check a print source such as the *Library of Congress Subject Headings* (LCSH). Ask the reference librarian where the LCSH is located. Usually, it will be near the card catalog or the on-line terminals. Look up your topic in the LCSH and copy any headings or key words that are related to your subject. Finding the right key word or combination of key words is the secret to successful research on computerized databases.

BIBLIOGRAPHIC COMPUTER SEARCH In addition to the resources available on-line, many libraries have other computerized databases to assist your research project. Some of these, such as ABI/INFORM (a general business database) or *InfoTrac* (database of general interest and current events), have no print equivalents. Your library may have one of the other popular computerized databases, such as the *Knowledge Index* or *DialogOnDisc*. Listed below are a few of the other commonly searched computerized databases:

- ERIC (Education Resources Information Center)
- NTIS (National Technical Information Service)
- SCI SEARCH (Science Citation Index)
- MLA (Modern Language Association International Bibliography)

PERIODICAL INDEXES Magazines, journals, and newspapers are called "periodicals" because most are published on a daily, weekly, or monthly basis. An *index* is just a list of citations, organized for easy reference. Indexes may be in print or computerized form, such as CD-ROM. Just as the index of a textbook refers you to topics, ideas, or names in that book, a periodical index refers you to articles published in a certain group of magazines, journals, or newspapers. Periodical indexes, such as the *Readers' Guide to Periodical Literature*, are usually monthly, quarterly, or annual publications that refer to articles published in hundreds of different periodicals.

The library contains hundreds of periodical indexes, in print or computerized format, each referring to a slightly different subject or group of periodicals. A *general* index such as the *Readers' Guide* refers to approximately two hundred popular magazines. A general computerized database, such as *InfoTrac*, draws from more than one thousand current magazines, journals, and current newspapers. A *specialized* index may focus on just one publication, such as *The New York Times Index*, or on just one subject, such as the *Art Index* which indexes approximately three hundred periodicals in the arts.

Below is a list of frequently used indexes. When you discuss your research project with your instructor or with a reference librarian, ask which indexes will be most helpful for your topic and which are available in computerized format:

- *Applied Science & Technology Index*
- *Art Index*
- *Book Review Index*
- *Business Periodicals Index*
- *Consumers Index*
- *Education Index*
- *Humanities Index*
- *InfoTrac*
- *Psychological Abstracts*
- *Public Affairs Information Service Bulletin*
- *Readers' Guide to Periodical Literature*
- *Social Sciences Index*
- *The New York Times Index*

GOVERNMENT DOCUMENTS The largest publisher in the world is the United States Government Printing Office (G.P.O.). It publishes countless articles, pamphlets, and books on history, government, and law. Many of the publications cover an astonishing variety of everyday topics and are written in nontechnical language for the general public. Your library may have a separate government documents section, and the documents librarian can help you gain access to the collection.

EVALUATING SOURCES As you collect both published and unpublished information, you should appraise your sources with a critical eye. Do not assume that every glittering statement you read or hear is valuable; only a handful of the dozens of sources you dig up will be true gold. Some will not relate specifically to your topic; others will be too superficial or too technical. Some will be out of date; others will be biased or simply inaccurate. Evaluate your sources based on the following criteria:

Sources should be relevant. The sources you select should be relevant to your subject, your purpose, and your intended audience. If your narrowed topic is still too general, all your sources will look relevant. In that case, narrow your subject even more. Sources must also be relevant to your purpose. If you are writing an argumentative research paper, for example, you need sources representing both sides of the issue. If you are proposing a solution to a problem, look for sources describing the problem or the solution. Finally, sources should be appropriate for your intended audience. The articles that Kate McNerny found in *Foreign Language Annals* were more appropriate for her academic audience than was the brief and superficial article from *Parents* magazine.

News broadcasts and documentaries typically identify people as "sources." How relevant, current, and reliable are the sources interviewed in the *Video Library*?

Sources should be current. As a rule of thumb, look for the most current sources—especially those on scientific or technical subjects. Research on AIDS is more accurate and complete now than it was in 1985. Current articles on turbocharged automobiles should be more informed than those written in 1970. Recent articles on child day-care programs will more accurately reflect current trends. Sometimes, however, older books and articles are important. If you are doing historical research about the Great Depression in the United States, you may want to read key documents from the 1930s. If your subject is Shakespeare, seventeenth-century literary criticism may be as valuable as twentieth-century analyses. In every academic discipline, some sources remain authoritative for decades. When you find that many writers refer to a single source, it may be valuable regardless of its date of publication.

Sources should be reliable. Check for possible biases in articles and books. Don't expect the National Rifle Association to give an unbiased report on gun-control legislation. Don't assume that representatives of right-to-life or pro-choice groups will objectively represent the full range of facts about abortion. Because at least some bias is inevitable in any source, locate and use a variety of sources representing several points of view. If you are in doubt about an author's point of view or credibility, consult experts in the field or check book reviews. *Book Review Digest*, for example, contains references to reviews that may indicate the author's reputation or reliability.

TAKING NOTES Taking careful notes from both published and unpublished sources is, of course, fundamental to accurate documentation. When a source appears relevant and useful, do the following:

1. *Record complete bibliographical information about it in the bibliography section of your research notebook* (or in your computer notebook). For *books*, you need authors, editors, titles, vol-

umes, publishers, places of publication, and years of publication. For *articles*, you need authors, article titles, magazine or journal titles, volumes and numbers or dates, months, and years of publication, and beginning and ending page numbers. As Kate McNerny did in her log, leave a space between each entry to record call numbers or locations of documents:

(Book): Simon, Paul. The Tongue-Tied American: Confronting the Foreign Language Crisis. New York: Continuum Publishing Co., 1980.

PB/38/. U655 East Wing stacks, main floor

(Article): Lambert, Richard D. "The Improvement of Foreign Language Competency in the United States." Annals of the American Academy of Political and Social Science March 1987 : 9-19.

H1/.A4 On shelf with current issues, 2nd floor.

If the source is unpublished—such as a telephone conversation, a letter, or a public document in the county courthouse—record all the information about it that your readers will need to identify and consult the source themselves. (See the Documenting Sources section in this chapter.) For printed sources, remember that the information you copy from a periodical index may be missing key information, such as the author's full name or page numbers for the article. *When you actually find each source, update your bibliographical information.*

2. *Record notes in the "Source Notes" section of your research notebook.* Identify each entry with the author's name and the title. If your notes fill two or more pages, put the author and title at the top of each page. Write on only one side of each page. Briefly *summarize* the main points made in the source, note specific information useful to you, paraphrase key ideas, transcribe interesting quotations, and jot down your own brief comments, questions, and memories. Place page numbers immediately following each paraphrase or quotation. Use direct quotation rather than paraphrase when the actual words in the source are more concise, authoritative, or persuasive than your paraphrase might be. *Be sure that direct quotations are accurate, word-for-word transcriptions from the original.*

3. *Photocopy important sources for later rereading and reference.* Make sure all photocopies clearly show authors, titles, and page numbers. (For some research projects, your instructor may request photocopies of every source you paraphrase or quote.) If you photocopy several pages, copy title pages or the magazines' covers and staple the copies together. Then you can underline key passages or make notes on the photocopies themselves.

Photocopying has distinct advantages. You can copy the relevant pages of a source so you don't have to lug thirty books home. (Leaving the sources in the library also helps other researchers.) Photocopies are good insurance against losing key information—in case the book or journal is checked out the next time you need it. Photocopies also allow you to reread sources *after* you have read other books or articles; often, on the first reading of a source, you're not certain what is important and what is not. Finally, photocopies allow you to recheck the final draft of your research paper against sources, to make sure that paraphrases, direct quotations, and page citations are accurate. You may save yourself an extra trip to the library to check a page number, a date, or a journal title. To avoid spending unnecessary amounts of money on photocopies, however, always read sources before making copies.

4. *As you read sources and take notes, record your own reactions and ideas in the "drafts and ideas" section of your research or computer notebook.* Be an active reader of your sources. When you agree or disagree with what you are reading, stop for a minute and jot down your ideas. When you think of a comparison, a process, a way to analyze or evaluate something, possible causes and effects, or examples from your own experience, *write out your ideas as completely as you can, right then, while they're fresh in your mind.* Don't get so absorbed in taking notes that you forget to record your own ideas. You don't have to collect twenty sources and *then* do a draft; instead, draft ideas *as* you collect information.

TEACHING TIP

To encourage your students to focus and clarify their research topics, try one of the following activities. First, have a brief early conference with each student on his or her topic and research plan. Often, teachers can help students narrow and focus problematic topics. Second, have students give what Bruce Ballenger calls a "press conference" on their topics: Ask them to take five minutes in class to "highlight the more surprising, interesting, or puzzling things they've discovered so far." Third, have students bring their notes and research logs to class and write 50-minute in-class versions of their essays in progress. Often, the pressure of writing an early rough draft in class helps students focus and organize their thoughts.

SHAPING

Once you've collected information for your research paper, you may feel overwhelmed by the task of shaping it into a coherent form. You can assert control over your data, however, and shape them into coherent form by reconsidering your purpose and thesis. *Reread your own notes and especially your draft sections from your research notebook.* Then, in the draft section of your notebook, answer the following questions:

Subject:	What is your general subject?
Narrowed topic or question:	What aspect of your subject is most interesting to you now? What question will you answer or explain?
Purpose:	Is your purpose primarily to inform, explain, evaluate, describe a problem and propose a solution, or argue a claim?
Working thesis:	What thesis, claim, or proposal do you want to impress upon your readers?
Audience:	Analyze your audience. How can you interest them in your subject? What aspects of your collected data are most appropriate for your audience?

Writing is the hardest work in the world not involving heavy lifting.
—PETER HAMILL, JOURNALIST

Writing a book is not as tough as it is to haul 35 people around the country and sweat like a horse five nights a week.
—BETTE MIDLER, SINGER, ACTOR, AUTHOR

As you shape, draft, and revise your research paper, you may continue to refocus your topic and question, refine your thesis, or revise your sense of audience.

SHAPING STRATEGIES Your goal now is to design some order, sequence, plan, or outline for your research paper. Forcing yourself to write an outline, however, simply may not work. You should have an idea from your previous papers about how your writing process works best, but if you're stuck, feeling frustrated, or overwhelmed, try several of the following strategies:

- *Review strategies for shaping* that are appropriate for your particular purpose. If you are arguing for a certain claim, reread shaping strategies in Chapter 10. If you are evaluating something or analyzing a problem and proposing a solution, review the strategies discussed in Chapter 8 or 9.
- *Explain to a friend or classmate* your purpose, audience, and working thesis. Then try to explain how you might proceed.
- *Try freewriting, looping, or clustering* to develop a plan.
- *Reread your notes and drafts* from your research notebook.
- *Take a break.* Let your ideas simmer for a while. Go for a walk. Work on assignments for another course. Go jogging or swimming. Let your mind run on automatic pilot for a while—the information and ideas in your mind may begin organizing themselves into an initial "sketch outline" without your conscious effort.
- *Try branching or treeing your main ideas.* On paper or at the chalkboard, begin with your topic and draw the trunk and main

branches of your topics. Try to explain your sketch or chalkboard drawing to someone.

Think of these activities as a circle—begin at any point, work in either direction, repeat them as necessary. When something starts to work, stay with it for a while. If you start to block or become frustrated, go on to the next activity.

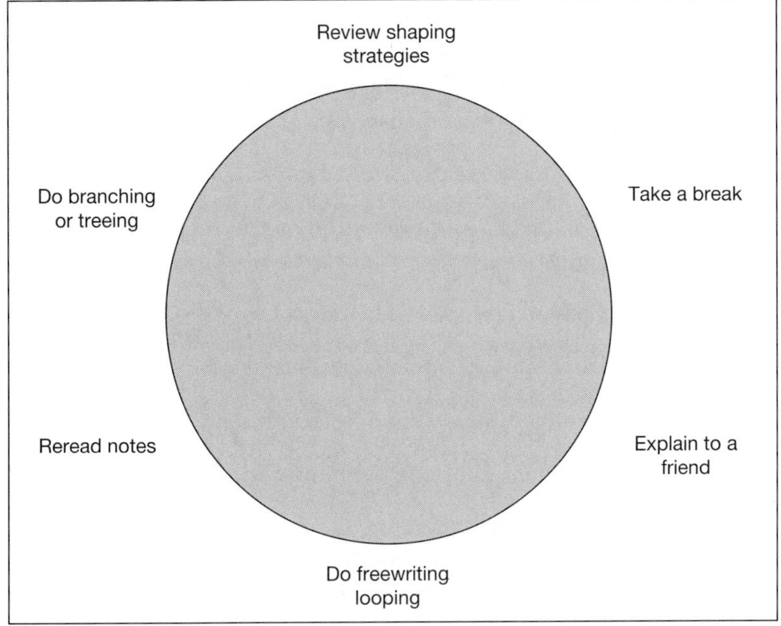

WORKING OUTLINE If the shaping activities helped you discover a basic design or plan, translate it into a working outline. If not, you may need to begin drafting in order to discover an outline. Kate McNerny decided to follow a pattern for writing an argument. Although she modified it considerably as she wrote, it helped her organize her ideas and source material so she could begin drafting.

Introduction: Comments—quotations from informal survey—why people feel they don't need to know a foreign language. Mention study on misconceptions of school aged children about Russian children.

I. Narration: Foreign language studies position in other countries as opposed to U.S.

Mention "glasnost" here?

TEACHING TIP

Requiring outlines, in this or other chapters, will help a few students but will frustrate many others. The writers in your class should know by now what shaping strategies work best for them. A short discussion of their preferences, however, may reinforce the notion that they should follow the composing strategies that have worked best for them in the past.

Example of French and Swedish requirements?

—Statistics on how many Americans are actually competent in another language.

Bill to require a state language?

U.S. position in world as far as power-trade.

II. Partition: American students should be required to study a foreign language throughout the 6 years of junior and senior high school. Study of a second language should also be encouraged. Reasons: language, culture, awareness, peace, trade, and business.

III. Arguments: To promote realistic understanding of other cultures.

Will help to improve diplomatic relations with other countries—peace cannot be achieved without this.

Change foreigners' attitudes of Americans.

Facilitate international trade and other business.

Enhance quality of education.

Without requirement, no incentive for many students.

IV. Refutation: Not necessary because other countries can speak English (This is more an argument against learning a language, not against a requirement.)

Not essential for quality education.

As requirement, would detract from other important subjects.

Not enough teachers to handle all students—use survey on Colo. schools.

Conclusion: Restate the problems created by current system: Offering 2–3 years of study doesn't lead to competency.

We misunderstand and are misunderstood.

Contrary to popular belief, we are not an isolated country.

A required study of languages will bring us one step closer to global understanding and peace.

ORGANIZING YOUR NOTES With a rough outline as a guide, reread your draft ideas, notes, and photocopies, and label them according to headings and subheadings in your working outline (for instance, Intro; I; Culture; II; Business; III; and so forth). (If you are using a computer notebook, print out all your files and label them.) Before you remove pages from the "source notes" section of your notebook or unstaple photocopied articles or sections of books, *make sure each entry or photocopy contains the author, title, and page numbers.* Now you are ready to arrange your notes and copies for use during drafting. Organize your notes into groups according to each section of your working outline. Reread each group, deciding which information should come first, in the middle, or last.

DRAFTING

At this point, some of the most difficult work is behind you. Congratulate yourself—there aren't many people who know as much as you do right now about your subject. You are an authority: You have information, statistics, statements, ideas from other writers and researchers, and your own experiences and observations at your fingertips. As you write, remember that you are communicating *your ideas* and what you are learning. Your sources become the evidence and support for your ideas. Remember that your voice and point of view should unify the information for your reader.

Many writers prefer to start a draft with the first main idea, leaving the introduction until later. As you write, you may discover a quotation, example, or narrative which doesn't fit anywhere else but which would be a perfect lead-in. Or you may already know how you want to start, using an idea that will help organize and direct your thoughts. As you draft, be guided by your working outline and your notes. Avoid copying passages verbatim from your own notebook ideas; instead, reread your notes and express those ideas in language that fits the idea you're working on.

If you get stuck, go back and reread what you have drafted so far or reread the source notes and ideas that you have assembled from your notebook and photocopies. Try to maintain your momentum by writing as quickly as possible. Don't be upset if the natural flow of your writing suggests a slightly different order or deviates from your working outline. Consider the new possibility. You may have discovered a better way to shape your material. If you are missing some fact or quotation, just leave a long line and keep writing. Later you can find the source and add the material you need.

TEACHING TIP

Although writers should choose a documentation format at the beginning of their projects so they know what bibliographical information is necessary, they do not need the specific details of documentation (usually) until *after* they have rough drafts. Covering this information too early in the research project sends a clear message that format is more important than thinking, learning, and writing.

USING SOURCES Proper use of sources requires both creativity and scrupulous honesty. On the one hand, you want to use other people's information and ideas when and where they serve *your* purpose and *your* ideas. A research paper is not simply a long string of quotations connected by a few transitions. On the other hand, the sources you cite or quote must be used fairly and honestly. You must give credit for other writers' ideas and information. You must quote accurately, cite your sources in your text, and document those sources accurately.

WHAT SOURCES TO CITE You must cite a source for any fact or bit of information that is not *general knowledge.* Obviously, what is "general knowledge" varies from one writer and audience to another. **As a rule, however, document any information or fact that you did not know before you began your research.** You may know, for example, that America spends more money on defense than it does on education. However, if you state that the defense budget for the previous year is greater than the total amount spent on education for the past forty years, then cite the source for that fact.

Knowing when you must cite a source for an idea, however, can be tricky. You do not need to indicate a source for *your* ideas, of course. But if you find a source that agrees with your idea, or if you suspect that your idea may be related to ideas from a particular source, cite that source. A citation will give your idea additional credibility: You show your reader that another authority shares your perception.

HOW TO CITE SOURCES In the text of your research paper, you will need to cite your sources according to either the Modern Language Association (MLA) style or the American Psychological Association (APA) style. **Remember:** Choose *either* the MLA style *or* the APA style and stick with it. Don't mix styles.

According to the MLA style, the in-text citation contains the *author and page number* of your source (Unks 24). No comma appears between author and page number. (If the author is unknown, identify the title and page number of your source. Underline book titles; place quotation marks around article titles.)

According to the APA style, the in-text citation contains *author and date* (Unks, 1985). Use a comma between author and date. If you refer to page number, it should appear after the author and date (Unks, 1985, p. 24). Use a "p." (or "pp." for more than one page) before the page number(s).

The in-text citation (either MLA or APA) refers readers to the end of your paper, where you give complete information about each source in a *Works Cited* (MLA) or *References* (APA) list. For illustration purposes, the following examples use MLA style. See Documenting Sources section (pp. 556–68) for examples of both APA and MLA styles.

Once you have decided that a fact, a paraphrase, or a direct quotation contributes to your thesis and will make a strong impression on your reader, use the following guidelines for in-text citation.

- *Identify in the text the persons or source for the fact, paraphrased idea, or quotation:*

As two foreign language teachers noted: "Like it or not, we are members of a world community consisting of hundreds of nations, and our fates are closely intertwined" (Long and Long 366).

Note: The parentheses and the period *follow* the final quotation marks.

- *If you cite the author in your sentence, the parentheses will contain only the page reference:*

According to Paul Simon, former member of the President's Commission on Foreign Language, the United States should erect a sign at each port of entry that reads, "WELCOME TO THE UNITED STATES—WE CANNOT SPEAK YOUR LANGUAGE" (1).

- *Use block format (separated from the text by a blank line, indented ten spaces, and double-spaced) for quotations of five lines or more:*

Educator Gerald Unks points out two instances in which a lack of language proficiency caused companies to initiate fatal marketing programs.

> When Pepsi-Cola went after the Chinese market, "Come Alive with Pepsi" was translated into Chinese in Taiwan as "Pepsi Brings Your Ancestors Back from the Dead." No Sale! General Motors sought to sell its Nova in South America, oblivious to the fact that "No va" in Spanish means "It doesn't go." (24)

Note: In block quotations, the final period comes *before* the parentheses containing the citation of your source.

- *Vary your introductions to quotations:*

Educator Gerald Unks claims that "only 15 percent of American high school students study a foreign language. Only 8 percent of our colleges require credit in a foreign language for admission (down from 34 percent in 1966)" (24).

"Only 15 percent of American high school students study a foreign language," according to educator Gerald Unks. And the problem is compounded because only 8 percent of our colleges currently have any foreign language admission requirements (24).

TEACHING TIP

To help your students avoid those "unidentified flying quotations," teach the "sandwich" approach to documentation. Quotations should be introduced by citing the author and sometimes his or her study or source. Then the quotation (the meat) follows. After the quotation, students should explain how the quoted material relates to their point. The Gerald Unks quotation in paragraph 9 of Kate McNerny's essay at the end of this chapter illustrates how to integrate quoted material into the writer's text.

In television reporting, human sources are identified by "tag lines" at the bottom of the screen. Help students to see that unidentified quotations in their essays would be as unhelpful as anonymous talking heads.

The problem is that high school students are not taking foreign languages, and most colleges no longer require a foreign language for admission: "Only 15 percent of American high school students study a foreign language. Only 8 percent of our colleges require credit in a foreign language for admission (down from 34 percent in 1966)" (Unks 24).

- *Edit quotations when necessary to condense or clarify.* Use three ellipsis points or spaced periods (. . .) if you omit words from the middle of a quoted sentence:

As two foreign language teachers noted, "We are members of a world community . . . and our fates are closely intertwined" (Long and Long 366).

If you omit words from the end of a quoted sentence or omit sentences from a long quoted passage, place a period after the last word quoted before the omission; follow it with three ellipsis points—for a total of four periods. (Be sure that you have a complete sentence both before and after the four periods.)

Paul Simon advises us that our nation's lack of language proficiency may have been a partial cause of our disastrous policies in Vietnam:

> Vietnam and the Middle East have taught us that our security position is not solely a matter of dealing with the Warsaw Pact countries or the giants among the nations. Before our heavy intervention in Vietnam, fewer than five American-born experts on Vietnam, Cambodia, or Laos . . . could speak with ease one of the languages of that area. . . . What if—a big if—we had had . . . a mere twenty Americans who spoke Vietnamese fluently, who understood their culture, aspirations, and political history? Maybe, just maybe, we would have avoided that conflict. (9)

Note: The first line is indented five spaces because in the source the quotation begins a new paragraph.

In some cases you may want to change the wording of a quotation or add explanatory words of your own to clarify your quotation. If you do so, clearly indicate your changes or additions by placing them within square brackets:

As Simon suggests, if only a few Americans knew Vietnamese then "maybe, just maybe, we would have avoided [the Vietnam War]" (9).

HOW TO AVOID PLAGIARISM Plagiarism is the act of passing off another researcher's or writer's *information, ideas, or language* as one's own. Whether intentional or not, plagiarism is a serious offense. In this class, the result may be a failing grade in both the research project and the course. In the working world, people have lost jobs and presidential candidates have been forced to end campaigns because they have been caught plagiarizing.

To avoid such consequences, be honest and give credit to the work of others by carefully documenting *all* facts, ideas, charts, diagrams, and actual phrases or sentences borrowed from your sources. Assume, for example, that an accurate quotation from your source would read as follows:

> "Most Americans take it for granted that English is the language of the United States and even imagine that every American speaks it fluently. According to the 1980 U.S. Census, however, 11 percent of Americans come from non-English-speaking homes, and over 1 percent of the U.S. population speaks English not well or not at all. No indicators suggest that these percentages will soon decrease" (Conklin and Lourie 3).

The most blatant form of plagiarism involves using *both* your source's information and your source's language (shown below in italics) without giving credit:

> It is ironic that *11 percent of Americans come from non-English-speaking homes*, and yet most Americans say they will never need to speak a foreign language.

A second form of plagiarism, equally serious, involves giving credit to a source for facts or ideas, but *failing to use quotation marks to indicate that you have borrowed the exact language from the source.* In essence, you are saying that these ideas and facts come from Conklin and Lourie, page 3, but that the language is your own. That, of course, is untrue:

> It is ironic that most Americans take it for granted that English is the language of the United States and even imagine that every American speaks it fluently (Conklin and Lourie 3).

Avoid plagiarism by documenting the passage as follows:

> It is ironic, as two researchers recently pointed out, that "most Americans take it for granted that English is the language of the United States and even imagine that every American speaks it fluently" (Conklin and Lourie 3).

To avoid plagiarism, don't randomly copy out interesting passages. Take accurate notes and transcribe quotations *exactly* as they appear in sources. Either put quotation marks around the exact words of the source or paraphrase the main ideas in your own words.

TEACHING TIP

Although students can resort to the essay files or the professional research paper services, allowing sufficient time for the project, requiring and checking a research log, conferring with students early about their projects, and requiring photocopies of all printed sources will eliminate most plagiarism cases.

What makes me happy is rewriting. . . . It's like cleaning house, getting rid of all the junk, getting things in the right order, tightening things up.
—ELLEN GOODMAN, JOURNALIST

REVISING

You have been revising your research essay since the first day of the project. You thought about several subjects, for example, but you chose only one. You started with a focus but revised it as you thought, read, and wrote more. You initially tested your ideas in the draft section of your research notebook, but you revised those ideas as you drafted. At this point, you are just continuing your revising; now, however, you have a complete draft to revise.

Start the revision of your complete draft by taking a break. Fix your schedule so that you can do something else for a couple of days. When you return and reread your draft, be prepared to be flexible. If there is something missing in your data, prepare yourself to track down the information. If a favorite source or quotation no longer seems relevant, have the courage to delete it. If an example on page 4 would work better as a lead-in for the whole paper, reorder your material accordingly. If the evidence for one side of an argument appears stronger than you initially thought, change your position and your thesis. *Being willing to make such changes is not a sign of poor research and writing. Often, in fact, it demonstrates that you have become more knowledgeable and sophisticated about your subject.*

After you have finished your rough draft, ask friends or classmates to give you their responses. Accept their criticism gracefully, but ask them to explain *why* they think certain changes would help. Would they help to make your purposes clearer? Would they be more appropriate for your audience? Don't be intimidated and feel that you must make every change that readers suggest. *You* must make the final decisions.

DOCUMENTING SOURCES Both the MLA and APA documentation styles require citation of sources in the text of your paper, followed by a "Works Cited" (MLA style) or "References" list (APA style) at the end of your paper. Use footnotes only for content or supplementary notes that explain a point covered in the text or offer additional information.

IN-TEXT DOCUMENTATION: MLA STYLE In the MLA style, give the *author's name* and the *page numbers* in parentheses following your use of a fact, paraphrase, or direct quotation from a source. These in-text citations then refer your readers to the complete documentation of the source in a "Works Cited" or "Works Consulted" list at the end of the paper.

As you cite your sources in the text, use the following guidelines:

If you cite the author in the text, indicate only the page number in parentheses:

> According to Vicki Galloway, Project Director for the American Council on the Teaching of Foreign Languages, a student's horizons will not be broadened by "grammar lectures and manipulative classroom exercises" (33).

If the author is unknown, use a short version of the title in the parentheses:

> Most students in the United States would be surprised to learn that the Communist Party in Russia actually sponsors rock concerts (A Day in the Life 68).

If the source is unpublished, cite the name or title used in your bibliography:

> In an informal interview, one university administrator noted that funding foreign language study has steadily decreased over the past ten years (Meyers).

If your bibliography contains more than one work by an author, cite the author, a short title, and page numbers. The following examples show various ways of citing a reference to Paul Simon, *The Tongue-Tied American*:

> In The Tongue-Tied American, Simon explains that students can earn a doctorate degree in the United States without ever studying a foreign language (2).

> As Simon notes, "it is even possible to earn a doctorate here without studying any foreign language" (Tongue-Tied 2).

> In the United States, one can earn a doctorate degree without studying a single foreign language (Simon, Tongue-Tied 2).

Note: Use a comma between author and title but not between title and page number.

If a source has two authors, cite both authors' names in the text or in the parentheses:

> A 1984 study sampling 536 secondary schools revealed that 91 percent did not require foreign language credits for graduation (Ranwez and Rodgers 98).

If a source has three or more authors, give the name of the author listed first in your bibliography followed by the abbreviation *et al.*, meaning "and others":

> Teachers should integrate the study of history, culture, politics, literature, and religion of a particular region with the study of language (Berryman et al. 96).

If a source has several volumes, precede the page number with the volume number and a colon, as indicated:

> Language and grammar can be taught with real-life contexts or scenarios (Valdman 3:82).

If you are citing a quotation or information from a source that itself cites another source, use the abbreviation "qtd. in" for "quoted in" to indicate that you have used an indirect source for your information or quotation. (If possible, however, check the original source.)

> As Sue Berryman et al. explain, "The course is developed as a world tour during which time the students take a vicarious trip . . . to become saturated in every aspect of a particular area of the globe" (qtd. in Simon 96).

If you cite two or more authors as sources for a fact, idea, or plan, separate the citations with a semicolon, as follows:

> Most recently, two prominent foreign language educators have published plans to coordinate foreign language studies (Lambert 9–19; Lange 70–96).

IN-TEXT DOCUMENTATION: APA STYLE In the APA style, give the *author's name* and *date* in parentheses following your use of a summary or paraphrase. If you quote material directly, give author's name, date, and page number. (Use "p." for one page and "pp." for more than one page.) These citations will direct your reader to your References list, where you give complete bibliographical information. As you cite your sources, use the following guidelines:

If you do not cite the author in the text, give author, date, and page in parentheses at the end of the citation:

> In a recent survey, New Jersey secondary school administrators "rated social studies objectives as contributing most to the attainment of high priority goals, and foreign language as contributing least" (Koppel, 1982, p. 437).

If you cite the author in the text, indicate the date in parentheses immediately following the author's name, and cite the page number in parentheses following the quotation:

> According to Vicki Galloway (1984), a student's horizons will not be broadened by "grammar lectures and manipulative classroom exercises" (p. 33).

If you cite a long direct quotation (more than forty words), indent the passage five spaces from the left margin. Omit the enclosing direct quotation marks. Place the period at the end of the passage, not after the parentheses:

> Educator Gerald Unks (1985) points out two instances in which a lack of language proficiency caused companies to initiate fatal marketing programs:
>
> > When Pepsi-Cola went after the Chinese market, "Come Alive with Pepsi" was translated into Chinese in Taiwan as "Pepsi Brings Your Ancestors Back from the Dead." No Sale! General

> Motors sought to sell its Nova in South America oblivious to the fact that "no va" in Spanish means "It doesn't go." (p. 24)

If you are paraphrasing or summarizing material (no direct quotations), you may omit the page number.

> According to Coxe (1984), many top American businesspeople agree that students who combine some business or economics training with fluency in Japanese have unlimited job possibilities.

Note: Although the APA style manual says that writers may omit page citation for summaries and paraphrases, check with your instructor before you omit page references.

If you have previously cited the author and date of a study, you may omit the date:

> In addition, Coxe points out that many top American businesspeople agree that students who combine some business or economics training with fluency in Japanese have unlimited job possibilities.

If the work has between two and five authors, cite all authors in your text or in parentheses in the first reference:

> Long and Long (1985) refer to two foreign language teachers who noted, "We are members of a world community . . . and our fates are closely intertwined" (p. 366).

> As two foreign language teachers noted, "We are members of a world community . . . and our fates are closely intertwined" (Long & Long, 1985, p. 366).

Note: In your text, write "Long and Long"; in parenthetical citation, use an ampersand: "(Long & Long)."

If a work has six or more authors, use only the last name of the first author and the abbreviation *et al.* followed by the date:

> Teachers should integrate the study of history, culture, politics, literature, and religion of a particular region with the study of language (Berryman et al., 1988).

If a work has no author, give the first few words of the title and the year:

> Most students in the United States would be surprised to learn that the Russian government has sponsored rock concerts (A Day in the Life, 1988).

If the author is a corporation, cite the full name of the company in the first reference:

> Foreign language study must be accompanied by in-depth understanding and experience of culture (University of Maryland, 1990).

If the source is a personal communication (letter, memo, interview, phone conversation), cite in text but do *not* include in your References list (personal communications are not recoverable data):

> As Professor Devlin (personal interview, September 21, 1991) explained, "Foreign language study encourages students to see their

own language and culture in a fresh perspective."

If you are citing a government document, give the originating agency, its abbreviation (if any), the year of publication, and (if you include a direct quotation) the page number:

> Newcomers to a foreign culture should "pay attention to their health as well as their grammar. What the natives regularly eat may be dangerous to a foreigner's constitution" (Department of Health and Human Services [DHHS], 1989, p. 64).

If your citation refers to several sources, list the authors and dates in alphabetical order:

> Several studies (Lambert, 1987; Lange, 1987; Long & Long, 1985) have documented severe deficiencies in America's foreign language preparation.

CONTENT OR SUPPLEMENTARY NOTES You may use footnote numbers in the text of your paper to refer to a "Notes" section at the end of the paper. If you have an important idea, a comment on your text, or additional information or sources *that would interrupt the flow of your ideas in the text*, you may use that idea or comment in your supplementary Notes section. During her research, for example, McNerny read about the movement to make English the "official language" of the United States. She didn't want to digress in her paper, so she described the controversy in a supplementary note at the end of the paper. Below is a first draft of that note:

> Twelve states currently have bills before their legislatures to make English the "official language." Proponents of these bills argue that immigrants need incentives to learn English. Many opponents from ethnic and civil-rights groups believe these bills are racist (McBee 64). If Americans were all educated in foreign languages, these bills would be unnecessary. Americans' ignorance and fear of foreign languages is probably a reason that these bills are so popular.

"WORKS CITED" LIST: MLA STYLE After you have revised your essay and are certain that you will not change any in-text documentation, you are ready to write your list of sources. Depending on what you include, it will be one of the following:

- A "Works Cited" list (only those works actually cited in your essay)
- A "Works Consulted" list (works cited and works you read)
- A "Selected Bibliography" (works cited and the most important other works)
- An "Annotated List of Works Cited" (works cited followed by a short description and evaluation of each source)

A Works Cited list alphabetically orders, by author's last name, all published and unpublished sources cited in your research paper. If the author is unknown, alphabetize by the first word (excluding *A*, *An*, or *The*) of the title. The first line of each citation begins at the left margin, and succeeding lines are indented five spaces. As a general rule, underline or italicize titles of books, periodicals, and newspapers, but use quotation marks to enclose titles of newspaper and magazine articles. Use the following abbreviations for missing information (other than an unknown author): N.p. (no place of publication given), n.p. (no publisher given), n.d. (no date of publication given), or N. pag. (no pagination in source). Double-space within and between all entries.

Below are examples of MLA style entries in a Works Cited list, organized by kind of source: books, articles, and unpublished sources. Use these as models for your own Works Cited list. For additional examples, see *MLA Handbook for Writers of Research Papers (1988).*

BOOKS: MLA STYLE

Order the information as follows, omitting information that does not apply:

Author's last name, first name. "Title of article or part of book." Title of Book. Ed. or Trans. Name. Edition. Number of volumes. Place of publication: Name of publisher, Date of publication.

A book by one author

Gould, Stephen Jay. Bully for Brontosaurus: Reflections in Natural History. New York: Norton, 1991.

Additional books by same author

Morrison, Toni. Song of Solomon. New York: Knopf, 1977.

———. Jazz. New York: Knopf, 1992.

A book with two or three authors

Conklin, Nancy F., and Margaret A. Lourie. A Host of Tongues: Language Communities in the United States. New York: Free Press, 1983.

Fairbank, John K., Edwin O. Reischauer, and Albert M. Craig. East Asia: Tradition and Transformation. Boston: Houghton, 1973.

[The names of well-known publishers are often shortened to the first key word. Thus, "E. P. Dutton" is shortened to "Dutton"; "Houghton Mifflin Co." is shortened to "Houghton"; and "Harcourt Brace Jovanovich, Inc." becomes simply "Harcourt."]

More than three authors

Comley, Nancy R., et al. Fields of Writing. New York: St. Martin's, 1994.

An unknown or anonymous author

Publication Manual of the American Psychological Association. 3rd ed. Washington: American Psychological Association, 1984.

An author and an editor

Austen, Jane. Pride and Prejudice. Ed. Mark Schorer. Boston: Houghton, 1956.

Editor of an anthology

Abbey, Edward, ed. Slumgullion Stew: An Edward Abbey Reader. New York: Dutton, 1984.

Editor

Myers, Linda, ed. Approaches to Computer Writing Classrooms. Albany: State University of New York Press, 1993.

A translation

Sophocles. Electra. Trans. David Grene. Greek Tragedies. Ed. David Grene and Richmond Lattimore. Vol 2. Chicago: U of Chicago P, 1960. 2 vols. 45–109.

A work in more than one volume

Morrison, Samuel Eliot, and Henry Steele Commager. The Growth of the American Republic. Vol. 2 New York: Oxford UP, 1941. 2 vols.

A work in an anthology

Blake, William, "The Tyger." The Norton Anthology of English Literature. Ed. M. H. Abrams et al. 6th ed. Vol. 2. New York: Norton, 1993. 2 vols. 37–38.

[Work appears in volume 2 on pages 37–38.]

Entry in an encyclopedia or dictionary

"Don Giovanni." Encyclopedia Americana. 1994 ed.

Government document

Machenthun, Kenneth M. Toward a Cleaner Aquatic Environment. Environmental Protection Agency. Office of Air and Water Programs Washington: GPO, 1973.

["GPO" stands for "Government Printing Office."]

Government document—unknown author

United States. Department of Health, Education, and Welfare. Infant Care. Washington: GPO, 1972.

ARTICLES: MLA STYLE

For all articles published in periodicals, give the author's name, the title of article, and the name of publication. For magazines, add complete dates and inclusive page numbers. For most professional journals, add volume numbers, issue numbers if appropriate, years of publication, and inclusive page numbers.

Article in a weekly or biweekly magazine

Hull, Jon D. "A Boy and His Gun." Time 2 August 1993: 22–27.

Article in a monthly or bimonthly magazine

Taliman, Valerie. "Saving Native Lands." Ms. Jan.–Feb. 1994: 28–29.

Morrison, Ann M., Randall P. White, and Ellen Van Velsor. "Executive Women: Substance Plus Style." Psychology Today Aug. 1987: 18–21, 24–26.

Unsigned article in a magazine

"Catching a Cold: It's Up in the Air." Science86 July–Aug. 1986: 8.

Article in a professional journal

Many professional journals have continuous page numbers throughout the year. The first issue of the year begins with page 1, but every issue after that begins with the number following the last page number of the previous issue. For such journals, give volume followed by the year.

Sady, Stanley P. "Prolonged Exercise Augments Plasma Triglyceride Clearance." Journal of the American Medical Association 256 (1986): 2552–55.

(For page numbers over 100, use only two digits for final page citation: 2552–55.)

If a professional journal begins with page 1, for each issue, cite the volume, issue, and year, *or* cite the volume, month, and year. In the following examples, the article is in volume 9, issue 1, published in January 1987.

Brodkey, Linda. "Writing Ethnographic Narratives." Written Communication 9 (Jan. 1987): 25–50.

Brodkey, Linda. "Writing Ethnographic Narratives." Written Communication 9:1 (1987): 25–50.

Article in a newspaper

Mundy, Alicia. "Attorney General of Social Work." The Wall Street Journal 5 January 1994: A14.

Unsigned article in a newspaper

"South Bronx Triumph: A Student at Harvard." The New York Times 12 January 1994: B8.

Editorial

Haavind, Robert. "Artificial Intelligence Has a Bad Name." Editorial. High Technology Dec. 1986: 4.

Unsigned editorial

"European Summit of Uncertainty." Editorial. Los Angeles Times 7 January 1994: B6.

Review

Molotch, Harvey. Rev. of *A Cycle of Outrage*, by James Gilbert. Science 15 Aug. 1986: 794–95.

Published interview

Lamm, Richard D. "Governments Face Tough Times." With Robert Baun. Coloradoan [Ft. Collins, CO] 30 Nov. 1986: B9.

UNPUBLISHED SOURCES: MLA STYLE

For unpublished sources, give relevant information that may help your reader *identify* or *locate* the source.

Computer software

Microsoft Word. Computer Software. Microsoft, 1992.

Film

Star Trek IV: The Voyage Home. Dir. Leonard Nimoy. With William Shatner and Leonard Nimoy. Paramount, 1986.

A Recording

Carey, Mariah. "Hero." Music Box. Rec. 1993. Sony Songs, Inc, Columbia Records, 1993.

Television or radio program

60 Minutes. CBS. KMGH, Denver. 30 Nov. 1993.

Letter

Ehrlich, Gretel. Letter to the author. 15 Mar. 1994.

Lecture or speech

Gridley, Rita. Lecture on Texas Folklore. U of Kansas. Lawrence, 8 Mar. 1993. [If known, use actual lecture title.]

Unpublished dissertation

Burnham, William A. "Peregrine Falcon Egg Variation, Incubation, and Population Recovery Strategy." Diss. Colorado State U, 1984.

Personal interview

Miller, J. Philip. Personal interview. 9 Sept. 1992.

Personal survey

Morgan Library Interlibrary Loan Questionnaire. Personal survey. 15 March 1994.

Pamphlet

Guide to Raptors. Denver: Center for Raptor Research, 1990.

"REFERENCES" LIST: APA STYLE If you are using the APA style, you should make a separate list, titled "References" (no underlining or quotation marks), that appears after your text but before any appendixes. Include only sources actually used in preparing your essay. List the sources cited in your text *alphabetically*, by author's last name. Use only *initials* for author's first and middle names. If the author is unknown, alphabetize by the first word in the title (not *A*, *An*, or *The*). In titles, *capitalize* only the first word, proper names, and the first word following a colon. If the entry is more than one line, start the first line at the left-hand margin and *indent* subsequent lines three spaces. *Double space* the entire References list.

Below are samples of APA style entries in a References list. For additional information and examples, consult the *Publication Manual of the American Psychological Association* (1984).

BOOKS: APA STYLE

A book by one author

Gould, S. J. (1991). Bully for brontosaurus: Reflections in natural history. New York: Norton.

Additional books by same author

Morrison, T. (1977). Song of Solomon. New York: Knopf.

Morrison, T. (1992). Jazz. New York: Knopf.

A book with two or more authors

Conklin, N.F., & Lourie, M.A. (1983). A host of tongues: Language communities in the United States. New York: Free Press.

An unknown or anonymous author

Publication manual of the American Psychological Association (3rd ed.). (1984). Washington, D.C.: American Psychological Association.

Note: In titles of books and journals, capitalize the first word, the first word after a colon, and any proper names. (American Psychological Association is a proper name.)

An author and an editor

Austen, J. (1956). Pride and prejudice (M. Schorer, Ed.). Boston: Houghton Mifflin.

A work in an anthology

Chopin, K. (1989). The story of an hour. In E.V. Roberts & H.E.

Jacobs (Eds.), Literature: An introduction to reading and writing (pp. 304–306). Englewood Cliffs, NJ: Prentice Hall.

Note: Titles of poems, short stories, essays, or articles in a book are *not* underlined or italicized or put in quotation marks. Only the title of the anthology is underlined.

A translation

Sophocles. (1960). Electra (D. Grene, Trans.). In D. Grene & R. Lattimore (Eds.), Greek tragedies (Vol. 2, pp. 45–109). Chicago: University of Chicago Press.

Note: The APA style usually uses the full name of publishing companies.

Government document

Machenthun, K.M. (1973). Toward a cleaner aquatic environment. Environmental Protection Agency. Office of Air and Water Programs. Washington, D.C.: U.S. Government Printing Office.

Government document—unknown author

United States Department of Health, Education, and Welfare. (1972). Infant care. Washington, D.C.: U.S. Government Printing Office.

ARTICLES: APA STYLE

The following examples illustrate how to list articles in magazines and periodicals according to APA style. **Note:** Do *not* underline or italicize or put quotation marks around titles of articles. Do underline (or italicize) titles of magazines or periodicals. If you cite a volume number, omit the "p." or "pp." before any page numbers.

Article in a weekly or biweekly magazine

Hull, J. D. (1993, August 2). A boy and his gun. Time, pp. 22–27.

Article in a monthly or bimonthly magazine

Taliman, V. (1994, January–February). Saving native lands. Ms., pp. 28–29.

Morrison, A.M., White, R.P., & Van Velsor, E. (1987, August). Executive women: Substance plus style. Psychology Today, pp. 18–21, 24–26.

Unsigned article in a magazine

Catching a cold: It's up in the air. (1986, July–August). Science86, p. 8.

Article in a journal with continuous pagination

Sady, S.P. (1986). Prolonged exercise augments plasma triglyceride clearance. Journal of the American Medical Association, 256, 2552–2555.

Note: Underline the volume number and do not include "pp." Also, APA style requires repeating all number digits: Write 2552–2555, not 2552–55 as in MLA style.

Article in a journal that paginates each issue separately

Brodkey, L. (1987). Writing ethnographic narratives. Written Communication, 9 (1), 25–50.

Note: Underline the volume number followed by the issue number in parentheses.

Article in a newspaper

Mundy, A. (1994, January 5). Attorney general of social work. The Wall Street Journal, p. A14.

Unsigned article in a newspaper

South bronx triumph: A student at harvard. (1994, January 12). The New York Times, p. B8.

Note: B8 means that the article appears in Section B, p. 8.

Editorial

Haavind, R. (1986, December). Artificial intelligence has a bad name. [Editorial.] High Technology, p. 4.

Unsigned editorial

European summit of uncertainty. (1994, January 7). [Editorial.] Los Angeles Times, p. B6.

Review

Molotch, H. (1986, August 15). A cycle of outrage. [Review of Gilbert, J., A cycle of outrage]. Science, pp. 794–795.

Published interview

Lamm, R. (1986, November 30). Governments face tough times. [Interview with Baun, R.] Coloradoan, p. B9.

Computer software

Microsoft word. Vers. 5.0 [Computer software]. (1992). Microsoft.

Film

Nimoy, L. (Director). (1986). *Star trek IV: The voyage home* [Film]. Paramount.

Recording

Carey, M. (Performer). (1993). Hero. Music box [Album]. Sony Songs, Inc., Columbia Records.

Television or radio program

60 Minutes [Television program]. (1993, November 30). KMGH Denver: CBS.

Lecture or speech

Gridley, R. (1993, March 8). Texas folklore in popular western fiction. Speech presented to the English faculty at the University of Kansas, Lawrence.

UNPUBLISHED SOURCES: APA STYLE

In the APA system, unpublished letters and interviews are personal communications and do not represent recoverable data. Therefore, they should *not* appear in a References list. Do, however, cite personal letters or interviews in your text. (See In-text Documentation: APA Style.)

EDITING AND PROOFREADING Edit your paper for conciseness, clarity, and accuracy of grammar, spelling, and punctuation. See your handbook for assistance in revising errors and improving usage. Check your direct quotations to make sure they are *accurate, word-for-word* transcriptions of the originals. Make sure that your in-text citation of sources is accurate. Proofread both the text *and* the Works Cited section. Finally, have someone else proofread your research paper for typos, spelling errors, missing words, or confusing sentences.

■ **POSTSCRIPT ON THE WRITING PROCESS** As your final entry in your research notebook, answer the following questions:

1. Reread your "research log" section. Compare your initial schedule with your actual progress. What parts of the research paper took longer than you anticipated? What took less time?

2. What was the most difficult problem you encountered while writing the research paper? How did you try to solve that problem?

3. What do you like best about the final version of your research paper? Why? What do you like least? Why?

FOREIGN LANGUAGE STUDY: AN AMERICAN NECESSITY

KATE MCNERNY

Kate McNerny's final version of her research paper appears below. Her purpose is to persuade students, administrators, and ordinary citizens that learning the language and culture of a foreign country is important, both to people as individuals and to America as a nation. In this paper, she uses facts, information, and her own experience to alert her readers to the seriousness of the problem. She argues that American schools should require students to study at least one foreign language during junior and senior high school.

McNerny follows the MLA style for in-text documentation, supplementary Notes, and Works Cited list. The marginal notations highlight key features of her research paper.

"Why should I learn a foreign language—everyone speaks English!" "I would never use another language—I never plan to leave the United States." "I had a hard enough time learning English!" These are only a few of the excuses people have given for opposing foreign language studies, and unfortunately they represent the ideas of more than a few American citizens. While other people agree that learning a second language can be beneficial, they still fail to see it as a necessity. Deep-rooted misconceptions regarding the value of foreign language study exist among Americans. Theodore Huebener's study, Why Johnny Should Learn Foreign Languages, shows how those misconceptions have, historically, led to a decline in foreign language study. In 1940, a committee of the American Youth Commission issued a report labelling foreign language studies as "useless and time-consuming" (Huebener 13). An even more appalling statement came from a group of Harvard scholars. They suggested that "foreign language study is useful primarily in strengthening the student's English. . . . For the average student there is no real need at all to learn a foreign language" (Huebener 14). With such attitudes, it is no wonder that students and administrators ignored foreign language programs during the 1940s and 1950s.[1] Even today, in an era of trade with Pacific Rim countries, with Russian *glasnost* or "openness," with increased cultural and economic exchange with China, students in our colleges and high schools are insufficiently educated in foreign language and culture. **(1)**

For her lead-in, McNerny uses quotations she collected in her informal survey.

McNerny presents historical background on the problem.

Ellipses points indicate omitted material from the source.

The footnote refers to the reader to the "Notes" page for McNerny's comment on the history of the problem.

Despite promising signs of changes, foreign language study still holds the weakest position of any other major subject in American secondary schools. A recent study of foreign language programs reports that "only 15 percent of American high school students study a foreign language. Only 8 percent of [American] colleges require credit in a foreign language for admission (down from 34 percent in 1966)" (Unks 24). Because available programs at the junior and senior high school level are generally limited in variety and scope, only a small percentage of those students that take a foreign language ever become fluent in it. A 1984 study that sampled 536 secondary schools revealed that most offered a foreign language, but 91 percent did not require foreign language credits for graduation (Ranwez and Rodgers 98). In contrast, many countries

Square brackets in quoted material indicate a word added by McNerny to clarify the sentence.

In-text citation for a source with two authors

require all students to learn at least one, and often two, foreign languages. In France, all students must study one modern language throughout their seven years in the lycée (secondary school). During the last four years of lycée, French children must also study Greek or an additional modern language. Swedish children spend almost one third of their secondary school class time on language studies (Huebener 26). **(2)**

Notice punctuation for in-text citation: source appears in parenthesis after *the quotation marks but* before *the period.*

The United States cannot continue to lag behind other countries in language capability. As two researchers noted, "We are members of a world community consisting of hundreds of nations, and our fates are closely intertwined" (Long and Long 366). It is time to change attitudes and to recognize that in order to successfully interact with its "world community," the United States must drastically change its foreign language policies. American students should be required to study at least one foreign language throughout their six years of junior and senior high school. **(3)**

McNerny's thesis

McNerny begins refutation of opposing arguments.

School administrators across the country oppose the idea of requiring foreign languages because they cannot see the contribution these studies make to the overall goals of the schools' curriculum. In a recent survey, New Jersey secondary school administrators "rated social studies objectives as contributing most to the attainment of high priority goals, and foreign language as contributing least," (Koppel 437). These officials fail to realize that language studies can add a valuable dimension to a social studies program. Educators can use a combined program to emphasize a global perspective in language and cultural studies. "The world looks and sounds different when one is 'standing in the shoes' of another, speaking another language, or recognizing another's point of view based on an alternative set of values" (Bragaw 37). This global-awareness is crucial in our increasingly interdependent world.[2] **(4)**

School administrators express concern about foreign language study's relevance to curriculum goals, but in addition, many students simply fail to see why they will ever need to use a foreign language. I used to belong to that group. I remember my mom always telling me, "Take French classes. Learn how to speak French so you can visit your cousins in France someday." At the time, during junior high, I did take French classes for a while, but then dropped them when my schedule became "too busy." Then, as my mom had promised, I got the opportunity to visit my cousins in France. For some reason, the fact that I couldn't speak French didn't really hit me—until I stepped off the train at Gare du Nord in Paris and couldn't find the relative who was supposed to meet me. After frantically searching the entire station several times, I had to break down and ask for help. At the information desk, a few completely butchered French phrases escaped my lips—only to be received by an unimpressed, unresponsive station attendant. He muttered something about dumb Americans. Then, with a wave of his hand, he gestured toward some unknown destination. I did survive that painful ordeal, but I vowed I wouldn't embarrass myself—and other Americans—again. **(5)**

When Americans travel abroad, they not only face a language barrier, but they may also face culture differences as well. Most foreign language courses today teach culture as well as language because the teachers realize that grammar and language are only a part of the barrier. In his resource book, Teaching Culture, H. Ned Seelye, Director of Bilingual-Bicultural Education for the State of Illinois, cites just one of many examples of culture shock that Americans may face:

McNerny introduces the author, the title of the book, and the author's credentials to lend authority to the quoted passage.

> At a New Year's Eve celebration in an exclusive Guatemalan hotel, one American was overheard telling another. "You see all these people? They're all my wife's relatives. And every damn one of them has kissed me tonight. If another Guatemalan man hugs and kisses me I'll punch him right in the face!" The irritated American was disturbed by two things: the extended kinship patterns of the group and the *abrazo de ano neuvo* as executed by the men (he did not complain of the female *abrazos*). Both customs—close family ties that extend to distant relatives and the abrazo given as a greeting or sign of affection devoid of sexual overtures—elicited hostility in the American who was bored by unintelligible language and depressed by nostalgia and alcohol. (85) **(6)**

At the end of the quotation, McNerny cites only the page number, since she has already introduced the author. Page number follows *the period in a block indented quotation.*

In order to prevent such linguistic and cultural misunderstandings, instruction in language and culture needs to begin early. In a recent study designed to reveal what children know about foreign language and culture, a group of intellectually gifted seventh graders wrote imaginative stories about the lives of Soviet children. While the students displayed some knowledge of communism and the Soviet Union, they also expressed serious misconceptions about the day-to-day lives of the Soviet children. The students believed that many Soviet children could not attend schools because they had to work in the fields. Many of the students did not understand that Soviet children could also be happy and enjoy their lives despite the political climate of their country (Long and Long 367). Even if most Americans never travel to another country or need to speak another language, they should be able to understand and appreciate different cultures. **(7)**

McNerny presents arguments for her thesis.

Recently, Soviet Leader Mikhail Gorbachev's policy of "glasnost" has created a promising change in Americans' attitudes. According to a report in Time magazine, Soviet studies are on the upswing in the U.S., and interest in languages is following along. At Vermont's Middlebury College, for example, almost 10% of the 1,900 undergraduates are currently majoring in Soviet studies, and a consortium of 18 Northeastern colleges has signed an agreement to exchange undergraduate students

McNerny paraphrases key information from article; she does not introduce the author here because she wants to emphasize the facts and trends rather than his authority.

with Soviet students from throughout the Soviet Union (Bowen 65). We have known for a long time that suspicion and hatred between countries often grows from the inability to understand each other. The students majoring in Soviet studies or participating in exchanges know that in order to achieve world peace, we must be able to communicate and empathize with our "enemies" as well as our allies. **(8)**

As a transition, McNerny uses a paragraph hook ("cultural understanding") to lead into this paragraph on international trade and the following paragraph on diplomacy.

A nationwide language study requirement not only would promote cultural understanding but also would strengthen the United States' international relations in business and diplomacy. International trade is continually increasing in the United States and has created a demand for businesspeople competent in foreign languages. Many top American businesspeople agree that students who combine some business or economics training with fluency in Japanese have unlimited job possibilities (Coxe 194). Company executives simply cannot expect to make efficient, sound decisions in their international markets without understanding and speaking the language of the country they are dealing with (Huebener 45). Educator Gerald Unks points out two instances in which a lack of language proficiency caused companies to initiate fatal marketing programs.

McNerny does not end her paragraph with a quotation; instead, she shows how this evidence supports *her* point.

> When Pepsi-Cola went after the Chinese market, "Come Alive With Pepsi" was translated into Chinese in Taiwan as "Pepsi Brings Your Ancestors Back from the Dead." No Sale! General Motors sought to sell its Nova in South America oblivious to the fact that "No va" in Spanish means "It doesn't go." (24)

These examples illustrate that business people need thorough competence in, not just rudimentary knowledge of, foreign languages. **(9)**

Language proficiency is important not only for business and trade, but also for diplomatic relations. Often, the United States attempts to help countries by showering them with money and technical aid but is unable to deal with their problems on a cultural or psychological level (Huebener 42). Thus, our "good intentions" are poorly communicated and often unappreciated or misinterpreted. "South America denounces 'Yankee Imperialism'; Cuba vilifies us; Panama is sullen. Our European allies are lukewarm" (Huebener 43). The image of the "Ugly American" can be traced directly to our lack of training in foreign language and culture. Ignorance of foreign language by our diplomats has been almost the rule rather than the exception (Huebener 53). If long-term language studies become an integral part of America's education systems, we could fill diplomatic positions with people who are linguistically and culturally sensitive to the people of that country. **(10)**

Even though McNerny has just cited Huebener twice, she cites the source again because this material is taken from a different page.

The need for required language study in the United States is urgent. The solution to the problem requires effort on at least two fronts: making students and school administrators aware that foreign language study is important, and obtaining the necessary funding for new programs. In the last few years, some educators have advocated required foreign language studies in the elementary grades (Jassey 159). Some have called for a reexamination of goals and teaching methods to meet social needs yet fit into the public school system (Galloway 32–35). Most recently, two prominent foreign language educators have organized a "national agenda" for improving language instruction and a national foreign language center to implement that agenda (Lange 70–96; Lambert 9–19). **(11)**

McNerny begins her conclusion, calling for local and federal administrators to support a foreign language requirement.

Although the plans and the strategy exist, often the funds do not. Some funds can be diverted from within school districts, but the federal government must take some initiative. The current presidential administration spends endless time and money developing national defense and supporting business interests. Since foreign language knowledge contributes strongly to success in both these areas, it would be practical for the administration also to support expansion of language studies. Instead, it continues to cut funding for special programs including language studies centers and international teaching facilities (Unks 25). Realistically, a foreign language requirement in junior and senior high school cannot be initiated without the support of both local school districts as well as the federal government. Americans must acknowledge the fact that they are not isolated from the rest of the world. Successful interaction in the "world community" relies on our ability, as a nation, to effectively communicate with and understand people from other countries. Understanding, communication, and world peace can hardly be achieved without language competency. **(12)**

NOTES

Content notes are placed on a separate page and double-spaced. Use raised footnote number and indent first line five spaces.

[1]One of the most disturbing facts is that although Heubener's study was done in 1961, very little has changed in almost thirty years. Except for slight changes in statistics, dates, and names of wars, Americans have remained strikingly insular in their attitudes toward foreign languages and foreigners.

[2]It is ironic that Americans not only hesitate to take a foreign language, but they also seem bent on keeping foreign languages officially "out of sight." Twelve states currently have bills before their legislatures to make English the "official language." According to a recent U.S. News and World Report article, proponents of these bills argue that multiple language use threatens to erode English as a unifying force, that immigrants need incentives to learn English, and that bilingual ballots merely postpone the melting pot process. Many opponents from ethnic and civil-rights groups believe these bills are racist (McBee 64).

In her notes, McNerny includes two ideas that would have been digressive in the text of her paper.

Americans' ignorance of foreign languages (and the fear that ignorance breeds) is an important cause for the popularity of these proposed "official language" laws.

The works cited list begins a new page. List entries according to author's last name. If no author is given, list by first word in the title. Double-space entries.

Indent five spaces after first line of each entry.

Book

Article from a journal with contiguous pagination

Article from a monthly magazine

For inclusive page number over 100, use only the last two digits in the second number (366–68).

WORKS CITED

Bowen, Ezra. "Iron Curtain Raising on Campus." Time 12 Oct. 1987: 65.

Bragaw, Donald H., and Helene Zimmer-Loew. "Social Studies and Foreign Language: A Partnership." Education Digest Dec. 1985: 36–39.

Coxe, Donald. "The Back Page." Canadian Business Feb. 1984: 194.

Galloway, Vicki B. "Foreign Language Study in the 1980s." Education Digest Oct. 1984: 32–35.

Huebener, Theodore. Why Johnny Should Learn Foreign Languages. New York: Chilton, 1961.

Jassey, William. "Aiming for a Foreign Language Requirement." Clearing House Dec. 1984: 159–61.

Koppel, Irene E. "The Perceived Contribution of Foreign Language to High Priority Education Goals." Foreign Language Annals 15 (1982): 435–37.

Lambert, Richard D. "The Improvement of Foreign Language Competency in the United States." Annals of the American Academy of Political and Social Science Mar. 1987: 9–19.

Lange, Dale L. "The Language Teaching Curriculum and a National Agenda." Annals of the American Academy of Political and Social Science Mar. 1987: 70–96.

Long, Delbert H., and Roberta A. Long. "Toward the Promotion of Foreign Language Study and Global Understanding." Education 105 (1985): 366–68.

McBee Susanna. "A War Over Words." U.S. News and World Report 6 Oct. 1986: 64.

Ranwez, Alain D., and Judy Rodgers. "The Status of Foreign Languages and International Studies: An Assessment in Colorado." Foreign Language Annals 17 (1984): 97–102.

Seelye, H. Ned. Teaching Culture: Strategies for Foreign Language Educators. Skokie, IL: National Textbook, 1974.

Unks, Gerald. "The Perils of Our Single-Language Policy." Education Digest Mar. 1985: 24–27.

Appendix: Writing Under Pressure

The main chapters of this text describe purposes for writing and strategies for collecting, shaping, drafting, and revising an essay. These chapters assume that you have several days or even weeks to write your paper. They work on the premise that you have time to read model essays, time to think about ideas for your topic, and time to prewrite, write several drafts, and receive feedback from other members of your class. Much college writing, however, occurs on midterm or final examinations, when you may have only fifteen to twenty minutes to complete the whole process of writing. When you must produce a "final" draft in a few short minutes, your writing process may need drastic modification.

A typical examination has some objective questions (true/false, multiple choice, definitions, short answer) followed by an essay question or two. For example, with just twenty-five minutes left in your Western Civilization midterm, you might finish the last multiple-choice question, turn the page, and read the following essay question:

> Erich Maria Remarque's *All Quiet on the Western Front* has been hailed by critics the world over as the "twentieth century's definitive novel on war." What does Remarque's novel tell us about the historical, ideological, national, social, and human significance of twentieth-century warfare? Draw on specific illustrations from the novel, but base your observations on your wider perspective of Western Civilization. Good luck!

Overwhelmed by panic, the blood drains from your face and your fingers feel icy. You now have twenty-two minutes to write on the "historical, ideological, national, social, and human significance of twentieth-century warfare." Do you have to explain everything about modern warfare? Must you use specific examples from the novel? Good luck, indeed! Everything you remembered about the novel has now vanished. Bravely, you pick up your pen and start recounting the main events of the novel, hoping to show the instructor that you at least read it.

You can survive such an essay examination, but you need to prepare yourself emotionally and intellectually. Following is some advice from senior English majors who have taken dozens of essay examinations in their four years of college. These seniors answer the question, "What advice would you give to students who are preparing to take an essay examination?"

Even though I'm an English major, I'm perfectly petrified of writing impromptu essays. My advice is to calm yourself. Read the question. Study key words and concepts. Before beginning an essay question, write a brief, informal outline. This will organize your ideas and help you remember them as well. Take a deep breath and write. I would also recommend *rereading* the question while you are writing, to keep you on track.

The first step is to know the material. Then, before you begin, read the instructions. Know what the teacher expects. Then try to organize your thoughts into a small list—preferably a list that will become your main paragraphs. Don't babble to fill space. Teachers hate reading nonsense. Reread what you've written often. This will ensure that you won't repeat yourself. Proofread at the end.

Organization is important but difficult in a pressure situation. Well-organized essays do have a tendency to impress the professor, sometimes more than information-packed essays. Organize your notes and thoughts about those notes as you study (not necessarily in a chronological order, but rather in a comprehensible order). Good luck.

Read the question carefully.
Get your thoughts in order.
Write what the question asks, not what you hope it says.
Don't ramble.
Give textual facts or specific examples.
Summarize with a clear, understandable closure.
Proofread.
Keep calm. Your life doesn't depend on one test.

My advice would be first to learn how to consciously relax and practice writing frequently. *Practice!!!* It's important to practice writing as much as possible in any place possible, because the more writing you do, the better and easier it becomes. Also, your belief that it *can* be done is critical!

Know the information that you will be tested over well enough that you can ask yourself tough and well-formed questions in preparation. You should be able to predict what essay questions your professor will ask, at least generally. I always go to the test file or ask friends for sample essay questions that I can practice on. Then I practice writing on different areas of the material.

The common threads in these excerpts of advice are to know your audience, analyze key terms in the question, make a sketch outline, know the material, practice writing before the test, and proofread when you finish writing. Knowing how to read the question and practicing your writing before the test will help you relax and do your best.

Know Your Audience

Teachers expect you to answer a question exactly as it is asked, not just to give the information that you know. Because teachers must read dozens of essays, they are impressed by clear organization and specific detail. As one senior says, teachers hate babble because they cannot follow the thread of your argument. Although they demand specific examples and facts from the text, they want you to explain how these examples *relate* to the overall question. In a pile of two hundred history exams graded by one professor, margins featured comments like "Reread the question. This doesn't answer the question." "What is your main point? State your main point clearly." "Give more specific illustrations and examples." Keep this teacher in mind as you write your essay response.

Analyze Key Terms

Understanding the key terms in the question is crucial to writing an essay under pressure. Teachers expect you to respond to *their* specific question, not just to write down information. They want you to use your writing to *think* about the topic—to analyze and synthesize the information. In short, they want you to make sense of the information. Below are key terms that indicate teachers' expectations and suggest how to organize your answer.

Discuss: A general instruction that means "write about." If the question says "discuss," look for other key words to focus your response.
Describe: Give sensory details or particulars about a topic. Often, however, this general instruction simply means "discuss."
Analyze: Divide a topic into its parts and show how the parts are related to each other and to the topic as a whole.
Synthesize: Show how the parts relate to the whole or how the parts make sense together.
Explain: Show relationships between specific examples and general principles. Explain what (define), explain why (causes/effects), and/or explain how (analyze process).
Define: Explain what something is. As appropriate, give a formal defini-

Teaching Tip

For your discussion of key terms, have each student bring to class one essay question or essay test question that they have been assigned. (If they do not have any current essay assignments, have them interview friends or roommates for possible questions. Have selected students write their questions on the board and then ask the class to explain the key terms in each assignment.

tion, describe it, analyze its parts or function, describe what it is not, and/or compare and contrast it with similar events or ideas.

COMPARE: Explain similarities and (often) differences. Draw conclusions from the observed similarities and differences.

CONTRAST: Explain key differences. Draw conclusions from the observed differences.

ILLUSTRATE: Provide specific examples of an idea or process.

TRACE: Give the sequence or chronological order of key events or ideas.

EVALUATE: Determine the value or worth of an idea, thing, process, person, or event. Set up criteria and provide evidence to support your judgments.

SOLVE: Explain your solution; show how it fixes the problem, why it is better than other alternatives, and why it is feasible.

ARGUE: Present both sides of a controversial issue, showing why the opposing position should not be believed or accepted and why your position should be accepted. Give evidence to support your position.

INTERPRET: Offer your understanding of the meaning and significance of an idea, event, person, process, or work of art. Support your understanding with specific examples or details.

MAKE A SKETCH OUTLINE

The key terms in a question should not only focus your thinking but also suggest how to organize your response. Use the key terms to make a sketch outline of your response. You may not regularly use an outline when you have more time to write an essay, but the time pressure requires that you revise your normal writing process.

Assume that you have twenty-five minutes to read and respond to the following question from a history examination. Read the instructions carefully, note the key terms, and make a brief outline to guide your writing.

- Answer *one* of the following. Draw on the reading for your answer. (25 pts)

1. Explain the arguments that the balance of power does and does not work in the nuclear age (discuss and illustrate both sides of the argument). Then take a stand—citing the evidence for your position.

2. Explain the arguments that the United Nations does and does not play a positive role in international relations (discuss and illustrate both sides of the argument). Then take a stand—citing the evidence for your position.

Let's assume that because you know more about the United Nations, you choose the second question. First, you should identify and underline key words in the question. The subject for your essay is the *United Nations* and its role in *international relations*. You need to *explain* the reasons why the UN does or does not have a positive effect on international relations. You will need to *discuss* and *illustrate* (give specific examples of) both sides of the controversy. Finally, you need to *take a stand* (argue) for your belief, citing *evidence* (specific examples from recent history) of how the UN has or has not helped to resolve international tensions.

Based on your rereading and annotation of the key words of the question, make a quick outline or list, perhaps as follows:

I. Reasons (with examples) why some believe the UN is effective
   A. Reason #1 + example
   B. Reason #2 + example

II. Reasons (with examples) why some believe the UN is not effective
   A. Reason #1 + example
   B. Reason #2 + example

III. Reasons why you believe the UN is effective
   Refer to reasons and examples cited in I, above, but explain why these reasons and examples outweigh the reasons cited in II, above.

With this sketch outline as your guide, jot down reasons and examples that you intend to use and then start writing. Your outline will make sure that you cover all the main points of the question, and it will keep your essay organized as you concentrate on remembering specific reasons and examples.

■ **JOURNAL EXERCISE** For practice, analyze at least one question from two of the following subject areas. First, underline key terms. Then, in your journal explain what these terms ask you to do. Finally, sketch an outline to help organize your response. If you are not familiar with the topics, check a dictionary or encyclopedia. (Do not write the essay.)

Biology

- Describe the process by which artificial insulin was first produced.
- What is reverse transcriptase and how was it used in genetic engineering?

- Humans—at least most of us—walk on two legs as opposed to four. How might you account for this using a Darwinian, Lamarckian, and Theistic model?

History

- Discuss the significant political developments in the English colonies in the first half of the eighteenth century.
- Account for the end of the Salem witchcraft delusion and discuss the consequences of the outbreak for Salem Village.

Human Development

- Discuss evidence for nature versus nurture effects in human development.
- Contrast Piaget's, Vygotsky's and Whorf's ideas on connections between language and thought.

Humanities

- How and why did early Christian culture dominate the Roman Empire? In terms of art and architecture, discuss specific ways in which the early Christians transformed or abolished the Greco-Roman legacy.

Literature

- Aristotle wrote that a tragedy must contain certain elements, such as a protagonist of high estate, recognition, and reversal, and should also evoke pity and fear in the audience. Which of the following best fits Aristotle's definition: *Hamlet*, *Death of a Salesman*, or *The Old Man and the Sea*? Explain your choice.

Philosophy

- On the basis of what we have studied in this class, define "philosophy." Taking your major subject of study (for example, biology, history, literature), discuss three philosophical problems that arise in this field.
- Write an essay explaining the following statement. Be clear in your explanation and use specific examples. "Egoism allows for prudent altruism."

Political Science

- Evaluate the achievements of the current administration's policy in Africa in recent years.
- Analyze the role of force in the contemporary international system.

Psychology

- Contrast Freud's and Erikson's stage theories of personality.
- What is meant by triangulation of measurement (multiple methodology)?

KNOW THE MATERIAL

It goes without saying that you must know the material in order to explain the concepts and give specific examples or facts from the text. But what is the best way to review the material so that you can recall examples under pressure? The following three study tactics will improve your recall.

First, read your text actively. Do not just mark key passages in yellow highlighter. Write marginal notes to yourself. Write key concepts in the margin. Ask questions. Make connections between an idea in one paragraph and something you read earlier. Make connections between what you read in the text and what you heard in class.

Second, do not depend only on your reading and class discussion. Join or form a study group that meets regularly to review course material. Each person in the group should prepare some question for review. Explaining key ideas to a friend is an excellent way to learn the material yourself.

Finally, use your writing to help you remember. Do not just read the book and your notes and head off for the test. Instead, review your notes, *close* your notebook, and write down as much as you can remember. Review the assigned chapters in the text, close the book, and write out what you remember. If you can write answers to questions with the book closed, you know you're ready for an essay examination.

■ **JOURNAL EXERCISE** Get out the class notes and textbook for a course that you are currently taking. Annotate your notes with summary comments and questions. In the margins, write out the key ideas that the lecture covered. Then write out questions that you still have about the material. Open your textbook for that class. Annotate the margins of the chapter that you are currently reading. Write summary comments about important material. Write questions in the margins about material that you do not understand. Note places in the text that the instructor also covered in class.

PRACTICE WRITING

As several of the senior English majors suggested, practicing short essays *before* an examination will make you feel comfortable with the material and reduce your panic. A coach once noted that while every athlete wants to win, only the true winners are willing to *prepare* to win. The same is true of writing an examination. Successful writers have already completed 80 percent of the writing process *before* they walk into an examination. They have written notes in the margins of their notebooks and textbooks. They have discussed the subject with other students. They have closed the book and written out key definitions. They have prepared questions and practiced answering them. Once they read a question, they are prepared to write out their "final" drafts.

■ **Journal Exercise** For an upcoming examination in one of your other courses, write out three possible essay questions that your instructor might ask. For each question, underline the key words and make a sketch outline of your response. Set your watch or timer for fifteen minutes and actually write out your response to *one* of your questions.

Proofread and Edit

In your normal writing process, you can put aside your draft for several days and proofread and edit it later. When you are writing under pressure, however, you need to save three or four minutes at the end to review what you have written. Often, you may be out of time before you have finished writing what you wanted to say about the question. At this point, one effective strategy is to draw a line ___________ at the end of what you have written, write "Out of Time," and then write one or two quick sentences explaining what you planned to say: "If I had more time, I would explain how the UN's image has become more positive following the crises in Israel and Iraq." Then use your remaining two or three minutes to reread what you have written, making sure that your ideas are clear, that you have written in complete sentences and used correct spelling and punctuation. If you don't know how to spell a word, at least write "sp?" next to a word to show that you think it is spelled incorrectly.

Sample Essay Questions and Responses

The following are sample essay questions, student's responses, and instructors' comments and grades.

> HISTORY 100: WESTERN CIVILIZATION Examination II over Chapter 12, class lectures, and Victor Hugo's *The Hunchback of Notre Dame*

ESSAY I (25 POINTS)

What was the fifteenth-century view of "science" as described in the *Hunchback*? How did this view tend to inhibit Claud Frollo in his experiments in his closet in the cathedral?

ANSWER 1

The fifteenth-century view of "science" was characterized by superstition and heresy. In the *Hunchback of Notre Dame,* for example, we see superstition operating when the king's physician stated that a gunshot wound could be cured by the application of a roasted mouse. Claud Frollo, a high-ranking church official, had a thirst for knowledge, but unfortunately it pushed beyond the limits of knowledge permitted by the church. When he worked in his closet on the art of alchemy and searched for the "Philosopher's Stone" (gold), he was guilty of heresy. Frollo read and mastered the arts and sciences of the university and of the church, and he wanted to know more. He knew that if he pressed into the "Black Arts," the Devil would take his soul. And indeed, the "Devil" of passion did. Frollo felt inhibited because many of the experiments he performed would have made him guilty of heresy and witchcraft in the eyes of the church. And this seemed to be the case in almost anything "new" or out of the ordinary. La Esmeralda, for instance, was declared "guilty" of witchcraft for the training of her goat. Her goat appeared to have been possessed by the Devil himself. When in fact, all the girl was guilty of was training the goat to do a few simple tricks. All in all, the fifteenth-century view of "science" was not one of favor, but of oppression and fear. Thankfully, the Renaissance came along!

An excellent response. Your focus on superstition and heresay along with the specific examples of the roasted mouse, the "Philosopher's Stone," and La Esmeralda's goat illustrate the fifteenth-century view of science and its inhibiting effect. Grade: A

ANSWER 2

The fifteenth-century view of science was that according to the Bible. God was the creator of all and as to scientific theory, the subject was moot. No one was a believer in the scientific method—however we do find some science going on in Claud Frollo's closet, alchemy. At that time he was trying to create gold by mixing different elements together. Though alchemy seems to be the only science of that time period, people who practiced it kept it to themselves. We even find King Louis IX coming to Frollo, disguised, to dabble in a little of the science himself. At

Give more examples from the novel and show how the fifteenth-century view actually inhibited Frollo. Otherwise, generally good response. (Why was creating the Earth such a religious "ordeal"?) Grade: B

Needs more specific illustrations from the novel. Frollo was inhibited by his lack of scientific method and the censure of the church. Underline title of novels: The Hunchback of Notre Dame. Grade: C

this time people were rejecting the theory of the Earth revolving around the sun because, as a religious ordeal, God created the Earth and man and they are the center of all things so there were no questions to be answered by science, because the answer was God.

ANSWER 3

According to The Hunchback of Notre Dame, the view of "science" in the fifteenth century was basically alchemy, that is being able to turn back metals into gold. Everything else that we would regard as scientific today was regarded as sorcery or magic in the fifteenth century. What inhibited Claud Frollo in his experiments of turning bare metals into gold was that, according to the laws of alchemy, one needed "The Philosopher's Stone" to complete the experiment and Claud Frollo was unable to find this particular stone.

ANSWER 4

State your ideas more clearly. Your response doesn't answer the question. Very limited in your examples of science. Grade: D

During the period that the *Hunchback* took place, the attitude toward science was one of fear. Because the setting was in the medieval world, the people were afraid to admit to doing some things that were not being done by a majority of people. The overall views during that period was to keep one's own self out of trouble. The fright may be the result of the public executions which was perhaps Claud Frollo's deterrent in admitting to performing acts of science which others are uneducated in. Claud Frollo was outnumbered in the area of wanting to be "educated" and he kept to himself because he feared the people. He was in a position that didn't give him the power to try and overcome people's attitude of fear toward science. If he tried, he risked his life.

BIOLOGY 220: ECOLOGY
FINAL EXAMINATION

ESSAY II (20 POINTS)

Water running down a mountainside erodes its channel and carries with it considerable material. What is the basic source of the energy used by the water to do this work? How is the energy used by water to do this work related to the energy used by life in the stream ecosystem?

Answer 1

The process begins with the hydrologic cycle. The sun radiates down and forces evaporation. This H2O gas condenses and forms rain or snow which precipitates back to earth. If the precipitation falls on a mountain, it will eventually run down the hillside and erode its channel. (Some water will evaporate without running down the hill.) The energy used by water to do its work relates directly to the energy used by life in the stream system. The sun is an energy input. It is the source of energy for stream life just as it is the source of energy for the water. Through photosynthesis, the energy absorbed by the stream is used by higher and higher trophic levels. So the sun is the energy source for both running water and the life in the stream. It all starts with solar energy.

Good response. Clear focus on the hydrologic cycle, photosynthesis, and solar energy and the source of energy for both the stream and its ecosystems.
Grade: A

Answer 2

Ultimately, the sun is the basic source of energy which allows water to do the work it does. Solar power runs the hydrologic cycle, which is where water gets its energy. Heat evaporates water and allows molecules to rise in the atmosphere where it condenses in clouds. Above the ground, but still under the effects of gravity, water has potential energy at this point. When enough condensation occurs, water drops back to the ground, changing potential energy to kinetic energy, which is how water works on mountainsides to move materials. As water moves materials, it brings into streams a great deal of organic matter which is utilized by a number of heterotrophic organisms. That is the original source of energy for the ecosystems, and also how energy used by water is related to the energy that is used by life in streams.

Very clear explanation of the hydrologic cycle, but respose doesn't explain how source of energy for the streams ecosystems is related, through photosynthesis, to solar energy.
Grade: B

Answer 3

The actual energy to move the water down the mountains is gravitation pull from the center of the earth. The stream's "growth" from the beginning of the mountain top to the base starts out with being a heterotrophic system. This is because usually there is not enough light to bring about photosynthesis for the plants and in turn help other organism's survival so the streams use outside resources for energy. Once the

Reread the question,. The basic source of energy is solar power, You almost discover the answer when you discuss photosynthesis, but after that, you get off track again. Grade C-

stream is bigger (by meeting up with another stream), it is autotrophic. It can produce its own energy sources. When the water reaches the base and becomes very large, it falls back to heterotrophic system because the water has become too deep for light to penetrate and help with photosynthesis.

HANDBOOK

A piece of writing is never finished. It is delivered to a deadline, torn out of a typewriter on demand, and sent off with a sense of accomplishment and shame and pride and frustration. If only there were a couple more days, time for just another run at it, perhaps then . . .

—DONALD MURRAY, TEACHER AND WRITER

SECTION 1

REVIEW OF BASIC SENTENCE ELEMENTS

If you are unfamiliar with grammatical terms, parts of speech, or basic sentence elements, check the definitions and examples in this section.

1a Sentence Structure
1b Nouns and Pronouns
1c Adjectives and Adverbs
1d Verbs
1e Phrases and Clauses
1f Articles, Prepositions, Interjections

SECTION 2

SENTENCE STRUCTURE AND GRAMMAR

This section shows you how to revise such common problems as sentence fragments, faulty parallelism, unnecessary use of passive voice, and lack of subject-verb agreement.

2a Fragments
2b Mixed Constructions and Faulty Predication
2c Dangling Modifiers and Misplaced Modifiers
2d Faulty Parallelism
2e Active and Passive Voice
2f Nominals and "Be" Verbs
2g Subject-Verb Agreement
2h Verb Tense
2i Pronoun Agreement
2j Pronoun Reference

SECTION 3

DICTION AND STYLE

This section contains tips on making your writing more precise, concise, and effective. You will learn to recognize and eliminate vague words, needless words, clichés, and jargon. At the end of this section, the Usage

Glossary explains distinctions between confusing pairs of words such as *affect/effect*, *advise/advice*, and *amount/number*.

3a Vague Words
3b Wordiness
3c Colloquial Language and Slang
3d Clichés and Jargon
3e Sexist Language
3f Denotation and Connotation
3g Usage Glossary

SECTION 4

PUNCTUATION AND MECHANICS

If you have problems using commas, semicolons, colons, or dashes, this section will help you pinpoint errors and fix them. The examples show you how to revise comma splices and fused sentences, how to punctuate dialogue, and how to use numbers, apostrophes, italics, and capitals.

4a Sentence Punctuation
4b Comma Splices and Fused Sentences
4c Commas
4d Periods and Semicolons
4e Colons and Dashes
4f Exclamation Points and Question Marks
4g Quotation and Ellipsis Marks
4h Underlining for Italics
4i Parentheses and Brackets
4j Apostrophes and Hyphens
4k Capitals and Numbers

The information in this Handbook will help you with the final stages of the revising process: editing and proofreading. Most writers and researchers agree that editing and proofreading should wait until the end of the writing process, when you are least likely to interrupt the flow of your ideas. During this final stage, you should clarify your sentences and correct any errors in grammar, usage, diction, spelling, and mechanics. As you edit, concentrate on polishing the surface blemishes in your writing, but don't get so locked in on punctuation or grammar that you ignore the meaning, organization, or development of your essay. Even when you are proofreading, you may find an occasional spot to add another bit of detail, take out a repetitious phrase, or sharpen a transition.

To be a good editor, you need to understand the *conventions* of language and *expectations* of the reader instead of memorizing rules. In fact, the "rules" of grammar, punctuation, and usage may vary from one occasion to the next. A sentence fragment or a substandard usage such as "ain't" may be appropriate for one situation but not for another. Moreover, the notion of "rules" tends to suggest that language is static or unchanging. In fact, the opposite is true: Vocabulary, acceptable usage, even grammatical choices depend on current conventions and expectations. What is acceptable for one occasion or audience may be totally inappropriate for another. If you are not aware of these conventions, all your hard work in collecting, shaping, drafting, and revising may be wasted. A sloppy job of editing can ruin the best of essays.

This chapter describes standard conventions of editing for formal American English usage. As you edit your writing, however, remember that your purpose and audience should be your final guide.

Why Edit and Proofread?

Most writers and readers agree that grammar, usage, spelling, and mechanics are less important than content and ideas. But writers should realize that readers react not only to the ideas in an essay but also to the clarity, accuracy, and even the surface appearance of the writing. Often, writers will say, rather defensively, "Of course there are a few typos and grammar problems in my essay, but readers can still get the message. After all, it's my *ideas* that count." Unfortunately, ideas count only if the reader *gets* them. If the reader becomes irritated by unclear sentences and errors in spelling or usage, your good ideas may never reach their destination.

Writers who say that surface errors are unimportant are either rationalizing or living in a fantasy world. In the real world, most readers react negatively if writing is not neat, accurate, and readable. If your friend or roommate leaves a scrawled note that says, "I borried your shert for too day—hope you do'nt mind!" you may worry about the "shert"—and look for a new roommate. If your bank statement has misspellings, crossed out numbers, or penciled-in debits, you may change banks in a hurry. If your doctor writes a note saying, "In my opinnion you should have bone serjury immediately!" you may rush to get another "opinnion" before agreeing to "serjury." The medium may communicate the real message: If the medium—your language—is flawed by surface errors, readers often suspect that the message is flawed, too.

Some readers believe that writers who do not edit or proofread are just lazy. Although you need time to polish your writing, effective editing and proofreading are not just matters of effort or willpower. Rereading your essay ten times will not necessarily resolve all the problems. Editing

TEACHING TIP

The best way to incorporate Handbook materials in a writing class is NOT to begin with Section 1 and assign every section. Instead, read students' drafts and determine which areas of grammar, usage, or punctuation will give them the most help. Then, during regular editing sessions for each essay, assign a small group of students to report on two or three *limited and specific* problems. Those students can then help other students as they edit each other's essays for those particular problems.

Easy writing's curst hard reading.
—RICHARD BRINSLEY SHERIDAN, DRAMATIST

The man snoozing in his chair with an unfinished magazine open on his lap is a man who was being given too much unnecessary trouble by the writer.
—WILLIAM ZINSSER, WRITER AND TEACHER

is often difficult because many of your errors really don't look like mistakes—primarily because *you already know what you are trying to say.* When you reread what you have written, you tend to recall the idea already in your mind instead of reading the words exactly as they are written on the page.

If you live with a friend or roommate, try this experiment. Sit in a neutral corner of the room and look at your desk. It looks relatively clean, right? A few books, papers, and pencils are scattered here and there, but you know where everything is. It has an order. It makes sense. The math book is on the corner of the desk—under the notebook, the sock, and the coffee—just where you left it last night. The psychology book is open to Chapter 4, right underneath the sweatshirt and the lecture notes that you're going to study after dinner. Stuff is kind of stacked up, but not really messy. Now look at your friend's desk. Everything looks disorganized, as if it were dumped upside down from a backpack. You count four books, two spiral notebooks, four dogeared sheets of paper, one cup of stale coffee, a broken ballpoint pen, and a T-shirt. It's a mess, right? And sometimes it really irritates you. *How can your roommate stand to live in such chaos?* But wait. Your roommate's desk has some order to it, too, just as yours does. You just can't see the order for the mess.

Unfortunately, the same is true for writing: In your *own* writing, all you see is the meaning—the order that is in your mind. In other people's writing, you see the errors first and then, only after careful reading, the meaning. The bedrock truth is that readers will more easily see your mess than your meaning. Your writing will be more effective if your readers aren't irritated about the mess that they have had to read through. Errors or surface distractions may even undermine your credibility as a writer. For some kinds of writing—letters of application or essays for classes—the result of a few errors may be more than irritation; you simply may not be admitted, get the job, or get a passing grade.

How to Edit and Proofread

The purpose of editing is, of course, to keep language problems from interfering with the ideas or message—to make language work for your purpose rather than against it. Editing usually requires that you read over your work several times, checking for errors and anticipating problems that your readers might have. However, because you literally may not *see* many "obvious" errors, have friends or classmates look over your draft for problems or mistakes. When you use other readers, however, explain your purpose and audience. Then ask them to use conventional proofreading and editing marks to indicate their suggestions. *Remember: Your editors' marks are suggestions.* If they mark errors you've simply overlooked, make the correction. But if they mark something that you don't understand, check the appropriate section in this Handbook. If you disagree with their marks or suggestions, ask them to explain *why* they are suggesting the change. *You are responsible for deciding whether and how to make the change.*

Begin your editing and proofreading process for each essay by *reviewing your previous essays.* What problems and errors did your peer readers notice or your teacher mark? If you are keeping a log in your journal of your problems in grammar, usage, punctuation, or mechanics, review your entries. If you typically have punctuation problems and wordy sentences, reread those sections in this Handbook and focus on those specific items as you edit.

To improve your editing and proofreading skills, learn the following proofreading marks and correction symbols.

Proofreading Marks

^,	Insert comma
embarassing (r inserted)	Insert letter or word
hot tub."	Insert quotation marks
south bound	Close up
¶	Begin a new paragraph
NO ¶	Do not begin a new paragraph
down his face ⊙	Add period
hop#back	Add space
peice of pie	Transpose letters
left will that	Transpose words
in a ~~large~~ sweat	Delete words
encounter, is	Delete punctuation
Los Angelos (e)	Replace a letter
deep ~~inhilations~~ breaths	Replace a word
Manure	Use lowercase
friday	Capitalize

The following paragraph by student writer Kenneth Clause illustrates how to use these proofreading marks.

My Home Town, LA Style

It is 11:00 p.m. on a chilly friday night. We are travelling South on the 405 freeway and have just entered Los Angeles city limits. A thick, damp fog rolls in from the ocean to blanket the city. Visibility is low. The vehicle discends through a sharp, banked turn and the headlights reveal the first glimpse of "it" looming in the distance. What my weary travelling companion from New York is about to encounter, is the most embarassing and horrifying beast known to residents of Los Angelos. I break out in a large sweat, realizing there are no exits left will that detour this formation. In a moment of desperation, I step on the accelerator. Perhaps I can speed by this depraved monument so my friend will not notice. Unfortunately, I'm too late. In that instant, he begins howling with laughter. We are suddenly upon it. The headlights reveal a heaping pile of Manure appears with a sign posted on the pinnacle that says, "Welcome to Los Angeles! A town where the grass is greener . . . on the other side of the hot tub. Well, no use in trying to hide any longer. I hit the brakes and pull the car over to the side of the road. Immediately, my jovial friend from New York opens the door and falls to the pave ment with tears of laughter streaming down his face The last thing he expected to see amoung the palm trees of California was a huge dungheap. The laughter of my merry schoolmate quickly ceases after a few deep inhilations. The foul stench of this revolting glob of dung is enough to make even his pollution-hardened lungs feel weak. Upon my request, we hopback in the car and head for home. After recieving such a shock to his senses, his only hope for revival a long shower and a peice of my dad's hot apple pie.

Editing Symbols

As you edit someone else's draft, use the following symbols to refer the writer to problems discussed in this Handbook. Your instructor may also use these correction marks to guide your own editing. Listed below are some of the most common symbols, with an explanation and reference to the section number in this Handbook.

adj	use adjective, 1c
adv	use adverb, 1c
cs	comma splice, 4b
d	revise diction (word choice)
dm	dangling modifier, 2c

frag	sentence fragment, 2a
fs	fused sentence, 4b
mm	misplaced modifier, 2c
//	revise faulty parallelism, 2d
p	punctuation needed, 4a-j
pn agr	make pronoun agree with antecedent, 2i
ref	pronoun referent problem, 2i
sp	spelling error
sxt	sexist language, 3e
sv agr	subject-verb agreement error, 2g
t	verb tense error, 1d, 2h
trans	needs transition
v	verb form problem, 1d
wdy	wordy—omit needless words, 2f, 3a, 3b
wc	revise word choice

Tips for Editing and Proofreading

1. Review sections of this chapter just before you begin editing. If you need to review basic grammatical terms, begin with Section 1. Otherwise, review appropriate parts of Sections 2, 3, or 4.

2. Practice your editing and proofreading skills first on others' essays. You will see others' problems much more readily than you will see your own. Becoming a good editor of their writing will, in turn, help you recognize your own problems more easily.

3. As you edit, look for one problem at a time. Concentrate, for example, just on punctuation, or just on subject-verb agreement, or just on diction or word choice.

4. Have a friend or classmate read your essay aloud. Listen as the person reads. If you notice something that is not clear, stop and revise the sentence. If the reader does not understand what he or she is reading, stop and revise.

5. If you are writing on a computer, reformat and print out your essay, double-spaced, in narrow columns, forty to forty-five spaces wide. Many obvious errors will jump out at you as you reread your writing in a new format.

6. For proofreading, place a ruler or a blank piece of paper underneath the line you are checking. If you are proofreading for typos, try reading backward, one word at a time, from the bottom of the page to the top.

Teaching Tip

Although some teachers use correction symbols as they respond to or evaluate student writing, use them sparsely and with discretion. Students will not make much sense of a welter of red abbreviations scattered over their pages. Also, avoid impressionistic remarks, such as "awk": the writer will probably have little clue why you found it "awkward" or how to go about fixing the problem.

Teaching Tip

Even under the best circumstances, peer editing can be problematic. Often students will receive insufficient, misleading, or simply wrong editing advice. To ensure maximum accuracy (and learning), try the following sequence: Before an editing session, review a *short* section from this Handbook; model your editing for those *limited problems* on an actual piece of writing; then ask students to edit each other's drafts primarily for *those specific problems.*

TEACHING TIP

This section is designed not to teach students traditional grammar, but to provide them with basic terminology to use during editing workshops. In most cases, the concepts are more important than the names: Students should know how to *use* correlative conjunctions ("both/and" or "either/or"), but they don't need to know the *term* "correlative conjunction."

SECTION I

REVIEW OF BASIC SENTENCE ELEMENTS

This section reviews the names and definitions of basic sentence elements. Other sections in this Handbook use the terms defined and illustrated in this section.

1A SENTENCE STRUCTURE

A sentence is a group of words beginning with a capital letter and ending with a period or other end mark; it has a subject and a predicate and expresses a complete thought. The *subject* is the word or group of words that is the topic or focus of the sentence. It acts, is acted upon, or is described. The *predicate* gives information about the subject: what the subject is, what it is doing, or what is done to it.

[SUBJECT]	[PREDICATE]
Piranhas	bite!
The McNeils	dig clams at the seashore.
Bubble gum	can cause cancer in rats.

Sentences may contain the following elements: subject (S), verb (V), direct object (DO), indirect object (IO), subject complement (SC), object complement (OC), modifier (M), and conjunction (+).

S V
Piranhas bite.

S V DO + DO M
Piranhas attack fish or animals in their waters.

S V IO M DO
Andrea gave Carlos two piranhas.

S V DO OC
Carlos considers Andrea a prankster.

S V SC
Andrea is a prankster.

Subjects may be nouns, pronouns, noun phrases, or noun clauses.

Verbs may be single words (*bite*) or verb phrases (*will have bitten*). Verbs may be transitive or intransitive; verbs have tense, voice, and mood.

Direct objects can be nouns, pronouns, noun phrases, or noun clauses. A direct object receives the action of a transitive verb. Direct objects usually answer the question "What?" or "Whom?" about the subject and verb:

Piranhas bit [whom?] *people.*

Indirect objects can be nouns, pronouns, noun phrases, or noun clauses. The indirect object answers the question "To whom?" or "For whom?" about the subject and verb:

Andrea gave [to whom?] *Carlos* two piranhas.

Complements occur in the predicate of the sentence following a "to be" or linking verb. Subject complements rename or describe the subject. Object complements rename or describe the object:

SC
Carlos is *upset.*

OC
Carlos named one piranha *Bucktooth.*

Modifiers describe or limit a subject, verb, object, or complement. They may be single words, groups of words, or entire clauses:

M
Piranhas have a *nasty* disposition.

Conjunctions are words that link words, phrases, clauses, or sentences. The word *conjunction* is derived from a word meaning "join together." (See Section 4a for additional examples of conjunctions.)

- *Coordinating conjunctions* (*and, but, or, yet, for, nor, so*) join equal sentence elements:

  Carlos is angry, *but* Andrea is laughing.

- *Correlative conjunctions* (*both . . . and, either . . . or*) also join equal sentence elements:

  Neither Carlos *nor* his aquarium fish are particularly happy about the piranhas.

- *Subordinating conjunctions* (*because, since, although, if, until, while,* and *others*) begin many dependent clauses:

  If Andrea plays another joke on Carlos, she may lose a good friend.

1B Nouns and Pronouns

A *noun* names a person, place, object, or idea. Nouns may be grouped in several classes:

- *Proper nouns* name specific people, places, or things (Abraham Lincoln, Cape Hattaras, Buick).
- *Common nouns* name all nouns that are not proper nouns (cat, ocean, helicopter).
- *Concrete nouns* name things that can be sensed (table, waves, coat).
- *Abstract nouns* name things not knowable by the senses (justice, pity, freedom).
- *Collective nouns* name groups (family, committee, team).
- *Compound nouns* are several words joined by hyphens to form a noun (brother-in-law, commander-in-chief).

A *pronoun* takes the place of a noun. Pronouns must meet three requirements:

- *Reference*: A pronoun must refer to a specific, identifiable word, phrase, or clause. This referent or antecedent occurs within the sentence or in a preceding sentence. (See Section 2j for examples of how to solve problems in pronoun reference.)

  Evelyn has the flu. *She* has missed two classes. [*Evelyn* is the referent for *she.*]

- *Agreement:* A pronoun must agree with or correspond to the noun that it replaces. A pronoun must agree in person (first, second, or third person), number (singular or plural), and gender (he, she, it). (See Section 2i for examples of how to solve problems in pronoun agreement.)

  Each girl should check on *her* friend. [*Her* agrees in person (third person), in number (singular), and gender (her) with the referent, *girl.*]

- *Case:* Pronouns must take the appropriate case (subjective, objective, possessive):

  Subjective pronouns (*I*, *you*, *he*, *she*, *it*, *we*, *they*, *who*) should be the subject or the complement in a sentence.
  They have the flu. [Subject]
  Who is sleeping there? It is *she*. [Complement]

Objective pronouns (*me, you, her, him, whom, us, you, them*) should act as objects in a sentence:
Evelyn gave *me* the flu. [Indirect object]

Possessive pronouns (*my, mine, your, yours, his, her, hers, its, our, ours, their, theirs, whose*) show possession:
I am sick as a dog with *her* flu virus.

Pronouns may be grouped in several classes:

- *Personal pronouns* (*I, me, mine, we, us, our, ours, you, yours, she, her, hers, he, him, his, it, its, they, them, theirs*) refer to people or things:

  She bought a cat for *him*.

- *Relative pronouns* (*that, who, whom, which, what, whose, whoever*) introduce clauses:

  Whoever fed the cat made a mistake.

- *Interrogative pronouns* (*who, whose, what, which, whom*) introduce a question:

  Which cat is the mother?

- *Reflexive and intensive pronouns* (*myself, yourself, herself, ourselves,* and so on) refer back to a pronoun or antecedent or intensify the antecedent:

  She says she paid for the cat *herself.* I *myself* suspect she just found it.

- *Indefinite pronouns* (*all, anyone, another, anybody, both, each, few, most, some, several, none, someone, something, such,* and so on) refer to nonspecific persons or things:

  Someone will turn up and claim the cat.

- *Demonstrative pronouns* (*this, that, these, those*) refer to an antecedent:

  On Tuesday morning, I must pay my bill. *That* will be a painful moment.

1c Adjectives and Adverbs

Adjectives are modifiers that limit, describe, or add information about nouns and pronouns:

Secretariat was my *favorite* horse. [modifies noun, *horse*]
Even standing still, he looked *dynamic*. [modifies pronoun, *he*]

Adverbs limit, describe, or add information about verbs, adjectives, or other adverbs, and they complete sentences:

He won *overwhelmingly*. [modifies verb]
The Kentucky Derby was a *very* important victory. [modifies adjective, *important*]
On that day, he ran *extremely* fast. [modifies adverb, *fast*]
Fortunately, he won the Triple Crown. [modifies whole sentence]

1D VERBS

The *verb* is the heart of most sentences. Verbs can set up equations or definitions ("A flotilla *is* a small fleet of ships"). They can describe states of being ("Fear and confusion *exist* in Lebanon"). They can explain occurrences ("The players *became* angry at the referee's call") or describe actions ("The candidate *defeated* her opponent"). When sentences communicate clearly, verbs often deserve the credit.

The great variety of verb forms creates a richness in the language. This richness, however, can create confusion. Some verbs are regular; others, irregular. In some cases, combinations of verb tense, voice, and mood may entangle sentences. The following explanations and examples will help you resolve problems in verb forms so that you can communicate precisely and vividly.

PRINCIPAL PARTS OF VERBS

Verbs have three principal parts: simple form, past tense, and past participle:

SIMPLE FORM (INFINITIVE)	PAST TENSE	PAST PARTICIPLE
live (to live)	lived	lived
go (to go)	went	gone

REGULAR AND IRREGULAR VERBS *Regular verbs* form the past tense and past participle by adding *-ed* or *-d* to the simple form:

SIMPLE FORM	PAST TENSE	PAST PARTICIPLE
count	counted	counted
dance	danced	danced
create	created	created

Irregular verbs can cause problems because they form the past tense and past participle by changing letters, sounds, or entire words. Check your dictionary to determine if a verb is irregular. If the dictionary gives only two forms (*catch, caught*), the past participle is the same as the past tense (*caught*). Below are some examples of the nearly two hundred irregular English verbs:

Simple Form	Past Tense	Past Participle
sing	sang	sung
begin	began	begun
break	broke	broken
drive	drove	driven
sink	sank, sunk	sunk
sleep	slept	slept
read	read	read
eat	ate	eaten
see	saw	seen
slide	slid	slid

Linking Verbs *Linking verbs (is, becomes, seems, looks*, and so on) equate subjects with predicates, so that the word or words in the predicate rename or describe the subject. A linking verb creates a subject complement (SC)—a word or words that complete the equation:

S V SC M
Lillian was president of the company. [Lillian = president]

S V SC
The storm seemed threatening. [Storm = threatening]

Auxiliary Verbs *Auxiliary verbs*, also called "helping verbs," combine with main verbs to show tense, voice, or mood. The verbs *be, do*, and *have* are common auxiliary verbs:

She is running a marathon. [auxiliary verb = *is*]
They did enjoy the dinner. [auxiliary verb = *did*]
He had left before she arrived. [auxiliary verb = *had*]

Tense *Tense* tells *when* a verb's action, occurrence, or state of being takes place. The six verb tenses in English are illustrated below with the regular verb *create*. The parentheses contain the *progressive* form (*-ing*) to show continual or ongoing action, occurrence, or state of being:

Present: I create (I am creating)
Past: I created (I was creating)
Future: I will create (I will be creating)
Present perfect: I have created (I have been creating)

The present perfect tense describes actions occurring or conditions existing at an unspecified time in the past and continuing into the present: *I have created several award-winning recipes for chili.*

Past Perfect: I had created (I had been creating)

The past perfect tense describes actions occurring or conditions existing before a specific time in the past: *I had created three different recipes for extra-hot chili before I won my first award.*

Future perfect: I will have created (I will have been creating)

The future perfect tense describes actions that have already occurred or conditions that will exist by a specific future time: *I will have created a new salsa recipe before the county fair begins.*

TRANSITIVE AND INTRANSITIVE Many verbs in English can be either transitive or intransitive, depending on the sentence. *Transitive* verbs take objects. As the prefix *trans-* suggests, they carry the action *across* to the object:

S V DO
Myrna developed the film.

S V DO
Michael sees the oncoming car.

Intransitive verbs do not take objects:

S V M
Myrna developed early. (*Early* is not a direct object; it describes when Myrna developed)

S V M
Michael sees in the dark. (*In the dark* is not a direct object)

VOICE Verbs have *active* and *passive* voice. *Active voice* means that the subject of the sentence performs the action. *Passive voice* means that the subject is acted upon. A passive-voice sentence uses a form of "be" plus a past participle. (For additional discussion of active and passive voice, see Section 2e.)

Active voice:	Eskimos *build* stone and peat houses.
Passive voice:	Stone and peat houses *are built* by Eskimos. [Contains a form of "be" + past participle: *are* + *built*]

MOOD Verbs have three *moods* that indicate a writer's attitude toward a statement. *Indicative mood* expresses a statement of fact or asks a question. *Imperative mood* expresses commands or directives. *Subjunctive mood* expresses a wish or condition contrary to fact:

Indicative:	She has perfect pitch. [fact]
	Why does she sing opera? [question]
Imperative:	Pay attention to the music. [command]

	Turn and face the spotlight. [directive]
Subjunctive:	I wish that I were more talented. [wish] If she were to catch a cold, she would not sing on opening night. [condition contrary to fact]

1E Phrases and Clauses

Phrases

A *phrase* is a group of related words that does not contain a subject or a predicate:

Prepositional phrase:	He wrote *on the computer*.
Noun phrase:	A *notebook computer* is handy.
Appositive phrase:	The Apple II, *the first popular school computer*, is the Model T of home computers. [An appositive phrase identifies or provides more information about the preceding noun or pronoun.]

A verbal phrase is a group of related words that contains a verbal: an infinitive (to talk), a present participle (talking), or a past participle (talked). There are three kinds of verbals:

Infinitives usually use *to + simple verb*; they function as nouns, adjectives, or adverbs:

Infinitive:	*To talk*
Infinitive phrase:	He planned *to talk for three minutes*. [infinitive phrase = direct object] *To listen carefully* was his first objective. [infinitive phrase = subject]

Gerunds are nouns made from the "-ing" or present participle form of the verb:

Gerund:	*Talking* got her into trouble. [*Talking* is a gerund; gerund = subject]
Gerund phrase:	*Talking during the lecture* got her into trouble. [gerund phrase = subject]

Participles are adjectives made from verb forms. As adjectives, they modify nouns or pronouns. They can use either the "-ing" (present participle) or the "-ed" (past participle) verb form:

Participle:	*Coughing* students may bother the teacher. [Participle modifies students.]

Whispered conversations may distract students. [Participle modifies *conversations.*]

Participial phrases: *Rustling their papers and snapping their notebooks closed,* they prepare to leave the lecture hall. [Participial phrase modifies *they.*]

Several students, *entranced by the final scene in the film,* write quietly for a few moments. [Participial phrase modifies *students.*]

Clauses

A *clause* is a group of words containing a *subject and a verb.* It need *not* be an entire sentence or a complete thought. Clauses can be independent (main) or dependent (subordinate):

- *Independent or main clause:* A group of words containing a subject and a verb that can stand by itself as a complete thought:

  We drank decaffeinated coffee.

- *Dependent clause:* A group of words that contains a subject and verb but cannot stand by itself as a complete thought:

  Because we drank decaffeinated coffee

- *Subordinate* clauses (sometimes called *adverb clauses*) are dependent clauses that begin with a subordinating conjunction, such as *because, if, although, unless, when, while, since, as, until, before,* and *after*:

  Although I drank coffee, everyone else drank tea.

- *Relative clauses* (also called *adjective clauses*) are dependent clauses that begin with *when, where, why,* or with relative pronouns (*who, that, which, whom, whoever, whomever, whatever*):

  Driving *when you are under the influence of alcohol* may result in a mandatory jail sentence. [Adjective clause modifies *driving.*]

  Free coffee, *which the bar serves after midnight,* is part of a campaign for responsible drinking. [Adjective clause modifies *coffee.*]

  The policeman gave a ticket to the woman *who was driving the red pickup truck.* [Adjective clause modifies *woman.*]

1F Articles, Prepositions, Interjections

Articles

Articles (a, an, the) often appear before nouns. They are modifiers that limit a noun. *A* and *an* are less limiting than *the:*

> I have *a* plan to solve our problems.
> I have *the* plan to solve our problems. [*The* suggests that the plan is more definitive.]

The article *a* appears before words that begin with a *consonant sound* (not necessarily a consonant): *a* kite, *a* hammer, *a* university, *a* one-sided victory.

The article *an* appears before words that begin with a *vowel sound* (not necessarily a vowel): *an* opening, *an* egg, *an* old shirt, *an* honor, *an* E.

Prepositions

Prepositions (*in, on, up, to, after, by, for, across, within,* and others) usually occur in prepositional phrases with a noun or pronoun that is the object of the preposition:

> *In* the hot sun *by* the edge *of* the water, a small turtle lay perfectly still.

Note that some words can function as either prepositions or conjunctions:

> We will row home *after* lunch. [preposition]
> *After* you finish your sandwich, we will row home. [conjunction]

Interjections

Interjections (*oh, alas, yea, damn, hooray, ouch,* and others) are words conveying strong feeling or surprise. Interjections occasionally appear in informal writing or in a dialogue:

> The Cardinals won the pennant (*yea!*) but lost the World Series (*boo, hiss*).
> *Alas*, their hitting was anemic.
> "*Oh*, she moped about it for days."

I've noticed a good deal, and there's no bird, or cow, or anything that uses as good grammar as a bluejay. You may say a cat uses good grammar. Well, a cat does—but you let a cat get excited once; you let a cat get to pulling fur with another cat on a shed, nights, and you'll hear grammar that will give you the lockjaw. Ignorant people think it's the noise *which fighting cats make that is so aggravating, but it ain't so; it's the sickening grammar they use.*
—MARK TWAIN, BAKER'S BLUEJAY YARN

SECTION 2

SENTENCE STRUCTURE AND GRAMMAR

When sentences don't follow standard American English conventions, readers may become aggravated, confused, or simply lost. While some deviations from established conventions barely distract the reader, others totally scramble meaning. If "sickening grammar" detracts from your meaning, your readers may react uncharitably. If you write a confusing sentence fragment, some readers will think, "This writer doesn't know what a sentence is." If you have a problem in subject-verb agreement, readers may think, "This writer didn't reread the sentence or doesn't know what the subject of the sentence is." If you write a sentence with a dangling modifier, the reader may think, "The writer doesn't know how comical this sounds." This section will help you avoid those embarrassing problems that confuse readers or invite them to think about your grammar rather than your meaning.

2A FRAGMENTS

Use sentence fragments only for special emphasis. A *fragment* is an incomplete sentence. A fragment may lack a subject or verb, or it may be only a dependent clause. *Test* for sentence fragments by taking the group of words out of the context. If the group of words cannot stand by itself as a complete thought, it is a fragment.

Revise sentence fragments by adding a subject or verb or by combining the fragment with the preceding sentence:

FRAGMENT: I still remember the championship basketball game when I scored forty points. *Breaking the existing conference record.*

Test: "Breaking the existing conference record" is not a complete sentence. It cannot stand by itself as a complete thought. Combine with previous sentence.

REVISION: I still remember the championship basketball game when I broke the existing conference record by scoring forty points.

FRAGMENT: At home I enjoy many water sports. *Waterskiing and sailing, which are my two favorites.*

Test: "Waterskiing and sailing, which are my two favorites" cannot stand by itself as a complete thought.

Revise to make one complete sentence.

REVISION: At home, I enjoy my two favorite water sports: waterskiing and sailing.

FRAGMENT: She stood in line for four hours in the freezing rain. *To get tickets for the rock concert.*

Test: "To get tickets for the rock concert " cannot stand by itself as a complete thought. Combine with previous sentence.

REVISION: To get tickets for the rock concert, she stood in line for four hours in the freezing rain.

FRAGMENT: After a tough class, I took a long shower, dried my hair, and put on my underwear. Then I walked into the living room. *Because no one was home.* Was I surprised to discover my mother talking to Reverend Jones!

Test: "Because no one was home" cannot stand by itself as a complete thought. It is a dependent clause or fragment.

REVISION: After a tough class, I took a long shower, dried my hair, and put on my underwear. Because I thought no one was home, I walked into the living room. Was I surprised to discover my mother talking to Reverend Jones!

FRAGMENT: At the end of the game, the frustrated fans began to throw snowballs on the field. *The score being 42-0.*

Test: "The score being 42-0" is not a complete sentence. Change *being* to *is* or *was*.

REVISION: At the end of the game, the frustrated fans began to throw snowballs on the field because the score was 42-0.

For special emphasis, however, sparingly used sentence fragments can be effective. In context, the following are examples of effective sentence fragments:

> When the river was dammed almost all of these things were lost. Crowded out—or drowned and buried under mud.
>
> —Edward Abbey

> Head off? Decapitation cases are rather routinely handled.
>
> —Jessica Mitford

> When I finally did fall asleep, I had that same hideous nightmare in which a woodchuck is trying to claim my prize at a raffle. Despair.
>
> —Woody Allen

TEACHING TIP

Sentence-fragment use varies according to the level of writing and the intended audience. In popular journalism, writers frequently use fragments; in academic journals, writers almost never use them. Bring samples of both kinds of writing to class to show how using an elaborate, formal sentence construction (such as extended parallelism) in a sports column is nearly as inappropriate as writing a fragment in an academic essay.

EXERCISE In the following passage, identify all sentence fragments. Then revise the passage to eliminate inappropriate fragments.

> (1) Most people think that a library is as quiet as growing grass, but often it is the noisiest place on campus to study. (2) The worst time being finals week. (3) Some of the chatter is from people who come to the library just to visit: "How did you like the party Saturday night?" (4) "Did you get the notes from chemistry?" (5) The chatter goes on continually, punctuated by coughs, gasps, and giggles. (6) Just when I start to panic about my calculus examination. (7) Someone across the table tells a joke, and they all start laughing. (8) They try to cover their laughter with their hands, but the sound explodes out anyway. (9) Irritating ten other students who are trying to study. (10) Sometimes I wish the library had its own police force. (11) To arrest those gabby, discourteous "party people." (12) I would sit there smiling as they handcuffed these party people and dragged them out of the library. (13) Ah, the sweet revenge of daydreams.

2B MIXED CONSTRUCTIONS AND FAULTY PREDICATION

MIXED CONSTRUCTIONS Occasionally, writers begin sentences with one structure and then switch, right in the middle, to another. Revise sentences with mixed constructions by choosing one structure and sticking to it:

MIXED: Because the repairs were so expensive is why I ended up selling the car.

REVISED: Because the repairs were so expensive, I sold the car.

MIXED: By getting behind in math classes is a quick way to flunk out.

REVISED: Getting behind in math classes is a quick way to flunk out.

FAULTY PREDICATION

Sometimes the predicate does not *logically* fit with the subject. Remember that the verb "to be" is an *equals sign*. Revise faulty predication by changing either the subject or the predicate:

FAULTY: Freestyle ski jumping is where skiers take crazy chances in midair.

Note: "Ski jumping" is an activity, not a place. It is illogical to say "ski jumping *is* where . . ."

REVISED: Freestyle ski jumping is a sport that encourages skiers to take crazy chances in midair.

FAULTY: My dog Noodles is the reason I'm feeling depressed.

Note: "My dog Noodles" is a specific animal, not a "reason." Missing Noodles, however, could be a cause for depression.

REVISED: I'm feeling depressed because I miss my dog Noodles.

FAULTY: Real intelligence is when you can say no to that third piece of chocolate cream pie.

Note: *Intelligence* is or equals a mental condition, not a *when*.

REVISED: Saying no to that third piece of chocolate cream pie requires real intelligence.

EXERCISE In the following passage, identify sentences with mixed constructions, faulty predication, or both, and then revise them.

> (1) After my sophomore year, I intend to transfer to Boston College. (2) Basically, I want to attend a school that has a city environment and a diverse population of students. (3) I suppose my sister Nadine is a big reason I want to transfer. (4) She wants me to move closer to home. (5) Also, by attending a city school will enable me to see plays, to visit museums occasionally, and to eat out at good restaurants. (6) Finally, I'd like to meet all sorts of students. (7) A good university is when a student can meet people from all walks of life. (8) Because Boston College has diversity is really why I intend to transfer.

2C Dangling Modifiers and Misplaced Modifiers

Dangling Modifiers

Modifying phrases must clearly describe, qualify, or limit some word in the sentence. When the modifying phrase occurs at the beginning of a sentence, the word that is modified must appear *immediately* following the phrase. Otherwise, the modifying phrase "dangles" or is logically "unattached" to the sentence. Such sentences are confusing and often comical:

FAULTY: Rushing to get to class on time, my shoelace broke.

Question: *Who* was rushing to get to class? The shoelace? Revise by indicating the person immediately after the comma.

REVISED: Rushing to get to class, *I* broke a shoelace.

FAULTY: Flying at 5,000 feet, the cars looked like tiny toys.

Question: Are the cars flying at 5,000 feet? *Who* is flying at 5,000 feet? Revise by indicating that person immediately after the comma.

REVISED: Flying at 5,000 feet, *I* saw cars that looked like tiny toys.

FAULTY: From birth until the first grade, one parent should be home with the children.

Question: Does the opening phrase, "From birth until the first grade," modify *parent* or *children*? Revise by placing the appropriate word immediately following the introductory phrase.

REVISED: From birth until the first grade, *children* should have one parent at home.

FAULTY: Sue practiced her freestyle stroke until she knew she could swim faster than Flipper, being a fanatical swimmer.

Question: Who is the fanatical swimmer—Sue or Flipper? When modifying phrases "dangle" from the *end* of a sentence, revise by placing the phrase next to the word it modifies.

REVISED: Being a fanatical swimmer, Sue practiced her freestyle stroke until she knew she could swim faster than Flipper.

Misplaced Modifiers

Place a modifying word, phrase, or clause immediately before or after the word it modifies. In the following sentences, notice how changing the placement of the word "only" changes the meaning of the sentence:

Only I tasted grandfather's pumpkin pie. [I was the only one who tasted it.]

I only tasted grandfather's pumpkin pie. [I only tasted it; Pete actually ate it.]

I tasted only grandfather's pumpkin pie. [I didn't taste any-

thing else; I didn't even taste Aunt Margaret's pecan pie.]
I tasted grandfather's only pumpkin pie. [Grandfather made only one pumpkin pie, and I tasted it.]

CONFUSING: He borrowed a computer from his professor with a faulty memory.

Question: Who or what has the faulty memory? Place the phrase "with a faulty memory" next to the word it modifies ("computer").

REVISED: He borrowed a computer with a faulty memory from his professor.

CONFUSING: The hamburgers have been horrible in the fast-food restaurants that I've eaten.

Question: Did the writer eat restaurants or hamburgers? Revise by placing the clause "that I've eaten" next to the word it should modify ("hamburgers").

REVISED: The hamburgers that I've eaten in fast-food restaurants have been horrible.

EXERCISE In the following passage, identify sentences with dangling modifiers and misplaced modifiers, and then revise each faulty sentence.

> (1) SP302, History of Film, is a worthwhile class to take. (2) Occurring on Tuesday night from 7:00 P.M. to 9:45 P.M., Professor Hancock teaches the class so that it coincides with dollar movie night at the campus theater. (3) Normally, a long class would be boring because of the Nod Factor. (4) However, Professor Hancock keeps everyone awake and entertains the students, being very energetic. (5) Her lecture on *Citizen Kane* was a particularly good example. (6) Unfortunately, the film began before she finished her lecture. (7) Rushing across the stage just as the film was beginning, an electrical cord tripped her up, causing her to lose her balance and fall. (8) She regained her composure in time to remind us that Orson Welles also wrote and performed the famous broadcast about the invasion of the Martians on the radio. (9) We certainly were relieved to get that important information!

2D FAULTY PARALLELISM

Repeated elements in a sentence that are similar in meaning or function should be parallel in grammatical form. The parallel form should, in turn, help to emphasize the meaning. Any repeated sentence elements,

TEACHING TIPS

As Shaughnessy explains in *Errors and Exceptions*, writers often make errors for perfectly understandable linguistic or cultural reasons. Writers are frequently told never to use "I," so after beginning a sentence with a modifying phrase, "Reading Mark Twain's famous novel" they quickly switch to a construction that avoids using "I": "Huckleberry Finn faces a moral dilemma." Correcting the source of the error is more effective than merely marking "dm" in the margin.

TEACHING TIP

Some teachers prefer to teach structural principles such as parallelism and subordination initially through sentence combining excerises: After students have combined kernels in a parallel structure, ask them why or how they were able to combine those elements. Practicing the function before applying the name, "parallelism," is an effective teaching strategy.

from subjects and verbs to prepositional phrases, may occur in parallel form:

Parallel clauses:	*I came, I saw, I conquered.*
Parallel adverbs:	He read *slowly* and *thoroughly.*
Parallel prepositional phrases:	She walked *through the archway, across the quadrangle*, and *into the library.*

Identifying and numbering the repeated elements may help you see the parallel elements in a sentence:

She walked
(1) through the archway,
(2) across the quadrangle
and
(3) into the library.

FAULTY: Walking, biking, and automobiles are the three most popular modes of transportation.

Test: Identify and number elements that should be parallel. "(1) *Walking*, (2) *biking*, and (3) *automobiles* are the three most popular modes of transportation." Revise, choosing one pattern for all three elements.

REVISED: Walking, biking, and driving are the three most popular modes of transportation.

FAULTY: Traveling abroad last summer, John increased his social awareness, his cultural knowledge, and overall sophistication.

Test: Identify and number elements that should be parallel. "Traveling abroad last summer, John increased (1) *his social awareness*, (2) *his cultural knowledge*, and (3) __________ *overall sophistication.*" Then revise, choosing one grammatical pattern for all three elements.

REVISED: Traveling abroad last summer, John increased his social awareness, his cultural knowledge, and his overall sophistication.

[or]

REVISED: Traveling abroad last summer, John increased his social awareness, cultural knowledge, and overall sophistication.

FAULTY: There are three commandments for college students: Thou shalt go to class; thou shalt read the text; and be sure to borrow your neighbor's notes.

Test: Identify and number elements that should be parallel. Since the first and second "commandments" set the grammatical pattern, the reader *expects* the third commandment to take the same "thou shalt" form.

REVISED: There are three commandments for college students: Thou shalt go to class; thou shalt read the text; and thou shalt borrow thy neighbor's notes.

FAULTY: She was angry not only because he was late but also he forgot the tickets.
Note: Compared or contrasted sentence elements introduced by "either . . . or," "both . . . and," or "not only . . . but also" must be parallel.

Test: Identify and number elements that should be parallel. "She was angry not only (1) *because he was late* but also (2) __________ he forgot the tickets." Revise to make (1) and (2) parallel.

REVISED: She was angry not only because he was late but also because he forgot the tickets.

EXERCISE In the following passage, identify and revise any sentences with faulty parallelism.

> (1) Alcohol abuse is a primary cause of spectator violence at college football games. (2) On average, the police department makes between five and ten arrests at each home football game. (3) These arrests are for property destruction, public intoxication, and occasionally when students conduct themselves in a disorderly manner. (4) When spectators consume too much alcohol not only do they hurt themselves but also act obnoxiously toward others. (5) Following a recent fight, ambulance attendants said that some drunken spectators or "animals" actually pelted them with sod while they tried to assist an injured man. (6) The attendants tried pleading, reason, and shouting, but to no avail. (7) To reduce these ugly incidents and restoring the enjoyment of the game, alcohol should not be sold at football games after the beginning of the second half.

2E Active and Passive Voice

Verbs that can have direct objects (transitive verbs) are in the *active voice* when the subject of the sentence *acts upon the object*:

TEACHING TIP

Teachers should be cautious about exhorting students to eliminate all passive-voice constructions or to follow computer program advice to reduce passives to some specified percentage. First, some passive-voice constructions are appropriate (see below). In addition, sometimes passive voice maintains coherence by retaining the same subject for successive sentences (see for example, the second sentence in "Teaching Tip" accompanying the Dangling Modifier section). Writers should not automatically change passive to active voice without considering the meaning, the coherence of the passage, and the intended audience.

The wolfhound bit Perry.

Wolfhound, the subject of the sentence, *acts upon the object, Perry*. The arrow shows that in the active voice, the action of the verb *bit* goes forward, toward the object, *Perry*.

Verbs that can have objects (transitive verbs) are in the *passive voice* when the *subject is acted upon*. The passive voice uses a form of *be (is, am, are, was, were, been, being)* followed by the past participle of the main verb (in this case, *bitten*):

Perry was bitten by the wolfhound.

The verb *was bitten* is transitive, but *Perry*, now the subject of the sentence, is *acted upon*. The arrow shows that the action of the verb goes backwards, so that *Perry* receives the action.

Notice the following *differences* between active and passive voice:

The *active voice* sentence, "The wolfhound bit Perry," uses two fewer words than the passive version, its action moves in a normal forward direction, and it clearly identifies the actor.

The *passive voice* sentence, "Perry was bitten by the wolfhound," uses two more words, and it inverts the direction of the action in the sentence. In some cases, the passive voice may omit the *actor* altogether: "Perry was bitten on Friday." In that case, the reader does not know who or what bit Perry.

ACTIVE VOICE

Usually, active voice is preferable because it is more direct, vivid, and concise than passive voice. Remember, however, that sentences must be judged *in the context* of the writer's purpose, audience, and focus.

Below are examples of passive-voice constructions that, in context, may be more effective in the active voice. To change from passive to active, move the actor (often identified in the "by" phrase) to the subject of the sentence:

Passive: Children's unruly behavior cannot be accepted by their parents. **Note**: The actor in the "by" phrase is *parents*. Change to active voice by making *parents* the subject of the sentence.

Active: Parents cannot accept their children's unruly behavior. [The active voice version places the actor in the subject of the sentence and has two fewer words.]

Passive: It is argued by the members of our class that the teacher grades too hard.

Note: The *actor* in the "by" phrase is *members*.
Change to active voice by making *members* the subject of the sentence.

Active: Members of our class argue that the teacher grades too hard. [This active voice version is more direct and has four fewer words.]

Passive: Under the current proposal, property taxes will be raised $1,000 dollars over the next two years.
Note: The *actor* is not identified in a "by" phrase; however, the *governor* actually proposed the tax increase. Change to active voice by making *governor* the subject of the sentence.

Active: The governor currently proposes to raise property taxes by $1,000 over the next two years. [The active voice version reveals who, in fact, is responsible. It adds information without increasing the length of the sentence.]

Passive Voice

The passive voice is appropriate when the actor is unknown or is less important than the action or the receiver of the action. Use the passive voice in the following situations:

When the actor is unknown:

When her sports car swerved off the road and into the river, Carolyn was killed. [We don't know who or what actually killed her.]

When you want to emphasize that some person or thing is helpless or is a victim:

The small Kansas town was leveled by the tornado.
Our football team was mauled by the Bears, 42-0.
The bag lady was mugged in broad daylight.

When the scientific experiment and the results should be the focus of the sentence or the passage (scientific writing typically uses the passive voice to lend objectivity to the findings):

The first recordings of humpback whales were obtained in 1952 from a U.S. Navy hydrophone installation.
The titration experiment was performed under careful laboratory conditions.

One typical *abuse of passive voice* occurs when writers omit the actor in order to conceal responsibility:

The tuition for nonresident students was increased by $500 for the upcoming academic year.

This sentence, which was written by university officials, omits the actor or the agency responsible for the change. Because tuition increases are unpopular with students, university officials may have deliberately omitted the responsible actor or agency to avoid confrontation or blame. Careful readers should recognize such deceptive uses of passive voice.

Caution: Don't assume that all verbs that follow the pattern, "be" verb form + past participle ["was ___________ed"], are necessarily passive voice. In the sentence "I was scared," for example, the verb "scared" can be either transitive or intransitive, depending on the context. **Only transitive verbs can be either active or passive voice:**

Transitive active:	A horrible Halloween mask scared me.
Transitive passive:	I was scared by a horrible Halloween mask.
Intransitive:	At the Cave of Horrors, I was upset and scared.
Transitive active:	The boss fired me.
Transitive passive:	I was fired.
Intransitive:	I was tired.

Test: To distinguish between intransitive and transitive passive, try adding the word *very*. If *very* cannot logically be used, the construction is passive voice:

I was [very] tired. [*Very* works; *tired* is intransitive.]
I was [very] fired. [*Very* doesn't work; *fired* is transitive passive.]

In addition, a good dictionary will indicate whether a verb is transitive, intransitive, or both.

EXERCISES Identify sentences containing passive voice. Change passive voice sentences into active voice:

1. People communicate using body movements.

2. A nod, gesture, or a glance can be interpreted by people in several ways.

3. A wave and a smile mean one thing, but a wave and a tear can be interpreted to mean something else.

4. In addition, some people may be irritated by a continual or intense stare.

5. We may also be intimidated by a person who talks to us at very close range.

Read the following passage and identify sentences that are in the active or passive voice. Then determine which sentences should be active voice and which should be passive voice. Revise the passage, leaving sentences as they are, changing active voice sentences to passive, or changing passive voice sentences to active—as appropriate for the context.

> (1) Writing on a word processor can transform the act of writing, but only if the writer has some rudimentary typing skills. (2) Unfortunately, many men have a sexist hang-up about typing so that their writing on a computer is inhibited. (3) Traditionally, it has been felt by most men that only females—i.e., secretaries—should type. (4) Only the macho Hemingways and Mailers of the world actually type their own novels and stories. (5) Now, however, many male business executives are caught by conflicting role-images. (6) It is socially acceptable for them to be computer literate, but it is still somehow demeaning to sit at a keyboard and practice the "female" skill of typing. (7) One more example of how notions about sexist roles can hurt men as well as women is thus provided by word-processing.

2F Nominals and "Be" Verbs

Nominals

Nominals (also called nominalizations) are *nouns* created from verbs. Nominals often make sentences less dynamic because they disguise or eliminate the action in a sentence. Frequently, nominals are nouns ending in *-ment*, *-ance*, *-ence*, *-ion*, and *-ing*. Each of the following nominals "contains" a verb: expectation (expect), description (describe), solution (solve), resistance (resist), government (govern), preference (prefer), meeting (meet). *For many purposes and audiences, you can make your writing more vigorous, dynamic, and readable by changing nominals into verbs*:

TEACHING TIP

As the examples below illustrate, reducing nominals and "be" verbs also helps to reduce wordiness (see 3b).

NOMINAL: Bill's *expectation* was to win the marathon.

REVISED: Bill *expected* to win the marathon.

NOMINAL: The owner's manual contains a *description* of how to adjust the timing.

REVISED: The owner's manual *describes* how to adjust the timing.

NOMINAL: On this campus, there exists some *resistance* among students to the tuition increases.

REVISED: On this campus, students *resist* tuition increases.

NOMINAL: *Dissatisfaction* with drinking-policy *decisions* is likely to be a major *contribution* to student *objections*.

Note: When repeated nominals obscure the meaning, rewrite the whole sentence, making the primary *actor* the subject of the sentence.

REVISED: Students object to the drinking policy.

"Be" Verbs

"Be" verbs *(is, am, are, was, were, been, being)* are effective for stating *conditions, definitions,* or *concepts:*

> Annie Dillard's *Pilgrim at Tinker Creek* is a literary classic.
> An "iconoclast" *is* one who destroys sacred images or seeks to overthrow popular ideas or institutions.

Often, however, "be" verbs create static, flat, or lifeless sentences. Where appropriate, make your writing more dynamic by replacing "be" verbs with action verbs.

Eliminate "be" verbs by changing passive voice to active voice, by changing nominals or adjectives into verbs, by selecting a more vigorous verb, or by combining sentences:

"BE" VERB: The classical mythology course that *is* offered by the English department *is* fascinating.

REVISED: The English department *offers* a fascinating course in classical mythology.

"BE" VERB: Star Wars *is* a high-tech defense system that may *be* a major deterrent to global nuclear war.

REVISED: Star Wars, our high-tech defense system, may deter global nuclear war.

"BE" VERB: The driving force for many workaholics *is* their fear of failure.

REVISED: Fear of failure *drives* many workaholics.

"BE" VERB: AIDS *is* a simple but lethal malfunction of the immune system. AIDS *is* a disease that can lead to the physical and mental destruction of its victim.

REVISED: AIDS, a simple but lethal malfunction of the immune system, can *destroy* its victim physically and mentally.

EXERCISE In the following passage, identify *nominals* and *be* verbs. Then revise the passage to make it more vivid, energetic, and concise by eliminating inappropriate nominals and "be" verbs.

> (1) As parents, we know that many young people love to ride motorcycles, motorbikes, and motorscooters. (2) Today, however, our ten-year-old kids have some attraction to those off-road three-wheelers. (3) Although kids get enjoyment from riding three-wheelers in the

hills, these vehicles can be the cause of serious injury. (4) Unfortunately, these young drivers—and their parents—do not receive sufficient education from salespeople about the potential dangers. (5) As a result, some activist groups are in opposition to the sales of all three-wheelers. (6) These groups want regulations for the industry in order to make riding safer for children and adults. (7) The efforts of these groups to reform the industry are commendable to every responsible parent.

2G Subject-Verb Agreement

A verb must agree *in number* with its subject. Remember: *-s* or *-es* added to a *noun* makes it plural: *whale, whales.* Adding *-s* to a present-tense *verb* makes it singular: *whales sing; whale sings.*

1. Many agreement problems occur when plural words come between a singular subject and its verb. To correct a subject-verb error, first identify the actual subject and then use the correct verb ending for that subject:

FAULTY: A list of campaign promises often hurt the candidate.

Test: Put brackets around any prepositional phrases. The subject of the sentence is never in a prepositional phrase. "A list [of campaign promises] often hurt the candidate." *List* is the subject and *hurt* is the verb. Read without the words inside the brackets and revise the verb.

REVISED: A *list* of campaign promises often *hurts* the candidate.

FAULTY: This company, with few skilled mechanics and electricians, do not guarantee any repairs.

Test: Put brackets around the prepositional phrase. "This company [with few skilled mechanics and electricians], do not guarantee any repairs." Read the sentence without the words in brackets and revise the verb.

REVISED: This company, with few skilled mechanics and electricians, *does* not guarantee any repairs.

2. Two subjects connected by *and* take a plural verb. "The sergeant and his recruits march double-time across the grounds." When two subjects are connected by *or* or *nor*, however, the verb agrees with the closer subject:

FAULTY: Neither the recruits nor the sergeant know how to march.

REVISED: Neither the recruits nor the sergeant *knows* how to march.

[or]

REVISED: Neither the sergeant nor the recruits *know* how to march.

3. Indefinite pronouns (*each, one, either, everyone, neither, everybody, nobody, no one, none, somebody, someone*) usually take a *singular* verb:

FAULTY: Each of the books cost twenty dollars.
Test: Remove the prepositional phrase: "Each [of the books] cost twenty dollars." *Each* is singular, so the verb should be *costs*.

REVISED: Each of the books *costs* twenty dollars.

FAULTY: Everybody in all three classes are going to see the film.
Test: Remove the prepositional phrase: "Everybody [in all three classes] are going to see the film." *Everybody* is singular, so the verb should be *is*.

REVISED: Everybody in all three classes *is* going to see the film.

4. A collective noun as a subject takes a singular verb. Collective nouns (*family, committee, audience, class, crowd,* and *army*) usually refer to a single *unit* or *group* of several individuals or elements, and thus they take a *singular* verb:

FAULTY: The audience at the concert whistle its approval.

REVISED: The audience at the concert *whistles* its approval.
Note: When referring to the action or condition of *several individuals* within a group, use the phrase *the members of* or the phrase *a number of* followed by the plural verb.
The members of the committee *argue* about the policy.

5. Even when the normal subject-verb order is reversed, the verb should agree in number with the subject:

FAULTY: For such a small dormitory, there is far too many students.
Test: Put the subject and verb in their normal order: Too many students *are* in the small dormitory. [*Students* is the subject, so the verb is plural: *are*.]

REVISED: For such a small dormitory, there *are* far too many students.

EXERCISE In the following passage, revise all errors in subject-verb agreement.

(1) If you have friends or a family member who smoke, I have some suggestions to help this person quit. (2) First, if the family are supportive, try talking openly about the facts. (3) There is a few public service agencies that will provide evidence demonstrating the link between smoking and cancer. (4) Next, investigate this person's behavior: What does this person do just before he or she smokes? (5) To quit smoking, the smoker must disrupt the patterns of behavior that leads to smoking. (6) An inventory of the activities and places that cause a person to smoke provide key information. (7) For example, if the person always smokes after dinner, suggest eating snacks over a two-hour period instead of having a sit-down meal. (8) If he or she always smoke in a certain chair in the living room, change the furniture. (9) Breaking any habit is always easier if you break the entire behavior pattern. (10) Of course, each of these smokers need to want to stop smoking.

2H VERB TENSE

Avoid unnecessary shifts in verb tense:

SHIFT: After they *ate* ice cream and cake for dessert, they *are* ready to relax.

REVISED: After they *ate* ice cream and cake for dessert, they *were* ready to relax.

SHIFT: Peter *ate* dinner before you *had offered* to cook tacos.

REVISED: Peter *ate* dinner before you *offered* to cook tacos.

SHIFT: At one point in the film, Gandhi *gathered* his followers together to discuss strategy. Suddenly, a British general *gave* an order to fire upon them. People then *scurry* around and *try* to protect themselves and their children from the hail of bullets.

Note: For summaries or accounts of artistic works, films, literary works, or historical documents, use the *present tense.*

REVISED: At one point in this film, Gandhi *gathers* his followers together to discuss strategy. Suddenly, a British general *gives* an order to fire upon them. People then *scurry* around and *try* to protect themselves and their children from the hail of bullets.

EXERCISE In the following passage, revise any unnecessary shifts in tense.

> (1) In Sophocles' play, *Antigone*, two characters are tragic figures: Antigone and Creon. (2) In the play, Antigone faced a choice of conscience. (3) Should she be loyal to her family and bury her brother, or should she have been loyal to the state and obeyed the edict of Creon, the King of Thebes? (4) She assumes that she knew the best way to handle the situation and willfully chooses her own death. (5) Creon also faced a choice of conscience. (6) Should he punish someone who has betrayed the state, even if that person is a member of his family? (7) Like Napoleon and General Custer, Creon thought primarily about himself and his public image. (8) In Creon's case, ego or "hubris" leads to tragic results for the people around him.

21 PRONOUN AGREEMENT

A pronoun must agree in number and person with the noun to which it refers:

FAULTY: One of the scientists signed their name to the report.

Test: Because the subject is never in the prepositional phrase, put parentheses around the prepositional phrase ("of the scientists"). Now look for another noun that could be the subject of the sentence. "One" is the subject of the sentence, and it is a singular noun. Change "their" to the singular form, "his" or "her."

REVISED: One of the scientists signed her name to the report.

FAULTY: Each of the students felt cheated on their test.
Note: *Each* is singular: *their* is plural.

REVISED: The *students* felt cheated on *their* tests.

FAULTY: Everyone brought their gift to the party.

REVISED: Everyone brought *his or her* gift to the party.
Note: Avoiding sexist language by using "his or her" can be wordy or awkward in some contexts. Rewrite the sentence with a plural subject and plural pronoun.

REVISED: The *guests* brought *their* gifts to the party.

Avoid shifts in person. Avoid shifting between third person (*people, one, they, he, she*) and second person (*you*):

FAULTY: When *you* come to the party, *everyone* should bring a friend.

Note: *You* is second person; *everyone* is third person. revise the sentence, using either second or third person throughout.

REVISED: When *you* come to the party, bring a friend.

FAULTY: A good party should make *people* feel at ease, so *you* can make new friends.

REVISED: A good party should make *people* feel at ease, so *they* can make new friends.

REVISED: A good party should make *you* feel at ease, so *you* can make new friends.

> *Vigorous writing is concise. A sentence should contain no unnecessary words, a paragraph no unnecessary sentences, for the same reason that a drawing should have no unnecessary lines and a machine no unnecessary parts. This requires not that the writer make all his sentences short, or that he avoid all detail... but that every word tell.*
> —WILLIAM STRUNK, JR., AUTHOR OF ELEMENTS OF STYLE

2J Pronoun Reference

A pronoun should refer clearly and unambiguously to its antecedent:

UNCLEAR: Joan told Bev that her bank account was overdrawn.
Question: Whose bank account is overdrawn?
REVISED: When Joan discovered that her bank account was overdrawn, she told Bev.

UNCLEAR: If people do not take care of their cats, we should turn them into the humane society.
Question: Who should be turned in—the cats or their owners?
REVISED: If people do not take care of their cats, we should report the owners to the humane society.

EXERCISE In the following passage, correct problems in pronoun agreement and reference.

(1) People use the term *best friend* to describe a person who has a special warmth and friendliness. (2) I still remember when Michelle Martin, one of my best friends, said that they really liked me, too. (3) I called her my best friend; we stood by each other. (4) One time at a party, I saw her talking angrily to another woman. (5) It turned out that she had dated Tom, the guy she was going with at the time. (6) Each of them felt cheated by their boyfriend. (7) Before I knew what was happening, they were screaming at each other. (8) When I tried to stick up for her, she took a swing at me, and so I swung back with my best left hook, popping her in the right eye. (9) As a result, I was suspended from school for a week. (10) It just goes to show that when you have a best friend, everyone expects that you'll help them if you can.

SECTION 3

DICTION AND STYLE

Effective writing hides a curious paradox. On the one hand, good writing contains vivid detail. Good writing does not merely assert that thus-and-so is true; it supports a claim or assertion with evidence. It re-creates an experience, shows exactly how the writer feels, or communicates precisely what the writer thinks. To accomplish this, writers *add* specific details, examples, facts, or other data. On the other hand, good writing is also concise. Good writers *take out* vague words, weak verbs, and empty language. Their writing is as lean and sinewy as a long-distance runner. As you edit your writing for diction (choice of words) and clarity of style, you should *add* specific examples but *remove* vague, imprecise language. Your details should be ample; your diction and style spare.

TEACHING TIP

Few pronouncements about writing are always true. As a teaching strategy, ask students to explain when Strunk's rule, "Vigorous writing is concise," might *not* be true. For example, written dialogue might be wordy and repetitious to capture the flavor of actual conversation. Also, native speakers of Spanish, who generally prefer elaborate prose, often find "concise" written English childish and simplistic. Would "conciseness" be appropriate, then, in a travel brochure written for Spanish-speaking tourists?

3A VAGUE WORDS

Replace vague words with more specific or concrete language.

1. The following *nouns* are vague or unspecific. Vague nouns encourage writers to *tell* rather than to *show* with specific details or examples. Vague nouns may also lead to wordy and imprecise sentences. In most cases, *replace* the following nouns with more specific words, details, or examples:

thing	factor	aspect
something	situation	difficulty
anything	type	feeling
something	way	beauty
someone	fun	people
some	trouble	deal
area	problem	place
case	field	character
manner	nature	appearance

VAGUE: During their freshman year, students worry about all sorts of *things*. [Be specific: What things?]

REVISED: During their freshman year, students worry about leaving their families, making new friends, and passing their courses.

VAGUE: I have taken courses in the *field* of statistics for two years, and it has changed my *feeling* toward studying in the *area* of mathematics.

REVISED: After taking statistics courses for two years, I no longer hate studying mathematics.

VAGUE: Meteorologists occasionally have a great *deal of trouble* in forecasting a *situation* where an upper-level disturbance becomes a *factor* in local weather. [Be specific: What kind of trouble? Be concise: Omit unnecessary vague words.]

REVISED: When an upper-level disturbance affects local weather, meteorologists occasionally miss a forecast.

2. The following *modifiers* are weak, vague, or unspecific. Replace them with stronger modifiers or add specific details:

very	a lot	pretty
really	good	bad
a few	certain	happy
many	nice	much
regular	similar	soon

VAGUE: I *really* liked *certain* classes in high school *very much*, but I just couldn't stand *a lot* of the *really boring* courses. [Be specific: What *certain classes*? Be specific: How or why were they *really boring*?]

REVISED: I really looked forward to learning about the turtles, snakes, and birds in the biology lab, but I couldn't stand just sitting still and practicing grammar hour after hour in French class.

VAGUE: Overall, *The Bill Cosby Show* is *pretty good*, but sometimes it gets *somewhat* unreal. [Be specific: What makes it *pretty good*? What makes it *unreal*?]

REVISED: *The Bill Cosby Show* has entertaining stories about family problems—I still remember the episode when Theo decides he just has to join the Blue Angels—but in many episodes, the family seems to resolve the conflict too easily and simply.

3. The following *verbs* are weak, vague, or unspecific. Where appropriate, replace them with more active, energetic, or vivid verbs. When these verbs occur with nominals or passive voice,

TEACHING TIP

Computer programs that "flag" vague or unspecific words alert students to *possible* changes in word choice. As long as students do not make the changes automatically—without thinking about context and meaning—such programs can effectively prompt them to reduce vagueness and add specific details.

change to active verbs or active voice. Always test your revision: In your context, is the change more effective, concise, or vivid?

deals with	take	get
involved with	relate to	go
has to do with	make	give

VAGUE: He gets some enjoyment from sky diving.

REVISED: He enjoys sky diving.

VAGUE: Her job deals with collecting rare species of lizards.

REVISED: She collects rare species of lizards.

VAGUE: Jogging along the path, she got involved with a rattlesnake in a serious way. [How exactly was she "involved" with this rattlesnake?]

REVISED: Jogging along the path, she was seriously bitten by a rattlesnake.

EXERCISE In the following passage, substitute specific and vivid words or phrases for all vague nouns, verbs, and modifiers.

> (1) When I was separated from my girlfriend, I missed her a lot. (2) Being alone sometimes gave me a pretty empty type feeling. (3) When I called her on the phone, we talked about all the nice times we spent together, not about all the very big fights we used to have. (4) Since there was no stress to deal with, we had a fun-filled, long-distance relationship. (5) I know that one aspect of this relationship will improve the way we get along, now that we're back together. (6) We always had difficulty talking in a serious manner about our future. (7) Now we are more involved with each other and can really talk about all sorts of things. (8) For anyone who is having troubles, I recommend this kind of separate situation because, in the long run, the relationship will be much happier.

3B WORDINESS

1. The following wordy phrases can be stated more concisely:

WORDY	CONCISE
due to the fact that	because
despite the fact that	though
regardless of the fact that	although
at this point in time	now
at the present time	now

until such time as	until
in the event that	if, when
at all times	always
there is no doubt that	doubtless
in a deliberate manner	deliberately
by means of	by
the reason is that	[omit]

2. The following phrases are redundant—they say the same thing twice or repeat unnecessarily:

Redundant	Concise
new innovation	innovation
disappear from view	disappear
repeat again	repeat
reflected back	reflected
circle around	circle
few in number	few
cheaper in cost	cheaper
oblong in shape	oblong
blue in color	blue
consensus of opinion	consensus
important essentials	essentials
resulting effect	effect
cooperate together	cooperate

3. Where appropriate, be more concise by omitting *there is, there are, it is,* and *this is* constructions:

WORDY: There are seven people living in that apartment.

REVISED: Seven people live in that apartment.

WORDY: This is the step that is crucial for getting a job.

REVISED: This step is crucial for getting a job.

4. Some *who, which,* and *that* clauses can be changed into modifying words or phrases:

WORDY: Cheryl Stickfinger, who is the mayor, is accused of embezzling city funds.

REVISED: Mayor Cheryl Stickfinger is accused of embezzling city funds.

WORDY: Then they each wolfed down a banana split that contained 500 calories.

REVISED: Then they each wolfed down a 500-calorie banana split.

WORDY: The police officer, who was frustrated about missing his promotion, started taking kickbacks.

REVISED: The police officer, frustrated about missing his promotion, started taking kickbacks.

EXERCISE Revise the following passage to reduce wordiness.

(1) One of the most recent new discoveries in medicine is the so-called diving reflex. (2) When people fall into water that is icy, their circulation slows down due to the fact that the water is so cold. (3) In addition, the metabolism of every cell that is in the body slows down, conserving oxygen. (4) In a recent case, Alvaro Garza, who is eleven years old, disappeared from view underneath the ice for 45 minutes. (5) When rescuers finally pulled him at long last from beneath the ice, he was unconscious, his body temperature was cold and below normal, and his skin was grayish-blue in color. (6) Regardless of the fact that rescuers could find no pulse or heartbeat, they began CPR (cardiopulmonary resuscitation) immediately. (7) Within a few days, Alvaro began to recover in a steady manner, and soon he was asking for a hamburger and French fries. (8) Although he may have some lingering effects from his ordeal that do not go away in a short period of time, the unexplainable miracle is that he survived.

3c Colloquial Language and Slang

Your audience and purpose should determine whether conversational language is appropriate. In informal or expressive writing, colloquial language (spoken language), slang, or trendy expressions may be vivid and effective. In conversation or informal writing, we may say that something is *cool, hip, gross, weak, sweet*, or *too much.* We may call a friend *dude*, a skateboarder a *thrasher*, or someone we don't like a *wimp* or *geek*.

In formal writing, however, you should avoid colloquial expressions and slang. Your readers may not know the expressions, they may find some slang offensive, or they may think "gross" is simply too vague to describe what really happened. Slang, in fact, tends to become a shorthand for a whole experience and thus invites *telling* ("This guy was a real geek") rather than *showing* ("Rudolph had messy hair, wore adhesive tape on his glasses, and always had one green and one orange sock sticking out of his polyester pants. He lived out of a forty-pound bookpack, watched *Dr. Who* on TV every day, and spoke like William F. Buckley").

3D Clichés and Jargon

Clichés

Some expressions are so commonly used that they have become automatic, predictable, trite, or hackneyed. The phrases in the left-hand column, for example, may have been fresh and original once, but now they are as stale as dirty dishwater and about as exciting as a secondhand sock. The expressions in the right-hand column, for example, are so predictable that we can easily guess the missing word:

tried and true	strong as an ________
needle in a haystack	dark as ________
easier said than done	heavy as ________
burning the midnight oil	cold as ________
didn't sleep a wink	busy as a ________
crack of dawn	happy as a ________
dead of night	white as ________
last but not least	quick as a ________
birds of a feather	blind as a ________
hit the nail on the head	sober as a ________
face the music	tough as ________
straw that broke the camel's back	gentle as a ________

Jargon

Jargon is the technical vocabulary of any specialized occupation, field, or profession. In technical or specialized writing, writers should use the vocabulary of their fields. In the following passage, the specialized vocabulary (*homeotic, mutant, rudimentary*, and *thoracic*) is entirely appropriate:

> In the cockroach *Blatella germanica*, a homeotic mutant produces rudimentary wings on the first thoracic segment. No modern insect normally bears wings on its first thoracic segment, but the earliest winged fossil insects did!
>
> —Stephen J. Gould, *Hen's Teeth and Horse's Toes*

Jargon, however, is also a generic label for impressive words used for their own sake. Any specialized vocabulary is inappropriate when used

Teaching Tip

Clichés exist in the eye of the beholder. Novice writers often think that their clichés are vivid and expressive, while readers find them childish and insulting. Avoiding clichés is a matter not of error but of etiquette. Teaching writers about cliché helps them learn about audience analysis and audience expectations.

not to *inform* but to *impress* an audience with the writer's intelligence. When writers use jargon inappropriately, they are not communicating—they're showing off.

Below is a jargon-filled parody, in legalese, of the simple, clear sentence, "Have an orange." This passage, by the editors of *Labor Magazine*, appears in Stuart Chase's essay, "Gobbledygook":

> I hereby give and convey to you, all singular, my estate and right, title, claim and advantages of and in said orange, together with all rind, juice, pulp, and pits, and all rights and advantages therein . . . anything hereinbefore or hereinafter or in any other deed or deeds, instrument or instruments of whatever nature or kind whatsoever, to the contrary, in any wise, notwithstanding.

Sometimes writers use jargon not to make *themselves* sound impressive but to promote the *subject* they're writing about. We commonly call the result "advertising." Here is a sample of a Nike advertisement for a walking shoe:

> Walking. To you, it's a simple matter of putting one foot in front of another. To Nike, it's an entire science.
>
> In fact, we have studied walking in one of the world's leading biomechanical labs. Our own. And as a result, we've designed a technically advanced shoe specifically for the walking motion. The EXW. We built it close to the ground for stability. With a tri-density midsole that supports and centers your foot. A vented toe area for cool comfort. Flex grooves that bend with your foot. And a Nike-Air cushioning system that makes you feel, literally, like you're walking on air.
>
> Now, all this technology may seem a bit much. But try on a pair. You'll see that the EXW doesn't make walking more complicated. It just takes it one step further.

Nike hopes the inflated language and technical jargon in this passage will make you feel better about spending fifty dollars for a walking shoe. "World's leading biomechanical labs," "advanced shoe specifically for the walking motion," "tri-density midsole," "vented toe area," and "flex grooves"—all this jargon does seem a bit much. We may ridicule such language, but remember that if the advertisement causes us to buy the shoe, the language is appropriate for the audience.

EXERCISE In the following passage, replace clichés with fresh, figurative language and eliminate or replace inappropriate jargon.

> (1) The television news media in America needs to be reformed. (2) The bottom line is that serious news has been lost as stations rush to entertain the viewer. (3) Trying to find an informative story on the evening news is like looking for a needle in a haystack. (4) The sta-

tion executives who finalize the programmatic output for the evening news believe that the average American is dumber than an ox. (5) As a result, viewers see in-depth stories about a sex scandal involving a local politician, but only a few seconds explaining why the stock market is scraping the bottom of the barrel. (6) Newscasters attempt to maximize their humor by telling jokes that go over like a lead balloon rather than informing the viewer about the latest decision-making process on armament restrictions. (7) If station programmers actually interfaced with the public occasionally, they would recognize the error of their ways.

3E Sexist Language

Do not use language that unfairly stereotypes people or discriminates against either women or men. Just as you would avoid racist terms, you should avoid language that stereotypes people's roles, occupations, or behavior by gender. Sentences such as"A doctor always cares for his patient" or "A secretary should always help her boss" imply that all doctors are men and all secretaries are women. Phrases such as *female logic, male ego, emotional woman*, or *typical male brutality* imply that all women are excessively emotional and all men are egotistical brutes. In fact, those stereotypes are not true. If you use sexist language, you will offend your readers. Even more important, your language should not encourage you or your reader to see the world in sexist stereotypes.

1. Avoid words that suggest sexist roles:

Sexist	Revised
man	people, person
chairman	chair, head
businessman	businessperson
policeman	police officer
mankind	humanity
congressman	representative
statesman	politician, diplomat
lady lawyer	lawyer
career girl	professional woman
coed	student
mailman	letter carrier
old wives' tale	superstition

Note, however, that some words that link occupation with gender are still appropriate. Most writers still use *actor* and *waiter* for men and *actress* and *waitress* for women. Other words, however, such as *stewardess* or *seamstress*, are often replaced with *flight attendant* or *garment worker*.

Resource Note

For a collection of essays illustrating the pervasiveness of sexist language in English, see Nilsen et. al., *Sexism and Language*.

2. Be consistent in your use of people's names. If you write *Ernest Hemingway*, then write *Emily Dickinson*, not *Miss Dickinson*. If you write *Lennon* instead of *John Lennon*, then write *Parton*, not *Dolly Parton* or *Dolly*.

3. Avoid using the pronouns *he*, *his*, or *him* when you are referring to activities, roles, or behavior that could describe either sex:

SEXIST: A doctor should listen carefully to his patient.
Note: Use plural if it does not alter your meaning.

REVISED: Doctors should listen carefully to their patients.

SEXIST: An effective teacher knows each of her students.
Note: You may use *his or her* sparingly, but avoid using the construction *s/he*.

REVISED: An effective teacher knows each of his or her students.

SEXIST: Everyone hopes that he will survive the first year of college.
Note: Often, you can revise the sentence by using first or second person or by omitting the pronoun.

REVISED: I hope to survive the first year of college.

REVISED: All of us hope to survive the first year of college.

REVISED: You hope to survive the first year of college.

REVISED: Everyone hopes to survive the first year of college.
Note: Do *not* mix singular and plural by saying, "Everyone hopes *they* will survive the first year of college."

EXERCISE Revise the following passage to eliminate sexist language.

(1) Everyone in college now is looking for that special job that will match his talents and yet bring him sufficient income. (2) Teaching is a low-paying but good career if you don't mind being a professor who spends his life reading papers, getting grants, and serving on committees. (3) A secretary or stewardess can begin her career with minimal training, but a nurse must dedicate herself to rigorous medical schooling. (4) In business and entertainment, girls can work right alongside the men. (5) In the entertainment field, many people dream of being a Bruce Springsteen or a Tina Turner, although most singers don't have Springsteen's talent or Tina's perseverance. (6) A businessman often works his way up the ladder and becomes chairman of the company. (7) Even staying at home and raising a family is a respectable career for either a man or his wife, though most men simply don't have the temperament to raise chil-

dren. (8) Whatever your chosen career, from mailman to congressman, hard work and dedication are the keys to landing and keeping that important job.

3F Denotation and Connotation

The *denotation* of a word is its literal or dictionary definition. Both *house* and *home* refer, denotatively to a structure in which people live. Many words have, in addition, a *connotations* or emotional associations that can be negative, neutral, or positive. *House* has, for most people, a *neutral* or sterile connotation, whereas *home*, for most people, has a *positive* connotation, suggesting warmth, comfort, security, and family.

Choose words appropriately for their connotative value:

INAPPROPRIATE: Dr. Aileen Brown, a *notorious* scientist, just received the Nobel prize for her work with superconductors. [*Notorious* people are usually famous for their *misconduct.*]

REVISED: Dr. Aileen Brown, a *famous* scientist, just received the Nobel prize for her work with superconductors.

INAPPROPRIATE: Beverly looked at her friend Steve and said, "Why don't you finish your dinner? You need the food—you're already a bit *scrawny* looking." [Steve prefers to think of himself as *thin* or *slim* rather than *scrawny.*]

REVISED: Beverly looked at her friend Steve and said, "Why don't you finish your dinner? You need the food—you're already a bit *thin.*"

INAPPROPRIATE: Lynn's father told Paul that the apartment was decorated *cheaply* but tastefully. [Paul's feelings may be hurt. He does have good taste in furnishings, and he did the best he could on his tight budget.]

REVISED: Lynn's father told Paul that the apartment was decorated tastefully but inexpensively.

Exercise The following groups of words have similar denotative meanings but vary widely in their emotional associations or *connotative* meanings. Rank the words in each group from most negative, to neutral, to most positive.

- social drinker, wino, lush, reveler, alcoholic, sot, party animal, elbow bender, inebriate, problem drinker, booze hound, bar hopper
- scholar, intellectual, four-eyes, walking encyclopedia, geek, savant, bookworm, genius, pedant, bibliophile
- thrifty, penny-pinching, frugal, miserly, tight-fisted, cheap, economical, prudent, stingy
- steady, loyal, stubborn, firm, unyielding, dedicated, obstinate, devoted

3G Usage Glossary

This glossary alphabetically lists words and phrases that frequently cause problems for writers. In many cases, writers disagree about the preferred usage in formal writing. If you are in doubt, check a dictionary, such as *The American Heritage Dictionary*, the *Random House Dictionary*, or a guide, such as Margaret Bryant's *Current American Usage*.

Because this glossary references only the most obvious usage errors, refer to a standard or unabridged dictionary for items not included.

a, an: Use *a* when the following word begins with a *consonant sound*: a book, a clever saying, a hat. Use *an* when the following word begins with a *vowel sound*: an apple, an old building, an honor.

accept, except: *Accept* is a verb meaning "to receive": "I accept the gift." *Except* is a preposition meaning "other than" or "excluding": "Everyone received a gift except John." Rarely, *except* is a verb meaning "to exclude": "The editor excepted the footnote from the article."

advise, advice: *Advise* is a verb: "I advise you to exercise regularly." *Advice* is a noun: "Please take this advice."

affect, effect: *Affect* is a verb: "The flying beer cups did not affect the outfielder's concentration." *Effect* is a noun: "His obvious poise had a calming effect on the crowd." Remember: If you can say, "The effect," then you are correctly using the noun form. Less often, *effect* is also a verb: "His behavior effected a change in the crowd's attitude."

all right, alright: *All right*, two words, is the accepted spelling. *Alright* is nonstandard, in the opinion of most experts.

already, all ready: *Already* means "by now" or "previously": "The essay was already completed." *All ready* means *completely prepared*: "The paragraphs were all ready to be printed."

a lot: *A lot* is always two words that mean "many." Wherever possible, however, *avoid* using *a lot*. Replace with more specific description. See Section 3a.

among, between: Use *between* for *two* people or things: "Let's divide the cake between the two of us." Use *among* for *three or more* people or things: "We should distribute the winnings among all the players." *Note: Between* is used for three or more items when location or a reciprocal relationship is indicated: "They found the treasure at a point equidistant between the three trees." "Through careful negotiations, a nonaggression treaty was reached between the four nations."

amount, number: *Amount* refers to quantity: "He saved a large amount of food for the winter months." *Number* refers to countable items: "She owned a large number of expensive sports cars."

anyone, any one: *Anyone* is a pronoun: "Anyone who likes Mayan art should hear the lecture." *Any one* is an adjective phrase modifying a noun: "He owns more Mayan art than any one person could possibly appreciate."

bad, badly: *Bad* is an adjective used in the predicate ("After a week of the flu, she looked bad") or before a noun ("She caught my cold at a bad time"). "She felt bad because she had a bad cold." *Badly* is an adverb: "He wrote badly because he had a high fever."

being, being that: *Being* cannot be used as a complete verb. "The seat being taken" is not a complete sentence. *Being that* is nonstandard: "Being that the bus was late, we missed the show." Use *because* or *since*: "Because the bus was late, we missed the show."

beside, besides: *Beside* is a preposition meaning *next to* or *by the side of*: "Peggi sat beside the senator." *Besides* is a preposition meaning *moreover* or *in addition to*: "Besides, the senator likes several people besides George."

can, may: In formal writing, use *can* for ability: "I can take out the garbage." Use *may* for permission: "May I have the honor of taking out the garbage?" Also use *may* for possibility: "If I have time, I *may* take out the garbage."

center around: Illogical: One can "circle around" but not "center around." Replace with "center on" or "focus on": "The controversy focused on the right of the worker to a safe, smoke-free environment."

cite, site: *Cite* is a verb meaning "to quote as an authority or to mention": "She cited Newcastle's blue law, which forbade card playing on Sunday." *Site* is a noun meaning "a place or location": "The church basement was, in fact, the site of Newcastle's first bingo game."

continual, continuous: *Continual* means "frequently repeated": "Most soap operas have continual interruptions for commercials." *Continuous* means "unceasing": "Throughout the broadcast, we heard a continuous buzzing sound."

could of, should of: Nonstandard. Use *could have* or *should have.*

data, media, criteria: The singular forms are *datum, medium*, and *criterion.* In formal writing, use plural verbs and pronouns with the plural noun. "Our data reveal a sharp increase in rapes and assaults since last year." "The media use their own criteria for sex and violence."

different from, different than: For prepositional phrases, use *different from*: "His chili recipe is different from yours." Although "different from" is preferred, sometimes "different than" results in a more concise sentence. "She is a different player than she used to be" is less wordy than "She is a different player from the player she used to be."

disinterested, uninterested: *Disinterested* means "objective or impartial": "As a disinterested third party, Marji resolved our dispute." *Uninterested* means "lack of interest": "We were uninterested in the outcome of the hall elections."

farther, further: *Farther* usually refers to distance: "How much farther are we going to jog?" *Further* refers to additional time, amount, or degree: "Furthermore, if you cannot hire me, I will go further into debt."

fewer, less: *Fewer* refers to numbers or countable items: "Fewer teenagers smoke than a decade ago." *Less* refers to amount ("less sugar") or degree ("less important"): "Teenagers spend less money on cigarettes than they did a decade ago."

hopefully: *Hopefully* means "with hope," or "in a hopeful manner": "Charlene waited hopefully for a letter from home." Most good writers still object to the colloquial usage of *hopefully* (meaning,"I hope," or "it is to be hoped"): "Hopefully, Charlene will get her letter from home." Change to: "I hope Charlene gets her letter from home."

imply, infer: *Imply* means to suggest without directly stating: "The news report implied that the president was seriously ill." *Infer* means to draw a conclusion: "I inferred from the news report that the president was seriously ill." Writers and speakers *imply*; readers and listeners *infer.*

its, it's: *Its*, like *his* or *her*, is a possessive pronoun: "The tree is losing its leaves." *It's* is a contraction of *it is*: "It's your turn to rake the leaves."

lay, lie: *Lay* is the transitive verb (lay, laid, laid) meaning "put" or "place." "Please lay the book on the table." *Lie* is an intransitive verb (lie, lay, lain) meaning "recline" or "occupy a place": "The books lie on the table."

like, as, as if: *Like* is a preposition: "A great race driver is like an opera singer—vain and arrogant." *As* can be a preposition ("His mission as a driver was to demonstrate his grace and courage"), but it can also introduce a clause: "Even at the end of the race, he looked as if he had just stepped off the cover of a magazine."

lose, loose: *Lose* is a verb meaning "misplace" or "be deprived of": "Good detectives never lose their nerve." *Loose* is an adjective meaning "free" or "not tight": "The psychopath got loose by climbing through the ventilating system."

principal, principle: *Principal* as an adjective means "major" or "main"; as a noun, *principal* refers either to a "chief official" or to a "capital sum of money": "The principal of the high school listed as his principal debt the $50,000 he owed on the principal of his house mortgage." *Principle* is a noun meaning "basic truth," "rule," or "moral standard": "He learned the principles of accounting and finance."

quote, quotation: *Quote* is a verb: "I quoted the passage from Thoreau's *Walden*." Do not use *quote* as a noun ("The following quote from *Walden*"); instead, use "quotation," "remark," or "passage": "The following passage from *Walden* illustrates Thoreau's politics."

that, which: *That* always introduces restrictive clauses; *which* introduces either restrictive or nonrestrictive clauses. Some writers prefer, however, to use *that* only for restrictive clauses and *which* only for nonrestrictive. "The hat that has the pheasant feather was a birthday present." The clause, "that has the pheasant feather" restricts, limits, and *identifies* which hat was the present. "The hat, which is nearly ten years old, was a birthday present." The clause, "which is nearly ten years old" is only incidental information; it does not specify which hat was the present.

their, they're, there: *Their* is a pronoun: "She is playing with their tennis balls." *They're* is a contraction: "They're really upset that she didn't even ask." *There* is an adverb or an expletive: "She's practicing over there. There are the tennis balls."

to, too, two: *To* is a preposition: "I am writing to Bev." *Too* is an adverb meaning "in addition" or "also": "You too can write her a letter." *Too* also is an intensifier meaning "very": "Dad expects me to write too often." *Two* is a number: "I have written two times this month."

used to, supposed to: Use the past tense ("used to") not ("use to"): "I used to go there every weekend."

SECTION 4

PUNCTUATION AND MECHANICS

The purpose of punctuation is to clarify meaning and promote communication. Commas, periods, semicolons, dashes, and other punctuation marks guide readers to meanings, just as traffic signals, double yellow lines, turning lanes, and one-way signs guide motorists to destinations. The conventions of punctuation create *expectations* in the reader. Just as you are surprised when a car runs a red light and nearly hits you, readers are surprised when writers fail to follow the conventions of punctuation.

Punctuation—or the lack of it—can change the entire meaning of a sentence. In actual conversation, pauses, inflections, intonation, gestures, and facial expressions do the work of punctuation. In writing, however, punctuation must provide these clues.

Read the following sentences. How many different ways can you find to punctuate each sentence? How does each version alter the meaning?

> Give the peanuts to my daughter Ella
> She said walk quietly
> Let's go see the lions eat Marcia.

"Sorry, but I'm going to have to issue you a summons for reckless grammar and driving without an apostrophe."

Sometimes writers unintentionally create confusion by omitting important punctuation. Notice how the appropriate use of commas in the following sentences prevents a possible surprise and clarifies the meaning:

CONFUSING: To keep the pipes from freezing the plumber advised us to run the water all night. [How exactly did the pipes freeze the plumber?]

REVISED: To keep the pipes from freezing, the plumber advised us to run the water all night.

CONFUSING: On the menu for lunch was ham and Sam was doing the cooking. [Is Sam on the menu?]

REVISED: On the menu for lunch was ham, and Sam was doing the cooking.

The guidelines for punctuation and mechanics in this section will help you avoid unintentional problems and clarify your writing. Review these guidelines as you edit your own and other people's writing.

TEACHING TIP

This section explains how basic sentence punctuation works. To avoid overwhelming students with the names of conjunctions, however, teachers may prefer to use simpler labels for each group: "and/but" or "BOYFANS" words for coordinate conjunctions; "because" words for subordinating conjunctions; and "however" words for conjunctive adverbs.

4A SENTENCE PUNCTUATION

Much of the confusion about punctuation occurs because connecting words often have similar meanings but signal different punctuation conventions. A stop sign, a red light, and a blinking red light, for example, all mean that motorists must stop, but each signals a slightly different procedure. In English, *but, although*, and *however* mean that a contrast is coming, but each requires different punctuation:

We won the volleyball game, *but* our best hitter broke her wrist.
Although we won the game, our best hitter broke her wrist.
We won the game; *however*, our best hitter broke her wrist.

Using commas and semicolons to punctuate sentences and clauses requires knowing the three basic types of connecting or *conjunctive* words.

Coordinate conjunctions: "Conjunction" means "join together"; "coordinates" are "equals." A coordinate conjunction joins equals together. The acronym BOYFANS will help you remember the coordinate conjunctions:

B	O	Y	F	A	N	S
but	or	yet	for	and	nor	so

Subordinating conjunctions: A subordinate conjunction joins a dependent or subordinate clause to an independent or main clause. The following are the most common subordinating conjunctions:

after	before	since	until
although	even if	so that	when
as	even though	than	whenever
as if	if	that	where
as though	in order that	though	wherever
because	rather than	unless	while

Subordinating conjunctions change an independent clause (IC) to a dependent clause (DC):

IC

Independent clause: He buys a newspaper.

Add a subordinating conjunction to create a *dependent clause*:

DC

If he buys a newspaper

DC IC

Complete sentence: If he buys a newspaper, he will see the story.

Conjunctive adverbs: A conjunctive adverb acts as a transitional phrase. Below are the most common conjunctive adverbs:

accordingly	however	meanwhile	still
also	incidentally	moreover	thereafter
consequently	indeed	nevertheless	therefore
furthermore	instead	otherwise	thus
hence	likewise	similarly	

If you are uncertain whether a connecting word is a conjunctive adverb, *test* by moving the connecting word to another place in the clause. Conjunctive adverbs *can* be moved; subordinating conjunctions (such as *if* or *because*) and coordinating conjunctions (BOYFANS words) *cannot.*

Conjunctive adverbs can be moved:

We won the game; *however*, our best hitter broke her wrist.
We won the game; our best hitter, *however*, broke her wrist.
We won the game; our best hitter broke her wrist, *however*.

Subordinating conjunctions cannot be moved:

Although our best hitter broke her wrist, we won the game.
Our best hitter, *although*, broke her wrist, we won the game.
[Obviously, *although* cannot be moved to another position in the clause.]

Coordinating conjunctions cannot be moved:

We won the game, *but* our best hitter broke her wrist.

We won the game, our best hitter, *but*, broke her wrist. [Moving a coordinating conjunction scrambles the sentence.]

Rules for joining independent clauses (IC) and dependent clauses (DC):

1. Join two independent clauses with a comma and a coordinating conjunction:

IC, BOYFANS IC.

The pizza is good, *but* the mystery meat is disgusting. [Use *both* a comma *and* a BOYFANS word]

2. Join two independent clauses with a semicolon and a conjunctive adverb:

IC, CONJUNCTIVE ADVERB, IC

The pizza is good; however, the mystery meat is disgusting.

3. Join two independent clauses (IC) with a semicolon:

IC; IC.

The pizza is good; the mystery meat is disgusting.

4. Join a dependent clause (DC) to an independent clause (IC) with a comma:

DC, IC

Although mystery meat tastes all right, it looks disgusting.

4B Comma Splices and Fused Sentences

Two common errors in joining independent clauses are the *comma splice* and the *fused sentence* (also called a *run-on sentence*). Revise by following one of the patterns in 1–3 above:

COMMA SPLICE: [IC, IC] I know that airplanes are safer than cars, I still have a fear of flying.

COMMA SPLICE: [IC, Conjunctive Adverb IC] I know that airplanes are safer than cars, however I still have a fear of flying.

FUSED SENTENCE: [IC IC] I know that airplanes are safer than cars I still have a fear of flying.

REVISED: I know that airplanes are safer than cars, *but* I still have a fear of flying.

REVISED: I know that airplanes are safer than cars; *however*, I still have a fear of flying.

REVISED: *Although* I know that airplanes are safer than cars, I still have a fear of flying.

EXERCISE In the following passage, correct all comma splices and fused sentences.

(1) For years, scientists have attempted to teach animals to communicate for the most part, their efforts have failed. (2) In the 1950s, psychologists failed to teach a chimpanzee to speak, the ape was able to grunt only a few words. (3) In the 1960s, however, a chimp named Washoe learned the sign language of the deaf. (4) Washoe came to understand hundreds of words, he used them to communicate and express original ideas. (5) As it turns out, the great apes have the capacity to learn language, but they cannot speak. (6) This research proved that humans are not the only animal capable of using language they are, however, the most sophisticated users of language.

4C COMMAS

COMMAS FOR INTRODUCTORY ELEMENTS

Use commas to set off most introductory elements:

Because I broke three flasks, I'm going to have a large bill for chemistry lab. [introductory dependent clause]

In the middle of finals week last semester, I became seriously depressed. [long introductory prepositional phrase]

Jogging home after classes, I see children playing in the schoolyard. [introductory participial phrase]

To save money, I often take the bus. [introductory infinitive phrase]

Incidentally, I hope my roommate will be here this weekend. [introductory adverb]

ITEMS IN A SERIES

Use commas to separate items in a series (a, b, and c). Generally, use a comma before the "and." In some cases, omitting the comma before the final item in the series may cause confusion:

CONFUSING: She rented an apartment with a convection oven, a microwave, a refrigerator with an icemaker and a garbage disposal. [Does the refrigerator have a built-in icemaker and garbage disposal?]

REVISED:	She rented an apartment with a convection oven, a microwave, refrigerator with an icemaker, and a garbage disposal.

EXERCISE Revise the punctuation in the following passage.

(1) Everyone can have fun outside in the wintertime by following some common-sense rules. (2) If you are going to be outside for several hours be sure to eat a nutritious meal before leaving. (3) On cold damp or windy days wear clothes that are warm and dry. (4) To stay warm protect yourself against moisture that builds up from the inside. (5) Most experts recommend dressing in layers. (6) The inner layer wicks moisture away from your body the middle layer provides thermal protection and the outer layer protects against rain or wind. (7) Curiously enough most people tend to put on too many clothes, underestimating their body's ability to exercise comfortably naturally and safely in cold weather.

NONRESTRICTIVE ELEMENTS

Nonrestrictive modifiers should be separated from the sentence by commas. Always *test* the phrase or clause. If it can be removed from the sentence without changing the meaning, use commas:

NONRESTRICTIVE:	Coach Hall, who was invited to the party, celebrated the victory.
Test:	The clause, "who was invited to the party," is incidental information. It does not restrict or specify which coach was celebrating. The two commas indicate that removing the clause from the sentence will not change the meaning: "Coach Hall celebrated the victory."
NONRESTRICTIVE:	Seattle, which has a reputation as a rainy city, is actually drier than New Orleans.
Test:	Remove the clause, and the meaning of the sentence is not altered. "Seattle is actually drier than New Orleans."
NONRESTRICTIVE:	Charles, the man in the gray suit, eats fried grasshoppers when no one is looking.
Test:	The appositive, "the man in the gray suit," can be removed from the sentence without altering the meaning.
RESTRICTIVE:	Demonstrators who hurled bricks were arrested by the police.

Test: The meaning is that *only those* demonstrators *who hurled bricks* were arrested by the police. The phrase *who hurled bricks* cannot be removed from the sentence without changing this meaning. Do *not* use commas to separate restrictive elements.

NONRESTRICTIVE: The class, which was taught by Anne Perkins, met at eight o'clock in the morning.
Note: This sentence says that the class met at eight o'clock, and Anne Perkins was, incidentally, the teacher. (Usually use *which* for nonrestrictive clauses.)

RESTRICTIVE: The class that was taught by Anne Perkins met at eight o'clock in the morning.
Note: This sentence says that *the particular class taught by Professor Perkins* met at eight o'clock. Other classes met at some other time. (Use *that* for restrictive clauses. Do not use commas.)

Unnecessary Commas

Do not use a comma to separate a subject and a verb:

FAULTY: My toughest class of the day, met at eight o'clock.
REVISED: My toughest class of the day met at eight o'clock.

Do not use a comma to separate compound subjects or predicates:

FAULTY: The Dean of Students, and the Chancellor decided to cancel classes. [compound subject]
REVISED: The Dean of Students and the Chancellor decided to cancel classes.

FAULTY: Because of the heavy snowfall, I stayed inside all afternoon, and popped popcorn. [compound predicate]
Note: When coordinate conjunctions do not join independent clauses or items in a series, a comma is usually not necessary (see Section 4a for appropriate use of commas with coordinate conjunctions):
REVISED: Because of the heavy snowfall, I stayed inside all afternoon and popped popcorn.

Coordinate Adjectives

Use a comma to separate coordinate (equal) adjectives. Test for coordinate adjectives: (1) insert an "and" between the adjectives and (2) reverse the order of the adjectives. If the meaning of the sentence remains unchanged, the adjectives are equal or coordinate:

EXAMPLE: It was a dull dark day.

Test: Insert "and"; reverse adjectives. It was a dull and dark day. It was a dark and dull day. Since the meaning of the sentence has not changed, these are coordinate or equal adjectives. Remove the *and* and add a comma.

REVISED: It was a dull, dark day.

EXAMPLE: The car had studded snow tires.

Test: Insert "and"; reverse adjectives. The car had studded and snow tires. The car had snow and studded tires. The meaning of the original sentence is changed; therefore, the adjectives are not coordinate. Do *not* separate with comma.

REVISED: The car had studded snow tires.

Dialogue

Use commas to set off a direct quotation or dialogue.

Direct quotation:

> The author points out, "One of the effects of embalming by chemical injection, however, has been to dispel fears of live burial."
>
> —Jessica Mitford

Dialogue:

> "We'll try it," the professor said to me, grimly, "with every adjustment of the microscope known to man."
>
> —James Thurber

In fiction or nonfiction, indent (begin a new paragraph) when the dialogue shifts from one person to the next:

> A white man finally came along and found her—a hunter, a young man, with his dog on a chain.
>
> "Well, Granny!" he laughed, "what are you doing there?"
>
> "Lying on my back like a June-bug waiting to be turned over, mister," she said, reaching up her hand.
>
> He lifted her up, gave her a swing in the air, and set her down.

"Anything broken, Granny?"

"No sir, them old dead weeds is springy enough," said Phoenix, when she had got her breath. "I thank you for your trouble."

—Eudora Welty, "A Worn Path"

Addresses, Dates, Degrees

Use commas to set off addresses, dates, degrees, or titles:

Addresses:	What Cheer, Iowa, is his home town.
Dates:	On December 7, 1941, the Japanese bombed Pearl Harbor.
Degrees:	Randall Beaver, D.D.S., is my orthodontist.

EXERCISE Revise the punctuation in the following passage.

(1) Dinosaurs which have been extinct for millions of years are making news again. (2) At a meeting of the Geological Society of America in November 1987 scientists announced a startling discovery. (3) Dinosaurs, that lived 80 million years ago, benefited from an atmosphere that contained nearly 50 percent more oxygen than it does now. (4) Gary Landis geochemist for the U.S. Geological Service and Robert Berner professor at Yale University reached that conclusion after analyzing, air bubbles trapped in bits of amber. (5) They found that the tiny, air bubbles contained 32 percent oxygen, compared with 21 percent in the modern atmosphere. (6) When asked whether a decreasing oxygen supply, could have caused the extinction of the dinosaurs, Berner explained "It was a very gradual change, and most organisms easily adapt." (7) "The large slow-moving dinosaurs probably became extinct" he said "following some cataclysmic, geological, event."

4D Periods and Semicolons

Periods

Use periods at the end of sentences, indirect questions, and commands:

Sentence:	The Statue of Liberty was officially rededicated.
Indirect question:	I asked my friend when he was going to stop taking pictures.
Command:	Wait until the ship moves into the picture.

Semicolons

Use a semicolon to join related independent clauses. Remember to test for independent clauses by using a period. If you can use a period at the end of each independent clause, and if the sentences are related, you may wish to use a semicolon. Remember, however, that semicolons are usually more appropriate in formal writing:

> Nowadays, says one sociologist, you don't have to have a reason for going to college; it's an institution. His definition of an institution is an arrangement everyone accepts without question; the burden of proof is not on why you go, but why anyone thinks there might be a reason for not going.
>
> —Caroline Bird

> I take a dim view of dams; I find it hard to learn to love cement.
>
> —Edward Abbey

Use a semicolon to separate items in a series that already have internal punctuation:

> We quickly meet the "good guys" of *Star Wars*: Luke Skywalker, played by Mark Hamill; Ben "Obi-Wan" Kenobi, played by Alec Guinness; and Han Solo, played by Harrison Ford.
>
> —Judith Crist

Do *not* use a semicolon to join dependent with independent clauses:

> Harrison Ford played the leading role in *Raiders of the Lost Ark*; which made him an instant star.

4E Colons and Dashes

Colons

Use a colon to introduce a list or an explanation. Colons often create formal, structured sentences:

> When you go to the grocery store, please get the following items: two boxes of frozen peas, five pounds of baking potatoes, and a package of stuffing for the turkey.
>
> There is only one guaranteed method to lose weight: eat less and exercise more.

Usually, a colon following a verb is unnecessary:

UNNECESSARY: The best way to lose weight is: eat less and exercise more.

REVISED: The best way to lose weight is to eat less and exercise more.

UNNECESSARY: I need: peas, baking potatoes, and stuffing.
REVISED: I need peas, baking potatoes, and stuffing.

DASHES

Use a single dash for an abrupt shift. Use a pair of dashes for an interrupting or parenthetical comment. Use a dash instead of a comma, colon, or parentheses when you want a sentence to have a more informal, colloquial flavor:

> At last a happy thought struck me—I would draw the fish.
>
> —Samuel Scudder

> Indeed, there are moments today—amid outlaw litter, tax cheating, illicit noise, and motorized anarchy—when it seems as though the scofflaw represents the wave of the future.
>
> —Frank Trippett

EXERCISE In the following passage, insert semicolons, colons, or dashes at the appropriate places. In some cases, there are several ways to punctuate the sentence correctly, so be prepared to explain your choice.

> (1) Yo-yo dieting the process of repeatedly losing and gaining weight is common today. (2) Instead of changing eating habits and exercise patterns, the yo-yo dieter uses three common strategies to lose weight taking diet pills, drinking diet liquids, and fasting outright. (3) The yo-yo dieter, however, needs to know the truth about dieting diet cycles decrease the muscle-to-fat ratio in the body and decrease the body's ability to lose weight during the next dieting cycle. (4) Quick-fix diets, in other words, will lead to rapid weight losses however, they will be followed by an even faster weight gain. (5) Ultimately, crash diets do more harm than good the body just wasn't designed to be a yo-yo.

4F EXCLAMATION POINTS AND QUESTION MARKS

EXCLAMATION POINTS

Use exclamation points sparingly, for stylistic emphasis:

I saw the sleek gray-haired manager standing near the dance floor, snapping his fingers and smiling. . . . I bet myself that he owned one of the few blow-dryers in Moscow. . . . He was watching the growing success of the only Western-style club in town and thinking: These kids! Right on! Crazy, but I love 'em!

—Andrea Lee

Bicyclists often ride as though two-wheeled vehicles are exempt from all traffic laws. Litterbugs convert their communities into trash dumps. . . . And then there are (hello, Everybody!) the jaywalkers.

—Frank Trippett

Question Marks

Use a question mark after a direct question:

What is your first childhood memory?

Do not combine question marks with commas or periods.

"What is your earliest memory?" she asked me. [Do *not* use a comma and a question mark: "What is your earliest memory?," she asked me.]

4G Quotation and Ellipsis Marks

Quotation Marks

Use quotation marks to indicate a writer's or speaker's exact words:

Marya Mannes says, "Woman, in short, is consumer first and human being fourth."

Use quotation marks for titles of *essays, articles, short stories, poems, chapters, and songs—any title that is part of a larger collection*:

"Television: The Splitting Image" is the title of an essay by Marya Mannes.

Use single quotation marks for quotations within a quotation:

James said, "I know I heard her say, 'Meet me outside the east door.' "

Ellipsis Marks

Use ellipsis marks (three *spaced* periods) to indicate material omitted from a direct quotation:

Marya Mannes said, "Woman . . . is consumer first and human

being fourth." [The ellipsis indicates that words are omitted from the middle of the sentence.]

Use a period *plus* three spaced periods to signal either omitted words at the end of a sentence or omitted intervening sentence(s):

Marya Mannes said, "Woman, in short, is consumer first and human being fourth. . . . The conditioning starts very early. . . ."

Punctuation With Quotation Marks

The following guidelines will help you to punctuate sentences with quotation marks.

Periods and commas go *inside* quotation marks:

According to biologist Julie Earwig, "Penguins are more densely covered with feathers than any other bird—nearly 180 feathers per square inch."

Colons and semicolons go *outside* quotation marks:

Recent data about the eagle's feathers may revise the old saying "light as a feather": the vaned feathers on a bald eagle weigh more than its entire skeleton.

Exclamation points and question marks go *inside or outside* quotation marks. They go *inside* if they are a part of the quoted material:

The award for the highest number of feathers, according to Earwig, "goes to the whistling swan with a staggering 25,000 feathers!" [The original sentence ends with an exclamation point.]

They go outside if they are not a part of the quoted material:

Is it true that, as Earwig claims, "the tiny ruby-throated hummingbird has 940 feathers"? [The original sentence ends with a period.]

4H Underlining for Italics

Use underlining to indicate words that should be set in italics.

Titles: "Down the River" is the most interesting chapter in Edward Abbey's *Desert Solitaire*. [Underline titles of books, magazines, films, paintings, newspapers—any work published separately. Use quotation marks for titles of chapters, articles, or poems—any title that is part of some collection in a book or magazine.]

Exceptions: Do not underline the Bible or titles of legal documents, such as the Deed of Trust or the United States Constitution.

Names: The most famous travel ships used to be the *Santa Maria*, the *Titanic*, and the *Queen Mary*. Now the great ones are the *Apollo* and the *Challenger*. [Underline names of ships, trains, aircraft, or spacecraft.]

Foreign words: He graduated *cum laude*, while his friend, who barely passed freshman mathematics, graduated *magna cum laude*. "*C'est la vie*," he thought. [Note, however, that some foreign words (*burrito, bourgeois, genre, clich é, junta*, and many others) have been incorporated into the language and do not need italics. Consult your dictionary if you are in doubt.]

Words or letters: *Suppose to* should have a *d: supposed to*. [Quotation marks are also used to indicate italics in handwritten or typed manuscripts.]

Note: Do *not* underline or put quotation marks around the title of your essay when it appears on a title page or the first page of your manuscript.

EXERCISE Revise the following passage, underlining appropriate words and titles.

(1) Tom Wolfe, author of The Right Stuff, has written a novel about a Wall Street broker in his newest work, The Bonfire of the Vanities. (2) This novel first appeared in twenty-seven installments in Rolling Stone magazine. (3) Wolfe's style has always been au courant, and Bonfire is no exception. (4) This novel features New York characters who run the gamut from drug pushers to the cunning and ambitious young lions of the investment world. (5) It is not a cliché; a to say that this book is difficult to put down.

41 Parentheses and Brackets

Parentheses

Use parentheses ( ) to set off additional information, examples, or comments:

Writing a film review requires that you carefully examine the criteria for your judgment (see Chapter 7).

Outside our lifeboat, let us imagine another 210 million people (say the combined populations of Colombia, Ecuador, Venezuela, Morocco, Pakistan, Thailand, and the Philippines), increasing at a rate of 3.3 percent per year.

—Garrett Hardin

Brackets

Use brackets [ ] to set off editorial remarks in quoted material. Brackets indicate that you, as an editor, are adding comments to the original material:

Original: After you hear my arguement, you will reelect Eastwood.

Edited: After you hear my arguement [sic], you will reelect [Mayor Clint] Eastwood. [As editor, you add information about Clint Eastwood and indicate by using "sic" ("thus it is") that the misspelling, grammatical mistake, or inappropriate usage occurs in the original source and is not your error.]

4J Apostrophes and Hyphens

Apostrophes

Use apostrophes for contractions, possession, and some plurals:

Contractions: It's too bad you don't agree.

Possession: The wind blew the student's notes across the front lawn. [The notes belonging to one student blew across the lawn.]
The wind blew the students' notes across the front lawn. [Several students' notes blew across the lawn.]
Your sister-in-law's accident was someone else's fault. [For compounds, make the last word possessive.]

Plurals: The 1980's [or 1980s] were the Yuppie years.
Eliminate unnecessary *which's* in your sentences.

Hyphens

Use hyphens for compound words, compound adjectives before nouns, some prefixes, and some numbers. When in doubt, always check a good dictionary.

Compounds: cross-reference; president-elect

Adjectives: a twentieth-century writer; the slate-blue sea; the three-year-old child
Note: When the compound adjectives follow a noun, omit the hyphen: *He is a writer well known only in Vermont.*

Prefixes: ex-President Reagan; self-motivation

Numbers: twenty-six; one hundred sixty-five; one-fifth

4K Capitals and Numbers

Capitals

Capitalize proper nouns and adjectives, professional titles, principal words in titles of books or articles, and regional locations:

Proper names: Judson Smith, Atlanta, Los Angeles, Missouri River, English, Swahili, American, Labor Day, Christmas, Hanukah, Wednesday, October [Do *not* capitalize seasons or terms: autumn, spring, summer, fall semester, freshman year.]

Titles: Senator Kennedy, President Lincoln, Professor Findlay, Associate Dean Natalie Renner, Uncle Don, Father [Do *not* capitalize family titles preceded by a pronoun: my mother, my uncle, our grandfather.]

Titles: *Gone with the Wind*, "The Short Happy Life of Francis Macomber," "The Triumph of the Wheel," "Star Wars" [Note that some style manuals suggest capitalizing only the first word in a title. If you are citing titles in a bibliography or list of works cited, check your style manual.]

Regions: the South, the Northwest, the Middle East [Do *not* capitalize directions: traveling east, walking due north.]

Numbers

Conventions regarding numbers vary. Generally, except in scientific or technical writing, spell out numbers of one hundred or less or numbers that require two words or less. If a passage requires many numbers, be consistent in your usage:

> This stadium seats fifty thousand people, but adding the end-zone bleachers increases the seating to fifty-seven thousand. [Hyphenated words count as one word.]
>
> Our chemistry lecture hall seats 425 students, but only 310 are enrolled this semester in Chemistry 201. [However, at the beginning of sentences, spell out numbers (Three hundred and ten stu-

dents are enrolled this semester) or rewrite the sentence (In Chemistry 201, 310 students are enrolled).]

EXERCISE Revise the following passage for proper use of apostrophes, hyphens, capitals, italics, and numbers. Use your dictionary to help you edit this passage.

(1) The advertisement shows a sky-diver floating down to earth, and the pictures caption says, "I take vitamin supplements every day, just to be on the safe side." (2) Self styled experts, from your local pharmacist to physicians from the mount Sinai school of Medicine in New York city, encourage the public to believe that vitamins are a cure all. (3) There are only thirteen known vitamin deficiencies (such as scurvy, which is a Vitamin C deficiency), but nearly sixty percent of the two hundred fifty two american's responding to our questionnaire believed in taking vitamin supplements. (4) These days, its almost patriotic to take vitamins—even your Mother says, "Don't forget to take your vitamins!" (5) During the 1980's, vitamins popularity rose an astonishing twenty nine percent, and revenue from vitamin sale's jumped to nearly three billion. (6) Although sales are generally higher in the west, some Eastern cities such as boston and Philadelphia have also shown dramatic increase's in sales. (7) If you want to learn more about vitamins, read The Vitamin-Pushers in a recent issue of Consumer Reports.

INDEX

A

A, an, 632
Abbey, Edward, 443
ABI/INFORM, 543
Abstract nouns, 596
Academic degrees, commas in, 644
Accept, except, 632
Active reading, 145-48
Active voice, 600, 611-13
  converting from passive, 612-13
Addresses, commas in, 644
Ad hominem fallacy, 408, 461
Adjective clauses, 602
Adjectives, 597
  commas with, 643
  compound, 650
Adverb clauses, 602
Adverbs, 597-98
  conjunctive, 638
Advertisement, summary and response to, 156-58
Advise, advice, 632
Affect, effect, 632
Agreement
  pronoun antecedent agreement, 596
  subject-verb agreement, 617-19
Alexander, Dennis, 296
Alexander, Vicki, 408
Allen, Gregory, 83
All right, alright, 632
Almanacs, 541
Already, all ready, 632-33
Alternating comparison-and-contrast structure, 339
Alternative pattern, outlines, 395
American Psychological Association (APA) style, 534, 552, 558-59, 565-68
  handbook for, 534
  in-text citations, 552, 558-60
  "References" list
    articles, 566-67
    books, 565-66
    unpublished sources, 568
Among, between, 633
Amount, number, 633
Ampersand in citations, 559
Analogy
  faulty comparison, 461
  in investigative writing, 239
  in observational writing, 87
  in remembering essay, 126
Analysis
  of audience, 27-28
  causal. *See* Causal analysis
  in evaluative writing, 337
  in explanatory writing, 255
  in investigative writing, 238-39, 241
  in summary and response essay, 184
Annotation, collaborative, 505
Anonymous author, citation of, 562, 565
Antecedent, of pronouns, 596
Anthology, citation of, 562, 565-66
Anyone, any one, 633
APA style. *See* American Psychological Association (APA) style
Apostrophes, 650
Appeals
  ad populum fallacy, 462
  in argumentative writing, 425-29
  to character, 427-28, 429
  combined, 428-29
  to emotion, 428, 429
  to reason, 426-27, 429
Appositive phrase, 601
Argumentative writing
  appeals for written argument, 425-29
  and audience, 419, 420
  claims for, 421-24
  collecting, 450-52
  drafting, 457
  examples of professional writers, 434-49
  outlines for, 453-55
  revision, 458-63
  Rogerian argument, 430-32
  shaping, 452-58
  student writing, 463-73
  subject selection, 450
  techniques for, 420-21
Arguments
  development of, 455-56
  in interpretive piece, 484, 508-9
  about story interpretation, 508-9
Arnold, Matthew, 524
Articles, 603
Articles (publications)
  APA style citation, 566-68
  MLA style citation, 563-64
  summary of, 204-6
Art works, evaluative writing about, 314-16
Atwood, Margaret, 8
Audience
  analysis of, 27-28
  and argumentative writing, 419, 420
  and drafting, 88
  profile of, 27
  and purpose for writing, 26-29
  and research paper, 525, 548
  and revision, 91
  -subject relationship, 27
  -writer relationship, 27
  and writer's role, 28
  and writing situation, 28-29
Authors, citation of

in-text citation, 556-59
in "References" list, 565
in "Works Cited" list, 561-62
Auxiliary verbs, 599

Background information, library research for, 541-42
Bad, badly, 633
Baker, Russell, 22
Bambara, Toni Cade, 20, 288, 496
Barthel, Joan, 209, 239
Bartholomae, David, 144
Begging the question, 460
Being, being that, 633
Bellow, Saul, 106
Berry, Wendell, 57, 366, 367
Berthoff, Ann, 80
Beside, besides, 633
"Be" verbs, 615-17
and passive voice, 612, 614, 616
revision of, 616
Bias, in articles/books, 545
Bibliographic databases, 543
Bibliographic reference sources, 231
Bibliography, 526
Bibliography section, research notebook, 530-31, 545-46
Biographical Dictionaries, 541
Biography and Genealogy Master Index, 541
Block comparison-and-contrast structure, 339
Block quotations, 553
Body paragraphs
in explanatory writing, 291-92
features of, 291
Books
APA style for citation of, 565-66
MLA style for citation of, 561-62
Brackets, 650
Brainstorming
for argumentative writing, 450
for explanatory writing, 283
method of, 125
for problem solving, 390-92
for remembering essay, 125
Branching
for argumentative writing, 452
for evaluative writing, 336
for explanatory writing, 284
for main ideas, 548-49
for research paper, 548-49
Brosseau, Nancy, 290, 302
Browne, Sonja H., 195
Burroughs, William, 60
Busch, Kristy, 401
Byron, Lord, 293

Can, may, 633
Capitalization, 651
Card catalogue, 231
Carlyle, Thomas, 144
Carson, Kit, 131
Case, of pronouns, 596
Causal analysis
in evaluative writing, 339-40
in explanatory writing, 289
in problem solving, 396
Cause-and-effect relationship
claims about, 422-23, 451
in explanatory writing, 261-63, 289
and *post hoc* fallacies, 294
Center around, 633
Character
appeals to, 427-28, 429
major/minor characters, 486
in short stories, 486
Character conflict map, for interpretive writing, 505-6
Checklists, 235
Chopin, Kate, 479
Christie, Agatha, 394
Chronological order
in evaluative writing, 339
in explanatory writing, 288-89
in investigative writing, 237-38, 241
in observational writing, 83-84, 89, 92
in problem solving, 397
in remembering essay, 126-27, 133
Circular arguments, 460-61
Citations. *See* Documentation in research paper
Cite, site, 633
Claims
in argumentative writing, 421-24
about cause and effect, 422-23, 451
in evaluative writing, 310, 343
of fact, 421-22, 451
narrowing claims, 450-51
pro and con arguments, 452, 464
about solutions/policies, 424-25, 451
about value, 423-24, 451
Classification
in explanatory writing, 287
in investigative writing, 239
in observational writing, 84-85
Clauses, 602
dependent, 602
independent (main), 602, 638
punctuation of, 638-39
relative, 602
semicolon to join, 645
subordinate, 602
Clichés, 627
Climax, of short stories, 486
Closed questions, 235-36
Clustering
for argumentative writing, 425
for evaluative writing, 336
for explanatory writing, 285
method of, 125
for problem solving, 393
for remembering essay, 125
Coherence, and paragraphs, 291
Colgrave, Sukie, 257
Collaborative annotation, in interpretive writing, 505
Collecting
argumentative writing, 450-52
computer tips, 81, 89-90, 181, 337-38, 397
evaluative writing, 334-37
explanatory writing, 283-86
interpretive writing, 505-7
investigative writing, 228-36
observational writing, 80-82
problem solving, 390-94
remembering essay, 125
research paper, 539-47
shaping, 181
summary and response essay, 174-79
in writing process, 33
Collective nouns, 596
and subject-verb agreement, 618
Colloquial language, 626-27
Colons, 645-46, 648

Combined appeals, 428-29
Commands, 644
Commas, 640-44
  addresses/dates/degrees, 644
  coordinate adjectives, 643
  dialog, 643-44
  direct quotation, 643
  introductory elements, 640
  nonrestrictive elements, 641-42
  and quotation marks, 648
  series, 640-41
  unnecessary, 643
Comma splices, 639-40
  revision of, 639
Common nouns, 596
Comparison-and-contrast structure, 338-39
  alternating, 339
  block, 339
Comparisons
  in evaluative writing, 338-39
  faulty comparison, 461
  in investigative writing, 238, 241
  in observational writing, 54, 55, 56, 84, 89-90, 92
  in remembering essay, 127
Complements
  object, 595
  subject, 595
Compound nouns, 596
Compound words, hyphens in, 650
Computers, 36-37
  databases, 542-43
  hypertext environment, 37, 38
  as networking tool, 37-38
  portable/notebook, 533
  as writing tool, 37
Computer software, citation of, 564, 567
Computer tips
  for collecting, 81, 89-90, 181, 229, 337-38, 397
  for conclusions, 240
  for double-entry log, 81
  for drafting, 455
  for editing, 295
  for freewriting, 81, 82
  for introductions, 240
  notebook for research, 533
  for revision, 510
  for shaping, 89-90, 397, 455
  for titles, 240
  "Wh" (reporter's) questions, 229
Conclusions
  computer tip, 240
  in evaluative writing, 340
  in interpretive writing, 509
  in investigative writing, 239
  in observational writing, 88
  in remembering essay, 131
  in research paper, 550
Concrete nouns, 596
Conflict, of short stories, 486
Conflict map, characters, 505-6
Conjunctions, 595, 638-39
  coordinating conjunctions, 595, 637
  correlative conjunctions, 595
  subordinating conjunctions, 595, 637-38
Conjunctive adverbs, 638, 639
Connections
  in remembering essay, 104, 105
  See also Relationships
Connotation, 631-32
Conrad, Joseph, 52, 86
Continual, continuous, 633-34
Contractions, apostrophe for, 650
Contrast
  in evaluative writing, 338-39
  in investigative writing, 238, 241
  in observational writing, 84, 89-90, 92
  in remembering essay, 104, 105, 127
Coordinating conjunctions, 595, 637, 639
Corporations, citation of, 559
Correlative conjunctions, 595
Could of, should of, 634
Council of Biology Editors (CBE) style, 534
  handbook for, 534
Coward, Noel, 334
Criteria, nature of, 310
Criteria analysis, in problem solving, 396

D

Dangling modifiers, 607-8
  revision of, 608
Dashes, 646
Data, citation of, 408
Databases
  bibliographic, 543
  on-line catalog system, 542-43
Data, media, criteria, 634
Dates, commas in, 644
Daybook. *See* Journal
Definition
  and claims of fact, 421-22
  in explanatory writing, 257-58, 287
  extended, 258
  formal, 257, 294
  in investigative writing, 238
  in observational writing, 85-86
  in remembering essay, 126
Denotation, 631-32
Denouement, of short stories, 486
Dependent clause, 602
Description
  in evaluative writing, 310
  in summary and response essay, 180-81
Descriptive details, 83
Descriptive process analysis, 260
Details
  descriptive, 83
  in observational writing, 54
  sensory, 54, 55, 56, 91
Devlin, Dudley Erskine, 173, 183
DIALOG, 231
Dialog, commas with, 643-44
DialogOnDisc, 543
Dialogue, in remembering essay, 131, 133
Diction
  clichés, 627
  colloquial language and slang, 626-27
  denotation and connotation, 631-32
  jargon, 627-28
  sexist language, 629-30
  usage glossary, 632-35
  vague words, 622-24
  wordiness, 624-26
Dictionaries, 541
  citation of, 562
Didion, Joan, 227
Different from, different than, 634
Dillard, Annie, 52, 66, 522
Direct objects, 595, 611
Direct quotation
  commas with, 643
  quotation marks, 647
Direct quotations

in argumentative writing, 456
block format, 553
condensed quotation, 182
editing of, 231-32, 554
in interpretive writing, 511
in-text citations, 553
introductions to, 553
lengthy, citation of, 558-59
omissions in, 554
in research paper, 553-54
in summary and response essay, 182, 187
taken from secondary source, 558
Disinterested, uninterested, 634
Dissertations, unpublished, citation of, 564
Doctorow, E.L., 54
Documentation in research paper, 527, 556-68
American Psychological Association (APA) style, 534, 558-59, 565-68
Council of Biology Editors (CBE) style, 534
in-text citations, 552
APA style, 558-60
MLA style, 556-58
Modern Language Association (MLA) style, 534, 556-58, 561-65
"References" list, 552
articles, 566-68
books, 565-66
unpublished sources, 568
stages of, 527
supplementary notes section, 560
"Works Cited" list, 552
MLA style, 560-65
Dominant idea
in observational writing, 88-89
See also Main idea; Thesis
Double-entry notes
computer tips, 81
format for notes, 81
and summary and response essay, 177, 189-90
Drafting
argumentative writing, 457
computer tips, 455
evaluative writing, 341
example of, 46-47
explanatory writing, 292-93
interpretive writing, 510
investigative writing, 240
nature of, 34
observational writing, 88-90, 90
problem solving, 399
remembering essay, 132
research paper, 551-55
summary and response essay, 186-87
Drafts and ideas section, research notebook, 532, 547
Drew, Elizabeth, 420

E

Editing
brackets in, 650
computer tips, 295
guidelines for, 593
importance of, 589-90
process of, 590-91
purpose of, 35
rationale for, 589-90
research paper, 568
symbols for, 592-93
Editorial, citation of, 564, 567
Editors, work by, citation of, 562, 565
Education Resources Information Center (ERIC), 231, 543
Ehrenreich, Barbara, 149
Either/or fallacy, 408, 461
Ellipsis marks, 647-48
for omissions, 554
Emotion, appeals to, 428, 429
Encyclopedias, 541
citation of, 562
ERIC (Information Resources Information Center), 231, 543
Essay map, 290
Evaluative writing
about commercial products/services, 312-14
about art works, 314-16
collecting, 334-37
drafting, 341
examples of professional writers, 319-32
in interpretive piece, 484
in interpretive writing, 508
about performances, 316-18
and problem solving, 389
revision, 342-44
shaping, 337-40
student examples, 344-56
subject selection, 334
techniques for, 310
Events
observational writing about, 59
remembering essay, 107-8
Evidence
in argumentative writing, 420, 458
in evaluative writing, 310, 343
in explanatory writing, 264, 293
in interpretive writing, 482, 511
for judgments, 310
in problem solving, 363, 364, 365
sources of, 154
in summary and response essay, 154, 187
Examples, in explanatory writing, 287
Exclamation points, 646-47, 648
Explanatory writing
analysis in, 255
collecting, 283-86
drafting, 292-93
examples of professional writers, 264-81
explaining "how," 259-61
explaining "what," 257-59
explaining "why," 261-63
in interpretive piece, 484
revision, 293-95
shaping, 286-92
student examples, 296-304
subject selection, 282-83
techniques for, 256-57
Exposition, of short stories, 486
Expository writing. *See* Explanatory writing
Expressions, figurative, 258-59
Extended definition, 258

F

Fact, claims of, 421-22, 451
Fallacies
ad hominem fallacy, 408, 461
ad populum fallacy, 462
begging the question, 460
circular arguments, 460-61
either/or fallacy, 408, 461
faulty comparison, 461
genetic fallacy, 460
hasty generalization, 459-50
logic errors, effects of, 459

post hoc ergo propter hoc, 460
post hoc fallacy, 294
red herring, 462
straw man diversion, 462
Farther, further, 634
Faulty comparison, 461
Faulty parallelism, 609-11
revision of, 610-11
Faulty prediction, 606-7
revision of, 607
Feature list, for interpretive writing, 507
Fewer, less, 634
Fiction. *See* Interpretive writing
Field research
for evaluative writing, 337-38
for explanatory writing, 286
Figurative expressions, in explanatory writing, 258-59
Figurative language, in short stories, 488
Film, citation of, 564, 567
First person
narrator, 487
writing in, 104
Fisher, Paula, 188
Fitzgerald, F. Scott, 240
Flashback, in remembering essay, 104
Flower, Linda, 25, 151
Foreign words, italics for, 649
Foreshadowing, in short stories, 486
Form, research paper, 525-26
Formal definitions, 257, 294
Fornes, Maria Irene, 8
Forster, E.M., 20
Fragments, sentence, 604-6
effective use of, 605
revision of, 605
Freewriting, 6, 21, 26
for argumentative writing, 419
computer tip, 81, 82
evaluative writing, 309, 338
explanatory writing, 256
for interpretive writing, 478-79
investigative writing, 203
observational writing, 54, 82
on problem solving, 361
remembering essay, 103
research paper, 524-25
Freire, Paulo, 153
Frost, Robert, 102
Fuentes, Carlos, 103
Furnish, Dale, 83
Fused sentences, 639-40
revision of, 639-40
Fussell, Paul, 85
Future perfect tense, 600
Future tense, 599

Gaines, Ernest J., 90
General indexes, 543-44
Generalization
avoiding overgeneralization, 408
hasty generalization, 459-60
Genetic fallacy, 460
Gerund phrase, 601
Gerunds, 601
Goldberger, Paul, 58
Goldman, Albert, 84
Goodman, Ellen, 556
Gorman, James, 319
Gould, Stephen Jay, 434
Government documents
citation of, 560, 562, 566
in library, 541, 544
Grossberger, Lewis, 211, 232, 238, 239
Guralnick, Peter, 59

Haas, Jim, 463
Hairston, Maxine, 35
Hamill, Pete, 548
Hansberry, Lorraine, 360
Harris, Sidney, 85
Hasty generalization, 459-60
Helping verbs. *See* Auxiliary verbs
Hemingway, Ernest, 4, 241
Heuristics, 228
See also Questions
Highet, Gilbert, 323, 339
Hoffman, Gregory, 126, 131
Hoffman, Roy, 14-17
Hooks, paragraph, 290-91
in evaluative writing, 343
in explanatory writing, 290-91
Hopefully, 634
Hope, Marjorie, 372
Houston, Jeanne Wakatsuke, 106
Hurston, Zora Neale, 522
Hwang, Sui Young, 407, 411
Hypertext environment, 37, 38
Hyphens, 650

I

Ideas section, of research notebook, 532, 547
If...then statements, 391, 408
Images
in observational writing, 54, 86-87
in remembering essay, 128, 133
Imperative mood, 600, 601
Imply, infer, 634
Indefinite pronouns, 597
and subject-verb agreement, 618
Independent (main) clause, 602, 638
Indexes, periodical, 231, 541, 543-44
Indicative mood, 600
Indirect objects, 595
Inductive logic, 426
Infinities, 601
Infinitive phrase, 601
INFOTRAK, 231, 543
Intensive pronouns, 597
Interjections, 603
Interpretations, in responses, 185
Interpretive writing
analysis of parts of story, 486-88
collecting, 505-7
drafting, 510
examples of professional writers, 488-503
purposes for, 483-85
and rereading, 477-78
responding as reader, 485
responding to short fiction, 485-88
revision, 510-12
shaping, 507-9
student examples, 512-19
techniques for, 481-82
Interrogative pronouns, 597
Interviews
for argumentative writing, 450
citation of, 564, 567
for evaluative writing, 336-37
for investigative writing, 233-34
for problem solving, 393, 394
for research paper, 539
In-text citations, 552-53
APA style, 552
format for, 553
MLA style, 233, 552
Intransitive verbs, 600
Introductions
in argumentative writing, 454

computer tip, 240
in evaluative writing, 340
in explanatory writing, 290
in investigative writing, 239
in observational writing, 87-88
in remembering essay, 131
in research paper, 549
Introductory elements, commas with, 640
Inverted pyramid, 236-37
Investigating. See Research
Investigative writing
about person, 209
collecting, 228-36
drafting, 240
examples of professional writers, 205-25, 242-47
multiple sources, use of, 206-9
purpose of, 203
revision, 241-42
shaping, 236-40
student example, 248-50
subject selection, 227
summary of book/article, 212-14
Irony, in stories, 488
Irregular verbs, 598
Italics, underlining for, 648-49
Its, it's, 634

J

Jargon, 627-28
Jong, Erica, 92
Journal, 10-17, 38-39
for explanatory writing, 282-83
professional writer on, 14-17
reading entries, 11
time line in, 505
write-to-learn entries, 11-12
writing entries, 12-13
Journal articles, citation of, 563, 566-67
Judgments, 310

Keller, Helen, 110
Key terms
in evaluative writing, 343
in explanatory writing, 256
in interpretive writing, 511
Kidder, Tracy, 282
Kiely, Robert, 329
Knowledge Index, 543
Koester, Jennifer, 193
Kozol, Jonathan, 219, 262
Krause, Steve, 401

Language
figurative, 258-59
use of. *See* Diction
Lay, lie, 634
Lead-in, in explanatory writing, 256, 290
Lectures, citation of, 564, 567
Lee, Andrea, 105, 127, 131
Lessing, Doris, 4
Letters
citation of, 564, 568
italics for, 649
Lewis, Karyn M., 156
Library, 230-32, 286
for background information, 541-42
bibliographic computer search, 543
DIALOG, 231
dictionaries, 541
encyclopedias, 531
government documents, 541, 544
librarian, help from, 541-42
microform room, 541
on-line catalog system, 542-43
periodical indexes, 231, 541, 543-44
reference sources, 231, 541
written sources, use of, 231-32
Library of Congress Subject Headings, 543
Like, as, as if, 635
Lincoln, Abraham, 322
Linking verbs, 599
Linton, Melaney A., 205
Lippmann, Walter, 202, 418
List, colon in introduction, 645
Literature, responding to. *See* Interpretive writing
Logic
errors. *See* Fallacies
inductive, 426
Logs
research, 529-30
three-column, 342
Looping
in argumentative writing, 452
in evaluative writing, 336
in explanatory writing, 285
method of, 125
in problem solving, 393
for remembering essay, 125
Loos, Anita, 124
Lose, loose, 635
Lyu-Volckhausen, Grace, 408

M

MacFadden, Brett, 512, 515
MacMillan, Julia, 512, 513, 515
McNerny, Kate, 537, 539, 568
Magazine articles
citation of, 563, 566
index to, 231
Main idea
in interpretive writing, 511
in remembering essay, 87, 104, 105, 132
of response, 154
of summary, 151
Major characters, 486
Malamud, Bernard, 90
Map
character conflict, 505-6
essay, 290
Marquez, Gabriel Garcia, 7, 131
Marshall, Paule, 56
Maynard, Joyce, 102
Meer, Jeff, 239
Meininger, Linda, 344
Memories. *See* Remembering essay
Metaphor
in investigative writing, 239
in observational writing, 86
in remembering essay, 126
Microform room, 541
Midler, Bette, 548
Milton, John, 418
Minor characters, 486
Misplaced modifiers, 608-9
revision of, 609
Mitford, Jessica, 270, 291-92
Mixed constructions, sentences, 606-7
revision of, 606
MLA style. *See* Modern Language Association (MLA) style
Modern Language Association (MLA) style, 534, 552, 556-58, 561-65
computerized database, 543
handbook for, 534, 561
in-text citations, 233, 552, 556-58
"Works Cited" list
articles, 563-64
books, 561-62

unpublished sources, 564-65
Modifiers, 595
misplaced, 608-9
vague, 623
Momaday, N. Scott, 106
Mood, 600-601
imperative, 600
indicative, 600
subjunctive, 600, 601
Morrison, Toni, 108, 131
Morrow, Lance, 238
Mowat, Farley, 70, 259
Muehlenhard, Charlene L., 204-5
Multivolume works, citation of, 557, 562
Murray, Donald, 10, 587

N

Nabokov, Vladimir, 342
Nader, Ralph, 360
Narration, 486-87
first-person narrator, 487
stream-of-consciousness narration, 487
third-person narrator, 487
National Technical Information Service (NTIS), 543
Networking, computer, 37-38
Newspaper articles
for argumentative writing, 450
citation of, 563-64, 567
New York Times Index, 544
Niebuhr, Reinhold, 366
Nocera, Joseph, 56
Nominals, 615-16
changing to verbs, 615
Nonrestrictive elements, commas with, 641-42
Notebook computers, 533
Notebook for research, 529-33
bibliography section, 530-31, 545-46
computer tip, 533
drafts and ideas section, 532, 547
research log section, 529-30
source notes section, 531, 546
Notes
double-entry, 81, 177, 189-90
during interview, 234
organization of, 551
for research. See Notebook for research
from sources, 545-47
supplementary, in research paper, 560
three-column log, 335
"Notes" section, of research paper, 560
Noun phrases, 601
Nouns, 596
abstract, 596
collective, 596
common, 596
compound, 596
concrete, 596
plural, 617
proper, 596
vague, 622
NTIS (National Technical Information Service), 543
Numbers, 651-52
hyphens in, 651

O

Object complements, 595
Objective pronouns, 596-97
Objectivity
and observational writing, 53
and revision, 90-91
Objects, observational writing about, 58
O'Brien, Edna, 5
Observation
in argumentative writing, 452
in evaluative writing, 335
in explanatory writing, 285
in problem solving, 393
in remembering essay, 104, 105, 133
Observational writing, 53-97
collecting in, 80-82
drafting in, 88-90
about events, 59
examples of professional writers, 62-77
about objects, 58
observing techniques, 54-55
about people, 56
about places, 56-57
revising in, 90-92
shaping in, 82-88
student examples, 93-98
subject selection, 78-79
Omissions, ellipsis for, 647-48
Omniscient narrator, 487
On-line catalog system, 542-43
On Line Public Access Catalogs (OPAC), 542
OPAC (On Line Public Access Catalogs), 542
Open questions, 235
Opinion, compared to evaluation, 309
Organizing. *See* Shaping
Orwell, George, 128
Outlines
alternative pattern, 395
for argumentative writing, 453-55
computer tips for, 455
point-by-point pattern, 395
for problem solving, 394-95
problem-solving pattern, 394-295, 397
for research paper, 549-50
for Rogerian argument, 454-55
step-by-step pattern, 395-96
for summary and response essay, 185-86
Overgeneralization, 408
Oxford English Dictionary, 541

P

Pamphlets, citation of, 565
Paragraph hooks
in evaluative writing, 343
in explanatory writing, 290-91
Paragraphs
body, parts of, 391
coherence and unity of, 291
See also Conclusions; Introductions
Parallelism, faulty, 609-11
Paraphrase
to avoid plagiarism, 232
citation of, 559
in summary and response essay, 181-82, 187
Parentheses, 649
in citations, 557-60
Participial phrases, 602
Participle phrase, 601
Participles, 601
Passive voice, 600, 613-14
and "be" verbs, 612, 614, 616
Past perfect tense, 600
Past tense, 599
Peer response
for evaluative essay, 341-42
for explanatory writing, 292-93
for problem solving, 398-99
People
investigative writing about, 209
observational writing about, 56

remembering essay, 106
Performances, evaluative writing about, 316-18
Periods, 644, 648
Person
first, 104
shifts in, 620-21
Persona
in investigative writing, 239
in remembering essay, 129-30
Personal communications, citation of, 559
Personal interviews, citation of, 564, 567
Personal pronouns, 597
Peterson, Jan, 242
Petrie, Neil H., 40
Petrosky, Anthony, 144
Petry, Todd, 131, 134
Photocopying, of sources, 547
Phrases, 601-2
appositive, 601
gerund, 601
infinitive, 601
noun, 601
participial, 602
participle, 601
prepositional, 601
verbal, 601
Places
in observational writing, 56-57
in remembering essay, 106-7
Plagiarism
avoidance of, 232, 555
forms of, 555
nature of, 554-55
Plato, 425
Plot
of short stories, 486
summary of, 511
Plurals
apostrophes for, 650
nouns, 617
Point-by-point pattern, outlines, 395
Point of view
in observational writing, 55, 91
in remembering essay, 133
Policies, claims about, 424-25, 451
Portable computers, 533
Porter, Katherine Anne, 310
Possession, apostrophe for, 650
Possessive pronouns, 597
Post hoc ergo propter hoc, 294, 460
Predicate, 594
Prefixes, hyphens in, 651
Prepositional phrase, 601
Prepositions, 603
Prescriptive process analysis, 259-60
Present perfect tense, 599
Present tense, 104, 511, 599
Primary sources, 539-40
Principal, principle, 635
Problem solving
collecting, 390-94
demonstration of problem's existence, 362, 362-64, 390
drafting, 399
examples of professional writers, 367-88
in interpretive piece, 484
outlines for, 394-95
proposing solution and convincing readers, 362, 372-76
revision, 399-401
shaping, 394-99
student examples, 401-14
subject selection, 388-90
techniques for, 362
Problem solving pattern, outlines, 394-295, 397
Process analysis, 259-61
chronological order in, 288-89
descriptive, 260
prescriptive, 259-60
Process of writing. *See* Writing process
Products, evaluative writing about, 312-14
Profile of audience, 27
Pronoun agreement, 620-21
revision of errors, 620-21
and shifts in person, 620-21
Pronoun reference, 621-22
Pronouns, 596-97
case of, 596
demonstrative, 597
indefinite, 597
intensive, 597
interrogative, 597
objective, 596-97
personal, 597
possessive, 597
reference of, 596
reflexive, 597
relative, 597
sexist, 630
subjective, 596
Proofreading
guidelines for, 593
importance of, 589-90
marks for, 591-92
research paper, 568
Proper names, capitalization of, 651
Proper nouns, 596
Proposals, in problem solving, 362, 394, 396-97, 408
Punctuation and mechanics
apostrophes, 650
brackets, 650
capitalization, 651
colons, 645-46
commas, 640-44
and comma splices, 639-40
dashes, 646
ellipsis marks, 647-48
exclamation points, 646-47
and fused sentences, 639-40
hyphens, 650
numbers, 651-52
parentheses, 649
periods, 644
question marks, 647
quotation marks, 647, 648
semicolons, 645
sentences, 637-39
underlining for italics, 648-49
Purposes for writing, 23-26
antithesis/claim/main idea, 25-26
audience based, 24-29
combinations of, 25
subject based, 24-25
writer-based, 24
Pyramid, inverted, 236-37

Q

Quammen, David, 162, 190-92, 264
Question analysis, for narrowing subject, 537-38
Question marks, 647, 648
Questionnaires
for evaluative writing, 336-37
for interviews, 235-36
for investigative writing, 234-36
for problem solving, 394

questions for, 235-36
for research paper, 539
Questions
begging the question, 460
closed, 235-36
for explanatory writing, 283-84
for investigative writing, 228-30, 234
open, 235
of questionnaires, 235-36
for research paper, 548
See also "Wh" (reporter's) questions
Quotation marks, 647-48
punctuation rules, 648
Quotations. *See* Direct quotations
Quote, quotation, 635

R

Radio programs, citation of, 564, 567
Random sample, 236, 427
Ranking lists, 235-36
Readers' Guide to Periodical Literature, 543-44
Readers. *See* Audience
Reading
active/critical reading, 145-48
and class discussions, 179-80
and evaluative writing, 336
and explanatory writing, 286
and problem solving, 394
rereading and interpretive writing, 477-78, 481
with writer's eye, 485-88
See also Summary and response essay
Reading log, and summary and response essay, 176-77
Reason, appeals to, 426-27, 429
Reasoning errors. *See* Fallacies
Recordings, citation of, 564, 567
Red herring, 462
"References" list, 552
articles, 566-67
books, 565-66
unpublished sources, 568
Reflexive pronouns, 597
Regan, Tom, 163-66
Regions, capitalization of, 651
Regular verbs, 598
Relationships
explaining, in short story, 508
in interpretive writing, 508
in remembering essay, 87
and transition words, 294-95
See also Cause-and-effect relationship
Relative clauses, 602
Relative pronouns, 597
Remembering
in argumentative writing, 452
in evaluative writing, 336
in explanatory writing, 285
in problem solving, 393
Remembering essay
collecting, 125
drafting, 132
events, 107-8
examples of professional writers, 110-22
freewriting, 103
people, 106
places, 106-7
revision, 132-33
shaping, 126-31
student writings, 134-40
subject selection, 124
writing techniques for, 104-5
Reporter's questions. *See* "Wh" (reporter's) questions
Rereading, and interpretive writing, 477-78, 481
Research
and argumentative writing, 452
evaluation of sources, 340-41
and evaluative writing, 336
for interpretive writing, 507
and problem solving, 393
strategies for, 286
Research paper
collecting, 539-47
documentation formats, 534
documentation of sources, 527, 556-68
drafting, 551-55
editing, 568
narrowing subject, 535-38
notebook for, 529-33
outline for, 549-50
preparation for writing, 527-28
purpose/audience/form as guides, 525-26
revision, 556
shaping, 547-51
sources, 526-27
student example, 568-74
subject selection, 535
techniques for writing, 524-25
timetable, 533-34
Response, 153-56
directions of, 154
example of, 155-56
shaping, 183-85
and supporting evidence, 154
See also Summary and response essay
Reviews, citation of, 564, 567
Revision
argumentative writing, 458-63
computer tips, 295, 510
evaluative writing, 342-44
example of, 47
explanatory writing, 293-95
interpretive writing, 510-12
investigative writing, 241-42
nature of, 34
observational writing, 90-92
problem solving, 399-401
remembering essay, 132-33
research paper, 556
of scene, 507
summary and response essay, 187-88
Richman, Phyllis C., 310
Rituals, of writers, 6-9
Rodriguez, Richard, 107, 131
Rogerian argument, 430-32
outlines for, 454-55
strategies in, 431
Rogers, Carl, 430
Rosenblatt, Louise, 148
Rosenfeld, Albert, 431
Run-on sentence. *See* Fused sentences
Russell, Pat, 518

S

Sagan, Carl, 87
Sample, random, 236, 427
Sanders, Scott Russell, 113
Scene revision, for interpretive writing, 507
Schedule, for research paper, 533-34
Science Citation Index (SCI SEARCH), 543
Scientific method, 426
SCI SEARCH (Science Citation Index), 543

Scudder, Samuel H., 62
Secondary sources, 540
Selby, Brooke, 137
Selective omniscient narrators, 487
Semicolons, 645, 648
 and independent clauses, 639
Sensory details, 54, 55, 56, 91
Sentence structure
 active and passive voice, 611-15
 adjectives and adverbs, 597-98
 articles/interjections/prepositions, 603
 basic elements of sentence, 594-95
 "be" verbs, 616-17
 dangling modifiers, 607-8
 faulty parallelism, 609-11
 faulty prediction, 606-7
 fragments, 604-6
 misplaced modifiers, 608-9
 mixed constructions, 606-7
 nominals, 615-16
 nouns and pronouns, 596-97
 phrases and clauses, 601-2
 pronoun agreement, 620-21
 pronoun reference, 621-22
 of short stories, 487-88
 subject-verb agreement, 617-19
 verbs, 598-601
 verb tense, 619-20
Series, commas in, 640-41
Setting, of short stories, 487
Sexist language, 629-30
 and pronouns, 630
 sexist/revised works, 629
Shange, Ntozake, 10
Shaping
 argumentative writing, 452-58
 collecting, 181
 computer tips, 89-90, 397, 455
 evaluative writing, 337-40
 explanatory writing, 286-92
 interpretive writing, 507-9
 investigative writing, 236-40
 methods of, 83-88, 180-81, 236-39, 287-300, 337-40
 observational writing, 82-88
 problem solving, 394-99
 remembering essay, 126-31
 research paper, 547-51
 summary and response essay, 180-85
 in writing process, 34
Shaw, George Bernard, 362
Sheridan, Richard Brinsley, 589
Ships, italics for names of, 648-49
Simile
 in investigative writing, 239
 in observational writing, 86
 in remembering essay, 126
Singer, Peter, 163-66, 432
Single quotation marks, 647
Situation for writing, 28-29
Skelton, Mark, 87, 88, 93
Sketching, 80
Slang, 626-27
Smith, Frank, 148
Smith, Lillian, 202
Software, citation of, 564, 567
Solomon, Jack, 168
Solutions, claims about, 424-25, 451
Solutions to problems. *See* Problem solving
Source notes section, research notebook, 531, 546
Sources in research paper, 526-27
 criteria for evaluation of, 545
 informal contacts for, 538-39
 library sources, 541
 photocopying, 547
 primary sources, 539-40
 proper use of, 552
 secondary sources, 540
 time for citing sources, 552
 unpublished sources, 539
 See also Documentation in research paper; Library
Spatial order
 in observational writing, 83, 89, 92
 in remembering essay, 126
Specialized indexes, 544
Stafford, William, 33
Statistical Abstract of the United States, 541
Steinbeck, John, 82
Steinem, Gloria, 8, 371
Step-by-step pattern, outlines, 395-96
Stevens, Mark, 314, 340
Stillman, Peter R., 36
Stone, Bridgid, 248
Story picture, for interpretive writing, 506-7
Straw man diversion, 462
Stream-of-consciousness narration, 487
Strunk, William Jr., 399, 621
Style, of short stories, 487-88
Subject
 -audience relationship, 27
 and purpose of writing, 24-25
 See also Claims; Main idea; Thesis
Subject complements, 595
Subject of sentence, 594
Subjective pronouns, 596
Subject selection
 argumentative writing, 450
 evaluative writing, 334
 explanatory writing, 282-83
 investigative writing, 227
 narrowing subject, 535-38
 in observational writing, 78-80
 problem solving, 388-90
 remembering essay, 124
 research paper, 535
 summary and response essay, 173-74
Subject-verb agreement, 617-19
 and collective nouns, 618
 and indefinite pronouns, 618
 and number, 618
 revision of errors, 617-18
 and two subjects, 617-18
Subjunctive mood, 600, 601
Subordinate clauses, 602
Subordinating conjunctions, 595, 637-38
Summary, 151-52
 examples of, 152, 183, 232
 purpose of, 151-52
 shaping, 180-82
Summary and response essay
 for advertisement, 156-58
 collecting, 174-79
 drafting, 186-87
 examples of professional writers, 162-70
 outlines for, 185-86
 response, 153-56
 revision, 187-88
 shaping, 180-85
 student writings, 188-97
 subject selection, 173-74

summary, 151-52
Supplementary notes, in research paper, 560
Surveys, citation of, 564
Symbols, in stories, 488

T

Tannen, Deborah, 192, 276
Television programs, citation of, 564, 567
Tense, 599-600, 619-20
 shifts in, 619
Text annotation, and summary and response essay, 176
That, which, 635
Their, they're, there, 635
Theme, of short stories, 488
Thesaurus, 541
Thesis
 in argumentative writing, 421
 in evaluative writing, 310
 in explanatory writing, 264, 294
 and purpose for writing, 25-26
 in research paper, 548
 See also Claims
Third-person narrator, 487
Thomas, David, 468
Thomas, Lewis, 260
Three-column log, 342
Thurber, James, 129, 131
Time line, for interpretive writing, 505
Timetable, for research paper, 533-34
Titles
 capitalization of, 651
 computer tip, 240
 of evaluative writing, 340
 of investigative writing, 239
 italics for, 648
 of observational writing, 87
 quotation marks, 647
 of remembering essay, 131
Tone
 in explanatory writing, 288
 in investigative writing, 239
 in remembering essay, 128-29
 in short stories, 488
Topic cross, for narrowing subject, 535-36
Topic. *See* Subject; Subject selection
Topic sentences, of paragraphs, 291, 292
To, too, two, 635
Toufexis, Anastasia, 214, 239
Transition words
 in evaluative writing, 343
 in explanatory writing, 290-91, 294-95
Transitive verbs, 600, 611, 612
Translations, citation of, 562, 566
Travers, Peter, 316
Trippett, Frank, 362
Twain, Mark, 33, 132

U

Underlining for italics, 648-49
Unity, and paragraphs, 291
Unpublished sources
 APA style for citation of, 568
 in-text citation, 557, 559
 MLA style for citation of, 564-65
 types of, 539
Unsigned articles, citation of, 563, 566
Unsigned editorial, citation of, 564, 567
Usage glossary, 632-35
Used to, supposed to, 635

Vague words, 622-24
 modifiers, 623
 nouns, 622-23
 verbs, 623-24
Value, claims about, 423-24, 451
Value judgments, 310
Verbal phrase, 601
Verbals, types of, 601
Verbs, 595, 598-601
 auxiliary, 599
 intransitive, 600
 irregular, 598
 linking, 599
 mood, 600-601
 principle parts of, 598
 regular, 598
 tense, 599-600
 transitive, 600
 vague, 623-24
 voice, 600
Verb tense. *See* Tense
Vidal, Gore, 4
Voice
 active voice, 600
 passive voice, 600
Voice of writer
 in explanatory writing, 288
 in remembering essay, 128, 133

Walker, Alice, 116, 131, 203
Warner, Charles Dudley, 361
Webster's Third New International Dictionary of the English Language, 541
Weekly, Kurt, 128
Welty, Eudora, 35, 488
White, E.B., 256, 258, 452
White, Stephen, 88, 96
"Wh" (reporter's) questions
 computer tips, 229
 in evaluative writing, 310
 in investigative writing, 228, 237, 241
 in problem solving, 390
 for research papers, 537-38
Williams, Sherley Anne, 24, 341
Wong, Elizabeth, 29
Woolfolk, Donna, 287
Wordiness, 624-26
 redundant phrases, 625
 revision for, 625-26
Words as words, italics for, 649
"Works Cited" list, 552, 561-65
 alphabetization of, 561
 in argumentative writing, 467-68, 472
 MLA, 560-65
  articles, 563-64
  books, 561-62
  unpublished sources, 564-65
World Almanac, 541
Wright, Keith, 401
Writer's block, 5
Writing
 energy and attitude for, 9-10
 personal dimension of, 21-22
 purposes for, 23-26
 rituals of writer, 6-9
 situation for, 28-29
 time and place for, 7-8

Writing courses, myths about, 5-6
Writing process, 33-36
  collecting in, 33
  drafting in, 34
  revising in, 34-35
  shaping in, 34

Y'Blood, Kent, 339, 354
Young, James, 372

Zimmerman, Paul, 383
Zoellner, Robert, 31

Alphabetical Reference to the Handbook

Active voice, **2e**
Addresses, **4c**
Adjectives, **1c**
Adverbs, **1c**
Agreement, **2g, 2i**
Apostrophes, **4j**
Articles, **1f**

"Be" verbs, **2f**
Brackets, **4i**

Capitals, **4k**
Clauses, **1e**
Clichés, **3d**
Colloquial language, **3c**
Colons, **4e**
Commas, **4a–c**
Commas for series, **4c**
Comma splice, **4b**
Complements, **1a**
Conjunctions, **1a**
Conjunctive adverb, **4a**
Connotation, **3f**
Coordinate adjectives, **4c**
Coordinating conjunctions, **1a, 4a**
Correlative conjunctions, **1a**

Dangling modifiers, **2c**
Dashes, **4e**
Dates, punctuation, **4c**
Degrees, punctuation, **4c**
Denotation, **3f**
Dependent clause, **1e, 4a**
Diction, **3a–f**
Direct object, **1a**

Ellipsis marks, **4g**
Exclamation points, **4f**

Faulty predication, **2b**
Fragments, **2a**
Fused sentence, **4b**

Gerunds, **1e**

Hyphens, **4j**

Independent clause, **1e, 4a**
Infinitives, **1e**
Interjections, **1f**
Intransitive verbs, **1d, 2e**
Italics, **4h**

Jargon, **3d**

Linking verbs, **1d**

Misplaced modifiers, **2c**
Mixed construction, **2b**
Modifiers, **1a**
Mood, **1d**

Nominals, **2f**
Non-restrictive, **4c**
Noun-pronoun agreement, **2i**
Nouns, **1b**
Numbers, **4k**

Passive voice, **2e**
Parallelism, **2d**
Parentheses, **4i**
Participles, **1e**
Periods, **4d**
Phrases, **1e**
Predicate, **1a**
Prepositions, **1f**
Pronoun agreement, **2i**
Pronoun reference, **2j**
Pronouns, **1b**
Punctuation, **4a–g, 4j**

Question marks, **4f**
Quotation marks, **4g**

Relative clause, **1e**
Restrictive elements, **4c**

Semicolons, **4d**
Sentence punctuation, **4a**
Sentence structure, **1a**
Sexist language, **3e**
Slang, **3c**
Subject, **1a**
Subject-verb agreement, **2g**
Subordinate clause, **1e**
Subordinating conjunctions, **1a, 4a**

Transitive verbs, **1d, 2e**

Usage Glossary, **3g**

Vague words, **3a**
Verb tense, **1d, 2h**
Verbs, **1a, 1d**
Voice, **1d, 2e**

Wordiness, **2f, 3a, 3b**